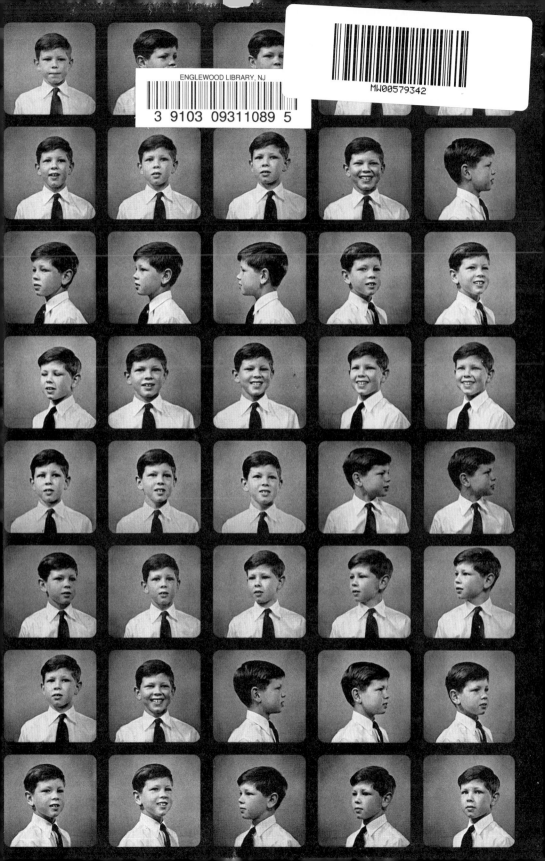

Nick Drake

Nick playing Sir Jakie Astor's Hammond organ at the Astors' home,
Hatley Park, spring 1968.

Nick Drake

The Life

RICHARD MORTON JACK

hachette
BOOKS

New York

Hachette Books
Hachette Book Group
1290 Avenue of the Americas
New York, NY 10104
HachetteBooks.com
Twitter.com/HachetteBooks
Instagram.com/HachetteBooks

First US Edition: November 2023
Originally published in Great Britain in 2023 by John Murray

All lyrics to songs by Nick Drake reproduced by permission of Bryter Music/Blue Raincoat Music.

Front endpaper photographs reproduced by permission of Bryter Music – The Estate of Nick Drake. Back endpaper photographs © Estate of Keith Morris/Getty Images.

Published by Hachette Books, an imprint of Hachette Book Group, Inc. The Hachette Books name and logo is a trademark of the Hachette Book Group.

The Hachette Speakers Bureau provides a wide range of authors for speaking events. To find out more, go to hachettespeakersbureau.com or email HachetteSpeakers@hbgusa.com.

Books by Hachette Books may be purchased in bulk for business, educational, or promotional use. For information, please contact your local bookseller or Hachette Book Group Special Markets Department at: special.markets@hbgusa.com.

The publisher is not responsible for websites (or their content) that are not owned by the publisher.

Print book interior design by Palimpsest Book Production Ltd, Falkirk, Stirlingshire

Library of Congress Control Number: 2023943887

ISBNs: 9780306834950 (hardcover); 9780306834974 (ebook)

Printed in the United States of America

LSC-C

Printing 1, 2023

To KVMJ
You are worth hundreds of sparrows.

Contents

PART THREE

PART FOUR

Foreword

THIS IS NOT an Authorised Biography. That term implies to me a straitjacketed affair, tailored by the estate, family, or subject themselves, to fit a desired image of the protagonist. This has not been the case with Richard Morton Jack's biography of my brother. But it is true that this is the only biography of my brother that has been written with my blessing.

When Cally Callomon – the manager of Nick's musical estate – and I published our own book about Nick, *Remembered For A While*, we meant this collection of fragments and memories to set a few records straight, and rectify some of the absurd myths that had grown up around Nick's life. But it also revealed the need for a more conventional biography – one that accurately told the story of Nick's brief life. This was certainly not a task that I could, or wanted to, undertake. But it posed a dilemma, because if such a biography were to be truly accurate, it would mean allowing access to hallowed grounds and household gods, and asking a stranger to 'tread softly, because you tread on my dreams'.

Nick's story has too often been overshadowed by the tragedy of his final illness. There was nothing romantic about it: like most mental illnesses, it was grim, repetitive and relentless, and it cruelly robbed him of his creative muse. It caused him despair – and a lifetime of grief for those closest to him. But if there is an interest in his short life, it surely lies in those years that led up to his illness, the years in which the seed of his talent was planted, nurtured and brought to full bloom in three albums of songs that have blazed a trail long after his sad death. It is these years that have never before been accurately analysed and chronologically documented.

Throughout the life of Nick's music, one of the miracles has been the nourishment and care it has received, both before and after his death, from strategic players, all of them outstanding people in their own right. Apart from our exceptional parents, and a fine housemaster at Marlborough who saw his potential despite his poor academic results, there was his meeting at Cambridge, almost by chance, with the fellow undergraduate and music scholar whose arrangements became integral to his songs, Robert Kirby; there was his introduction to his producer, the remarkable Joe Boyd, who despite all setbacks has never ceased to champion his music; and there was his master sound engineer, John Wood, who became a good friend to him, and has protected both Nick and his work ever since.

Thanks to Joe Boyd, Nick was signed to Chris Blackwell, world famous for his Island record label, and thanks to Island, a quarter of a century after Nick's death, its Creative Director, Cally Callomon, took on the mantle of Manager of the Nick Drake Musical Estate, which, at his suggestion, we have called Bryter Music. It is Cally who has expertly guided Nick's music ever since, and it is to Cally in large part that Nick owes his posthumous fame. And now Nick owes him the discovery of another key player in his saga – that of the storyteller. In Richard Morton Jack, Nick has, I do believe, once again struck gold.

Cally met Richard many years ago through a joint love of record collecting, and gradually became aware of his rare ability to combine a copious knowledge of the history of music with a forensic facility to sort out fact from fiction. When Richard stated his desire to write a biography of Nick, Cally realised, after cautious reflection, that here was a man who could be trusted to sift through all the myths, seek out the buried facts, and present an accurate record of his twenty-six years on Earth.

I was, perhaps, more hesitant, fearing the intrusion and the re-opening of a wound that never heals. But I put my trust first in Cally, and then, as I started to know him, increasingly in Richard – not only in his obvious love of his subject, but in his sensitive objectivity. I knew there would be no bending of the facts to fit a personal agenda, and I also knew that I could, without compunction, give him introductions to many contacts who have in the past been reluctant to talk about Nick.

What neither Cally nor I had realised was quite the lengths of investigation Richard was prepared to go to – just how many contacts he would follow up and speak to, how many tiny pieces of evidence he would uncover and place in order, making a coherence of Nick's life that, almost half a century after his death, we could never have believed possible. I have no idea how enormous his database must be, but the important point is that he has sorted through all of it, culled everything of importance, and produced a book of page-turning interest. I find I have learned many facts about my brother's life that I never knew.

In life one should never say 'never' – but I cannot see myself ever visiting this story again. I now feel satisfied that it has been told as fully and accurately as, at the moment, it possibly can be. I am grateful to Richard for having peeled back layers of confusion and inaccurate information. I am equally grateful to him for having indeed trodden lightly on my dreams. For me the rest is silence. For you, I hope, this book will lead you to listen, or perhaps re-listen, to its subject's creations: the songs of Nick Drake.

Gabrielle Drake
January 2023

Remember this when you are full of woe
There is a time when every sigh must end;
So often do we think of Time as foe
We do forget that Time can be a friend –

Prologue

SHORTLY BEFORE I p.m. on Monday, 25 November 1974, Rodney Drake happened to ring home from the local garden centre. Aged sixty-six, he had retired four years earlier and was engaged in winter preparations for his roses. His wife, Molly, answered – though it could just as easily have been their Karen housekeeper,* Naw – and asked him to return at once to their house, Far Leys, in Tanworth-in-Arden, thirteen miles north of Stratford-upon-Avon, Warwickshire.

It was a fifteen-minute drive and she came out of the house to meet him. 'I could tell by her face what had happened,' he wrote in his diary a few hours later. 'Naw had looked in on Nick at 11.45, found him lying across his bed and called to Molly, who went in and found him dead.' An empty pill bottle was close by.

Nick, their twenty-six-year-old son, had been based at Far Leys since the spring of 1971, following a sharp decline in his mental health, and his illness had come to define his parents' lives. By now the three low-selling albums he had made were well in the past – the last had been completed over three years earlier – and though he had made attempts to write and record in recent months, his muse had seemingly vanished.

That was one plausible reason for his despondency, but no one understood what had made this promising young man – a popular schoolboy, a champion athlete, an open-minded traveller, a Cambridge undergraduate, a superb musician, a unique singer-songwriter – so

---

* The Karen people are indigenous to the Thailand–Burma border region. Persecuted by the Burmese, they were loyal to the British, particularly during the Second World War.

I

introverted, unsettled and unhappy. Family, friends and doctors had done their best to reverse his decline, to no avail. He had been prescribed different medicines but took them haphazardly, and at best they controlled his symptoms rather than eliminating them.

He had spent part of the previous month in Paris and shown glimmers of improvement, but in recent days he'd been silent, surly, restless, inactive and indecisive – all the characteristics his parents and sister Gabrielle had come to associate with the worst of his illness. Enough was enough, he had evidently decided on impulse.

Eventually the local GP, Dr Ackroyd, arrived and explained what was already clear: Nick had died some hours earlier. An ambulance was sent away and Rodney and Molly gave statements to a sympathetic policeman, PC Howell. They told him that the contents of the pill bottle – a prescribed anti-depressant, Tryptizol – were missing. 'Later, undertakers Dyson Richards arrived to remove our poor old Nick after we had said goodbye to him,' Rodney wrote. 'We were left in a daze of grief, wondering how and why it had all come about . . .'

Rodney, Molly and Gabrielle would never cease to ponder those questions, but their grief was softened not just by time, but by a curious phenomenon. The artistic recognition their cherished son had craved was growing and growing. Articles about him began to appear, his work was repackaged and sold more and more copies, fans from Britain, Europe, America and even further afield turned up at Far Leys to learn more about him, and his family did their best to explain who the magically gifted, frustratingly unfathomable Nick had been.

PART ONE

I

A Very Cosy World

THE DRAKES MOVED into Far Leys in late May 1952, when
Gabrielle was eight and Nick was nearly four. A large but not
cavernous mock-Georgian house built in the early twentieth century,
its asking price of £10,000 was above their budget but it was precisely
what Molly had been hoping to find upon settling in England after
many years out East.

Tanworth-in-Arden had been plain Tanworth until the nineteenth
century, when it was renamed to avoid confusion with the market
town of Tamworth in Staffordshire, on the other side of Birmingham.
The area had once sat in the ancient Forest of Arden; by the 1950s
it was long since denuded. Far Leys took its name from the
surrounding meadows, but it wasn't in deep countryside – the train
that carried Rodney to work in Birmingham, fifteen miles away,
could be glimpsed in the distance.

The heart of the village was its pretty green, bordered by the
handsome fourteenth-century limestone church, St Mary Magdalene,
and the Bell Inn. Bates Lane, where Far Leys stands, was off the
village centre and the house was set back from the road, making it
secluded without being isolated. A short, gravelled driveway led to
its front door, flanked by pillars.

Inside was a hallway with a large study to the right. In recent
years it had served as a doctor's surgery and a playgroup classroom
but was used by the Drakes as a lumber room, then as 'the music
room'. Leading off it, and overlooking the sweeping lawn to the
back, was the drawing room. A passageway led to a compact dining
room and a pantry, with the kitchen at its end.

Upstairs were a nursery, a dressing room, three bedrooms and
two bathrooms. Nick's cosy, square room was tucked away down its

own very short corridor, between his sister's and parents' rooms. A tall bookshelf was set in an alcove to the right of the door, and a window (with animal-print curtains, when he was a child) was opposite; to the right were twin beds, a desk and chair, and a circular window overlooking the side of the house.

Until he was eight he shared his room with his bespectacled Karen nanny, Naw Rosie Paw Tun, known as 'Nan'. She had accompanied the Drakes back to England in 1951 and was more like a family member than an employee. 'It was like having three parents, really – Mummy, Daddy and Nanny,' according to Gabrielle.[1] 'Mummy was always very glamorous, Father was the most wonderful sort of strong person, and Nanny was Nanny. She was always there in a crisis and was the calm centre to our lives.'

Tanworth was safe, with few cars, and Gabrielle and Nick soon got to know everyone, at least by sight. The vicar was Canon Dudley Lee, the tiny post office was presided over by the gossipy Mrs Chattaway and her daughter-in-law (nicknamed 'the Chats' locally), the Ivy Stores was run by old Mrs Tibbles, and the closest thing to a celebrity was 'Gentleman' Jack Hood, landlord of the Bell and the 1926 British welterweight boxing champion.

There was a village school, a garage and filling station, a green-grocer, a butcher and even a boot-mender. Local characters included Pip Patterson, who wore plus-fours and foraged in hedgerows for material to smoke in his pipe, and Mr Onions, who hosted summer fêtes in his large garden. 'We lived in a very cosy world,' as Gabrielle's childhood friend and neighbour Joanna Lodder summarises.

Reunited with their possessions – most notably the grand piano, which took pride of place in the drawing room – the Drakes settled into their new and, to an extent, alien life. For Rodney it was a welcome return to his homeland after two happy and productive decades abroad, despite the challenges of the war and its aftermath. Molly's homecoming was perhaps more nuanced: she was English and had been educated in England but had barely lived there as an adult.

Her formidable father, Sir Idwal Lloyd, had graduated from Gonville and Caius College, Cambridge, before rising through the Indian Civil Service to become Deputy Commissioner in Rangoon,

Burma – the province's second-in-command. He and his wife Georgette were well-established figures in its expatriate community, and Molly was born there on 5 November 1915. Her real name was Mary but she was always known as Molly, or 'Mol-Mal' to her family. A shy child, she had an easy – if uncomfortably hot – early childhood.

When the First World War ended she and her glamorous older sister Gwladys – born in May 1912 and nicknamed 'Gad-God' – were sent to boarding school in England. They did not meet their younger sister Nancy – born in November 1918 and nicknamed 'Nan-Non' – until she joined them in England, aged five. Thereafter Molly had a lifelong affinity with her. The girls barely saw their parents from one year to the next. It was not an ideal family dynamic but notions of duty and resilience were ingrained, even as the Raj tottered.

Rodney had also been born into what was then called the 'upper middle class', on 5 May 1908, a year after his sister Pamela. The son of Ernest Drake, a Harley Street doctor, and his wife Violet, he grew up in Redhill, Surrey, and was educated at Marlborough College* in Wiltshire. Thereafter he trained as an engineer with the London and North Eastern Railway (LNER), before moving to Rangoon in 1931 to work as an assistant engineer for the Bombay Burmah Trading Corporation (BBTC). Able, game and decent, he quickly established himself as another stalwart of the expat community and was often turned to for advice.

Molly sailed to Rangoon upon leaving school, arriving in December 1933. She and Rodney met at one of the many entertainments that kept the British amused, and they recognised a deeper compatibility beneath their superficial differences. For all Rodney's conviviality, he was thoughtful and empathetic, while Molly's self-effacement was a cover for her keenly observant mind. Both were artistic and enjoyed writing – Rodney's stories and songs tended to be humorous, while her work had a more existential, even fatalistic bent.

They married in the Cathedral Church of the Holy Trinity in

---

* Pronounced 'maulbruh'.

Rangoon on Wednesday, 14 April 1937, when he was twenty-eight and she twenty-one, and spent a happy honeymoon in rural Burma. Molly, however, struggled to adjust to married life and shortly after their return to Rangoon suffered a breakdown. Her father had recently retired, so it was decided that she should return to London and stay with her parents in Chelsea. For a time she was unable to face the outside world, but regained her strength and returned to Rodney after a few months. She had no more such episodes, and Gabrielle surmises that her father's unwavering support gave her lifelong equanimity thereafter.

Rodney and Molly were in New York on BBTC business when war broke out in Europe in September 1939. It was inevitable that the Japanese would eventually invade Burma, to sever the Allies' access to its rubber and to China, so Rodney joined the Artisan Works Company, using his engineering training counter-intuitively to blow up bridges. It was dangerous work and the order to retreat brought no more safety for Molly: she and Nancy – who had married Rodney's friend Chris McDowall – trekked through malaria-infested jungle to safety in India, where they nervously awaited news of their husbands.

Rodney had been appointed Embarkation Officer at Shwegin, tasked with loading ragged and enfeebled Allied troops onto decrepit ferries that sustained heavy fire as they sailed for India. There it was monsoon season; they slept in the open, and many, including him, caught dysentery. He finally staggered into Delhi in April 1943. His dysentery was replaced by hepatitis, but he never complained of the horrors he had witnessed and experienced, reflecting Molly's lifelong mantra (as recalled by Gabrielle): 'Never be a moaner or a groaner.'

Upon his recovery, the BBTC tasked Rodney with setting up a sawmill in the hill station of Jhelum, in the Himalayan foothills. Gabrielle Mary Drake (known as 'Gay', 'Birdy' or 'the Bird' to the family) was born on 30 March 1944, and when the Japanese were routed in May 1945 her parents moved back to Rangoon, settling at 11 Mission Road. Nancy and Chris also returned to the city, and life resumed its earlier routine, with wartime sufferings taken as read and not dwelt upon.

When Burma's post-war administration was set up, Rodney's tact, charm and administrative talent were recognised in his appointment to its House of Representatives. He also faced the complicated task of rebuilding the BBTC's business as its manager and chief engineer. 'It was an arduous assignment, with the ravages of war to be repaired and numerous military and civilian requirements to be met,'[2] stated a later profile of him, and in the immediate post-war years he was required to travel widely.

Family was his top priority, though, and Nicholas Rodney Drake was delivered by Dr Pereira in Rangoon's Dufferin Hospital at 7.15 a.m. on Saturday, 19 June 1948. His birthweight was a solid 9 lb and Molly remained in hospital with him for eight days. Like his bright, outgoing sister, he was cherished from the moment he appeared. 'When he was born Nicholas looked exactly like Seymour Hicks,'[*] wrote Molly in a wry journal of his infancy:

> He could hold his head up at birth. The second day of his life he looked the image of his grandfather, Idwal Lloyd.[†] At birth his hair was very thick and almost black and grew low on his forehead. He was rather a nice nectarine colour, but in spite of his weight his legs were terribly thin. This was soon remedied. I breastfed him for just under six months. He was a very greedy baby. No table manners at all.
>
> Nicholas was easy to wean and made no fuss about any new foods . . . He first smiled on 18 July 1948 after his 10 p.m. feed, the cause being his Daddy's spectacles. By seven months he could move all over the place by means of a swimming action along the floor. He took his first steps at thirteen months. His sister was four years old when he was born. He found her an unfailing source of amusement.

Gabrielle was less enchanted at first, having been longing for a sister. However, this soon 'gave way to delight in this bouncing baby with jet-black hair which grew in a Regency-style quiff'.[3]

'Nicky', as he was called in childhood, spent his first months in Mission Road, where his hair turned first blond and then the deep

---

[*] Sir Edward Seymour Hicks (1871–1949), a celebrated comic actor-producer.
[†] Born in 1878, Sir Idwal had died in a nursing home in Hampshire on 6 March 1946, leaving an estate valued at £3,359 (approximately £100,000 in 2022).

brown it would remain. He was vaccinated and circumcised by the family doctor, James Lusk,* and christened into the Church of England by the Bishop of Rangoon on 28 November, with Nancy and Chris acting as godparents, alongside Molly and Rodney's friends John Shelley and Hope Hughes.

The Drakes loved Burma but, prompted by the ongoing turmoil, in early 1949 Rodney accepted the BBTC's offer to become director (and joint chairman) in Bombay. Before taking up the post he had six months' leave, which the family spent in England, arriving by sea on 23 April. It was Nick's first visit to his homeland, though he was too young to know it. Returning in October, they set up home in Bombay, decamping after humid working weeks to a mud-floored seaside cabin in the suburb of Marve Beach, where Nick learned to swim at a very young age.

It was a happy pattern, but Rodney and Molly were realists. Britain's glory days in the East were over, and they had no desire to replicate Molly's experience by packing their children off to school in England. By Gabrielle's account, her parents 'found the thought of separation from each other, if she accompanied the children back to England, intolerable'.[4] In any case, the prospect of early retirement – the convention if you worked out East – did not appeal to Rodney's energetic nature. It was therefore fortuitous that, in the summer of 1951, he was headhunted to join an agricultural engineering firm in the Midlands, the Wolseley Sheep Shearing Machine Co., Ltd.

They once again packed all their possessions and steamed home aboard RMS *Caledonia*. Having recently turned three, Nick would be too young to remember Burma or India, and was ineligible for most of the entertainments on board. His seven-year-old sister took enthusiastic part, though. 'I was a dreadful exhibitionist,' she later said.[5] They reached Liverpool on 20 August 1951. In Gabrielle's words, 'With our return to England, the prelude to Nick's and my lives ended and we started the process of becoming proper people.'[6]

Wolseley was based in Birmingham, so while house-hunting the Drakes stayed in the Glebe Hotel in nearby Barford. Gabrielle and

---

* James Wallace Lusk MBE, MD, ChB was the uncle of Nick's first biographer, Patrick Humphries.

Nick had no difficulty assimilating to British life, and she recalls being enchanted by novelties like 'seeing snow for the first time and being able to drink water straight from the tap . . . I remember thinking that was extraordinary.'[7] The family celebrated her eighth birthday at the Glebe on 30 March 1952, by which time Rodney had undertaken to buy Far Leys from a local stockbroker named Jim Smith.

Molly delighted in creating a comfortable, elegant domestic world for her family. In particular, she oversaw the installation of a new and immaculate kitchen whose centrepiece was a cream-coloured Aga. 'She deeply loved her husband and her children and creating a home for them became her primary purpose in life,' as Gabrielle puts it.[8] Nan greatly assisted her in accomplishing this. According to Gabrielle,

> having been nanny in England to other retired colonial families, she knew more about 'Home' – an austere post-war England – than either Molly or Rodney did themselves. She it was who guided Molly through the complexities of post-war rationing, and helped her set up a household without servants, something Molly had never known before in her married life.[9]

In September 1954 the household was joined by Nan's niece Naw Ma Naw, who was born on 27 August 1914 and travelled from Burma to make a new life in England. Gabrielle: 'Naw came to us having lost all her family in Burma except for one daughter, who died – to her great grief – during the first year she was with us, so that, unlike Nan, she had no family save us.' She remained a gentle constant in their lives and, like Nan, called Molly and Rodney 'Mummy' and 'Daddy'.

'Even though she was the same age as my parents, it was like having a third child for them,' explains Gabrielle. 'She was quiet and reserved compared to Nan, but they were a great double act. Nan was more of a nanny and Naw more of a housekeeper.' In the short term they attended to a lot of the minutiae of Gabrielle and Nick's lives, but they weren't taken for granted and, as Gabrielle puts it, 'Being uncivil to them was a worse crime than being uncivil to our parents.' Joanna Lodder's younger sister Janie was often at Far Leys and says that above all Nan and Naw 'gave Rodney and Molly *time* – to read, to write music and poetry, to garden'.

Much of Rodney's time was, of course, devoted to his new job. Founded in 1889, Wolseley had made huge profits by mechanising the laborious sheep-shearing process, but when the wartime demand for its machinery dried up, the firm seemed in danger of – at best – stagnating. In Rodney it was hoping for a leader who would transform its fortunes with energy and innovation. He worked hard to do so, launching a variety of new products including the popular 'Merry Tiller' garden rotavator, and the board recognised his success by appointing him sole managing director in October 1953.

At home he rejoiced in his large and varied garden, keeping chickens (rationing still being in force) and tinkering in his workshop, where his children often visited him. Although Nick and Gabrielle's age and gender difference made them imperfect playmates, they had a harmonious relationship as they grew up. For her, 'I suppose it was a typical sort of brother-sister relationship, really – annoying elder sister, annoying younger brother – but I certainly loved him dearly.'[10]

Far Leys was a home Rodney and Molly wanted to share, whether through drinks, dinners, children's parties or their annual Christmas Eve celebration (with carols led by the village choir). They slotted into a local social circuit including well-meaning and conventional couples such as John and Pam Lodder, Cyril and Biddy Hughes, Charles and Margharita Chatwin and Evan and Mildred Norton. 'My parents became great friends with them as soon as they met in 1952,' says Guy Norton, who – having been born in November 1939 – was a generation older than the Drake children but knew the family well.[*]

> Molly and Rodney were exceptionally respected in the area. He was the best possible example of an English gentleman, upstanding but warm and non-judgemental. He was hardworking but it would have been anathema for him to have been seen to be striving. Modesty was much more his style. He had the stiff-upper-lip demeanour of

---

[*] He was, however, a close friend of the Chatwins' son, the writer Bruce Chatwin (1940–89), with whom he was about to start at Marlborough, and whom Nick knew peripherally.

his generation but was unquestionably a loving father and would never have made himself unapproachable to his children. Molly was warm, intelligent and attractive, and would have been a wonderful person to find yourself next to at a dinner party.

They were cultured and well-read, not small-minded. There were a lot of suburban snobs around but Molly and Rodney were accepting of everyone. They would never have dreamed of calling anyone 'common', as others did. There was no front with them, they were absolutely natural, with nothing flashy about them – they lived comfortably and elegantly without being rich.

Indeed, the Drakes owed their affluence to Rodney's talent and hard work; there were no inherited means on either side, let alone a sense of entitlement about their lifestyle. 'It was never extravagant,' according to Gabrielle. 'It was comfortable without being lavish or overblown.'[11]

Rodney and Molly's ostensible roles – breadwinner and housewife – don't reflect the respect they held each other in and the strength they drew from each other. 'They had a balanced marriage – they were equal in force,' continues Guy. 'It's inconceivable to me that they would ever have shouted at one another, or even disagreed other than very politely.' Gabrielle says that 'their marriage gave my mother the deepest emotional happiness, fulfilment and security':

> It was certainly something *she* believed. As children, my brother and I were always aware of two facts: firstly, our parents deeply loved us; and secondly, my parents loved each other *even more* than they loved us. I think this gives any child a feeling of security and freedom. It certainly did to me.
>
> There was no lack of physical demonstration of their affection; we were not the frigid family so often imagined to be the norm in the English upper middle classes. My mum was incredibly tactile, though maybe a bit reticent in front of strangers, as one was in those days. The joy of her was that she was so available for a hug, and to others outside her family. I always thought that my dad thought so too, and that she taught him to be tactile. My dad, though he loved it if one flung one's arms around him, was always just that tiny bit embarrassed, whereas my mum, if she hadn't instigated the physical

contact (more likely), revelled in it. As children Nick and I both relished this, especially as she looked so beautiful, always wore scent and smelled divine.

All who knew the Drakes vividly recall their warmth and hospitality. 'They engulfed you when you went to see them,' Guy summarises. 'Far Leys reeked of happiness, that's why I loved going there. To an outsider, the Drakes seemed to be the perfect family.'

2

A Totally Warm And Communicative Kid

— ~ —

RODNEY DID NOT continue to write songs after returning to England, though he happily accompanied himself as he sang at the piano. Much more influential on Nick's nascent musicality was Molly. Aside from running the household, her main pastime was writing songs. Some were humorous or for children, some were more personal and philosophical, but – crucially – from earliest childhood Nick absorbed the sound of her singing, composing and practising them all.

Although she wasn't embarrassed to be heard working on them, or to perform them in front of family and close friends during the musical soirées their circle often hosted, she did not discuss them or the emotions that underpinned them, and Gabrielle and Nick didn't ask. 'Music was a private joy, as was her poetry,' as Gabrielle puts it:[1]

> All her life, both provided a retreat and a place from which to draw inner strength. And though she was happy to play and sing her songs to friends and family, their composing was always an intensely private affair, and she would sit for hours alone at a piano, working out words and music.

In doing so she was greatly assisted by Rodney's early adoption of home recording, typifying his fascination with gadgets and technology. Gabrielle: 'One day he staggered in to the house after work, carrying what looked like an enormous green trunk: it was an early reel-to-reel recording machine. It must have been one of the first pieces of domestic recording equipment on the market – real state-of-the-art stuff';[2] 'Understanding, as he always did, the private nature of her creative work, my father would set up the machine and leave her to record her songs on her own.'[3]

Despite her devotion and availability to her children, Gabrielle and Nick took it for granted that Molly was to an extent inscrutable. For Gabrielle she was 'something of an enigma . . . There was always a part of my mother that remained unknowable, unattainable and her own. All of us – especially my father – understood this. It was no mystery to us.'[4] She concealed her depths from those who didn't know her intimately, to whom she could seem distant, if ever gracious and friendly. 'I knew she was musical but had no idea that she wrote and sang songs,' says Guy Norton.

Although her home recordings were carefully preserved, it didn't occur to Molly to seek a professional outlet for her material, and none of her work was circulated in her lifetime. Nonetheless, Nick grew up regarding songwriting as a perfectly normal and worthwhile activity. 'Nick was composing songs at a very early age,' recalls Gabrielle. 'When he was three or four, two of his great passions were cowboys and food. I can remember two songs he wrote then – one was about a cowboy in a book [by Lois Lenski] called *Cowboy Small*: "Oh Cowboy Small, oh Cowboy Small / All the other cowboys call Cowboy Small." The other was about celery and tomatoes.'[5] Nick also had a cowboy outfit, and a teepee pitched in the garden.

His imagination was beginning to spark: shortly before his fourth birthday he amused Molly by insisting that a flower smelled yellow. He lacked local playmates in the short term but was contented and self-contained. While Rodney was at work and Gabrielle was at school, he and Nan might head to Birmingham (which was favoured over Coventry for shopping), potter around the village or play in the garden. 'He'd spend a very long time in the garden by himself, wandering around,' said his father.[6] His mother remembered: 'His sister was always saying, "Oh, can't we have someone to tea?" and "Can't we do this? Can't we do that?" Nick didn't mind, he was perfectly happy amusing himself and getting on with his own pastimes.'[7]

He also spent a lot of time in the nursery, which contained a wireless and a wind-up gramophone. 'There was music going on in the family the whole time,' as Molly put it.[8] 'We were all into music in a very big way. Every time any music started, Nick as a tiny child would stand and conduct, and we always used to say, "He's going to be a famous conductor!"' For Rodney, 'Any form of music was interesting to him. We had certain records which were favourites of ours, and some of those attracted him very much. I remember *The Swan of Tuonela* by Sibelius – I told him the legend . . . It rather frightened him, I think.'[9] His mother added that he 'sang himself to sleep every night'.[10]

Molly was determined to encourage his nascent musicality and began to teach him piano as soon as he was able, though he was initially resistant (especially disliking finger exercises). In the summer of 1953, just before turning five, he joined Gabrielle at Hurst House, a friendly private day school on the outskirts of Henley-in-Arden, five miles away. That July his teacher, Judith Jones, wrote: 'Nicky has spent a satisfactory first term. He appeared worried at first, but having adjusted himself to the new life and routine he settled down happily . . . He writes figures and letters well.'

The Drakes shared the school run with the Hicks family, who also lived in Tanworth. Diana was a year younger than Gabrielle: 'Molly sang as we bumped along in her little Morris Minor, which always smelled sweetly of her scent. The greatest treat was to stop for the famous Tudor Ices on the way home. [Rodney] was very entertaining, quizzing us on current affairs and telling (and asking for) stories.'[11] At a bend in the road on the way out of Danzey they passed a tree with a huge fungus growing out of it; Molly soon had them singing 'Shall we see the mushroom tree?' to the tune of an old nursery rhyme.

Diana's brother Andrew was a year older than Nick, but they became playmates. He recalls Nick as 'a totally warm and communicative kid whom everyone liked':

> He was gentle and kind, and joined in and asserted himself without any lack of confidence but avoiding being pushy. He was never aggressive and always without malice . . . He was not the most boisterous among us but he was sociable, joined in all the fun and got messy like everyone. He was happy, healthy and normal . . .[12]
> We'd fight and fall in the muddy stream and have fun without any restraint. In summer we played in the extensive garden behind [Far

Leys]. The lawn sloped down to the fields and a marshy stream flowing out of a pond on the other side of the road, where Nick and I would happily get ourselves covered in mud.[13]

The boys also devised indoor games, one of which involved dashing along the upstairs corridor together before throwing themselves onto a mat and sliding the remaining distance down the polished floor. On one occasion they got the timing wrong and Nick landed on Andrew's leg, breaking it. 'Molly and Nick visited me, prostrate in my bedroom. They brought me some presents – activity games and a Noddy book – and signed my plaster. I distinctly remember Nick saying that I had been very brave . . .'[14]

Molly and Rodney's emphasis on good manners was clear:

> With adults his behaviour was impeccable, his goodbyes and thank yous perfectly rehearsed, always addressing Mr or Mrs Double-Barrel by name. Even unbroken, his voice had a hint of the low huskiness we hear in his singing. He was the handsome, delightful child that every parent would want their own to be.[15]

Nick's best friend at Hurst House was Joanna and Janie's cousin Dave Lodder. He was three months Nick's junior and lived with his family in an old farmhouse named Whitley, in Henley-in-Arden. 'I loved visiting Far Leys,' he says.

> Their household was different to ours – Whitley was a farm, there were five children and we tended to live in the kitchen (the one room that was always warm – we didn't have central heating like the Drakes). Far Leys was very comfortable, with deep carpets throughout. They even had a room just for drinks!* It had a sink, a cupboard full of glasses and dozens of soda syphons which we were allowed to make fizzy orange from. There was a routine, but Rodney and Molly weren't strict – nor did they have any need to be.

Janie was a few months older and also appreciated the calm, elegant atmosphere at Far Leys. 'Molly loved arranging flowers, making the house pretty and welcoming. Rodney never appeared

---

* The pantry.

to raise his voice and was immensely kind and had concern and interest in all we did.' Family lore had it that Nick was insistent as a child that he wanted to marry Janie. To her,

> He was always self-contained but didn't seem unusually intelligent or precocious. I wouldn't say he was ever mischievous, and I think Molly and Rodney might have been a little over-protective of him. A lot of Dave's and my playing involved bikes and streams, and he wouldn't be allowed to join in certain games.

Nonetheless, most of their activities involved being outdoors in all weathers. Much of their time was spent in the garden at Far Leys. 'On one side was a croquet lawn, which Nick and I used to have imaginary swimming races up and down,' continues Dave.

> When the Drakes' gardener was mowing we took it in turns to run as close as we could in front without getting hit. We built a den in the corner from which we could see the road and watch the rare person who walked down it, in the knowledge that they couldn't see us. There was an orchard containing a hut [in fact a traditional Burmese 'spirit house'] built by Nan and Naw, with a thatched roof that was caving in. That was a great place to play. We once hid in the bushes with an airgun and waited for a bird to come to the bird table. Eventually a bullfinch showed up and we shot it. (I don't recall who pulled the trigger.) We were very proud of ourselves, but Nick's parents weren't at all impressed, so we then felt guilty and tried to justify it by saying they ate all the buds off the fruit trees.
>
> In the holidays we'd cycle to each other's houses, then go off on our bikes with a picnic and have adventures. They were great days – everything seemed so exciting. We climbed trees, hunted for bird's eggs, built dens in hay bales (it scares me to death thinking how dangerous that was) and sometimes went fishing. In the winter we went tobogganing and found a frozen pool. Nick had read somewhere that if you spread your weight around, you wouldn't go through ice, so he lay on top of the toboggan with his arms and legs stretched out. Needless to say, it went straight through and into the freezing water.

Rodney and Molly always took an interest in their children's activities. For example, recalls Dave,

Around the time that Roger Bannister ran his four-minute mile [on 6 May 1954] Nick and I decided we wanted to do it too, so Rodney measured out exactly one mile on the village sports field and timed us as we ran it. When I stayed overnight he would sometimes produce his huge tape machine in the evening and record us fooling about. That was a huge excitement.

Nick showed an impish sense of humour. 'There was a field next to Far Leys with a horse in it, and he told me that if I jumped onto its back it would run around the field. I did so and it took off like a rocket, with me clinging on for dear life as it galloped towards the barbed wire.' On another occasion, 'Rodney had bought a new Rover, so Nick and I sneaked into the garage and got into it. Nick was showing off all the features, and without me knowing he heated up the cigarette lighter, then told me to touch it, so of course I burned my finger. Rather a mean joke!'

Nick sometimes saw his cousins Grania ('Gogs'), Lois ('Losa') and Virginia ('Gingey'), the daughters of his aunt Gwladys. Grania and Lois were a generation older than Nick and didn't know him well, but their half-sister Virginia was much closer in age and occasionally came to stay at Far Leys, where she found him excellent and intrepid company.

Once we'd been climbing out of windows and he got stuck on a ledge fairly high up. He told me to go and get help, but I was so afraid to admit that we'd been doing something naughty that he'd been up there for ages when I finally told them.

Above all, his cousins remember the Drakes' gaiety. Nick was quick to laugh – as Molly put it, 'He had a very great sense of humour, he was a great laugher.'[16] Of course, his youthful sense of humour was not sophisticated. 'Once he and I went to the village telephone box, which had a directory in it,' says Virginia. 'We looked up all the people we could find whose surname had "bottom" in them and tried to call them. We thought it was the funniest thing in the world, we killed ourselves laughing.'

In the main, however, Nick's wry, ironic sense of humour took after his father's gentle sense of the absurd. 'Rodney was very funny,' says Virginia. 'We used to go on a family Christmas outing to Bertram Mills Circus at Olympia in London, and he would lead the way through the crowd, holding his umbrella over his head with his bowler hat on top of it. I remember that more than the circus.' Gabrielle confirms that 'Nick didn't do rollicking humour, and nor did my dad'. As Virginia puts it: 'Nick had a hoarse little chuckle, low-key but infectious. The family jokes would always bring that out. I can hear it now.'

Nick's self-effacement stood in contrast to his sister, who knew from the age of eight that she wanted to be an actress. His own stage debut came as a rat in a school production of *The Pied Piper of Hamelin*, but his talent was better deployed aged seven in late 1955, when he was cast as Ralph Rackstraw in Gilbert and Sullivan's *H.M.S. Pinafore*, performed in the Memorial Hall in Henley. 'He was the romantic lead, which he railed against mightily,' says Gabrielle. 'He had this beautiful soprano voice (obviously why he was chosen) but had great difficulty taking large enough breaths to sing whole phrases. This was what I remember him and Mum struggling with!'

By the mid-1950s the Drakes were firmly established in the area and Wolseley was steadily growing under Rodney's leadership. In 1958 he secured its long-term future by merging it with the Hughes Cushion Tyre Company (headed by his friend and neighbour Cyril Hughes) to create Wolseley-Hughes. 'He was fantastic at managing people – calm, diplomatic, friendly,' reflects Guy Norton.

As his obituary stated many years later, 'Rodney Drake combined, to a most unusual degree, exceptional skill in all aspects of mechanical engineering with a high order of administrative ability and financial acumen.'[17] This was borne out by his becoming a council member of the Birmingham Chamber of Commerce (a post he held for fifteen years) and chairman of the Midland branch of the Institute of British Agricultural Engineers.

He was no workaholic, though. As the effects of the war receded and rationing ended, the Drakes benefited from the economic boom. In particular, summer family holidays were sacrosanct. They visited Ireland, France, Germany, Spain, Holland and Italy, as well as spots around the UK such as Guernsey and Scotland. In August 1956, for example, they drove to the west coast of France. 'Nick and I made up a lovely new game called water volley,' wrote Gabrielle in her journal. 'One person had his or her back to the waves and sometimes a wave took you by surprise and knocked you over . . . Then Nick saw masses of crabs and started screaming, so Mum had to come and fetch him.'

The Drakes kept in touch with a variety of so-called Old Burma Hands, as well as hosting tennis parties on their lawn or visiting local friends. 'Our mothers did French classes together and became good friends,' says Jeremy Harmer.

My first recollection of Nicky (as he was called then) and Gabrielle is them coming to play tennis and have a dip in our little stand-up pool. Molly was sweet and kind, with a beautiful smile and speaking voice, and Rodney simply seemed the perfect gentleman. They appeared to inhabit a wonderfully leafy, enclosed world.

3

Recognised As Efficient

URST HOUSE HAD been an idyllic introduction to school life,
but Rodney and Molly were determined to give Gabrielle
and Nick what they considered the best education possible, which
meant moving on to boarding school. Aged twelve, Gabrielle had
gone to her mother's austere alma mater, Wycombe Abbey, some
eighty miles away in High Wycombe, and in early May 1957 it was
the eight-year-old Nick's turn to be sent away.

His parents decided against the local Arden House (where many
of his Hurst House contemporaries, including Dave Lodder, were
headed) and settled on Eagle House in Sandhurst, Berkshire, whose
skimpy magazine, *The Eagle*, boasted at the time that among its alumni,
'holders of many important posts and distinctions are represented'.

It did not reflect emotional coldness on his parents' part. It was
simply the convention for boys of their background, and means, to
go to preparatory ('prep') school until the age of thirteen, 'public'
school until eighteen, and then to university (which really meant
Oxford or Cambridge) if they were up to it. Uprooting Nick from
his happy home for months at a time was collateral damage that had
to be borne (at a cost of eight guineas a week) to maximise his
chance of fulfilling his potential, becoming as rounded an individual
as possible, and ultimately working as a doctor, a lawyer, an engineer,
a soldier, a diplomat or any of the other respectable callings typical
in his family circle.

Eagle House was a feeder for Wellington College, the tough,
military-oriented public school next door, and therefore placed strong
emphasis on discipline. The school was small, with ninety-five boys
overseen by eight masters and one mistress, but occupied a twenty-
acre site that allowed for plenty of outdoor activity.

According to its prospectus,

> As character-training must play such a large part in true education, we endeavour to teach them to be well-disciplined, good-mannered and public-spirited in their outlook. We hope too that the chapel services, which are designed to appeal to boys of that age, will help them to acquire a firm Christian basis to their lives. At the same time, it is our duty to train the boys to put their talents – intellectual, physical and cultural – to the best possible use . . . We try to prepare boys for a full life and to teach them to stand on their own feet, whilst at the same time preserving a friendly, homely atmosphere.

Talk of a 'homely atmosphere' was carefully calibrated for parents like Rodney and Molly, as access to their sons was strictly limited. 'Boys are allowed out three times a term, on Sundays, from 11.45 a.m. to 6.15 p.m. . . . There is no special half-term, but parents are invited to the Christmas entertainment and the sports finals at the end of the Michaelmas and Summer terms.' A good deal of trust was involved in handing Nick over, but (as the prospectus proudly concluded): 'The school is recognised as efficient by the Ministry of Education.'

Wearing his uniform of a blazer, blue pullover, grey flannel shirt with red tie and blue corduroy shorts, Nick was driven the hundred miles to Eagle House for the start of the Summer term.* 'On the drive up to the main building were two leering stone eagles, which clearly communicated "Abandon hope, all ye who enter here" to me,' recalls his contemporary and friend Chris Cobley. The foreboding atmosphere was exacerbated by the school's proximity to Broadmoor, Britain's best-known high-security psychiatric hospital, whose eerie siren was tested every Monday morning.

The school's pipe-smoking Headmaster (and proprietor) Paul Wootton greeted the Drakes in the entrance hall, where big-game trophies hung alongside pictures of the Queen and Winston Churchill. Having said goodbye to his parents, Nick was shown to

---

* At that time it was perfectly common to join or leave private schools at the beginning or end of any term.

his dormitory and began his new life. The regime was basic by modern standards. 'Pastoral care was non-existent,' says Chris.

> It was a harsh environment from the moment we woke up every day, shortly before seven. We chucked on a dressing gown and trooped down to a cold changing room, where we stood naked in shivering lines by a freezing shower. Every three seconds a master clapped his hands, one little boy got out and the next went under.

No one was permitted to leave the dining room before finishing their (by general consensus revolting) food; one boy remembers being forced to eat a rotten egg and promptly vomiting. 'We were not well-fed and were permanently cold,' says Chris. 'We sat on radiators to warm up, so we all had chilblains and chapped knees, as we wore shorts all year round. There wasn't a culture of bullying, but a lot of teasing went on.'

As another of Nick's contemporaries, Hugh Dunford Wood, puts it:

> It was probably a regular prep school for those days. You quickly developed a carapace and had two characters – home and school. A sense of humour got you through an awful lot. The atmosphere was very much that you kept your head down and assimilated whatever happened to you.

Nick swiftly adapted. 'He was a very strong character at school, they always said in the reports we got,' his father said.[1]

'I am well pleased with the way in which he is shaping,' Mr Wootton wrote to Molly and Rodney on 15 May.

> We have put him in our bottom form but one, with two other new boys . . . I am most impressed by his general manner and demeanour and I feel confident that whatever his attainments, he will at least be a most popular member of the school. I do hope you hear cheerfully from him.

Gabrielle does not remember her brother being homesick, and the letters he sent home suggest he was happy, though he perhaps wrote them under a degree of scrutiny. A typical example, written on 30 June 1957, shortly after he'd turned nine, ran exactly as follows:

Thank you for sending my watch it is very useful. In chapel this morning it was so hot that a boy fainted and he looked rather funny because you see he is in the chior and he looked like a tin soldier falling out of the chior stalls because he was so stiff. Last night it was so hot that we were aloud to take all are blankets off including are sheets and we wern't really soposed to but our dorms second let us take are pyjamas tops of. It has been very hot latley. Just now a boy has split a bottle of ink. Well I must go now because I have got to rite to granny. Love from Nicky.

The school took its academic obligations seriously, though Hugh remembers: 'There were some oddballs on the staff, leftovers from the war who didn't know what to do with themselves. They certainly didn't need a teaching qualification – just to be able to chuck a cricket ball and stay one chapter ahead of the boys in lessons.' Corporal punishment was unquestioned – Mr Wootton meted it out with a Jokari paddle – and the staff could be intimidating. Chris says: 'Mr Huxtable, who became the deputy head, was terrifying, and Mr Ash literally ground his teeth when he was angry. "Butch" Keating, the maths teacher, used to chuck the board-duster at people, which was pretty dangerous, but we took it in good part.'

Although the world of the school was fundamentally odd, especially in comparison to Far Leys and Hurst House, Nick muddled along. 'He wasn't exactly what you'd call gregarious, he didn't make friends with everybody, but he had a few friends and they were very good friends,' said his mother.[2] 'Our relationships were close,' Chris confirms, 'as we spent all our time together. In some ways we were closer than siblings – but we barely knew each other's first names, and certainly wouldn't have called each other by them. Everyone used surnames.'

None of Nick's contemporaries recalls him with anything but fondness. Oliver Stapleton says he was 'a straightforward person, tall, gangly and quiet'. For Chris he was 'graceful, unusually beautiful and slightly whimsical, with a daydreamy quality', while Hugh calls him 'sweet and shy – but suave. He was handsome and seemed bright and quietly confident, as well as being good at games. He was a golden boy, I wanted to be like him one day.'

Indeed, his quiet confidence soon began to pay dividends. Alongside academic achievement, music, sport and drama were valued at Eagle House, and he acquitted himself well at all of them without ever pushing himself forward. At the end of his first year he was awarded the cup for 'General Efficiency'. Chris Cobley won it another year and explains: 'It was for boys who kept their heads down and got on with life (and perhaps were fools enough to put their hands up and volunteer for things).'

In Nick's spare time he could read or participate in art, carpentry, gardening and other activities. Messing around outside also formed a major part of daily life. 'In break time we would play with our Dinky toys (which were almost all of a military sort) at "Dinky Base", a group of Scotch pines amongst whose roots generations of children had dug tunnels and made dens,' says Chris. Legend had it that an enormous rock in the grounds concealed the entrance to a secret passage, and much time was devoted to seeking it. Ian Fleming's James Bond books were banned, so the boys buried a few in a tin in the woods and occasionally exhumed them in search of racy passages. They also invented their own blend of hockey and golf, which they called 'holf'.

The main sports were rugby (Michaelmas), hockey (Lent) and cricket (Summer), at all of which Nick did well, consistently playing for the school. Tall for his age, he was marked out as a promising runner in his first year's edition of *The Eagle* and praised as an outstanding athlete the following year ('Drake ran in the senior division in spite of his being under age'). In the summer of 1959, when he was ten, he played cricket for the Second XI, but it was not a game for which he ever had much enthusiasm.

He fared better in rugby: in its coverage of the 1960 season, *The Eagle* referred to 'Drake's length of stride' and 'some thrilling running', as a result of which he was awarded another cup. Boxing was compulsory and Nick did well enough at it, though he didn't enjoy it. He also swam strongly and shot on the school's range; these activities were overseen by Sergeant Pye, a stickler who packed miscreants off to run around the grounds with their arms above their heads.

Nick was in the choir, and piano playing became more important to him as the 1950s progressed. 'We plugged on, and then he went to school and had some proper lessons,' his mother said. 'And it was one of the proudest days of my life when he said to me: "Oh, Mum, I'm glad you made me go on, because now it's my favourite thing."'[3] At Eagle House he was taught by a Mr Bean, and the ability to read music would stand him in good stead in years to come, though he never took grade exams. Gabrielle remembers him being keen on the hugely popular pianist Russ Conway, and aged eleven he wrote home to announce that 'Stapleton is being nice this term and we have good fun playing the piano. We have decided to go into the business when we grow up (in music)!'*

They were perhaps inspired by the example of their fifty-one-year-old French master, John Watson, a hobbyist songwriter whose outmoded composition 'Looking High, High High' (echoing the school's motto, 'Sublimiora Petamus': 'Let us seek higher things') came second in the 1960 Eurovision Song Contest.[†] Eagle House did not encourage enthusiasm for popular music, but permitted the boys to watch the British heats on the BBC that February, much to their excitement.

Pop was certainly not frowned upon at Far Leys: although Rodney and Molly were by nature conservative, they were by no means reactionary. Nick was starting to develop critical faculties and kept a log ('My Gramophone Records', with a family of ducks on its cover) of his growing collection. His grudging entries in the 'Remarks' column ranged from Ray Charles's 'Don't Let the Sun Catch You Cryin'' (*'Can't remember'*), Johnny Restivo's 'Dear Someone' (*'Utterly pointless'*), Sammy Turner's 'I'd Be a Fool Again' (*'You already are!'*) and Johnny Shanly's 'Makin' Love to You' (*'Soppy and utterly wet'*), to Floyd Robinson's 'Tattletale' (*'Not Bad'*) and Neil Sedaka's 'Forty Winks Away' (*'Quite good'*).

As for classical music, he felt that Prokofiev's *Peter and the Wolf* – a school production of which he had recently appeared in – had a '*Good Story*' and Gilbert and Sullivan's *The Gondoliers* had '*Very*

---

* Oliver himself remembers nothing of this.
† The song was performed by Bryan Johnson. Mr Watson had other songs recorded by Alma Cogan and Diana Dors.

good tunes'. His highest praise, however, was reserved for his mother's home recordings. Under 'Title of Piece', for 'M. Drake' he wrote *'There are Lots of them'*, and his critique read: *'Very good indeed'*.

Nick wasn't writing songs but he had started to devise his own pieces on the piano and occasionally made recordings of himself. On one occasion he solemnly announced that he would now play Beethoven's Moonlight Sonata, paused the tape, put on a record of it by Wilhelm Kempf, then resumed the recording. It was a solid gag – but involved wiping a precious poetry recital by his sister.

Despite Rodney's fondness for machinery, the family had no television until 1961, though Nick had plenty of other things to do when at home. Reading and music-making were the two main standbys, but he frequently saw friends and was closely involved in building a go-kart with his father. Over Christmas 1960 he went skiing for the first time, staying with his family in a hotel in Little Klosters, and towards the end of the holiday he began to keep a staccato diary that gives a vivid insight into his life aged twelve and a half:

> Mucked about in garden . . . Gay went to dance. Me too young
> – swiz . . . Have to go to dentist . . . In afternoon saw *Man in the
> Moon* in cinema. Kenneth More v. good . . . Went to pantomime
> – *Sleeping Beauty*. Rather wet first half, quite good second half . . .
> Went to Oxford to see *Charley's Aunt*. V. good . . . Went to church
> in morning. To Leamington in afternoon to see Meema*. Mucked
> about with tape recorder, recorded a few things . . . Went skating
> in the morning . . . Composed music in afternoon . . . Went round
> to Hughes to watch tele [*sic*]. Saw *Lassie*.

Short though it is, the diary strikes no note of discord in his happy, conventional existence. Peter Carey, whose parents were also Old Burma Hands, was the same age and stayed at Far Leys on several occasions.

> I registered his quiet and gentle character, but the overwhelming
> memory I have is a feeling of intense childhood jealousy, because he

---

* Rodney's mother Violet, who had been a widow since October 1955.

was living at an altogether more stratospheric level in terms of clothes, lifestyle and possessions. I looked enviously at his designer jeans and suede shoes, contrasting them with my much less modish appearance.

Nick's family knew all too well how particular he was about his appearance. He was short-sighted and had to be fitted for glasses whilst at Eagle House, but always disliked wearing them or being photographed in them, and wanted his hair to be just the right length. 'He was frightfully keen on everything being exactly the way he wanted it to be,' recalled Molly.[4] 'I'll never forget the time we went to buy him a pair of bedroom slippers. We went to about fifteen shops until we found exactly the ones he'd got in mind. I think he was very meticulous, and he got what he wanted.'

His final year at Eagle House began on 16 January 1961.

Got up. 7 o'clock seemed awful . . . Have stinking cold . . . Sausages for breakfast . . . Tuck . . . 50 mins maths prep . . . Naval officer for lecture and two films of Navy . . . Thunderstorm . . . Had v. bad nightmare about hook-nosed man . . . Rained. No hockey. Swiz . . . Saw film called *Crimson Pirate* . . . Choir practice. Hope voice will break.

In keeping with most childhood diaries, the entries became increasingly sparse before ceasing altogether as of 2 February.

Nick's personality was coming into focus as he approached his teens. He was neither rebellious nor sanctimonious and was naturally able at a variety of things. He tended to keep his own counsel, however, and came across as passive. Over the course of his Eagle House career he won all the school sprinting titles in the junior, middle and senior sections, as well as being its champion hurdler, yet never gave the impression of much caring. As his final rugby report stated, 'What he lacked was an aggressive spirit' (though his imperfect vision may have been partly responsible).

His classroom performance was solid and undistinguished, with his silence being noted. 'A steady and workmanlike term,' commented his English teacher that year. 'He is unimaginative but does produce intelligent essays.' His History was deemed 'Satisfactory, but he is still "dumb" in class'. Nick's friends also found him quiet, though he was well-liked. 'Nick was always affable,' says Hugh Dickens, whose parents lived abroad. 'My mother died in 1960 and he was very kind to me about it all.'

Nick Stewart began at Eagle House in 1961 and was given the next-door peg to him in the changing room.*

> At that age four years is a gulf, so I was probably an aggravating little tick to him, but he wasn't condescending. He had a calm, quiet authority about him, as well as a winning smile. He was on the rugby team and the hockey team and was good at athletics, but he wasn't blustering or chest-thumping. He seemed a nice, well-grounded boy.

As well as having his decency and sporting and musical abilities recognised, Nick had come to be perceived as authoritative and responsible. 'He didn't really like responsibility and so on, but he always got shoved into it,' according to his father.[5]

> He didn't push himself [forward] at all, but he liked doing things well, there's no doubt about that. In the early days he tried very hard – in fact he always did try hard, old Nick. He didn't really like being in charge of things and organising things – but if he did anything he liked to do it well.

To his surprise and without aspiring to it, he was appointed Head Boy for his final term, Michaelmas 1961. 'He didn't seem energetic or proactive, he seemed to drift through life,' remembers Chris Cobley. 'I suspect he looked like the ideal advertisement for the school and would have impressed prospective parents.'

His letters home continued to indicate a cheerful engagement with all the school had to offer. Though Eagle House – like all prep schools of its time – did not provide its charges with easy lines of emotional communication to adults, there is no evidence to suggest he was ever bullied or abused.

His father felt that 'When Nick was dissatisfied with something, you could tell immediately',[6] and Gabrielle says: 'I really don't

---

* Nick went on to work for Island Records, putting together the *Heaven In A Wildflower* compilation, released in May 1985.

remember Nick being unhappy there – our parents often took us out for weekends together, and surely if he had been in distress it would have manifested itself in some way.' For Oliver Stapleton, 'Eagle House certainly wasn't a torture chamber, and I don't remember Nick being cold or hungry or miserable there. I seem to remember that he enjoyed it. I didn't have any inkling of him having problems, anyway.'

Having passed his Common Entrance exams, Nick was given a place at his father's alma mater, Marlborough College. In December he took the lead role ('Jack Pincher, of Scotland Yard') in *The Crimson Cocoanut*, a 1913 farce by 'Ian Hay' (John Hay Beith) concerning an anarchist plot to blow up the Bank of England. On that high note – seemingly the last acting role he ever undertook – he departed Eagle House, donating a cup for 'Standard Sports' as a parting gift. 'Scholastically it has been a relatively uneventful year,' the school magazine delicately stated, their sole award being the second scholarship to Felsted. None of Nick's contemporaries went on to Marlborough with him, and he never saw or communicated with any of them again.

In his final, mildly hyperbolic Headmaster's report, Paul Wootton described Nick as 'a splendidly keen, hard-working and reliable boy':

> These are attributes which have enabled him to make a first-class job of the office of Head Boy and which will ensure his future success. He has had a splendid career here in every way and has every reason for facing the future with confidence. Quite apart from his accomplishments he is a delightfully natured boy who leaves many friends behind him and will assuredly make many more in the future.

Nick had certainly had an objectively successful career at Eagle House, but he didn't make a strong personal impression on his teachers or schoolmates. Asked to recall him twenty-five years later, Wootton could only write: 'As regards music, I only remember him for his fine voice as a leading member of our chapel choir. Athletics was a sphere in which he was outstanding, in the course of what was (apparently) a very happy and normal career at the school.'[7]

'I don't recall him being artistic or musical,' says Nick Stewart. 'If you'd asked me at the time to guess which boy would go on to become an introspective folk singer, he would have been the last person I'd have named. He was a really decent fellow and destined for success, but I would have assumed he'd end up achieving something more conventional.'

4

A Rather Dreamy, Artistic Type Of Boy

$\sim$

I N THE RUN-UP to Christmas 1961 the Drakes and the Lodders decided that their respective sons should learn ballroom dancing – as good a way to keep them out of mischief as any. 'The instructress was called Mrs Pritchard,' says Dave. 'She held classes in Tanworth village hall, but Nick and I had private lessons. The trouble was, she quite obviously only wanted to dance with him. He was effortlessly good at everything.'

Perhaps in response to the many years they had spent out East, Rodney and Molly always strove to make Christmas at Far Leys special. A tree appeared in the drawing room, the house was hung with holly and mistletoe, and there were outings to the pantomime in Birmingham and the circus in London. On Christmas Eve the village choir sang carols in the hall in front of local guests, whose children sat on the stairs, as a prelude to drinks before the late service in St Mary's.

Molly's widowed mother, Lady Lloyd, would be present and correct, visiting from Oxford. 'She was long a widow and lived frugally on a small pension from the ICS,' says Gabrielle. 'She was a formidable example of the women of the British Raj, both incredibly difficult and deeply generous. She wrote tough letters in every direction if she spotted what she thought to be an infraction of The Rules.' Also present were her and Nick's aunt and uncle, Nancy and Chris McDowall. 'They couldn't have children of their own, but were very close to us. Nancy and Chris played violin and piano respectively, so they'd spend happy hours with Nick in the music room, occasionally recording their efforts as a trio.'

Nick was given another diary for Christmas, and began to write in it on New Year's Day, 1962.

Snow very powdery . . . Wrote thank-you letters till lunch . . . Dave called in and asked me to stay the night . . . Fed hens . . . Went tobogganing . . . Helped Naw with beds . . . Cleared ice away from drains . . . Went to oculist – new glasses necessary . . . Went to Solihull cinema, saw *Breakfast at Tiffany's* . . . Went to drinks with Chatwins . . . Worked on go-kart . . . Got Gay up and went for a bicycle ride with her . . . Went to ice rink . . . Went to Meema's for tea – saw *Bronco* on TV and she gave me £1 . . . Went 20 mph up Bates Lane on my bike . . . Went to Stratford for a haircut – too short . . . Mucked about with airgun . . . Went up to village on bike and bought sweets at Tibbles.

These quintessential schoolboy pursuits marked the end of one phase of his life. On Friday, 19 January, his parents drove him ninety miles south to Marlborough College, just off the centre of the Wiltshire market town from which it took its name. Founded in 1843, it sits beside an ancient hill named the Mound, and centres on 'Court', a large yard surrounded by buildings, akin to an Oxbridge college. The school does not have an enclosed campus, meaning that many of its buildings are integrated with the town, and a busy main road runs through it. It was long established as one of the country's leading independent schools, and Nick had the security of knowing his father had enjoyed his time there.* Its profile wasn't grand or aristocratic, with most pupils drawn from families similar to Nick's, and it was well run and academically demanding without sacrificing a broader sense of education.

Nick arrived alongside around 160 other nervous thirteen-year-olds from all over the country. At a time when many public schools were old-fashioned, it was their good fortune that a progressive Headmaster, John Dancy, had taken over the previous year. Nick therefore found himself in an environment whose ethos was broadly sympathetic to modern adolescence, rather than in conflict with it.

'Nick and I started at exactly the same time,' says Colin Tillie. 'I first saw him in the school outfitters, where our mothers were buying

---

* Nonetheless, the regime in Rodney's day was harsh, as is made clear in *Summoned by Bells* by John Betjeman (a couple of years his senior there): 'Doom! Shivering doom! Inexorable bells . . .' (Betjeman (2006), p. 441).

us jockstraps while we stood around in acute embarrassment. We established that we were going into the same Junior House, and went on there together.' The house in question was Barton Hill, where around forty boys spent their first eighteen months. Their Housemaster was 'Tubby' Middleton, a well-liked maths teacher, and the intention was to provide them with a soft landing, away from older boys.

Life at the bottom of the school was far from luxurious, though. 'We slept in an impersonal dormitory – no posters or anything like that,' continues Colin. 'There were no bathtubs – to wash you took an iron basin and filled it from a tap, which might be lukewarm if you were lucky. The loos were outside, and very basic – a whole row of cubicles with no doors.' In winter the younger boys were tasked with breaking the ice on them for the Seniors.

'When you left, I found myself rather bewildered, and went up to the library and read,' Nick wrote home on his first Sunday.

> Then Mr Middleton called all the new boys into the library to talk to them. He's very friendly and nice and the first thing he said was, 'Your parents pay a hell of a lot for you to come here, so for God's sake enjoy yourselves!', which was, I thought, a very good piece of advice.

As at Eagle House, he quickly assimilated this daunting new environment. His diary recorded (before petering out the following week):

> Middleton showed us around . . . Went to my form room, copied down timetable, unpacked trunk, read in library, went to be weighed . . . Had choir practice . . . Learnt to slide down banisters during Lower Chapel . . . Played billiards . . . Played hockey . . . Had first piano lesson . . . Laid tables as orderly . . . Went for a bike ride . . . Mucked around by stream . . . During evening chapel played ping-pong and won . . . Didn't do very well in German dictation.

'He's a very quiet boy, but I think he's settled in easily enough; he never appears to be unhappy,' Mr Middleton wrote to the Drakes. This is borne out by the letters Nick sent them at the start of his

Marlborough career.* Their content is quotidian – they discuss matches and cake, or request money or items of games kit he'd omitted to pack – and their tone is jaunty and affectionate, in emulation of his father's manner.

His self-contained yet amiable persona stood him in good stead. 'Marlborough was austere,' continues Colin. 'It was tricky if you were a shrinking violet, but whilst Nick wasn't an extrovert, he didn't come across as shy.' He soon made friends. Simon Crocker's first impression was of a 'tall, very gentle guy who smiled a lot, a guy who seemed to be enjoying himself'.[1] Chris Rudkin was even taller and says, 'We were kindred spirits from the start, slightly on the edge of things, and I think we recognised a certain fragility in each other. I knew I could confide in him completely and safely. He was a great listener and offered support when I was feeling fragile.'

Upon arrival all newcomers were given an IQ test, and Nick's was measured at 116. 'A score of 116 or more is considered above average,' the school explained to his parents. 'A score of 130 or higher signals a high IQ.' He was no scholar but was regarded as having academic promise and put into the Remove, a stream reserved for the more able boys.

Simon says Nick 'didn't come across as especially bright or intellectually curious. Like most of us, he got by without being obviously ambitious in any direction.' Chris, however, feels that 'He was academically bright, and certainly left me way behind. He could catch on to ideas quickly and was definitely a reader.' In his first few weeks his teachers suspected he was maintaining a sensibly low profile, but they came to be frustrated by his taciturnity. As at Eagle House, his reports consistently described his classroom manner as 'quiet', 'reserved', 'reticent' and 'withdrawn'.

Despite Nick's reserve, once Mr Middleton had got to know his new charges he appointed him Head of House at Barton Hill. 'When he went to Marlborough he said, "Well, thank goodness, anyway, I shall have no responsibility when I first get there" – but of course the first thing that happened was he was made Head Boy of his

---

* There was a tendency to hoard in the family, and much of the correspondence survives.

Junior House, so there he was with responsibility all over again, which he didn't want!' said Molly.[2] Nonetheless, Mr Middleton reported that he 'did the job with commendable patience and good sense, managing to get his own way without fuss or friction. He has a quiet but nonetheless strong personality.'

He remained good at games, but music was where he made the strongest initial impression on his peers. 'There was a piano in Barton Hill and it was obvious straight away that he was very musical,' says Chris, while Simon adds: 'He would easily pick out tunes we'd all heard on the radio. He clearly had an ear for music even aged thirteen.' He continued to take piano lessons, but perfecting classical pieces was never his passion. 'I'm taken by a lady called Mrs Howe,' he wrote home on 29 January. 'She's not a bad old girl and reminds me a bit of Granny. The only trouble is that she talks all the while I'm playing and makes it rather difficult to concentrate.' She was cautiously impressed by him, reporting at the end of term: 'He is musical and shows keen interest. I think he has it in him to become quite a competent performer.'

As well as joining the choir (his voice still being an unbroken treble) he took up the clarinet. 'In our first term we could have free music lessons, to help us find the right instrument,' explains Simon. 'I started learning the clarinet but didn't make much progress. Nick picked it up one day and effortlessly played it ten times better than I could. I actually found it quite annoying.'

Their teacher was the eccentric Ted Dowse, known to the boys as 'Eddie', who had a profound impact on Nick's musical development. Robert Peel, head of Marlborough's Wind Department, described him as 'never one to dress even presentably' and 'the friend and confessor to generations of Marlburians in his apparently chaotic teaching room'.[3] With his encouragement Nick joined the wind orchestra, known as 'Brasser', and the Dance Band, which specialised in old standards.

It was compulsory to join the cadet corps, and Nick was not slow to realise that playing in its band was preferable to square-bashing. Chris says that a 'favourite trick of Nick's was to play around with the rhythms'. His sense of humour wasn't immediately apparent, but his peer group was coming to regard him as droll.

In the summer of 1962, just a few months after starting at Marlborough and still aged thirteen, he sat his first two public examinations: O-levels in French and Latin. Results were only recorded as pass/fail and he passed both, but French was never his forte. He had a chance to improve it in August, when his family went to the South of France with their old friends the Careys. Peter had recently turned fourteen too, but found it hard to establish a rapport with Nick.

One occasion sticks in his mind:

We had gone to one of our favourite beaches, at Brégançon – an achingly beautiful setting, with golden sand and rocky pine-covered promontories sliding into the warm indigo of the Mediterranean. It was a picnic atmosphere but Nick was not into the scenery or the sea or the family gathering. Instead, there was an *otherness* about him. For almost the entire time we sat together he had his knees pulled up and his head resting on them. He was there but not there at the same time. It was as though one were sitting next to a black hole.

Nick spent the following Easter on a French exchange with Dominique Saint-André Perrin (to whose family Gabrielle had recently been an au pair). Parisian youth culture initially intimidated him, as he informed his parents: 'I was carted off to meet a whole lot of creeps. Everybody looked at least twenty and I felt rather out of place. They're now dancing away in the drawing room. I was very relieved to get away and write this letter.'

He soon revised his opinion of the 'creeps' and had an early taste of the sort of evening he would come to enjoy:

We went to an Alfred Hitchcock thriller, which was very good indeed. After it we went along to a café and had a drink and I had a very interesting talk with a chap about jazz. We left at about 1.45 a.m. and they strolled off down some side street, shouting and laughing . . . It turned out that we were at one of their flats. We stayed there until about 3.15 a.m. It wasn't too bad, as they had some good records. Somehow word got round that I played the piano so I was forced to play it in the drawing room. Eventually we took a taxi home and I got into bed at about 4 a.m.

Dominique's family also had a place in Veauchette, five hours' drive south. There Nick rode ('My horse, which was very big, galloped off at the most horrifying pace. How I managed to stay on I can't imagine'), shot at pigeons ('we didn't kill any') and became adept at the esoteric practice of 'putting chickens to sleep . . . You tuck its head under its wing and sway it from side to side. Soon it drops off into a deep sleep and you leave it on the ground.'

Shortly after he returned home, Rodney's mother − Nick and Gabrielle's beloved Meema − died in a care home in Leamington following a fall. She was ninety-one.* As well as mourning her, in the summer of 1963 Nick had another six O-levels looming. 'I was at Oxford and Nick was having difficulty with maths, so I offered to tutor him,' says Guy Norton. 'I suppose we did ten or so sessions. He was delightful − eager to learn and easy to teach and get along with. We formed a friendly bond.'

Boosted by the effervescent Guy, Nick managed to pass the dreaded Elementary Maths, as well as English Language, English Literature, History, and − to his astonishment − German, failing only Physics with Chemistry. Having tasted independence on his French exchange, he set about planning a summer cycling holiday around Cornwall with his old pal Dave Lodder (who was at another public school, Uppingham, in Rutland). It was an early indication of his wanderlust and desire to be independent - though ultimately Dave went without Nick, who had Dominique to entertain at Far Leys.

Before the new academic year Nick bade a sad farewell to his much-loved Nan, who was returning to Burma for good.† There was change at Marlborough too − in September he joined his Senior House, C1, where he was to spend his remaining three years. Despite its utilitarian name, C1 is a handsome red-brick building that dominates Court, the centre of the College, and was the original building when it was founded. Its conditions were basic but it had the great benefit of Dennis Silk as its Housemaster.

Nicknamed 'Den' by boys and parents alike, Mr Silk took over

---

* Her estate was valued at £11,572 (around £190,000 in 2022).
† She sailed on 22 October, but Nick wouldn't be home again before then. He never saw her again.

at the same time Nick joined. Aged thirty-one, he was a newlywed and young for the position, giving him a better understanding of modern teenagers than his older colleagues. A committed Christian, he taught English and was a close friend of Siegfried Sassoon, but was more sportsman than scholar. Although Nick didn't always take him seriously, Mr Silk had his measure and always fought his corner, describing him at the time as 'essentially a rather dreamy, artistic type of boy'.[4] 'Den was a wonderful people person who took a lot of trouble with us all,' as Colin Tillie puts it.

Marlborough grouped subjects into so-called sides, and Nick was placed on the 'History side'. 'The cool guys tended to do the History side, which meant History, English and maybe French,' says his contemporary Michael Hodge. 'There wasn't anything like the choice you have now for subjects.' After some discussion, and despite Nick's lacklustre classroom performance to date, he was placed in the History Fifth, a stream reserved for promising boys. This opened up the possibility of applying to Oxford or Cambridge, a notion that his mother was (in Gabrielle's words) 'tremendously keen on', in part because her adored father had gone to Cambridge.

Now that Nick was no longer a Junior, he was expected to take more responsibility – for his timetable, his prep, his possessions, his behaviour. Despite his Housemaster's best efforts, at first he found the adjustment uncomfortable, both socially and academically. Mr Silk summarised the boys' daily routine as 'work, work, games, prep, house prayers, more prep, bed. We bored them silly!'[5] Inevitably, he soon settled in, though he was in the midst of puberty and adolescence. Over the autumn of 1963 he underwent a growth spurt, reaching a full height of six-foot-two. According to his sister, 'Nick suddenly shot up, growing several inches in one term. At that point he turned more into himself – everyone thought he had "outgrown his strength".'

'Nick and I became friends in House Classroom, where we went to do our prep and muck about before we had our own studies,' says Andy Murison.

I always thought he was bright, but he had an ethereal, distracted air. Other than his enjoyment of music he showed no evidence of energy at all, but nor did he ever seem down in the dumps. I don't think he ever started a conversation, but he was perfectly engaged when others did. We'd talk about objective subjects and he'd give his logical judgement, but he wouldn't talk about his feelings. He didn't say much but was charming and mysterious.

'He was a taciturn, reserved chap, friendly enough, but always kept something back, so he wasn't easy to get close to,' confirms Mick Way, a talented pianist who shared Nick's love of music. 'He was popular but always slightly on the edge of everything. I certainly never saw him roar with laughter – he might make a sardonic remark, but he wasn't sarcastic. You were never quite sure what he was thinking.'

Nick was a natural sportsman, unusually long-legged as well as co-ordinated and graceful. He enjoyed hockey, and his Housemaster hoped he might eventually play on the rugby First XV for two years instead of the customary one, but he was ambivalent about games and never developed an interest in them as a fan. Part of the reason was an instinctive dislike of camaraderie, but the main problem was his short-sightedness, about which he was self-conscious and secretive.

Music was becoming his main priority, though he was losing enthusiasm for piano lessons. 'I've got the same old cow teaching me as I had before,' he griped to his parents on 13 October. 'She's hurriedly put me onto the most lifeless piece that ever survived and stamped out any enthusiasm that I had.' Beatlemania had recently erupted, partly accounting for his diminished enthusiasm. 'All the music teachers were longing for him to be a player in the orchestra and Nick didn't want to disappoint them, but he was obviously gripped by the new music,' as Mr Silk later put it.[6]

Unsurprisingly, several of Nick's friends wanted to play 'the new music' themselves. 'Marlborough wasn't obstructive towards people who wanted to form bands,' says Dave Wright. 'I joined one called Les Blousons Noirs (we wore black clothes), playing Dave Clark covers and so on, not very well.' Nick, however, did not rush to join one, though spots in them often became available. In fact, he didn't appear to be engaged with the wider life of the school at all.

'I don't ever remember Nick contributing to the school magazine or being in a play or anything else,' says Simon Crocker. 'He never pushed himself forward. He wanted to be in the background.'

'There is evidence of an all-round lack of drive, almost of sleepiness,' Mr Silk told the Drakes at the end of the year. 'In class he needs to adopt a more dynamic approach, joining in discussions and volunteering answers much more readily. He has a reasonably good mind, but at present it is not being over-taxed.' At Easter 1964, however, he found Nick's demeanour more distant than ever. 'I can't remember him offering of his own volition a single contribution to a discussion,' he sighed. 'His essays are thin and dull and the remedy will take some implementing. He reads happily enough but does not appear to acquire any views.' This tendency towards passivity appeared to be gaining primacy just when he was expected to start showing signs of drive towards admission to Oxford or Cambridge.

By contrast, Ted Dowse stated that he had 'shown great interest and made very good progress indeed' on the clarinet. Nick's musical interests expanded over the course of 1964, with the US folk revival offering special stimulus. 'Nick and I were both mad about music, but I was more interested in the Top Twenty and he had more sophisticated tastes – he liked jazz and was an early Bob Dylan enthusiast,' says Dave Wright. Several of Nick's contemporaries credit the esoteric Jeremy Mason, a self-described 'poseur' at the time, as the first of their number to pick up on Dylan. By his account, however, 'Nick listened to modern American jazz, R&B, Delta blues, Odetta, Dylan . . . He broadened my musical horizons, there's no doubt about it.'

In keeping with his enthusiasm for modern jazz, Nick's interest in the clarinet waned. Fortunately, Mr Dowse was happy to encourage him to switch. 'I told my music teacher about wanting to take up the sax, and he said it would be just about alright now, especially if I took up the alto,' Nick wrote home on 5 July. 'So I've had one lesson with him, which was great fun. He has now given me some pop music to transpose into the right key for the sax so that I can play it next week with him accompanying me on the piano. I look forward to that.'

'Another term of excellent progress!' Mr Dowse enthused in his summer report – but the rest of it made for demoralising reading. 'I fear that he hardly has the imagination to master medieval history, and his memory is astonishingly weak,' wrote the formidable Head of History, Dr Peter Carter, placing Nick twenty-first out of twenty-one in his set. His Housemaster's report reiterated Nick's detached persona: 'He needs to join in more in community exercises, in things which demand initiative directed towards the common good. He is by no means a selfish person, just a little too hermetically sealed.'

Mr Dowse lent him a battered alto for the summer, and his parping and tooting was much in evidence at Far Leys over the ensuing weeks. That August the Drakes went to Holland, but their holiday was cut short when Rodney suffered a heart attack. It was cruel timing. He was fifty-six and approaching the peak of his career but had to cut back on commitments, as well as pay closer attention to his health thereafter. He downplayed his sufferings to Nick and recovered well, but could never again commit his previous level of energy to his work.

Back at school in September 1964, Nick was a sixth-former, thereby qualifying for a study. His was at the end of a corridor, and he shared it with Mick Way. 'Psychologically we felt slightly off the radar,' says Mick, and they set about making the room their own. 'The walls are rather bare, so could you possibly send me that sketch of a cock that I bought in the Louvre,* and also that Paris painting Gay gave me a little while ago?' Nick wrote home. 'Would it be possible to send any spare *Vogues*, as they sometimes provide good material for decorating walls? And if you could manage two of my LPs, *The Freewheelin' Bob Dylan* and *The Five Faces of Manfred Mann*, that really would be terrific.'†

Nick and his peers were constantly in and out of each other's studies, killing time by chatting, snacking, listening to records and occasionally working. Being at close quarters with Nick didn't make Mick feel any closer to him, though. 'You'd have to prise out an

* *The Cock* by Bernard Buffet.
† Released in the UK in November 1963 and August 1964 respectively.

opinion. In a circle of four or five he would step slightly back, so he'd simultaneously be part of it and not part of it. I don't think any of us really understood him.'

Fortuitously, Mick had a cheap Spanish guitar, which Nick began to play at the start of term. 'I don't think he'd ever picked one up before,' says Mick. 'I could play quite well by ear and showed him the basics.' Dave Wright has a similar memory: 'I remember sitting down and teaching him C, A minor, F and G7th . . . A few days later he was better at it than I was. He was a proper musician. He played by ear, and he was good.'[7]

Nick was sixteen years and three months of age, and felt an immediate affinity with the instrument. Self-expression had never come easily to him, and now it had a ready outlet. He had unusually large, broad hands with slim wrists and long fingers that allowed him to get round the notes whilst using his thumb for the bass string, and his instinctive co-ordination and dogged focus meant that he quickly mastered fingerings. He assimilated everything in Bert Weedon's hugely popular *Play in a Day* primer and began playing what he later termed 'lots of Dylan things'.[8]

'Within three months he was way ahead of me,' says Mick, and by the end of term he had decided he needed a guitar of his own. In December he spent everything he had – £13 (around £200 in 2022) – on a second-hand nylon-stringed classical, manufactured by Estruch, in the Sound of Music in Marlborough High Street. 'Nick was always frugal with his money presents, saving up for something he really wanted,' explains his sister, but the outlay horrified his parents.[9]

He was working towards A-levels in History, English and 'Latin Translation with Roman History', a fiendish course devised by Dr Carter himself, but was far more attentive to the guitar. His Christmas report only served to amplify the sense that his priorities were in the wrong order.

'He has got to do something about his reticence,' insisted Mr Silk, who was his English teacher as well as his Housemaster. 'One can fire questions at him until one is blue in the face and he will gaze dreamily back and say nothing. At present his suitability for University is very much in question. An absolute revolution must take place in his work next year.' On a personal level, things were warmer: 'He cuts far more ice in House than I thought he did last term, and I am hopeful that he will end up as a really considerable leader here. Certainly one could not ask to meet a nicer boy.'

Molly and Rodney understood that Nick was a slow developer and were unfussed by his generation's penchant for long hair, pop music and boundary-pushing. A measure of this is the fact that he was not slow to invite his schoolmates to Far Leys. 'Nick's parents were delightful and friendly, very welcoming,' says Dave Wright. 'I always got the impression that they enjoyed meeting his friends.' Andy Murison also visited Nick at home and saw no hint of a generational clash: 'I never saw any sign of difficulty in his upbringing. His parents seemed relaxed and gentle.'

As his enthusiasm for the guitar grew he gravitated towards Jeremy Harmer, who was in the year above him at Marlborough and spent time at Far Leys over the holidays:

> I'd started writing songs aged fourteen, and when Nick started playing
> I occasionally went over with my guitar. I don't remember him
> playing sax or clarinet on those occasions, only guitar. We'd sit in
> the music room and mess around with his family's reel-to-reel tape
> recorder. It was the first one I'd ever seen.

Nick was well used to recording himself speaking or playing the piano, clarinet and saxophone, but when he began playing the guitar the tape recorder took on a new dimension. As he single-mindedly taught himself songs, he could record, listen, rewind, erase and re-record at will, a process that greatly helped his development. 'He was quite a perfectionist and was always erasing songs that he deemed inferior,' recalled Rodney,[10] while Molly added: 'He would play and play and play in the early days.'[11]

While Nick practised in the music room, his parents fretted about his prospects for Oxford or Cambridge. Rodney wrote to Mr Silk on the subject over Christmas, and he replied on 6 January 1965: 'If all goes well, I would hope that Nick might make it to one of the humbler Cambridge colleges, where they would take note of his non-intellectual qualities. The work must keep on improving.' Nick took this to heart and – for a time – increased his efforts. However, it had become clear that, in an unusually strong cohort, he was not academically motivated.

Outside the classroom he gave up the cadet corps in favour of 'conservation detail', which involved maintaining old school buildings. He and a few others were tasked with repainting Mount House, a bow-windowed Georgian building on the corner where the main road ran through the heart of the school. Most of their time there, however, was spent fooling around. 'They were the funniest afternoons,' says Simon Crocker. 'I just remember us spending the whole time laughing. We liked a black sense of humour, certainly.'

Amidst the mirth, Jeremy Mason says Nick 'was always cool – which more or less means he didn't say a lot. I was more talkative. I think part of the reason we became good friends was that he was a good listener.' As the boys became more image-conscious, Nick's friends began to conflate his self-containment with the notion of 'cool'. When they were hanging out in each other's studies,' says Andy Murison, 'Nick would suddenly up and leave, but it didn't worry me – I thought it was unusual, even eccentric, but perhaps cool. Being cool was quite important, so I rather admired this "take it or leave it" behaviour, at an age when boys like to be popular.'

By his mid-teens, according to Dave Wright, Nick had settled upon a personal style from which he barely departed in years to come: 'He had a decent length of hair, a donkey jacket, tight trousers and Chelsea boots.' Michael Maclaran, another schoolfriend, adds:

> He was tall and stooped forwards, holding his head quite low in his shoulders as if there were always a cold wind blowing. As was typical in those days, he was always pushing the clothing and appearance regulations to the limit . . . However, he didn't do this in an extrovert way and got away with more than some 'rebel' types, to the quiet admiration of his peers.[12]

'We would smoke and drink, but Nick wasn't a troublemaker,' continues Andy. 'The only time I remember getting into trouble with him was when we went out for a lovely dinner with his sister and a friend of hers in early 1965 . . .' This incident took place on Saturday, 13 February, when Gabrielle visited for the weekend with her friend Sarah Buchanan. 'We were all infatuated with Gay – she had a starstruck audience whenever she came to Marlborough,' says Colin Tillie, so an opportunity to spend the evening with her was much coveted. Nick asked Dave Wright and Andy to join them for dinner at a nearby pub, the Bell at Ramsbury, where the girls also treated them to beer, wine and liqueurs.

'Nick was in excellent form – I've never seen him so gay and forthcoming,' Gabrielle wrote to Molly and Rodney (who were in India) a couple of days later.

> I think all the boys thoroughly enjoyed themselves – no shyness or any nonsense of that kind . . . Nick was very *au fait* and adult-seeming – as indeed they all were. They all said that as Silk wasn't there it didn't matter what time they got back . . . Apparently, quite contrary to what they said, House Captains [i.e. school prefects] had been tearing their hair out and ringing up police.

The following morning the girls gatecrashed his Dance Band practice ('Nick was rather pulverised with embarrassment, but it was fun – he seemed to be doing very well. Didn't spare us a look, I need hardly say!'). That evening brought a reckoning with Mr Silk, who put Nick on 'sweats' – long early-morning runs – as a punishment.

The weekend was a rare encounter between brother and sister, for whom heart-to-heart exchanges had never been the norm. By Gabrielle's account,

> By then I was leaving [drama] school and concentrating on my own life, which was becoming very exciting; I lost touch a little with his problems and dilemmas. And at that time he seemed to be doing quite well; he was wonderful at sports, though he hated them, and was the kind of person who was quite capable of being Head Boy.[13]

Nick, however, was unfussed by conventional measures of schoolboy success and was hedging his bets as to his longer-term future. 'I've been going into the matter of my career recently,' he told his parents the same month. 'Advertising seems to be top of the list at the moment. Den's found out a bit about it for me. I'm going to see the careers master about it this evening.' The idea wasn't pursued, and Cambridge remained his ostensible goal. Mr Silk was encouraging Nick to apply to Fitzwilliam House – the very definition of one of the 'humbler' colleges.* It helped that Mr Silk was a friend of its sport-loving Admissions Tutor, Norman Walters, who relied on a network of such contacts to supply what he considered the right sort of candidates. 'Fitzwilliam used to be nicknamed "Fitzmarlborough" because so many Marlburians went there,' says Jeremy Harmer.

'I would be most grateful if you would send me application forms for Fitzwilliam, as I am very anxious to try for admission to the college,' Nick wrote to Mr Walters from Far Leys at the start of the Easter holidays in 1965. 'I am 16 years 10 months and would very much like to come up in October to read History.' He was certain not to get in on purely academic grounds, but the hope was that, given the glimmers of improvement in his work, his athletic ability and a recommendation from Mr Silk (perhaps the pre-eminent Cambridge sportsman of his generation), might just swing it.

His friends did not consider him an obvious candidate. 'I was surprised when I heard about Nick's plans to go to Cambridge, because . . . Why would he?' asks Dave Wright. 'In those days there was far less of an expectation that you would go to university, and Nick didn't strike me as any more interested in his studies than I was.' For Andy Murison, who was also applying to Fitzwilliam, 'Nick was very still, and I think people therefore assumed that his waters must be very deep.'

---

* Fitzwilliam House had been set up in 1869 for students who couldn't afford full access to the trappings of life in a Cambridge college. In the 1950s moves began to be made for it to be granted full collegiate status, which finally took place in 1966. Then, as now, candidates applied to specific colleges rather than the University itself.

5

No One Can Claim To Know Him Very Well

O VER EASTER 1965 Nick accompanied the Harmer family on a skiing holiday in Verbier, Switzerland. They drove out, with the boys' guitars in the back. 'I felt a bit nervous about him joining us because we certainly weren't close friends and he could be hard to communicate with, even at that age,' says Jeremy. 'In the evenings we would sit in the bar and try to entertain the guests, singing pop and folk songs in the Peter, Paul and Mary vein.' These were almost certainly Nick's first public performances as a singer-guitarist, and Jeremy candidly describes their efforts as 'awkward chords, unoriginal fingerings'.[1] Nonetheless, Nick was clearly not shy with his guitar.

Rodney and Molly collected him from the Harmers' in Stratford on 25 April. 'We were able to get a good account of their adventures in much more detail than we ever should've been able to from Nick,' Rodney wrote to Gabrielle that week.

> We found Nick looking tremendously bronzed and fit, having obviously had a marvellous time. Evidently Jeremy and Nick made a good name for themselves with their guitars, playing in the hotel as well as the local nightclub. Mrs Harmer says everyone in the hotel came to listen to them on the last night. After lunch we made them give us a performance and we really were very impressed. They sang in harmony, played very well and obviously had several numbers extremely well worked out – they sang 'Puff the Magic Dragon', the Beatles tune 'And I Love Her', 'Where Have All the Flowers Gone?' and a number of others.

Nick and Jeremy briefly continued their collaboration back at Marlborough, entertaining a small crowd outside C1 on Commemoration Day in late May. Jeremy's mother had her camera to hand

and took the earliest known photograph of Nick with a guitar as the duo ran through their repertoire. By the summer of 1965, says Mick Way,

> Nick was concentrating on the guitar to the exclusion of almost anything else. I was still strumming away on open chords but he had started developing his own style. We had a crappy old Dansette and I had *Back Country Blues* by Sonny Terry and Brownie McGhee, which we played a lot. He also liked Robert Johnson. Complicated finger-picking is what we liked and tried to emulate − things that were hard to break down. We played together quite a bit, but then he'd go into reveries and be off in a corner, doggedly practising and not communicating. He just got his head down until he'd got it. The word would be 'obsessive', even then.

Folk-singing, however, was not going to impress Fitzwilliam, so in a bid to burnish Nick's credentials Mr Silk appointed him a 'Captain of Classroom', responsible for supervising younger boys in C1's crowded communal study hall. He wasn't an obvious choice as far as his friends were concerned. Andy says he was 'not in the least officious or disciplinarian', and indeed, controlling a roomful of rowdy fellow adolescents proved beyond him, leading to further censure. He was young to be sitting A-levels and found the work-load towards History at Cambridge onerous. 'However hard I work, only half of it ever seems to get done,' he complained to his parents, while Mr Silk remained frustrated by his lack of focus. 'He was reasonably industrious but his heart was not really in anything academic except English. A very dreamy pupil.'[2]

His appetite for team games was evaporating, so he turned to athletics, which came easily to him. 'Marlborough had quite an athletics tradition and lots of people would turn out to watch the matches, so boys on the team were to an extent school heroes,' says Michael Hodge. 'It was good, as games were over quicker for us.' Andy Murison and Chris Rudkin were also on the team, which was captained by Mark 'Foggy' Phillips, whose only memory of him is 'as a good athlete'.[3] Nick excelled at hurdling and relay races but sprinting was his forte; he eventually broke the school's hundred-yard record with a time of ten seconds flat, running 'upright and like a ship in full sail', as Mr Silk put it.[4]

He was more enthused by his musical activities, though, and that term he formed a jazz group comprising himself (alto and tenor sax), Adrian Hutton (piano/vocals), Jeremy Harmer (bass) and Simon Crocker (drums). 'We play rather more sophisticated stuff like "Summertime" and "Misty", and a few vocals like "Sit Right Down and Write Myself a Letter",' he told Molly and Rodney. 'Just your sort of vintage, really!'[5]

Oldies, however, had dwindling appeal. In March the innovative jazzy R&B outfit the Graham Bond Organisation had released their first album, *The Sound of '65*, which electrified Nick and his friends and drew them to Soho, the home of British R&B. They began to visit its clubs, watching Georgie Fame, Chris Farlowe, Inez and Charlie Foxx and others at the Flamingo or the Marquee, and having their eyes opened by their surroundings. 'Soho had the first pizza restaurant I'd ever seen, just up from the Flamingo, and I remember Nick and me getting accosted by a lady of the street and bartering with her, then running off,' says Dave Wright.[6]

At the end of a full and enjoyable term, Nick sat his A-levels more or less cold. Having just turned seventeen, he knew he could always have another go if he had to, unappealing as the prospect was. The start of the holidays on 20 July distracted him from the impending disaster of his results, though his report sounded a warning. 'The sense of urgency is not there,' wrote his History teacher. 'I wish him luck in the exam, but I fear his chances of success are not very high.'

In the meantime, he and Dave Wright had cooked up a plan to hitchhike around Europe on a shoestring. They caught a train to Dover in early August and set sail. 'Nick was shyer than me, perhaps a bit less gung-ho, but perfectly confident and resourceful,' says Dave. 'Our plan was to sleep in youth hostels, but we hadn't realised that you can't make plans when you're dependent on hitching to get around.' Nick did not take his guitar, but nonetheless:

> We were unable to get anyone to give us a lift in Northern France, so we took the train from Paris down to Avignon and tried our luck there. Eventually someone told us about a cave you could sleep in, so we headed there for the night – and it was revolting. From there

we just hitched and bumbled along the Côte d'Azur, having a great time. At one point Nick stood on some urchins in the sea and I tried to remove them. A year later he joked to me that I'd done a bad job, because he still had them in his foot. Finding somewhere to sleep was always the challenge. On one occasion we crept into an unfinished shop and slept on its concrete floor. We slept on the beach at Cannes, and another time a blonde girl picked us up and said we could sleep in her garden at Cap d'Ail. Nick got a nasty surprise when he put his hand onto a tree in his sleep and got covered in ants.

Like many young men of their generation, they were enamoured of Françoise Hardy, but their running joke was that everywhere they went they were pursued by Sonny and Cher's 'I Got You Babe'. They made it through Switzerland and Italy and into Germany but, recounts Dave, 'When we couldn't get a ride together in southern Germany we split and came home separately. It was a lot of fun.' Not all teenagers would have embraced a foreign adventure of this sort, with limited funds and no itinerary; the fact that Nick cheerfully did so speaks clearly of his independence, resourcefulness and confidence on the brink of adulthood.

The trip had been a hoot, but the laughter stopped when Nick's exam results reached Far Leys. He had scraped through History (with a D) and English (with an E), but failed Latin Translation with Roman History. This fell far short of the minimum standard of three C grades expected by Cambridge. It was swiftly decided to keep him at Marlborough until the summer of 1966, in order for him to retake the exams and, it was hoped, mature in the interim.

'Everything seems to have happily settled down into the good old termtime monotony,' he wrote home on 26 September 1965. He was now sharing a study with Andy Murison and Martin Scott. 'We didn't sleep in it but were in close proximity when we did our prep, listened to music and so on,' explains Andy. 'Nick had a Donovan poster on the wall. He was interested in the Beatles' innovations and especially loved "Yesterday".* Martin had a record of

---

* 'Yesterday' was included on *Help!*, which had been released on 5 August.

whales singing to each other, which we would listen to on his headphones.'*

'I bought records that Nick liked,' says Jeremy Mason, who startled his friends by painting his entire study – including his possessions – white. He recalls the artists in question including Astrud Gilberto, Jimmy Smith, Segovia and Odetta ('Auction Block' being a particular favourite of Nick's), as well as John Hammond's *Big City Blues*, Bob Dylan's *Bringing It All Back Home*, Booker T & the MGs' *Green Onions*, Miles Davis's *Kind of Blue* and John Coltrane's *Giant Steps*.

Nick was now in the demanding History sixth form, presided over by the rigorous Dr Carter and containing several of the school's cleverest boys. He dropped History – supposedly what he was hoping to study at Cambridge – but continued to work towards the rigorous Latin Translation and Roman History, as well as English and the General Paper. The latter was intended to indicate a rounded mind but was not taken seriously by universities. Playing it safe, Nick also applied to sit the entrance exam to St Peter's College, Oxford, 'where the field would not be all that strong', Mr Silk assured Rodney that month. They declined Nick's candidature, however, leaving Fitzwilliam his sole hope.

'Well, as usual there are lots of exciting events to recall after yet another thrill-packed week at Marlborough Coll.,' was the mordant opening to a letter home on 24 October, in which his weariness of both study ('The work is plodding on and is not particularly inspiring') and games ('I had to face two rugger matches last week') were plain. Molly and Rodney can't have failed to notice his change in tone when he turned to his shambolic jazz group, in which he played saxophone ('the musical side of life seems to be thriving at the moment'). Soon afterwards Gabrielle wrote to say she might be able to secure them a gig in a club in Malvern over Christmas, via contacts she'd made that summer; Nick replied with cautious enthusiasm, but it didn't come to anything. Gabrielle's acting career had been gathering momentum and she was now renting a top-floor

* *Whale and Porpoise Voices*, recorded by William E. Schevill and William A. Watkins (Woods Hole Oceanographic Institution, 1962).

London flat at 5 Cyril Mansions in Prince of Wales Drive, Battersea
– a short hop over the river from Chelsea and the King's Road. It
was a huge asset to Nick, to whom she was always happy to offer
her spare room. London was, inevitably, more alluring than
Marlborough and the nature of her work meant she was often away,
so he could accommodate friends too.

On Friday, 29 October, he and Jeremy Mason watched the Graham
Bond Organisation at the Manor House Hotel in North London.
Their heroes did not disappoint:

> I can remember Nick standing with a cigarette, watching Ginger
> Baker doing a drum solo on 'Camels and Elephants',* and he was
> so impressed he'd poured a pint of beer all the way down his front
> before he noticed. We got their autographs after the show and stayed
> at Gabrielle's flat.[7]

In Nick's final year at Marlborough the sight of him hunched
over his guitar in his study became familiar to all. He took to writing
out the words to contemporary standards in a notebook, giving a
good idea of his repertoire. Several were known to him via Peter,
Paul and Mary ('Stewball', 'All My Trials', '500 Miles', 'Early Mornin'
Rain' and 'Freight Train'), one was probably familiar via Joan Baez
('East Virginia'), and two were by Paul Simon ('A Most Peculiar
Man' and 'Leaves That Are Green').[†] His Housemaster well remembered his zeal, later remarking that 'his music was his life'.[8] At the
time, however, he characterised his response as: 'Drake, for God's
sake put that bloody instrument away!'[9]

'Producing a very pleasant sound indeed,' glowed Eddie Dowse's
clarinet report at the end of 1965. 'Developing into a very useful
instrumentalist.' His other teachers were exasperated. 'He gives me
the impression of being about a year younger than he actually is,'
wrote the Headmaster, while Dr Carter was dismissive of his prospects for Cambridge:

---

* The final track on the group's second album, *There's a Bond Between Us*, released
in December 1965.
† First released on *The Paul Simon Song Book*, in August 1965, and later on Simon
and Garfunkel's *Sounds of Silence*, released in the US in January 1966.

Although he has done his best, he has never done better than approximate the equivalent to a borderline A-level pass. He is especially vulnerable in the General Paper, where only his interest in music will help him much, as on most contemporary or abstract problems he has very little to offer. The fact is, for one of his ability he has been aiming unrealistically high.

The relentlessly sanguine Mr Silk reiterated that 'Good A-levels could still get him into Cambridge next year', though he felt obliged to add: 'I cannot say that his study has been a great success: too many illegalities have flourished there.'

One evening over Christmas at Far Leys Gabrielle and Nick recorded 'All My Trials',* leading them to discuss devising 'some sort of act together — but it never materialised'.[10] Nick's main focus over the holidays was on getting his driver's licence, but his reluctance to address his poor eyesight meant he ploughed through a stop sign, ensuring failure. He went on a Scottish skiing trip with Andy Murison ('The skiing was no good and it was bloody cold'), then saw in 1966 with Dave Wright, who recalls:

> We went to Trafalgar Square, where everyone was revelling, jumping in the fountains and so on, and got drunk. When it was time to go home there were no cabs or buses anywhere to be seen, so we walked all the way back to my sister's place in Primrose Hill. We didn't get there until about 4 a.m., by which time we'd sobered up.

On New Year's Day Nick travelled to the Masons' family home in Essex. 'I had an Oscar Wilde party,' says Jeremy. 'It was enormous fun.' He remembers girls being drawn to Nick's effortless charisma, and his evident lack of interest in them. In particular, he says, 'A very bright girl called Bo, who was staying with us, fell for him. She kept changing her clothes to get his attention, but he didn't pay her any. Nick never seemed to notice when girls took a fancy to him.'

Several of Nick's friends observed this. 'Towards the end of our days at Marlborough most of us had girlfriends, but I never knew

---

* A touching, if morbid, spiritual popularised by Joan Baez (on her November 1960 debut album) and Peter, Paul and Mary, among many others.

Nick to,' says Dave. 'I don't think he was gay, though, and he certainly wasn't one of those people who was interested in the younger boys as a girl-substitute.' For Mick Way, 'He would never have joined a conversation about who fancied who, but that's not to say I think he was gay. I'm sure that would have emerged to some extent at school, and I never saw any sign of it.' Andy adds: 'Nick was charismatic without being assertive. I can imagine him driving girls mad by never making a move.'

Ever with an eye to improving Nick's Cambridge prospects, in January 1966 Mr Silk made him one of C1's 'House Captains' – a prefect – and also saw him appointed Secretary of the Athletics Club. Although none of Nick's friends remember him being much interested in literature, it was decided that he should now apply for Cambridge's English course. As such, a special timetable was devised that allowed him to spend more time reading in his study than would normally be permitted.

He responded well: 'Being a Captain really does make quite a bit of difference, since my bedtime is now fairly unlimited,' he wrote home on 23 January. 'I now feel that I'm doing things which interest me, and that not only makes life more enjoyable but is also rather more likely to produce acceptable A-level grades.' A fortnight later he told them, 'Life here seems to be really rather tolerable at the moment. I'm almost enjoying my work at times, and that's something I don't think you've heard me say during the last two years.'[11]

He continued to play a lot of solo guitar as well as sax and piano in bands, switching his focus from jazz towards R&B. 'There was a film show on Saturday and nobody seemed to be prepared to provide music before it, so I was asked to organise something,' he told his parents in late January.

> I formed a small group and after one practice we went on and attempted to play. The result, as you may imagine, was pretty good chaos. For want of someone better, I had to sing myself and I need hardly tell the trouble that was likely to cause. In one number I completely forgot the words of the last verse, and we ground to an embarrassing halt in the middle of the song! Fortunately, Simon was in the group so we were able to laugh a lot of it off.

Undeterred by that fiasco, he informed his parents in February: 'I've abandoned that group which came to such grief in its one and only performance and have now started another one.' This time he took it more seriously. Simon:

> Nick wasn't a ball of energy or ambition, but if he wanted to achieve something he'd put effort into it. We'd get up at 6 a.m. to rehearse in the Memorial Hall. He was the musical leader, but it was my job to arrange the rehearsals, get everyone out of bed and so on. He certainly wouldn't have done that! We rehearsed a fair bit – Nick was insistent on us playing his arrangements correctly. We strictly played R&B, mostly learnt from Pye singles – 'Hi-Heel Sneakers', 'Hoochie Coochie Man', 'Parchman Farm' and so on. Nick liked Mose Allison.[*]

Their equipment was cobbled together but they managed to sound respectable in rehearsal. Nick sang and played piano, harmonica and occasional sax; it's noticeable that he seems not to have considered playing the electric guitar. 'To begin with I did the singing, but soon found that playing the piano and harmonica and singing at the same time was a bit too much, and anyway my voice isn't really up to it,' he explained to his parents. Attempts to find a replacement came to naught, so he persevered[†] – but before they could perform, they needed a name. 'I came up with The Perfumed Gardeners,' says Simon.[‡]

> It wasn't intended seriously – we all found it mildly funny, but I hardly had it painted on my bass drum. It was more a scratch band than anything organised or ambitious, and the line-up fluctuated. We played a grand total of maybe four times, to a captive audience before the film show on Saturday nights. Nick sang from the piano confidently and well. It wasn't his style to belt songs out, but he put them

---

[*] In early 1966 Nick wrote out a list of songs they either played or considered playing. In addition to those Simon mentions, it includes material recorded by the Beatles, the Rolling Stones, the Who, the Yardbirds and the Pretty Things.
[†] Simon Crocker says: 'A guy called Chris Davison wanted to play with us, but he was in the year below and we thought he was a little too keen and poppy for us. I just remember him as a small guy with a large guitar. He later changed his name to Chris de Burgh. The arrogance of youth! We would have been lucky to have him.'
[‡] Named after *The Perfumed Garden of Sensual Delight*, a fifteenth-century erotic text by Nefzawi, translated by Sir Richard Burton in 1886.

across compellingly; his way of handling them was original and made people pay attention. I have no idea how good or bad we were, but I'm told that people were excited to hear us and thought we were really good.

In his Easter report Mr Silk said 'his group make a very delectable sound', but wistfully added: 'No one can claim to know him very well.' The reliably downbeat Dr Carter felt that Nick's 'passive attitude is not only hard to break through but singularly unconducive to constructive criticism'. His English report called his essays 'undistinguished, with too many descents into journalese, too much repetition of obvious points. He oversimplifies and tends to overstate the case he is making', while his classes for the General Paper apparently found him 'wrapped in his own thoughts, seemingly oblivious of anything going on around him. I presume he regards the whole exercise as a waste of time, but I wonder what he would be doing otherwise.'

The answer, of course, was playing his guitar and hanging out in London, which was his priority over the holidays. The closest station to Far Leys was Hampton-in-Arden, which reached Euston (via Coventry) in about ninety minutes. However, he managed to pass his driving test in April and was rewarded with the use of Molly's old Morris Minor, nicknamed 'HOB' after its number plate. Although he promptly had an accident that cost Rodney a painful £150 to put right,[*] HOB gave him the freedom to make the two-and-a-half-hour journey to London – one he would come to know intimately.

Based in Gabrielle's flat, he passed his days playing guitar or hanging out with schoolfriends including the urbane Mike Hacking, generally considered the coolest Marlburian of their generation. 'Nick was in awe of Mike – we all were,' says Simon Crocker, while Colin Tillie states:

> Mike was a godlike figure to us all. He was our age but seemed older and more sophisticated. As well as being the nicest guy in the world he was extremely good-looking and advanced sexually. He was exactly the sort of person who'd have an older girlfriend who drove a little sports car.

[*] A little over £2,000 in 2022.

'My parents lived abroad, so I was often alone in London, which set me a little apart from my contemporaries,' concedes Mike, who did in fact have an older girlfriend who drove a little sports car. Her name was Désiree Burlison-Rush, known as 'Desi', and she was born in April 1940. 'Desi was seven years older than me, a friend of my older sister's,' he explains.

> She was small and quite pretty – some might say witch-like – with pale skin, high heels and long dark hair covering her eyes and running all the way down her back. She was a bit of a player in London, a high-powered secretary, super-efficient and organised, maybe a little neurotic. She was possessive but very kind.

Desi lived in a fourth-floor flat in Sloane Street, Chelsea, where Mike and his friends were often to be found, and she would also pop down to visit him at Marlborough, to general envy. She took a liking to the affable, taciturn Nick, and was quick to recognise and encourage his musical talent, while he felt comfortable around her. Perhaps having an older sister made him more assured than he might otherwise have been, or perhaps his own lack of sexual energy made him easy for her to relate to, but they became good and lasting platonic friends despite the significant age gap.

Nick had revelled in his relative independence in London, and reluctantly returned to Marlborough for his final term on Tuesday, 26 April 1966. 'The thought that in two months' time it'll be the end of Marlborough rather than just the end of term seems to make everything just about tolerable,' he told his parents. Mick Way had at least bought John Renbourn's newly released debut solo album, which greatly impressed Nick. '"Plainsong" on that was the big one!' says Mick. 'We thought Renbourn was the greatest. By then Nick was playing fingerstyle, with finger and thumbpicks we'd both bought. He was experimenting but I don't remember him constantly retuning at school.'

Although Nick had yet to show evidence of any personal ambition to go to Cambridge, on 12 May he filled in his formal application to read English at Fitzwilliam. Unconvinced it would be successful, at much the same time his father wrote to his friend Arthur Tite, a dealer in miniatures, regarding a possible career for

Nick in the art world. The idea was not pursued, and later that month Rodney – who had just turned fifty-eight – suffered another heart attack.

'Well, this is a fine state of affairs, is it not – the old man crocked up again,' he wrote to Nick on 30 May, again downplaying concerns on his account. His convalescent bed overlooked the garden. 'Yer Ma is planting some new roses, judging from the sounds emanating from the beds, and, again judging by ear, Gay, who has been stretched out on the terrace in her bikini like a fish on a cold slab for the whole afternoon, has been dragooned into doing some watering.'

Pleasantries aside, he had something important to impart:

> Afraid it sounds as though music is a bit of a casualty this term – but it's all in a good cause. No doubt you find Latin in particular a tiresome distraction from the proper pursuit of living . . . Nevertheless, I do think that it is essential when one is young to learn to discipline one's mind and body to do things they don't want to. One of the several important benefits derived from the process is an increase in the powers of concentration (an important matter in the case of N.R.D.?) – and you'll need that, whatever you go in for.

Mr Silk was under the impression that Nick was beavering away in his study, but his friends say he was more likely to have been playing his guitar. 'The really alarming thing is that I have an A-level in about a week's time,' Nick replied to his father in early June. He was suffering from a heavy cold, but that wasn't the only reason for his poor performance on the day. Along with his lack of preparation, 'I don't think he could take stress, and exams were probably something he found stressful,' suggests Andy Murison.

'I've decided that running is perhaps more stupid than rugger, which is saying something,' Nick went on, but he had to participate in the Wiltshire Athletics Championships, held at Marlborough on Saturday, 18 June. For all his apathy, he performed outstandingly in his section, coming first in both the 100-yard dash (with a time of 10.4 seconds) and the 220 yards (22.8 seconds).* His success was recorded in the *Wiltshire Gazette and Herald* the following Thursday

---

* Approximately 90 and 200 metres respectively.

(as 'M. Drake'), alongside a photo of him beaming in his kit. It was perhaps the last time he ever wore it.

By his exasperated Housemaster's account, Nick was

> a most talented athlete who was never really deeply interested in breaking records which were well within his grasp. He is probably one of the best sprinters we have had at Marlborough since the war, and yet he would much more often than not be found reading when he should have been training.[12]

'Reading' was probably a euphemism, but his athletic success was a vital plank in his Cambridge application. 'Fitzwilliam was trying to lift its profile and wanted to compete with the bigger colleges, so an outstanding sprinter would certainly have been attractive to them,' says Andy.

Nick turned eighteen the day after the Championships, so he and Dave Wright decided to celebrate in style. 'We sneaked out of the house at around 10 p.m. on Saturday night, nipped down the High Street towards the A4, stuck out our thumbs and found our way to Wardour Street,' says Dave.

> I don't remember who we watched, but it was brilliant.* We were conscious of the need to get back, so after an hour or so we made our way to Chiswick and got a ride as far as Slough. We tried to pick up another lift there, but there was no one coming at all. We stood by the side of the road as the sun came up and realised we were in quite a serious situation. Suddenly a police car slowed down. We told the policeman the truth and he said, 'You'll never get a lift from here. I'll take you somewhere where you can.' He did, and someone took us all the way back to Marlborough. That was a one-off, not a regular thing, but we were all planning how we could escape to Swinging London when we left school.

In the short term Nick made sorties of a more local variety. Jeremy Mason recalls them going for long, tobacco-fuelled walks alongside the local railway line, and says, 'Almost every day after lunch Nick and I used to scamper off to a splendid café down the

---

* The blues singer Jimmy Witherspoon was on at the Marquee that night.

High Street, which had a bay window, so we could see if anyone was coming. We'd sit there smoking Gauloise Disque Bleu cigarettes.' A friend in the year below, Rich Robbins, adds:

> In the summer term of 1966 Nick, Dave Wright, Martin Scott and I used to get up at 5 a.m., creep out of the house, take a couple of javelins from the athletics track and go to the Savernake Forest, which is lovely at that time of year. We'd set snares for rabbits and try to hunt, but never got anything. A couple of hours later we'd creep back and roll up for breakfast with everyone else.

Nick was under no illusions about the fragile status of his retakes and Cambridge application. 'If I'm lucky I might get in for '67 on my A-levels, but on the other hand they might want me to take University Entrance [i.e. Cambridge's own exam], in which case Den suggests I go to a crammer for a term,' he told his parents during his exams. 'I don't know how that idea seems to you.' Thus did he plant the seed of another disappointing set of results.

The Perfumed Gardeners had a last hurrah one Saturday night in July. By Simon's account:

> We did the most amazing version of 'St James Infirmary'. That's the tune I remember us blowing the walls out with, and everyone was amazed, because normally at school there were four people playing popular little tunes, but we suddenly had an eight-piece really playing . . . Nick was a natural performer. He was bloody good: he was the band leader, he projected well, he was a confident performer.[13]

Jeremy Mason well remembers the performance: 'Nick suddenly put down his saxophone, went over to the piano and on his own played a thing called "Parchman Farm"*– and it was an absolute tour-de-force.'[14] Nonetheless, the boys had no intention of pursuing the group beyond school.

Nick was delighted to have the end in sight. 'We were told we must not do anything on the last night of term,' according to Jeremy. 'It was the absolute cardinal rule.'[15] As such, he, Nick, Dave Wright

---

* 'Parchman Farm' was written by Bukka White, but Nick probably knew and performed Mose Allison's adaptation.

and their like-minded friend John Du Cane hatched a plan. 'We decided to celebrate by sneaking out of our houses and breaking into the music rooms with booze and smokes,' John explains. Unsurprisingly, they overdid it and got caught. 'My abiding memory is of Nick with a bottle of sweet white wine, probably Graves, absolutely out of it, completely cold, by the music block,' says Dave.[16]

Nick departed for good the next day, with a filthy hangover and his Housemaster's rebuke ringing in his ears. His final report contained sentiments that were by now wearily familiar to his parents. Most damningly, his report in English – the subject he was hoping to read at Cambridge – stated: 'He seems to have fearful difficulty in identifying the point of a question, so his essays move aimlessly and vaguely around the subject without ever getting to grips with it.'

His Headmaster's parting statement was blunter.

> He told me (I think) when he said goodbye that he was thinking of going to a crammer's with a view to University entrance. After reading these reports I would like to express the strong opinion that, unless his A-level grades show marked improvement this year, he should not pursue the idea.

As ever, it fell to Mr Silk to sound a positive note. 'It certainly looks as if the writing is on the wall so far as University is concerned, but no one will have gone down fighting harder than he,' he stated unconvincingly. 'I shall always feel that it was his inability to communicate in class that was the real stumbling block, and that is something one simply could not impart to him.' Cambridge might no longer be in prospect, but he assured the Drakes that 'There are many fine things for a person with his delightful personality to succeed in outside the realms of school and University.' In conclusion, he reiterated: 'Everyone has liked him, though few have really known him.'

Despite Nick's tendency to be reserved and taciturn, none of his schoolfriends considered him to be anything other than well-adjusted at Marlborough, and all enjoyed his gently ironic wit. 'Nick was happy and friendly at school, very much one of the lads,' states Michael Maclaran. 'He was excellent company, with a great sense of humour, and very good at sharing laughter. He certainly wasn't depressed or gloomy or a loner.' Jeremy Mason echoes this: 'Nick was an absolutely normal bloke at school – he didn't stand out or make an impact, he was just very likeable, very agreeable, never difficult or demanding.' Simon Crocker adds: 'I don't remember him in any way being moody, introspective or difficult.'[17]

He had not fulfilled the academic promise discerned in him at the outset of his career, but he had excelled on the athletics track, consistently developed musically and made a large number of friends. 'Nick wasn't obviously anything in any particular direction at school,' reflects Andy Murison. 'I feel that I knew him as well as anybody did there – which perhaps wasn't especially well. I could never quite work out who or what the real Nick was. To paraphrase Dorothy Parker, was there a "there" there?'

6

A Genuine Late Developer

～—

Eager as Nick was to press ahead with an independent life, he remained mired in the Cambridge application process. Just after leaving school in mid-July 1966, he was interviewed at Fitzwilliam. He was not enthused by the ugly, unfinished college on the city's outskirts, but he made a favourable impression on Norman Walters, largely owing to his athletic prowess. According to another candidate, John Venning, Walters 'manipulated admissions in certain ways in order to fill the college with the sort of undergraduates he thought it needed – he wanted a dynamic mix of people not selected purely on the basis of academic achievement'. Before he could offer Nick a place, however, he needed the results of his retakes.

In the interim Nick was concerned only with the short term. 'The summer we left school Nick, Mike Hacking, Chris Rudkin and I had a grand plan to drive a Land Rover to Gibraltar and Morocco, then all the way to Nairobi – until we worked out how far it was,' says Dave Wright. Instead, Nick embarked on a less ambitious road trip through France with three other schoolmates: Michael Maclaran, Hugh Griffith and Jonathan Clague. They weren't among his closest friends, but all were music lovers and Michael was a fellow Perfumed Gardener.

Having mustered at Far Leys and loaded their bags, a tent and Nick's guitar into HOB, they set off. 'Nick and I were the two with recently acquired driving licences; the others had most of the luggage on their knees in the back seat,' by Michael's account.[1] 'Driving a heavily laden and underpowered car was a nightmare, and included such dramas as losing both wing mirrors at once in a head-on near collision and scraping the entire contents of a traffic island in our path as we ploughed on, wheels locked.'

The boys slept anywhere they could, as Nick and Dave had the previous summer. 'Wherever we went the evenings were often the same, with groups of people gathering around bonfires under the stars, on beaches, in woods or at campsites, to hear Nick sing and play his guitar,' continues Michael.

> At St-Tropez, amongst the luxury yachts and private beaches, it was often getting light by the time last night's party was ending – and Nick would still be strumming away . . . Despite the many people who would gather, most of them well lubricated, the sessions never became raucous singalongs; he didn't play to the crowd.

As Michael watched Nick, it struck him that he 'played beautifully and people would clap at the end of each song, but he never looked up or seemed in any way to solicit their applause or adoration'. It was as if he were playing for himself, and the appreciation of others was incidental.

After some 750 hard miles, the inevitable happened: 'The car finally broke down near the top of the climb towards Grenoble. Short of mechanical skills, we stared under the bonnet. Someone spotted a broken spring, which was miraculously replaced by an identical one from a nearby piece of farm machinery.'[2] Rodney would have been proud. The ailing HOB then managed another 150 miles south to Lédenon, where Jeremy Mason's parents had a holiday home.

The exhausted, sweaty boys arrived on Friday, 5 August, to find John Du Cane already there, and passed a merry weekend enjoying their newfound freedom. That evening they strolled a mile through the dry heat, Nick bearing his guitar. 'All the young of the village used to walk to the main road and sit on a wall at a junction of the roads,' explains Jeremy. 'Nick was a great hit. He played "Michael, Row the Boat Ashore",* "House of the Rising Sun",† all that sort of singalong folk stuff – and I remember them all singing along.'[3] Back at the house, says John, 'I remember us lying out at night gazing at the starry sky . . .'

---

* A much-recorded African American spiritual; Lonnie Donegan had a Number 6 UK hit with it in 1961.
† A traditional American folk song, hugely popularised by the Animals in 1964.

The next day, Jeremy recalls, was passed 'lying in the sun, looking very white, trying to be cool wearing dark glasses, swimming under the Pont du Gard, reading Oscar Wilde aloud and drinking'.[4] A surviving colour photo shows the pasty group by the water, Nick in his prescription glasses, seemingly oblivious of a bikini-clad lady passing behind them. (It's one of only two known photos of him wearing glasses.) That evening the Masons took them to watch the celebrated El Cordobés at a bullfight in Nîmes, before the boys sallied forth again.

'We were asked to an enormous village fête,' says Jeremy.

It consisted of trestle tables, where we were persuaded to drink pastis without any water in it, which we duly did. We got so drunk we ended up running along the tops of the tables and jumping into strange people's arms. We then asked them all back to the house – I said, 'Come back and have a drink! Nick will play his guitar some more!' My mother came downstairs to shoo them all away. She said, 'I could hear this cacophony approaching, led by you and Nick . . .'[5]

Washing up after dinner on Sunday evening, the conversation turned to drugs. Jeremy recalls: 'Nick sort of said, "Oh well, you know, it's one of those things one tries." My mother got quite cross . . . This was the summer of 1966, long before the Beatles admitted to taking LSD or anything.'[6] It was not, however, an announcement of any imminent intention; as Jeremy interpreted it, 'Nick's view was that one could relate to it and deal with it, and it wasn't a problem. But at that time he was obviously thinking exclusively about marijuana.'[7] For all Nick's apparent willingness to flirt with drugs, Michael says: 'I can definitely state that there were no drugs on our trip.'

The boys left the Masons on Monday, 8 August, making the gruelling return trip to Far Leys in the long-suffering Morris. The claustrophobic journey didn't lead to ructions, though. 'We seldom had a cross word and parted on the best of terms,' says Michael – but Nick never saw any of them again. Back home he played guitar and reconnected with Dave Lodder and other local friends whom he had barely seen whilst at Marlborough.

One evening he went to a party in the nearby village of Wootton

Wawen, the home of the Maynard-Mitchell family. Returning in the small hours, he played the piano, sang and decided to tape himself tipsily burbling. The result is the longest recording of his speech to survive. Amongst verbiage and non-sequiturs, he slurs:

Um, good evening – or should I say good morning? The time is twenty-five to five and I think I've been sitting here for some time now, actually. It's after a party which I quite enjoyed . . . In fact, there weren't as many people there as I expected there to be . . . There weren't nearly as many as one might have thought, which was . . . which was a pity.

In fact, I think I must have drunk rather a lot, although it didn't seem so at the time (I thought myself quite sober) – but when I leapt into the car to drive home after my merry abandon I found the task extremely difficult. And it was extremely fortunate that there was nothing else on the road because, looking back at it, I seem to remember I had a mental brainstorm, although I didn't realise it at the time, and I think I drove the whole way home on the right-hand side of the road, which is something of course which comes from driving in France too much, which is what I've been doing recently, as you probably know.

And in moments of stress such as was this journey home, one forgets so easily . . . the lies, the truth and the pain . . . And so . . . I'm wavering from the point. What I was trying to say is, um . . . When I sat here I had an extremely pleasant time on the piano, actually. I was playing the piano and sort of singing, and I rather fear I might have kept people awake upstairs . . . One hopes not, but it was pleasant, and it's extremely pleasant sitting here now, because I think there is something extraordinarily nice about seeing the dawn up before one goes to bed, because there's something uncanny about it when it suddenly becomes light, because one connects darkness with going to bed, surely . . . And when one is still up when the new day begins it is something of an intriguing experience, I always find.

I can look out of the window now, and that tree over there is green, whereas before one goes to bed, just when one goes to bed, that tree should be black, surely! Everything should be black before one goes to bed, but that is surely the essence of the Romantic.

Anyway, I think I'm straying from the point. I should probably stop talking now because, um, if I don't I shall start sort of relating life-histories and things, which will be frightfully tedious. So it's here that I'll sort of say goodnight, you know . . . Goodnight!

With a quiet chuckle, the recording ends. For Gabrielle it is 'a cod piece of broadcasting':

> an imitation of those 'intimate' radio broadcasts with the speaker doing his best to make the listener feel he or she was receiving valuable philosophising on a one-to-one basis. I think Nick was sending this (and himself) up. The tone of his voice is one he used when mocking himself, and his little laugh at the end is indicative.

Although its content is throwaway and Nick certainly did not intend it to survive, it offers some insights. Most importantly, it preserves his deep, husky speaking voice and hesitant manner of delivery, bordering on a stammer. His accent and use of the pronoun 'one' and phrases like 'merry abandon' and 'frightfully tedious' place him in a rarefied social stratum. His references to enjoying the party and being disappointed at the poor turnout confirm the gregarious-ness that his friends recall from this period. The admission of drunkenly driving home on the wrong side of the road before waking the other occupants of the house suggests typical teenage insouciance, and his casual misquotation of Rupert Brooke's 'The Old Vicarage, Grantchester' ('Deep meadows yet, for to forget / The lies, and truths, and pain') and reference to 'the essence of the Romantic' speak of his literary taste.

Nick had another 'moment of stress' when his exam results arrived. He had hauled his English grade up to a B, but got Es in British Constitution, Latin Translation with Roman History and the General Paper. They were far from sufficient to merit a place at any decent university, and in theory torpedoed any hope of getting to Cambridge. His parents, however, immediately set plan B in motion – sending him to a crammer in Birmingham in order to sit Cambridge's entrance examination, subject to Fitzwilliam's approval.

Accordingly, in early September he filled in his UCCA form, a government requirement for anyone wishing to attend university. It required him to give a brief account of his achievements to date, so he wrote: 'House Captain at school [no doubt aware that this title sounded more distinguished than it was], member of various musical societies, played in the school orchestra, concert band, dance band etc. Also interested in art, Goya and modern art in particular. School athletics colours, played in hockey XXII and rugger XL [*sic*].' He then added, as if an afterthought: 'Head boy at prep school.'

Nick sent the form on to Dennis Silk, who set about writing a 'Confidential Statement' about his former pupil. 'Nicholas Drake is a boy who has taken a long time to mature academically,' he tentatively began.

> His IQ, measured when he first came to the school, was high enough to make us hope for a much more dynamic approach than he showed for several years . . . Suddenly, in his last year, after one rather poor set of results at A-level, he began to go forward fast and the mirror of this is the B he obtained in English this year, where he had only managed an E the year before.

It was thin gruel, and little weight can have been attached to his next remark: 'I strongly feel that given the chance to read English at the University he would be a very good candidate indeed.'

Casting about for strings to add to Nick's bow, he somewhat desperately added that he 'has always had a feel for the theatre and comes from an acting family',* before perceptively remarking, 'He loves music and plays several wind instruments and would, I think, secretly like to be good enough to make his living in music.'

Having remarked upon Nick's athletic talent (and lack of ambition in that direction), he concluded: 'He is a genuine late developer who is only now growing into his academic potential . . . He could give a lot to the community as well as getting a lot. He is a most delightful person to deal with.' It was an affectionate and generous portrait of an inscrutable individual with a long track record of academic lethargy. Nonetheless, Norman Walters agreed to have him sit the exam towards the end of the year.

---

* Nick did enjoy the theatre, as did his whole family, but Gabrielle was their only connection to acting.

Nick's personal statement notably omitted any mention of guitar playing, which remained his major occupation. He was fascinated by acoustic players such as Davy Graham, Bert Jansch and John Renbourn, as well as American blues, but also enjoyed rock. He was well aware that his old heroes Jack Bruce and Ginger Baker had split from Graham Bond and formed a new band with Eric Clapton. Accordingly, he went to a deafening gig by Cream at the Marquee Dance Club in Birmingham on Saturday, 10 September.

The following Wednesday found him visiting Chas. E. Foote, Ltd, sellers of 'New and Reconditioned Band Instruments' in Denman Street, London W1, where he bought his first serious guitar, a Levin, helped by money he had received for his eighteenth birthday.* At a cost of £53 11s., with an accompanying case for £9 10s. and a capo for 10s. 6d., the total outlay was £63 11s. 6d. It was a significant sum, equating to around £900 in 2022, yet he knew it was essential to his musical development. 'Levins were easily the best entry-level guitars you could get,' explains Wizz Jones, a well-known figure on the folk scene of the day. 'They were Swedish copies of Martins (which no one could afford).'

He spent much of September playing it in London, where he had Gabrielle's flat largely to himself, before reluctantly enrolling at the Birmingham Tutorial School at the end of the month. Located at 67 Harborne Road, it was a Victorian house reconfigured as a warren of small classrooms, commonly known as 'Bantock's'.

Raymond Bantock had founded it in 1923, since when it had manoeuvred innumerable local youths into schools and universities that had seemed beyond them. He set about making preparations for Nick, opening one letter to Mr Walters with the unpromising line, 'I wrote to you on 29th September concerning Jonathan Drake'.

Fortuitously, Dave Lodder was also booked into Bantock's for retakes that autumn.

Neither of us took it very seriously, as far as I remember – Nick didn't seem bothered about going to Cambridge. I'd go to the Drakes'

---

* The handwritten receipt states it's a Levin Deluxe, a semi-acoustic instrument, but that might be an error; photographs taken in the ensuing months show Nick playing the LS-18 model.

in the morning and he would drive us there while we chatted away about this, that and the other. He was a reckless driver and always went flat-out – he used to belt round corners. One morning he drove far too fast out of a junction and ploughed into a car that was full of eggs. He was okay, as was the lady driving the other car, but I was thrown into the windscreen and banged my head, and there were eggs everywhere.*

Perhaps inspired by their childhood escapades, Nick continued to show his reckless side.

Another morning as we drove down Bates Lane there was a guy walking towards us and Nick suddenly said, 'Watch this!' and swerved across the road into a giant puddle and absolutely drenched him. It could easily have been someone he knew or who recognised the car, but we roared off, killing ourselves with laughter. So he had a streak of evil in him! Our route took us through the back streets of Moseley, and we used to drive past a men's hairdresser with 'Hair Stylist' printed in its window. Nick decided to make an appointment (which tells you something about him – I would never have wanted to have my hair 'styled'). He was so appalled and furious with the results that I had to persuade him not to return that night and put a brick through its window.

Sometimes after we got back we'd go to the music room at Far Leys and he'd play his instruments – guitar, sax, piano, clarinet, he could play anything – but it was all wasted on me. It was clear that he was becoming more and more focused on music, but in no way did it seem obsessive, and it wasn't obvious that he was music-mad from our conversations.

Nick sat his Cambridge papers in November, having given every appearance of intending to fail. Bantock's certainly had low expectations. 'Test papers produce marks in the low 50s, but this, I would say, is an optimistic estimate,' wrote Mr Bantock to Rodney and Molly.

---

* Following this accident – far from Nick's first or last – Rodney undertook to 'pay insurance, registration & major repairs not due to bad driving'.

I found Drake considerably deficient in knowledge of current affairs, of English literature at large, and especially of modern literature. Furthermore, I found his approach to essays lacking in penetration and originality. His views, when formed, seemed to be average and conventional . . . I feel that if he has failed to make the grade in this examination, it will be due almost entirely to his above-mentioned insufficiency of knowledge and his inability to formulate new ideas and original lines of argument.

With this depth-charge in the post, Nick drove to London. He stayed at Gabrielle's flat and (courtesy of her contacts) spent a few weeks earning good money as a stagehand for *Man of Magic*, a musical about Harry Houdini at the Piccadilly Theatre. Otherwise, he hung out with schoolfriends at Desi Burlison-Rush's flat, where music was the lingua franca. Innovations in pop were rife, with recent albums such as the Beach Boys' *Pet Sounds*, the Byrds' *Fifth Dimension*, the Yardbirds' *Yardbirds*, the Beatles' *Revolver*, Donovan's *Sunshine Superman* and the Incredible String Band's self-titled debut all reflecting a thrilling expansion of ideas and possibilities.

Not least of these was the influence of pot, which Nick was determined to try. 'He and I went on a mission down Portobello Road to buy grass (definitely grass, not hash), and eventually managed to get some in a pub,' says Mike Hacking, who had spent the previous few months in New York's demi-monde. 'We weren't sure it was the real thing, but we went back to Sloane Street and smoked it. That was the first time Nick ever smoked dope.' Dave Wright was there too: 'I remember Nick laughing as he rolled a joint and telling us that his parents had warned him about the dangers of drugs in the big city.'

The city was in full swing and the fabled UFO was about to open, but long nights in psychedelic clubs weren't Nick's style.* In fact, a poem he wrote at this time entitled 'Delusions Of Night Life' indicates a quasi-puritanical contempt for the trendy nightspots that had lately sprung up all over London:

* UFO (pronounced 'Yoofo') opened on Saturday, 23 December. Although it seems Nick never went there, in the dying days of 1966 he did join another subterranean club, Blaises, in South Kensington.

Forced, jerked rhythms and sweating eyes,
Hysterical enjoyment and unnatural benevolence.
How can man so delude himself?

Another, shorter poem, 'An Influenced View Of Life', also takes a lofty view of his fellow man, albeit acknowledging dope as its basis:

What does it matter?
From this soaring, neo-immortal seat,
Under this seemingly heaven-sent influence
One can look down on the swarming futilities of life.
Why should it matter?
Why must one return to the shallow qualities of pretentious lying?
Why must it matter?

Setting aside the jejune wording and sentiments, a certain detachment and fatalism can be detected in the poems. No one at Marlborough had detected any creative impulse in him, yet shortly after leaving he had started to write. He was not yet framing his words as lyrics, though; improving his guitar technique remained his focus.

'Desi's flat was where we used to listen to him playing,' says another schoolmate, Nic Ratiu. 'I remember him being intrigued by harmonics at that time and explaining to me that when you pluck two strings at once you can get a completely new sound – he was experimenting with that and trying to develop it.' Mike also remembers Nick being happy to share his enthusiasm:

I used to strum away too, and he was always very encouraging to me, which is funny because he was so much better. I used to think he played much better than he sang, and fear I might have told him that once, which is awful, because of course he saw his guitar and voice as one whole.

There were girls on the scene, not least Desi, but no one recalls Nick taking anything other than a friendly interest in them. 'Four girls shared a flat on the floor below us, but if he saw one of them on the stairs he'd just nod and keep going,' says Mike. 'He really didn't relate to girls – I don't remember him ever having a girlfriend or even flirting. I would say he was asexual. He wasn't a physical person – if you hugged him he wouldn't warm to it, he wouldn't engage, his arms would stay by his side.'

On Saturday, 10 December, he joined Les Cousins* at 49 Greek Street in Soho. Describing itself as 'London's folk and blues centre', it was the city's leading venue for aspiring acoustic guitarists and singers, who would crowd into its small subterranean space to hear each other and exchange musical tips and gossip. The singer-songwriter Bridget St John describes it as 'a small, crowded music-soaked basement: one flight of steps both entrance and exit, one somewhat noisy fan for ventilation, no dressing room, no backstage, strong coffee in industrial-thick mugs, a raised platform, a stool, and two mics with the audience seemingly only inches away'.

Saturdays were all-night sessions at which audience members could get up and sing. It's possible that Nick did so at this time; his friends don't recall him being shy about performing, and he had at least one other gig. 'At one point I was so broke I got a job washing up in Borscht 'n' Tears in Beauchamp Place and arranged for Nick to play guitar there while people ate,' says Mike.†

Nick was in London, probably asleep, when a letter with a Cambridge postmark arrived for him at Far Leys on Wednesday, 14 December. With his advance permission, Rodney opened it. It was from Norman Walters at Fitzwilliam. 'Dear Drake,' it began, 'I am happy to say that, as a result of your work in the Group Entrance Examination, we are able to offer you a place to read English beginning next October.'

It was a tremendous vindication of the long campaign to get Nick in, and Rodney replied on his behalf at once, with palpable exhilaration: 'I need hardly say that we are delighted to hear you are able to offer him a place, which he accepts, of course, with great pleasure.'‡

There was a sting, though. As Mr Walters wrote: 'In view of the

---

* Pronounced as if 'Les' were the English name, and 'Cousins' the English noun.
† There's no evidence that Nick ever attended London's other leading folk clubs, Bunjie's and the Troubadour, either as an audience member or a performer.
‡ Of the 196 boys in Nick's year at Marlborough, 52 went to Oxford or Cambridge.

requirement in the English Tripos* for translation from French into English, I should be grateful if you would let me know what arrangements you will be able to make to deal with this side of your work between now and coming up.' Rodney was able to parry this with ease: 'He will be spending six months, from the beginning of February '67, at the Université de Marseilles, Aix-en-Provence.'

---

* The University's term for a course of study leading to an undergraduate's degree examinations.

7

Young And Discovering The World

'NICK'S MOTHER RANG my mother, asking what I was going
to be up to over the first few months of 1967,' says Simon
Crocker. 'She explained I was going to learn French in Aix, so they
arranged for him to come along too.' When it emerged that Jeremy
Mason had separately organised to do the same, the three boys agreed
to travel together on Saturday, 11 February. Enrolling for a brief and
undemanding course as foreign students at the Université d'Aix-
Marseille was a standard way for young English people to kill a few
months between school and university. The course had no academic
entry criteria nor any exams at its end, so it promised to be a pleasantly unpressured way to kill time away from home, under the
fig-leaf of improving their French.

Nick spent the early weeks of 1967 working as a stagehand and
squirreling away a decent sum to see him through the months ahead.
Gabrielle didn't see much of him, but they did spend an evening
together in February, when she took him to a preview of *Fiddler on
the Roof*.* 'I remember being so proud walking down the Haymarket
with him because he looked so good – six foot two or three and
these broad shoulders, narrow waist, long legs . . .'[1]

The night before his departure Nick left HOB at Far Leys and
returned to London on the train, carrying a suitcase and his guitar.
Rodney subsequently found that the car's petrol tank was completely
empty and thus had to summon the local mechanic, who – he wrote
to Nick – 'was vastly tickled by what he regarded as a very shrewd
piece of budgeting on your part'.

The boys arranged to meet in Victoria Station. Having located

---

* *Fiddler on the Roof* opened at Her Majesty's Theatre on 16 February.

Jeremy, who was bidding a protracted farewell to his recent fiancée, Simon says: 'We got on the train, looked at each other and thought, "What the hell are we doing?!" . . . We'd all had relatively sheltered lives at school, and suddenly we were out in an unstructured life.'[2] It had been six months since the end of Marlborough and they'd barely seen each other since.

> Our hair was starting to grow and we were emerging from our school selves. I'd say Nick and I were good friends, if not close, and I didn't know Jeremy very well. They shared interests in philosophy, classical music and other things I wasn't so interested in then, so they had a connection there.

After sailing to Calais, reaching Paris and waiting three hours for their connection to Marseilles, it was almost evening when the weary trio finally reached Aix. It was dark and the town was cold, awaiting the mellowing of spring. 'Our parents, for some extraordinary reason, had not fixed up anywhere for us to stay,' says Jeremy. 'They had been told that it would all be arranged once we got to the university. We went to the university and they were completely uninterested.' Eventually they were packed off to stay with a local family who spoke no English.

On Monday morning they formally registered, a process that involved (according to Nick) 'filling in the biggest pile of forms you've ever seen, all of which were naturally in French and extremely complex'. On Tuesday they presented themselves at an address recommended by the accommodation office:

> We had come to absolutely depend on this one prospect, so there we were at 9 in the morning, looking the very epitome of respectability, when a woman appeared and informed us in the most light-hearted fashion that the flat had been taken even before we had arrived in Aix.

There was nothing for it but to trudge around the local letting agencies, making enquiries in schoolboy French. It was a crash course in taking responsibility. 'Most of them had nothing to offer, except for this one that sent us round to the "Résidence Sextius", a huge block of rooms which have only just been completed,' continued

Nick. The modernist block was in fact still a building site, ten minutes' walk from the town centre, but he had learned to be economical with the information he sent home. The boys took two cheap rooms opposite one another; Nick shared one with Simon while Jeremy slept in the other, which doubled as a communal sitting room. 'They were cells, really,' says Simon. 'They had a bed and a couple of chairs but no sheets, no towels and so on, so we had to go off and buy those as cheaply as we could.'

'One of the first things was to get it looking homely and cool – we were determined to be cool,' adds Jeremy.

> We went out and bought some pictures and books, but most of it was done purely for effect. We got Baudelaire's *Fleurs du Mal*, Dostoevsky's *The House of the Dead* and Oscar Wilde's *Picture of Dorian Gray*, but Nick didn't read much in Aix, as I recall – he was more interested in his guitar. He was in charge of the music and we had an eclectic collection of records including Dylan, Dave Van Ronk and Bert Jansch.

'I'd brought my Dansette but no records,' says Simon. 'I bought Donovan's *Mellow Yellow* album and Nick played it incessantly and taught himself some of the songs on it. We also had the *Bert and John* album, and solo albums by them [Jansch and Renbourn] which Nick must have picked up there.' Jeremy also recalls them listening to Bach's Brandenburg Concertos, John Mayall and Jefferson Airplane.*

Having set up their base, they began to explore. For Nick Lewin, whom Nick soon encountered,

> Aix was a sleepy little hick town with a great university in it. It appeared to be miles from anywhere but was actually brilliantly placed for the Riviera, Italy, Spain, Morocco and so on, and full of young people like us, who weren't sure what they were going to do. We were rather snooty about the locals – they seemed to be about fifteen years behind the times – but it was wonderful to be so far from the familiar.

---

* *Surrealistic Pillow* had been released in America on 1 February; it is likely that Nick was influenced by Jorma Kaukonen's solo showcase on that album, 'Embryonic Journey'.

It was an eye-opening environment in several ways. Anglo-French relations were tense and the gendarmerie targeted English students, frequently asking them to produce their papers. 'We never carried our ID, which we were supposed to have on us at all times, and often pretended to be either Irish or Scandinavian to avoid being harassed by the police,' explains Simon. In addition, recalls Jeremy, 'There were racial tensions in the air – we'd see the occasional fight and hear about Arabs stabbing each other.'

More mundanely, he adds that 'Aix was the first place where I saw printed T-shirts or had pizza,' while Simon says: 'We didn't have much money – we subsisted on cheap wine, bread and great blocks of cheese. Pizzas were a great discovery in the backstreet restaurants/ cafés – filling and cheap. We also discovered lager and yoghurt – staples now, but not then.'

With his domestic arrangements made, Nick was supposed to be immersing himself in learning. 'I intend going to lectures on French grammar and speaking, as well as some philosophy, which in this case deals with existentialism and in particular with Albert Camus,' he assured his parents. 'There is also a course on Surrealist poetry, which I might try and cope with later on.' These were genuine – if peripheral – interests of his, but, admits Simon, 'We gave up studying pretty quickly. No one was checking on us so we welcomed the opportunity of not having to do any work.'

The boys slept through much of the morning before venturing forth. 'The English used to meet every day in one or other café for coffee and gossip, making plans and so on,' Simon explains. 'Jeremy and I introduced ourselves and made connections, while Nick hung back and listened and watched. However, his silence was compelling and people were drawn to him.' As Nick told his parents, 'Life here seems to revolve largely around moving from café to café – very pleasant in its way.'

True to form, he gravitated towards the less boisterous among the English crowd, though he primly told his parents:

The majority of them seem to be rich young Londoners who have been sent out here for want of something better to do, have at no stage had any intention of learning French, and are constantly bored stiff. All nice guys, but not the sort of type who help one improve one's French.

'We were all young and discovering the world and who we were,' reflects Jo Dingemans. 'There were a lot of English in Aix, as well as Americans dodging the draft and the occasional Swede selling drugs. A lot of students congregated in a café called Les Deux Garçons in the Cours Mirabeau (the main street), doing *The Times* crossword and letting their coffees last.' She soon encountered Nick, who struck her as 'gorgeous – not a pretty boy but a slender, distinctive persona with that round-shouldered stoop tall people have. His smile transformed his face. He was reserved rather than shy, a very attractive young man.'

James Calvocoressi says: 'He didn't strike me as shy or withdrawn – he was modest but perfectly outgoing.' Nick Lewin recalls him constantly putting Herb Alpert and the Tijuana Brass on the jukebox in Les Deux Garçons and calls him 'part of the gang': 'He was quiet and shy but also charming – and very funny, in his way.' Derek FitzGerald remembers his idiosyncratic style, at a time when many were brightly dressed:

> I never remember him wearing anything colourful or flashy – he'd be in a dark jacket and jeans. He was great company but held things back. He struck me as an amused observer of life rather than an active participant in it. He and I used to play an awful lot of table football. He was forward and I was back. He was very good at it – he had a very strong wrist and absolutely fired the balls. We'd play long tournaments against the local French boys, sometimes for money.

Any winnings were welcome. According to Nick Lewin: 'We had small allowances from our parents, which we always had diffi-culty collecting from the bank – they would say it hadn't arrived and so on.' It didn't help that there was a strict limit on how much sterling could be taken abroad – £50 (around £700 in 2022). As such, they tended to pass the evenings in each other's digs rather than going out.

Nick also spent much of his time playing his guitar at Résidence Sextius, refining his style and sound late into the night. 'It went from a schoolboy thing to something he did more and more', by Jeremy's account. 'He sat for hours on his bed. I knew then he was getting pretty serious about it. He used to loosen the strings – completely, as I recall . . . He would strum away and tighten them up as he went.'[3] Jeremy drew Nick in February 1967, the image clearly conveying Nick's immersion in his task.

Familiar chord patterns and tunes began to emerge from his improvising, and it dawned on Simon that he was devising original material: 'Up until that we'd all been doing cover versions, just mucking around – and here was Nick obviously doing something seriously. It wasn't surprising, but one was surprised at how good they were.' It's not known what Nick's very first song was, and he never spoke clearly about his metamorphosis into a songwriter. The closest he came was the vague statement: 'It was one of those periods in time when I was uncertain what to do with myself. I hadn't thought for myself and it was only when I did that I began to write properly.'[4]

James Calvocoressi's flat in Rue Manuel was something of a social hub, and Nick was happy to bring along his guitar. 'One knew immediately that he was a cut above your average teenager doing a Bob Dylan impression,' says James,[5] adding that, 'All the times I heard him play he was happy and comfortable and enjoyed the attention and respect that his obvious talent commanded.' Derek adds: 'He would play old classics but was also starting to write his own songs and would throw those in too. It was obvious to everybody that he was exceptional.'

If Nick weren't playing, James had a ready alternative: a portable Philips tape recorder.

> I'd taped some records with it (Beatles, Stones, Cream etc.), which provided a good soundtrack to whatever was happening, but I didn't have any intention of recording anybody or anything and I don't think I even brought any blank cassettes – but people often remarked upon it and it intrigued Nick.

Occasionally everyone piled back to Résidence Sextius, which Jo remembers as 'modern and bare – I don't remember furniture. Nick had a single bed that also acted as a sofa.' The group would listen to music, drink wine, smoke dope and chat into the night. On one occasion the talk turned to spiritualism. 'Childishly, we had a big session of table-turning, which Nick did get very involved in,' recalls Jeremy.[6] 'He rustled up some uncle he didn't know existed and actually rang his parents from a café (which in those days took three hours) to ask, "Did this uncle exist? Why did I not know about him?"'* Jo was also there: 'After the séance finished, rather dramatically, we were followed by this big black dog, which we never saw again. It really shook us up.' ('I had never heard of the "black dog" in connection with depression at that time,' she adds, 'but have always thought "Black-Eyed Dog" was about the aftermath of that séance.')

On the afternoon of Friday, 24 February – barely a fortnight after reaching Aix – Nick, Simon and Jeremy made their way to the Masons' house in Lédenon, scene of much jollity the preceding summer. Simon drove on a decrepit moped he'd acquired, while Nick (with guitar) and Jeremy hitchhiked. Upon arrival over six hours later, says Jeremy, 'It wasn't as magic as we remembered it from the previous summer. We cooked out of tins and stayed for three or four days, but it wasn't really very enjoyable.'[7] Nick had managed to borrow a tape machine – James is emphatic it wasn't his – and Simon recalls that cold weekend being 'certainly the first time we recorded some of his songs. I can clearly remember holding the microphone while he sang into the tape recorder.'[8]

Back in Aix Nick continued to find fault with his compatriots, largely owing to his loathing of boorishness. 'I am getting to find the English group rather tedious, which is probably a good thing,' he told his parents on 3 March.

> Although individually they are mostly very nice, as a group they are thoroughly nauseous. I have made one or two contacts with French people, though not nearly as many as I'd like to . . . I have met one or two female French students, which is of course rather pleasant . . . I'm finding the lectures a bit tough and think I shall probably

---

* Nick kept the scrap of paper on which he scrawled down his mother's reply: she'd managed to dredge up a great-uncle of hers who'd died in Worcestershire the previous September.

stick to the actual French lessons for a while, and perhaps keep going on the philosophy lectures, which I find easier than the rest.

He was implying a strong engagement with his course but music was his focus, and he began to seek public outlets. 'I'm looking around for an opportunity to start playing my guitar in public,' he continued. 'I went to a jazz club in Aix the other night and stood in for about half an hour with some other students. I mostly played piano, but also had a go on an alto. My saxophone playing proved, regrettably, to be somewhat rusty.'

The club was in the cellar of La Tartane restaurant and was run by a French student named Jean-Louis Pujol, who also put on folk nights there and played guitar. He got talking to Nick and went back to Résidence Sextius one evening. 'I simply copied Renbourn, Jansch and others, but Nick had gone way beyond that,' he says. 'He was inventing his own style, using his own tunings, always experimenting – brilliant. I think he was aware that he was talented, that he had found something in himself.'

A Californian student named Robin Frederick had a regular gig at La Tartane. One night in early March, she says,

> Nick and his friend Jeremy came up to me after I finished a set. Jeremy introduced himself and went on to say that his friend 'would like to know if I'd be interested in working with him' . . . It seemed odd that he asked on Nick's behalf, when Nick was standing right there. I assumed he meant performing, singing, something like that, and I said 'Yes'.

Before they could play as a duo they needed to assess one another's ability. 'The first time we met up to play music was in Nick's room,' says Robin.

> This was the first time I heard him play. I noticed how fluid he was and the interesting ways he played with timing, playing some songs faster than I was used to and others with extra bars between sections. There were quite a few of his friends in the room as well. I got the sense that it was more like a performance for them than the two of us working up material to do together.

Indeed, she recalls, 'He didn't strike me as being shy about playing. He knew he was good and, like a proud bird, he liked to display his feathers.'[9]

As the night wore on, they worked through their separate repertoires.

> We played songs back-and-forth but didn't sing together . . . I remember his beautiful voice – intense, quiet, and honest . . . I don't recall him singing any original songs. He may have been writing then but didn't feel ready to share any with me. He was doing songs by Bob Dylan, Bert Jansch and other contemporary songwriters. I remember singing 'Changes' by Phil Ochs, which he liked a lot.[10]

Soon afterwards Nick and Jeremy turned up on her doorstep in the small hours, having managed to lock themselves out of Résidence Sextius. The next time, Nick was alone.

> He always brought his guitar and always wore a velveteen jacket – I remember thinking how cold he must be. It was difficult to sing with him because he often played with the timing or phrasing of songs that I knew. I could never anticipate when he was going to do that, so it never seemed to me that we were working up the songs for a set. After a couple of these evenings we just played songs for each other. I think that's when he learned my song 'Been Smoking Too Long'.

Robin 'got the feeling Nick was absorbing everything around him – music, lyrics, sights, sounds, people – quietly taking it all in. Although he was shy and reserved, he had a powerful presence that seemed to draw people to him. Certainly he was physically beautiful and that, plus his natural quietness, made it easy to embroider a tapestry of fantasies around him.'[11] As ever, he gave no sign of noticing or caring. Perhaps this was studied insouciance (Robin felt he was 'determined to look cool'[12]), but his friends agree that he simply wasn't interested in romance.

'Nick's stillness was attractive to some girls, and he liked their company, but it never went anywhere,' reflects Simon. 'He wasn't red-blooded, he was passive around them, and there was no woman-ising on his part. I wouldn't have known what "asexual" meant back then, but I think in retrospect it could well have applied to him.' One night Simon had company:

There was a French-Moroccan girl who liked hanging around the English crowd, and I slept with her. The next day Nick told me she was notorious for having the clap, which sent me rushing off to the chemist in a panic. I escaped unscathed, but never knew whether he was simply making it up to tease me. He thought it was hilarious. He did have a dark sense of humour at times.

Nick, Simon and Jeremy hadn't set out to be in Aix together, and as the days turned into weeks they drifted apart. 'We weren't really a trio there – we all did our own things most of the time,' says Jeremy. 'I'd started drawing, Nick was playing the guitar more and more . . .' One important difference was that Simon and Jeremy weren't dope smokers. Nick, however, did not struggle to find those who were. 'Aix was very near to Marseilles, where the dope came in from North Africa, so it was easy to buy if you wanted it – people would sidle up to you in cafés,' explains James Calvocoressi. However, Simon clarifies: 'I didn't see Nick smoking any more than anyone else.'

Within a fortnight of arriving Nick was arranging to spend the Easter break in Morocco – an ambition that had been thwarted the previous summer and had perhaps been an ulterior motive in his agreeing to go to Aix in the first place. However, he told his parents on 3 March, 'My plans are by no means certain, since the fellow who offered to take me is one of the English students, who is at the moment in either Paris or Geneva and no one is quite sure whether he's coming back.'

No sooner had he posted the letter than the fellow in question, Mike Hill, returned. 'The trip was my idea,' he explains. 'It was an ad hoc group – I was at the university in Aix but met Bob when I visited Paris, and he was keen on coming.' 'Bob' was the outgoing Rick Charkin, so nicknamed because his hair resembled Bob Dylan's. He was studying in Paris and had met Mike there through a mutual girlfriend. 'We drove down to Aix in his dark blue Cortina GT,' he says. 'It wasn't small, but it had a finely tuned engine and went fast.'

Mike was impatient to get going. There was one space left in the car but Simon was planning to slip back to London for a party and Jeremy's fiancée was due to visit, so Nick roped in another young Englishman living in Résidence Sextius, Julian Raby, who was just seventeen. The motley quartet cruised out of Aix on the morning of Tuesday, 7 March. Term hadn't yet finished, but Nick had no desire to be stranded when it did. In departing so abruptly, he had to discard a plan with Robin: 'Nick asked me to meet him at a café and then never showed up. I was furious. And hurt . . . I never saw him again.'[13]

'Leading the expedition was one Mike Hill, heir to some five titles and endowed with private means of fairly notable proportions,' Nick wrote to his parents upon his return.[14] He added that Rick was 'a really great guy who at first gives the impression of being thick as boots but is in fact very intelligent, and is going up to Cambridge next Oct. to read science'. To Rick's subsequent bafflement, Nick chose not to mention that he was also bound for Cambridge; it was as if he were unwilling to admit it to himself.

By Nick's account, Julian was 'a sort of far-gone intellectual who has a classical scholarship to Oxford'. In response, Julian says, 'I was certainly far-gone but perhaps more of an antiquarian nerd than an intellectual! I was not going to Oxford with a classical scholarship and would certainly not have claimed any such thing, so perhaps Nick larded things for his parents' consumption.'

'None of us were especial friends but we were united by a sense of common adventure,' he continues. 'Nick was always amiable, but it was difficult to get through to him – we were almost in parallel universes. Mike was a forceful, extroverted guy who had no vibe with him at all, as I recall.' According to Mike, 'Nick had a gentle manner, but along with that went a degree of privacy. That said, we weren't all having deep conversations, we were living for each day, and he was a decent travelling companion in every way.'

Julian well remembers Mike's Cortina: 'He'd souped it up by adding a little metal bar between the accelerator and the brake, so he could do both simultaneously on corners. He wanted to get through Spain at breakneck speed.' They tore towards Granada, arriving at lunchtime on Wednesday the 8th. 'Granada provided our first taste of Moorish civilisation, and I must say I was immensely impressed,' Nick related. His ensuing description could have come from *The Perfumed Garden*: 'One can so clearly imagine the great fat Moorish rulers lounging around there, surrounded by their oozing, silken females.'

Next they traversed the narrow mountain roads to Malaga. 'Since Mike rather fancies himself as a would-be rally driver, there was a certain amount of hanging on involved,' Nick told his parents. 'I think we must have set up a few records.' Reaching Gibraltar on the evening of Thursday the 9th, they discovered they weren't allowed to take the car in, so strolled across the border on foot. Having drunk and explored their fill ('There's a fabulous deep, deep cave halfway up the rock, with dim lighting and beautiful choir music drifting around – I just sat there for about an hour in a complete trance'), on Saturday, 11 March, they drove to Algeciras and caught a ferry to Tangier, eight miles across the Strait of Gibraltar.

'The weather was brilliant by now, and we had a delicious crossing, sunbathing on the 1st class deck (our tickets being 4th class!). It was rather nice to be sailing out of Europe for the first time in 15 years.' Their reverie was interrupted as soon as the ferry docked: 'We were set upon by an Arab trying to make money out of us. This was something we were to encounter just about every two minutes for the rest of our time in the country.' They checked into a fleapit hotel and explored, spending the evening in a café named the Dancing Boy, 'an extraordinary place where all the Arabs sit around smoking their marihuana [*sic*] pipes, drinking mint tea and listening to the band. Star of the show is a boy dressed in white silk, who sings and occasionally hops up and does a dance.'

'I've been really bitten by Tangier and find it quite fascinating,' Nick wrote separately, on a postcard home. 'Just as I always imagined African towns, with noisy marketplaces, beggars, snake-charmers – the lot. We've been into one or two really Arabic cafés, which have great atmosphere and *incredible* music.' The crowds, heat, smells and sights made a deep impression on him, but it was the music that affected him most. 'Moroccan music scored a major hit with me, although it's probably not every European's cup of tea,' he emphasised. 'I find it to be the most mournful, but at the same time one of the most dignified, forms of music that I've ever heard.'

When not out and about, Nick played his guitar – in his hotel room, on balconies, up on the roof – often providing the soundtrack to the effects of the local hash. 'We smoked a fair amount, but it wasn't a constant thing,' says Rick. 'It was probably camel dung half the time, anyway. We certainly weren't buzzed out of our heads, and Nick was no more into it than the rest of us.'

Rumours were swirling around Tangier that the Rolling Stones were in town. Nick had never been a die-hard Stones fan, but he was steeped in R&B and certainly didn't disdain them. Julian confirmed their presence on the penultimate night: 'Smoking hash made me feel remarkably sick. I was looking out of a tiny window over a narrow alley when I saw the Stones' party passing, in sheep-skins and bell-bottoms, like a medieval apparition.' Mick Jagger, Keith Richards and Brian Jones were there, as well as a court including Anita Pallenberg, Cecil Beaton, Robert Fraser, Christopher Gibbs and Michael Cooper.

Urged by his companions, Nick took his guitar when they sallied forth the next evening. 'Hoping to make contact with them, we went down to their hotel, the celebrated El Minzah,' he wrote home.

> Having seen them going in, looking quite extraordinary even by their own standards, we marched in and I made a request to play in the bar. After I had been turned down very politely, Bob, whose nerves seem to stop at nothing, proceeded to ring up the Stones' suite and ask if they might be wanting a little musical entertainment! This was unfortunately refused in a similar fashion, and it was decided that my fortune should be made elsewhere. So we made a quick tour of the nightclubs, asking if I could play.
>
> Fortunately, one of those which accepted the offer was the Koutoubia Palace, Tangier's most exclusive nightspot, which is done up in the style of a Moorish palace. I couldn't help feeling a little out of place, but all the same I played for about a quarter of an hour. The reception was extraordinarily good and we all got stood rounds of drinks, which was rather pleasant.

It's notable that – albeit egged on by his friends – Nick had the confidence to perform spontaneously.

The following morning Mike whisked them the 370 miles to

Marrakesh. Nick was stunned by the countryside en route and told his parents: 'I think that is probably where I shall move to after making my proverbial million.' After pitstops in Rabat and Casablanca, they reached Marrakesh in the evening. He was overwhelmed by its souk, calling it

> a huge, crowded gathering place where one finds musicians, magicians, soothsayers, acrobats, snake-charmers, dancers, and various other oddities which I am unable to find a name for. Best of all was a set of African drummers and dancers, who produced about the most infectious rhythms I have ever been infected by.

By coincidence the Stones were also in the crowd, making a field recording. Urged by Rick, they revived the idea of getting Nick to play for them. Having established that they were staying in an old French colonial hotel, La Mamounia, they went there that evening. Upon discovering that they were in its grand dining room, says Julian, 'Rick went in with Nick and told them how great Nick was at the guitar. Nick then played for them while Mike and I stood around in the lobby.'

Again, it's striking that Nick was willing to perform alone and at close quarters in front of such an intimidating audience. Rick does not recall what he played, but when he stopped, continues Julian,

> Mike and I were summoned in and we all sat down. It was a large room with a long table immediately on the left, deserted but for the Stones and their entourage. Mick Jagger was at the head, and in my memory Nick sat at the opposite end. It was like a scene from *The Decameron*, with food everywhere, which they invited us to help ourselves to. We were very grateful, because we were starving. They were bombed out of their minds yet clearly impressed by Nick. At the end of the encounter Mick said to him, 'You must come and see us when you're back in London,' which I doubt he said to everyone.

Young musicians all over the world would have envied Nick, yet by Julian's account, 'He was so congenitally mellow that it seemed normal for him. He seemed to internalise it all.' His own vague account to his parents ran: 'I went in and did them a few numbers. We in fact got quite chatty with them, and it was quite interesting learning all the inside stories.' None of the boys had cameras, but Mike says he 'had a portable tape machine on the trip and recorded odds and ends, including our encounter with the Stones. A number of years ago I found my old tapes and chucked them all away . . .'

The following morning the quartet motored south, intending to reach the northernmost tip of the Sahara before looping back. They were making decent progress, with Mike at the wheel, Nick in the passenger seat and Rick and Julian in the back. By Nick's account, they were 'covering large distances in fairly short spaces of time, and eventually began to come into what one thinks of as "African" countryside – bush land, gulches, etc.'.

Rocketing through scrubland sixty miles beyond Ouarzazate, disaster struck. Julian:

We were driving at 120 km/h along a straight road that turned to the left and then went uphill. Mike took the corner at immense speed, but almost immediately another car appeared over the hill, so he veered off to the right, the car flipped and we just *flew* off the road.

'A lot of gravel had been blown across the road and we skidded off, turned over, bounced on the roof of the car, and eventually ended up on all four wheels in the middle of the bush land,' recounted Nick with the benefit of a few weeks' distance.

It was rather hair-raising really, but we all succeeded in climbing out quite unscathed, bar a few bruises . . . The windscreen was smashed and the roof completely caved in about 6 inches in front of my nose – so, had I not had the [safety] belt on, one can imagine the sort of mess there might have been.*

Dazed and confused, they took stock. No one was hurt and, amazingly, Nick's guitar was undamaged. They succeeded in pushing the Cortina back onto the road, only to find that its steering and

---

* It is notable that Nick chose to share the story with his parents at all, especially given his own history of dangerous driving.

headlights were shot. 'Eventually some Bedouins came towards us on camels,' says Mike. 'At first we thought it was a mirage. They inspected us and rode on. Finally a car stopped.' Rick hitched a lift to Ouarzazate; four long hours passed before the lights of a taxi appeared in the gathering darkness, with Rick in the back. They slowly followed it back towards Ouarzazate, only for the driver to stop short, wishing to pass the night in his village.

'We were received with great hospitality, provided with an excellent meal at the village tavern, and after being taught how to play Moroccan cards were eventually allowed to kip down on the floor of the local surgery,' Nick related. By Mike's account, this was another gentle moderation of the facts: 'We were put up on marble slabs in the mortuary. Thankfully there were no occupants who weren't alive, but it wasn't the longest night's sleep.'

At dawn they rumbled on to Ouarzazate, where a mechanic patched up the car sufficiently for them to make the epic four-hundred-mile drive north to Meknes, where proper repairs could be carried out. The exhausted Mike handed the driving over to Nick, and they set off in the afternoon haze, with no windscreen and the roof crushed on the passenger side. They stopped halfway to spend the night in a hotel in the small city of Ksar-es-Souk (now known as Errachidia).

Rick got chatting to the proprietor's teenage son in the adjoining café, and boasted that Nick had recently played guitar for the Rolling Stones. The boy understood him to mean that Nick was a member of the Stones, and Rick, 'determined not to miss such an opportunity, quickly informed the fellow that I was Mick Jagger on a quiet, private holiday', Nick wrote home. 'No one was quite sure what he looked like, so they all happily convinced themselves that there was a celebrity in their midst.'

Julian was also caught up in the prank: 'The local boys asked us to sign a single, with a picture of the Stones on Hampstead Heath on the cover. Thankfully their faces were too small to see properly, so Nick signed as Mick, I signed as Charlie, and so on.' Thereafter they were fêted, as Nick explained:

We were given free dinner, rooms in the hotel, breakfast, as well as an invitation to go swimming at a nearby oasis with the proprietor's son and have a couscous lunch with him afterwards. However, the whole thing had by now become thoroughly embarrassing, and we were feeling extremely guilty, so we decided to push off after breakfast.

Entering the car via the windscreen, they lumbered into Meknes and left it with a mechanic. It was unclear how long the repairs would take, so they decided to hitchhike the forty miles to Fes. As Nick told Molly and Rodney, it 'happened to be the time of the Moroccan fiesta, the main feature of which seems to be chopping up every goat in sight, alive or dead'. They decided to hitchhike on to the Algerian coast, but 'after taking about 2 days to travel 20 miles we gave up the ghost and ploughed back once more to Meknes, deciding instead to go westward and hit the sea somewhere near Rabat'.

Venturing ninety miles northwest to the seaside city of Kenitra, they rented a shack on the beach. Three days later they headed back to Meknes, confident that the car must be ready. They were disappointed, however, and struggled to obtain the £75 – around £1,000 in 2022 – needed to pay for the work in any local banks. 'We ended up having to stand over them right through the night until 11 o'clock the next morning to make them finish the job,' wrote Nick. The fiasco had cost them ten days, and by its end they simply wanted to return to Aix, where the Summer term was about to start.

Nick found the home journey 'absolute hell . . . every conceivable thing went wrong with the car'. When they finally made it to the ferry port in Tangier, karma awaited them. 'We were surrounded by police,' says Rick. 'We had appeared in the local Meknes newspaper as the Rolling Stones, and the fact that Nick played the guitar convinced them, so they tried to bust us for dope.' Thankfully they had none with them and their protestations were eventually heeded.

A beady-eyed young Scotsman named Colin Betts – a self-described 'meretricious hippie tramp'[15] – picked them out in the boarding queue. 'When I saw Nick leaning on a battered Ford Cortina I could tell from the hair, clothes and glimpse of a guitar that we had much in common,' he wrote, and as soon as the ship set sail he introduced himself.

I'd been busking around the UK, Ireland and Europe for four years. Nick must have thought that was cool, because we bonded over tunes by Dylan, the Beatles and the Everly Brothers. Our voices worked together and we both knew all the words — as did half the hippies, despite being from all over the world. They joined in, a few danced or played percussion . . . I was impressed and captivated by Nick's musicality, eloquence, wit, charm and humour and can only assume he vaguely admired my radical credentials.

Colin was hoping to catch a lift through Spain and into the South of France, where he planned to spend the warm months. Sure enough, he was invited to squeeze into the Cortina for the nine hundred miles to Aix. She almost made it, but as a final insult her engine boiled over three miles outside town. At least the weather had improved. The trip hadn't been significant ('It was an amazing adventure, but we weren't a close group — there were no shared excitements or ideas,' says Julian) but it undoubtedly broadened Nick's horizons, not least through the hypnotic sounds and rhythms of North African music, which he had immediately begun to assimilate into his already wide range of influences.

In his long letter home of 6 April — prefaced by apologies for having not let his parents know of his whereabouts — he made no further pretence at engagement with his studies. 'The students here come and go much as they please, since the Institute shows very little interest in them on the whole. If it provides any consolation, I did in fact improve my French a lot more in Morocco than I have done in Aix.' There was no more talk of French grammar lectures, philosophy or Camus.

8

A Natural Progression

J EREMY AND SIMON noticed a change in Nick post-Morocco. 'He became more serious, I think,' says Simon,

> and to a degree lost some of his light-heartedness. In the English crowd there were some guys who burned the candle at both ends, and Nick was quite taken with them. They were the well-cool cats, the Chelsea kids, sons of rich people, pretty hip. There was a kind of split in Aix, and Nick did get sucked into the slipstream. And certainly, yes, that was the camp where there were more drugs.[1]

Jeremy recalls returning to Résidence Sextius shortly after Nick's return and being startled to find him with a broken guitar he'd found somewhere. 'He set light to it and hung it from the ceiling of the apartment, going, "Wow". I was going "Wow" too, but I was sure he had been smoking a joint.'[2] On another occasion, he says, 'I distinctly remember coming back to the flat and finding Nick in my bedroom and the room barricaded. The bed had been moved to the balcony – I was under the impression that he had been told that when you were tripping you thought you could fly.'[3]

Although it is possible that this was the result of Nick having been spiked, this is the closest any of his good friends can come to asserting that he ever deliberately took acid, but Derek FitzGerald is unconvinced, stating: 'I don't remember anyone taking LSD in Aix.' Simon didn't see evidence of it either, but adds: 'I'd be surprised if Nick never took it. He wasn't reckless, though – in fact, he was careful in many ways. He would have been aware of the parameters if he took it.'

It seems that Nick's travels had served to increase his determination to master the guitar and develop as a writer, and perhaps to assimilate the Arabic sounds he'd been so struck by. Colin Betts was crashing on Julian Raby's floor at the time, and later wrote that he heard Nick 'practising through the walls and ceilings every day and night of the week – marvellous stuff'.[4]

Robin Frederick had left while Nick was in Morocco, so Jean-Louis Pujol was glad to encounter him in the street.

> I told him to come back to the club and sing, that he would make some money. He said he would but never showed up, and the next time I bumped into him he made excuses. I can only assume he didn't want to be held to an obligation – a specific time and place, an organised set. I think he wanted to be free to do as he pleased.

Nick preferred to supplement his modest parental allowance by busking. 'When you needed money you could sing outside the many cafés in the Cours Mirabeau,' explains Jean-Louis, himself a veteran busker. 'Nick sang familiar songs – Dylan, Donovan and so on, the things passers-by would recognise. I don't think he sang his own songs there.' Colin was eager to busk with him, anticipating that his self-assurance and Nick's talent would prove a lucrative combination. They did so only once, however.* Nick occasionally improvised twelve-bar blues with Simon on harmonica and Jeremy manning the basket, but the lovelorn Jeremy decided to abandon Aix in April, leaving his friends with a room apiece in Résidence Sextius (and freedom from his romantic woes).

After days of solitary guitar playing, Nick continued to go wherever the nocturnal action was. Ben Laycock, an old friend of Derek FitzGerald, Nick Lewin and others, had just returned from India and visited for a couple of days in April. 'We were partying away, and Nick, whom I'd never met, was being quiet in a corner,' he recalls.

> Various people, including me, had a shot at playing guitar, then someone said, 'Nick can play!' so he sang 'God Bless the Child' by Billie Holiday – and then came the explosion (in my head, at least). I'd never met anybody of my age who could do *anything* that well,

---

* Simon: 'Colin kind of latched on to us . . . My recollection is that Nick was mildly entertained by him, nothing more, and that we didn't especially like or trust him. We were always paying for him and soon got disenchanted.'

just magically get these sounds out, those strong fingers flying across the fretboard . . .

Before he departed, Ben urged Nick to get in touch when he returned home.

Simon was finding Nick increasingly self-contained and focused on his guitar. 'We gradually went our own ways and latterly spent relatively little time together,' he says. The banging and drilling in Résidence Sextius was often excruciating, so any opportunity to be elsewhere was welcome. In mid-April Jo Dingemans invited Nick to spend the weekend with her in the seaside town of Cassis, an hour's drive away, where she had the use of a flat. 'Four of us went in a VW Beetle and Nick wrote a song there as the sun came up,'* she recalls.

Its title, 'Strange Meeting II', references Wilfred Owen's poem, which also has a broadly supernatural theme, but rather than a harrowing encounter in the underworld, Nick's lyric concerns a beautiful girl glimpsed in a 'summer sea-dream haze' one night on a 'distant beach'. She echoes the intangible 'glimmering girl' in W. B. Yeats's 'The Song of Wandering Aengus' more than anything in Owen's poem, while the intricate guitar part – in the recording he made of it the following month – is in Bert Jansch's style.

On another occasion Jo, Nick and Simon made their way to St-Tropez, where Nick had enjoyed himself the previous summer. 'We saw Brigitte Bardot walking past with a leopard on a chain,' says Simon. 'Later we went to Vroom Vroom – *the* St-Tropez disco – and watched her dancing very near to us, surrounded by good-looking young Frenchmen.' Nick liked the town's atmosphere and prospects for busking, so he decided to quit his course and move there.

He wrote a candid letter home on 30 April:

I'm afraid you may be feeling fairly starved of news concerning my life in Aix, but there has in fact been very little worth telling you about, since very little of note has happened. I've made a lot of

---

* Two of Nick's other early songs were titled 'Joey In Mind' and 'Joey'; if either or both were inspired by Jo, she was unaware of it.

friends and learnt to speak quite a bit of French, and my life has been quite enjoyable in its own way, but I can't think of any particularly positive events that have taken place. I'm in fact quite glad that I'm moving on elsewhere. I've now moved out of my room in the Résidence Sextius and am kipping in the flat of a friend until I get sufficiently organised to go down to St-Tropez.

The flat was in Rue Roux-Alphéran, where Jean-Louis visited him: 'It was dark and smelled of dope, which wasn't my thing.' Nick spent long hours there, tirelessly practising and refining his songs. On 15 May he ran into James Calvocoressi: 'I asked Nick if he would like to commit some of his songs to tape and he leapt at the idea.' They agreed to make the recording in the small kitchen in James's flat, whose stone floor helped with the acoustics. James placed his tape machine on the table, pressed RECORD and said: 'Live from Rue Manuel – the fabulous Nick Drake!'

Nick played a dozen songs over the ensuing thirty-seven minutes, offering a clear insight into his repertoire. He began with a brace of well-worn standards: 'Get Together'* and 'Cocaine Blues',† delivered with fluency and confidence. Next came 'Here Come the Blues' by Jackson C. Frank‡ and 'Tomorrow Is a Long Time' by Bob Dylan.§ At that point he claims, 'I can't think of any other songs to do. What could I do that might be interesting? Did I do "Milk and Honey" [another Jackson C. Frank song] the other night?' He then plays it. Next James suggests, 'Do that one the American girl did,' to which Nick replies, 'I'm not sure I'm in a state to sing it – I'm so damned sober.' Nonetheless, he does sing 'Been Smoking

---

* Written by Dino Valente and popularised by the Kingston Trio.
† Written by the Reverend Gary Davis and much covered in the 1960s; among others, Nick would have known the version on Davy Graham's December 1964 LP *Folk, Blues and Beyond*. (There is no evidence to suggest that he ever had cocaine running all around his own brain.)
‡ Frank's sole, self-titled album was released in the UK in December 1965, and had a powerful influence on aspiring singer-songwriters all over the country. None of Nick's schoolfriends remember it, so it's likely he encountered it (or learned its songs) after leaving Marlborough.
§ Written by Bob Dylan but not yet released by him. Nick would probably have known versions by Joan Baez, Judy Collins, Ian and Sylvia, and Odetta.

Too Long', after which he says: 'I'd just like to make my apologies for the music which precedes this, it's the most piss-awful session . . . Nails are a bit too short.'

He then tackles the traditional American folk song 'Kimbie',* before throwing in an unfamiliar number, with no announcement or comment. Its title was 'Leaving Me Behind', and James was unwittingly making the first surviving recording of a Nick Drake original. Centred on a descending guitar figure, played consistently without strumming while his voice contributes the melody line, it's a candid meditation on personal helplessness in the face of unstoppable outside forces, and does not seem at all deficient in its company. There's nothing callow or affected about the song; it's a crisp statement of resignation, and a prophetic recognition of Nick's own ambivalence towards the music business: 'Success can be gained, but at too great a cost.' For an eighteen-year-old with much to look forward to, its repeated declaration, 'For them there's a future to find / But I think they're leaving me behind', is unsettlingly fatalistic.

Next Nick lightens the mood with 'Strolling Down the Highway', the opening track on Bert Jansch's May 1965 debut. It seems almost fluffy in comparison. 'The capo's completely fucked,' he says as he finishes, then announces 'another song I learned very recently, which means I'm likely to forget the words'. He swallows the word 'learned', however, as it is in fact 'Strange Meeting II'. He ends it with a chuckle, saying, 'As I thought, I forgot the words.'

'Did you write that?' asks James in admiration. After a pause Nick admits, 'Yes, I did, actually. That's my surrealist song. It's crazy, I don't know, it's a sort of funny dream.' Again, it's an impressively complete statement, not at all outclassed by the material surrounding it. After a brief rendition of the gospel standard 'Amen', the tape ends with 'If You Leave Me Pretty Momma',† which illustrates Nick's skill as a blues guitarist as he smoothly incorporates various licks into a rounded whole.

---

* Better known as 'I Wish I Was a Mole in the Ground', it's also included on Jackson C. Frank's album.

† Written by Dave Van Ronk and included on his debut, *Dave Van Ronk Sings Ballads, Blues and a Spiritual* (Folkways, 1959), also containing 'Black Mountain Blues' and 'Betty and Dupree', which Nick tackled elsewhere.

It's noticeable that he doesn't play any traditional British songs on the tape, only American; he seems never to have been much interested in British folk. The whole session finds him singing softly and unaffectedly, in a high register at odds with his deep speaking voice. The chat between songs (and, in some cases, during them) is good-humoured; Nick is clearly enjoying himself. 'I can't remember what the object of the exercise was, as Nick never asked for the tape and I couldn't possibly have made him a copy,' says James, who simply hung on to it.

The same tape also contains five minutes of Nick playing at a nocturnal gathering in James's flat at around the same time. He noodles, plays fragments of songs and interacts with others. 'Been Smoking Too Long' gets another airing, and Jo asks him to play 'the one you wrote – I heard it in Cassis', at which Nick laughs and says, 'I can only play that when I'm high.' He also plays 'Black Mountain Blues'* (with harmonica accompaniment, perhaps from Simon) and 'Michael, Row the Boat Ashore', on which a girl (probably Jo) harmonises. It's a carefree document of a group of young people enjoying themselves, and again emphasises the confidence with which Nick played and sang in public.[5]

Nick hadn't completed his course, but whatever faint academic spark he'd possessed had died out since he'd started writing songs. Developing as a musician and writer was now his sole ambition. On 20 May he packed his suitcase, picked up his Levin and strolled down the highway towards St-Tropez. As ever, the guitar was not an enticement to motorists; to his amazement, the person who finally offered him a lift was the grandmother of the family upon whom he'd briefly been billeted upon arrival in Aix three months earlier. It neatly bookended his short time there.

In St-Tropez he was thrown on his own resources. 'I was given a contact on one of the yachts but went onto the wrong one, which was rather embarrassing, and was unable to find the right one,' he explained on a postcard home. 'I spent the night in a station waiting room where I didn't sleep at all.' Thereafter he checked into a hotel and eked out his funds whilst trying to hustle a gig in a restaurant

---

* Popularised by Bessie Smith.

or nightclub, armed with a couple of contacts from Jo. However, he told his parents, 'They wanted me to bash out songs at the top of my voice and I shan't be prepared to do that until I'm really broke.'

He soon ran out of options and patience, so hitched a lift to Paris with a party of tourists and made his way back to England, reaching London on the evening of 25 May. After visiting Soho to buy new Martin medium guitar strings, he went on to Far Leys. Gabrielle's career had gathered steam in his absence – she was about to appear in *Coronation Street* and was the subject of press speculation about replacing Diana Rigg in *The Avengers* – but she was there to welcome him back, alongside their parents and Naw. His hair had grown in France, even if his grasp of French was much the same. 'He did not one stroke of work but had a wonderful time, I think,' was Molly's assessment.[6]

After dinner he casually produced his guitar and played three songs – 'Strange Meeting II', 'Bird Flew By' and 'Rain'. It was the first inkling his family had that he was a songwriter. 'It was thrilling and unexpected, and yet at the same time totally expected,' recalls Gabrielle. 'It was somehow a natural progression, because it was something that we'd grown up with, with my mum composing all the time and my parents playing on the piano . . . but nevertheless exciting.'[7] Elsewhere she said: 'I remember being terribly impressed at what he had written. He was perfectly "ordinary" then . . . Quite happy to sit down and play songs he'd written, to me, to our parents.'[8]

If Molly was struck by any similarity between Nick's songs and her own, she is unlikely to have remarked upon it. The extent to which she continued to write beyond Nick's childhood is hard to ascertain, as is his attitude towards her work as he became a song-writer himself. Gabrielle recalls him once saying to her, 'Your songs are so naïve!' and her replying: 'Yes, but they are my own.' He doesn't appear ever to have sought her opinion on his material and they never collaborated, but there are striking similarities between their outputs, superficially different though their traditions were.

'It would be foolish to say Nick's songs sound like his mother's,' Nick's arranger Robert Kirby contended many years later.[9] However, he added, 'some of the harmonies, some of the melodic lines, and the way the harmonies fit against them . . . You can see where Nick came from.' Nick's producer Joe Boyd was also startled when he first heard Molly's compositions: 'There, in her piano chords, are the roots of Nick's harmonies. His reinvention of the standard guitar tuning was the only way to match the music he heard as he was growing up.'[10]

Nick had mentioned travelling to Istanbul, but – perhaps reminded by his parents of the need to improve his French – he quickly returned to France, alone. Colin Betts described bumping into him in St-Tropez in June, busking around the harbour cafés, 'trailing around a Jewish-American girl called Emily Stone' and attempting to blag his way into a Terry Reid gig.* Colin's possibly unreliable account places Nick in Aix the following afternoon, tripping on acid supplied by Emily. Colin says Nick gave another tab to him – his first – and that the two of them proceeded to jam on their guitars in front of an appreciative crowd before having a running race back to Résidence Sextius and parting the next day with 'a swaying hug that [ended] in wet eyes'.[11]

Nick was living in a cheap hotel in Paris by the time he turned nineteen on 19 June. 'Have found myself a job playing in a night-club,' he wrote home a few days later. 'Not particularly lucrative, but it passes the time . . . Haven't been doing anything in particular, though have seen quite a few films.' Jo Dingemans was also there: 'I think he was busking and playing small gigs,' she says. Convinced of his talent, she did her best to further his prospects. 'I helped set up a private concert for him, with a friend who did most of the organising, to try and get him a record contract. I'm not sure who was there, but there were record producers and so-called "cool" people.' Unfortunately, however, Nick 'flatly refused to play – I think he found the whole thing too much.'

When he came home in July his oeuvre – as detailed in the back of an old notebook – consisted of 'Leaving Me Behind', 'Strange Meeting II', 'Day Is Done', 'Rain', 'Blossom Friend', 'Come To The Garden', 'Bird Flew By' (an especial favourite of his mother's),

---

* Born in November 1949, Reid is a British singer-guitarist. In June 1967 he was singing with Peter Jay's Jaywalkers.

'Forgotten Dream City', 'Girl Above' and 'Just Another Girl'.* The last three seem not to have survived,† but the others share a wistful edge and lyrics touching on the seasons, the weather and doomed romance.

By general consensus he tended not to write words without music, but his creative process is opaque. He was always guarded about his songs until he felt they were complete; only then would he play them to others. From the start of his life as a writer he held himself to exacting standards, and his surviving material is uniformly well-constructed and distinctive. It's likely that the lost songs simply didn't meet his own criteria for circulation, though of course he might have recycled elements of them.

Back in Tanworth, Nick happily reconnected with Dave Lodder, who'd been hitchhiking around Europe. 'A group of us would go to parties or gatherings in each other's houses,' says Dave. 'The only obvious difference between us was that Nick was so cool. He cut a different figure to everyone else – tall and self-contained and didn't say a lot. All the girls ran around him.' For Dave's sister Liv, however, 'He was lovely to look at but somehow not super-attractive, perhaps because he didn't seem accessible. He had a sort of super-cool loucheness to him.'

According to Liv, Kirstie Clegg was 'definitely the most attractive girl on that scene, a real trophy for anyone'. Her family had settled in Wootton Wawen, six miles from Tanworth-in-Arden, in 1961. In the summer of 1967 she was seventeen and had just left boarding school. 'I'd met Nick at parties here and there, but my first dealings with him came when he rang me up and asked if I wanted to join a group of people going to a club in Birmingham,' she says. This was the Penthouse, in Constitution Hill, accessible only via a fur-lined lift. Nick was a member.

---

* Nick gave three of these titles as 'Leaving Me Behind (The Tramp)', 'Bird Flew By (Bird's Eye View)' and 'You And The Blossom', but in later lists they had changed.
† The lyrics for 'Just Another Girl' do survive, and concern a failed romance in which a 'Face that once shone in the light / Now has faded in the night', leading him to the conclusion: 'So go your way, I'll go mine / Life will continue just fine'.

Nick's compositions, summer 1967.

We met at Far Leys and set off in his car – he was always an absolute maniac behind the wheel! When we got there it was pretty obvious that it was me he was interested in. Later we sat in the music room at Far Leys and he played his guitar. I certainly didn't stay the night, but we started seeing more of each other and became a couple.

As Gabrielle puts it, 'Blonde, petite, gentle but more daring and adventurous than Nick, Kirstie led him into adulthood. By her own confession, she knew little about music, but would listen to Nick for hours, sitting on his knee whilst he played his guitar around her.'[12] Kirstie herself recalls:

I was pretty left-wing while most people I knew were more conservative, and Nick was a bit different too. He didn't talk a lot (I took him to one party where he didn't speak to anybody at all) and I was more inclined to blurt everything out, but our silences were comfortable, not awkward. We were at ease with each other and he was tactile and affectionate – he'd always put his arm around me.

He was gentle, with a twinkle in his eye. 'Wry' is a good word for him. He'd make asides rather than jokes – he definitely wasn't a 'joke' person. He was laid-back but enthusiastic about things he liked. Life was certainly for living at that stage as far as he was concerned. One night I was woken up by pebbles hitting my window – it was Dave and Nick on the steps below. I think they'd had a bit to drink and wanted me to go out with them. Unfortunately, they woke my parents up too. My dad was furious until he realised who it was. He always liked Nick. Everyone liked Nick.

Kirstie was the closest to a girlfriend that Nick ever came, but their relationship wasn't serious:

We only really saw each other when we were both at home – we'd go out to the pub together, or to a club, or the cinema, or bowling. We never wrote to each other or went away together or gave each other anything. Our feelings were unspoken. I wouldn't know if he wrote anything for me.* There was always a side of him that stood apart – I think there has to be if you're creative.

---

* Molly later said that 'Joey' was written about Kirstie.

As Liv reflects, 'Going out with someone in those days didn't mean you shared an awful lot, it was quite superficial. Nonetheless, I think they had more of a connection than they realised.'

One connection they didn't share was smoking dope. Nick was now a regular smoker, though it was far from a constant habit and not something he did at home. 'I don't remember him smoking a lot of dope, but he could be pretty spaced-out, so he was probably stoned on those occasions,' Kirstie suggests. Nick wasn't reckless, but Dave felt that he was less risk-averse than most in their circle; when a local friend mentioned he'd been given a small packet of speed and didn't know what to do with it, Nick enthusiastically proposed they take it (which they proceeded to do, in a Birmingham club). Speed was never his drug of choice, though. Naturally reticent, he found hash a useful tool for smoothing uncomfortable or tedious edges from social situations, as well as putting him in the frame of mind to play and write, and he gravitated towards others who smoked. Unsurprisingly, most of them were also music lovers. From now on these factors would govern almost all the friendships he made or pursued.

Inevitably, most of these were based in London, which held more appeal for him than Warwickshire. As the summer of 1967 progressed Nick drove there for days or weeks at a stretch in 'BAB', a temperamental white Vauxhall Viva that his parents had given him to replace the exhausted HOB. 'He was spending more and more time in London,' confirms Dave. 'Perhaps he found us provincial, though he didn't make us feel that way.'

He based himself in Gabrielle's flat and reconnected with old schoolmates as well as newer friends such as Derek FitzGerald and Ben Laycock, who recalls:

> I think we were probably quite proud, in a ghastly way, of having a new friend who was so extraordinary, and I think we probably couldn't wait . . . not to show him off, because he wasn't asked to show, but . . . 'Here's our new friend, dig this, man!'[13]

They swiftly assimilated him into their like-minded circle, which included Alex Henderson, Sophia Ryde, David Ward, Christopher Sykes, Robert Abel Smith, Julian Lloyd and Victoria Ormsby-Gore.

They'd known each other for years and in several cases grown up or gone to school together, but Nick's reticent yet amiable personality was a perfect fit for them.

Alex describes himself as 'the most extroverted member of the group, perfectly happy to make a fool of myself'. He had immersed himself in the nascent counterculture in 1966, watching early Pink Floyd shows and quickly joining UFO, but he attended more conventional gatherings too. 'I went to lots of deb parties and met Sophia at one of them. She was outgoing and popular – neither a retiring mouse nor a raging extrovert. She loved music and was interested in art, as was I, and we got together.'

The delicately beautiful Sophia (pronounced to rhyme with '*fire*') was born on 19 May 1948, exactly a month before Nick. 'She was outwardly gentle and soft, but inwardly tough,' says Robert, who grew up alongside her. 'She was lovely on the outside and the inside, though.' For David, 'She was shy and self-conscious but had a strong character. She was lovely and caring, but not an angel of mercy-type figure.' If Nick took a special shine to her, no one noticed, including her. 'When I first knew Nick he was completely normal and quite jolly,' she says. 'He was always pleasant, in fact – I never saw a nasty side to him.'

'He wasn't shy around us – we all had the same way of thinking,' says David. 'He wouldn't say a lot but he had a way of summarising a situation in a nutshell, often in an ironic or amusing way, that would make everyone sit up. I thought he was highly intelligent.' Alex agrees: 'I thought he was extremely intelligent and knowledgeable – you could always have an interesting conversation with him. He was circumspect, didn't suffer fools, but all of us were like that. We thought our gang was great.'

Their lives centred on Chelsea, which was still affordable for young people despite being the epicentre of 'Swinging London'. 'Nothing existed for us much beyond Chelsea,' as Alex puts it.

It was a small place, there were no smart shops, everyone was within easy walking distance. We were always skint (apart from David*), but

---

* David was grandson to the 3rd Earl of Dudley.

Chelsea was cheap in those days. Nick had an old car and wore more or less the same things every day: a dark jacket, a collared shirt, slightly short trousers, Chelsea boots. They looked like school clothes he'd outgrown.

Nick's sole concessions to the prevailing psychedelic trend were a paisley neckerchief and a pair of pale corduroy lace-ups. Alex continues:

> He didn't wear the latest Carnaby Street stuff, but there was a certain vanity to his look. It was studied, but that was hardly unusual. Being cool was important then. Shaking hands when we saw each other would have been too formal, but none of us hugged – that would have been uncool. I'm a tactile person, but Nick was physically self-contained.

He spent idyllic, stoned summer days and nights hanging out with this new and ready-made friendship group. 'We were grown-ups, but quite childish ones,' Alex reflects. 'In those days it was novel to enjoy being young, rather than simply leaving school and turning into your parents.' Far from partying and clubbing, says Sophia, 'We didn't do very much. We weren't wine drinkers – people weren't in those days – and I can't think what we ate. It was more a case of sitting around, smoking dope and listening to records.' Robert adds: 'We were all into music – the latest Byrds, Doors, Jefferson Airplane, 13th Floor Elevators, whatever it might be. All we did was endlessly go round to each other's places to hang out.'

'We were stoned quite a lot of the time,' agrees Ben, but as far as any of them remember, Nick's drug use was limited to hash. Sophia: 'Some of us tried acid, but it wasn't a "thing" within our group. I only took half a tab once, and I think it's perfectly possible that Nick didn't ever take it.' 'I was a fairly adventurous drug taker,' Alex says, 'and he never asked me if I could get hold of anything stronger than dope.' By Julian's account,

> We'd smoke hash – the question was whether it was Red Leb or the Pakistani black stuff. Grass wasn't nearly so easily available. We'd smoke spliffs, then get madly hungry and drive off to the Noor Jahan in Bina Gardens, where we'd sit and giggle and eat huge quantities of biryani or whatever.

They weren't idle, though. Nick was constantly polishing his songs and working on new ones, Julian was a photographer's assistant, Alex was a teaboy at a film company, Sophia was working in Harlequin Records in New Bond Street, and Ben was managing a restaurant named Rupert's in Park Walk ('even though I had no clue what I was doing'). Rupert's became a regular haunt of Nick's, as did the borrowed house Julian was sharing with Alex in Stokenchurch Street.

As well as listening to records, guitar playing was a prominent aspect of all their gatherings. 'Everything was based around music, and Nick wasn't frightened of playing to his mates,' says Alex. 'The only thing that set him apart from the rest of us was his ability on the guitar, because he really was extraordinarily good. Ben and David were in awe of his playing – and they were pretty good too.' As Sophia puts it: 'Nick was in a different league to everyone we knew.'

Their respect for his musicality only deepened when it emerged that he was also a gifted and prolific songwriter. In the absence of other obligations his creativity was blooming, and his canon was growing to include 'Blue Season', 'Joey In Mind', 'Outside', 'Blues For JA' and 'Magic'. Of these, only the wide-eyed, wistful 'Magic' is known to survive; the first four exist only as lyrics and in the lists he kept.

'Blues For JA' may have been an instrumental, and it's not known what the initials stood for. The words to 'Blue Season' are an appeal to autumn and winter to give way to spring and summer, very much in keeping with the zeitgeist, while 'Joey In Mind' is a lover's lament. 'I'll leave for my terrace and tea laced with rum / And wait for the day when Joey will come,' run the words, enigmatically concluding with a promise to fellow sufferers: 'Together we'll sit in this Sunday rain / And dream of Joey or Mary Jane'; he would return to both names, and the seasons and the weather remained common motifs in his songs.

In 'Magic' he casts himself as an outsider ('I was born to love no one / No one to love me'), and hints at a Romantic identification with childhood that others have allowed themselves to forget. As with 'Blue Season', its imagery touches on contemporary hippie themes ('Dream with the sun and the skies' or 'sail away / Into a land of forever'), but the persona it conveys is detached and isolated.

This notion is developed in 'Outside', which comes across as a pledge to withdraw from the world if its demands grow too heavy. Like 'Leaving Me Behind', it displays a greater degree of self-awareness and personal honesty than his other early material.

Assuming he sang them to his friends, their jaded, equivocal words didn't come across as alarming, just as another facet of his dazzling talent and enigmatic personality. In any case, it wasn't his lyrics that drew the attention in the first instance – it was his playing. David Ward says that Jansch and Renbourn remained strong influences on Nick, but vividly remembers his restless exploration of his instrument in pursuit of his own style. 'He increasingly found new harmonics by exploring tunings when he wrote, and occasionally showed them to Ben and me.'

David's first cousin, Micky Astor, was also a gifted musician who enjoyed jamming. 'By 1967 I wasn't really playing guitar, I'd moved on to flute and double bass, but I liked what Nick was playing – his ideas, his harmonies, his cross-rhythms. I was particularly interested in the sounds he was getting by lowering his strings and opening the tuning.' Nick relished the opportunity to incorporate wider instrumentation into his arrangements, and he and Micky began to extemporise together.

Nick's main base was Gabrielle's flat, but Julian and Alex were happy for him to be at Stokenchurch Street whenever he wanted. Alex:

> One day I'd forgotten my keys, so I was knocking and peering through the window at Nick. He was cross-legged on the floor, listening to [the Byrds'] *Fifth Dimension* through headphones, oblivious. It gives you an idea of his interest in his social life at that time that he had one hand on the telephone in case it vibrated, because he didn't want to miss a call.

He had good reason to monitor it: despite eschewing Jo Dingemans's attempt to further his career in Paris, he was quietly determined to make professional headway in London. Although Nick kept his ambitious streak hidden, Alex remarks that 'A lot of successful people have a level of obsession that runs deeper than in most of us, and that makes them hustle. I think Nick was like that with his music, although we didn't see that side of him.' Julian had also inferred 'a definite sense that he was on a mission with his music. That's what drove him and where his future lay', while for David 'the immaculate precision and the dynamics of his perform- ance swiftly convinced us that a growing public recognition was inevitable'.[14]

Ben wholeheartedly agreed: 'I thought he needed to be managed, so I offered my services, even though I didn't know what I was doing.' One idea he had was to introduce Nick to an old friend of his family, Rory McEwen – a celebrated folk singer and impresario, as well as the presenter of the influential 1963 folk and blues TV programme *Hullabaloo*. 'I thought,' says Ben,

'If I introduce Nick to him, he might know what to do . . .', so I took Nick to his studio in Tregunter Road, where Nick played him a few songs. Rory got him at once and said, 'You're amazing – but I'm not really involved in the music business anymore . . .' In my memory, he suggested Nick try Chris Blackwell at Island instead.

Another contact Nick made at this time was the glamorous Chinese-American Calvin Mark Lee, a PhD in pharmaceutical chem- istry who'd signed the controversial cannabis law reform advert in *The Times* of 24 July. Alex Henderson remembers Calvin haunting the cafés that dotted the King's Road, and imagines Nick met him in one of those. Not a musician himself, he was involved with David Bowie and on the lookout for other talented young artists, either to help or to seduce. For Angie Barnett (who would later marry Bowie), Calvin was 'very beautiful, very sensitive, very clever . . . He would easily walk up and take a likely candidate into that soft, sweet, snare of his.'[15] The details of his friendship with Nick are opaque, but it seems likely that Calvin too attempted to kindle interest in his songs.

Nick did not introduce his new friends to his schoolmates, but still hung out with them at Desi Burlison-Rush's flat in Sloane Street. When she realised he was shifting his focus onto original material and hoping to make professional headway, she began to act as his unofficial agent, helping him assemble a list of contacts spanning independent producers (Denis Preston at Lansdowne, Denny Cordell at Straight Ahead Productions), A&R men (Bunny Lewis at Decca), publishers (Steve Rowland at Hansa Productions) and label owners (Chris Blackwell). It's also possible that Nick tried to follow up on the interest Mick Jagger had shown in March, but the Stones were having a tumultuous summer, with Jagger and Keith Richards having been briefly jailed for drug offences on 30 June.

'Desi was a forceful and confident person, not easily intimidated, and it would have been exactly like her to look for ways to help Nick with his career,' says Mike Hacking. He remembers her downstairs neighbour helping too: 'Freda Hilton, who lived on the second floor, was an agent for Alan Price, Tom Jones and a few others. She had parties with stars there and would invite Desi and me plus our friends, including Nick. She gave him advice about his music career.' Nick duly wrote letters, offering to meet or leave a demo tape with anyone who might be interested, with the more dynamic Desi chasing them up.

At the end of August he heard back from Hansa, a German-owned music publisher based in Denmark Street, the heart of London's 'Tin Pan Alley'. They wanted four of his songs: 'Rain', 'Day Is Done', 'Leaving Me Behind' and 'Bird Flew By'.* As such, they sent a boilerplate contract to him at Desi's address, 62 Sloane Street, dated 31 August, offering him a nominal shilling to assign them the copyrights, with the promise of royalties should anyone record them. It was better than nothing, if not by much.

At nineteen, Nick was too young to sign it himself, so he passed it to his father. Rodney was well used to scrutinising legal documents and annotated it. Next to a section that gave Hansa 'the right to make additions and adaptations and alterations in and to the words and/or music of the said work(s) and such changes of title as they may desire', he wrote: 'Can change anything'. This struck at the heart of one of the essentials of Nick's creativity – the need to be in control of his work – and he boldly decided not to proceed.† In any case, he was more interested in recording the songs himself.

---

* For unknown reasons the contract referred to 'Rain' as 'My Love Left With The Rain'; 'Day Is Done' as 'The Day Is Done'; and 'Bird Flew By' as 'Life Flies Away'.
† Asked about Nick in May 2020, Steve Rowland, Hansa's British director at the time, replied: 'I have absolutely no recollection of the writer or songs in question.'

Nick spent the weekend of 6 September at Hatley Park, the Astors' family home outside Cambridge. Also there were Ben Laycock and Christopher Sykes. The intention was to make music; a photo taken on that occasion shows him at the family's Hammond organ, cigarette in mouth. 'Christopher played the clown centre stage and Nick was highly amused by his antics,' says Micky's younger sister Stella. 'We had tremendous laughs together.'

As well as being a joker, Christopher was a gifted pianist. One night, he says,

> I was fooling around on the piano – my party trick was to improvise a slow blues with verses about each person in the room. Out of the blue whilst playing, I sang 'There was a man who lived in a shed / Spent most of his days out of his head . . .' It wasn't about Nick, but he found it very funny.

Nick incorporated the line into a bittersweet song he was germinating, to which he gave the working title 'Sad Story For Christopher' in tribute.

The weekend was the last of a memorable summer. Ahead of starting at Cambridge, Nick submitted to a general medical examination by a Dr Stratford of 10 Belgrave Square. 'You seem to be a splendidly fit young man with no outstanding problems,' ran the ensuing report, which concluded: 'We would be failing in our duty if we did not point out that smoking carries three times the coronary risk by the time you are 40 or so, to say nothing of bronchitis and lung cancer.' The practice separately reported to Rodney, as the health insurance policy holder, adding the bizarre remark: 'Quite frankly, he struck us as being a slightly limp young man, which I suppose is common to all our sons in this day and age.'

Back at Far Leys Nick had the reality of Fitzwilliam – and his course's daunting reading list – to face up to. There was a consensus among all who'd lately encountered him that he had a special musical gift and an obvious future as a musician. He had found his voice as a songwriter, one international company had signalled interest in his work, and he was waiting to hear from others. As such, university did not seem an obvious next move. 'I knew music was in his

Molly Drake (1915–93).

Rodney Drake (1908–88).

Molly, Rodney, Nick and Gabrielle at home in 1954.

Far Leys, Tanworth-in-Arden, Warwickshire: the Drakes' home from May 1952.

The drawing room at Far Leys, where Molly spent a lot of her time
writing songs at the piano as Nick grew up.

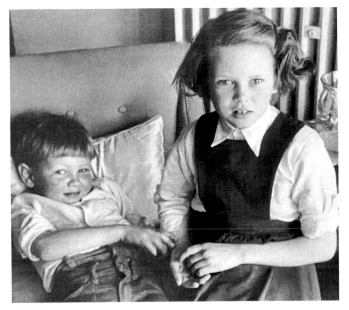

Nick and Gabrielle, shortly after moving into Far Leys. Despite the four-year age gap, they were close siblings.

Naw Ma Naw (1914–88), the Drakes' much-loved Karen nanny–housekeeper, who joined the family in September 1954.

Molly and Nick buying school uniform in London, April 1957. Already image-conscious, Nick is concealing a balloon behind his back.

Eagle House in Sandhurst, Berkshire, where Nick began boarding
in May 1957, aged eight.

Definitive schoolboy humour in
Nick's autograph book, August 1960.

Let the wind
go free
Wherever you be
For holding it in
Was the death
of me!

N. R. Drake

8/8/60.

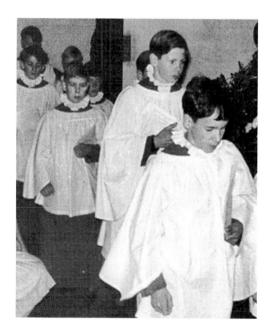

Nick towering over his
fellow choristers at Eagle
House, December 1961.

C1, Nick's house at Marlborough College, Wiltshire, from 1963 to 1966, with the dining hall to its right.

Nick looking stolid with his saxophone in Marlborough's Combined Cadet Force band, June 1964.

A rare sight: Nick helping in the garden, 1963.

Dennis Silk, Nick's unfailingly supportive Housemaster.

Nick in his athletics kit, 1965. Despite being a gifted sprinter, he was far more interested in playing the guitar.

On holiday in France (1964), a country Nick visited often throughout his life.

Michael Hacking, by
common consensus the coolest
Marlburian of his generation.

Andy Murison was a close
friend at school and Nick's
contemporary at Cambridge.

Mick Way showed Nick the
basics on the guitar in the
autumn of 1964.

Jeremy Mason, a schoolboy
aesthete who shared literary and
musical enthusiasms with Nick.

Dave Wright also loved pop
music and bummed around
Europe with Nick in the
summer of 1965.

Simon Crocker played in bands
with Nick and travelled with
him to Aix-en-Provence in
February 1967.

Nick's childhood friend Dave Lodder, with whom he attended a crammer in Birmingham in the autumn of 1966.

Kirstie Clegg, Nick's on-off girlfriend from 1967.

Désiree Burlison-Rush, one of several women with whom Nick had close platonic friendships.

Nick with Jeremy Mason at Amiens station, en route for Aix, February 1967.

Nick at Far Leys in the summer of 1967, just after his return from adventures in France and Morocco. He was now a prolific songwriter.

soul, so I thought it was a bit odd that he was going to Cambridge instead of pursuing it full-time,' as Kirstie puts it.

Over September Nick spent time with Kirstie and other friends, apathetically read some texts, and continued to play and write. His family wanted to preserve his songs to date, but his self-effacement wasn't the only obstacle. 'We all had great difficulty in rescuing them because he'd record a thing and then of course he'd go and record something else over the top of it,' Rodney later explained.[16] 'But I managed to get him to do this long tape once, and as soon as he'd finished it I snatched it away from him and hid it away from him in a drawer so that he couldn't use it again.'

As the beginning of term approached Rodney drafted a document concerning Nick's finances. By his calculation academic fees would amount to £260 per annum and basic living expenses to £240. He offered to double the total by depositing £1,000 – around £14,000 in 2022 – in Nick's account for the year ahead, undertook to cover insurance and road tax for BAB, and explained that Nick's means-tested grant from the Local Education Authority (£50, payable in three tranches) would be his as well.

'The only items which I will be prepared to consider adding to the above are special expenses connected with the promotion of your career,' he concluded, adding, with characteristic prudence and humanity: 'This arrangement is conditional upon your promising to tell me if you get into financial difficulties.'

Molly and Rodney were all too aware that Nick did not relish the prospect of exchanging the independent, cosmopolitan life he'd led since school for a parochial and academic one, and understood that he was starting at Cambridge with the intention of pursuing music seriously in parallel. It had frustrated them to see him coast through Marlborough, and they were hoping that he would widen his interests at university, rather than focus on his guitar to the exclusion of almost all else. By offering a generous package that would obviate the need for him to earn in his vacations, they were suggesting a middle way: he could embrace Cambridge in term-time and pursue music beyond it.

PART TWO

9

Casting Around

※

RODNEY AND MOLLY drove Nick to Fitzwilliam for the start of term, Tuesday, 3 October. It was located far down Storey's Way, a long and mainly residential road a mile from the heart of the University.* Such parts of the college as had been built were designed by arch-modernist Denys Lasdun. 'We arrived at a brutalist desert,' says John Venning, a Cornishman who also started as an English undergraduate that term.

> Fitzwilliam was an architectural eyesore, not generously endowed and very much a second-class citizen compared to the older colleges. It was out on a limb geographically, well outside the centre of town,† on Cambridge's only hill.

'The entrance was inauspicious, an archway about the size of a small shopfront,' adds another new undergraduate, Ed Gilchrist, a Liverpudlian. The accommodation was meagre, and surely reminded Nick of Résidence Sextius. The room he'd been assigned was on the ground floor of Block A. 'It was a boring reddy-grey brick building,' says Ed, which, John explains,

> had to be built according to government regulations for new university buildings. Some new universities had used the available space creatively, but we simply had shoeboxes. The rooms were solo, with a desk, a desk chair, an armchair and a divan bed that could be a sofa by day.

---

* In 1967 the entrance to the unfinished college was off Huntingdon Road, described by Nick's contemporary John Venning as 'the utilitarian backside of the building, utterly ugly and devoid of inspiration'.
† W. H. Smith's newspaper delivery advert in the *Varsity Handbook* specifically excluded Fitzwilliam.

There was a wooden wardrobe with some drawers in it, a pinboard and a long window with curtains. Bathrooms and loos were communal.

Gabrielle thought Nick's room was 'mean and horrid' on her sole visit. 'There were five bedrooms on our corridor,' says Ed.

> Straight ahead as you went in was A3, occupied by a larger-than-life rugby lad named Chris Hughes. Nick was in A2, to his left. Opposite was a doorway that led to the bathroom and shower. A1 was occupied by another quiet, sporty lad named Colin Fergusson. To the right as you went in was A4, occupied by a friendly and studious guy named Nick Salmon, and I was in A5. Opposite me was the 'gyp room', where we could make tea or coffee.

John explains that 'in theory, the people you shared your floor with formed a social unit,' but Nick had no interest in doing so.

He looks stolid in the college's matriculation photo – a group shot of his intake at the start of their first term. He is wearing the prescribed jacket, tie and gown, his hair below his ears but not long; it had recently been cut. On his face is a half-smile that hints at reluctance to resume life in a regulated, all-male institution.[*]

Upon starting every undergraduate was assigned a 'moral tutor'. Nick's was Ray Kelly, a popular Yorkshireman who had been a French don but was now College Bursar. 'Your college was supposedly *in loco parentis*, so your moral tutor would see you termly to discuss your reports and so on,' continues John. 'You were meant to get permission from him to do certain things, such as go beyond a certain distance from Great St Mary's Church. Such rules already seemed ludicrous, and it was totally common to climb in and out of your college, for example.'

Although bound by archaic traditions and rules, Cambridge was not immune to the changes sweeping society in 1967. That Michaelmas the Union had its first female President, Ann Mallalieu, and – despite widespread interest in Prince Charles, who had joined Trinity College – anti-establishment feeling was almost mainstream. 'Politics in Cambridge has undergone a major change recently,' stated the *Varsity Handbook*, which most new undergraduates owned. 'Previously it was

---

[*] There were no mixed colleges at Cambridge until 1972; Fitzwilliam admitted its first female undergraduates in 1979.

an activity associated with careerism, debates and tea-parties. Now it is dominated by student power activists.'[1] Nick was no firebrand, but nor did he exude entitlement. Although his education and accent set him apart from many of his peers, he was neither a snob nor rich, and his manner was ever gentle and courteous.

He was one of fifteen undergraduates reading English in his year at Fitzwilliam, a reflection of its desire to grow and make a mark on the University. 'This number was almost unheard of in any college, let alone one that was not distinguished or wealthy,' explains John, who was one of the two Exhibitioners (or sponsored Scholars) in their subject's intake. Andy Murison was also meant to be starting at Fitzwilliam (reading Economics) but had broken his leg in Australia and had to miss the first term. Nick seems to have taken one look at everyone else and withdrawn.

From John's perspective this was a missed opportunity:

> If Nick had taken the time or trouble to get to know the under-graduate body at Fitzwilliam he would have realised that it was a broad and interesting group. For example, there was a film society run by Tim Rayner which showed all sorts of underground movies by Kenneth Anger and others, which were virtually impossible to see at the time, and Derek Bishton and Nick Clarke founded *Broadsheet*, a University-wide arts magazine.

His lack of engagement with his peer group in college made him a subject of curiosity. For Derek he 'was the epitome of cool – he always wore Cuban heels (which made him even taller), blue jeans, a blazer and white shirt. I was in complete awe of him, so our conversations were one-sided.' David Punter, who was also reading English, 'thought he was supremely self-confident. Whereas I seemed to be preoccupied with finding the right things to say and be in order to fit in, I thought he genuinely didn't feel the need to care.'

The Cambridge system centres on tutorials called 'supervisions', for which undergraduates are typically paired up. Organising their timetable would have been a challenge under any circumstances, but was greatly complicated by the fact that the overweight and over-worked Norman Walters had collapsed and died in June. 'The college was reeling when we went up,' continues John.

It was faced with the obligation to teach English to forty-five undergraduates, with the man in the centre unavailable and no supervisions
in place. Its response was to cast about frantically, and upon arrival
we were summoned as a body to a meeting at Queens' College,
where a research fellow named Dominic Baker-Smith [later a distinguished scholar of Tudor humanism] had been persuaded to take on
our direction. Dominic told us that we would be last in line for his
attention, before putting us in pairs and sending us off in various
directions. It was an enormously deflating experience, but it allowed
Nick to maintain a very low profile indeed.

None of Nick's supervisions took place in Fitzwilliam. Instead, he
was initially taught by Dominic or by Maurice Hussey, a Chaucerian
scholar at Downing College. Occasionally the year group congregated
for a class, but no one recalls Nick contributing, and attending lectures
seems not to have occurred to him. His supervision partner Martyn
Moxley recalls of their first session in Queens': 'Nick and I waited
silently outside until beckoned in. I remember at the time wondering
where he had disappeared to by the second. Certainly it was already
known he was creatively busy, not to say a law unto himself.'

Most of his time was spent playing guitar in his room, and his
creativity was lent impetus shortly after reaching Fitzwilliam. On
Monday, 9 October, less than a week after he had gone up, Desi
managed to have a meeting with Island Records, after which she
excitedly rang Far Leys. 'She said she had taken your tape round to
Chris Blackwell (have I got the name right?) and that she was present
when it was played and that they were "delighted" with it,' Rodney
wrote to Nick from his office in Birmingham the next day. 'I imagine
that she will be writing to tell you about this. So that all sounds
very promising and I wonder what the next step will be? As you
may imagine, Mum and I celebrated with an extra drink!'

With this in prospect, Nick chafed all the more at the strictures
of Cambridge. It's a measure of his closeness to his parents that he
continued to write home at all – a notion more or less alien to his
contemporaries – let alone to speak his mind to them. 'I don't see
that it's going to be the fantastic existence that people like to make
out,' he grumbled in a letter of 17 October.

From what I've seen of the social life so far, it's just great if you happen to like talking about games and getting drunk with the chaps every night . . . As yet I've met virtually no one in Fitzwilliam, and from what I see around me I'm not sure that I terribly want to. Terrible attitude, of course, but I don't seem to be cut out to be one of God's gifts to the community life. The main trouble with Fitzwilliam is that it's so far out. It's easier now that I have a bike, but it's still rather a long way from the centre of things.

Using his bicycle, Nick did make efforts to visit friends in other colleges. Following their escapades in Morocco, Rick Charkin had just started at Trinity. Nick established where his room was and knocked on its door. Given that they'd spent a month at close quarters that spring, Rick's bemusement was understandable: 'Nick hadn't mentioned that he was going to Cambridge, so it was a pleasant surprise.' He also went to St Catharine's to look up his fellow Old Marlburian Colin Tillie, who recalls having 'a cup of tea in his room as he sat strumming his guitar', but their friendship did not last.

'The various intentions I had on coming up here don't seem to have come to much as yet,' he admitted to his parents after a fort-night.[2] A vague plan to take up karate foundered because there was no club available, and he was making no attempt to pursue athletics, to the college's disappointment. 'Several people came around and tried to get him interested, but he wouldn't have anything to do with it,' Rodney later explained.[3] 'We quite understood,' added Molly, 'because supposing you're a very good runner and you get to a university, they make you do that the whole time, you've got no time to do anything else at all – you've got to be practising and training and all that.'[4]

He was more interested in musical possibilities: 'There is a Classical Guitar Society,* but it is on rather an unsatisfactory system . . . I

* 'The Society provides the opportunity to learn classical guitar,' reads *The Varsity Handbook* (1968); 'Professional tuition given each Saturday of full term, in the Bateman Room, Caius', going on to characterise the Asian Music Circle as follows: 'Meets frequently for talks, listening to tapes and records, and, most important of all, for hearing live musicians from all parts of Asia.'

think I may join the Asian Music Circle.' He mentioned seeking opportunities to play guitar in public but told his parents:

> My guitar is out of action at the moment, since the shop has had to send up to the factory for a new part. This of course does not greatly help my state of mind. While it's been away I've been writing quite a few words, but am in the deeply frustrating position of not being able to set them to music.

In the absence of his instrument, he did at least have a distraction: 'My Chinese friend Calvin is up here for a couple of days, doing a bit of lecturing, and it is naturally a relief to find someone so interesting and unusual for a change.'

Perhaps spurred by the damage to his Levin, at around this time Nick made the momentous decision to buy a Martin D-28 guitar too. It was a huge step up in terms of quality and outlay. 'There's no way I could've ever afforded a Martin in 1967,' states Wizz Jones.

> They were imported from America and cost at least £300 [the equivalent of around £4,000 in 2022], maybe more if they were new. Owning a Martin meant you were either a very successful musician, very rich, or had a well-paid day job. Paul Simon had one and that really impressed us all. Even Bert Jansch didn't have one!

How Nick afforded it is a mystery, though Gabrielle emphasises that he 'was always pretty good at saving up for something he really wanted'. Perhaps he was feeling flush after receiving his funds for the year ahead, and decided he'd rather have the instrument and live frugally. He doesn't appear to have mentioned it to his parents, instead indicating that he was engaging with academic life: 'It seemed reasonably easy to put my brain back in action, which was lucky, and the work in fact seems to be about the most acceptable thing about the place so far.'

His course encompassed topics as broad as Chaucer, Shakespeare, Literature from 1625 to 1798 and French translation, and he was supposed to attend two supervisions per week and come up with an essay or translation for each. 'During the day our corridor was quiet,' recalls Ed Gilchrist, who was reading Engineering, and he and Nick both welcomed diversion when they were supposed to be working.

I occasionally bumped into him in the gyp room, and we would chat about day-to-day things. He could have seen me as a rough-and-ready northerner, but he wasn't at all prejudiced. He seemed genuine. When I went into his room he would sit on his bed and I would sit on the chair next to his desk, and we'd be within eighteen inches of each other.

Nick's preferred topic of conversation was, of course, music.

His way of talking about it one-on-one was thoroughly engaging and charming. He explained the ins and outs of the way he tuned (or retuned) his guitar – it was as if he didn't really believe in 'normal' tuning. He would start by playing for me, then visibly disappear into his own world. It was always something he'd come up with, and when I heard his first album I recognised phrases that he'd been playing, if not complete songs. He was putting together those songs in that room in Fitzwilliam.

I once managed to persuade him to chat in my room, but he seemed agitated and I realised it was because he was without his guitar. I would constantly hear it – if he was in and there was no guitar, I'd wonder if there was something wrong! He told me that some nights the sounds from the neighbouring room would keep him awake or interfere with his playing. I'm not sure if that contributed to him not being there much, but it probably explains why he would wake up late – our bedders [the women employed to clean college rooms each morning] would sometimes knock on his door and get no answer and move on. But Nick wasn't the only one who liked a lie-in. I have no recollection of him taking anyone to his room for the night, but that doesn't mean he never did.

Ed barely saw Nick other than on their corridor. 'When he wasn't in his room he was hardly ever in college. We were supposed to eat in, but only Formal Hall was compulsory, so he'd go to that every week – you had to wear your gown. I never saw him in the college bar – I recall him going in and out a lot.' John Venning calls him 'a mystery man': 'From our staircase David Punter and I could look across to Nick's. We would often see him nipping off and wonder where he was going.'

Rick Charkin was Nick's closest companion in his early days at Cambridge. 'If you weren't interested in the academic side of life, you had a lot of time on your hands, so we often gathered in each other's rooms,' he says. 'We weren't around girls much in term-time – it was a predominantly male environment. There was a lot of listening to Sibelius and rolling joints. I found Nick easy to communicate with and not noticeably different from the rest of us.'

Rick introduced Nick to two other new Trinity undergraduates, Paul de Rivaz and Joe Cobbe, who had both been at school with him at Haileybury. 'Rick was boisterous, even a little outrageous, but Nick was always quiet,' says Paul. 'I have no memory of him leading a discussion. He was one of the gentlest people I'd ever met. He was always calm – it was impossible to imagine him being angry or unpleasant.'

As for Joe,

Rick took me to Fitzwilliam to meet Nick because we were both guitar players. He was shy, he didn't like looking at people, but he had a quirky sense of humour with lots of quiet irony. I remember him joking about rugby a few times – he certainly wasn't a fan of it or the culture that went with it. He didn't go out much, he spent most of his time in his room, playing guitar and writing songs. In our first term we probably spent five or six long afternoons there, playing guitar together. He had a large-bodied, very resonant Martin, which must have cost a small fortune. It was probably the first one I'd ever seen and I found it difficult to play – I had a little Boosey and Hawkes Spanish guitar, which I'd bought for £6 in 1963.

He patiently taught me finger-picking and was happy to show me how he did things, but I couldn't keep up – he was a marvel. The first thing he taught me was his own arrangement of 'Angi' by Davy Graham, which was wonderful. I shamelessly copied it. He was a wonderful blues guitarist, too, and a very competent pianist – on a couple of occasions he played piano in a hall somewhere in Fitzwilliam while I played guitar. He was focused on his own songs rather than other people's, but he did play me records by Davy Graham, Bert Jansch, John Renbourn and others, which were new to me as I was much more interested in rock.

Nick was a regular visitor to Trinity, where the boys listened to records as they idled in one room or another, or Nick might play his guitar. 'Many of us were more interested in Bob Dylan than in going to lectures at nine in the morning, so he certainly wasn't out of the ordinary in that respect,' says Rick. 'What was extraordinary was his guitar playing, which was weirdly wonderful, more so than his singing.' Paul was also amazed at his talent: 'He could play all sorts of things wonderfully. He was so clearly brilliant that we all just assumed he'd eventually make an album – his songs seemed "oven-ready" even then.'

Sometimes, says Rick, 'We'd go to the Corner House, a cheap Greek restaurant, for moussaka and chips, or the Copper Kettle, a café opposite King's, for Chelsea buns. We occasionally went to the cinema to watch underground movies, and sometimes we'd meet in the Criterion.' One evening in that cavernous, basic pub Nick met another first-year undergraduate, Brian Wells, who was reading Medicine. For Brian, the Criterion was where 'the "heads" congregated – people who had long hair, were listening to Pink Floyd through headphones,* going to Andy Warhol movies and smoking hash'.[5]

Born in November 1948, Brian had grown up on airbases around the world and boarded at Framlingham College in Suffolk. Like Nick, he had been apathetic about applying to Cambridge. He had spent the year since leaving school in America, working in Ohio as a local radio DJ and in a car factory, where his workmates steeped him in soul and R&B. That summer he'd driven to California and become a regular dope smoker. His outlook was more worldly and sceptical than most undergraduates', and Nick immediately took to him, even though he was living with a bad grooming decision. 'Before I went up I had my hair cut off after my dad told me I looked like a vagrant. I spent the whole of my first term kicking myself, because I thought I'd be rejected by the cool crowd.' He was at least wearing pink corduroy jeans.

His first impression of Nick was of someone

---

* Pink Floyd's debut album, *The Piper at the Gates of Dawn*, had appeared in August.

taller than most, with long hair, a warm smile, an easy laugh and a refined sense of the ridiculous in an atmosphere thick with tobacco smoke and noisy drinking, with people calling each other 'man' (which I was used to from the States). He looked exactly as he does on the cover of his first album – same shirt, same jacket – just a bit more cheerful.

They quickly found mutual ground:

I had few friends in my college, Selwyn, which was rather ecclesiastical, and Nick didn't like his. I forgot about my short hair and talked enthusiastically about the radio station I'd worked for. I was able to tell him about a lot of American soul that hadn't come out in the UK, and we discovered we both liked a number of the same things, from *Blonde on Blonde* to Vaughan Williams. That evening we made a plan for him to come over to Selwyn, where I had a Dansette.

Nick duly visited Brian's room, where they smoked a joint and listened to records.

I was really into Sam and Dave, Wilson Pickett etc., having seen their roadshows in the States. Donovan's *Sunshine Superman* album was on constantly, and Nick loved Tim Buckley (especially 'I Never Asked to Be Your Mountain') and the Doors (especially Jim Morrison), but I thought West Coast rock was dreadful.* I don't remember talking about earlier musical enthusiasms – I think he'd moved on from listening to Davy Graham and co., but he could still play a flash version of 'Angi'.

Sometimes Brian made the trek to Nick's room, which was decorated with Indian prints he'd retrieved from Gabrielle's flat on a visit to London.

He would spend literally hours on end in his room playing guitar. Sometimes he'd play a simple riff over and over until he'd got it just

---

* Buckley's second album, *Goodbye and Hello*, had been released in America in late September. The Doors' debut had been released in America in January, and their second album, *Strange Days*, was released that October. Like all hip American albums of the time, they were swiftly available on import in the UK.

right. There were a lot of rugger-buggers at Fitzwilliam, and he found them pretty annoying. I was once there while he was playing his guitar and a pair of feet suddenly appeared at the window – the drunk guys above were dangling someone out, but Nick just raised his eyebrows and kept playing.

Brian played too, but knew his limitations.

I had worked out a little lick in 'Corrina, Corrina' [a 1920s American standard popularised by Bob Dylan] and Nick complimented me on it – it's the only nice thing he ever said to me about my guitar playing – but I didn't need to teach it to him as he had already worked it out. Fitting into someone else's playing and jamming wasn't really his thing, although he was pretty adaptable.

He also saw Nick in other colleges, and quickly understood that he 'was quite a loner. People would toast crumpets in their rooms and he would show up, make polite small talk, have a cup of tea and disappear.'

Five weeks in, Nick had made a few friends but felt far from settled. 'My views on Cambridge seem to undulate continually from good to bad,' he wrote home on 12 November.

At the time of writing it doesn't seem too bad, although I'm still not particularly knocked out by the people I meet. However, I think most people going up to university suffer from misconceptions about the types they will meet there. Thinking they are going to find a place brimming over with interesting and enlightened people, it doesn't take them long to discover that the average student is in fact extraordinarily dull.

In the same letter he told his parents that 'I haven't yet played my guitar in public, since I haven't found a suitable place', and added: 'I would certainly enjoy being a psychologist, by the way, since it always interests me to try and understand other people. I only wish I could understand myself!'

Rodney and Molly were unimpressed by his lack of *esprit de corps*. After some reflection, his mother replied on 29 November, gently but firmly urging self-examination:

Darling Nick, I was rather grief-stricken to hear your condemnation of all things pertaining to Fitzwilliam. It seems your disappointment and disillusion are complete . . . Your entry into Fitzwilliam was, we know, governed to a small extent by Den's good report of you – by his telling them that they were getting in you not only a fine athlete but also one who was a good mixer and popular with his colleagues. And what have they got? A toffee-nosed recluse? It could appear that way.

Nick doubtless weighed her words, but songs were emerging from his relentless playing in Fitzwilliam, and they counted for more. Set to a mellow tune, 'Time Has Told Me' was a cryptic meditation on the constraints of others' expectations, and became the first thing he tended to turn to when asked to play. 'Way To Blue' was a sombre expression of yearning for transcendence. 'The Thoughts Of Mary Jane' was daintier, another tribute to a mysterious, mystic female, though its words speak of the impossibility of fathoming someone else's inner workings or motives. Its title was, perhaps, a wink towards the influence of dope. 'Time Of No Reply' has a similar theme of difficulty in communicating, with Nick even likening himself to a tree, finding peace and reconciliation in stillness and silence.

When he wanted an alternative, he couldn't reconcile himself to his college and sought hipper, dope-smoking company elsewhere. Rick and Brian were always glad to see him; they watched the Incredible String Band in the Union Chamber on 19 November, and Rick contributed a line (he forgets which) to another song Nick was working on, 'Saturday Sun', a jazzy blues concerning the nature of time and memory. Nick also continued to hang out with Joe Cobbe, who – being a good electric guitarist – had befriended fellow Trinity man Pete Carr, the bassist in a university band called 117.

Starting life as the Fix in 1965, 117 – its name inspired by numerology – had played widely around Cambridge over the previous couple of years, then taken a psychedelic turn as 1967 came around. Their singer was James Fraser, a choral exhibitioner at Gonville and Caius (universally known as plain 'Caius', pronounced 'keys'). He became Nick's local source for hash, though Joe says, 'I would hate people to think that Nick just sat around getting stoned. He didn't. He smoked a bit, it didn't seem to affect him much, and he was definitely not a heavy user.' Rick agrees, adding: 'I never saw any evidence of Nick taking harder drugs,' and Brian confirms this: 'I got into amphetamines in my first year. That wasn't Nick's thing. Hash was the only drug we ever took together.'

When Joe was invited to join 117 Nick was assimilated into their circle, centring on Caius. James introduced him to his good friend and fellow Caian Pete Russell, and they became friends too. Nick had finally found the 'interesting and enlightened people' he had been hoping for. 'Pete was well ahead of the curve in terms of thought, meditation and so on,' says James. 'He was totally at home with that sort of stuff by 1967 – he'd got the message and was very good at passing it on.' By late 1967, explains Pete, 'The underground movement in London was closely reflected in Cambridge. Hair started to grow longer, pot started to come in, concerts of experimental music began to happen, it got a little more political.'

Nonetheless, London was where Nick preferred to be, and he habitually broke University rules by hopping onto trains there. He was always sure of a warm welcome from Ben, Alex, Sophia, David and co. 'He'd come round to Stokenchurch Street with his guitar, we'd talk and listen to records,' says Julian Lloyd. 'I can picture him that winter in an armchair by the fire, playing his guitar with those big hands, always looking down, deep in himself.'

'David and Nick used to play together phenomenally,' Ben remembers, adding that Nick was perfectly happy to pass around his prized new Martin but

> The problem was, it was really hard to play if you weren't Nick. He had huge, strong hands, and had the strings higher off the frets than normal. He used to show me tunings and so on, and was complimentary about my playing too – but I'm sure he was just being nice. One evening he played 'Time Has Told Me', and at the end we all said, 'Wow!' He had a habit of breaking off before he'd finished, and said something about it being 'just strumming'. I remember thinking, 'I wish I could strum like that!'

Most of his songs from 1967 suggest the influence of poets such as Blake, Wordsworth and Yeats, whom he enjoyed reading for pleasure. Writing essays about them was another matter. Brian describes Nick's attitude towards his studies as 'more than averagely lazy' and his Michaelmas 1967 report from Maurice Hussey – written in November – observed:

> It has taken a month of extremely dull essays to reach the point at which he has begun to show a little vitality and intellectual initiative. I don't expect him to blossom very daringly but there is no doubt that he has found it difficult to start at this point of the syllabus.[6]

As Nick muddled towards the end of term, Victoria Ormsby-Gore, Stella Astor, Christopher Sykes and others were working hard to mount a series of fundraising concerts to be held at the Roundhouse – a draughty former tram shed in Camden, North London – in the run-up to Christmas, under the name 'Circus Alpha Centauri'.* Ticket sales were being handled by Indica Books, epicentre of London's underground, and interest was running high because the fabled Country Joe and the Fish were due to play their first British dates there, leading to rumours that other San Francisco luminaries would appear too.

'It was pretty ramshackle, we were all trying to think of anyone we could to fill up the bill,' says Victoria. She therefore asked Nick if he would be interested in performing on the 'folk and blues night', Thursday, 21 December. Having decided not to accept an invitation from his family friend Peter Carey to join a skiing party, he accepted – but the prospect was intimidating. Until now he had almost only ever played in private, and his nerves were not soothed by the fact that his heroes Bert Jansch and John Renbourn were to appear the same night, as part of Pentangle.

When term ended on Friday, 1 December, he returned to London and visited Chris Blackwell in Island's Oxford Street office, taking

---

* According to the *International Times* of 15 December 1967, the purpose was 'to raise money for an art centre for underprivileged children', but *Melody Maker* of 23 December reported that the organisation had 'been formed to promote avant-garde pop music, theatre and the arts generally'.

his guitar with him. 'I liked him immediately,' says Chris. 'He was gentle and had a special aura that he made no attempt to project. He was simply the sort of person you cared for as soon as you met. I'd liked his tape and he played me something and I liked that too.'

Unfortunately, however, after releasing records in a wide variety of genres over the past five years – bluebeat, calypso, jazz, folk, blues, pop, easy listening and even adult humour – Island had recently decided to focus on underground rock. Chris felt that they had taken a misstep that October by releasing *London Conversation*, the debut by a gifted nineteen-year-old singer-guitarist named John Martyn.*

> The whole point of a label is to give credibility to its artists, and I had learned from John's album that the worst thing I could do was sign someone, then not give them the guidance or leg-up they needed. All my attention was going on Traffic and Art (soon to be Spooky Tooth), so I explained to Nick that I couldn't take him on at that point. I wasn't fobbing him off, but I asked him to come and see me again in six months' time.

If Nick was dispirited, at least he had Circus Alpha Centauri to distract him. Perhaps partly to allay his nerves, Micky Astor agreed to back him on double bass and flute: 'I don't think we had any formal rehearsal – we were always hanging around in flats playing in those days, and we had sufficient musical communication to do the gig without intense preparation.'

They showed up on the cold night in question to find chaotic scenes. 'It was a rolling show, with people milling about – a "happening" rather than a formal, seated performance,' says Victoria. 'Nick was extremely shy beforehand, crumpled with nerves, but we all encouraged him.' Micky remembers it as 'very hippie, with people rushing around backstage and so on'.

There was certainly no soundcheck. Nick wandered around the cavernous auditorium before his slot and bumped into his

---

* Robin Frederick, Nick's friend from Aix, had become friendly with John in London over that summer and contributed the song 'Sandy Grey', which she later said was inspired by her feelings for Nick.

schoolmates Dave Wright and Chris Rudkin, who were there – like most of the audience – to see Country Joe and the Fish. Characteristically, he had not told anyone about the show, let alone asked them to come along and support him. 'The place wasn't packed to the brim and Nick came over to say "Hi",' says Dave. 'He seemed very stoned – probably to help him fight stage-fright.'

Eventually his time came. By his mother's account, 'He'd never really appeared in public before. I remember him saying to me that he suddenly found himself [in front of] five hundred people and said to himself, "What the hell am I doing here?" Anyway, he went ahead . . .'[7] Micky recalls:

> It was just the two of us, me standing on his left, playing his songs, without massive lights. I found it very hard to hear myself play onstage in those days, so I'd taken the end off a stethoscope and put the tube into the body of the instrument to amplify it. Nick was incredibly nervous and I remember getting the giggles because his legs were shaking so much that his trousers vibrated.

Chris Rudkin confirms: 'He was nervous as he played – his body language was hunched and distant, and I'd seen him in enough everyday settings to judge. The Nick onstage wasn't the Nick I remembered from school.'

The audience wasn't there to watch Nick, needless to say, and he was easily the least familiar name on the bill. Nonetheless, continues Micky, 'I guess we played for fifteen minutes and we went down well.' No setlist survives, if one ever existed, but by all accounts Nick was now focused exclusively on his own songs, and they're likely to have played 'Magic', 'The Thoughts Of Mary Jane', 'Time Has Told Me' and 'Day Is Done'.

Victoria was running around but did manage to watch Nick:

> Onstage you could see that he wanted to be invisible – he was dressed in black, as if to minimise his presence – but he played amazingly and sounded beautiful. Compared to a lot of the people who did or didn't turn up, he was wonderful. Despite his nerves, he believed in his talent and there was a part of him that really wanted people to hear his songs. That night was a clear chance to step forward. He

could easily not have turned up, but he steeled himself to do it because he wanted to move things on for himself.

He made a powerful impression on at least one audience member: Ashley Hutchings, bassist and leader of the underground rock band Fairport Convention. They weren't busy that night, so Ashley had seized the chance to watch Country Joe and the Fish. Wandering around the venue, he happened to catch the start of Nick's set and made his way to the front:

> The thing that struck me first of all was his demeanour and his charisma – I didn't take the songs in. He sang well, he played well enough, the songs were interesting. But it was Nick the figure-on-stage which really registered. That is what made a really strong impression on me.[8]

Apart from Nick's presence, he noticed that 'At that time, all the singer-songwriters, like John Martyn, sang with American accents, so to hear this very English-sounding music really stood out.'[9] Far from psychedelic excess, he felt that Nick 'contrasted so nicely with what was going on at the time – there was a lot of extravagance, and he stood very still and he performed very simply.'[10]

Fairport had yet to release anything, but they had recently signed up with the American producer-manager Joe Boyd. It wasn't Ashley's habit to act as a talent scout, but when he spotted Nick on the floor of the Roundhouse after his set, he approached him. 'I said how much I had enjoyed it, and did he have any plans? He said no, he was casting around. I said, "Well, I'm with Fairport Convention, we're signed to Joe Boyd, and may I mention you to him?"'[11]

10

A Remarkably Original Singer

A LITTLE OVER a fortnight earlier, on Sunday, 3 December 1967, the *Observer* magazine had run an article entitled 'Who's Who in the Underground'. It profiled Joe Boyd alongside the Beatles, the psychedelic artist Nigel Waymouth, the co-founder of *International Times* (the UK's only major underground newspaper) Barry Miles, and the BBC's champion of left-field music John Peel. Joe was only twenty-five but his credentials were remarkable. He had promoted blues artists in America, distributed folk, blues and jazz records, tour-managed blues and gospel legends in the UK, overseen the sound at the Newport Folk Festival in July 1965 (including Bob Dylan's step-change for popular music by 'going electric'), and helped launch the British wing of the innovative Elektra label, with the aim of breaking American stars like Judy Collins, Phil Ochs, Tom Paxton, and Tom Rush (with whom Joe had roomed at Harvard in 1961), as well as sourcing local talent.

He signed the Incredible String Band to Elektra in the spring of 1966, but was sacked shortly after their debut album appeared that September. In need of an income, he resolved to put on a weekly night in a Tottenham Court Road basement. This became UFO, doyen of London's underground clubs. He produced Pink Floyd's debut single for EMI, released in February 1967, and made more waves in July with the Incredible String Band's second album for Elektra, the hugely influential *The 5000 Spirits or the Layers of the Onion*.

Really, though, he wanted to form his own production company. To his regret, he had signed the Incredible String Band directly to Elektra instead of retaining the rights to their recordings and licensing them. He had an idealistic vision of a business that would provide an all-encompassing service – management, recording, publishing, promotion and live agency – to acts he believed in. Fortunately, his friend and fellow US expat Tod Lloyd was in a position to make it happen.

'Joe was a force: a strong, charismatic guy who didn't get mad at people or get engaged in personal animosities,' he says.

> He had his eye on what he wanted to achieve and how best to accomplish it, so that put him above the fray. Everybody liked him – he was positive and sensible, more of a businessman than a hippie, yet sympathetic to the underground movement. Thanks to an inheritance I actually had some money, unlike everyone else I knew, and one night in Joe's flat at 90 Westbourne Terrace I asked him, 'What would you do with $10,000?' He proceeded to tell me exactly what he would do and I told him, 'Well, I have $10,000!' . . .

They named the company Witchseason after the 'beatniks out to make it rich' in Donovan's 'Season of the Witch', but the reference was purely ironic – personal enrichment was not the goal. After hearing Fairport at UFO in late July 1967, Joe snapped them up, largely on the strength of their eighteen-year-old guitar wizard Richard Thompson. For him, 'Joe was about six feet four, handsome and inescapably clean-cut. He looked like a cross between Ivy League and hippie.'[1] He also signed the relentlessly inventive South African jazz pianist Chris McGregor and his group, indicating the catholic nature of his taste and the roster he wanted to build.

With backing and artists in place, Joe needed a sympathetic record company to work with: 'I was twenty-five and thought I was hot shit – I felt validated by having found the Incredible String Band and Pink Floyd.' German-based and deep-pocketed, Polydor was disrupting the British record industry by offering artists and producers more leeway and higher royalties than the established major labels. 'They seemed to be handing out labels like candy – Reaction to Robert Stigwood, Marmalade to Giorgio Gomelsky, Track to Kit Lambert and Chris Stamp – and I wanted one.'

He therefore approached Polydor's UK boss, the equally urbane Horst Schmolzi. Horst didn't offer Joe his own imprint, but he proposed to pay advances, and press and distribute Witchseason's recordings on existing Polydor labels. In return, it would have autonomy and its distinctive logo (designed by Adrian George) – a witch on a broomstick – prominently visible. Joe agreed, and set about making recordings, as well as touring with the Incredible String Band.

Also with Polydor's backing, he started Osiris (Visions), which sought to market the eye-boggling posters his friends Nigel Waymouth and Michael English had created for UFO and others. Its delivery boy was an ambitious teenager named Phil Dudderidge. 'Joe seemed to be a grown-up to me,' he says.

> He was an impressive personality – there was something of the Svengali to him, but nothing malign. He had a charisma that belied his age and always seemed busy. He was offhand, but charming if he wanted to be. He was more of an aesthete than an old-time hustler, and he loved his artists and their music – the last thing he'd do was rip them off.

Despite being thanked on its poster, Joe couldn't make it to Circus Alpha Centauri because he was recording the Incredible String Band's hugely anticipated third album and moving offices. Witchseason had outgrown Westbourne Terrace, so they'd leased space at 83 Charlotte Street, W1. It wasn't at the heart of the music business, or even salubrious, but it was in the centre of town. They moved in over Christmas. 'Joe's office was at the front,' says Huw Price, who had run the door at UFO and was now handling live bookings for Witchseason. 'There was a long corridor running down the building, with my office leading off it, then two more offices at the end, for Tod Lloyd and for Danny Halperin, who did artwork, amongst other things.'

Good as his word, Ashley Hutchings enthusiastically handed over Nick's number. Joe accepted it politely but without enthusiasm; he tended to find British singer-songwriters ersatz in comparison to their American counterparts. 'I was generally hostile to singer-songwriters as a breed,' he explains. 'I could see that they represented the future in some fashion, but it was only the crazy outliers who weren't following Dylan, Simon, Jansch etc. too slavishly that interested me.'

Joe respected Ashley's taste, though, so amidst the chaos of his new surroundings he rang Nick in early January 1968 to request a demo. If Nick had been excitedly awaiting his call over Christmas at Far Leys he didn't let on, but he turned up the next day, wearing his overcoat against the cold. They barely spoke; Joe simply remembers a first impression of someone 'tall and handsome with an apologetic stoop' hand-delivering a tape.[2] 'I don't know if it was recorded especially for me, but I doubt it. I listened to it in a quiet moment that evening. It had home recordings of "The Thoughts Of Mary Jane", "Time Of No Reply", "Magic" and "Time Has Told Me".'

Joe was stunned by the quality of the songs and Nick's delivery. 'I played it three times, straight through. From that moment I knew I wanted to make a world-class record with him, with the best possible musicians supporting him.' Unlike most of the aspiring musicians who came Joe's way, Nick wasn't obviously influenced by anyone else. 'It was Nick's melodies that really impressed me,' Joe reflected in 1974:[3]

> There was also a considerable feeling of sophistication and maturity about his songs and the way they were delivered. While the tape was in the office I was playing the songs to someone who came in, and he made a remark to the effect that they sounded like Donovan, and although a lot of people went on to echo that sentiment, it was one that never occurred to me, because I really did feel that I was listening to a remarkably original singer.

In an era of excess and whimsy, Joe felt that there was 'something uniquely arresting in Nick's composure': 'The music stayed within itself, not trying to attract the listener's attention, just making itself available. His guitar technique was so clean it took a while to realise how complex it was. Influences were detectable here and there, but the heart of the music was mysteriously original.'[4]

Unlike the straight recordings he had already made with artists such as Sydney Carter, Alasdair Clayre, Shirley Collins and Dave Swarbrick, here Joe envisaged a creative role for himself as producer; he heard spaces in the songs that could be adorned by sympathetic musicians and sensitive arrangements. This surprised him: 'A month earlier, if somebody had said to me, "You're going to record an artist, and you're going to put strings behind him," I would have said, "You're nuts!" I was very against, in a way, that kind of aesthetic, of a singer with strings.'[5]

Serendipitously, *The Songs of Leonard Cohen* was hot off the presses in America, and Joe – ever attuned to the zeitgeist – had an early copy. He admired John Simon's arrangements and imagined creating something similar. As he later put it, 'Nick had these incredible songs with these amazing harmonic progressions and these wonderful guitar parts which immediately struck me as the spines of fantastic arrangements that had yet to be written or made or played.'[6] Joe was also mindful of Joshua Rifkin's arrangements on Judy Collins's *In My Life*, which he had had a hand in recording in London in mid-1966.

He rang Nick again the next morning and asked him to return at his earliest convenience. Nick came later that day, and Joe threw various questions at him. Had he made other recordings? Played many concerts? How much more material did he have? What was he up to at the moment? In his diffident way, Nick explained how things stood; as he spoke, Joe recalls being transfixed by his strong hands and long fingers. Joe explained that he thought his songs would lend themselves beautifully to string arrangements and suggested they get together again a few days later.

It was precisely the break Nick had been hoping for since returning from France five months earlier. With a head full of new possibilities, he drove Julian Lloyd to Minffordd in Wales, where Derek FitzGerald had been lent a seaside cottage. Julian remembers:

> We travelled overnight in Nick's old white Vauxhall. He drove assertively – he had a certain amount of dash to him and was completely undaunted by the snowy mountain road as we approached Harlech.* By then dawn was breaking, and I remember us being suddenly struck by the sight of the sea as we left the snow behind and things became multi-coloured again. It was just the three of us there – macrobiotics were quite a big thing so we didn't eat much, we just

---

* This may have been a result of Nick's poor eyesight, and his reluctance to wear glasses or contact lenses.

chatted, listened to music and went for walks. We went to Portmeirion*
one day and looked around. There were speakers hidden in the trees
playing birdsong, which we had a good laugh about.

Julian took numerous photos that week. A couple find Nick
framed in the cottage's doorway, grinning bashfully. One afternoon
they made their way to the vast Harlech Beach, where he captured
Nick swathed in his familiar black overcoat. In one shot he grins
with the ruins of Harlech Castle far behind; in another he's puffing
on a joint, close-up, looking preoccupied; in a third he's striding
along in the pale lace-ups he occasionally favoured.

Back in London Nick and Joe had a third meeting at which Nick
spent the evening playing through his whole repertoire. Joe focused
purely on the music[†] and found the experience 'just incredible': 'I
mean, it was just so many great songs, that were so different from
each other, and there were so many rich possibilities that were
opening up as I was listening to them.'[7]

On this occasion he observed: 'From the first time I met him he
stuttered, he was apologetic, he was hesitant in all things, in all
situations. And in a way it was only when he had a guitar in his
hands that he seemed physically confident.'[8] Joe observed the different
tunings and chord shapes Nick employed for each song, and by the
end of the evening had decided he was a better player than Bert
Jansch, John Renbourn, John Martyn and Robin Williamson. 'I
thought Nick was obviously a genius,' he states simply.

Nick and Joe were never close friends, partly because Nick was
six years Joe's junior and lacked his cosmopolitan ease, partly because
Joe was so busy, but they did have things in common. Joe came
from a social milieu Nick could relate to; he had attended a boarding
school (Pomfret, in Connecticut) and gone on to Harvard, so he
understood the pressures Nick felt from Cambridge and – to an

---

* The exterior location for the surreal cult TV drama *The Prisoner*, which was
currently appearing on ATV.
† 'Not playing the instrument myself, I've always tuned out when people gush
about Martin D-28s, Guilds or whatever. I just remember how they sounded, not
what make they were or how they looked.' (Joe Boyd, interview with RNZ
Music, June 2019.)

extent – his parents, who would later comment on their passing physical resemblance, both being tall, elegant, long-haired and possessed of a detached manner that could seem aloof; Joe was dynamic and energetic but not easy to be close to.

'He paid little attention to anything he considered irrelevant to the current project,' according to Rose Simpson of the Incredible String Band.[9]

> His glossy outside layer seemed to repel all encumbrances without effort and I never saw him angry, although he must often have been irritated beyond forbearance as he tried to keep together the disorderly lives of so many musicians and their attachments. He had a way of looking smiley and bland while making a cutting remark. It was difficult to retort without seeming petty . . . Life alongside Joe was either skin contact or arm's length, with no comfortable familiarity in between.

Most importantly, Joe shared Nick's passion for good music of every sort and was able to communicate directly with him about his material. He ended the meeting by telling Nick what he must already have inferred: he wanted to sign him to Witchseason and work towards an album. The offer was for 50 per cent of Witchseason's net royalty income after studio costs had been recouped. 'There might have been a lump payment of £50 on advance – which was a lot of money then,' says Joe (the equivalent of around £700 in 2022). 'When Elektra signed the Incredible String Band they already had a following and a career and they got £33 each. It would have been astonishing for any production company or label to pay a big advance to an unknown in 1968, unless it was someone with pop star potential.'

Nick was still too young to sign the contract himself, so Rodney would be required to do so on his behalf. The paperwork was slow to materialise; a handshake was good enough for Nick and Joe. 'As soon as Nick met Joe Boyd, almost at once he was offered this recording contract,'[10] Molly later said, expressing the view that it was all too fast. But Nick had no desire to delay; Witchseason seemed tailor-made for him. Firstly, its holistic approach spared him having to navigate the choppy waters of the music business. Secondly, at Witchseason the artist was pre-eminent: he would get to record his music at his own pace with a sympathetic producer he admired. Thirdly, there was the possibility of another income stream, organised in-house. As Joe explains: 'I was excited about Nick's publishing too – I thought lots of people would want to record his songs.'

Joe understood Nick's obligations to Cambridge and told him to stay in touch, to keep writing and maybe find some opportunities to perform, and that he would arrange a preliminary recording session in a few weeks' time.

11

My Musical Friend

ᴬ

NICK RELUCTANTLY RETURNED to Fitzwilliam on Tuesday, 16 January 1968, taking with him a roll of Osiris (Visions) posters Joe had given him. 'We were desperate to get rid of them!' Joe remembers,[1] and Nick gave or sold them to friends, sticking a Jimi Hendrix one on the outside of his door. As ever, much of his time was spent in his room, but he reconnected with Brian Wells, Rick Charkin, Joe Cobbe, Pete Russell and others, and soon after the start of term James Fraser had a proposal for him: '117 wanted to put on a multi-media event, which we were calling "Under the Influence", and we were trying to fill up the bill, so I asked him to play.'

Fresh from his success at the Roundhouse, Nick accepted, and – without mentioning Joe – explained that he was interested in finding someone to help set his songs to strings and other instruments for the show, scheduled for the evening of Friday, 23 February. James liked the idea, and a name immediately sprang to his mind: 'Robert Kirby was a first-year choral exhibitioner in Caius and had become a good friend of mine the previous term, so I suggested they collaborate.'

Robert was a couple of months older than Nick, having been born in Bishop's Stortford on 16 April 1948. His father was a cabinet maker and his mother a housewife. He described his background as 'upper-working/lower-middle class, a boy from the countryside, a bumpkin',[2] but his childhood was comfortable and secure. He was a boisterous child but took music seriously and was a chorister from the age of seven. 'We were a musical family – there was always music in the house,' says Stuart, his only sibling, who was born – like Gabrielle – in 1944. 'Robert was a musical all-rounder and took

144

the highest grades in his Royal College of Music exams. He was always going to be a musician.'

The Kirbys were determined for their boys to fulfil their potential and placed great emphasis on their schoolwork. Like his brother, Robert earned a so-called 'County Scholarship' to the local public school, Bishop's Stortford College, which he took up in the autumn of 1959. Bright and sporty as well as musical, he threw himself into the life of the school. 'He was always amiable,' says John Williams, a fellow County Scholar and musician. 'He was often in trouble, but in the nicest possible way.'

'The school had a strong musical tradition,' continues Stuart, and Robert had the good fortune to be taught by Christopher Bishop. 'Robert and John were the last two A-level music students I taught before going to work as a producer for EMI,' recalls Christopher. 'Robert was a large boy, terrifically likeable and ebullient. If there was something fun going on, off he would go and be part of it. He really loved music – he played the horn well but singing was his main thing, and he had a great voice.'

Robert also liked pop, being a Beatles devotee and (in late 1964) forming the Four Apostles, a folk quartet that performed locally and toured Germany singing US standards, many of them popularised by Peter, Paul and Mary. They had a residency in a folk club in Hampstead whilst still at school, but classical music was where Robert's future seemed to lie, and he excelled to the extent that Mr Bishop not only recommended he read the subject at his old Cambridge college, Caius, but also apply for a Choral Exhibition. He was duly awarded one, starting in October 1967. Before going up he participated in amateur theatrics, grew a moustache and extravagant sideburns, and travelled around Europe, making a pilgrimage to Mozart's birthplace in Salzburg.

Caius came as a shock: 'At school I was regarded as brilliant at music. As soon as I got to Cambridge I had to fight very hard to be even regarded as moderately good.'[3] He quickly met his fellow Exhibitioners, including Marcus Bicknell, who says: 'He was pear-shaped even then, an extrovert, self-confident and great company, with a slightly scatological sense of humour. He liked a drink and was in the pub much more than the rest of us.'

The enterprising Marcus had gone up the year before and founded Fab Cab – short for 'Fabulous Cabaret' – a group of Caius choristers who sang a capella arrangements of pop songs at parties. They had been talent-spotted that June, leading to a contract with Polydor, who saw commercial potential in their attempt to bridge choral music and pop. Robert took the place of a departing member, so he didn't participate in their first recordings, as the Gentle Power of Song (as Polydor renamed them for their recordings). Nonetheless, explains Marcus,

> [Robert] started writing and adapting most of our new material. He loved music theory and was always spouting forth about Bach's fugues and the way they twisted around on themselves. He was starting to move away from classical – he had pop vocal harmonies in his brain and liked a lush style.

The group was riding high in January 1968. On 23 December 1967 they had appeared on the Christmas special of BBC1's hugely popular *Dee Time* to promote their album of Christmas songs, *Peace*, and its accompanying single, 'Constant Penelope',* and at the start of the new year they'd recorded a second album for Polydor, this time featuring Robert. As such, when he met Nick he was a major label recording artist with several of his arrangements awaiting release.

At the outset of his second term Robert was a widely known and liked character in Caius. All who knew him there seem to have fond memories of him – such as the time he paraded around a party with a chili pepper up his nose, only to develop a painful nasal infection the next day. 'He was a scream – jolly, bright, musical,' says his fellow Exhibitioner Antony Evans. 'He was always out for a laugh, smoking, drinking and carousing, and he was kind-hearted and generous-spirited, never catty or nasty.'

His friend Mark Wing-Davey describes him as 'open and enthusiastic, with no sense of an agenda. He was a dope-smoker but certainly wasn't "cool" in terms of outward signifiers, like James Fraser or Nick Drake. Outwardly he seemed quite conservative, in

---

* The viewing figure has been estimated at 18 million, possibly including the Drake family.

that uneasy straddle between being a public schoolboy and someone who was yet to find his cultural feet.' Another member of Fab Cab, Alan Fairs, says Robert had 'all the good bits of Falstaff, with no lack of confidence or ambition'.

Unfortunately, however, Robert was not enjoying the demanding Music course, which he found staid. The first composition he'd submitted as part of his studies had been returned with 'a line struck right through it, and my lecturer wrote "Corn Flakes commercial" underneath. But I was delighted – I thought, "Is this really good enough to be in a Corn Flakes commercial?"'[4] As Alan puts it: 'Musicology wasn't his thing – he wanted to write and make music himself.' James knew this when he pointed Nick towards Robert's room, Q4 in the college's ancient Tree Court.

Having knocked and entered, recalled Robert, Nick 'offered some muttered introductions, mentioned [James Fraser's] name and said that he had written some songs and wanted them arranged for strings that could be used locally for live gigs.'[5] Robert's first impression was that 'One immediately noticed an aura of gravitas. He was six-foot-two, good-looking, quietly well-spoken, smiling a lot.'[6] He was also struck by Nick's clothing: 'In the early days he always looked immaculate. He was always wearing a dark jacket, dark jeans, open-collared shirt, long hair.'[7]

By Robert's account, Nick had not brought his Martin but

picked up my rather naff Spanish guitar and proceeded to make it sing like never before or since. He played 'Day Is Done', 'Time Of No Reply' and 'Magic' on guitar. He then played 'Way To Blue' and 'Saturday Sun' on my old upright piano, which was rented from the local music shop and tuned rather infrequently. I was astounded by the sheer inventiveness and absolute quality of his songs.[8]

As Joe had also understood at once, it wasn't only Nick's songs that were remarkable, but his musicianship. 'Nick was an absolutely phenomenal guitarist,' Robert stated in early 1975.[9] 'He was very adept at highly complex double-picked rhythms, with the thumb on the bass string and the other fingers working on as many as four tunes at a time. He was a master of counterpoint.' He later added:

He was the first guitarist I'd seen who used all six strings . . . As a classically trained musician I could see a lot of skill there – there would be counterpoint going on within each string, countermelody, there would be a tenor part, a bass part, an alto part – just on the guitar.[10]

The fluency of his playing struck Robert too:

It was faultless, it was immaculate. I was very keen on Eric Clapton, Jeff Beck, George Harrison, I think they were possibly my favourite lead guitarists, but Nick was just phenomenal, he was stunning, he was a greater guitarist than any I've mentioned. Even though I come from the generation of Jansch, Renbourn, Davy Graham, who again were immaculate guitarists, I think Nick had better, greater technique than any of them.[11]

Nick's singing made less immediate impact on Robert: 'To be perfectly honest, I was not immediately taken by his voice – I was a choral scholar – but I was by his lyrics.'[12] Nonetheless, he added, 'To start with I thought the voice was a bit weak, but that was just my immaturity. I soon saw it was the perfect way to deliver the lyrics and vocals of those songs – very understated.'[13]

He was impressed that Nick's influences went beyond the obvious touchstones of the day:

I loved Jansch, Renbourn, Graham, but Nick was better than them at the blues. He could either do it in a complex sixties rock style or he could make it sound like the original black Americans before the war. He had studied it a lot, he really had. Like a lot of people at the time, he used to go to Dobell's and Collet's for his records. He used to talk about some quite esoteric forties and fifties players. He knew their music inside out.[14]

Robert also noticed how conversant Nick was with the classical tradition:

He talked about other types of music. We talked about a fair bit of classical music – I seem to remember Fauré's *Requiem* was one that we mentioned. Nick was quite well up on nineteenth-century French literature – very well up. I think that was how the conversation got on to Fauré and the string sounds there.

Robert readily agreed to work on the songs. Nick regarded their collaboration as equal, but did not mention his connection with Joe, let alone the fact that they were both technically Polydor artists – another indication of his increasing tendency to compartmentalise. For the time being Robert knew only that Nick wanted to experiment with backings for a concert in February, and he was delighted to have some high-quality original material to work on as an antidote to the dry matter of his degree.

Nick brought some albums to their next meeting. Robert remembered him offering four specific points of inspiration: *Pet Sounds* by the Beach Boys (with arrangements by Brian Wilson), 'Morning Glory' by Tim Buckley (from *Goodbye and Hello*, arranged by Jerry Yester), *The Magic Garden* by the 5th Dimension (with arrangements by Jimmy Webb) and the guitar playing of Django Reinhardt. Robert also remembered Nick enthusing about Mose Allison, whose distinctive blend of jazz and blues permeated some of the songs he was writing.

As for Robert, 'Mozart was my favourite composer, but the Beatles ran him a close second.'[15] Unsurprisingly, his favourite arranger was never in doubt: '"Day Is Done" was the first of Nick's songs I worked on, and I can unashamedly say that the quartet was strongly influenced by George Martin's work on "Eleanor Rigby".'[16]

Nick and Robert got along well, despite their different personalities. For Robert, Nick 'was fairly quiet and introverted but he had a great sense of humour – he laughed and joked, but not in a sort of belly-laughing way . . . There was some sort of refinement about him, he just seemed that little bit distant.'[17] Having started to get to know each other and their respective tastes, they embarked upon the laborious process of building arrangements around Nick's intricate guitar parts.

Robert: 'He was extremely patient as I boringly dissected each one – writing down exactly how any complex chords were voiced.'[18] He wasn't being pedantic; he understood how intricate the songs were and how important it was to respond to their nuances: 'Sometimes a low string would be higher than the string above, and you could easily miss something from a lower string that was very important, and I wanted to be certain of how the harmonic progression was going, so it would be very important for me to write down exactly how he played each chord and every bar . . . That sometimes annoyed him, I think, because it took a long time – but I had to do it.'[19]

Robert first scored for a string quartet, then they worked in other instruments. Far from being left to his own devices as Robert worked, Nick was intimately involved. The system tended to be that Robert threw out ideas and suggestions as he went, which Nick assessed and responded to. His ability to read music served him well. Robert recalled:

> He could see the parts that I was writing down, he could tell what I was writing, and quite often [as he played] he would say, "And how about if the flute plays this here, or the violin plays this here?" if he had an idea of a counter-melody.[20]

Not every song ended up being arranged. For instance, they agreed that 'Saturday Sun' was fine as it was; Robert likened it to Ketty Lester's 1962 hit 'Love Letters', much of whose power derived from its relative minimalism. He notated the guitar part for 'Blossom Friend', but they didn't take it further: 'I don't think it would've fitted in with any of the albums.'[21] Nick evidently took the same view of several other early numbers, which did not survive in his repertoire beyond this time.

The concert date was fast approaching, so at their third meeting, according to Robert, he taped Nick playing songs on guitar and piano for him to work from when Nick wasn't around: 'I had a 1959 Series 3 Ferrograph valve mono tape-recorder [on which] he recorded "Way To Blue", "Magic" and "Saturday Sun".'[22] Shortly afterwards, Alan Fairs and others found themselves in Robert's room:

> He put on this recording he'd just made of Nick and we were all spellbound. We were all musical and still had high hopes of having a hit with 'The Gentle Power of Song', so it was as if the almighty had sent Nick to show us that we weren't anywhere near as great as we thought we were. As we listened to this wonderful thing he'd created, Nick leaned against the wall by the window in an almost apologetic attitude. The memory of that moment, and of Nick's stillness, is vivid in my mind after over half a century.

The duo met regularly to discuss each song minutely, and the songs evolved as they worked. For example, Nick originally played 'Way To Blue' on the piano, and 'Time Of No Reply' started faster than their joint version ended up. Robert drew on different influences according to the song:

> In some of the arrangements I tried to get a bit of an Impressionist feel, but there again, say on 'Way To Blue', I tried to handle it completely as a baroque song, like Handel or Bach . . . It was almost like a Bach chorale; it was a religious song, I thought, a spiritual song.'[23]

His guiding principle was that the arrangement should always serve the song, never swamp it: 'I was very much at that time into Handel and this was part of my Handelian phase. With ['Way To Blue'] I tried to write a proper baroque concerto grosso. It was always put there to support his melody and lyric, not to get in the way of it.'[24]

They mostly worked in Robert's room, which Nick found more congenial and had the advantage of a piano, but Robert visited Fitzwilliam too: 'Nick's first-year room was full of books, absolutely packed with books, as I remember, particularly nineteenth-century French poetry, which I was interested in a bit at the time as well, because I was interested in the songs of Debussy and Ravel, so we would talk a bit about Impressionism.'[25]

Marcus Bicknell often witnessed them working away.

> I first encountered Nick playing his guitar in Robert's room. His playing was fluent and relaxed, in the way you have if you've played an instrument for long enough. He would sit there finger-picking for many minutes before his voice came over the top. I had a very commercial ear and thought he was fantastic. His songs had shape, form and meaning, and the effect was absolutely beguiling. I didn't spend time alone with him – Robert was always there.

The stout, owlish extrovert and the tall, enigmatic introvert made for an odd pairing but, as Marcus puts it, 'the interesting thing was the way Nick latched onto Robert – there was a palpable bond between them. Maybe Robert changed his manner around Nick –

I doubt he lit a fart in his presence.' (Others recall Robert's ability to say 'the Bishop of Bath and Wells' whilst belching.) Their backgrounds were close enough for them to have many common references, and Nick didn't give the impression of being embarrassed by his relative affluence. 'People talk about him hating public school and rebelling against Cambridge – I don't think any of that is true at all,' said Robert.[26] 'I think in many ways he was the epitome of a public schoolboy and fitted in perfectly at Cambridge – but we all had a bit of a cynical attitude at the time.' The bedrock of their friendship appears to have been a recognition of each other's profound love of music, and the sensitivity that underpinned it.

Although Nick spent a good deal of time with Robert, there was a limit to how much he chose to share of his creativity. 'I never saw him in the process of actually writing a song,' said Robert. 'Whenever I heard a song, it was finished.' As such, he could only guess at their genesis:

> I think he would probably come up with a tuning and a mood on the guitar first, or maybe at the same time as he had an idea as to what the lyric was to be about. And then, I would think, once he'd got the support pattern on the guitar, he would know what kind of lyric he could write. This is the way I would think he wrote them, but it's merely guesswork . . . He seemed to leave it to yourself to work out what you thought they meant . . . I might have had an entirely wrong idea of a song and he wouldn't have tried to put me right.[27]

Elsewhere, he speculated further as to the beginnings of Nick's songs:

> He would come up with strong guitar phrases, harmonic sequences, tunings. He would have these parts in his head for a long time, and then, as lyrics came, he'd got a library of parts that would go with them. It makes it sound a bit mechanical, but I believe that's the way they came. I'm sure there must have been plenty of songs when he was sitting there and a lyric came, and then he wrote some music for it, but all of his experimentation came with the guitar. He took the guitar to extremes.[28]

When Robert required more recordings to work from, Nick asked Paul de Rivaz to cart his Grundig reel-to-reel tape recorder from Trinity to Caius and do the honours. As was Nick's habit, on the tape he modestly suggests his performances are sub-par, blaming a new string and stating: 'I'm afraid this is proving to be rather an unprofessional tape altogether at the moment . . . party due to intoxication.' (He probably meant from hash, rather than alcohol.) His performances are in fact immaculate, taking in 'Rain', 'Day Is Done', 'Mickey's Tune' (the only surviving rendition, which he refers to as the 'nameless one'), 'The Thoughts Of Mary Jane', 'Magic' (two versions, with different rhythms), 'Blossom Friend' and a largely instrumental 'Time Has Told Me'.

His playing is punctuated by muttered suggestions such as that he wants 'as expansive a sound as possible' on 'Rain', that he sees 'Day Is Done' as 'a generally sort of string quartet song', and wants the arrangement on 'Magic' to be 'as sort of *celestial* as possible'. He describes 'The Thoughts Of Mary Jane' as 'a little impulse song – might be worth doing simply if the backing works out well', and calls 'Blossom' 'corny' in part, while the pretty 'Mickey's Tune'* seems almost a parody of contemporary hippie pop, referencing daisy chains, a fairground, a merry-go-round and 'floating away on the breeze'. Nick also plays an unnamed solo guitar piece, commenting: 'It would be nice to have an instrumental . . . rather nice to have a solo violin.'

When he had finished recording, Paul agreed to leave his machine with Robert (whose own was presumably inferior or out of action). To his surprise, when Robert returned it the tape was intact, presumably because he had finished transcribing it. Paul explains: 'I didn't record over it – even if Nick didn't become famous, I knew I would want to hear it again because I thought he was so good.'

When not working with Robert, Nick had time on his hands and was only too happy to spend it away from Cambridge. On Saturday, 10 February, Stella Astor drove from London in search of him, together with Victoria Ormsby-Gore and Christopher Sykes.

---

* Micky Astor, to whose first name the song's alternatively spelled title is likely to refer, is nonplussed by it.

The situation was complicated by the fact that Christopher had dropped his first tab of acid just before setting off. 'We bumped into Nick in the street by utter fluke, whereupon a rather intense undergraduate of our acquaintance, straight off the squash court, said hello,' says Stella. 'The gear-change was too much for Christopher, who freaked and fled, with me – his minder – close behind. Nick found it hilarious.'

Having recaptured him she asked Nick to Hatley Park for the night, so they made their way to Fitzwilliam for him to gather some overnight things. 'He seemed relieved to get out, as he didn't have any mates among the other undergraduates in his college,' says Stella. 'He said on the whole they just liked getting "pithed" (his description) on a Saturday night – and we thought drinking was definitively uncool.' Victoria, meanwhile, remembers Nick complaining that 'stoned' meant 'drunk' at Fitzwilliam: 'He kept saying, "I can't believe it, it's so grim here, there's no one to talk to, everyone's a rugger-bugger, there's nobody I have anything in common with at all . . ."'*

At Hatley they embraced their definition of 'stoned', though Stella adds: 'Had my father [Major Sir John Jacob Astor VII] known, we would have incurred the wrath of God.' Unable to ignore Christopher's bizarre behaviour, 'Dad eventually asked him point blank if he was on drugs,' continues Stella. 'Instead of going through the roof, mercifully he felt the kindest thing was for Christopher to be put to bed, which we pretended to do.' After dinner Christopher, who was slowly coming back to earth, rejoined them. 'We went for a moonlight walk,' says Stella. 'It was frosty and still and Christopher did a brilliant, bizarre and very funny imitation of an Ice Warrior from *Doctor Who*. These were some of the daft things Nick was party to.'

The following day Stella drove Nick to London, where Calvin Mark Lee had tickets to watch Françoise Hardy taping an episode of BBC2's long-running *International Cabaret*, compèred by Kenneth

---

* Nick's contemporaries at Fitzwilliam dispute this characterisation of the college and regret that he did not make efforts to find friends among them.

Williams.* He and Calvin arrived late and were squeezed in at the front, though he characteristically wrote to his parents on 12 February: 'You might recognise me by my hands, behind which I hid for most of the programme for fear of being spotted by a passing camera.' The intention was to recreate the atmosphere of a nightclub in the studio, so audience members were given a champagne substitute that Nick compared to washing-up liquid.

At the end the well-connected Calvin introduced Nick to Françoise, but a plan for them to have dinner at Rupert's – the restaurant managed by Ben Laycock – fell through as she had to go out with her agent. Nick was smitten, though, telling his parents: 'I've never really thought much of her before, but seen close to in the flesh I must admit she's quite something.'

Turning to his musical endeavours, he wrote:

> My musical friend, a guy named Robert Kirby, is working quite hard on arrangements for some of my songs, and seems to be pretty competent. He's a rather splendid fellow, and looks rather like Haydn or Mozart or someone, being rather short and stocky, with long wavy hair and rimless spectacles. However, he's quite hip to my sort of music, being quite a proficient folk singer himself.

For the first time since starting at Cambridge, Nick was feeling fulfilled: 'It may surprise you to hear that during the last few weeks I've been extraordinarily happy with life, and I haven't a clue why!' They surely inferred that he was excited about Joe's interest, his collaboration with Robert and their impending performance. 'It seems that Cambridge can in fact do rather nice things to one if one lets it, and I'm not sure that I did let it before,' he continued. 'I think I've thrown off one or two rather useless and restrictive complexes that I picked up before coming here.'

It seems that he had made peace with his lack of academic enthusiasm. 'I'm doing sort of 17th, 18th Century poets, people like Swift, Pope, Blake, etc., who have quite a lot to offer in their way, but they seem to be very difficult to write about,' he remarked, prompting Gabrielle to add: 'Perhaps it's a case of "those who can, do, those

---

* It was shown in colour on Monday, 11 March, and appears not to have survived.

who can't, criticise".' He hadn't joined any societies, let alone sports teams, but – inspired by Pete Russell – he and Brian Wells were initiated into Transcendental Meditation on Saturday, 17 February. Upon discovering they had been given identical secret mantras, they laughed the idea off.*

It was now less than a week until Under the Influence. 'We ended up booking a lecture theatre called Lady Mitchell Hall,' explains James Fraser. 'The upside was that it was large and had a sound system and projection, the downside was that it was all seated.' Robert was doing the best he could to complete the arrangements, but it was a tall order. As well as his obligations as a chorister and to his course, he was busy with Fab Cab, whose repertoire he kept up-to-date by arranging the latest hits. He slipped in a vocal setting of 'Saturday Sun' alongside their usual selection of favourites by the Beach Boys, the Beatles and the Mamas and the Papas, making it the first time anyone other than Nick is known to have performed one of his songs.

'He's done a rather beautiful string quartet arrangement for "Day Is Done" and is now working on "Time Of No Reply",' Nick told his parents, who were evidently familiar with the songs.[29] 'Naturally, it's a rather lengthy process, and I don't know whether he'll be able to get enough done.' On Thursday the 22nd, the day before the concert, Robert was in London performing with Fab Cab on BBC1's *Late Night Line-Up*, then switched gear back in Cambridge to make final preparations.

He had scratched together a group of student classical musicians, but they – like his arrangements – were not tried and tested. 'I had played violin in a casual string quartet in my first term, so Rob thought of me,' says Mark Wing-Davey. 'The group was assembled for the concert – there was no sense of it being a permanent thing. We had a short rehearsal, maybe on the day.' As Robert recalled of such performances: 'On the day of the concert we would run through the act twice.'[30]

---

* Nick seems not to have made a habit of meditation, though Pete remembers meditating with him on a subsequent occasion at Gabrielle's flat. He kept a prospectus for Maharishi Mahesh Yogi's summer course, due to take place at the University of Keele in Staffordshire between 16 and 25 July 1968, but it seems he did not attend.

Mark felt that 'Nick's songs were certainly a lot less clichéd than the songs I was writing at the time':

> They were lyrically engaging and certainly weren't driving. They had a dreamy, woozy quality that was lovely. It felt like they all came from the same palette rather than ranging widely. Robert's arrangements weren't taxing – they were largely chordal – long notes without much melody and not especially dynamic. They were supportive to Nick, but not partnering.

University regulations required Under the Influence to be presented under the auspices of an established society, so James arranged for the free-spirited, quasi-philosophical Heretics, originally founded by Bertrand Russell in 1906, to lend it their name. At a cost of five shillings per head, the bill offered 117, the Antonio Renaldi Septet (a light-hearted jazz quintet* led by James's friend Mike Weissmann, later Schutzer-Weissmann) and 'Nick Drake and Robert Kirby', billed as if a duo. The local Arts Lab showed old movies, poet John Fielding gave a reading, and a light show was provided by 'The Rainbow Explosion' – a pseudonym for Pete Russell (aided by a strobe owned by Brian Wells). A stripper named Penny Blue was due to come up from London, but the University authorities forbade it.

The show began at 8 p.m. Brian recalls that 'the MC was a long-haired character in Jesus [College] called Rick Hopper, who sang in the Pineapple Truck† and wrote articles about music in the weekly university newspaper, *Varsity*.' Nick was supported by strings, two flutes, an organ and Robert's French horn. Robert explained that he sat 'in the middle of the stage on a stool, in his jeans, with his guitar, and [the musicians] arranged behind him in a semicircle', while he positioned himself 'in the front row of the audience, in the middle, and conducted the orchestra from there – sitting down, sort of thing'.[31]

Nick played five songs with arrangements, in the sequence 'Time Of No Reply', 'Magic', 'Rain', 'Day Is Done' and finally 'Way To

---

* Their running joke was to make outlandish excuses for the two missing players.
† The University's only other psychedelic rock band, they had supported the Incredible String Band at the concert Nick had attended in November.

Blue'. He probably played some others alone. As became his habit, the running order was taped to his guitar. Mark remembers that Nick 'seemed hunched and introverted. I think his interaction with the audience was limited to saying the name to each song before we played them.' Joe Cobbe, who was appearing with 117, says that

> Nick played for forty-five minutes or so. I thought he was brilliant, but the crowd was restless. They didn't boo or heckle, but I think they were more interested in hearing rock music and he was so understated. I don't remember the details – I was almost certainly stoned out of my head.

Brian was there and doesn't remember Nick being shy or reluctant, and Robert never considered him the weak link on such occasions: 'Nick always played perfectly in time, his guitar was always perfectly in tune; he always did the songs exactly the same way. There were no problems [with him] at all, but the musicians were amateur, so the overall effect wasn't as good.'[32] Although Robert stated that 'Day Is Done' was 'never changed' – 'note for note, that was the same from when it was written right the way through' – some of the arrangements bore traces of haste and inexperience. Of his first stab at 'Way To Blue' he said: 'The instrumental section in the middle was totally different, really bizarre.'

In keeping with regulations for University buildings (and in comic contrast with the happenings it had been inspired by), Under the Influence came to an abrupt end shortly after 10.30, while 117 were still playing. 'The coppers turned up and someone pulled the plug in the middle of one of my solos!' says Joe. As the audience left and the musicians packed up, Rick Hopper enthusiastically approached Nick. Brian recalls: 'He said he thought someone called Joe Boyd might be worth approaching about management – so Nick had the satisfaction of replying that he was already being managed by him.'

Exposure and acclaim had not been Nick's goals at Under the Influence; he simply wanted to know how his songs would sound with strings. Rough though the results had been, it seemed obvious that he and Robert should continue to work together, and they agreed to give another joint performance before the end of term, to be organised between them.

In the meantime most of Nick's playing continued to be done in Fitzwilliam, alone and in private; he appears never to have played alone in Cambridge's colleges, clubs or folk venues, although he occasionally accompanied Fab Cab to gigs. 'We went out at thirty quid a pop singing a capella Beatles and so on,' says Marcus. 'I managed the business side of things and drove us to gigs – Nick was interested in any bookings I could get for him and came along with us to a handful.'

Songs continued to come. 'Strange Face' opened with a powerful, hypnotic repeated guitar phrase, requiring fast and precise finger-picking of the sort Nick excelled at. Lyrically it touched on the same ambiguities as other songs he wrote at this time, appearing to be addressed to a superior being – even an alter ego – with the enviable ability to transcend worldly woes: 'But while the earth sinks down to its grave / You sail to the sky on the crest of a wave'.

'Fruit Tree' was a meditation on art not being recognised during its creator's lifetime, and the cold comfort of posthumous renown, especially for those who had died young. It echoes Thomas Gray's 'Elegy Written in a Country Churchyard', and – like other songs Nick was writing – was strongly existential. For Gabrielle,

> I can see Nick understanding the phenomenon from the point of view of other artists he had studied that he might have associated himself with. He was reading English, and if you think of Keats and Shelley and Byron . . . I'm not sure that at the time I would neces-sarily have thought it was because he saw himself [doomed to join their number].[33]

Joe Boyd remembers asking Nick about it: 'He muttered something about it being more about Buddy Holly or artists and poets like Thomas Chatterton [than himself].'[34]

'Sad Story For Christopher' had become 'Man In A Shed', a superficially jaunty tale of unrequited love with an undercurrent of isolation, carrying the implication that Nick felt cut off from others and could only implore them: 'Please stop my world from raining through on my head'. If the girl who 'lived in a house so very big and grand' was a specific person, he is unlikely to have made his feelings clear to her. For Stella Astor, at whose big and grand house the song germinated, he was nice-looking but not sexually attractive; he wasn't flirtatious and always seemed self-contained. 'I liked him but there was this distance, this chasm between us,' she says. 'There was no spark.'

Another new composition Nick's friends remember him playing at this time is 'Mayfair Strange', which he soon renamed plain 'Mayfair'. 'I was living with a friend in a tiny flat in Park Lane and he visited us there, so perhaps it was inspired by that,' suggests Sophia Ryde. Of all his songs, it's the closest to his mother's work and, in contrast to the rest of his material, it feels like a vignette intended for others to sing. One home recording features the only surviving instance of him whistling, and Ben Laycock remembers: 'He was worried it was a bit too much like the Kinks.' In fact it bears a more obvious debt to the newly released 'Skip-A-Long Sam' by Donovan.

Nick became a familiar sight in Caius, working with Robert by day or joining other members of the college as they gathered in each other's rooms by night. 'He was part of a small group with me, Robert, Mike Weissmann, Chris Jones and one or two others,' says Pete Russell. Nick was the only public schoolboy among them, but it was hardly noticed. 'It wasn't a competitive group – there was no hierarchy or pecking order,' says Chris, who, as a Liverpool schoolboy, had watched the Beatles playing at lunchtime in the Cavern. 'I think that's what he liked about our company. I remember his far-back, frankly quite posh accent and lovely, crystalline laugh. He was, of course, very handsome and cool, and we were all aware of his talent.'

They were bonded by enjoyment of dope, conversation and – above all – music. 'It was an informal musical appreciation society, with the accent on "informal",' says Pete. Mike was especially influential. He had gone to the Quintin School in North London and was a couple of weeks younger than Nick, but seemed older and worldlier than his peers. He had gone up to Cambridge to read Chinese but switched to English, an indication of his wide-ranging mind. 'Mike was small in stature but charismatic,' according to Pete.[35]

✓ Time of no reply   0
✓ Day is done   1
✓ Leaving me behind   0
✗ Mickey's Tune
✓ The Thoughts of Mary Jane   1
   Blossom Friend   0
✓ Time has told me   1
✗ My love left with the rain   0
✓ Sad Story for Christopher   0
✓ Fruit – Tree   1
✓ Made to Love Magic   0
   Just Another Girl   1
✓ Mayfair Strange   1
✓ Saturday Sun   0
✗ Strange Meeting
✗ Bird Flew By
   Outside   1
   Blue Season   0
   Find the man with ——   0
   Cello Song

Nick's compositions, circa summer 1968.

'People tended to pay attention to what he said. He had this amazing and eclectic collection of records – he would play Bach by the Leonhardt-Consort followed by Jaki Byard, William Byrd juxtaposed with Motown. He was our mentor.'

Mike had an outstanding hi-fi system and happy evenings were spent in his room, directly above Caius's gate on Trinity Street. Dope was hidden in its rafters, accessible through a trapdoor. One night it fell to Nick to retrieve some, and he plummeted straight through the ceiling.* 'A lot of people have an image of Nick as being somehow abnormal or distant,' Robert said of Nick in this period. 'He wasn't, he was perfectly easy to be friends with. One could talk to him, have a conversation, do what you would with anybody else. One could talk of normal things, and in fact very seldom did I talk about what you would call "deep" things with him.'[36]

'He was quiet, but I wouldn't say he was shy,' adds Pete. 'He could be light-hearted and certainly wasn't deadly serious. A good word for him is "contemplative". We had interesting conversations.' Chris agrees that he 'didn't come across as moody or miserable':

> it's more that there was a sense of isolation about him. He was a classic introvert: somewhat withdrawn, softly spoken, not loquacious. Despite being introverted, he was engaging and likeable and had a magnetic personality. What he did say would cut through and make sense; there was a zen-like minimalism to his utterances.

He would sometimes play his guitar at their gatherings, though by all accounts he did not tend to carry it around with him, probably owing to the distance from Fitzwilliam. Chris says: 'He might play a song or two, and we would be respectfully quiet as he did (not least because it was so lovely to listen to), but he wouldn't play song after song.'

Chris wasn't the only one of Nick's Cambridge friends to observe a tendency he had shown at school:

---

* According to his son Joe, Mike claimed that Nick had been in search of wine, but 'perhaps this was Pa's euphemism for pot'.

Occasionally in a group setting one would become aware of the fact that he had silently upped and left. This added to his mystique considerably, and wasn't taken as unfriendliness. It was no doubt due to copious amounts of cannabis smoking – at times he would become overloaded by this and have to extricate himself to clear his head and walk back to his college.

Brian describes himself as 'peripheral to the Caius gang' – he barely knew Robert at Cambridge – but well remembers Nick's habit of extricating himself from a social group. 'He wasn't one for sitting round and just shooting the shit. [A gathering] would run out of steam and then he would look nervous and say, "Right, I've got to go." And you knew that he wasn't going to anything, he just wanted to withdraw . . .'[37]

On such occasions it's likely that he was itching to return to his guitar, but he and Brian still spent a good deal of time together. In hindsight, Brian reflects that 'We were pretty arrogant, and dismissive of a lot of people':

We had a definite sense of superiority to people riding off to lectures on their bicycles. When Nick's was stolen and I spotted it next to the Senate House, he laughed at the idea of retrieving it. In those days you could get away with doing very little work at Cambridge, even as a medic. We thought it was cooler to wake up late, smoke a joint and go for breakfast in the Copper Kettle at 11 a.m. A lot of the time we'd sit in cafés or pubs, watching people and making humorous observations with a sting to them.

Their people-watching sometimes left them in hysterics.

We were in the Bun Shop one lunchtime, possibly stoned, and I noticed a guy with red hair who looked extremely menacing. I said to Nick, 'Don't look now, but that guy over there looks really nice, maybe you should go over and say hi.' When Nick looked at him we both laughed until we cried. Another time we were in the Arts Lab and watched a chubby guy called Bruce Birchall (who was involved with theatre in Cambridge) struggling to brush his long hair because it was so tangled. The brush kept getting stuck and we started laughing, so he looked over and snarled, 'It's not fucking funny!' After that we occasionally said 'Bruce!' to each other in some awkward situation or other.*

In early March, as the end of term neared, Robert and Nick agreed to put on another evening performance, this time in Caius, where several of the required musicians were based. Robert booked the Bateman Room, a high-beamed, wood-panelled space with stained-glass windows. 'People could reserve it for meetings or performances of various sorts,' says Marcus Bicknell. 'It had chairs and a dais, so it was good for recitals.'

Robert wanted this performance to be recorded, so he contacted another Caius undergraduate, Peter Rice. 'I'd joined the Tape Recording Society in my first year and got involved in making recordings around the University. We didn't charge for our time, just for the tape used.' He had recently made a tape for Fab Cab, at Marcus's behest, and thus knew Robert: 'Two or three weeks later he contacted me. My understanding was that he wanted to have his arrangements recorded – there was no suggestion that it was Nick's idea or that it was for a recording company.'

Rehearsal time was again scant. 'I met Nick for the first time on the day, to discuss what equipment, cables etc. would be needed, and we probably did a soundcheck in the Bateman Room,' continues Peter. 'Nick wasn't amplified but his guitar and voice balanced well. I played guitar and had recorded lots of singer-songwriters around Cambridge, but when I heard him I immediately thought he was better than most of them. His playing was exceptional.'

The performance wasn't advertised but it was free, meaning the room contained around fifty people, many of whom had wandered up after dining in hall. Unlike Under the Influence, Nick was the only act. He hadn't publicised it at all: 'He didn't tell me about his performances or else I'm sure I'd have gone,' says Andy Murison. Being a member of Caius, Chris Jones was present, and says: 'There was a lovely, informal ambience to it.'

Musically, however, it was substandard. 'Robert was making

---

* 'Bruce Birchall *was* theatre in Cambridge,' adds John Venning. 'He dressed in an ultra-bohemian way and was always surrounded by acolytes, so his fury at being mocked would have been spectacular.'

changes on the spot and his arrangement for "Magic" wasn't finished, so Nick played that alone (and very well),' explains Peter.

> The other four performances – 'Time Of No Reply', 'Rain', 'Day Is Done' and 'The Thoughts Of Mary Jane' – were musically terrible, with the instruments out of tune. At one point there's laughter – something must have happened, like some music falling off a stand. It was a bit Morecambe and Wise.*

Part of the problem was that Robert was unable to conduct properly because he was also playing instruments, including a bright red Farfisa organ borrowed from 117.

Despite the shambolic presentation, the recording captures Nick's composure. 'He wasn't nervous,' according to Peter. 'He introduced the songs and his singing voice was clear and strong. If anything, there was a hint of trying to project too much.' Peter didn't tape the entire evening:

> Tape was expensive and sometimes Nick took as long tuning as he did playing the song, so the recording stops and starts. The musicians also played some pieces by Robert that didn't feature Nick, which Robert didn't want recorded. In due course I gave the tape to Robert, who had commissioned it.

Robert was not proud of the results: 'It was crap. The reason the orchestra is naff is that the string bass is following Nick's voice and not his guitar (nor, strictly speaking, my beat). Everyone else does.'[38] With no false modesty, he felt the highlight of the evening was Nick's solo piece: 'I think the treasure on the tape is to be reminded how Nick played guitar on "Magic" – a very standard, traditional, fast folk-picking style.'

As term neared its end, Joe Boyd contacted Nick and arranged to make some recordings with him in mid-March. It had been two months since they had met. In the interim Joe had (among other things) completed work on the third Incredible String Band album, attended MIDEM, the music industry's annual conference in Cannes

---

* Robert suspected the laughter was prompted by his straining for a high note on the French horn.

(where Fairport had played a showcase gig), finished work on Fairport's debut single and album, visited South Africa with saxophonist Dudu Pukwana and flown to the US to organise an Incredible String Band tour. The relative amateurism of the Bateman Room performance was not likely to impress him.

Determined to ensure his studio performances were as polished as possible, Nick wrote a note to Peter Rice, requesting that he make a solo recording of him to listen to and learn from in the coming days. 'We made an arrangement for a Saturday or Sunday morning in his college room, but when I turned up it was obvious he'd forgotten,' says Peter. 'There were various people in there, male and female, and I got the impression it was a smoking party.' If so, it was most unusual for Nick to host such a gathering; as Marcus Bicknell puts it, 'There wasn't a Nick who was a party animal.'

The haggard Nick eventually emerged, muttered an apology and suggested they try recording in the gyp room. He was not on form, vocally or instrumentally, and, as Peter adds:

> There was a noisy extractor fan and other sounds from outside, so we agreed to find another time and I lugged the equipment off again. A friend of mine said we could try to record in his room in Peterhouse while he was away for the weekend. He was a Scholar, so he had a bedroom and a separate sitting room – I was in the bedroom with the tape recorder and Nick was in the sitting room.
>
> Nick was very clear as to how he wanted the recording set up: two mikes with no mixing afterwards, so it would sound the way someone would experience it if they were sitting six feet away. I got the impression that he knew something about tape recording, but microphone placement is a different thing (I was using STC 4038s). To get comfortable he recorded a couple of songs by other people – 'Blues Run the Game' was one. He then played the five songs he'd performed at Caius, and a couple he said weren't yet finished.

After playing each song Nick came through to listen.

When he put on the headphones he handed me his guitar, which I played, but the tuning was very odd – G was an F sharp. When I'd finished the whole thing, I shouted to him from where I was but got no reply, so I went through and saw that he'd left without saying anything.

Such apparent discourtesy would have dismayed his mother, but Peter put it down to awkwardness, and left the tape in Nick's pigeon-hole just before the end of term.*

* The recording is lost.

12

Happy Moments

— ⁓ —

Nick based himself at Gabrielle's in London for the Easter vacation, though they saw little of each other.

> He was very secretive. We got on OK and I loved him dearly and always wanted success for him, but I could never say that we had deep, intimate conversations in which we revealed ourselves to each other. I didn't know what he was doing during the day, because I was very busy rehearsing most of the time and was never all that curious. In retrospect that sounds harsh . . . but at the time he was doing his first album he was happy and I felt he was fine.[1]

Aside from her work, she was preoccupied by a new relationship with the South African-born painter Louis de Wet. Universally known by his surname, de Wet was described at the time as 'a strange mixture of unique artist, intense philosopher and overbearing egotist'.[2] He and Nick were separated by an eighteen-year age gap and had very different personalities, but each had a fervent devotion to their art that provided a mutual understanding.

'I was plunged into an entirely different world,' Gabrielle remembers, 'and a whirl of newness and excitement and being in love, so I was less and less at the flat and less and less involved with Nick at that time – but there was no need to worry about him then.' Naturally, there would be occasional disagreements. 'I'd be cross with him if he was untidy or didn't turn up on time – we'd have a row about something as an ordinary brother and sister would.'

> I would row quite easily and get over it, but Nick couldn't. It would matter much more to him. We had one awful incident – I felt so awful. I think I had been away for the weekend and he'd come

to the flat and he couldn't find the keys and had had to go and find the landlord. We had a furious row about it.[3]

From her perspective it was simply an echo of the sort of silly arguments they'd occasionally had as children, but to her shock Nick started sobbing; she had underestimated how upsetting he found confrontation.

His social life was a mystery to her:

Nick never really introduced me to his friends – I always inkled that it was because he was rather ashamed of me, so I felt somewhat inferior when I *did* meet his trendy friends. On one occasion we went out for dinner at a restaurant called 235 Kings, in the King's Road, and I felt he was embarrassed by me – but I think it was probably more to do with his compartmentalising syndrome.

Gabrielle never knew Nick to bring a girl back for the night, or felt that he aspired to intimacy of any sort. She didn't think he was gay but inferred from his body language that he had 'sexual hang-ups I didn't have'.

Nick continued to see Kirstie Clegg from time to time. 'People say he might have been gay or bisexual, but I never saw evidence of it,' she says. Their romance remained vague:

He dotted in and out of my life quite a bit. We briefly got back together in London when I was training to be a teacher. That was his move – he got back in touch and used to come over to the flat I was sharing just next to Whiteleys [the shopping centre on Queensway]. We used to go out for walks quite a lot. My flatmate Lynne Rankin was seeing Jimi Hendrix, who was also there sometimes, but I don't remember him and Nick meeting, and I don't remember Nick ever having his guitar with him – but music was becoming more and more important to him. He was already going down a lonely trail.

On the agreed date in mid-March – one day in the week of the 18th – he strolled with his guitar from Prince of Wales Drive to Sound Techniques, a converted dairy at 46a Old Church Street, which stretches south from the Fulham Road to the river. It had been Joe Boyd's preferred recording studio since early 1966, and he had formed a close working relationship with its co-owner and chief engineer, John Wood, as they worked on various folk recordings, as well as Pink Floyd's first single. Most Witchseason recordings were made there. One day in early 1968, says John, 'Tod Lloyd was in Sound Techniques with me on an early Fairport session and said, "You just wait until you hear Nick Drake!" That was the first time I heard his name.'

Born in Sevenoaks in November 1939, John had begun his recording career at Decca in January 1960. There he learned the art of stereo mastering before moving to the Top Rank label and the independent Levy's Sound Studios, where his ingenuity was tested creating soundalike covers of hits for budget releases. The chief engineer there was Geoff Frost, with whom he decided to launch a new studio and workshop in the winter of 1964. As John puts it, 'Sound Techniques was simply a jobbing independent studio with a constant turnover of different sessions and projects, so I really learned my craft.'

Joe liked John's plain-speaking manner and fastidiousness, and the studio's location, but most of all he liked its atmosphere and sound. By his account,

> The control room looked down on the studio from a box above one side while the offices were built over the opposite side. It looked awkward, but the differing ceiling levels meant that you had three different acoustics in the same studio; you could move things around until you found the sweet spot for an instrument or a singer.[4]

In the process of recording the second Incredible String Band album the previous year Joe had discovered his knack for mixing, something he likened to 'an endlessly fascinating jigsaw puzzle . . . like watching a print in the developing bath'.[5] 'From that point on, in a funny sort of way, I think Joe and I were learning from one another,' reflects John. 'I wasn't acquainted with the folk/underground world, so I needed to adapt and learn to incorporate my more classical approach into the projects Joe was working on.' A curious dynamic evolved. By Joe's account,

The normal deference of engineer towards producer didn't seem to apply . . . When other producers hired him as an engineer, they were appalled at the way he sassed them back . . .[6] John does not suffer fools gladly, and that was the way I learned how to work, and I relied on it . . . I liked the fact that I'd say, 'Let's do this', and John would say, 'You what? You must be out of your fucking mind!' And then I'd have to think about how certain I was about wanting to do something. I found it a great way of working.[7]

John does not deny this:

Most of the time a producer tells an engineer what to do, but we had a different sort of relationship. His technique as a producer wasn't what was normally expected at that time, and sometimes he seemed not to be paying attention at his end of the mixing board while tracks were being put down, but to be reading the *Herald Tribune* instead. This appearance of detachment sometimes made artists feel insecure or fed up, and I would tend to stand up for them rather than him.

This is not to suggest any lack of respect between the two. John was well aware of Joe's unusual qualities, not least a lack of ego rare in a record producer:

He didn't try to put his stamp on a session – he was very focused on the material and trying to capture things live. He saw the talent in people straight away and was much more concerned with the act than most producers (and would indulge his artists to a greater degree than most). The Incredible String Band and Fairport weren't brilliant in the studio at first, but Joe was convinced they had great things in them, and maintained from the very start that Richard Thompson would come to be regarded as one of the country's top guitarists. His other great quality was choosing the right people to play on a record – that's a skill I really learned from him.

John ran a tight ship, and everything was ready when Nick arrived at Sound Techniques for the first time. 'Nick was wearing (as always) dark clothes, and had hunched shoulders, so he stooped forward,' John recalls. 'He was neither over-friendly or stand-offish. I'd say he was quietly efficient.' He sat down and played 'Mayfair', 'Time

Has Told Me', 'Man In A Shed', 'Fruit Tree', 'Saturday Sun', 'Strange Face', 'Magic', 'The Thoughts Of Mary Jane' and 'Day Is Done'.* All were delivered immaculately with no second takes.

Joe was delighted at this confirmation of his talent, and at the quality of his latest songs. As Tod had anticipated, John was taken aback by Nick's talent and professionalism. 'I was certainly impressed – you couldn't not be. Nick clearly knew the material well and played it perfectly.'

John agreed right away that 'the songs were going to sound even better if they were augmented': 'The reference in my head, certainly, was Judy Collins's *In My Life* LP, which we'd recorded in Sound Techniques in 1966.' It was decided there and then that 'Magic', 'The Thoughts Of Mary Jane' and 'Day Is Done' should be the first three songs to be arranged. Nick did not mention that he had already been working on them with Robert, so Joe asked his friend Peter Asher (formerly of the pop duo Peter and Gordon, and a close associate of Paul McCartney) if he had any suggestions. Peter recommended Richard Hewson, with whom he played in an informal jazz trio.

Aged twenty-four, Richard had orchestrated a single by the French pop star Michel Polnareff but was a largely unknown quantity and hence relatively inexpensive. Joe dimly recalls going with Nick to meet him in Swiss Cottage; Richard has no recollection of ever encountering him. Either way, he was commissioned, and it was agreed that when his arrangements were ready they would reconvene at Sound Techniques.

If Nick had reservations, he did not express them. Over the next few weeks he resumed his gentle social round, meeting schoolmates, Cambridge friends or his London crew, but never mixing them. Brian Wells does not consider this an accident: 'I never knew how deep any of Nick's friends or friendship groups were. He would compartmentalise and he was vague and remote about them.' He has subsequently come to regard this as revealing: 'He was quite defended (which would be the technical term). Compartmentalising

---

* A tape containing the first six of these – presumably run off for Nick – ended up in the possession of Beverley Martyn, who hung on to it.

is to do with being defended. It's to do with not letting others in and controlling the boundaries; it's to do with being self-consciously mysterious, even a bit narcissistic.'[8]

'There was a small element of mystery surrounding Nick, because we only had one life but he had several,' reflects Alex Henderson.

> I never once met any of his Marlborough or Cambridge friends. We were aware at the time that he kept the different parts of his life very separate, and we would comment on it to each other, but not to him. He wasn't the sort of person you'd take the piss out of – not because he didn't have a sense of humour, but because you were instinctively aware that he was sensitive and you wouldn't want to upset him.

Mike Hacking has similar memories:

> By 1968 Desi had moved to another flat, in Pavilion Road. It had a relaxed atmosphere and a roof terrace. Nick would visit from time to time but never mentioned any other friends or introduced us to any of his music contacts. He would just drop in when he was in need of a safe haven. We seldom went out to do things and it was always unstructured – but things *were* unstructured in those days. He'd sit, chat, have something to eat, smoke some dope and play his guitar.

Nick's old friend Dave Lodder visited him in London that spring.

> I felt our friendship was petering out and I wanted to instigate it again. He suggested I come up to stay and go out for the evening. He was ironing his shirt as I arrived, which amazed me – men didn't iron shirts back then! – but it shows the pride he took in his appearance. We went to an all-night club [presumably Les Cousins] down a steep flight of stairs, with about twenty people in it, and singers playing songs on guitars. We were there from about 10 p.m. until 5 a.m. Nick was hugely into it, but it wasn't my scene. There was no natural light or fresh air – I couldn't wait to get back to the countryside.

On 30 March Nick went to the Speakeasy with Ben Laycock and Alex to watch Tim Buckley, which Ben remembers him loving. 'He was perfectly normal throughout this period,' he says.

He was thrilled to hear my little Japanese stereo system with head-phones, and he enjoyed being on the back of my motorbike – but he must have been the worst pillion rider ever. He tended to lean the wrong way going round corners – he'd be too busy looking at things or daydreaming. We were usually off scoring dope from a lovely Trinidadian bloke called Owen in Castelnau.*

The consensus among Nick's friends is that his dope intake was moderate. 'I don't remember him smoking any more than anyone else,' says Sophia, and Brian agrees:

> He wasn't smoking a lot of dope. I mean, he really wasn't. Nick wasn't into instant gratification in the way someone like I was, or someone who becomes an addict is. He was the guy who would have a puff on a joint and pass it on . . . Quite often he'd say, 'No thanks'.[9]

'In my experience he didn't smoke any more dope than the rest of us,' says Julian Lloyd:

> but we didn't understand the potential dark side of recreational drugs. The possibility that spliff could be damaging never entered our heads. I myself got paranoid on dope in 1968, and my solution was to smoke more of it, which obviously didn't help. It just goes to show that we didn't really understand what we were doing.

Over Easter Alex asked Nick to join him, Sophia, David Ward, his girlfriend Sarah Coates, Ben Laycock and his girlfriend Rose Cuninghame on a week-long jaunt to Dalmaclare, his mother's cottage on the Isle of Mull, off the west coast of Scotland. 'We drove up in convoy through the night, in a fleet of Minis, and caught the early morning ferry from Oban,' says Alex.

> The cottage had a porch overlooking the sea. We'd go for walks, go to the beach if it was sunny, maybe spend a day buying provisions and having a pub lunch in Tobermory, eat fresh fish, play back-gammon, sit around, smoke dope, listen to records on the little portable record player, sing songs . . .

---

* Castelnau is the long road connecting Hammersmith Bridge and Barnes Village in southwest London.

For Sophia, 'It was magical':

There was no electricity, so when it got dark everything was lit by candles and gas lamps. I used to borrow albums from Harlequin to listen to at home, so I could recommend things to customers. We liked Love, Traffic, the Byrds, Tim Buckley, the Appletree Theatre . . .*

When they finally turned in, says Alex, 'Nick slept in a tiny cubby-hole at the top of the stairs, in what we called "the sea-captain's bed". He was far too tall for it – we all remember the sight of his feet poking out of the door.'

While Nick was in Scotland, Richard Hewson informed Joe that he had completed his three arrangements, so a booking was made at Sound Techniques for the evening of Thursday, 11 April. It was an important moment for Nick, wary as he was of his songs being adorned without his involvement. Upon arrival he found Richard, who was conducting, and various string and woodwind musicians looking over their parts as John Wood set up microphones. The musicians were booked through Richard, as was standard practice at the time, and they were not attuned to the spirit of Nick's songs. 'They were in their forties or fifties and pretty jaded,' says John. It seems that a session guitarist was also among their number, suggesting that Richard assumed Nick was purely a vocalist.

It was theoretically the first session towards Nick's album, but as they began recording, John was struck by the fact that he didn't seem fazed by performing live with accomplished pros for the first time. Nonetheless, it quickly became obvious that his unique quality was not coming across.

'Magic' felt like a mainstream MOR ballad, with the gently strummed guitar swamped by the other instruments. 'The Thoughts Of Mary Jane' featured the flute refrain that would appear on *Five*

---

* Traffic's *Mr Fantasy* had come out on Island in December 1967. *Forever Changes* by Love (released in the US the same month), *The Notorious Byrd Brothers* by the Byrds (January 1968), and *Playback* by the Appletree Theatre (March 1968) were swiftly available as imports in Harlequin, ahead of their British releases.

Leaves Left, suggesting that Nick had to some extent communicated with Richard, but his singing on it was cloyingly winsome, as if trying to adapt to the arrangement. No acoustic guitar was audible; instead, an electric is strummed. 'Day Is Done' felt ponderous, and again made no feature of his guitar.

'Joe's weak point as a producer was in choosing arrangers,' contends John.

> Richard Hewson was no good for Nick and I just couldn't get a handle on his arrangements, or how to balance them. Nothing seemed to work, and Nick was getting more and more frustrated as time went on. He clammed up and it became obvious that it wasn't working for him. Eventually someone suggested that the strings should be played without vibrato, which was a load of rubbish. The session limped to an end, and after the musicians left we listened back to the best takes.

The arrangements weren't inept, but they simply didn't gel with the songs; instead of integrating with them, they sat on them. It sounded as if Nick were bending his performances to accommodate them, which was clearly the wrong way round. For Joe they were 'competent, mediocre and slightly fey, distracting from the songs rather than adding to them'.[10] He hoped the session could be salvaged via mixing, as scrapping it would be a painful expense to absorb, but John was convinced it was a lost cause.

Nick was in an awkward position, but – emboldened by Joe and John's muted response – up in the control room he admitted to being unconvinced too. At an impasse, says John, 'At the end of the evening Nick told us about Robert. Joe and I found it hard to believe that a nineteen-year-old student would be up to the job.' Joe was indeed sceptical:

> I said, 'Oh, sure, has he ever done anything, has he ever done any work?' And he said, 'No, but I think he'd be quite good . . .' And there was something in the way Nick said it. Nick was very, very definite when he knew he was on firm ground, and you could tell that it was a firm idea that he had.[11]

Joe was picking up on something Nick's parents and sister had always known: 'Beneath his shy exterior, Nick was strong-willed.'

'I had a gut feeling that his judgement about Robert would be sound,' says Joe, but he made no immediate promises. Polydor wanted to know what its money was going on, so he played the Hewson recordings to them. Far from sharing Nick, Joe and John's dissatisfaction, they were enthused by their dainty, commercial sound. 'Someone at Polydor had the idea of dressing Nick up in a velvet suit and having him do Tom Jones/Engelbert Humperdinck stuff!' laughs Tod Lloyd.

Nick did not know Joe well and was still learning how Witchseason functioned and what his place in it was. Joe's stock had never been higher than in April 1968. The Incredible String Band's new album, *The Hangman's Beautiful Daughter*, was selling faster than anyone had predicted and ultimately reached Number Five in the charts – an unheard-of achievement for such esoteric music. They had just played several dates in large venues around Britain, which Joe was organising (whilst navigating the duo's 'robust dislike of each other'[12]) and he was finishing jazz albums with Chris McGregor and Dudu Pukwana, while Fairport's debut awaited release. He had also just signed an American band based in London named the New Nadir and another singer-songwriter, Beverley Kutner (who had been on the same bill as Nick at Circus Alpha Centauri).

Joe was eager to foster creative friendships between his artists, so Nick took to hanging out at Sound Techniques from time to time. He met Beverley – or Bev, as she was universally known – at a demo session for her in April. 'He was there at Joe's invitation,' she says. 'He was solitary and I think Joe wanted people to be friends with him – he liked putting like-minded people together.'

Born on 24 March 1947 and raised in Coventry – not far from Nick, but in very different circumstances – Bev had already had a busy career. She had studied drama, played on the folk circuit, released a single for EMI as part of the Levee Breakers in June 1965, lived with Bert Jansch (she features on the cover of his second LP, *It Don't Bother Me*, released in November 1965) and been one of the first two signings (alongside Cat Stevens) to Deram, Decca's 'progressive' label, in September 1966.

Disappointed by false promises of pop stardom, she had embarked on a romance with Paul Simon and toured the US with Simon and Garfunkel for several months in 1967, where – thanks to Paul – she was sneaked onto the bill at the Monterey Festival in California on 16 June. That same month, she recorded a brief spoken part on Simon and Garfunkel's 'Fakin' It'.

Upon returning to the UK she was dropped by Decca, returned to playing in folk clubs and found she was pregnant. Penniless and without a record deal, she was at a low ebb, but Tod and Joe came to the rescue, helping her find a place to live, giving her a weekly retainer and undertaking to record her when she'd had her baby. Her range of contacts and experiences went far beyond Nick's, and he did not easily befriend women, but Bev was creative, caring and self-doubting, and he felt an affinity with her, without sexual tension on either side. 'You couldn't not like Nick – he wasn't cocky or smarmy or off-putting in any way,' she says. 'You were careful with him, gentle with him.'

Nick returned to Cambridge in late April with no clear path towards his album – but Joe was committed to bringing out the best in his material, however long it took.

> The way I worked with Nick was very different from the way I worked with the other artists. With them we tended to go in and do a record in a concentrated period of time, but with Nick we worked slowly. We went in, did a couple of tracks, listened to them, thought about what we wanted to do with them, worked on them a bit more, put down a few more tracks, waited a month, waited six weeks, thought about it some more . . .[13]

This approach suited Nick perfectly, both because of the demands of Cambridge and because he didn't yet have an album's worth of songs he was happy with. He and Robert continued to spend time together, but – perhaps bruised by their Bateman Room performance, and with 'Prelims', or first-year exams, looming at the end of May – their collaboration was not as intense. Nick was in no rush to tell Robert of his association with Joe, or the possibility of recording their arrangements.

As Nick's Summer term got underway, Witchseason was having

difficulties with Fairport. At the start of May – a few weeks before Polydor was to release their album – they replaced their singer Judy Dyble with Tod Lloyd's old friend Sandy Denny. While that drama played out Joe was again touring America with the fractious Incredible String Band. The date for Nick's next session had been set for Friday, 10 May, but because Joe was away, Tod was producing – the only time he did so for Nick – alongside John Wood.

With the tacit agreement that the Hewson recordings would be set aside, this was effectively the first session for his album. Nick slipped away from Cambridge with his guitar and recorded 'Man In A Shed' (accidentally introduced by John Wood on one of the two takes as 'Man In A Shirt'), 'Mayfair', 'Time Has Told Me' and 'Saturday Sun'. At one point Tod attempted an experiment: 'Nick used to make a little rhythmic noise with his mouth whilst playing guitar, and I tried to record just that and use it as an overdub.' This went no further but exemplifies the open-minded attitude Witchseason took to working with him.

After the session Nick proceeded to Far Leys, perhaps with the idea of revising for his exams. They didn't count towards his degree but failing them would involve tedious college sanctions and re-takes in October, casting a shadow over the summer. On Saturday, 11 May, Diana Hicks – with whom Nick and Gabrielle had shared school runs fifteen years earlier – got married in Tanworth. Her brother, Nick's childhood friend Andrew, caught up with him that evening but their exchange made him feel 'a bit conventional and boring, Nick all studied cool and glamour . . . He kept a distance, not quite engaged.'[14]

His Cambridge supervisors also found him distant and disengaged: Joan Black, who was teaching the Shakespeare paper, reported that

> Mr Drake has been a disappointing student. He contributes little to discussion. He seems to find difficulty in expressing orally the character of his response to the text set, and this is confirmed by his written work, which though punctual and adequate in length, is vague, rather scrappy and invariably inconclusive.[15]

Iain Wright, a young research fellow at Queens', was overseeing the seventeenth- and eighteenth-century aspect of his course. 'Still very

immature essay style – very much 6th form type of work, rather ver-
bose, rather "literary", rather afraid to commit itself,' he commented.[16]

Dr Kelly reviewed the reports with Nick, who was immune to
their barbs. He had come to regard his course as nothing but an
impediment to his music and started to entertain thoughts of dropping out. 'We had supervisions together at Queens' in the summer
of our first year,' says Derek Bishton.

> Neither of us was very interested in *Sir Gawain and the Green Knight*
> etc., and while we were waiting for one supervision to begin he
> confessed that he didn't think he was going to carry on with his
> studies. I was shocked, because for me getting to Cambridge was
> like being the first man on the moon, but Nick was so laid-back
> about it all.

On one occasion that term Nick left a pile of books in Brian
Wells's room in Selwyn and never bothered to collect them.
Eventually, says Brian,

> I took them back to the English Faculty Library, saying, 'Sorry these
> haven't been returned sooner, the person who took them out has
> had a nervous breakdown.' It was bullshit, but the librarian said, 'I'm
> so sorry to hear that and of course it will be fine.' Nick thought that
> was very funny.*

He had prepared minimally for Prelims and had no goal beyond
passing them. Wearing his gown, as tradition required, he sat five
papers in various locations, covering his syllabus to date, then enjoyed
so-called May Week in June – the round of parties, plays, concerts
and sporting competitions that follow exams at Cambridge every
summer. Rick Charkin remembers them going to see the newly
released *2001: A Space Odyssey*, which blew young minds wherever
it was shown, and Robert emphasised that Nick was good company
at this time:

> He was always quiet, but we went out to pubs, drinking, and to
> parties . . . I can remember punting, swimming, getting in the car

---

* Joan Black was then assistant English Faculty librarian, so this might have been
a double bluff on her part.

and just looning off on the spur of the moment, talking about anything at all . . . I can remember him trying to chuck me in the river, me trying to chuck him in the river.[17]

May Week placed heavy demands on Robert as a singer, both in and out of college, and the Gentle Power of Song had their second (and last) album to promote. *Circus* appeared in late June; coincidentally, the other pop LP Polydor UK issued that week was Fairport's debut. Witchseason had recently run an advert in the US trade magazine *Billboard* stating that Nick was also a Polydor artist[18] – the first public acknowledgement of his connection to Joe – but Joe was growing frustrated with Polydor, not least because they had never sent him a contract along the lines Horst Schmolzi had set out in 1967.

Horst had, in fact, been too liberal in general, and Polydor decided to replace him. 'By the summer of 1968 Horst had been recalled to Germany and there was a new regime in London who wanted me to sign a much less generous contract,' explains Joe. 'I went out to Hamburg to appeal to him, but there was nothing he could do.' In the meantime, Joe stalled on Polydor's new contract but continued to settle bills with their advance money, aware that a reckoning lay ahead.

Nick received his Prelims results just before the end of term. As with all the exams he'd sat before, he had performed poorly. He was placed in the Third Class, accounting for the bottom 12 per cent of his subject's cohort across the University. His best mark was 52 per cent in French translation, his worst 36 per cent in Literature from 1625 to 1798. The latter was also by some distance the lowest mark anyone in his college year group scored in that paper, a surprise given the evident influence of the Romantic poets on his own writing. It seems that he enjoyed and absorbed their work without finding it easy to formulate or articulate a critical response to it.

He wasn't fussed, though; he had passed and that was all that mattered. Robert's results were similar, but Caius was stricter with dilatory students, Choral Exhibitioners or not. He was warned that he would be sent down unless his performance improved markedly over the following year. Such concerns seemed distant at the outset of the vacation, with three straight months of free time to look forward to, and Robert's focus was now on collaborating with Marcus Bicknell on a production of *Through the Looking Glass* by Cambridge Ballet Workshop, which premiered on 23 July.*

Nick's parents collected him from Fitzwilliam and drove him and his possessions back to Far Leys, but he did not intend to pass the summer there. As his mother put it, 'He didn't spend much time here in the holidays, so at that stage we weren't terribly in touch with him.'[19] For his father,

> I think we were rather outside the sort of life he believed people should lead. He was always very nice to us and kind to us, but I think he thought that we represented part of society which he didn't want to identify with. The alternative society was a different thing altogether. He was never hostile in any way towards us, or anything of that sort, but I don't think he thought in those days there would be any object in sitting down and arguing with us about it.[20]

Nick preferred to be in London, where the agenda in his circle tended to be smoking dope and listening to music at home. He remained happy to play and sing at their gatherings but, says Alex Henderson,

> He was private about his music-making and we wouldn't have asked him about his songs, lyrics or arrangements. Because he was a great acoustic guitarist and Dylan, etc. were around, he has been cast in this 'folk singer' mould, but I always thought of his music in broader terms. His tastes were certainly broad – he loved *The Hangman's Beautiful Daughter* and Pentangle's first album,† but listened to a lot of classical too.

He occasionally went to David Ward's flat in Pont Street to play guitar. 'We had a long chat there late one afternoon about life, music and so on,' remembers David's old friend Martin Wilkinson.

---

* Cambridge Ballet Workshop was the brainchild of Marcus Bicknell's mother Mari.
† *The Pentangle*, released by Transatlantic in May 1968.

He was willing to listen to my thoughts on early blues musicians, if not to talk about his own music. Eventually we walked up to a low-key restaurant in Worlds End, where we met some other people. As soon as we arrived, Nick clammed up. If anyone said something to him, he smiled and looked away. It was as if he were socially deaf and dumb all of a sudden. Dope was probably being smoked, which increased the social acceptability of not saying much, but it was still striking.

Nick hadn't told his friends that he was working towards an album, but he muttered something vague to Julian Lloyd. 'He felt he had a career opening up before him and it occurred to him that he might need some publicity photos,' Julian recalls. 'I offered to take them as a friend – there was no commission.' They set off from Stokenchurch Street early one morning in mid-July.

We drove to Selborne in Hampshire, where my parents lived, to take some pictures. We just went for the day. We collected a large blanket from my parents' house – they had bought it on honeymoon in Spain and we used to use it for picnics. It felt right, given the nature of the time. Nick carried the blanket through orchards and fields to some woodland at the foot of a little valley, opposite a hill next to a farmhouse on an estate there. You can see the barley is ripe. He wrapped himself in the blanket for some of the photos. It was all spontaneous and simple – in one he's holding some mushrooms he'd just picked. I developed the black-and-white shots in my darkroom at Stokenchurch Street and sent the colour ones off to be processed.

The expedition was a whim and Nick didn't pursue the idea of using the results. In fact, says Julian, 'He never saw the pictures, and nothing happened with them.'

The group occasionally ventured out. 'One day we were going out for a picnic from Stokenchurch Street when I realised that I'd forgotten something, so I ran back to the house, the door slammed on me and I cut myself on the glass,' says Victoria Ormsby-Gore, who had recently paired up with Julian. 'There was blood streaming down my arm, but rather than moving away Nick definitely stepped forward to help. He was incredibly sweet, getting me a handkerchief and making sure I was all right.'

At another point that summer the gang decamped to Wiseton, the Laycocks' family home in Nottinghamshire. 'We drove up in David's old minibus, which had no seats, and we all rolled around in the back, falling on top of each other,' says Sophia Ryde. Ben and David were considering putting a band together and jammed away in the stables there, but Nick didn't participate. Instead, recalls Ben, 'He was a good and competitive croquet player.'

Nick also visited Hatley Park, where Donovan's *A Gift from a Flower to a Garden* provided the soundtrack. 'He especially loved the melody of "Skip-A-Long Sam", which always reminds me of him,' says Stella Astor. 'My Chilean friend Adriana Santa Cruz came down and rather liked him. She was a great fan of soul sounds and Motown, which he also enjoyed. She danced around but he just smiled and didn't join in. They were happy moments. He certainly wasn't depressed in those days.' One day Stella's parents presided over a spontaneous picnic, with a horse and cart; a photo taken at it shows Nick opening a bottle of champagne, though Sophia says: 'I hate that picture – that wasn't him at all.'

Nick had drifted away from his schoolfriends. 'From around 1968 he became elusive,' says Chris Rudkin. 'I remember us trying to find out if he was okay, but never really knowing where he was or what he was doing.' He occasionally hung out at Pavilion Road, but the energy there had changed, as Mike Hacking explains:

> I was breaking up with Desi, which wasn't easy. Nick continued to be friends with her – she cared for him, she fed him and looked after him when he was in need of it. He had a deeper relationship with her than with the rest of us, I think, but it wasn't romantic.

Nick got to know Bev better over the summer of 1968:

> Joe would encourage us to hang out, taking us to galleries and concerts. Nick was very interested in hearing me talk about Bert Jansch, John Renbourn and Davy Graham. One afternoon we went to an Indian classical concert [by Nazir Jairazbhoy]* at the home of some Indian friends of Tod's. It was very hot and we all sat in the

---

* Joe had recently recorded an album for Polydor that featured him: *Classical Indian Ragas* (1967).

garden. He would occasionally say something witty, but rarely, as he was so shy.

Bev initially found him odd but warmed to him: 'I grew to love this fragile young man like a brother, and feel protective of him.'

Nick and Kirstie were still vaguely involved, but she found him unfathomable and the end of their relationship that summer was not dramatic. 'One night we went to a party somewhere and then he went back to Far Leys, which was only a few minutes away. Maybe he was planning to come back, but Dave took me home instead and that was that.' Kirstie and Dave began a serious relationship, but Nick didn't mind. For her,

> Nick was fun and we had a good time, but he wasn't committed. I could never really read him, and I think my lack of understanding of him meant we couldn't go on. He was affectionate but self-contained and rather aloof, so our communication felt superficial. He was off in his own world a lot of the time, and I knew that I wasn't in that world.

Witchseason was an important part of his world, and he frequently dropped into its office, even if work towards his album was proving slow. In August Joe was recording with the Incredible String Band and Fairport, as well as dealing with the collapse of Osiris (Visions). Recognising that he had too much on his shoulders, he hired Anthea Joseph to help manage and publicise his acts, especially Fairport. Born in October 1940, she had helped run the Troubadour in Earl's Court and been an ally and friend to Bob Dylan during his stint in the UK in 1963. More recently she had been working as EMI's publicist in Dublin. A 'strikingly tall woman, long black hair down to her hips, white, skull-like face, a deep, posh voice',[21] she defined her role as being Witchseason's 'in-house nanny'.[22]

She began there on Monday, 5 August, and described its premises as 'hardly spacious accommodation':

> It was one of those Georgian houses – you went up a rickety stair-case, you came to our floor. There was very little furniture, and everything came off the back of a lorry. Very few chairs, so people spent a great deal of time sitting on the floor. Joe had an office, I

had an office, then we had a sort of open-space bit which people congregated in.[23]

It was hardly the Beatles' Apple, but had its own cast of characters. Familiar figures were Joe's assistant Marian Bain (Joe: 'She was the best assistant you could ever imagine. Everyone loved her – she was softly spoken, not effusive, but totally helpful and efficient'); Phil Dudderidge, who was now driving the Incredible String Band; Huw Price, who organised the acts' live schedules; Danny Halperin, who designed artwork; and a revolving troupe of girls on reception. Nick knew all these people but maintained his gnomic reserve around them.

Rose Simpson of the Incredible String Band retains an image of him as 'a shadowy figure sloping through the Witchseason office', and Huw says: 'My main memory of Nick is of looking up from my desk and seeing him walking down the corridor, dark-haired and skinny as a beanpole, shy and terribly well-spoken.' For Anthea, forming a relationship with him was almost impossible: 'By the time we met him it was almost as though he was bricked-up. There was a wall round him.'[24]

This might be partly attributable to his feeling supernumerary. He was an unproven quantity to everyone but Joe and Tod, having not released any music or given any performances beyond one at the Roundhouse and two at Cambridge, and his refined speech and detached manner marked him out amidst the camaraderie of staff, musicians and hangers-on there. Nonetheless, from her first days in Charlotte Street Anthea remembered Nick's habit of materialising there.

For her he was 'this tall, thin, very beautiful young man who didn't speak':

> He could just about say 'Hello' to you, once he'd decided that you were a human being. He'd come in and he'd sit, just sit, doing nothing, reading the paper, watching the world go by . . . He was always very still – and isolated. He could be in a room, surrounded by people sitting on the floor, shrieking with laughter and saying, 'Here, what do you think of this?' and playing a verse of something – there'd be Fairport there, the String Band, all sorts of people falling

in and out of the building – and Nick would be still, completely on his own. He would be there – he was always *over* there – but not part of it.[25]

Also popping in and out of the office was Bob Squire. Joe had met him in the summer of 1967 upon knocking on the door of a shabby flat above a hair salon in Princedale Road, Holland Park, to enquire about a green Morris convertible for sale outside. By Joe's account it was opened by 'a seedy-looking man in a string vest and braces, a roll-up dangling from his mouth, two days' growth of grey-flecked stubble and dark, thinning hair'.[26] Having bought the car he befriended Bob, an archetypal dodgy geezer with a heart of gold.

For Phil Dudderidge, Bob was

a bit of a Fagin-like character, in his forties – double my age at the time. He was an old East End gangster-type – 'a bit of a hound' was the expression he used about himself – and he liked playing up to that image. He had useful connections in the motor trade and was always making a buck from me, but I got streetwise under his tutelage.

Joe soon roped him in to drive his acts (and supply their vehicles), as well as to fulfil other practical tasks, and he took to ribbing Nick about his reticence.

Over the course of 1968 the flat Bob shared with his wife June, their teenage tearaway Vernon and their baby Jason became a social focal point for Witchseason's array of talented youngsters. 'He used to host gatherings in the evenings, with dunghills of hashish, endless cups of sickly sweet tea and long games of liar dice,' recalls Adrian George, who did design work for Witchseason. After a tiring day in the office or the studio Joe would sometimes head over. For him, 'The pressures of coming up with new songs, finishing mixes in time for release dates or juggling cashflows seemed to evaporate' there.[27]

Bob kept everyone amused with a stream of anecdotes and esoteric slang while Jimmy Smith, Brother Jack McDuff, Lord Buckley or the first Dr. John album, *Gris-Gris*, played. 'His flat was tiny and (with hindsight) an absolute dump, but we were hippies, unlike him, and didn't notice,' says Phil. 'He was a magnet for people, a source of hash as well as card games. I think we were all a little in thrall to him.'

One night Joe took Nick along. 'I didn't spend a huge amount of time with Nick socially,' he later recalled, 'but I was very pleased that he enjoyed the atmosphere at Bob's. He wouldn't say much but he loved playing liar dice – and he was very good at it, because the whole point is that you don't give anything away.' For Tod, 'I don't know how at ease Nick ever was in the company of other people, but I think he felt most at home playing liar dice at Bob's. He was always welcome there.' Joe adds: 'He loved Nick, he adored Nick . . . His attitude was, "Come on Nick, speak up! Don't just sit there – what's the matter with you?", and he'd punch him in the shoulder and he would gee him up, and Nick would respond, Nick would become more animated.'[28]

'We called Bob "the old goat",' says Bev.

> He was a character – surprisingly well-read, full of words of wisdom. They were poor people, Bob did whatever he could to keep them afloat. We played kalooki – 13-card rummy. Whoever lost had to make the tea, Nick included. Bob was very particular about tea. It had to be made through a strainer. There was always fun and cama-raderie there, always a spliff going around, and Nick enjoyed Bob's wind-ups, he made Nick snigger. Nick could surprise you with his dry sense of humour. He chose his moments – after playing loads of games of cards he'd drop the odd one-liner or give you a look. He would have encountered people there he'd never have come across in his other milieux.

Adrian remembers 'various terrifying friends of Bob's from his Soho days, whose names we were never told':

> One of them wore a suit and tie, unlike the rest of us, and had a habit of meticulously wiping down everything he touched with a handkerchief. The whole atmosphere was very like *Performance*, these all-night games where rich people, poor people, thugs, embryonic rock stars and draft dodgers all mingled. I look back on it with a strange mixture of nostalgia and fear.

For Joe, long summer nights at the Squires' were a welcome distraction from his major dilemma. He had agreed a date in September to sign with Polydor but was increasingly convinced they weren't the right fit, not least because they hadn't put much effort into promoting Fairport. Walking away and seeking an alternative, however, would leave him with a bill he couldn't hope to pay. It was therefore fortuitous that he bumped into Chris Blackwell at Morgan Studios in Willesden, northwest London at the start of that month, as he put the finishing touches to Fairport's second album.*

Joe and Chris had met a few times and knew exactly who each other was. They got talking. Island's pivot towards rock was paying off handsomely, but Chris had the foresight to realise that the small company's staff – which handled Traffic, Spooky Tooth and Free, among others – shouldn't be its only source of new talent. He had therefore agreed a production deal with Chris Wright and Terry Ellis of Chrysalis (who managed Jethro Tull) and was open to other such arrangements.

'I told Chris about my situation with Polydor,' explains Joe.

> He was initially interested in Fairport – if they were available, he wanted them. By then Nick was just as big a deal for me as Fairport or the Incredible String Band. I was *very* excited about him and told Chris about him right away, but he didn't mention having heard him before.

They agreed to talk further over dinner in an Italian restaurant off Kensington High Street, where Chris jokingly castigated Joe for not having come to him in the first place.

> I told Chris I was receptive to being lured away from Polydor, but that I needed an umbrella deal whereby Island would always have first refusal on anything I recorded. He said he would take on Witchseason and pay Polydor's expenses to date, which were around £10,000 [around £130,000 today]. The deal was literally [worked out] on a napkin.

---

* Sound Techniques had booked free time at Morgan in lieu of an unpaid bill.

It was a perfect solution. Island presented none of Polydor's corporate barriers, and Chris relished taking an unconventional approach to the music business – though it was an error to mistake his casual dress and unruffled manner for insouciance. He gave Joe a cashier's cheque for the full amount and Joe went to Polydor's office off Bond Street as arranged. A photographer was present to record the belated contract-signing for the trade press, but rather than posing with pen in hand, Joe announced that he had changed his mind. The mood soured and the German delegation reminded him that he owed them a large sum. He then produced the cheque (what he calls 'a dramatic and satisfying moment') and – after a few days' token resistance – they had no choice but to cash it.

Chris enjoyed hearing about the meeting and was delighted to add Witchseason to his roster. As he puts it, 'Joe was very talented and had great taste.' Island's sales manager David Betteridge, who had been with the company since the beginning, adds that 'Joe was honourable, you could trust his word – and I wouldn't say that about many people in the business back then.' Although Nick wasn't directly signed to Island, he was now working towards a release on the country's hippest label.

Chris had mainly wanted Fairport, and had his eyes on the Incredible String Band in the longer term, but was delighted to have Nick too:

> I remembered him well and was thrilled to be able to have him on Island, but with Joe looking after him. I felt that Joe had done the initial work with him that I hadn't been able to, like getting the material finessed and putting him in the right studio with the right engineer – and John Wood was a master.

Nick, however, hadn't been in the studio for four months, partly thanks to the deadlock with Polydor and partly to Joe being so busy. Among Joe's other preoccupations that summer had been helping to arrange London's most hotly anticipated underground gigs of the year: two all-night shows by the Doors and Jefferson Airplane at the Roundhouse on Friday and Saturday, 6–7 September, barely nine months after Nick's own appearance there. Nick admired both bands, and especially Jim Morrison, and eagerly went to the first night with Ben, Alex and Sophia.

'Nick was in great shape that night, he was thrilled to be there,' says Ben. The start was long delayed, so the DJ, Jeff Dexter, played records to entertain the 2,000-strong audience as they milled around or sat on the floor. Ben continues: '"The Weight" by The Band was being played over the PA before the gig started, and Nick was insistent that I listen to it and said: "This is absolutely the best thing around."'

Nick's friends had realised that he was involved with Joe, and Alex recalls him shyly introducing them that night: 'We were probably slightly in awe of him – he was American, he was older, he was involved with cool and interesting people, and he belonged to a different part of Nick's world.' The Doors came on first and finally started to play at 11.30 p.m. 'During the concert I was standing right at the back and suddenly became aware of Nick at my side,' says Sophia. 'It was a lovely moment.' The show was being filmed by Granada TV, which perhaps partly accounts for his skulking. Unfortunately, however, the resulting film, *The Doors Are Open*, does not include footage of the audience.

The following Wednesday – 11 September – Nick finally had another session, devoted to experimenting with 'Strange Face', which he had painstakingly polished in recent months. After laying down a guitar track, other instruments were added – a second guitar (also played by Nick), congas and shakers (played by Remi Kabaka), and double bass and cello by unknown musicians. It was an unusual attempt to shape one of his songs in the studio, rather than adhere to a set arrangement.

The session was Nick's sole commitment since the end of term, causing his father gently to query why he hadn't used the summer vacation to gain experience of playing live.[29] The answer appears to be that, whilst Nick was well able to perform alone, he simply didn't enjoy it or see the benefit in doing so. Instead, he ended the break by motoring down through France alone. His destination was de Wet's house in Castagniers, outside Nice, which he reached on Thursday, 19 September.

'Made quite good time, with BAB behaving very well,' he wrote on a postcard home that week. 'I really like the house and it has a lovely view . . . I've been swimming, sunbathing etc., and in general I'm eating, sleeping and feeling very well indeed.' He didn't mention guitar playing, but the bulk of his time was surely spent doing just that. The summer had passed in an undemanding haze, but as the month drew to a close he had to drive home, pack and confront his second year at Cambridge.

13

Developing A Purely Professional Approach

~

Almost all Fitzwilliam undergraduates were obliged to live outside college after their first year. Nick's digs at 56 Carlyle Road – a rundown terraced house incongruously named 'Handley Villa' – were at least conveniently located. Turning left out of its front door, he followed the curve of Chesterton Road until the Jesus Lock footbridge took him over the River Cam, on to Jesus Green and quickly into the middle of town. Turning right took him on a brisk ten-minute walk to Fitzwilliam, though he limited his visits to compulsory weekly dinners.

He was now paired with John Venning for supervisions with Chris Bristow, who taught English Literature 1700–1830 on the top floor of a Victorian house in West Road. Chris retains an image of Nick as 'a slim, ethereal person' who 'was always waiting outside when I arrived. I have no idea why he was so punctual, as I would have expected him to be late.' John was taken aback to find him waiting when he arrived for their first session:

He was looking out of the window, exactly as he does on the cover of his first album. I tried to make conversation but he offered no real comeback. He had not done the essay and said nothing in the supervision. Chris was easy-going and muttered something about perhaps making sure to do one for the following week.

Whatever Nick replied, he remained serenely indifferent to his studies and to the University. He did not relish encounters with his landlady, a spinster named Winifred Reed, and kept the curtains to his front ground-floor room closed.* Behind them he read, listened to music and – above all – played his guitar. Over in Caius, a contemplative new undergraduate named Paul Wheeler was feeling similarly listless. 'There was a sherry party for newcomers at which I was rather formally introduced to Robert Kirby, because I wrote and sang songs,' he says. 'As soon as we met, he said I must meet Nick . . .'

Paul was born in January 1949, grew up in Purley, South London, and attended the local Whitgift School. A prodigious consumer of jazz and folk, he became a regular at Les Cousins from 1965 and began to play the guitar and write songs. Upon leaving school he went to Paris in April 1967, nominally to study at the Sorbonne, but when Caius awarded him a scholarship in English he had another year to fill, so did the TV production course at Ravensbourne College of Art in Bromley.

Whilst there he played around London's clubs. 'I thought the Incredible String Band were the next great thing after the Beatles,' he says, and in the spring of 1968 he met John Martyn at a small gig of theirs in Kingston. John had been born Iain McGeachy in Surrey in September 1948 and had a comfortable upbringing in Glasgow before drifting back south during the folk boom, reinventing himself, earning a reputation as a guitarist and songwriter and signing to Island. 'My first impression of John was a mixture of endearing bumbling cherub (I recall him swilling and spilling his beer) and acutely perceptive worldly warrior,' according to Paul.[1]

They became fast friends, their social life centring on John's flat in what he called 'Suburbiton', and they had a joint residency at Les Cousins between May and August. 'We'd also do the all-nighters on the weekends, alongside people like Davy Graham, Bert Jansch, John Renbourn, Martin Carthy and Linda Peters,' Paul explains. 'I got to know most of them but didn't meet or hear of Nick, and didn't recognise him when I did meet him.'

On 11 July, John recorded his second album, *The Tumbler*, nominally produced by Al Stewart. Paul played second guitar, co-wrote

---

* 'We had to live in digs with resident landladies approved by the University,' explains John Venning. 'They were supposed to report us if we misbehaved, or lose their licences.'

'Fly On Home' with John and contributed the inscrutable liner notes. Released in early October, the LP was an impressive calling card as he arrived in Cambridge. Like Nick before him, however, his dream of instantly finding like-minded souls evaporated. 'I was disappointed by how unpractical Cambridge was – there were lots of ideas around but most people were more interested in being critical than creative.' Sitting around dissecting albums, books and films wasn't his idea of fun, however articulate the company, and it didn't help that he wasn't a dope smoker.*

A few days into term Robert introduced Paul and Nick backstage at an open audition for Footlights, the University's amateur theatrics club, which owned its own premises in the centre of town. Despite its prominent association with comedy, it was not only looking for clowns; talented musicians and songwriters were welcome too, not least to provide entertainment between sketches at their regular cabarets, known as 'smokers'. Nick wasn't seeking a place in the troupe, and probably went along at Robert's suggestion.

'My first impression was that Nick was bright-eyed and smiley, certainly not withdrawn,' says Paul.

> Robert was pleasant but struck me as an establishment figure, straight and eager and concerned about status in a way Nick and I weren't. I detected a toughness beneath his jolly exterior, as if it were also a tool for opening doors. I wouldn't say that he and Nick were the same sorts of people. Nick didn't come across like a public schoolboy, but a fellow traveller. I felt, 'At last! Someone in Cambridge I can relate to.'

Nick had his Martin with him. 'It was unusual to see a Martin, but it was very much the instrument he deserved to be playing,' says Paul – but he wasn't much interested in guitars and doesn't remember Nick being so either, so they didn't discuss the subject. As they waited backstage, Paul remembers Nick playing 'Time Has Told

---

* Paul avoided other drugs too: 'I have never taken LSD because I'm aware of being the sort of person who would be in danger of not returning from a trip. I was always surprised by how casually other people took it, but Nick certainly didn't take it with me, and I was not aware of him ever taking it.'

Me': 'I think he had designed it to be his signature introductory song.'

After the show – which Paul describes as 'sixth-form comedy with musical interludes' – Nick suggested that he drop round to his digs.*

> It was dowdy and pokey compared to my room in Caius, or ones I'd seen in other colleges. It was untidy and anonymous – most people made statements with posters or other decorations in their rooms, but his felt temporary. I thought, 'No wonder he spends so much time in Caius.'

Paul flicked through Nick's record collection, a classic icebreaker of the day.

> It was a mixture of familiar stuff by Bert Jansch, John Renbourn, Davy Graham, Tim Buckley, Bob Dylan and so on. I remember him playing 'Sad-Eyed Lady of the Lowlands' and being surprised that he was so enthusiastic about it, because Dylan wasn't on a pedestal for me. He told me he liked its length and reflective, sinuous quality. He didn't especially like rock but he loved 'Song for Our Ancestors' by the Steve Miller Band,† whom I'd never heard of. I think its appeal was that it was a soundscape, which was a new concept. I don't remember him ever expressing an interest in Brazilian music, but people often had token records – something flamenco, something Indian, something by Bach, etc. – so if he had anything South American it was probably *Getz/Gilberto*.‡ In general we didn't listen to the most popular artists, but the Beatles were overarching.
>
> I was keen on British jazz, so Nick would certainly have become aware of the Don Rendell–Ian Carr Quintet and others through me, if he weren't already. I introduced him to the *Blues Project* compilation on Elektra, which was very influential in those days

---

* There is nothing to suggest that Nick ever again performed at Footlights.
† The opening instrumental on *Sailor*, released in the US in early October 1968 and immediately imported into the UK. Miller's singing style on other tracks is strikingly similar to Nick's in places.
‡ Released in March 1964, Stan Getz and João Gilberto's self-titled album, which also featured vocals by Astrud Gilberto, popularised bossa nova worldwide.

but had somehow passed him by, and we discussed the integrity of English singers who sang in their 'natural' accents, like Colin Blunstone.

As they listened to music and chatted they began to recognise each other as kindred spirits. 'I think – like me – he felt uncomfortable with the critical and analytical aspects of Cambridge and was more interested in being creative.' For Paul, 'His company was enjoyable and full of ready humour and laughter.' He doesn't recall him brooding: 'When you saw him, it wasn't: "Oh dear, here comes Nick, poor guy." Rather, it was: "Great, here's Nick!"'[2] On one occasion Paul described accompanying John Martyn to the BBC: 'I said that I'd watched Alan Freeman through the glass, and that as he spoke into his microphone his leg was bobbing up and down and made him look like a puppet. For some reason Nick found the image so funny that he laughed out loud.'

Paul came to regard Nick as 'sensitive but streetwise, humorous and observant, quick and nimble (both physically and mentally), but also capable of detachment and despair'. Their love of music was an obvious bond, but they could relate on other matters, not least the fact that they were reading the same subject, limited though Nick's interest in it was. 'People assume Nick was deeply interested in literature, but that wasn't the case. He was keen on Blake, but he didn't read a great deal and I don't have memories of him stuck in a book.'

Nick often visited Paul and others in Caius but, says Paul, 'He didn't bring his guitar. I played an Epiphone Texan and he would play that.' Paul was privy to Nick's latest material as soon as he was ready to share it. His composition 'Three Hours' had a noticeably more complex guitar part than most of his work to date. Paul detected in it 'a North African style – the influence of the Incredible String Band. Nick certainly took them seriously.'

No one recalls Nick jotting down observations or ideas in notebooks, and none of his lyrics survive in draft form. The faintly ominous imagery in 'Three Hours' was perhaps influenced by Leonard Cohen, but Paul questions whether Nick intended any of his words to be considered deeply:

When I first heard Nick's songs I thought, 'Oh right, he's driven more by the sounds and the rhythms of the words than by what they mean' . . . I'm certain [he] would choose certain phrases for the expression conveyed in the sibilances and vowel sounds, rather than the actual meaning of the words. 'A troubled cure for a troubled mind' trips off the tongue but doesn't mean much – to me, anyway.*

Nick's mother was precise in her own lyrics and admitted:

The first time I heard Nick's, I couldn't understand them and it rather irritated me, but now, what does it matter if you can't understand them? The more you listen to them, the more it comes through, not as actual meaning, but as something that you get under your skin.[3]

Robert tended to agree:

The music and the words are welded together in such a way as to make the *atmosphere* in all his songs the most important facet. I know that was Nick's primary purpose – I don't think, for example, that he was hung up about his lyrics being 'great poetry' or anything. They're there to complement, to compound a mood that the melody dictates in the first place.[4]

Like others before him, Paul was quick to note Nick's technique and perfectionism:

Speaking as a guitarist, it's his right hand that's interesting. Synchronising your fingers, most guitarists only use two fingers on the right hand. Nick used his whole hand, and used it in a very interesting way. Even just sitting round in people's rooms, if he played through a new song he'd written he would always get it absolutely right. There was always a sense of professionalism. He never played a bum note.[5]

Robert also marvelled at this, recalling that even in songs 'where there's a very complicated guitar part', it

---

* Jeremy Mason remembers Robert Kirby later telling him that the 'Jeremy' referred to in 'Three Hours' was him, but – as with Betty, Giacomo, Mary Jane, Hazey Jane and Joey – it is unclear that Nick intended the name to refer to a specific individual.

was always note-for-note the same. He might vary tempi sometimes, but every string, every fingernail connected at the same micro-second, each time he did it. All five of the fingers on his right hand could be used equally for playing a melody – the thumb would come up and do the tenor part on the D and A strings. But he wouldn't just get the notes right, he would control the tone and timbre. He'd got the technique of a virtuoso classical guitarist.[6]

Paul's schoolfriend Iain Dunn was in his second year reading English at Corpus Christi College and began to see a good deal of Nick too. He felt the energy in Cambridge had changed over the past year: 'We'd had the Summer of Love, and 1968 was the year of Revolution. So, from it all being peace and love and freedom, the agenda for the next academic year, if you like, was revolution.'[7] By his account, however, 'I don't think Nick was ever involved. I don't think he had the slightest interest in political agendas or what was going on.' Indeed, strongly though Nick felt about issues such as apartheid, Vietnam and the criminalisation of dope smokers, he never took an active interest in politics or current affairs.

'Nick would come round to Paul's room simply to sit around and play,' continues Iain.

> They'd play each other songs and I would sit in the background . . . Most of the stuff I remember Nick playing ended up on the first album . . . As soon as I heard him play [I realised] he was obviously a very able guitarist . . . They would play songs together too, but that would just be jamming, blues and stuff, for fun.

Marcus Bicknell also remembers Nick and Paul playing together in private, but for him 'It didn't gel; Nick was too much his own man.'

Iain came to understand that there was a limit to how well he would ever know Nick:

> He was very nice, incredibly nice, but he wasn't at all outgoing. I think 'detached' is probably the word. You wouldn't see him around that much. I don't even know where his rooms were – you were never invited. I think he quite liked the idea of there being an air of mystique about him, but I think he was also genuinely, incredibly shy, and found himself to be quite remote from other people. I wasn't

quite sure if this was a conscious image he was developing or whether it was just the way he was, and came to the conclusion that it was a bit of both.

Chris Jones well remembers Nick's image circa late 1968:

He looked striking, like a Romantic poet. He tended to dress in dark, sombre colours – nothing bright. He often wore a roll-neck, and in winter what used to be called a 'greatcoat'. He cut quite a famous figure in that – part of his mystique was the sight of him coming down the street in it.

For Robert, 'There was a suggestion that he cultivated this "loner" image, and that it took over. I think certainly at Cambridge it was a cultivated image.'[8] Paul, however, adds that Nick 'looked smart from a distance but was casual and scruffy up close. Most teenagers play a role to a certain extent. Nick had a certain studied air, as did I, but he certainly never came across as pretentious.'

Nick continued to conceal his myopia from his friends, and only wore his glasses alone in private. At other times he wore contact lenses, though he often didn't bother unless driving. Paul, who saw as much of him as anyone at this time, says he 'was unaware that Nick had poor eyesight. Thinking about it, perhaps not being able to see very well contributed towards the image he projected of being disassociated from what was going on around him.'

Dope played its part too. 'Even though I didn't smoke, he'd happily light a joint in front of me,' says Paul.

There was always a pleasant look on his face when he did so. It became so habitual that he forgot he was doing it. I would've told him that I thought it was a bad idea, but you have to consider his dope smoking in the context of the time, and I think it's a slur to suggest that he was constantly stoned. He certainly wouldn't smoke when he was driving, for example.

In contravention of University rules, Nick kept BAB in Cambridge in his second year and Paul remembers outings led by him: 'Soon after meeting Nick, we drove to the coast one evening. It was quite a long way. He was a skilful driver, slightly risky but not flamboyantly so. We walked on the beach, listened to the waves, then drove back.' Robert recalled similar excursions: 'We'd all pile in . . . I remember the first time I heard "Three Hours" was at Madingley – the American cemetery [four miles northwest of Cambridge]. We'd gone out there one night, and it was scary just to hear him play that there.'

BAB's main use was to facilitate Nick's double-life, making it easier to nip to London and back. When driving alone he'd listen to music on headphones plugged into a portable cassette recorder, but Paul often provided company. He was quick to introduce Nick to John Martyn:

> They first met when we went from Cambridge to Surbiton and visited John's flat.* John was disarmingly outgoing, very different to Nick and me. He was the sort of person who would stop someone in the street and ask why they were wearing a particular tie. He could get away with that.

Nick certainly knew of John's association with Island and might have seen him perform at Les Cousins, but there was another link by the time they met. In September Jackson C. Frank had played a gig alongside John at Chelsea College of Art and encouraged Bev to leave her baby, Wesley, with a childminder and come too. Bev hadn't encountered John before and was 'knocked sideways by this angelic-looking hippie child with bare feet and flowing hair who played a beautiful guitar . . .'[9] He invited her up to sing a couple of songs and they quickly became inseparable: 'It was one of those intense meetings that seem like magic. We couldn't bear to be out of each other's company in those early days.'[10]

Bev knew little of John's early life: 'I knew nothing of the bad reputation he had in Glasgow; he didn't mention that he had a background of violence and a criminal record, and I didn't realise that his English accent was assumed.' Beneath the charisma and charm John was volatile and prone to excess, though those sides of his personality were largely latent in 1968. For Tod Lloyd, 'Life

---

* John later said he first met Nick at a party hosted by Joe Boyd, and also at a party in a village outside Cambridge.

was an uphill struggle for Bev – some of her problems were her doing, some were other people's. She had a great talent, but it was a disaster on just about every level when she got together with John.'

Engulfed by new love, she quickly suggested to Joe that John be incorporated into the album she was working on: '"Bad scene," was all he said. He must have known of John's reputation and was trying to warn me off, but I was in love.' Chris Blackwell had in fact already asked Joe to add John to Witchseason's roster:

> In theory he was a perfect Witchseason artist. I just didn't rate him that highly. I don't think I had any particular animus towards him at that point, I'd seen him live once or twice, possibly met him, but just didn't think his music was that great. I was never clear whether Chris had told John that I passed on taking him on – we never discussed it, that I recall. But certainly John and I were always instinctively wary of each other.

According to Paul, at their first meeting 'John indicated that he knew who Nick was, but Nick didn't [reciprocate]. Perhaps a seed of jealousy was there on John's side from the start – not just about Beverley, but for the sort of "cool" Nick had.' Several other observers – not least Bev – have commented on John's envy of Nick. 'I think Nick threw John,' Joe suggests, 'because on the one hand John was jealous of his guitar playing, but on the other hand Nick's personality was so meek that he was clearly no threat on his territory.' John himself conceded: 'To be honest, there was always a slight element of rivalry.'[11]

For Bev, 'Paul was similar to Nick – talented and sensitive – but John was more of a rough diamond, he'd had a tougher background.' John was indeed earthier and more outwardly confident than Nick, but perhaps intellectually insecure in relation to Nick and Paul; he took to claiming that he too was at Cambridge, reading Theology. Still, Bev feels that John's response to Nick was fundamentally benign: 'When John first met Nick he recognised his talent and that he was a lovely person.' John himself said that Nick first struck him as a 'very quiet lad': 'Extremely personable and charming when necessary. Handsome to a devastating effect . . .

When I first met him he was rather more urbane than he became, always charming, delicately witty.'[12]

Nick had gone from knowing no one who could play guitar to his standard to meeting two others at once. He, Paul and John were all the same age, just twenty, and shared a preoccupation with improving their technique. As such, they often spent time playing together in London. Like Nick, John had always experimented with the instrument, as if inherently dissatisfied with it, and was intrigued by Nick's innovative tunings.

> He used seconds quite a lot, very strange tunings, diminished as well, so when you applied just two fingers you'd change the thing in a very radical way . . . He had the most beautiful fingers when he played, and they were made even more beautiful by the fact that the shapes that he'd play were not those you would normally see when other people played.[13]

Paul emphasises that their interest in unusual tunings was far from unique: 'The Incredible String Band, Joni Mitchell and others were playing with tunings, and there would be a lot of earnest discussion about them. Everyone was fiddling around with them, and of course the guitar was an instrument that allowed it.' For him, 'John saw himself as a flashy guitarist more than Nick did and made sure he came across to audiences that way.' In contrast, Nick regarded his guitar as more of a companion and tool for writing songs than a vehicle for virtuoso display.

Paul knew that Nick was working towards an album on Island, and of course that John was already signed to them, but he wasn't angling for a deal of his own; writing fiction was his ambition. Nonetheless, he was a fine songwriter too, and Nick admired his work. '"Julie Was Saying Goodbye" was a favourite of both Nick and John Martyn,' Paul recalls. 'I wrote it in the summer of 1968, before I met Nick. It uses a C tuning, which I shared with him.'

Unlike Nick, Paul Wheeler had a long-term girlfriend, Diana Robertson, who occasionally visited from London for the weekend. She got along well with Nick too. 'Nick always looked more or less the same – beautiful but fragile, like a twig that would easily break,' she says. 'He had a lovely smile, but it was rare. He was quiet, but not because he was out of his head. He thought before he spoke. He had a peaceful, gentle energy – he was the sort of person children and animals would feel safe around.'

Nick and Paul encouraged each other's ambivalence about Cambridge and spent much time together over the course of the academic year. Being a Scholar at an ancient college, and a protégé of the revered Caius don and poet J. H. Prynne, Paul had an entrée that Nick lacked. As he puts it, 'People automatically introduced me to like-minded people.' One was Mark Lancaster, who had recently been appointed 'resident artist' at King's.

'I was introduced to him at a party,' says Paul.

> He was well-connected – he was a friend of David Hockney and had been at the Factory with Andy Warhol – and not an academic at all. He was modest and humorous and had a dream job at King's. I don't think he even had to paint; he just had to be around.

A decade older than Paul and Nick, he was nonetheless generous and open with them (as he had been towards Bryan Ferry at Newcastle University a few years earlier).

> Part of Mark's task was to find the most interesting people he could and introduce them to each other. He had one of the most amazing rooms in Cambridge, with a large, semi-circular window overlooking King's Parade and the whole south front of the Chapel, and it acted a little like an old-fashioned salon, with central social figures. Nick and I had a rather silent tea with E. M. Forster there. Forster sat, quietly smiling. It was the opposite of an animated conversation, but not awkward. The only exchange I recall was when I asked him if, having lived in India, he was interested in Indian music and he said: 'I'm sure they were up to something . . .'*

Forster's approach to conversation was similar to Nick's. 'Nick wasn't a conversationalist – I didn't think he felt the need to be –

---

* 'Forster retired to King's for his last years and was a local landmark,' as John Venning puts it. On 10 June 1970, Molly wrote to Nick, remarking upon Forster's recent death and stating: 'I remember you were very impressed with him when you met him at Cambridge.'

but if you said something that rang bells with him, he would always react,' says Iain Dunn.

> My memory of that is always to do with rueful laughter. If you hit on something – the Faculty, some tutor who was a total lunatic or something – he would laugh, and he was certainly aware of issues that were around. But I don't ever remember him particularly insti-gating that. I think songwriting and performing, in the sense of playing the songs in someone's room, were, for him, the easiest form of communication.[14]

Mark Lancaster introduced Nick and Paul to albums including *Roots* by the Everly Brothers and Randy Newman's debut.[*] The latter became a favourite with Nick. Newman didn't fall neatly into any contemporary category and suggested an appealing model for Nick's career, being fundamentally a writer whose work was widely covered, obviating the need to tour or self-publicise. Nick was especially struck by the slow, heartfelt 'I Think It's Going to Rain Today', which featured a delicate string arrangement by Newman of just the sort he had been striving for with Robert.

Within Caius, Paul was absorbed into the group that gathered around Mike Weissmann, who was similar to Mark, only younger.

> Mike was exactly the sort of eccentric connoisseur I'd hoped to find in Cambridge, the sort of figure you'd find in Evelyn Waugh. He had amazing, arcane knowledge – he knew interesting little res-taurants, artists and shops and so on – but was affable with it, not a show-off. He had contacts in the most unlikely and disparate worlds, at a time when the notion of having a smorgasbord of contacts was very appealing. I think that's what Nick also accumulated, whether consciously or not. Not wanting to be pinned down by one identity was typical of the time.
>
> We would congregate in Mike's room for listening sessions, but not just anyone could turn up – he would refuse entry to cer-tain people. He was like a DJ and played an incredible breadth of

---

[*] *Randy Newman* had been released in America in April 1968, its British release following in July; *Roots* was an early foray into country-rock, released in December 1968.

music – Bach followed by Charlie Parker followed by Jaki Byard – and we'd just sit there, blown away by it all. It was amazing to switch from William Byrd to the Miracles, and there were rumours that Mike had written a scholarly comparison between Smokey Robinson and medieval mystics. Robert said that Mike had a copy of the elusive Beach Boys *Smile* album, although I never got to hear it. He was an arbiter of taste, so if we had a new album we'd take it there as if for approval. He'd listen carefully and if he didn't like it he wouldn't pass comment, he'd just say 'Tea?' and walk out.

One album that emphatically passed the test was Van Morrison's *Astral Weeks*, which was released in the US that November, heavily imported into the UK, and became another touchstone for Nick.*
They enjoyed live music too, says Paul:

We had a thing about going to evensong in Caius – Mike, Nick and I would sit in the gallery at the back. I also remember going to a Gustav Leonhardt concert in London with Mike and Nick. Leonhardt was a hero of ours, through Mike. For us it was like seeing Brian Wilson – in other words, someone we'd listened to a lot.

However, Paul says that often Nick was 'noticeable because he was elusive. Even living across the river made him seem less present, when we were all in Caius.' Still, his friends occasionally visited him. 'A group of three or four of us would hang out there – he had a good sound system,' says Pete Russell. 'Sometimes we'd go for a walk. The mood was usually contemplative.'

Stimulating female company was harder to come by. Cambridge was almost entirely male; there were twenty men's colleges to three women's, and access to either was restricted. As Iain Dunn summarises, 'There were an awful lot of men chasing not very many women.'[15] Nick, however, remained serenely uninterested. 'He was very attractive to women, who found him even more compelling than his male confrères did,' says Chris Jones. 'My girlfriend at the time, Lynn Humphreys, was very taken with him.' Paul adds: 'His

---

* *Astral Weeks* was not released in the UK until September 1969.

main attraction, so I was told, was that he didn't seem to know he had an attraction.'

Rick Charkin concurs: 'Girls used to really love him, and he never did a bloody thing, he never lifted a finger.'[16] Nick was not a virgin, but Brian Wells suggests: 'His interest in women was more aesthetic. We were all chasing girls, but Nick was admiring them in a different way.' Alex Henderson goes further: 'I would almost describe him as asexual. I think he had a romanticised, even poetic notion of women rather than a carnal one. He certainly wasn't ever going to be a serial shagger.'

'He wasn't a horny guy, but I always assumed he had got his leg over,' says Brian.

> I once talked to him about my sex life and he was interested, not repulsed. One of the few intimate conversations we had was one night in my second year when he woke me up in my college room at about 2 a.m., drunk. He'd met a town girl and told me, 'I really thought I was going to fuck Gaynor tonight.' That was the word he used, and it stuck in my mind because it was so rare to have any sort of locker-room talk from him. I commiserated and he borrowed my bike to cycle back to his place. He took a candle, which he placed on a huge red physiology textbook, and I watched him wobbling off with it on the handlebars, shielding the flame.

On Friday, 15 November, Brian watched Family at the Cambridge Union with Nick, but often got the sense that he had preferable company elsewhere.

> I was more than a loyal 'buddy', but very aware that I wasn't cool, and not much of a musician, so perhaps not his first choice of companion when it came to 'cool music people'. I certainly wasn't in the same league as Paul, and Nick could be dismissive or make me feel belittled. I felt a bit like a younger brother around him – good company if there was no one more appealing around, but he'd let me know if he wasn't in the mood for whatever it was.

He didn't share the details when he went off to see Joe Boyd, and I knew he was secretive. One evening he and I went to a party

in Chelsea where Alice Ormsby-Gore embraced him.* I knew she
was with Eric Clapton and felt strongly that I wasn't part of that set.

Witchseason and his friends weren't the city's only draws for Nick,
though: 'He would usually return with a lump of hash and say, "I
am now in a position to turn you on . . ."'

For much of Nick's time in Cambridge he maintained a cloistered
existence in Carlyle Road, relentlessly polishing his songs and devising
new ones. At his next Sound Techniques sessions, held on Monday
and Tuesday, 11 and 12 November, he revisited 'Time Has Told
Me', 'Day Is Done', 'Saturday Sun', 'Man In A Shed', 'Fruit Tree'
and 'Strange Face', and introduced three more – 'Three Hours',
'Clothes Of Sand' and 'Joey'.

In its finished form 'Three Hours' was the longest track he ever
recorded (albeit only a few seconds longer than 'Poor Boy') and as
close as he came to anything psychedelic, with its hypnotic, conga-
driven instrumental break. 'Clothes Of Sand' (as yet simply noted
as 'New Song No. 2') was a surreal love song, echoing 'Strange
Meeting II' in its address to an elusive, even evanescent subject. Like
several of his songs to date, it posed rhetorical questions and drew
on Nick's preferred imagery – the sea, the moon, the seasons. 'Joey'
took a similar approach, addressing a mysterious girl whose world-
liness evidently outstripped his: 'Where she may come from, where
she may go / Who she may run from, no one will know'.

Danny Thompson was there to play double bass. Nine years older
than Nick, he was tall and commanding, a veteran jazzer and session
musician and a member of the popular Pentangle, whom Nick
admired. Like Bob Squire, he made no concessions to Nick's reserve.
'Most people, myself included, were too careful, wary of disturbing
Nick's silences,' according to Joe.[17] 'Danny would slap him on the
back, tease him in rhyming slang, make fun of his self-effacement
and generally give him a hard time. Nick would crack a hesitant
smile and be relaxed and laughing by the end of the session.'

Like most of the musicians Joe asked to play with Nick, Danny
was left to devise his own parts. By his account, Nick 'was not very

---

* Alice, who Nick knew peripherally, was Victoria's younger sister.

communicative about anything musically': 'They were my bass lines, there was nothing written for me. He was watching as I played, he had a grin on his face. There was that instant rapport that a musician has with another musician who realises that that's what he wants.'[18]

Joe had come to understand that, whilst Nick was taciturn, he would clearly communicate anything he considered important.

> He was full of comments. He spoke quietly and he sometimes hesitated before speaking, but he would always make his views known, like 'I'm not sure about that take, I think we'll have to do it again', something like that. And we'd do it, because we had huge respect for Nick and his taste and his vision for his music, so we would always listen to what Nick had to say.[19]

John Wood had recently moved to Suffolk, so he dropped him back in Cambridge after the session: 'He was easy to chat to (unless I was going too fast). I asked him who the "Man In A Shed" was and he indicated that it was his father.' (John assumed it referred to Rodney's tinkering in his workshop at home, unaware that the title and opening lines were in fact by Christopher Sykes.) Most of their talk was about music. 'The most striking thing about Nick to me was how musically literate he was. I've never worked with anyone else of that age who had that level of musical understanding and ability, as well as such a wide taste and knowledge of music.'

Nick was back at Sound Techniques the following Monday, 18 November, working on 'Time Has Told Me', 'Day Is Done', 'Saturday Sun', 'Man In A Shed', 'Fruit Tree' and 'Strange Face'. Danny was there, as was the pianist Paul Harris,* over from New York. His credentials aligned neatly with Nick's tastes: he had played with Tom Rush, John Sebastian, Tom Paxton, Richie Havens and others, and had recently arranged 'Touch Me' for the Doors. Joe had asked him to contribute to 'Time Has Told Me', and he became increasingly intrigued as he heard Nick's songs. 'Paul spent hours

---

* Paul later overdubbed piano onto 'Man In A Shed' in New York. John Wood: 'When Joe got back with the tape we found that the piano was out of tune. It was still just about usable, but I gave him stick for it.'

talking to Nick,' by Joe's account. 'He kept scratching his head, as if trying to figure out what planet this kid was from.'[20]

Work on the album continued in Nick's absence. The saxophonist and flautist Lyn Dobson – who had played with Georgie Fame and Manfred Mann and was now with the Keef Hartley Band – added flute to 'The Thoughts Of Mary Jane', and Richard Thompson also contributed to that track, and to 'Time Has Told Me'.* By his account,

> I was never in the studio at the same time as [Nick]; I added my parts separately to a tape. Joe said, 'Listen to this, start playing along and at some point we will start recording.' I got no instructions on how to play; they wanted to see how I reacted. It was a good approach . . . I added my guitar where I felt there was space . . . I got a session fee of £9 or £10.[21]

Nick and Richard had much in common, at least superficially. They were of similar ages – Richard was ten months younger – and shared a thoughtful disposition, a wry sense of humour and a remarkable gift for guitar playing and songwriting. In particular, they drew inspiration from classical music as much as folk, jazz or pop. 'Much of my guitar style comes from people like Debussy, which is by no means as outlandish as it sounds,' Richard said at the time.[22] Nonetheless, they never became friends, despite intermittently encountering each other. 'In an era when a lot of people didn't say much, myself included, Nick stood out . . . So my acquaintanceship with Nick was mostly restricted to averted eyes and half-smiles.'[23]

Anthea Joseph, who encountered them both frequently, speculated that wariness might have underpinned their response to each other, specifically with regard to Joe. 'It was that sort of late teenage "He's mine!", "No he's not, he's mine!" . . . Richard was no slouch

---

* Fairport had recently finished work on their second album, which was being released in time for Christmas sales alongside the Incredible String Band's *Wee Tam and The Big Huge* (and the Beatles' 'White Album', the Rolling Stones' *Beggars Banquet* and the Jimi Hendrix Experience's *Electric Ladyland*). Meanwhile, Richard's stirring 'Meet on the Ledge' – on which he took a cryptic lyrical approach akin to Nick's – was about to appear as a single.

intellectually at all, but Nick having been to university and being slightly older . . . They did get jealous.'[24] Linda Peters,* who was dating Joe, suspected the same: 'They were young and slightly competitive . . . I'm sure they saw each other as rivals – they were the two golden boys, Joe was daddy, kind of thing.'[25]

Nonetheless, they respected each other's musicality. Nick would not have wanted another guitarist on his songs unless he considered him an equal, and Richard regarded Nick as 'quite extraordinary': 'He played immaculately and uniquely on acoustic guitar, which isn't an easy instrument to play in a flawless way. You get buzzes, you get fret noise. Not with Nick. He'd really worked at it very hard.'[26]

Nick was supposed to gain permission to spend the night away from Cambridge but never bothered. Eventually he was caught out, as his Moral Tutor Ray Kelly recalled: 'I was on the verge of doing what we normally did: hospitals and the police. You had to find out. So I rang the parents.'[27] Molly and Rodney quickly established where he was, urged him to return, and reassured Dr Kelly that he was on his way – but it was another clear sign that his mind was not on his degree.

His academic performance remained perfunctory. John Venning continued to see him for supervisions with Chris Bristow:

I gradually twigged that he turned up early each time. On one occasion I was twenty minutes early, to escape the rain – and there he was. On another occasion I was there deliberately forty minutes early – and there he was again. There was never any interaction. We would wait together in silence, and I couldn't help wondering what his days consisted of, if he was turning up in such good time. The mystery is why he continued to turn up at all, because he had nothing to offer when he did. I effectively got one-on-one supervisions – Chris and I would natter on and make the occasional attempt to involve Nick.

'It was very hard to get anything out of him,' agrees Chris. 'He only really spoke when challenged to, and only seemed interested

---

* Born Linda Pettifer in Glasgow on 23 August 1947.

in Romantic or early nineteenth-century poets.' He saw no academic spark in him, and remarks:

> At the time there were still a large number of people at Cambridge for reasons that had nothing to do with intellectual ability (quite a lot of them at Fitzwilliam, I might add). I would have tolerated him submitting one in two essays, maybe one in three – but not none at all.

It surely came as no surprise to Dr Kelly that Chris's end-of-term report bordered on the contemptuous:

> A Mona Lisa smile seems to be the main stock-in-trade; what's going on behind it I have little means of knowing. Nothing, possibly, although I suppose a mind is at work in the few thin essays I've had from him. There may be personal reasons for this lack of industry, but I haven't been able to find any. Could it be sloth?[28]

Instead of crafting more substantial essays, Nick had been working on another new song, the last he would write for the album. Built on a gentle, insistent riff, with a dramatic chord change and evocative, inscrutable lyrics, 'River Man' represented another advance in his art. As ever, he did not play it for others until it was finished to his satisfaction. 'He first played it to me in my room in Caius and I was very struck by it,' says Paul.

> I thought, 'This is completely different . . .' He was excited by it – he knew it was a step forward. I think he found himself in that song, found a pose he felt comfortable in. His other songs of the time were clever but didn't feel like a part of him to me.*

In a literal sense, the Cam seems an obvious reference point – as Paul points out, 'Nick crossed the river a lot, and it had a symbolism in Cambridge.' Otherwise, its words are opaque. Is it a meditation on the futility of life? Is the 'lilac time' (perhaps a borrowing from Alfred Noyes's 1904 poem 'The Barrel-Organ') mentioned simply because Nick liked the sound of it? Or was he referring to early

---

* John Martyn also said 'River Man' was his favourite of Nick's songs (*Trouser Press*, January 1978).

summer in Cambridge, when the scent of lilacs was heavy in the air around Fitzwilliam?* Is the 'river man' himself a deity, even Charon? Or is he the ferryman in Herman Hesse's *Siddhartha* (a hugely popular book in the late sixties)? And is 'Betty' a simulacrum of Nick?

As a writer himself, Paul knew better than to ask.

> The references in its words didn't chime with me and I didn't ask him about them. I think, if anything, the influences on it came from Mose Allison and the concept of Ol' Man River. I detected a wry quality in 'River Man', as with Mose Allison, and Nick was a wry person.

Even if Nick meant anything specific in his songs, he wasn't in the habit of expounding them. Iain Dunn, who was privy to some of them as soon they were written, understood that they were not up for discussion: 'You didn't sit there and dissect the songs, or say, "Well, that was nice, but wouldn't it be better if . . .?" That was it. Each song was a statement, and it was left. It wasn't like conversation.'[29]

Nick wrote 'River Man' knowing that he wanted it arranged – surviving early recordings indicate spaces for strings – and he asked Robert to work on it as the term came to an end. In December Nick again based himself in London, and recorded demos of 'River Man', 'Three Hours', 'Joey', 'The Thoughts Of Mary Jane' and 'Time Of No Reply' at Sound Techniques on Friday the 20th. This was Joe's first hearing of 'River Man': 'I thought it was great – but then, I thought most of Nick's songs were great. I certainly felt it was important that it be on the album.'

As his album took shape, Nick became convinced that Cambridge was a waste of his time and that he wanted to leave right away. His old friend Andy Murison was one of the few people with whom he discussed his dilemma.

> I didn't try to dissuade him. He obviously wasn't enjoying Cambridge and said that his going there had been his parents' wish, and that he

---

* 'I always associate the smell of lilacs with Cambridge exams,' says John Venning. 'Taking a break from study and walking around suburban Cambridge – e.g. Storey's Way – was accompanied by heavy lilac scents.'

was simply following the accepted path, which seemed less and less appealing to him, but that his parents considered the music business too uncertain to leave Cambridge for. I remember telling him that having a manager and a record contract probably amounted to much the same prospects a degree would.

Nick broached the subject over Christmas at Far Leys. Civil as their discussions were, Molly and Rodney were concerned that his single-mindedness about his music was inhibiting his wider development. The notion of it causing him to abandon university dismayed them. As they talked, Rodney suggested that his life at Cambridge was 'passive', by which he meant that Nick was not taking enough advantage of what was on offer, and 'escapist', which he might have intended to encompass Nick's dope smoking.

His remarks did not come from a position of contempt towards Nick's chosen field; as their local contemporary Joanna Lodder says, 'Nick and Gay's careers were outside the conventional local circle, but their parents were always so supportive of them. I'm not sure any of the other local parents would have embraced and enjoyed their children being artists in the same way.' Rodney and Molly simply wanted what they sincerely believed was best for him, and Nick understood that.

Joe was one of the only other people to whom he mentioned his desire to drop out, but he did not encourage him to do so, as he had perhaps hoped: 'I recommended he stay there and keep his options open.' They had now known each other for a year, but their relationship was hard to define. They weren't exactly friends, but – as with all Witchseason artists – their affiliation went beyond the strictly professional. For Joe, 'Nick was difficult to have a close personal relationship with. He had a stammering way of speaking to me and was always shy and quiet around me, but I had tremendous affection for him and felt protective of him.'

At Anthea Joseph's recommendation, Joe had recently signed an Irish counterpart to the Incredible String Band, Dr. Strangely Strange, who were crashing with him in Lots Road while they recorded at Sound Techniques in early January 1969. Nick was fitted in on 4 January, and worked on ''Cello Song' (as he had renamed 'Strange

Face'), 'River Man', 'Mayfair', 'Day Is Done' and 'Saturday Sun'. 'Day Is Done' was one of the first things Nick had recorded in Sound Techniques; the fact that it was still being honed almost a year later speaks of Joe's faith in him at a time when few records were made as slowly. For him, Nick's sessions were a pleasure: 'He never made a mistake in the studio . . . He never sang out of tune, he never missed a guitar note.'[30]

Danny Thompson was there to play double bass, and Clare Lowther to contribute to ''Cello Song'. A graduate of the Royal Academy of Music, she had studied with Jacqueline du Pré and played for Margot Fonteyn and Rudolf Nureyev, and did not find it a challenge to reproduce the counter-melody Nick had previously hummed. By her account,

> The session was around 6 p.m. The studio was quite dark. I saw the producer seated and another person standing, hovering near him. I played through the track. I think the 'wave-like' theme was suggested to me, but as the song progressed I was able to make my own contribution . . . I left promptly without hearing the track back.

For her it was simply another pop session: 'I did not pay particular attention in any special way – I didn't even know what the track was for.'[31]

Nick had long since abandoned other songs from 1967, but it is striking that he remained loyal to 'Mayfair'. Perhaps he was fond of it as an echo of his mother's style, perhaps it was deemed a likely candidate for cover versions, or perhaps there was talk of it being a single. No one is quite sure, although there's a consensus that by 1969 it didn't sit comfortably alongside his other material, structurally or lyrically. Besides, Joe had never much cared for it.

After a week of unusually foul weather back in Cambridge, Nick wrote to his parents on Thursday, 23 January.

> Cambridge has been quite pleasant this term, but here I am, becoming increasingly sure that I want to leave soon. I'm sure that our various conversations have made clear my general feelings . . . As far as performing is concerned, I am certainly no more than amateur. However, with regard to my songwriting, I can only progress from

the stage that I have reached so far by developing a purely professional approach . . . I know for a certainty that I must make this progression with my music in order to achieve any sense of fulfilment in my present life.

I hope you can perhaps appreciate that the idea of having my music as a 'vacation hobby' for another year-and-a-half is not a particularly happy one. It seems that Cambridge can really only delay me from doing what at the moment I most need to do . . . I am constantly getting hit by thoughts such as the ones in this letter. I suppose my time here has provided some sort of groundwork, but I feel that my achievements here are so unimportant in comparison to the things that I would have a chance of achieving if I left.

Nick didn't want to seem ungrateful for his place at Fitzwilliam and the efforts others had put into securing it, but music was much more than a 'hobby' for him, as his use of the verbs 'must' and 'need' indicate. Having discussed the matter at length with Molly, Rodney sent him a considered reply the following week. 'Obviously it is a step which we have to consider carefully, because it is an irrevocable one,' he began, going on to pose two vital questions: 'Are you more or less likely to succeed at your chosen career if you leave now? Secondly, what advantage unconnected with your career may you be throwing away if you leave now?'

He continued candidly:

We are slow developers in our family and you, I believe, are no exception to this. I would go so far as to say that you will surprise yourself in the next two years by the changes and development that will occur in your personality, your understanding and your outlook. In addition to this, any career involving self-employment demands a high degree of self-discipline and a will to overcome one's weaknesses, and making the effort required to tackle problems which do not come easily. I think you have a long way to go here.

You believe that the problem of turning yourself from an amateur into a professional can be solved merely by transferring yourself from Cambridge to somewhere where you are surrounded by, and under the influence of, professionals in your chosen field. From what you say I take it that you must believe that it was the prospect of returning to Cambridge for 8-week periods during the year that prevented you, in the long summer vac, from getting into the swim, so to speak, and of starting to acquire the professionalism which you are rightly seeking.

But I doubt this very much and I would regard as far more likely reasons your reticence (which you must overcome), your difficulty in communicating (which you must overcome), and your reluctance to plunge in and have a go (which you conceal from yourself by self-persuasion that more *solo* practising and *solo* listening are required before the move is made) . . . If I am right in what I say, and the real trouble is that you have not yet overcome your weaknesses (and God knows we all have them), then you may well find that you have thrown over Cambridge simply to continue indefinitely on the outskirts of what you are looking for.

At Cambridge you have a chance to fight your weaknesses and overcome them (and fight like hell you MUST), to discipline yourself from inside, and take a more active interest in your fellows (another weakness of yours – I am being very blunt, aren't I?) and generally to prepare and develop yourself to make a real success of what you want to do. And, in the meantime, your creative powers will be developing, not stagnating, do please believe me.

On the second aspect – what advantages unconnected with your career may you be throwing away – there is not a great deal to say except that it is a rounded personality which is most likely to lead its owner on a happy and full road though life. To specialise too early and to have interest in only one activity makes Jack a very dull boy . . . One and-a-half years may seem a long time to you. Allow me to assure you it is not – but it is a terribly important time in the *development* of you as a person into something that you are going to *start* to be at about the age of 23.

The winning of a degree may seem to bear little significance to you, and the argument that it is a safety net if you come a cropper with your music will doubtless evoke the response that a safety net is just what you don't want. I would say to you, however, that the self-discipline which it involves, apart from anything else at all, is a priceless asset in whatever you want to tackle during the rest of your

life. So there we are, Nick – there's my view. I urge you to resolve
to see Cambridge through and make a success of it.

It was indeed a blunt statement, but Nick knew it was written out
of love, recognised the truth in it and did not take it amiss. He
agreed not to leave immediately but had his limits, and did not vary
his activities by participating in, say, sport or the life of his college.
Rodney had written nothing that any concerned parent wouldn't
have thought under the circumstances, but he and Molly perhaps
didn't grasp the intensity of their son's commitment to his music,
or – as they later conceded – his brilliance.

14

The Record Of The Year

NICK CONTINUED TO divide his time between Cambridge and London. His next session was held at Morgan Studios on Friday, 14 February, halfway through term. Joe and John were both present to work further on 'Time Has Told Me', ''Cello Song' and 'Man In A Shed'. At the same session Nick recorded further takes of 'Three Hours' and ''Cello Song', with Chris Wood (of Traffic) on flute and his friend Rebop Kwaku Baah on congas. However, recalls Brian Wells, 'Nick told me it had been a nightmare getting the conga player to do it in the way he wanted,' and the tracks were put aside until Rocky Dzidzornu – a Ghanaian percussionist who'd played on the Rolling Stones' *Beggars Banquet* the previous year – overdubbed the congas a few weeks later.

Nick's power of veto was an accepted aspect of the album's gestation and caused no upset. 'I just kept throwing ideas at him, or throwing him in the studio with various different people, and sometimes he would respond and sometimes he wouldn't,' explains Joe. 'There were some things that happened and he'd say, "I don't like that," and we'd just drop it. And there were other things where he said, "Oh, that sounds all right . . ." It was a very enjoyable process for me.'[1]

The songs requiring orchestrations remained in limbo. When the subject arose, Nick reiterated that he wanted to use the arrangements he and Robert had put together. Joe saw the sense in doing so, and Nick finally broached the subject with Robert:

Nick said that he had already recorded some of the songs – I believe he told me that he'd done them with arrangements which weren't to the style that he'd imagined they were going to finish up like, and the initial request was, could he use [our] arrangements?[2]

He was, of course, delighted for them to be considered, but the decision did not rest with Nick. 'I needed to look Robert in the eye and discuss it all,' says Joe. 'If I was going to take this leap of faith, I needed to know that he wasn't some stoned, flakey kid.' Robert was certainly stoned some of the time, but when Joe drove to Cambridge to meet him he was impressed by his musicality, as well as his natural personality and easy interactions with Nick.

When Joe agreed to try out the arrangements, Nick went further, as Robert recalled: 'I think it was then Nick who stood up for the fact that I should come and conduct and MD the sessions, as I knew the arrangements intimately.' Joe agreed to this too. 'I was very excited,' said Robert.

> I'd come to university to read music and I'd always imagined that my future would be Handel's *Messiah*, Gilbert and Sullivan . . . I was going to be a schoolmaster, I couldn't think what else you could do . . . But here suddenly, 'Oh, just a moment – musicians can do arrangements?' And it was all a minor explosion in my head.[3]

To ensure their arrangements were as polished as possible, Robert sought showcases for Nick around Cambridge with ad hoc backing groups. Ed Bailey was another Choral Exhibitioner in Caius and a gifted cellist, so he was roped in.

> If I was free I would play, because I liked Robert and we were fellow Caians, but above all because I was really impressed with Nick. I thought he was brilliantly talented – we all did. His material was noticeably better than other composers' material (including Robert, and I recall him writing some good songs).
>
> Robert knew instrumentalists from all over Cambridge, so the group was drawn from several colleges. We weren't always the same players, as we all had competing attractions and obligations. There were five or six of us at most, sometimes only four. We rehearsed, not on a frequent or regular basis but for each particular gig . . . We may well have rehearsed in the Bateman Room and the Senior Parlour in Caius, and in St Michael's Church. We were never a 'group' as such – we never had a name, nor were there any promo photos.

Robert occasionally played French horn, but Ed says

Nick was concerned that he should not be swamped by the backing group, even in interludes when he was not singing, and that a brass instrument would alter the whole dynamic. My impression is that he felt we could be too loud, although I am sure that we were all conscious that his singing and playing were on the quiet side. I recall him asking if I thought his playing and singing blended with the backing, and I told him that in any ensemble it could be really difficult, if not impossible, to judge from within the group how you would sound to the audience.

Ed did not find Nick easy to communicate with:

He was always quiet, a real contrast to Robert. He rarely came out of his shell. He could have pushed himself on the music scene in Cambridge a lot more, but my memory is that he was never that keen to become 'known'; he was far more interested in his composition and guitar playing. Robert, on the other hand, had a wide acquaintance and put it to use for Nick. I felt that Nick never had the courage of his own talent. Robert once asked me to tell Nick how good I thought he was, I assume in order to boost his confidence.

It is possible that Robert also wanted Nick to be reassured of the validity of the whole concept of performing with other musicians. 'At times Nick seemed to rely on Robert, at others he would draw away from him,' says Ed.

On more than one occasion I had the distinct feeling that he felt uneasy having us playing behind him – Robert told me that Nick was far from certain that he needed a backing group and would have happily been just a solo artist. There were occasions in rehearsal when Nick played songs that we did not then perform.

Their performances were sporadic; Ed recalls playing at a private house in Grange Road and in a postgraduate college, Clare Hall. There was no advertising or publicity and being paid was not the object of the exercise.

We would play a few arrangements by Robert, then Nick would play some songs on his own, then we would all play something else together. Nick was always precise – neat playing, no general strumming, and pretty clear articulation of the words. I don't remember him retuning at any great length between songs.

The arrangements would change from gig to gig, as Robert tweaked them. While Nick would accept much that Robert wanted to do as arranger and fixer, there were times when he was quietly insistent that things should go as he wanted. He wasn't particularly tolerant of bad performance, and I like to think that I never let him down. Nick was a reluctant performer – I don't mean that he was nervous or didn't enjoy playing, but that he didn't seem to like being the centre of attention. Any talking from the stage was done by Robert, not him.

Robert had been striving to devise an arrangement for 'River Man' but just couldn't get it right.

Dave Brubeck's 'Take Five' aside, that was the only time in my life I'd heard a piece of music consistently in 5/4. I could not for the life of me work out how to write a piece of music that didn't stagger along like a spider missing a leg – how you crossed over and missed the bar lines . . .[4] Nick and myself agreed that I was not able to arrange such a complex song.[5]

Nonetheless, Nick began to play it at their gigs. By universal consensus, it was something special, even by his standards. Ed says: 'I recall looking out over the audience during one performance [of it] and being struck by how spellbound everyone's faces were.'

Paul Wheeler played regularly around Cambridge, but never shared a stage with Nick. One evening Iain Cameron – a first-year undergraduate in Selwyn – heard Paul at the Cambridge Union. Iain had also been a teenage regular at Les Cousins and had played a few gigs with Linda Peters after leaving school, before joining a West Coast-inspired band named Tintagel in January 1968. With them he shared stages with Fairport, Tomorrow, Brian Auger and others, and even played at the Royal Albert Hall. Like Paul, therefore, he was an experienced performer by the time he started at Cambridge.

I was so taken with Paul's music, which was very much what I was listening to before I got to Cambridge – good, blues-based, songwriter-guitarist stuff – that I went up to him afterwards and said, 'Loved your songs! I play the flute – maybe we could hook up?' I would go round to Paul's room in Harvey Court and we'd blow.[6]

On one occasion in early 1969 he found Paul already had company.

This time there were rather more people hanging out than usual. Paul and I played a bit and then this rather quiet and very striking-looking young man played some of his songs. One of these was 'River Man', which completely took my breath away . . . It was extraordinary – the beauty, the invention, the meaning coming in and out of focus, the technical accomplishment, the timbres and sonorities . . . Although Nick was cool and somewhat aloof, he had no trouble in projecting himself and his work musically to the eight or ten people in the room.[7]

Nick also performed a brand-new song, as Iain recalls:

The first time I met him, in Paul's room, he played 'One Of These Things First'. I thought the guitar lick was borrowed from 'The Mandolin Man and His Secret' by Donovan, but I didn't say so. Afterwards Paul and Nick discussed it and Paul pointed out that it had certain similarities to 'The Way You Do the Things You Do' by the Temptations, specifically in the lyrics.[*]

On another occasion the action was taking place in the room of another friend of Paul's, Ian MacCormick, an undergraduate at King's.[†] Nick was there with Paul, who introduced him. By Ian's account,

After a few moments to check his tuning (or to let the intervening hubbub hush), this tall, elegant person – at whom all the women

---

[*] 'Penthouse Pauper' by Creedence Clearwater Revival (from their January 1969 album *Bayou Country*) is another possible source of lyrical inspiration.
[†] Paul: 'Under the pen name Ian MacDonald, many years later he wrote about Nick in the academic style which Nick and I had both found so stultifying.'

were now intently gazing – began to play, craned over his small-bodied guitar and staring at the carpet, his long fingers moving unerringly across the fretboard while he sang low in a breathy, beige voice: 'Time has told me you're a rare, rare find / A troubled cure for a troubled mind . . .'

My eyes met those of another friend, a pianist with a jazz penchant. He silent-whistled: *What have we here?* 'Wow!' chorused the gathering at the end of the song . . . Nick whoever-he-was finished another bout of tuning and began to play again. In 5/4. Not many folk guitarists play in 5/4. And he sang: 'Betty came by on her way / Said she had a word to say / About things today / And fallen leaves.' Few present are likely to have forgotten that afternoon.[8]

Nick's effect on such audiences was not lost on him, but the only public performances he gave were arranged by Robert. There was strength in numbers at these, and they placed limited demand on him; as Paul puts it, 'All he had to do was sit in the right place and play along with the strings when Robert told him to start.' On Friday, 21 February, Nick made his way to the Pitt Club, at 7a Jesus Lane. It was a bastion of male undergraduate entitlement; according to a contemporary account, 'Cambridge retains a manner that is quite aristocratic and this is nowhere more apparent than in the Pitt Club. Named for the statesman and housed in a beautiful building that dates from 1826, the Pitt is one of the most exclusive clubs in Cambridge.'[9]

'Marion Stevens was at Girton and *the* glamour girl of the '67–'68 intake at Cambridge,' says Brian.

> I'd see her at lectures or we'd have the odd chat, and she was always pleasant, lively and intelligent. She had a Hooray Henry boyfriend who drove an Aston Martin, and she moved in those sorts of circles. He threw a twenty-first birthday drinks party for her at the Pitt Club, and Nick and Robert played with strings as a sort of cabaret. I was there because I did the sound.

Nick was not relaxed in the Pitt Club, despite his privileged background. Ed Bailey recalls Robert having to cajole him into agreeing to the date, part of the inducement being the fact that they were to be paid: 'It was a daytime party, and a far cry from my undergraduate parties.' Brian says, 'I remember them playing "Time Of No Reply", "Saturday Sun", "'Cello Song" (with no congas) and "Way To Blue", which particularly blew me away.'

Paul Wheeler, meanwhile, was struck (as ever) by 'the orderliness of Nick's performance'. Nick's songs were sandwiched between works by the baroque composers Willem De Fesch and Tomaso Albinoni, all conducted by Robert. Nick declined to play anything alone, perhaps put off by what Ed calls 'the general opulence of the occasion – the food, champagne and even a stripper'.

The Caius circle was disdainful of the rarefied aspects of Cambridge typified by the Pitt Club, but Mike Weissmann found a way to put an ironic spin on them by reinventing a college society named Ye Ancient Order of Gonville Loungers, supposedly first founded in 1459. 'The Loungers had come and gone over the years, and most recently it had been a sporty sort of club,' explains Paul. 'We felt that it was funny to raid that world – with the Loungers we felt as though we'd broken into it . . .'[10] Its flippancy appealed to us – the concept of following in the footsteps of lazy people in the ancient past.'

Mike's rules allowed for one member from another college, known as 'The Oddefellowe', designed so as to include Nick. They were required to 'lounge' by the college's Gate of Humility regularly and 'observe how strange creatures ye Lord hath made'. 'If you didn't turn up you were fined,' explains Pete Russell.

> Mike used the fines to pay for a lavish breakfast each month, which we took it in turns organising, with the chef at Caius helping us put together exotic menus. We'd each invite a guest or two and sit around in a small dining room in Caius with waiters serving us.

As Robert put it, 'All you did was have a seven-course meal at ten o'clock on a Sunday morning.'[11] They also had occasional Loungers' outings, such as punting by night, which Paul calls 'a completely different experience. Seeing the lights of the colleges dimly twinkling was very peaceful.'

In early March Nick had flu and was confined to Fitzwilliam's sick bay. It was bad timing. Not only did it prevent him from joining

Paul and Robert in attending an avant-garde performance by John Lennon and Yoko Ono at Lady Mitchell Hall on Saturday the 2nd, but he also urgently needed to find somewhere to live for the next academic year. He had been offered a room in a house owned by Trinity at 65 Chesterton Road, near his current digs, only for it to be withdrawn when they found they needed it after all. 'I am sure that eventually we will be able to find something suitable for you, and this letter is just to stop you worrying about the matter,' Fitzwilliam's Chief Clerk assured him,[12] but the prospect of having to live outside the centre of town again dismayed him.

Accommodation wasn't the only challenge Cambridge was presenting. After the brief Easter vacation, during which he wanted to complete his album, he would be sitting Part I of the dreaded Tripos. After eighteen months of doing the bare minimum of work, it was – in the words of his supervision partner John Venning – 'the brick wall towards which he was fast heading'. His end of term reports offered little cause for optimism. 'Very silent,' began Clare Campbell, who had supervised his work towards the Literary Criticism paper. 'Obviously sensitive and thoughtful, but lacks the confidence to express what he means clearly in discussion; better on paper. Attendance irregular.'

'He has been very quiet,' echoed Laurel Brodsley, a young American research fellow who was supervising him for the Shakespeare paper. 'He does his work, has ideas but doesn't express them fluently and, because he is shy, he doesn't respond quickly to new ways of looking at things.' Jill Mann, who was overseeing the medieval aspects of his curriculum, crisply stated: 'Mr Drake's translation is fair, but he does not seem to go beyond the glossaries for information, and his knowledge of Middle English is probably still not very extensive.'

Chris Bristow, who had been supervising Nick's study of Romantic and Victorian literature, offered him a lifeline of sorts:

The Tripos wasn't meant to be only about criticism, but all forms of literary endeavour. As such, you could submit your own creative work in lieu of a given paper, and if it was deemed to be at or above the standard of the worst of your other papers it would count towards your result. I knew Nick was writing songs and told him this, but he didn't take me up on it and never showed any of his writing to me. Looking at his words since, I think he had a lyric gift and that he shared a detached, evanescent, free-floating quality with writers of the post-Romantic period, who were seeking a new way to relate to the world.

At the end of term Nick gave his old friend Jeremy Harmer — who was studying at the University of East Anglia, sixty miles beyond Cambridge — a lift to Warwickshire. They hadn't seen each other in years, but Jeremy says: 'There was instant ease and communication. We chatted amiably in the car.' Jeremy had kept up with his own musical enthusiasm and was also in the process of making an album with chamber arrangements by a friend — but he had been unable to find a record deal and was recording it privately.* After a couple of hours, he says, 'We stopped outside Woodstock to have a pee in a copse, then stood admiring the stars. I remember being conscious that it was a magical moment, and how full of promise the world seemed.'

Nick had another magical moment a few days later: between 10 a.m. and 1 p.m. on Thursday, 3 April, after well over a year of writing, playing and tweaking, the arrangements for 'Way To Blue', 'Fruit Tree', 'The Thoughts Of Mary Jane' and 'Day Is Done' were recorded. Nick and Robert had stayed the night at Gabrielle's and turned up at Sound Techniques in good time. Robert remembered it as 'a beautiful studio with windows up in one wall, too high to see out of, the control room bolted up at one end and a staircase at the other end'.[13] Paul Wheeler was there too, 'at Nick's invitation. It was quite a contrast with the party atmosphere of John Martyn's sessions. It was formal and organised, with session musicians and sheet music, and I didn't stick around for long.'

John Wood had booked the players via the London Symphony Orchestra and explains: 'I preferred people who weren't used to playing pop sessions, as you tended to get more out of them.' Robert recalled the strings being led by the hugely experienced violinist

---

* He pressed *Idiosyncratics and Swallows' Wings* in a run of ninety-nine copies, which were sold around the UEA campus in 1969.

David McCallum and the players being 'professional and businesslike'. He had much to prove, but by his account: 'The atmosphere was laid-back and relaxed . . . [As at Cambridge] we kept it to exactly the same format of an octet, but we'd got Danny Thompson playing bowed bass with the octet, reading the parts that were there.'[14]

Robert was impressed by John and Joe: 'John did fashion the sound, but in the first place it was Joe who put the team together to get that sound. I think they made a very good pair.'[15] When John finished placing microphones he joined the impatient Joe in the control room. The first song they tackled was 'Way To Blue', which Joe and John had never heard. Nick had initially written it for his own piano accompaniment, but he and Robert had since agreed – perhaps owing to the influence of Randy Newman's 'I Think It's Going to Rain Today' – that its impact would be greater if he simply sang to the strings.

Joe and John were dubious. 'It was very unusual for an artist to play along with classical players, let alone sing,' says John. Having got levels from each instrument, allowing Joe to hear snippets of the arrangement, John gave Robert the nod. 'Suddenly John pushed up all four faders on the board and we heard this part and we both were knocked back in our seats,' remembers Joe. 'We thought, "This is exquisite, just amazing!"'[16]

Next the woodwind players ran over their parts before the whole ensemble taped 'Day Is Done', 'The Thoughts Of Mary Jane' and 'Fruit Tree'. 'We did those four tracks live with Nick in one three-hour session,' explained Robert.

> Nothing was overdubbed, so Nick's playing guitar, we're doing the quartet and the string bass with him. Most of the time was spent getting a decent string sound – he would play his part in exactly the correct tempo each time there was a take . . .[17] I was astounded by Nick's professionalism. He was always in tune, perfectly tuned . . . If I was standing at the front going, 'We'll take it from bar 37,' he was perfectly precise every time.[18]

Joe was not a demonstrative man, but when it became clear that the arrangements were not only adequate but masterful, 'I almost wept with joy and relief.'[19] At the end there was a general sense of triumph, though Nick remained phlegmatic. 'Nick was not really the type to go overboard with praise and I was never sure what he thought of my somewhat rococo embellishments,' Robert reflected thirty years later.[20]

Up in the control room, recalls Joe, the subject of 'River Man' came up and Nick explained that Robert felt unequal to the task. 'I have a vivid memory of being disappointed that Robert wouldn't tackle "River Man",' he says. He and John could clearly see that the song required the best possible treatment. John says: 'When Nick said he envisaged a Ravel/Debussy/Delius feel, I suggested Harry Robinson, with whom I'd worked on various film soundtracks.'

Harry Robinson (né Robertson) was born in November 1932. By 1969 he had a long career behind him as an arranger for stage, film, TV and records, as well as being – coincidentally – an early business associate of Chris Blackwell. Joe arranged for him to be sent a tape of the song, and shortly afterwards he and Nick took a cab to his house on Barnes Common. By Joe's account, 'Having heard the tape, Harry was already intrigued when we arrived. Nick played the song through, then strummed chords as the tape played, showing Harry the textures he wanted for the string parts. I had never heard him so articulate or so demanding. Harry made notes and nodded.'[21] It was a process Robert was familiar with, and they agreed to reconvene at Sound Techniques when it was ready.

In the meantime Nick was in theory preparing for his exams in mid-May; the topics he was to be examined upon included Literary Criticism, French Unseen Translation, and English Literature and Its Background 1300–1642. It was a lot to take on board in such a short time but, inevitably, his focus was on his album.

Artwork had now became a priority. On Monday, 14 April, Nick met the witty, energetic and direct photographer Keith Morris at Witchseason. Ten years Nick's senior, he had studied at Guildford School of Art, where he described his approach as 'the process of communication; an attempt to fuse observer and observed'.[22] The emerging underground offered plenty of photogenic subjects and he had come to Joe's attention when he photographed the Incredible String Band. His friend Mark Williams, the chief music writer on *International Times*, says: 'If he thought you were stupid, acquisitive or self-interested he'd treat you accordingly, but if he respected you then you quickly became friends.'

When Keith arrived, Joe played him some of Nick's recordings and Danny Halperin gave him a broad brief. Nick said barely anything, but Keith's impression was of someone 'shy and boyish and likeable'. He was struck by Nick's lack of concessions to the style of the day: 'The way he dressed, you could never believe he ever had any other clothes. You imagine the Incredible String Band in all their finery, and Nick was nondescript in a dodgy blazer.'[23] The two of them went around the corner and 'had a non-alcoholic extended lunch and I said, "Have you got any ideas you want to do?" I always work better bouncing ideas off people, and between us we came up with a number of ideas.'

On the morning of Wednesday the 16th Keith drove them to Wimbledon Common, where he took colour shots of Nick sitting or lying in the grass, looking alternately pensive and good-humoured.[*]

> I never tried to force things on him. I was quite happy to go with what he threw at me, try and work it different ways. I think, in a funny sort of way, Nick knew what he was doing visually. He was very much the sucked-in cheeks. He posed naturally . . . Vain is a bit strong, but Nick knew what he wanted to look like.[24]

They wandered into a derelict house just off the Common, where Keith shot him by an upstairs window, then drove to Battersea, where Keith had identified the Morgan Crucible[†] plant in Church Road as a promising location. He wanted to juxtapose Nick with workers leaving at close of business, exemplifying his interest in fusing observer and observed. The concept echoed the opening line of Max Ehrmann's 1927 poem 'Desiderata' (a hugely popular text of the time), 'Go placidly amid the noise and the haste . . .', as well as Nick's membership of the Loungers.

---

[*] One of these was used inside the gatefold for the July 1971 *Nick Drake* compilation in America (Capitol SMAS 9307). Most of the others appear to be lost.
[†] Then one of the UK's leading manufacturers of industrial and electrical engineering products.

They arrived in good time and waited. Eventually people began to emerge, and Keith shot thirty-five frames.

> The idea was fairly simple. We wanted a neutral background, not a confused background, i.e., a wall. Nick would be there, static in an observer position, and we were going to get people walking past, running past, going past however they happened to appear. We got there around going-home time and recorded people, some in droves. The one we ended up using had the one person, who was running for a bus, as I recall.[25]

The fourth and final location, Keith's studio in Gunter Grove (off the Fulham Road), was a short distance over the river, and in Nick's usual stamping ground. He posed in low light at the end of a table, looking cheerful, quizzical or despondent, presumably at Keith's direction. By then they had got into a rhythm. 'When I first met him in the office, he was totally monosyllabic,' according to Keith, but 'I got more into Nick the more I knew him . . . The more you found out about Nick, the more likeable he was.'[26]

Following the session, Nick reluctantly drove back to Cambridge for the summer term. He was finding it hard to motivate himself. 'We were walking by the river one sunny afternoon and he said hello to a guy he knew who was also doing English, who was sunbathing with his girlfriend,' says Brian Wells. 'He told Nick that he'd finished revising and as we walked away Nick said to me, "I haven't even started!" I think at that moment he realised he really needed to get his act together.'

Nonetheless, two final recording dates had been set for early the following week. On the evening of Monday, 21 April Nick presented himself at Sound Techniques. Fourteen musicians awaited him, alongside Harry Robinson. It was Nick's turn to be apprehensive; he had not yet heard the arrangement for 'River Man'. In another indication of Nick's confidence where his music was concerned, John Wood remembers him asking for it to be tweaked as it was performed – there were certain figures he wanted played as longer notes instead – and Harry graciously assenting.

There was unanimous agreement that the result was another triumph, nodding both towards Frederick Delius and John Barry, and serving the song immaculately. Joe says: 'I saw Harry many years later and he said, '"River Man" was so wonderful, all of us together in one room – I felt like Nelson Riddle with Frank Sinatra."'

The following morning Joe and Nick (but not Paul Wheeler, for reasons he doesn't recall) attended John and Bev's wedding at Hampstead Register Office. The reception took place in the nearby basement flat they had recently moved into, at 40a Denning Road. They had barely known each other six months and it was a haphazard affair. 'Everyone sat around rolling joints and Joe saved the day by getting hold of champagne and glasses,' recalls Bev.[27]

Another regular on the folk circuit, the Welshman John James, was chatting to Nick in the crowded sitting room when

> the girl next to us lit a ciggie, blew at the match and put it back in the box. Next thing, BANG! The whole bloody box went up. Screams, laughter, poor Nick white as a sheet. Cue Joe, arm around Nick, 'I think it's time to go . . .' And up the steps they went.[28]

They headed for Sound Techniques, where Danny Thompson overdubbed double bass onto 'Three Hours' and 'Saturday Sun', and percussionist Tristan Fry contributed to the latter. Tristan was part of the London Philharmonic Orchestra and a seasoned studio musician whose credits include the Beatles' 'A Day in the Life'. Initially he was booked to play vibes on 'Saturday Sun', but happened to have a drum kit in his car and played that too, making it the only track on the album with drums.

At the end of the session, the album was, at last, fully recorded. 'It was made with care and was maybe a little indulgent, but it was mainly Nick and guitar, and the arrangements were done at the same time, so it wasn't too expensive,' explains Joe.

Mixing was a smooth procedure, partly because John had been so thorough whilst recording and partly because he was always candid about anything he didn't like; in Joe's words, 'with John, you got all the bad news, all the time'.[29] This could make him seem unduly negative but was actually a symptom of his commitment to achieving the best possible result. Joe therefore knew and was grateful for the fact that 'With John you knew no nasty surprises were awaiting when it came to mix'.[30]

For Joe, 'The whole process of creating music is partly a process in which elimination is as important as what you present,'[31] and the next decision was what to leave off. It was decided to omit 'Mayfair', 'Joey' and 'Time Of No Reply', the latter because Robert and Nick felt its arrangement was too similar to 'The Thoughts Of Mary Jane' (which Nick preferred).*

Next, Joe and John worked out the running order for each side with a crude but efficient system of their own. 'We'd cut up strips of paper proportionate in length to each song, then divide them into two columns and juggle them around until they matched and we liked it,' explains John. '"Time Has Told Me" was always going to be the opener and "Saturday Sun" the closer. Usually the weakest song went next to last, but that didn't apply in Nick's case, with "Fruit Tree".'

Masters were cut at Apple in Savile Row under John's close supervision and sent straight to the manufacturers, Phonodisc Ltd, who took around a week to create test pressings. Danny Halperin, meanwhile, was drafting artwork in close collaboration with Island's production and marketing manager, Tim Clark. At this stage the album's title was to be *Saturday Sun*, so the cover was prepared with that in mind. Keith had quickly developed the fruits of his shoot with Nick and submitted them to Witchseason. 'I remember him bringing the contact sheet of the session into the office,' says Joe. 'We both went for the shot with the blurred man and said, "That's the one!" I think Keith really caught the measure of Nick,† in a funny way, as the man who stands still while the rest of the world rushes by.'[32]

Ultimately, though, it was decided that a colour shot would have greater impact, so 'the running man' was relegated to the back and for the front Danny selected a cover shot of Nick looking down from an upstairs window in the abandoned Wimbledon house. He

---

* Nothing was omitted for reasons of space; the running time of Nick's finished album was 41:43, while Dr. Strangely Strange's was considerably longer, at 49:21.
† Whether Keith intended the pose to encapsulate Nick is moot; they barely knew each other, and he shot variants of the image with Ian Whiteman for the first Mighty Baby album later that year and of Richard Thompson for *Henry the Human Fly* in 1972.

wanted the photo to speak for itself, without a busy background or complicated lettering, so set it against plain green: 'Very often and quite correctly an image of the artist or artists concerned is all that is necessary if presented intelligently,' he stated.[33]

It was decided that a gatefold was warranted; in addition to wanting to use photos taken by Keith in three different locations, all at decent size, Joe says, 'We wanted to show what a strikingly individual lyricist Nick was, so we liked the idea of printing *some* lyrics, even though there wasn't room to print them all.' The words to 'Three Hours', 'Saturday Sun' and 'River Man' were therefore placed next to a large, contemplative image of Nick in Keith's studio.

There were signs of haste, though: 'Three Hours' was titled 'Sundown', 'Giacomo' was spelled wrongly and included a verse Nick had omitted from the recording, while 'River Man' also included an extra verse.* Further omissions and errors appeared in the credits on the back, where Tristan Fry's name was misspelled, Lyn Dobson's name was omitted, and the order for 'Day Is Done' and 'Way To Blue' was reversed (as it was also on the first batch of labels). 'Deadlines for printed matter were earlier than deadlines for master tapes,' explains Joe. 'Many times an album was already at the printer's while I was still juggling running orders, artists might be changing their minds about titles, etc. – and Nick might have given us a set of lyrics that had changed when he recorded the song.' All in all, he admits, 'We were in a hurry and not a lot of thought went into the sleeve.'

Island received test pressings in early May and immediately despatched one to Nick in Cambridge. 'My room was above Bowes & Bowes bookshop in Trinity Street,' says Chris Jones.

> One afternoon Robert, Mike Weissmann and I were there, consuming certain aromatics, when Nick turned up, chucked an advance copy of his record onto my bed and said, 'That's my album.' We all said, 'Wow, great!' and put it onto my old Dansette right away. I can still remember hearing 'Time Has Told Me' and 'River Man' playing for

---

* 'Betty fell behind awhile / Said she hadn't time to smile / Or die in style / But still she tries / Said her time was growing short / Hadn't done the things she ought / Where teacher taught / And father flies'.

the first time. We listened closely and were very appreciative. The responses were fraternal and congratulatory.

Nick's flawless and distinctive guitar playing was apparent right from the unconventional opening chords to 'Time Has Told Me'. The more austere tracks ('Way To Blue', 'Fruit Tree') were balanced by jaunty ('Man In A Shed') or dainty ('The Thoughts Of Mary Jane') ones, and his detached yet wry, quietly self-assured personality came across strongly, with little sense of striving for effect. The album transcended its recording history by being strikingly coherent, despite touching on several genres. Certain lyrics were callow, perhaps, but outweighed by powerful and memorable imagery else-where. For someone aged twenty the assurance of the whole was remarkable.

Hearing the fruit of their labours together was an important moment for Nick and Robert, especially in the company of the esteemed Mike (even if a song Robert hadn't arranged was widely considered the standout). The experience of writing, recording and directing four arrangements for the album had in fact caused Robert to rethink his whole future: 'When I got the cheque for doing Nick's stuff, it seemed a positive thing to do – to get on with a career as an orchestrator . . .'[34]

Nick was delighted with the album, by all accounts, but he did have one reservation: he didn't want it to be called *Saturday Sun*. 'As we listened, Nick said he needed to come up with another title but couldn't think of one,' recalls Chris.

> Just at that moment I was handling a Rizla packet, and up popped the warning slip, saying 'Only 5 Leaves Left'. I handed it to him and said, 'There you go – there's your title.' He muttered something in his usual way, and that was that. Since then I have seen various interpretations of the title, some of them pretty far-fetched, but I can say for sure that's where it originated.

Among other interpretations, the phrase could be taken to refer to the last pages of an old book; according to Robert, 'It has a sort of autumnal ring about it, leaves and the end of autumn. But at the same time, a certain kind of person who used those cigarette papers would know what it was about. It was a bit of an in-joke.'[35] Nick swiftly passed the idea on to Joe, who says: 'I liked the title *Five Leaves Left* right away. Hip, enigmatic, dope-referencing – what could be better?'

Nick also played the test pressing to Paul Wheeler. 'I was surprised when I heard it,' he says.

> I was used to hearing the songs unadorned, so it seemed a little over-done. I thought the arrangement on 'River Man' took the song into outer space and placed it within a flow of classical music that was beyond the scope of Robert's arrangements, which felt conservative and influenced by George Martin. For me, the general impression the album created was sentimental, which wasn't my impression of Nick. I thought he was dreamy, but not sentimental. He was great company at that time, often light-hearted, with a lovely sense of humour. I can picture him throwing his head back and laughing. *Five Leaves Left* seemed weighty and serious in comparison, so I didn't feel it presented the person I knew. It seemed too monumental.

Iain Cameron had similar reservations:

> The inside feeling among the cognoscenti was that the arrangements and production were not a hundred per cent sympathetic to the spirit of the songs and the performances as we knew and loved them. There was a feeling that it was slightly overdone, hadn't quite got the delicacy required . . .[36]

James Fraser had been travelling around India since leaving Cambridge the previous summer, but was back in time to hear *Five Leaves Left* and recalls 'a general sense of people not being too keen on the orchestrations, and not being sure how much they enhanced Nick's songs – they made them sound too classical.'

A copy of the test pressing found its way to John and Bev's flat, and John James was there when John put it on: 'He liked the first track, "Time Has Told Me", but skipped through the rest, saying "Nothing else jumps out".' This may well have been a figment of envy, but Bev had misgivings too: 'It was a bit overdone . . . It was like saying, "For [your songs] to work, you've got to have all this stuff behind you."'[37]

Nick surprised Jeremy Harmer by bringing the test pressing to his tiny basement room in Randolph Terrace, Maida Vale.

I don't know why he decided to make that effort – perhaps he had a residual respect for the fact that we'd played guitar together at the start. Either way, we listened to it all way through on my mono Hacker record player. I didn't realise how bloody good he had become. I remember him quietly, elegantly beaming with pleasure. He took it with him when he went, leaving me ripped apart by wonder at his talent – and sheer jealousy.

Once Danny had added the title to the artwork (omitting the word 'only' for fear of copyright infringement), the album was approved for manufacture. Joe then belatedly sent Nick a three-year contract with his publishing wing, Warlock Music. Nick passed it to Rodney, who wrote to him from work on Tuesday, 6 May:

However carefully an agreement is drawn, it won't work unless the two participants trust each other, whilst conversely, however badly an agreement is drawn it will still work if there is trust. One has to make up one's mind about people oneself and one gets better at it as one goes on . . . Anyway, I think it's all a very fine effort on your part.

Nick, of course, did trust Joe, frenetic though he was. As well as completing Nick's album he had recently finished recording the third offering from Fairport and was working on the next Incredible String Band record. He wasn't arrogant, but had good reason to be confident:

Up to the spring of 1969 I saw my trajectory as Pink Floyd, the Incredible String Band and Fairport, with sidelines into making other records with acts that I didn't have a strong connection with (Alasdair Clayre, Shirley Collins and one or two others). I thought, 'If I believe in something, it will succeed.' I was probably over-confident, but until then everything had happened the way I'd envisaged, and I thought *Five Leaves Left* would simply be the next success off the Boyd production line.

At the end of the first week of May he flew to New York with John Wood. They had booked time at Vanguard Studios to mix the

Fairport album, an innovative step towards blending rock with trad-itional British folk, featuring outstanding songs by Sandy Denny and Richard Thompson. In between sessions he was arranging for the Incredible String Band to play a string of summer dates (including the vast Woodstock festival in upstate New York) and for Fairport to play at the Newport Folk Festival – a dream come true for them.

On the night of Sunday, 11 May, Fairport played in Mothers nightclub, Birmingham. After the gig Sandy returned to London by car while her bandmates (and their gear) squeezed into their Transit van for the tedious journey. At around 4 a.m. their exhausted roadie nodded off at the wheel on the outskirts of London, and the van left the road at 70 mph. Their drummer Martin Lamble and Richard's American girlfriend Jeannie Franklyn died at the scene and the others were injured to varying degrees.

The dreadful news reached Witchseason early that morning. Anthea called America to tell Joe, who immediately arranged to fly home. 'We are all in a state of shock because this tragedy is just unbelievable,' she told *Melody Maker* later that day. The accident weighed down the buoyant atmosphere at Witchseason for the summer ahead. Not least was the question of Fairport's future – they weren't only a dynamic artistic force but a vital contributor to the company's turnover.

Nick didn't know Fairport well but had met them all at various times and owed his career to Ashley Hutchings. The aftermath of the catastrophe formed part of the background to his Part I exams, which took place over the week of 19 May. 'Here's wishing you all the best of luck,' his father wrote to him. 'Take it easy and remember you can't do better than your worst, or worse than your best, or whatever the saying is.' He did turn up for each paper, but was not especially invested in their outcome.

His thoughts were coloured by the generally held assumption that *Five Leaves Left* would be a hit, critically and commercially. 'I think it must have influenced his thinking that Joe and I both thought he had made a great record, and that it would therefore create a lot of interest,' says John Wood. 'Before it came out my wife Sheila and I played it to various people, and they all agreed. Everybody thought it would be a storming success.'

With exams over, undergraduate life at Cambridge was again taken over by May Week. In particular, various colleges put on lavish, all-night 'May Balls', cynically described in that year's *Varsity Handbook* as '10 guineas' worth of desperate enjoyment'.* Brian recalls that

> On the afternoon of the Trinity Ball Nick and I went to watch the orchestra rehearsing, and I was struck by him saying, 'Imagine how much hard work those musicians have all put in, eight hours' practice a day, all their lives, in order to earn a tenner playing third fiddle in front of a bunch of pissed students.' That evening Rick Charkin and I borrowed some waiters' uniforms from an Indian restaurant and gatecrashed it. Nick wasn't with us – he would never have done anything so uncool.

As Robert put it, 'Everyone talks about the sixties and flower power, but the May Ball was very much what it would have been like before the war.'[38] It wasn't Nick's scene, but he agreed to perform with backing musicians at the Caius Ball on 10 June. 'I arranged the bookings, which is how Robert and Nick came to do a spot there,' says Marcus Bicknell. Headlining were bluesman John Mayall, humorous poets the Liverpool Scene and pop quartet Tuesday's Children. The bill was bulked out with undergraduate acts: White Unicorn and Horn both featured Iain Cameron, the North West London Contemporary Jazz Five was the latest name for Mike Weissmann's jokey band, and the moribund Fab Cab were present and correct, as was Paul Wheeler.

Nick was billed alone, with the programme stating: 'Nick Drake's forthcoming LP, already hailed in the press as the record of the year,[†] was produced by Joe Boyd (producer of the Incredible String Band and Fairport Convention). Robert Kirby arranged some of the tracks on the album and his orchestra will be accompanying Nick tonight.' Borrowing the PA system Brian used for his sideline as a mobile party DJ, Nick performed in the college library in the small hours,

Projentime

---

* Approximately £150 in 2022.
† This was pure hype: *Five Leaves Left* had yet to be mentioned anywhere in the press, including the University's own weekly paper, *Varsity*.

backed by an octet including Iain on flute and soprano saxophone, Ed Bailey on cello, Colin Fleetcroft on double bass* and Steve Pheasant (of Horn) on flute. In addition, Robert recalled some girls from New Hall being involved, decked in feather boas.

Robert described the library as 'really a sitting-out/rest room'.[39] It was, according to Ed, 'an out-of-the-way venue that would not attract that many people, there always being competing attractions'. Nick's audience was therefore small but not humiliatingly so; Iain estimates it as around forty. They played the four songs Robert had arranged for *Five Leaves Left* and Nick played a few others, alone or with Iain. 'We played "Mayfair" as a duo, with me extemporising on soprano saxophone,' he says. 'I remember the girl I took with me to the ball saying she hadn't enjoyed my playing on that one!'[40] According to Robert, 'After every third song we stuck in classical bits – the slow movement of Leopold Mozart's Trumpet Concerto and the Albinoni Adagio and Fugue.'[41] It was the last time Nick played live with musicians behind him.

As an antidote to the exclusive May Balls, between 8 and 11 June a group of enterprising undergraduates – including Marcus – mounted the open-air Cambridge Free Festival on Midsummer Common, just over the bridge from Nick's digs in Carlyle Road. It offered gratis performances by artists including David Bowie, King Crimson, Mighty Baby, Brian Auger and Family (most of whom were in fact in Cambridge to play at May Balls). The University was represented by Paul, Henry Cow, Horn, White Unicorn and others – but Nick was notable by his absence, even though he had an album to preview. His non-appearance wasn't a result of stage-fright, but an acceptance that he and his music were unlikely to connect with an audience in such circumstances.

One sunny afternoon Nick made his way with his Martin to Bodley's Court at King's to meet another player, Howard Gannaway, at Rick Charkin's suggestion. Once they'd settled on the grass by the river, Howard played his arrangement of the Doors' 'Light My Fire'. 'Nick said something polite and appreciative, then began to play himself. I remember feeling like my insides had turned to

---

* Colin later said he had no recollection of having played with them.

water, he was so good. He didn't sing, but I didn't get the impression that he was shy about playing – he came across as strong and self-confident, just not very talkative.'*

Nick's exam result was published on Friday, 13 June; he had again been placed in Class III. It was far from distinguished, but at least he had passed, qualifying him for the rest of his degree course. Fitzwilliam was unimpressed by his showing, tersely summarising on their brief annual report to Warwickshire's Education Authority: 'His ability is not great and he lacks confidence.'[42] He was unfussed, though, just pleased to be free from having to do remedial work over the summer.

Robert, alas, had not squeaked through. 'When Robert failed his Part Ones he had nowhere left to turn,' as Ed Bailey puts it. 'Caius said he could only come back for his third year if he read Theology, which he turned down,' is Chris Jones's bizarre recollection. His school mentor Christopher Bishop was 'amazed and sad when I heard that he'd chucked his place at Caius. The story I was told was that he was throwing jazzy chords into the harmony parts he was writing as part of his academic work, and his supervisor got upset.' Whatever the precise cause, Robert would not be returning to Cambridge in October.

Term ended on 18 June, when several more of Nick's friends left for good. Rather than pursuing a conventional career, Marcus had accepted a job as a booker with one of London's leading live agencies, Terry King Associates. Chris Jones was heading back to Liverpool to teach, while Mike Weissmann returned to London and also became a teacher, at the Lycée in South Kensington. Nick's days of working up arrangements with Robert, playing the odd concert and hanging out with like-minded souls in Caius were over – but with the summer ahead and his album due to be released in little over a fortnight, he wasn't nostalgic.

---

* Howard adds: 'I was incredulous to see *Five Leaves Left* in a shop a few weeks later – Nick hadn't mentioned that he had made an album that was about to be released.'

15

Lost In The Shuffle

—◦—

NICK TURNED TWENTY-ONE on Thursday, 19 June 1969, a milestone his parents marked by giving him a one-volume complete Shakespeare and a cheque for £750 (around £10,000 in 2022). Gabrielle had had a party in the Savoy Hotel when she turned twenty-one in 1965, but that wasn't Nick's style. He was now legally free to do as he pleased, twenty-one still being the 'age of majority' in the UK. On the threshold of adulthood, his personality was little changed from early childhood: detached, self-contained, quizzical, quietly humorous. He had no difficulty making friends, though: as Julian Lloyd puts it, 'Nick was fun to be with, a good companion, and very popular. Everybody liked him very much.'

After his birthday he based himself in London for the summer. His family and friends were nothing but supportive of his music, but he chose to keep quiet about *Five Leaves Left* until the finished article was in his hand. This strategy might have been aimed at burnishing his cool – as David Ward puts it, 'Nick came across (not in an arrogant way) like someone who had already made it' – but it's as likely to have been a symptom of his reserve and tendency to internalise.

The album was delivered to Island – who had just moved offices from Oxford Street to Basing Street, in Notting Hill – and thence to Witchseason shortly before its release on Friday, 4 July.* 'I remember the whole office being excited when a pack of finished copies arrived from Island, but I don't remember any sort of launch celebration,' says Joe, who immediately took a few round to Nick at Cyril Mansions. Gabrielle happened to be there too: 'I was never

---

* Island's press ads erroneously gave the date as Thursday, 3 July; the cassette release followed in December.

The newly built Fitzwilliam College, Cambridge, termed 'a brutalist desert' by one of Nick's contemporaries. Nick's room is second from the right on the ground floor.

A bemused Nick in his college's matriculation photo, October 1967.

Brian Wells and Nick found common ground at Cambridge and remained friends for the rest of Nick's life.

Rick Charkin, with whom Nick travelled in Morocco in the spring of 1967 and gladly reunited at Cambridge that autumn.

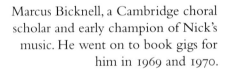

Marcus Bicknell, a Cambridge choral scholar and early champion of Nick's music. He went on to book gigs for him in 1969 and 1970.

Nick at Far Leys at Christmas 1967, a few days after making his live debut at the Roundhouse in London.

Joe Boyd, the expat underground impresario and producer who thought Nick was 'obviously a genius' upon first hearing him in January 1968.

Robert Kirby, another Cambridge choral scholar, who Nick also met in January 1968. They immediately began to arrange Nick's songs.

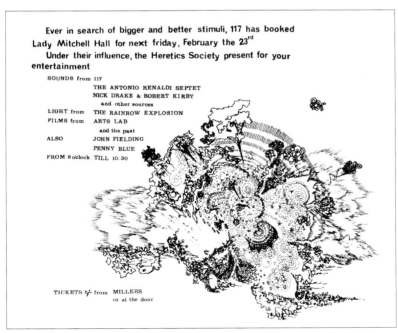

A flier for 'Under the Influence', the concert in February 1968 at which Nick and Robert first performed together.

Ben Laycock, who introduced Nick to his circle in London in the summer of 1967.

The artistic, music-loving Sophia Ryde, whose company Nick often sought.

Alex Henderson, at whose London flat Nick often hung out and stayed in the late 1960s.

David Ward, with whom Nick would sit up late playing guitar.

Nick gently placing a croquet hoop over a puppy. He was a formidable player.

Julian Lloyd and Victoria Ormsby-Gore. Julian took the first promo photos of Nick, and Victoria helped organise his Roundhouse appearance.

Sound Techniques, Chelsea, in which Nick recorded all three of his albums.

John Wood, its co-owner and chief engineer, who took care of Nick both in and out of the studio.

THE INCREDIBLE
STRING BAND
   Elektra Records

FAIRPORT
CONVENTION

NICK DRAKE

THE CHRIS
McGREGOR GROUP
   Polydor Records

*Independent Production
& Personal Management*

**WITCHSEASON
PRODUCTIONS LTD.**
83 Charlotte St.
London, W.1
01-636 9436

Joe Boyd Tod Lloyd
Danny Halperin Huw Price

Nick is announced as both
a signing to Joe Boyd's
Witchseason roster and a
Polydor artist in *Billboard*,
25 May 1968.

Anthea Joseph, who
joined Witchseason in
the summer of 1968
and did her best to
further Nick's career.

Chris Blackwell met
Nick in the autumn
of 1967, added him
to Island Records a
year later and allowed
him artistic freedom
thereafter.

Paul Wheeler, a fellow singer-songwriter Nick met in Cambridge in October 1968, with whom he had much in common.

Mike Weissmann, whose wide-ranging artistic tastes influenced Nick at Cambridge.

Gabrielle and her partner Louis de Wet were consistently supportive and understanding of Nick.

Caius May Ball

Tuesday
10th June 1969
10pm till 6am

Nine and a half guineas

Apply to S J Clarke Caius

The poster for the Gonville and Caius May Ball on 10 June 1969 – the last time Nick performed his arrangements live.

Nick happily posing on Wimbledon Common on 16 April 1969,
as the finishing touches were put to his first album.

Nick loitering outside the
Morgan Crucible plant in
Battersea later the same day, as
its employees departed.

The first Nick Drake album,
'Five Leaves Left', available
July 3.

The new Fairport Convention,
'Unhalfbricking', available
July 3.

The first Dr. Strangely Strange,
'Kip of the Serenes', available
July 3.

Like Fairport Convention, both Nick Drake and Dr. Strangely
Strange co-produced their albums with Joe Boyd.
Nick Drake wrote all the songs on this first L.P.
The unusual string arrangements were played on the session by
Danny Thompson, Paul Harris and Richard Thompson.
Dr. Strangely Strange are greatly admired by the Incredible
String Band, who have done so much to help them.

island ISLAND RECORDS LTD. BASING STREET LONDON W11. TEL 229 1229

Island's first press ad for *Five Leaves Left*, giving the wrong day of
release and inaccurate background information.

Nick in rural Nottinghamshire in the summer of 1969.

actually introduced to Joe, although it was my flat. He disappeared off into Nick's bedroom.'

She was aware that her brother had been making recordings but was unaware that anything like a finished album was in the offing. 'As I was about to go out to work Nick came into my room, said "There you are" and threw down this record, which was *Five Leaves Left*, onto my bed. I had no idea it had reached that pitch.'[1] Paul Wheeler had a similar experience: 'The first time I saw a finished copy was in the Battersea flat. Nick didn't present it, he placed it on a sofa as if it had materialised on its own.'

Nick's own response to the finished album is not known, but its release was the culmination of a huge amount of determined effort on his part. Rodney and Molly seem never to have described their first sight or hearing of it either, but in later years Rodney confessed that 'We didn't appreciate the music as much then as we appreciate it now . . . I don't think either of us realised how good it was.' Nonetheless, he told Nick in a letter that they considered it 'a delightful work of art'[2] and proudly spread the word.

Nick diffidently showed it to his close friends. 'None of us had any idea that he was even recording *Five Leaves Left* – we were amazed when he showed us the finished album,' says Ben Laycock. 'We were all terribly excited and rushed out to buy it,' adds Sophia Ryde. Upon playing it, continues Ben, 'We adored it, we thought it was fabulous, unbeatable, we were thrilled for him.' Victoria Ormsby-Gore remembers him 'being very pleased by compliments for it', but Sophia emphasises that he 'wouldn't talk about it and we wouldn't play it when we were all together'. They played it a lot when he wasn't around, though. For Julian, 'It seemed different to most music of the time – it had its own sound and feel,' and David recalls: 'We all thought it was lovely and was going to go gold.' Simon Crocker happened to spot it in the window of the Chelsea Record Centre in the King's Road.

> I was amazed and delighted and rushed in and bought it with all the money I had. It was impressive that he was on Island – that was a seal of cool approval, unlike EMI or Decca. I was even more delighted when I heard it, because it was so good. I loved its austerity.

Robin Frederick had briefly known Nick as a novice songwriter in Aix two and a half years earlier. She was astounded to see a copy of his album in an import bin in Tower Records in California:

I was thrilled that Nick had made a record. I rushed home and played it. I was seduced by its beauty but also a little perplexed. On the cover was my friend, still wearing the same jacket and jeans he wore in Aix, still sure of his image. But on the album was someone I hardly recognised. The voice seemed to float in some strange way, detached from the guitar rhythm. The playing was rock solid as always, but more complex, and there were those amazing cluster chords. In less than twenty-four months, Nick had somehow rocketed light years ahead of the rest of us.[3]

Island released two other Witchseason productions – *Unhalfbricking* by Fairport and *Kip of the Serenes* by Dr. Strangely Strange – alongside *Five Leaves Left*. This meant they could build window displays around them and make their advertising spend stretch further. Ads for the albums ran in *Time Out*, *International Times* and *ZigZag*, the short puff for *Five Leaves Left* stating that Nick had 'co-produced it' and sloppily adding: 'The unusual string arrangements were played on the session by Danny Thompson, Paul Harris and Richard Thompson.'

This was amended in the version that appeared in the 5 July issue of the country's top-selling music weekly, the hugely influential *Melody Maker*:

There's nothing unusual about the fact that Nick Drake writes his own songs and plays good guitar – you've heard that before about hundreds of new artistes. Listen to the record because of the great playing by Danny Thompson, Paul Harris and Richard Thompson and the amazing string arrangements – then you'll find out about the singer and his songs.

The music press that week was dominated by Brian Jones's drowning, shortly after midnight on 3 July,* and the free concert

---

* The press reaction disgusted Nick: 'I thought the way they treated Brian Jones's death was obscene,' he was quoted as saying in *Jackie* of 30 May 1970. 'They seemed completely blind to the fact that he was a human being.'

the Stones were playing in Hyde Park on Saturday the 5th. (Alex Henderson and Nick Lewin went together and don't recall Nick being there.) In other news the Beatles were reportedly preparing two new albums at once, the Jimi Hendrix Experience were splitting and the Royal Albert Hall's week-long 'Pop Proms' – featuring Led Zeppelin, Fleetwood Mac, the Who, the Incredible String Band and others – were a sell-out. The release of a collection of subtle acoustic material by an obscure newcomer with no live profile went entirely unremarked, and Nick took no steps to stimulate interest in it.

'It was always a problem working out what to do with Nick,' says Tod Lloyd, who was partly responsible for publicising *Five Leaves Left*. 'He was really shy yet eager to succeed. There was a curious tension there.' Joe was baffled by his lack of engagement with the imperative for promotion: 'It's hard to imagine a situation today where an artist wouldn't ask any questions, or wouldn't have something to say, or would have no clear position regarding his career – but Nick really didn't. He was very clear about his music, but almost totally indifferent about everything else.'[4]

Part of the problem was that responsibility for his career was unclearly divided between Witchseason and Island, leaving space between them for Nick to be overlooked. In addition, Joe admits to a degree of complacency: 'Pink Floyd and the Incredible String Band had sold themselves, I'd quickly had people requesting interviews with them, and the same happened as soon as Sandy joined Fairport, so it didn't occur to me to put pressure on Island to promote Nick.'

Muff Winwood, whose roles at Island included handling radio and TV exposure, explains: 'We didn't handle print promotion in-house – decisions about interviews and so on would have been made by Witchseason without involving us. We had much more day-to-day involvement with our own acts.' It didn't help that there was no press officer at Witchseason. 'Witchseason didn't do much promo – that was Island's job,' says Joe, 'and even though Chris loved the record they didn't quite know what to do with it, and Nick wasn't exactly a sparkling interview for the press department.'

The task of concocting a press release fell to Island's Vivien Holgate, who tapped out three vague and inaccurate paragraphs to accompany review copies of the LP: 'After a conventional education Nick delayed his University entrance in favour of a round-the-world hitch-hiking trip, but only reached as far as Central Europe before having to return for health reasons. His songwriting, he says, benefited a lot from the trip – short though it was.'

Emphasising his enigmatic quality, she wrote that

> He lives 'somewhere in Cambridge', close to the University (where he is reading English) because he hates wasting time travelling, does not have a telephone – more for reasons of finance than any anti-social feelings – and tends to disappear for three or four days at a time when he is writing.

She concluded by declaring: 'His future plans are very open and undecided, definitely slanted to a musical career, but as he explains: "There is so much I want to learn before I finally decide what I want to do." Whatever musical field he favours, the talent of Nick Drake is undoubted.'

Chris Welch, an influential writer on *Melody Maker*, took heed.[*] As he recalls:

> I found a copy of *Five Leaves Left* among the weekly pile of new releases delivered to our office in Fleet Street. I was struck not only by the cover picture but by his sensitive songs, all delivered in an understated, highly personal style. Record companies and their PRs were begging us to cover their products on a daily basis but there was nothing much to explain who Nick Drake was, or why and how he'd made this intriguing album.

Beguiled, he called Anthea Joseph to set up an interview.

> She was normally friendly and communicative, but said curtly that she didn't want to arrange an interview with Nick – it wasn't appropriate at this stage in his career. Frankly, I was astonished – it was almost as if she were afraid of what I might say or how I might present him. I'm still sorry I never got to meet him and ask him a few polite, kind questions.

---

[*] Chris had been at the Caius May Ball to review John Mayall (*Melody Maker*, 21 June 1969), but didn't catch Nick's performance.

The truth was that Nick didn't want to give interviews, or indeed play live. Anthea was well aware of how unconventional an approach it was:

> He was incredibly lucky to fall into Witchseason's hands, and then Island's, where this sort of thing was indulged. I mean, any other record company that might have signed him at the time wouldn't have pursued him past the first album, and the fact that he wasn't going to do any gigs or interviews – nobody else would have tolerated it. It was a commercial waste of time.[5]

Nick played no confirmed gigs at all for well over two months after the release of *Five Leaves Left*.[*] This baffled his peers. 'You had to go out there and work hard at it, selling yourself at gigs, making a living,' says Bev.

> John was doing the university circuit, carting all his guitars and pedals around on trains, sleeping on people's floors. Nick always seemed reluctant to perform, even though no one ever considered the idea of making a record without promoting it, because it was understood that nobody would buy it (and even if there were any royalties, it took time for them to come through).

As John Wood put it: 'Once you commit yourself to making records, you commit yourself to appearing in public.'[6]

Nick, however, was taking it easy. His parents were visiting old friends in Sweden in July; he wrote to them on Tuesday the 22nd:

> This is really just a note to say that everything is in good shape here at Far Leys, where I am at the moment. I came up on Saturday. Robert Kirby also came up for a couple of nights, to try and put some musical ideas together, and went again this morning. Unfortunately, we didn't achieve anything, but the weather is fine here now and I think he enjoyed some pleasant relaxation.

---

[*] He does seem, however, to have appeared unbilled at Les Cousins, at least on one occasion. Bridget St John remembers encountering him there that summer. Stifled in the basement as they awaited their turns to play, they came up for air at the same time: 'Nick and I walked a little way up the street and sat silently side by side on the kerb outside a pub – both nervous, preoccupied, no need for words.'

This was Robert's only stay at Far Leys, and his impression was that Nick 'was quite happy to go home. He got on with his family.'[7] Neither Nick nor Robert mentioned the fact, but they were together at Far Leys for the moon landing on Sunday, 20 July, and presumably watched it that evening.

'I shall probably go back to London tomorrow,' Nick told his parents, before getting round to mentioning that 'The record seems to be doing all right. I have a good friend who runs a record shop in Bond St.* and is going to give me a big display in one of his windows, which is very useful, and I got one quite nice review.'

This was a reference to the earliest – and most perceptive – critique of *Five Leaves Left*, which had appeared in *International Times* on 18 July. 'Unfortunately, Drake's voice is going to be repeatedly compared to that of Donovan,' began Mark Williams. 'But Don would be nowhere without his songs, and Nick will get nowhere without his. They are beautiful, gentle breezes of cadent perfection, which carry along reflective poems like dancing, golden leaves.'

A rave in the country's most significant underground paper was a major validation for Nick, but few other reviews trickled out over the ensuing weeks. *Melody Maker* vaguely described the album as 'poetic' and 'interesting', *Top Pops* said it was 'attractive', 'poetic' and 'pleasant', and *Disc and Music Echo* felt 'his guitar work is soft, gentle and tuneful, his voice highly attractive, husky and bluesy', but called his songs 'uncertain and indirect'.† Other than these superficial remarks, it seemingly attracted no press attention at all over the summer.

Given Nick's low profile, it wasn't surprising. A dizzying number of albums were appearing almost every week, making it hard for reviewers to give those by obscure newcomers more than one cursory play. Around the time of *Five Leaves Left* debut albums also appeared by a slew of male singer-songwriters including Ian Anderson, John Bromley, Marc Brierley, Duncan Browne, Jimmy Campbell, Keith

---

* Harlequin Records, 119 New Bond Street, whose manager, Gordon, Nick knew through Sophia, who worked there.
† On 26 July, 9 August and 23 August, respectively.

Christmas, Mike Cooper, Gary Farr, Andy Fernbach, Tim Hollier, Gordon Jackson, Dave Kelly and Robin Scott. In that context, it's easier to understand why the originality and commercial potential of *Five Leaves Left* were overlooked.

Still, it seems perverse that Nick wasn't interviewed anywhere; his work was of obvious interest if only on account of being produced by Joe and coming out on Island, both considered to be marks of prestige. 'No one was pushing Nick hard enough,' admits David Betteridge, the label's sales manager.

> Joe had a production deal with us, so there was a barrier that wouldn't have existed if we'd been using our in-house A&R.* I don't mean that to knock Joe, I think he's fantastic, but he was a producer and not a marketeer. Nick needed a proper manager to fight his corner (though God knows who that would've been!). Then perhaps we would have gone out and done more. As it was, he got lost in the shuffle.

Muff Winwood:

> Joe's acts weren't as visible to us as the ones directly signed to Island. I never socialised with Nick, and I'm not sure that any of us did. I don't ever remember him coming to the office at the time that he was first involved with us. We all thought his music was fantastic, but it was just delivered to us. I was simply given the album and asked to do what I could [to promote it].

It was a time of extraordinary growth for Island, which both helped and hindered Nick's prospects. 'We were a small label that had effectively spent the whole of the sixties in apprenticeship and then within six to eight months we had all these acts suddenly breaking – Fairport, Free, Jethro Tull, King Crimson, etc.,' continues David. July also saw the release of the hugely anticipated album by Blind Faith, whom Chris Blackwell co-managed, while the indefatigable Jethro Tull's second album, *Stand Up*, was released three weeks after *Five Leaves Left* and quickly climbed to Number 1.

---

* In other words, if Nick had been directly signed to Island by the label's in-house Artists and Repertoire team.

Demand for it took the company by surprise and much of its effort went into satisfying it.

Island didn't expect a similar take-up for Nick, who had no reputation to build on. 'I don't recall any conversations about going big on him,' says David.

> We simply took him on and underwrote the sessions because of our agreement with Joe, and never anticipated big sales. It wasn't all about sales, though – Witchseason acts were important ingredients in our success even if they weren't huge sellers individually, as they helped the image of the company in general. We knew Nick was a great guitarist and a talented songwriter, but I must admit that we didn't recognise his genius at the time, and perhaps missed our opportunity to do more with him.

Tim Clark also stresses how enthusiastic they were about Nick: 'We were very conscious that he was a special artist. We were all really sold on his artistry and potential, and there was that sense of excitement in having an artist we all believed in.' Nonetheless, they didn't manufacture many copies of *Five Leaves Left*: 'I suspect we printed 3,000 sleeves and pressed an initial run of 1,500 discs. We would typically print more sleeves than records, then re-press very quickly (which we could) when we sold out or came close.'

Persuading even a few hundred people to buy the album was far from easy, though. The underground was a small and penurious sector of the market, with brutal competition for new releases. Barry Partlow was one of the Island reps responsible for getting it into shops, and found even that a struggle: 'There was very little reaction to *Five Leaves Left*, with just a few of the specialist shops taking a copy or two – and that was based on Island's reputation more than anything . . . If the London scene didn't propel Nick, then we were struggling in the sticks.'[8]

Another vital factor in record promotion was airplay, for which competition was fierce. Singles were an obvious route to the BBC's precious 'needle time' because programmes that played album tracks were fewer and more specialised. Just one spin from a mainstream DJ like Tony Blackburn or Terry Wogan could reach millions of listeners. It is therefore puzzling that no single was released to help establish Nick. He was in a tiny minority of Island album artists who had no single released in 1969,* though several of his songs – including those left off *Five Leaves Left* – could plausibly have attracted attention on that format.

'Meet on the Ledge' by Fairport was unconventional, after all, but had done much to enhance their reputation in hip circles, and their even more offbeat 'Si Tu Dois Partir' – an accordion-driven Bob Dylan cover, whimsically translated into French – had been released on 11 July and become an unlikely Number 21 hit, earning the band a spot on *Top of the Pops* and boosting *Unhalfbricking* to Number 12.

'I have to criticise us for what we didn't do – for example, not releasing a single,' says David, but Tim counters that 'Breaking an artist without a single was perfectly plausible, and some artists or managers actively requested that no single should be released.' Muff remembers that 'We often discussed 45s in the office but it would have been Witchseason's decision, not ours. I suspect Joe wanted Nick to be an album act, because his music was sophisticated and might not have come across on a single.' As Joe puts it:

> Those decisions were never made in a vacuum by either side, it was always a dialogue. If Island's promotion people had said to us, 'We think this will make a great single and we think it's a great idea to release it,' it would have happened straight away. But they never did. In hindsight, I think Island didn't release a single by Nick because he seemed clearly an 'album artist' and no one track jumped out as a potential chart hit.

For Chris Blackwell (who was touring America with Blind Faith when *Five Leaves Left* was released), 'Promoting Nick on the radio was a challenge because none of the songs on the album stood out as obvious for airplay, and in any case Island didn't have strong connections with presenters and producers on folk-type shows.'

---

* The only others were Dr. Strangely Strange, Tramline and White Noise. There is in fact an unused serial number in Island's catalogue (number WIP 6063) from exactly the time a single from Nick would logically have been issued, though there's no evidence that it was intended for him.

Nonetheless, the BBC was supplied with a copy of *Five Leaves Left* and Pete Ritzema (pronounced *rightzeemer*), a young producer on Radio 2's late-night arts programme *Night Ride*, diligently listened to it.

Impressed, he invited Nick to come to their Maida Vale Studio 5 to record some songs for the show on Tuesday, 5 August. It was quite a break – *Night Ride* went out every weeknight, with a remit to showcase esoteric music and culture, and had a large national audience. It had a rotating series of presenters; the episode Nick was on was to be hosted by John Peel. John and Nick didn't meet, though, as Nick pre-recorded 'Time Of No Reply','Cello Song', 'River Man' and 'Three Hours' in his absence, with Mike Harding engineering.*

'He was a gloomy fellow – very, very quiet,' according to Pete.[9]

> I remember being slightly disappointed because I thought he would come in and improvise, but he wasn't up for that. Rather than do free-flowing, spontaneous versions of the songs, he just did the arrangements as they were on the record. He was very concerned that he didn't have the strings [on 'River Man'] – he wanted to do it like the record, which is understandable, so he left gaps for the string arrangements, while he'd just strum away.

A surviving off-air recording confirms how faithful Nick was to the album versions – but what Pete didn't know was that Nick never deviated from the finished guitar parts of any of his songs.

Nick's session had a secondary purpose: musicians featured on BBC programmes had to be evaluated for future broadcasts, so it served as his audition. 'Attractive vocal quality somewhat reminiscent of Donovan,' was Pete's assessment. 'Quite professional behaviour on the session.' Most remarks from the eight-strong internal panel were positive ('at last something that holds one's interest from the start', 'excellent guitar work', 'pleasant voice', 'a quiet voice which none-theless rivets one's attention', 'good intonation and diction'), although

---

* Not to be confused with the Mike Harding who presented many folk programmes on the BBC. There is no evidence that John Peel championed Nick's work during Nick's lifetime.

some were less effusive ('good of its kind but of limited appeal', 'voice moody and rather down and a little bit uninspiring', 'not a general-appeal contribution'). The panel was headed by senior producer Jimmy Grant, who summarised: 'Material good and he plays well. Unanimous pass.'

The programme, which also featured the writer Iain Sinclair, was broadcast at five past midnight on 6 August.* One night owl who tuned in was a seventeen-year-old schoolboy named Nick Kent, who says: '"River Man" stopped me in my tracks – and when John Peel mentioned that Nick Drake was on Witchseason it made him stand out even more, because Fairport were my favourite band at the time.' There was kudos attached to appearing on a Peel broadcast, and surely certain people explored the album as a result, but it made no measurable difference to sales. At least Nick was paid, receiving the standard fee of 15 guineas.

He seems not to have undertaken any other promotional work whatsoever. For the most part he hung out with friends as if the album didn't exist. Gabrielle was moving out of Cyril Mansions and into de Wet's unconventionally decorated house and studio at 28 Campden Hill Gardens, Holland Park (which he called 'La Porte Grise Ouvrant'). As such, Nick's BBC paperwork was sent to 3 Aldridge Road Villas in Notting Hill, a downmarket address where several of his friends recall visiting him. Brian Wells says the flat was occupied by 'a skinny hippie girl who used to flutter around Nick. She was knitting a cushion cover and had a pet monkey that he complained shat everywhere.'† It's possible she was an acquaintance, or that he had taken a room in her flat via an advert; Paul Wheeler also visited but doesn't find it strange that he never knew her identity:

---

* Nick's contribution was re-broadcast on *Night Ride* of 25 September (alongside a session from the intense hard rock band High Tide). It was subsequently wiped, in accordance with BBC policy, though a partial off-air recording has since surfaced.
† Several other of Nick's friends recall the monkey. Alex Henderson says it was 'always up the curtains', and Robert remembered that 'as soon as the turntable would start spinning the monkey would jump on top of it. Then we would sit and watch it go round and round.'

Not knowing such things was part of the mystique of the time. Wandering around and knocking on people's doors was what we all did in Cambridge. In London we would drift from one flat to another and not think to ask who owned them. Part of the zeitgeist was to be on the move, or in a state of flux – where you lived, what you were doing, who you were with.

Alex Henderson had recently moved into his own place with Sophia:

I was lucky enough to be able to buy a one-bedroom flat at 12 Edith Terrace, off the Fulham Road, which became the unofficial head-quarters for our group. It was on the first floor, with a kitchen and living room painted green, and a small office space off it with wooden steps leading up to another little bed.

It was another crashpad for Nick, who Alex says 'lived there on and off, not paying any rent, just as a mate'.

Alex says he was a perfect guest.

He was good company and had other things going on, so it wasn't as if he was hanging around all the time. He didn't really have possessions, so there wasn't much for him to make a mess with, and we had a cleaning lady anyway. Above us was an Aussie called Bill Staughton, who owned a great restaurant in the Fulham Road called The Hungry Horse. Nick used to call it 'The Hungry Head' because we'd eat there when we were stoned. We'd wander up there, laughing away, and were always given a warm welcome. Nick was giggly in those days.

Nick also dropped in on David Ward in Pont Street, where they'd play their guitars together. Nick was working on new songs and on one occasion in the summer of 1969, recalls David, he let his guard down in an unusual way: he played him a new composition called 'Things Behind The Sun', cautioning that it wasn't finished.

One weekend he joined Alex and Sophia, Ben Laycock and David at the home of their friend Tom Poole in Gloucestershire. A photo taken there shows Nick in a lane, about to puff on something, a beatific smile on his face as Sophia wanders towards him. 'On the same day Alex happened to ask Nick what his father did and he said, "He makes electric fences,'" recalls Sophia. Electric fencing was indeed one of numerous products marketed by Wolseley-Hughes, but it is striking that his friends didn't already know – though they had come to realise how separate he kept the elements of his life.

Derek FitzGerald wasn't living in London, so he saw less of Nick, but they did catch up that summer:

> I was staying in Stratford so I phoned Nick, who happened to be at home. He drove out in his car to collect me and brought me back for dinner. His parents were absolutely charming and we had a lovely time, sitting outside on a beautiful evening. We all discussed what he should do next with his life, but in a friendly, conversational way, nothing serious.

Nick's resolve to leave Cambridge was in fact hardening, but he didn't discuss it with most of his friends. 'I was totally unaware of him thinking of leaving Cambridge,' says Sophia. 'He never mentioned it.'

His path ahead was unclear and Joe wasn't around to discuss it; he was spending August in America, where the Incredible String Band were touring (including a set at Woodstock on Saturday the 16th) and John and Bev Martyn were making an album together, against his better judgement. 'Joe and John never really got on,' remembers Bev. 'They were just too competitive, as John would just try and take over any situation he was in.'[10] Having rehearsed their songs in Woodstock – where Bob Dylan took a shine to Bev during a random encounter, causing John to assault her for the first time[11] – they recorded them in New York, with Paul Harris acting as musical director and John Wood present and correct at the controls.

Dylan, meanwhile, travelled to the UK to play at the Isle of Wight Festival on the final weekend of the month. Billed as 'the biggest show of the century', it was his first major public performance in over three years and attracted around 150,000 fans. Among them were Nick, Robert Abel Smith, David and Sarah, Ben and Rose, and Alex and Sophia, who all took the car ferry together. Also in their party was Alex's mother. 'She enjoyed the company of the younger generation,' he explains. 'She was rather eccentric and brought some grouse down from Scotland, which she cooked for us.'

Her contribution went beyond being (and providing) game: she'd had the foresight to book three caravans away from the main site, so their party had somewhere to sleep without having to pitch tents amidst hordes of others. According to David, 'Sarah and I shared a caravan with Nick, but we didn't move around as one big group all weekend – we'd go off and do our own things.'

A mind-bending array of acts was on offer, including some of Nick's favourites (The Band and Family) and some of his labelmates (Free and Blodwyn Pig). He cheerfully wandered the site with his friends, marvelling at its scale, smoking dope and absorbing the vibes. In the evenings they gathered at their base, where Sophia remembers him playing guitar by the campfire.

Of course, the weekend was building up to the main event on Sunday, 31 August. 'Our whole reason for going was to see Dylan, but he was terribly disappointing, at the end of a long day,' sighs Sophia.[12] 'He came on after Richie Havens, who was wonderful.' The next day Nick returned to Far Leys to wash and catch up on sleep. Gabrielle happened to be there too, and was taken aback by his demeanour: 'Nick came home elated and declared that now, finally, the world would change and peace would prevail. It was one of the few political statements he ever made.'[13]

When Joe got back to London, Nick met him to discuss his future. He was disheartened that *Five Leaves Left* wasn't selling better, not least because so many had believed it would. Joe felt it too: 'I was crushed when it didn't sell but, unlike Nick, I had lots of other projects to keep me busy.' Nick's prospects of a breakthrough weren't helped by the fact that not a single foreign territory had picked it up.

'There would sometimes be an intermediate stage of exporting albums, and if that went well a local pressing would follow,' explains Joe.* 'North America was an important source of income for Island,

---

* Copies were exported to Scandinavia. 'This is a boring album,' wrote Mats Olsson in the Swedish newspaper *Arbetet* on 9 September 1969. 'It's suitable for a candlelit room on a dark autumn evening when the TV is broken and you aren't able to listen to Blodwyn Pig.'

and Chris would negotiate separate deals for different acts. I was back and forth to America the whole time and I did what I could to get *Five Leaves Left* released over there . . .'

Island's Tim Clark explains that 'The licensees called the shots, so the fact that *Five Leaves Left* didn't come out in any other territories was because none of them regarded Nick as a sufficiently commercial proposition.' David Betteridge puts it even more starkly: 'There was no buzz about Nick. Our licensees piggybacked on us and wouldn't have wanted an act that we hadn't been able to break at home.'

Joe didn't encourage him to drop out of Cambridge, but he did want to get on with making another album, irrespective of the response to *Five Leaves Left*: 'At that time I think I can genuinely say that I wasn't over-concerning myself with thinking about how much the records were going to sell, or practical considerations. It was more of an excitement about the music.'[14] The slow gestation of *Five Leaves Left* was not a luxury Nick could have twice, though. He would need to focus hard on songwriting in the coming months.

In order to do so efficiently, he explained, he needed a London base of his own, somewhere he could create in peace whether or not he left Cambridge. Joe agreed that he should find somewhere suitable, and undertook to cover its rent and his basic living expenses. His only stipulation was that it should have a phone: Witchseason needed to get hold of Nick more easily. As Joe remembers, 'I started paying him a weekly cash advance of fifteen pounds – everything was in cash at Witchseason! – against publishing royalties. That was viewed then as pretty generous and risky.' (£15 in 1969 is around £200 in 2022.)

He remained convinced, however, that Nick's songs would provide rich pickings for other artists: 'I was bullish about all the covers he was going to get. For example, when I heard Roberta Flack's first album [*First Take* (released in June 1969)] I immediately thought "Time Has Told Me" would be perfect for her, and sent an acetate of it to Atlantic.' She did not oblige, alas.

With Joe's backing, Nick set about finding a suitable place. Following the premature end to his Cambridge career, Robert was renting a flat with Marcus Bicknell at 136 Cranley Gardens in Muswell

Hill, North London. Nick could have joined them, says Marcus, but he didn't want flatmates. Instead, through an agency named Hampstead Homefinders, he took a room elsewhere in North London. 'Danehurst' was a large, turreted Victorian Gothic corner house at 112 Haverstock Hill, at the junction of Parkhill Road and England's Lane, where Hampstead runs downhill into Camden Town. At the turn of the century it had been the London home of the High Sheriff of Middlesex, but it had gone down in the world and was now divided into accommodation for sixteen people.

Danehurst, the Victorian Gothic house in Haverstock Hill
in which Nick lived from September 1969.

Located at the back of the ground floor, to the right of the stairs, Room 7 was bigger than a bedsit but not exactly a flat; the agency carefully described it as a 'flatlet'. It didn't have its own bathroom but did have a kitchenette facing the door, as well as a bay window overlooking the unkempt garden and a door down into it. It didn't

258

have its own telephone extension either, but there was a communal phone – number: 722 3145 – in the hallway, just outside his door. He did little to make it homely; Gabrielle recalls his familiar Indian prints and Bernard Buffet print of a cockerel being the only decorations, and his bed in the corner almost the only furniture.

Despite the house's large number of occupants, there was no sense of community; these were transient times. The anonymity suited Nick, who was perhaps mindful of the Romantic notion of the artist in his garret. Part of its appeal was probably that it was unlikely to become any sort of social hub; in Chelsea he would have been much more vulnerable to unplanned visits from his friends. This didn't necessarily reflect an anti-social tendency, more the seriousness with which he intended to work.

John and Bev lived a mile up the hill, hardly near enough to have influenced Nick's choice. 'I don't think being near to John and Bev would have been a deciding factor,' Paul Wheeler says. 'They were always pleased to see him, he was a welcome presence, but I didn't get any sense of there being a special relationship between the three of them.' If anything, it was more likely that he chose Danehurst for its relative proximity to Robert, with whom he intended to continue collaborating.

Although the arrangement laid bare his ambivalence about his degree, Nick didn't keep it secret from his family. 'It's impressive that Nick should have his flat rent paid by Witchseason,' de Wet wrote to Gabrielle from the South of France in September.* 'I hope that this doesn't stop him going back to Cambridge, though. With the character he's got, Cambridge could one day furnish him with a retreat and – who knows? – a shelter from a world he may feel a growing isolation from as he grows older.'

---

* In the same letter de Wet referred to following up on Nick's interest in meeting his friend Christopher Logue, whose 1959 poetry and jazz EP *Red Bird* had been a favourite at Marlborough, but Gabrielle doesn't recall a meeting taking place.

PART THREE

16

No Backward Glances

~

AFTER CAREFUL CONTEMPLATION Fairport had decided to regroup and carry on, so Huw Price of Witchseason organised the revamped band's first major concert, a hugely anticipated evening at the 2,500-seat Royal Festival Hall on London's South Bank on Wednesday, 24 September 1969. 'The post-accident Fairport had a limited repertoire, so we needed to fill the first half,' says Joe. John and Bev agreed to open, and Joe took the opportunity to kick-start Nick's live career by adding him to the bill too.

He had no safety in numbers: the logistics were unrealistic for him to play with backing musicians, so he would face the audience alone. 'People weren't certain if he was going to turn up,' according to Keith Morris,[1] while Anthea Joseph recalled that when he did appear he was 'sick with fright. He was shaking all over.'[2] As the audience members filed in, Joe was gratified to see how conscious they were of the event's emotional charge. 'There was a hushed atmosphere in the Hall. Everyone sat still until the main act came on, whereas usually there'd be people coming and going, buying drinks, talking and so on. I put John and Bev on to open, then Nick, as he clearly couldn't open a show.'

The supportive ambience on both sides of the curtain was ideal for Nick as he quivered backstage, first listening to John and Bev and then to Joe – resplendent in his favourite red boots – introducing him. He came on to warm applause in his familiar jacket, shirt and jeans, holding his guitar. Wisely, his parents hadn't told him they would be there. 'We dared not show ourselves because we were afraid it would absolutely throw him,' recalled Molly. 'We crept in – we were at least thirty or forty years older than practically all the rest of the audience. One almost wanted to leap up and say, "That's my son!" But we were quiet as a mouse.'[3]

Watching from the wings, Joe was almost as nervous as Nick. He knew that breaking him would be much easier if he could carry off live performances, but had never seen him give one. To his great relief, 'He was magnificent. He didn't say a word to the audience, he tuned his guitar and he just played, and he was absolutely mesmerising.' According to audience member Steve Burgess, 'Nick sang his songs with a pervasive, frightened melancholy, staring intently at the boards, too introspective to say one word to the sympathetic audience.'[4] Victoria Ormsby-Gore remembers that his nerves seemed to evaporate as he went on: 'When he played he seemed lost in another world and sounded wonderful.'

Iain Cameron says, 'He played well up to standard – I remember "Things Behind The Sun" going down especially well.' Of that song, Joe says, 'I was astonished, as I hadn't heard it before and thought it was brilliant.' He remembers Nick playing 'The Thoughts Of Mary Jane' and 'Three Hours', and it seems likely that his thirty-minute set also included 'Time Has Told Me', 'River Man', 'Fruit Tree' and "Cello Song'.

'As each song was rewarded with huge applause, I could feel the affection surging towards the stage,' says Joe.[5] Ben Laycock also thought he played beautifully, but was 'disappointed that he didn't say a thing'. Robert Kirby had the same memory: 'He had one guitar and had to retune after each number, and he didn't tell jokes, [which was] the way you got by when you retuned in the folk clubs.'[6]

Nonetheless, Gabrielle was struck by her brother's effortless presence:

> I've read all these reports about how Nick shambled onstage at the Festival Hall. I was there, I'm a performer, I know something about it. It's true he didn't do the pre-chat. He just came and sat on a stool and played – and he electrified the audience . . . He was a charismatic figure, there were no two ways about that.[7]

His proud mother drank in the response: 'You could see all round, all the faces, everything – nobody coughed, they really were quite spellbound.'[8]

'I hadn't heard Nick before, so I don't know that much about his history,' Lon Goddard admitted in his thoughtful *Record Mirror* review of the concert, calling him 'an accomplished guitarist with extreme dexterity and a rather breathy voice':

> His picking was complicated yet clear and concise, while the original material was built mainly on his own self-constructed chord sequences. The unique thing about the overall aspect was that his songs didn't drift into patterned and predictable attempts at atmosphere by endless descending minor chords; the union of his perfect rhythmic picking and the odd choice of notes on the vocal scale gained a near-classical effect. Best of the set were 'The Thoughts Of Mary Jane' and 'Things Behind The Sun'.[9]

The moment Nick finished 'Things Behind The Sun' he slipped offstage, leaving applause and calls for an encore ringing around the auditorium. 'I was there with a few people who knew him and we all stood up and clapped madly,' says Keith Morris.[10] 'He did very well, all by himself,' was Rodney's verdict. 'He got a lot of applause, and he just got off the stool, waved his guitar to everybody and wandered off. And they couldn't get him back again.'[11] Molly summarised the whole performance as 'Nick just came on, played, got up and went out. There was no showmanship of any sort at all.'[12] Afterwards, she recalled, he said 'it was the most terrifying thing and the most thrilling thing he'd ever done'.[13]

Joe was jubilant: 'All the Witchseason people were backstage in the interval and Huw came up to me and said, "I'm going to book Nick a tour! He can make this work!" I got carried away, I thought, "Great, let's book him around the world!"'[14] Lon Goddard concluded his review by stating, 'Nick is at present studying at Cambridge, but I think public demand will put an end to that shortly and set him off with a heavy performing schedule.'[15] That night it seemed entirely plausible.

Eager to maintain momentum, Witchseason booked Nick's next gig for the Friday of the following week, 3 October. It took place in the Upper Room Folk Club, held above a mock-Tudor pub in North Harrow named the Goodwill to All. The other featured act was Folkomnibus, a pair of callow local schoolboys named Bruce

Fursman and Andy Whetstone, who sang songs by Donovan, the Incredible String Band, and Simon and Garfunkel.

According to Bruce, 'There was no stage as such – a narrow central aisle ran between the chairs up to a darkened space at the top end of the room, near the bay windows that overlooked the street.' The audience slowly drifted in with drinks from the bar downstairs; Bruce says there were around thirty people, who struck him as 'grown-up and of another generation'.

As Folkomnibus stood playing in matching pink shirts, Bruce saw Nick standing 'at the very back of the small room, where it was at its darkest', but didn't know who he was. As they finished and carried their instruments down the aisle they noticed him 'with his hands raised in front of his chest, clapping purposefully and enthusiastically':

> When we got to the back he remarked, 'You've played all my songs!' with a gently teasing smile. He was very tall and had a strong phys-ical presence. The energy around him felt positive and benevolent. We felt he was relaxed before his performance, unlike us.
>
> We didn't exchange many words. He looked with fascination at my ten-shilling mandolin and held it like a newborn baby in his long fingers, slowly turning it and admiring the fine woodwork! He gently strummed the eight strings and fingered the fretboard. Meanwhile the compère announced that they were honoured and delighted to have Nick Drake with them, and mentioned Fairport Convention and John and Beverley Martyn. Andy and I were impressed to hear him talked about in the same breath as Fairport.

As the audience applauded, Nick made his way forward and sat on the chair provided. 'The nearest punter was probably less than a metre or so away, which might have been unnerving for someone as shy and private as Nick,' continues Bruce. 'Except for his mesmerising voice and beautiful music, and the few cars that passed outside, there was a reverential silence in that little attic room. He hunched low over his guitar, his hair covering his eyes, maybe acting as a shield between him and the silently watching audience.' As at Cambridge, Nick had no difficulty in performing for atten-tive audiences.

A couple of reviews of *Five Leaves Left* belatedly appeared in the aftermath of the Royal Festival Hall show. The huge-selling *New Musical Express* covered it in its 4 October issue. 'I'm sorry I can't be more enthusiastic, because he obviously has a not inconsiderable amount of talent, but there is not nearly enough variety on this debut LP to make it entertaining,' carped Gordon Coxhill. 'His voice reminds me very much of Peter Sarstedt, but his songs lack Sarstedt's penetration and arresting quality. Exceptions are "Mary Jane" [*sic*], a fragile little love song, and "Saturday Sun", a reflective number on which the singer also plays a very attractive piano.'*

Its final contemporary review came the following week in the *Daily Telegraph* – seemingly the only non-music newspaper, national or local, to have covered it. Maurice Rosenbaum wrote that Nick had made 'an excellent LP of his own songs',

> on which his own slightly hypnotic guitar is backed by Richard Thompson, Danny Thompson, and Paul Harris. His voice is slow, reflective and warm, and although the verse structure tends to melodic monotony, there is no mistaking the quality and the promise of 'River Man', 'The Thoughts Of Mary Jane', 'Man In A Shed' and other items on this disc.[16]

At much the same time Island issued *Nice Enough to Eat*, a budget-priced sampler LP that included 'Time Has Told Me' – a last-minute substitution for 'River Man' (perhaps because Nick opened his performances with it). It was somewhat lost between Traffic's 'Forty Thousand Headmen' and King Crimson's '21st Century Schizoid Man', but the album was a huge seller, sitting in the top twenty for weeks on end, and was where most people first heard of Nick at the time.

Five Leaves Left wasn't a hit but Nick had cause for optimism as the autumn progressed. His name was spreading and Joe was eager

---

* Sarstedt's self-titled debut album had come out in February and reached Number 8 in the UK, fuelled by the kitsch Number 1 hit 'Where Do You Go To (My Lovely)?' Nick is unlikely to have taken the criticism to heart; the previous issue of the same paper had stated that *Astral Weeks*, one of his favourite albums, featured Van Morrison 'sounding for all the world like Jose Feliciano's stand-in'.

to forge ahead with live bookings and more recordings. He had to make his mind up about Cambridge, though. Combining his creative process with academic obligations had, perforce, been the model for *Five Leaves Left*, but it was not one he wanted to repeat, especially with an increased academic load. In theory Danehurst was a pied-à-terre while he completed his degree, but once he'd moved in, the notion of returning to Cambridge was less appealing than ever.

Term began on Tuesday, 7 October. Nick had not exerted himself to find digs, and to his dismay the room he'd been allocated, at 239 Hills Road, was two miles from the city centre and three miles from Fitzwilliam (albeit close to the railway station). Adding to his sense of estrangement, his social circle was much reduced. He quickly reconnected with Brian Wells, who had spent the long vacation working on an oil rig and only just picked up *Five Leaves Left*: 'I first saw it in a shop in Cambridge and remember noticing that the title wasn't *Saturday Sun* anymore.'

The Caius gang had dispersed but Pete Russell was doing postgraduate studies (supervised by Stephen Hawking), so Nick and Brian spent the evening in his room. The term ahead weighed heavily on Nick. 'He didn't fit easily into the university scene and wasn't suited to it,' says Pete. 'He clearly had musical talent and his love lay in that direction, not in his studies.' The mood wasn't gloomy, though. 'We listened to *Abbey Road* together for the first time,' says Brian. 'We really got into the medley and laughed at "Her Majesty" at the end.'

Nick was less jolly as he made the trek back to his new digs. Had Fitzwilliam been able to provide more congenial accommodation, he might have seen the year through. As it was, he decided he couldn't face it. The next day he went into college and informed Ray Kelly that he had resolved to drop out (or 'withdraw', as the University preferred it). He summarised his reasoning in an interview a few months later: 'I had never been entirely satisfied with the place. I felt I could be doing something much more worthwhile elsewhere. All the time, I was more or less involved in the London music business; I knew that was where I wanted to be.'[17] As his mother later put it, 'I think he felt, having brought out *Five Leaves Left*, that if he went slogging on at Cambridge for another nine months he would just miss the peak, miss his chance, miss his foot-hold in the world.'[18]

Nick agreed to meet Dr Kelly in Fitzwilliam to discuss the situation on the morning of Monday, 13 October. He then rang Far Leys to tell his parents, making it clear that he neither expected nor wanted further financial support from them. It wasn't an easy conversation, and the following afternoon his father wrote him a letter that typified his restraint and common sense yet carried a weight of feeling. 'Of course, we were both terribly disappointed to hear of the decision you have reached, but we have said all there is to say on our side and no doubt you have weighed up all the pros and cons very carefully,' he began.

He then restated his own position one last time:

> Well, Nick, it does seem an awful pity and I still feel that you may live to regret it bitterly, and it is my duty to say that to you. To us, of course, it seems a tragedy now – to you perhaps it will do so one day. I think it probably could. Have one more think about it . . .
> In your own interests I feel I must make this final appeal to you.

His affectionate sign-off made it clear that there was no anger or coercion underpinning his words: 'Whatever happens, we are so hoping you will be able to come to see us soon and the sooner the better. (And whatever you've decided we shan't have a go at you.) Very much love from us both, Dad'.

Rodney was not so much preoccupied by the value of a lowly degree, or the inference possible employers might draw from Nick's abandoning the course, as by the harm dropping out might do to Nick's personal development and the self-reproach he might feel in years to come. As Nick did not lightly disregard his parents' advice or good opinion, he resolved to request a year off when he met Dr Kelly, rather than abandoning Cambridge altogether.

In the interim he caught up with Paul Wheeler, who hadn't seen him since June, having been busy putting on a play at the Edinburgh Festival. Paul was not shocked by Nick's desire to leave: 'I don't remember him being anguished about the decision. If anything, he probably saw it as a fuck-you to the establishment – but I'm sure he communicated a different version to his parents.'

They went to see the controversial *Easy Rider*, which had just come out in the UK and implied the death of the sixties dream.

> Nick was shocked by its ending, which we hadn't seen coming. He was still sitting after everyone else had left the cinema and was still shaking his head when he finally stood up. It sticks in my mind because it was unusual for him to show such a strong reaction to something.

Wanting to see the film, however, was consistent with an aspect of Nick's personality that Paul had already observed:

> He was very conscious of what was happening – he'd know if there was some new fashion in clothes or in music or in the arts or the cinema and stuff like that – 'Have you seen this? Have you heard that? Have you heard what so-and-so's doing?' – and he would often be ahead of the game. So for all his detachment and dreaminess he was actually on the ball a lot of the time.[19]

As if to validate Nick's choice to drop out, Witchseason had arranged for him to appear at another major Fairport concert, at Croydon's Fairfield Halls on Friday, 10 October, just after the start of term. Joe's Harvard room-mate Tom Rush had been scheduled to fill the first half of the bill, but Nick and Bridget St John – whose sparse, melancholy debut album had appeared on John Peel's Dandelion label in August – were substituted at short notice. It had been a beautifully sunny day and another capacity audience – of 1,800 – gathered.

The complex's cavernous main auditorium was a very different proposition to the claustrophobic Cousins, where Nick and Bridget had previously met. She remembers 'a dressing room for each of us . . . a huge stage with enough room for choirs and orchestras, Fairport's audience masked by myriad stage lights'.[20] She and Nick went on one after the other, each marooned on the huge stage. Bridget watched him from the wings, and recalls 'hair mostly obscuring his face, his body curved over his guitar, eyes closed for the most part – a body immersed in the performance of his work. And I felt that, like me, he was uncomfortable in-between songs, not knowing what – if anything – to say: awkwardness created by the expectation of filling silence.' Nonetheless, she says, 'Both of us felt good about our performances.'

For Sandra Grant of the *Croydon Advertiser*, Nick and Bridget

> were too similar in outlook, and thus each robbed the other of impact. Both sang sad, personal songs in rather deep, hushed voices, interspersed with the slightly amateur incoherencies one associates with this sort of performer. But both are pleasing enough artists, with above-average skills at the guitar and composition. Drake, a Cambridge undergraduate, wore youthful cords, an open-neck shirt and jacket, and a rather anxious expression.[21]

An unnamed scout for *Record Retailer* simply stated that 'Drake sounded pleasant but unmemorable',[22] a comment that bluntly encapsulated the challenge he faced in putting across his complex songs and taciturn persona to large audiences.

Far from offering words of support to the newcomers, the *éminence grise* of British folk reviewers, Karl Dallas of *Melody Maker*, was dismissive, even denying them their own identities: 'There's only one question in my mind after having heard the Fairport Convention's superlatively excellent performance at the Fairfield Halls last Friday,' he wrote. 'Why the hell did the organisers make us sit through almost an hour of sheer tedium before the interval, instead of letting Fairport have the whole show to themselves?'[23]

'At the time his words were devastating,' recalls Bridget – but assimilating criticism or unappreciative crowds was a vital attribute for a travelling performer. Thus far Nick had played to sympathetic audiences in Cambridge, supportive gatherings in a couple of London folk clubs and a rapt Royal Festival Hall. The reaction in Croydon gave him a taste of the indifference most audiences showed support acts. To win them over you needed more than good songs; you had to project, to engage, to put on a show. As well as being a singer, John Martyn was practically a stand-up comic, and Sandra Grant's review of Fairport in Croydon praised Sandy Denny's 'chatty introductions between numbers'.

Back in Cambridge on Monday, Nick put his proposal for a sabbatical to Dr Kelly. As he had probably anticipated and even hoped, the answer was a flat 'no'. Dr Kelly subsequently wrote to Rodney stating:

> I explained to him that, whilst the University could allow this sort of thing for either academical or health reasons, neither the University nor the college would be able to consider leave of absence on the grounds which Nick was suggesting – i.e. to follow up professionally his interest in folk music . . . The decision to withdraw had to be definite and final – there could be no going back on it.[24]

After their meeting Nick returned to Hills Road and wrote to Dr Kelly straight away:

> Contrary to all good advice, I have decided that it would be best for me to leave Cambridge at this stage and devote myself to my musical activities. I don't feel that I would be able to devote enough time to my Cambridge life to make another year here worthwhile. I'm very sorry to be doing this at such short notice, and I hope it won't cause problems. I would be very grateful if you could let me know of any complications concerning college fees etc. Thank you for taking an interest in my case this morning, and I appreciate that the grounds I presented would not be sufficient in the eyes of the authorities to warrant a year off.
> Yours,
> Nick Drake[25]

Fitzwilliam gave him a final opportunity to change his mind by the end of the week. Nick, however, was resolute, so Dr Kelly reluctantly wrote to him once more on 21 October, formally acknowledging his withdrawal and concluding: 'You know that I do not agree with your decision but I should like to reiterate my good wishes for the future.' He then notified the Warwickshire education authorities and returned their £50 grant cheque for the year ahead.

Convinced that Nick was making a grave error, Rodney made a final appeal to Dr Kelly:

> I am well aware that you thought this a bad mistake, and of course I did too, but there seemed no way of altering his views, and it

21 October, 1969

    I write now to acknowledge formally your letter of 13 October informing me that you have decided to withdraw from College in order to devote yourself to your musical activities. You know that I do not agree with your decision but I should like to reiterate my good wishes for the future. I will write further about College fees as soon as I am in a position to do so.

                Yours sincerely,

                R. Kelly
                Tutor

N. R. Drake, Esq.,
Far Leys,
Tanworth in Arden,
Warwickshire.

Fitzwilliam's formal acceptance of Nick's 'withdrawal'
from Cambridge University.

became clear long ago that the usual last resort of a parent in such circumstances – the withdrawal of financial support – would have no effect, and in fact Nick himself has insisted that he must go it alone from now on. Of course, there is no doubt that his music is everything to him and I am sure it will continue to be in one form or another. The argument that a degree would be a safety net did not appeal to him.

I know that he was greatly torn in reaching his decision – much more so than he appeared – and I have a feeling that he will soon be greatly regretting it, if he is not already doing so. If only his success at the Festival Hall had not come when it did, or if he could have put off the decision for a month, I think we might have turned him back . . . I suppose there is no question of his place still being vacant anyway for the rest of this year, and for him to be able to take it up again next term, if we can persuade him? Do forgive me for asking this.[26]

Dr Kelly's reply was courteous but unequivocal: quite apart from not meeting the University's residency requirements, by missing the term's work Nick would face an 'impossible handicap' for the second part of the Tripos in May 1970. The only comfort he could offer Rodney and Molly was to repeat that he had

urged him, once he had taken his decision, whichever way it went, to give himself wholeheartedly and without any backward glances to the course of action he had chosen. He told me that he realised the importance of doing this and I think now that he has made his choice he will have the determination to work and plan for the future on the basis I indicated.[27]

Nick's departure did not surprise his fellow English undergraduates at Fitzwilliam. 'None of us thought the choice was strange, because his genius was obvious from *Five Leaves Left*, which became part of the theme music for the year ahead,' says John Venning.

Cambridge certainly hadn't been a total waste of time. Nick had had the remarkable good luck to meet Robert Kirby and had forged other important friendships – principally with Paul Wheeler and Brian Wells – and the city itself appears to have informed his songs and creative sensibility. He had been able to spend a large amount of time in inspiring surroundings, listening to music and refining his songwriting with minimal outside pressure, and the University had given his life an overarching structure that had assisted the creation of *Five Leaves Left*.

Having himself left prematurely, Robert didn't question Nick's decision for a moment:

> Nick had an ambitious streak, he knew what he wanted. He wanted success as a singer-songwriter-performer, and he was convinced that he had the talent to do it. He *did* have! And he worked very hard . . . He lived totally and solely for his music – his guitar playing, his lyrics – that was his sole *raison d'être*. While we were at university we'd go to pubs or go punting and have a bit of a laugh, but it always very quickly got back to the music. I don't think there was ever really a lot of doubt that Nick would leave and pursue the career, because really he *had* to. He realised he had to maintain the impetus of *Five Leaves Left* and get another album out as quickly as he could – and a better album.[28]

17

Two Different Worlds Coming Together

———

A S OF MID-OCTOBER 1969 Nick was based in London, a full-time singer-songwriter with complete responsibility for his own upkeep and welfare, outside the accustomed framework of family, school or university. The prospect didn't intimidate, him, though: as Paul Wheeler puts it, 'The whole point of the way of life Nick chose after Cambridge was that it had no structure.'

His focus was on coming up with new material and he approached the task single-mindedly, as if to vindicate the course he had taken. His social life was a low priority, for better and for worse; as Joe Boyd puts it, 'From a social point of view he went from being surrounded by people his age, people who cared about him, to living alone in a bedsit in Hampstead.'[1] For his mother, 'He was gregarious, almost, and then he suddenly said, "This is no good" and went off to Hampstead. He decided to cut off from all his friends, and that he was just going to concentrate on music.'[2] As Rodney put it, 'He shut himself off in this room and it was rather difficult to get at him.'[3]

Mindful of Nick's unfinished education and tendency to intro-spection, his father took to sending him articles from *The Times*, the *Listener* and other sources, hoping to discuss them when they met. As he added in one covering note, 'You never read the papers!'[4] Whether or not Nick appreciated the gesture, he kept the cuttings. His parents encouraged him to visit Far Leys as often as he liked, but he rarely did so, seeking to stand on his own feet as much as possible. His cousin Grania suggests that

> The music milieu was very different to his family background, and
> perhaps he found it difficult to reconcile the two. He came to a

drinks party in my flat in Kensington but didn't fit in. I should never have asked him – my friends weren't remotely like the people he was used to.

He did not prioritise building a live profile. It is revealing that one of London's most popular underground music venues, the Country Club, was just up the road from Danehurst (at 210a Haverstock Hill), and though such singer-songwriters as Bridget St John, Roy Harper, Gary Farr, Shelagh McDonald, Cat Stevens and Elton John all played there during his residence, Nick never did.

He was, instead, fixated on his next album, which he knew from the start he wanted to have more coherence than *Five Leaves Left*. 'Nick talked a great deal about concept albums, which were [coming] out at the time, and wanting to use instrumental overtures and links between tracks,' said Robert.[5] Nick specifically referred to the Beach Boys' *Pet Sounds* and the 5th Dimension's *The Magic Garden* in this regard, and the DJ Jeff Dexter recalls him admiring Neil Young's solo debut, both sides of which open with instrumentals.

He already had a few pieces worked out – he and Robert had devised the beautiful instrumental that would ultimately be titled 'Introduction' at Cambridge that summer, and friends remember him playing 'One Of These Things First' and 'Hazey Jane I' at the same time. Over the latter part of 1969 he added to them 'Hazey Jane II', 'At The Chime Of A City Clock', 'Poor Boy', 'Fly' and 'Northern Sky', as well as the instrumentals 'Bryter Layter' and 'Sunday', which joined 'Introduction' to form a vital part of his conception of the album. He was unwilling to discuss the material's genesis, though. 'I couldn't tell you what my songs are about,' he remarked the following spring. 'It's a very private feeling, writing songs – often so private that I wouldn't want to tell anyone how I came to write the song.'[6]

He had written much of *Five Leaves Left* without a thought to arrangements, but approached the new album differently. 'I had something in mind when I wrote the songs, knowing that they weren't just for me,' he later explained in a rare interview, referring to the wider instrumental backing that was part of their conception.[7] To help with the process, he had an upright piano in his room at Danehurst, mimicking the set-up in Robert's room in Caius.*

Robert had found a job selling instruments and accessories at the London Music Shop in Great Portland Street, where his affability and musical knowledge were valued assets. He was also hustling for work as an arranger, with *Five Leaves Left* his main calling card. Apart from ad jingles, his first commissions were on *Zero She Flies* by Al Stewart (produced by Joe's good friend Roy Guest) and *Just Another Diamond Day* by Vashti Bunyan (produced by Joe himself). Nick's new material remained his top priority, though, and they spent a good deal of time working on it together.

He would often visit Danehurst and remembered 'bare floorboards, a record player, a few books, a guitar, a single bed, posters on the wall. He got more minimalist as time went on.'[8] Nonetheless, he recalled the gestation of Nick's second album as a 'very happy period, a very up period . . . As far as Nick was concerned, it was, I think, the happiest time I remember – having a laugh, a good social time.'[9]

Their new arrangements were not being written with a view to live performance, so there was no restriction to their scope. 'We were certainly listening to *Astral Weeks* heavily at that time – the string bass playing, the violinist,' says Robert. 'It's funny, that's got a track about walking around Ladbroke Grove ["Slim Slow Slider"], and Nick's got "At The Chime Of A City Clock". There are similarities.' Robert probably had in mind the possible reference to Hampstead Heath in the line: 'Travel to a local plain / Turn around and come back again.'

Their collaboration remained harmonious, even if they had the occasional difference about how best to serve each song. 'We had disagreements about things, but there was never any aggravation,' as Robert puts it. He recalled them listening to Atlantic and Stax records while they worked on 'Hazey Jane II', and described 'Sunday' as 'a driving song':

---

* No home recordings appear to exist of 'Hazey Jane II' or 'At The Chime Of A City Clock', so it is not known how they sounded when he played them alone.

You're meant to listen to it while you're driving. Nick and I had this great thing where we used to drive around on Sunday. There's one section towards the end of the instrumental, a low-string chord, which is meant to be when you drive on a motorway on a nice day with the window open and a lorry passes you.[10]

On one occasion Brian Wells was visiting from Cambridge when Robert arrived. They all smoked a joint, but he underestimated how intent Nick was on the task at hand:

Robert and I were a little stoned and chatty, yacking about whatever, and Nick got a bit irritated with us and snapped, 'Can we do some music now?' He was irritated that I was there, that he didn't have Robert's full attention. I felt a bit awkward that I'd sort of intruded on what was meant to be a 'professional' situation.[11]

Sometimes Nick would go to Cranley Gardens. 'He would often come by, work with Robert, play some music, smoke hash and crash for the night,' says Marcus Bicknell.

If they were working and I was at home, I would be welcome to watch and listen. I'd pop my head around the door and be beckoned in. Robert would have come up with three or four ideas for a song, then he'd play them through on the piano when Nick came, and they'd discuss them and choose what worked best. Their collaboration was equal – it wasn't a case of Nick telling Robert what he wanted.

As Robert put it, 'It was just the same procedure [as at Cambridge], he would come round and say, "I think I want some strings on 'Chime Of A City Clock', and 'Poor Boy' brass . . ."' Robert sometimes made informal recordings of Nick in Cranley Gardens: a couple of surviving renditions of 'Northern Sky' taped there (and kept by Robert) indicate that Nick originally intended it to have a prolonged instrumental opening, perhaps with an arrangement created with Robert.

Marcus found Nick easy to interact with as the album gestated.

He seemed cheerful enough when he came over, and never ill-at-ease. There was usually a joint on the go, but never anything stronger when I was around. I can remember him tucking into bread and jam in the kitchen and taking a strong interest in trying to descale our dirty old kettle. That was an ongoing thing, so he must have been mechanically minded to some extent.

Part of Nick's resolve in leaving university had been to cut himself off, but he occasionally visited friends in Cambridge. On one occasion he and Paul were in Market Square there when Paul mentioned that his girlfriend Diana had just got a job as an assistant to John Lennon. 'He reacted with a look of almost terrified interest (highly unusual – that's why I remember it),' says Paul. 'He asked if I'd heard "Cold Turkey", and said how shocking the song was. I wondered what had happened to make him so receptive to its honesty and raw intensity.'

He suspects that Nick was taking Lennon's lurch away from the Beatles (and what they had represented as he grew up) and towards radical politics and self-examination almost personally: 'Nick wasn't overtly political, but the influence of the Left was implicit for him without going on marches. He had taken the utopian dream of 1967 very much to heart.'

In London he remained an occasional presence at Bob Squire's nocturnal card games (where, according to Richard Thompson, John Martyn 'was famous for cheating. Just famous for it'[12]). 'I remember him as a figure stretched out on a pile of cushions at the back, like a giant cat with a baby face,' says Adrian George.

> He seemed catatonic but would occasionally be prodded into life when a joint reached him or he was given a cup of tea or a piece of cake, at which he would repeatedly say 'thank you' in a quiet voice. He was completely silent most of the time, but terribly sweet and polite. His gentleness really shone out in that context.

Another haunt was a dank basement flat on the corner of the Cromwell Road in South Kensington, where he spent late nights with Tony Hill Smith and Barry Johnston of the harmony pop group Design. 'We met Nick through mutual friends,' says Tony.

> I had a colonial family background and we had all gone to private schools and had the same accent, experiences etc., so we could relate

and communicate easily. I always found him friendly and likeable, and thought of him as a stray cat; he moved around a lot. He usually had his guitar with him and we would stay up singing and playing. We'd have a cup of tea or a glass of wine, but didn't smoke much dope with him – we might occasionally have shared one joint between the three of us, if anything.

One evening I'd just written a thing called 'Coloured Mile' and brought it up. 'What colour is a mile?' asked Nick, which sent us off into what colour is a frown, a smile, and so on, until someone said 'a lady', whereupon Nick said, 'Ladies are silver.'

He was interested in our vocal harmonies and intrigued by my way of playing guitar. I was nowhere near the player he was but had a twelve-string that I played upside down, and he liked weird chords. So did I, in fact – when Nick played an original chord I always asked exactly what it was, and he was happy to show me.

Perhaps his most frequent home-from-home was the Martyns' basement flat, described in a contemporary article as 'comfortable enough, with books and records scattered about, a chair on the floor without any legs, and a divan propped against the wall'.[13] 'I have happy memories of Denning Road,' says Paul Wheeler. 'John and Bev were always welcoming and the atmosphere was relaxed. There was a constant stream of visitors – John attracted people wherever he went, and always found someone he was interested in.'

'We had some warm and happy times there,' says Diana Soar, whose boyfriend Andy Matheou ran Les Cousins.

I thought, perhaps naïvely, that John and Bev were set for life, like Andy and me. In those days John was sweet, like the angelic face you can see on the front of *Bless the Weather* [released November 1971]. We'd get stoned and do silly things like listen to the static on the radio, waiting for the notes to change.

All the Martyns' friends concur that Nick was closer to Bev than to John. 'I think Nick's friendship with John was really all about Bev,' Joe contends.

She was a mother hen, very kind and concerned that Nick be fed and not sink into a stoned torpor. Nick appreciated the warmth and welcome of their flat, and I think he was stimulated by John and appreciated how clearly he admired his playing and songwriting – but it was Bev that he was more fond of and drawn to, for sure.

Joe remembers her 'making Nick chicken soup, chiding him about his hair and sometimes even washing his clothes'.[14]

'In my mind the closeness of John's relationship with Nick has been mythologised,' says Paul. 'At the time I remember John being offhand about him. Nick was used to being looked after, after having servants at home, going away to school and then Cambridge. I think certain women, including Bev, helped him with that.'

By Bev's own account,

I never went to his place – it wouldn't have been the done thing for a married woman in those days – but he often came to ours. He would turn up at the right time for dinner – he didn't cook much for himself, but John was good in the kitchen and often made a chili con carne or whatever. John used to say, 'He's looking thin, we need to feed him up.' I suspect food was the last thing on his mind, but he never refused it, and he wasn't a fussy eater. I mean, Joe hated mushrooms, but Nick wolfed down anything you gave him. He was polite, always said 'Thank you' at the end. He liked watching Wesley toddling about and laughing at his inquisitiveness. He liked his inno-cence. He occasionally babysat and recorded himself on a tape machine while Wesley slept.

Evenings at the Martyns' would usually evolve into spontaneous, dope-fuelled jam sessions. Jeff Dexter lived round the corner and was a regular:

There were many late-night sing-songs there, so I was lucky to get more of Nick than most. We'd sing Beatles songs, Everly Brothers songs, Buddy Holly songs . . . Everyone wanted to hear Nick but he was often too shy unless he could feel really comfortable, with someone like Bev – then you'd hear the best of him. Nick and Bev sang and played together all the time.[15]

'I was occasionally invited, so I'd take along my flute,' says John Altman, a saxophonist-flautist who often acted as an accompanist at

Les Cousins and other clubs. 'About the time Nick was working on his second album he would try out new songs, with other people joining in or making suggestions. I remember him playing "Poor Boy" in Denning Road.' Andy Fernbach, another young singer-guitarist, lived opposite and was often present too. 'I remember Nick being fascinated by how I'd managed to work out how to play slide guitar in a normal tuning,' he says, adding: 'John was quite hard to be around because his ebullience could be overpowering. Nick was always polite and quiet around him.'

One afternoon at the Martyns' the talk turned to gigs, about which Nick remained wary. As far as he was concerned, organising them was Witchseason's department. Seizing the initiative in his usual style, John spontaneously telephoned Andy Matheou and insisted that Nick play a headline set at Les Cousins as soon as possible. A paid spot there was a vital step on the way to making your reputation, so Andy – described by Diana as 'a mercurial, magnetic, big-hearted guy' – was a powerful figure on the acoustic scene.

Happy to oblige John, and already an admirer of Nick, Andy suggested Friday, 14 November. John was committed elsewhere that night, so he enlisted John James, who was also hanging out in Denning Road that day, to play too, and act as Nick's minder: 'Nick and I looked at each other . . . He looked like he was thinking, "How the hell do I get out of this?" John was very persuasive.'

'Nick, a fine songwriter. John, equally fine in what he does. Adm. 5s.,' ran the vague copy in the ensuing *Melody Maker* small ad. It was spotted by two sixteen-year-old schoolfriends, Herman Gilligan and Paul Weinberger, who had bought the *Nice Enough to Eat* sampler LP and enjoyed 'Time Has Told Me' enough to buy *Five Leaves Left* and then venture into Soho for their first ever gig. Arriving at opening time, 7 p.m., they made their tentative way down the steps but found the place empty except for Andy.

By Herman's account,

> The room was bare except for chairs and church pews against both the far and the left-side wall. At the near end, beside the door to the stairs, was a primary school-like raised wooden stage area on which stood a single microphone stand. Beyond this austere performance

room was a wide opening into another, slightly smaller, room with a rudimentary refreshment counter.

They bought some coffee and hung around.

'The next person to come in was a very tall, imposing, long-haired young man, who said nothing, just looked around and seemed as perplexed about the set-up as we were.' Recognising him as Nick, Herman and Paul complimented him on his album and found him 'polite and respectful but not talkative or self-promoting. He just stood there between us, obviously not going to initiate any further chat.' Paul asked if he knew what music was playing. To their bafflement, 'He just replied, "The Band," and slowly walked off.'*

As the club began to fill the boys sat cross-legged on the floor, directly in front of the stage. Unlike a lot of venues of its time, Les Cousins's focus was squarely on music. 'I suppose people could find a back corner to chat, but it really wasn't that kind of milieu,' says Diana, who often performed there herself. 'The club was too small and packed to have ongoing conversations, and it would have been intrusive as people sang.'

John James played the first set, followed by a break. Just before the music resumed, recalls Herman, 'Someone came bounding into the room, pushed through the crowd to get to the stage and said something like, "Hi, I'm John Martyn. I'm actually playing a gig around the corner but wanted to introduce you to my friend Nick Drake."† Nick then made his way up. Paul remembers him 'sitting on a stool with his guitar, looming over us':

we could have just about reached out and touched him. He was a huge, enigmatic presence, helped – not hindered – by the fact that he didn't say a single word before he started. He was everything I wanted to be and plainly never could be.

His playing was superb, with everything intricately finger-picked,

---

* They later realised that he was referring to The Band – an act they hadn't heard of.

† On 2 December the boys approached John Martyn at the Hayes Folk Club. According to Herman, 'John waxed lyrical about Nick's music and asked me if I'd enjoyed the gig. "Loved it," I replied, to which John smiled and said, "Good lad."'

never simply strummed. It sounded to me like two guitars at once. His voice was mellow, pitch-perfect and confidently projected, yet he only ever appeared to be whispering. He mumbled 'Thank you' after each song, retuned and played another. He played most of *Five Leaves Left* and probably a few more, then stood up with his guitar and was gone.

John James recalls:

Nick did thirty minutes. I sat on the edge of the stage, legs up on the guitar cases, knees jammed under the piano keyboard for the whole of his set. At half-time I reckoned it was better for him to go back on after the break and me to finish the night off – but I found him at the bottom of the stairs, guitar in case, on his way out.

Later that night Diana encountered Nick in the Greek restaurant above Cousins. 'Andy's parents ran it, so we would all drift up there after sessions and sit at the back,' she says. John Martyn had joined the party:

He loved a big gesture, so he'd insisted on opening champagne. Nick was sitting next to me. We both had reserved personalities, so neither of us said very much. We were just staring at the same glass on the table, and eventually Nick said to me, 'How do the bubbles keep on coming?' It was a moment of connection.

Andy and Diana became two of the few people Nick befriended after moving to London. Diana – who was very often at Cousins – emphasises that 'Nick didn't only play at the club when he was advertised. Andy would call people up if someone dropped out, or they might do a spot between other people's sets.* It was ramshackle and ran on a lot of goodwill.' Ramshackle it may have been, but a den of iniquity it was not. 'Dope wasn't permitted, and I never smelled it being smoked there. The club could have been closed down.'

They smoked it elsewhere, though. 'One time Andy and Nick came up to the room I was renting in a roof in Swiss Cottage,' she continues.

---

* Several bills for Les Cousins and elsewhere in the latter part of 1969 and 1970 announce John Martyn and 'guests' or 'special friends'.

I was doing a jigsaw, which Nick thought was funny, and I made us all lemonade. We went off to score some dope from an ex-boxer/ semi-villain called Gerry, who ruled the roost in a flat behind King's Cross. Nick and I were in his awful old car and Andy was on his moped. I remember Nick giggling because Andy was a large guy and he looked so ridiculous in his huge duffel coat on that tiny bike.

On Saturday, 15 November, the day after his slot at Cousins, Nick visited Far Leys, where the talk turned to drugs. Rodney – upon whom the meaning of the phrase *Five Leaves Left* had not been lost – was concerned that Nick's largely solitary existence in London would lead to increased dope smoking. He wrote to him the following Tuesday. 'I thought the enclosed article on meditation might be of some interest,' he began, but his main purpose was graver.

> Your remark to me that 'you are not smoking as much as you used to' clears the way for me to write this to you. I have been very greatly saddened for some years by my awareness that you were smoking pot, and have contemplated it in great fear.
>
> You asked if I had ever heard of anyone doing themselves any harm by the habit. I think in order to answer this question one has to consider the perhaps more significant one of why any particular individual takes to it . . . The really damaging and hopeless and degrading effect of these stimulants and sedatives comes into play when a man resorts to them as a refuge from his daily problems. The man who resorts to pot as the solution to his problems becomes bemused, befuddled and vegetable-like. How do I know this, you say? Because I saw it *again and again* in the East.
>
> I have believed all along that you are basically a strong person and that you are determined to find your own way through life and be the sort of person you want to be. However, it's the old business of 'to thine own self be true'; the man who starts deceiving himself has had it.

Nick may have regarded the letter as evidence of the generation gap, and perhaps it put him off spending more time at Far Leys, but – though he seems not to have replied – he carefully kept it with his parents' other correspondence.

He dropped into Witchseason each week to collect his cash advance. One day Joe took the opportunity to discuss his live career with him, emphasising that he simply had to play gigs if he wanted to sell more records and make more money. 'Few acoustic artists counted on record income for anything – they mostly made their money from gigs. I thought eventually we could maybe promote him in a small hall on his own terms, but he had to sell some records first,' he says.

Nick agreed that Huw Price would organise some low-key club appearances, with Bob Squire driving him when possible. 'We booked him a few dates – they weren't concerts as such, just appearances,' continues Joe.

> The idea was to see if he could make money and gain fans working small venues as a solo artist. My vague memory was that there were six or seven dates. I think there were days between most, so much of Bob's driving was back-and-forth to London, but there were some contiguous dates where they had to stay locally.

One booking was for a folk night held above the Haworth Arms at 449 Beverley Road in Hull, East Yorkshire. On the cold Thursday afternoon in question Nick ventured the two hundred miles north alone, carrying his Martin on the train. In the audience was Michael Chapman, a local singer whose own debut album, *Rainmaker*, had come out in May 1969, and his partner Andru; Bridget St John had recommended *Five Leaves Left* to them and they were eager to see its creator in action. They were with a few like-minded friends but by Michael's account it was mainly a 'silver tankard and finger-in-the-ear crowd' who wanted 'sea-shanties and singalong songs'.[16]

'It was more of a trad jazz venue and the crowd was ambivalent, there more to drink,' adds Andru.

> Only a few of us wanted to listen. There were some floor singers before Nick came on. He looked slight and delicate, very different to Michael. I can't imagine him with a chainsaw in his hands! He barely lifted his head and didn't introduce his songs or say anything, but we were enthralled by his performance. He played one longer set rather than the usual two.

Nick had never taken an interest in traditional British folk and, Michael continues,

> The folkies did not take to him. They completely missed the point, they didn't get it at all – they wanted songs with choruses. They just didn't get the gentleness, the subtlety . . . It was actually quite painful to watch. It was obviously not in his nature to perform, especially to a crowd like that. He should never have been there. But, back then, if you played acoustic guitar on your own and played your own songs, folk clubs were the only places that you *could* play.
>
> After the gig Andru noticed him standing alone under a streetlight and said, 'Never mind those arseholes, the people who know and care about music were enthralled. Are you waiting for a ride to your accommodation?' (They hadn't even bothered to provide anything.) 'Get in the car, come with us.'

Andru explains that 'Singers were often reliant on the kindness of strangers, so we invited him back to our place in Louis Street. It wasn't far but we'd driven, as the trawlermen used to look out for hippies to attack.'

According to Michael: 'At our apartment guitars, wine and dope appeared. I thought I knew more than a few guitar tunings, but Nick left me for dead.'[17] They went to bed in the small hours, Nick crashing on a mattress in the front room. 'Michael and I weren't early risers, and by the time we got up the next morning Nick was gone,' recalls Andru. 'He didn't leave a note, he had just disappeared and probably made his way back to the station.'

Michael's music was just as hard to categorise as Nick's, but he was a hard-travelling mainstay of the folk circuit and worked relentlessly to raise his profile. For him, 'Nick's name was never around':

> Whenever I went down to London, I'd drift along to Cousins to check out the opposition, nick a lick, maybe pinch a gag or a bit of patter – but I never saw Nick there. Me and Al Stewart, Roy Harper, Ralph McTell, we were all out working the circuit – but that gig in Hull was the only time I ever saw Nick.

Paul Wheeler suspects Nick underestimated how hard it would be to forge ahead in the teeming, competitive field he had chosen:

I don't think he quite realised what he was letting himself in for, going away from the languor of Cambridge into the professional London folky guitar scene. The musicians he was associating with [John Martyn, Andy Fernbach, John James, Bridget St John, Michael Chapman, Fairport and the Incredible String Band among them] really slogged, not just up and down the A1 but around the world, fighting for audiences until they got them – and that was not what Nick was doing. Those guys were tough. I'm not saying he was naïve, but I think he thought he could latch onto that world without going through the slog.

Allan Taylor was another constant on the circuit and says it was 'tough trying to make an impression in those days, firstly because there was so much competition and secondly because there were many clubs that did not appreciate singer-songwriters – these were the traditional clubs, and they were very critical of us. I think Nick had a hard time with this.' Bev agrees, adding, 'The reality of life for us was that people would be rowdy in clubs, and you had to accept that. Nick's upbringing had shielded him from a lot of reality and he wasn't used to being confronted with difficulty. It was two different worlds coming together.'

Allan identifies another possible problem:

Most of us aspiring singer-songwriters were from working-class backgrounds, with accents to match. What I remember most about Nick (apart from his music) was his accent. We thought he was awfully posh – not in a bad way, because he was such a nice guy, but obviously coming from a posh background.

Marcus Bicknell was working for the small Rondo Promotions agency, based in Kensington. In addition to the dates organised by Witchseason, he says, 'I put any halfway suitable gigs Nick's way as a mate, without ever being his manager or agent or having an exclusive agreement with him.' An ad in *Melody Maker* of 20 December 1969 listed among Rondo's acts the John Dummer Band, Audience, Andwellas Dream, Smile (who morphed into Queen), Dave Kelly and – almost as an afterthought – Nick Drake. Marcus was especially involved with another public school-educated act, Genesis, whose first album had come out on Decca that April but gained no more traction than *Five Leaves Left*. 'I understood Nick's position about gigs from Peter Gabriel, who was similarly introverted and reluctant to perform,' he says.

One of Rondo's specialities was supplying entertainment for working men's clubs in the Midlands, with the run-up to Christmas being especially busy. 'Typically, they had simple stages projecting into a sea of tables,' explains Marcus.

> Most of the time we'd send them MOR or pop acts, but as they hosted shows every weekend, occasionally they'd get underground or progressive acts. It was very much a bearpit atmosphere, and not ideal for Nick. At least he was paid – he would have got something like £10 plus petrol money for each one [around £125 in 2022].

On Sunday, 14 December, Marcus booked Nick and Genesis to play at the end-of-season dance for the rugby team fielded by a local company, Guest, Keen and Nettlefolds Screws and Fasteners, Ltd, in their Sports & Social Club in Thimblemill Road, Smethwick, outside Birmingham (about thirty minutes from Tanworth). It was the first of several gigs Nick played with Genesis, but he never travelled or socialised with them. On this occasion, Marcus drove him up from London in his Mini.

Dinner was still being cleared when Nick came on stage at around 9 p.m. 'He placed his chair in the left-hand corner and, without a word, proceeded to play,' according to Rob Jones, who was sixteen at the time.[18]

> He had a small but attentive audience in front of the stage; the rest of the people in the hall continued to arrange chairs, clean up after the meal, or just chat among themselves. You could tell he was feeling the strain against the constant chatter in the background . . . After five or six numbers he just packed away his guitar in its case and walked off, without a word. There was muffled but appreciative applause from a few of us who were near the stage.

Nick had in fact played for as long as expected. Backstage Tony Smith, one of the organisers, recalls 'trying to assure him that the unruly reaction had nothing to do with his talent, but was due to the effect of alcohol'.[19] Perhaps Nick should have counted himself lucky; after his set the doors were opened to the public and a posse of skinheads materialised. As Tony puts it, 'Unfortunately there was a rowdy element in the audience who did not appreciate the talent before them . . . Genesis had to play such hits as "The Hokey-Cokey" to appease them.'

Marcus describes the ensuing atmosphere as 'terrifying', and he and Nick fled as soon as they could. 'Nick and Marcus knew it was going to be the pits – but it was a gig,' recalled Robert.[20] 'It was a riot, anyway – it wasn't Nick particularly they were moaning about, it was just pints of lager being thrown everywhere. They came back to Cranley Gardens afterwards. Nick was laughing and joking about it – and he'd got paid!'

It seems he returned to the Midlands on Friday, 19 December to play at the Christmas Dance held by the Apprentice Association for another major local employer, Alvis, in their Sports and Social Club in Holyhead Road, Coventry. The main attraction was the Big Idea, a popular rock band from the area. The apprentices were, of course, drunk and boisterous. Patrick Garrett, the Big Idea's roadie, says that on such occasions 'audiences became a single entity and were unforgiving of acts that didn't fit. We, of course, had each other for support when gigs went wrong – but I don't want to think about a solo artist . . .'

John Martyn remembered the fallout well, calling the gig 'one of the things that contributed to [Nick's] utter detestation of the whole [live] thing':

> In those days 'Purple Haze' was 'in', and there he was singing 'Fruit Tree' and all these gentle, breezy little ballads. I can just imagine them swigging back the Carlsberg Special and giving him an awful, hard time. I know that that gig lived forever in his mind – he'd talk about it quite regularly.[21]

Elsewhere John said: 'That really destroyed him . . . I think that was a major blow to his confidence. I remember him being depressed about that for days and days.'[22]

Nick told Molly about what appears to have been yet another Midlands booking at this time:

He'd gone up to play at some factory, in the canteen, in Wolverhampton, and they'd all gone on talking and drinking and crashing their glasses about and things and nobody had listened to him at all. The only time he told us he laughed about it, but I think it had upset him frightfully. I think he felt, 'Well, what is the good? They don't want my sort of music . . .' They should have had someone who'd have kind of jollied them all along.[23]

Although such gigs were unlikely to further *Five Leaves Left*, Joe remained frustrated and perplexed by its low sales. 'Leonard Cohen barely performed, yet his records were selling like crazy,' he says.

I envisaged Nick occupying the same position in Britain, but failed to appreciate that Leonard was a huge beneficiary of FM radio, which we didn't have. Things were much more categorised in 1969, and Nick's blend of folk, blues, jazz, strings and more wasn't what people expected when they dropped a needle on a new record. *Five Leaves Left* was hard to grasp right away, so I didn't expect it to be a hit – but nor did I expect it to vanish.

Alex Henderson remembers Nick explaining, 'The idea with *Five Leaves Left* was that word-of-mouth would spread like bushfire, helped by a few live performances,' but Joe was coming to realise this was unrealistic. Island chose to include it in their back-page advert in the Christmas issue of *Melody Maker*, alongside releases by Fairport, Free, King Crimson, Spooky Tooth, Quintessence, Blodwyn Pig, Renaissance, Mott the Hoople and Jethro Tull, but it didn't find its way under many trees.*

In planning his next album, Nick tacitly agreed with Joe that – without compromising his essence – they would aim it at a broader audience. He wouldn't be sitting his Cambridge Finals in May 1970, but he'd have an album out instead – and with any luck a successful one. As 1969 ended and the songs and arrangements came together, Robert recalled: 'Nick was quite high on it. The first [LP] had got his name known, and I think he felt this was going to be the one. We were told this was going to be the one . . .'[24]

---

* It was also released on cassette in December, with a generic pink cover design and (presumably in error) the sides reversed.

18

People Didn't Really Listen

~ ~

A s NICK FINESSED his new material Joe had been producing Fairport's pioneering new album, *Liege & Lief*, which set traditional folk to contemporary rock arrangements. Shortly before its release in early December 1969, Ashley Hutchings and Sandy Denny announced that they were separately leaving the band. Whilst dealing with this crisis Joe was also making albums with the Incredible String Band, Geoff and Maria Muldaur and Vashti Bunyan, and restructuring Witchseason.

His intention had always been to provide as large an umbrella as possible for his acts to shelter under – 'I do like to be totally involved with the artists I record,' he said at the time[1] – but not nearly enough money was coming in. As he encapsulates it, Witchseason 'was struggling with too many nice reviews and too few sales'.[2] At the start of the new decade he renegotiated the terms of his deal with Island, giving them first refusal on Witchseason recordings for the next four years (outside the US and Canada) in exchange for a lump sum for every finished master he delivered.

The arrangement assured the company's future to an extent, but also created an incentive for it to deliver as many albums as possible.

> The cross-collateralisation in my deal with Island was brutally simple. We used the advances to pay studio costs, royalties and overheads, and the money was recouped by Island from royalties owed to us. We never really got to that point, though – advances always ran ahead of royalties. Paying Fairport royalties would clean me out, so my response was to make more records and hope to have a hit. The bills kept coming, so I was spending more and more time in the studio to try to pay them – I'd owe five grand to the travel agent,

pay them two to keep them quiet for a while, then before I knew it the debt was back up to five.

Unsurprisingly, Joe became frazzled. 'He was always being pulled in several directions at once,' says John Wood, who was unconvinced as to the wisdom of Joe's 'total involvement' policy.

Part of the problem with Witchseason offering an all-round service to its acts was that they were nannied – no one forced any of them to do anything they didn't want to. In fact, Joe was very supportive of them when they didn't want to do things. Some of Joe's acts were sloppy in performance, but I don't think he would ever have told them to tighten up. To be successful, artists have to have a work ethic. Maybe some of them felt that their middle-class status meant they were exempted from getting their hands dirty – John Martyn was the only Witchseason artist who really didn't get along with Joe, and he was from the least comfortable background.

Ultimately, though, the problem was that they simply weren't selling enough records. 'I valued the creative relationships I had with the Witchseason artists so highly that I was always willing to rob Peter to pay Paul in order to keep the show on the road,' says Joe. 'Even though *Five Leaves Left* hadn't sold, tracks like "Three Hours", "River Man" and "Time Has Told Me" were why I made records, regardless of whether they were hits.' He wasn't profligate but his commitment to quality was expensive. 'Joe was never one to count cost,' continues John. 'He was interested in making the best possible records. To him, even a one per cent difference in the quality of the end result was worth paying extra for.'

The result was a slow puncture:

At the start of 1970 I was swamped with production, management, travel, financial woes etc. Instead of shrinking, I went through a double-or-quits phase. I wanted to get rid of the obligation to be a manager, so I was either encouraging people to go with other management or else hiring people into Witchseason to effectively manage so I wouldn't have to have the day-to-day responsibility.

For a start he appointed Susie Watson Taylor, a friend of John and Bev's who he felt 'had a rare grasp of what I was trying to do', to act as 'personal manager' to them, the Incredible String Band and Nick. Nicknamed 'Susie What's On TV' at Witchseason, she was also friends with Joe's girlfriend Linda Peters, who remembers her as 'beautiful and clever and posh'. Joe says:

> The model had worked perfectly with Anthea Joseph and Fairport, so why not with her and Nick? Assigning Susie to Nick was a sign that it was time to treat him as an active Witchseason artist who needed managing, that he wasn't just someone I made records with. She adored him, but I doubt she had much to do as his manager.

Joe hired Brenda Ralfini, who had been handling Bob Dylan's British copyrights, to run Warlock Music. He remained convinced that Nick's material – and that of his other signings – had commercial potential for others, and it was vital for publishing income to increase in the absence of sufficient record royalties. He also created an in-house live agency named Werewolf, run by Huw Price, whose immediate tasks included organising a launch concert for John and Beverley's delayed *Stormbringer!* album and separate tours for the trimmed-down Fairport and Sandy's as-yet unnamed new group.

Amidst all this activity, Joe met Nick to hear him play through his new songs, much as he had two years earlier, in January 1968. The experience reaffirmed his conviction in Nick's artistry. He felt the magic was

> partly in the structure of the songs, partly in the intelligence of the lyrics, because I think the two go together . . . He wasn't observing other people, he was mostly observing himself, which is what makes his songs so interesting – his acute observations of his own predicament, which are full of humour and irony.[3]

Especially ironic was 'Poor Boy': 'Nick played it through to me on a semi-acoustic guitar – the jazzy approach was very much his conception, but I put the other parts of it together in my head. I immediately thought of [Leonard Cohen's] "So Long, Marianne" and could hear those girls' backing voices.' They agreed to begin recording the album in February, with a view to releasing it in the spring. 'I couldn't wait to make another record,' recalls Joe. 'I looked forward to being in the studio with Nick more than with any other artist.'[4]

It was already understood that the songs would incorporate wider instrumentation than *Five Leaves Left*. 'Nick was a weak artist in a recording context,' states Tod Lloyd. 'I don't mean his talent, just the means he had of putting himself across, so when *Five Leaves Left* didn't sell, the thinking was, "Let's throw a bucket of stuff at the next one."' For John Wood,

> It was a shock when *Five Leaves Left* fell by the wayside with a tremendous thud. We were dumbfounded that no one bought it. With the second album there was a definite move towards making a more approachable, broadly appealing record – a concerted attempt to make it palatable to a wider audience, hence the electric guitar, electric bass, rhythm section and so on.

Robert was also clear on this point, summarising: 'This was going to be the one with a single on it.'[5]

It made obvious sense for members of Fairport to play on it. They had just moved into a draughty, disused pub named the Angel in Little Hadham, Hertfordshire, which their newly recruited bassist Dave Pegg – known to all as 'Peggy' – cheerfully describes as 'a dump'. As he explains,

> Joe suggested Nick visit the Angel to run through the material with us. Dave Mattacks and I spent a couple of days sitting around with him as he played and sang us the songs. I was amazed by the fluency of his guitar playing. Although Richard [Thompson] played on the album, I don't remember him taking part at the Angel, and I can't remember if Nick stayed overnight – but we didn't go to the pub or anything. We were worlds apart, really.

Dave Mattacks remembers 'sitting in [Peggy's] room running through the songs, Peggy with a small bass amp on "one" and me with a pair of sticks and a practice pad. I recall Nick being very shy.'[6] Peggy agrees: 'He was quiet and didn't exude confidence in what he was doing. I found him serious – not unfriendly, but there to get a job done. There was no discussion or analysis of the songs, we simply learned them and worked out our parts.'

Nick continued to play intermittent gigs. On Saturday, 17 January, he, John Martyn and the Bristol country-blues guitarist Mike Cooper shared a bill for an all-night show at Les Cousins. At all-nighters, recalls the sideman John Altman,

> The audience gathered along one side, with benches right in front of where you played. As it got later, people started going to sleep on them, so it would feel as if you were playing to a bunch of corpses. People would loom out of the darkness and appear onstage, and I never knew who would be next. I'd play all night, but Nick got rather lost in the throng.

Ian Anderson, another country-blues exponent from Bristol, sometimes compèred all-nighters at Cousins, and sang some of his own songs. By his account, Nick was 'fucking awful',[7] 'a really nervous, undistinguished singer-songwriter who sent the audience to sleep',[8] and 'simply wasn't that noticeable – his music was definitely not outstanding among that of many other similar people around and his performance skills were frightful. Quite why he attracted a record deal is a mystery.'[9] Elsewhere he has remarked:

> It would be very easy to not remember seeing Nick Drake . . . Whatever you think of his records, he really was a dreadfully dull live performer with absolutely nothing memorable about him at all, other than not being very good. I'm sure I was only awake because I was either MC-ing or waiting to play.[10]

Reactions that negative appear to have been in a minority. Jerry Gilbert, *Melody Maker*'s folk editor and a regular at Cousins, felt that 'Nick's performances were always very accomplished. I don't recall huge amounts of shaky fingers and bum notes or anything at a Nick performance. I think once he got himself into the song, he lost himself in his own world.'[11] One night he appeared there alongside Dr. Strangely Strange, whom he barely knew despite their mutual ties to Joe. 'We all greatly enjoyed his set,' recalls the trio's bassist-keyboardist Ivan Pawle. 'I remember standing around on the street outside afterwards, Tim Goulding particularly saying how good it was to Nick, and Nick being terribly self-critical . . .'

Leo O'Kelly of the Irish folk duo Tír na nÓg was also a regular at Cousins. He never met Nick but says: 'Even then there was a mystique and an excitement about just spotting him.' Paul Wheeler suspects there was an element of self-consciousness to Nick's persona:

> I think that he knew that an enigmatic presence was part of his identity and was in reaction to the kind of singer-songwriters who did make a point of chatting to the audience and so on. If you wanted to build a reputation in the clubs you had to have 'an act', you had to work out a set, pace the songs, prepare jokes for certain places and have responses ready for hecklers. That simply wasn't Nick.

However, Iain Cameron – a regular at Cousins since 1966 – did not regard his lack of patter as problematic there. 'The audience was rightly completely captivated by the music – fine original songwriters, high virtuosity – and didn't really care about the repartee. Indeed, many would have signed up to an "authenticity" ethic which would have been antagonistic to anything that looked too rehearsed on the verbal front.'[12] Instead, it seems that the problem was that Nick's material was insufficiently arresting upon first hearing. 'I saw him at Cousins a couple of times and he went over my head,' says Wizz Jones. 'It was only later, when I listened to his records properly, that I realised what a clever and original player and writer he was.'

On 24 January Marcus Bicknell booked Nick alongside Genesis at Ewell Technical College in Epsom, Surrey. 'It was an important venue for up-and-coming acts,' says its social secretary for that year, Lindsay Brown. Topping the bill was the keyboard-driven hard rock trio Atomic Rooster, who seem ridiculously inappropriate alongside Nick – but, explains Lindsay, 'Eclectic bills were totally normal.'

'At Techs people didn't really listen,' says Genesis's lead guitarist Anthony Phillips, who was only seventeen at the time.

> Nick performed just him and his guitar, and it was a very crouched, husky performance . . . When you're playing this quiet acoustic stuff to people who are just shouting, it kills the songs. You had to stamp on people with volume unless you were a name. It was difficult enough for us, let alone for him.[13]

Lindsay counters that 'It was a music-loving audience – they were stoned, not drunk. They didn't go along to go potty, they wanted to hear an evening of interesting and varied music, not a "rock concert" as such. Nick was good, his songs were amazing.'

On Wednesday, 4 February, Nick was with Genesis at Queen Mary College in the East End of London. Anthony Phillips recalls: 'One of our most popular acoustic songs was a very sixties-sounding thing called "Let Us Now Make Love". Nick obviously liked that very much – I remember him coming up to me when he heard that I wrote it and saying, "Dangerous!"'[14]

The following day Nick joined Fairport for a couple of dates on their short national tour. There was no souvenir programme but its promoter, NEMS, printed a double-sided souvenir poster offering forthcoming dates and brief biographies. Nick, it said, has 'worked on the college circuit and in various folk clubs around the country. He is working on his next album for Island, which will be recorded during February, released in early spring.'

The first concert was at Liverpool Philharmonic Hall, in front of 1,700 people. Paul Donnelly was in the audience, and his memories chime with those who saw Nick elsewhere: 'He came on and said nothing audible, either before or between songs. I remember "'Cello Song" and "Three Hours", mainly because they were two of my favourites. When he'd finished he just got up and walked off.'[15] Also on the bill was Roger Ruskin Spear and His Kinetic Wardrobe, a robot-based multimedia act by a former member of the Bonzo Dog Band; at the end of Fairport's set Roger joined them onstage for a raucous rock'n'roll medley, but Nick was nowhere to be seen, and Roger barely remembers him.

The following evening's show took place in a packed Manchester Free Trade Hall, whose capacity was over 2,500. Audience member Dave Burrows noted Nick's 'gangly, loose-limbed gait as he walked on and off the stage', 'some great guitar playing and a husky, reson-ant voice'.[16] Steve Greenhalgh recalled:

> He perched on a high stool, never said a word and started playing. Unfortunately, the booze was flowing freely amongst his potential audience who, for the most part, continued talking. After a couple

of numbers (one of which, I think, was 'River Man') he stopped playing, vacated the stool and slipped off the stage, carrying his guitar gingerly by the neck.[17]

If the audiences weren't rapt, Fairport were: 'We always watched his sets from the wings because we were in awe of his talent and wanted him to succeed,' says Peggy.

> He was very well received, the audiences liked him . . . He didn't have any spiel, but the songs were strong enough to get people's attention – and in those days people were into listening to music, anyway. He didn't have much stage presence, he was the opposite of somebody who tries to gee the audience up, but the fact that he was that way [meant] people had time for him, because the music and his voice were so good.

Probably coinciding with this concert, Nick made his only known television appearance, on a short-lived early evening magazine programme named *Octopus*.* Made in colour by Granada in Manchester, its title referred to its extensive reach: it described itself as being 'about new developments, be they in music and the arts, scientific research or literally anything that's happening today'.[18] Its director, John Downie, characterises it as 'short, fast, and ever so slightly out-of-control – a waft of weed not too many rooms distant'.

Nick's booking came about through its co-presenter Andrew Fisher, a friend of Gabrielle and de Wet's. John simply remembers 'a tall guy with a guitar whose studio presence was fairly peremptory', and says he was filmed 'with basic lighting and a two camera set-up – face/figure and close-up guitar'. He performed ''Cello Song' (with no cello) and was not interviewed; the fact that he played a song from *Five Leaves Left* implies that he was mindful of the need to promote that, rather than preview anything newer.

Back in London he appeared at least twice in the newly opened

---

* The first edition of *Octopus* was broadcast on 7 January 1970, the last on 29 July. It was shown throughout the north of England and in some other regions, but appears not to have survived. Other musical acts featured on it included Love, Mighty Baby, Taste, the Bonzo Dog Band, Quintessence and Bridget St John.

Crypt Folk Club in St Martin-in-the-Fields, Trafalgar Square, where a liquid light show caused psychedelic inks and bubbles to dance over him as he played. 'I remember him hunched over his guitar like he was too big for it, picking hypnotic, almost impressionistic melodies that went on for quite a while before he started singing,' says Nick Sibley, who was in the audience.

> His voice was hypnotic too. The atmosphere was friendly and supportive, but he did take ages tuning between songs and didn't try to develop any rapport, unlike most performers. He was adored by the small audience, though. We were silent throughout and the lights made it even more of a mystical experience.

He continued to play gigs organised by Marcus, and was presumably glad of the income. On Saturday, 14 February, he and Genesis were the unlikely entertainment at Leicester University's Valentine's night dance, and on Friday the 20th they played at a fundraiser named The Cannon Ball at the private Hurlingham Club in Fulham, London. On that occasion the boorish audience heckled Nick. This was probably the gig Robert later referred to as the 'famous one where the microphones didn't work and he carried on playing',[19] adding: 'I think they were Hooray Henrys whom he would have expected to have listened, and they weren't in the slightest bit interested – "Get off!", that sort of thing. That did sour him.'[20]

Bruised, the following evening he opened John and Bev's *Stormbringer!* album launch at the 900-seat Queen Elizabeth Hall on the South Bank. Gabrielle was there, as was David Sandison, who had just joined Island with responsibility for press and promotion, after working at Philips Records and for Leslie Perrin, doyen of pop PRs. Unfamiliar with Nick, shortly before the concert he'd taken *Five Leaves Left* off a shelf in their Basing Street headquarters. 'From the opening notes of "Time Has Told Me" to the last chord of "Saturday Sun", I was held by the totally personal feel of the music, the words and the vague feeling of intruding on someone's phone conversation,' he wrote the following year.[21] He therefore went to the QEH with high expectations.

For Paul Wheeler, however, the evening was fundamentally flawed:

'It wasn't much of a concert – it was still novel to have folk music in such venues, and there was no staging and minimal lighting. Really, it was just a case of transposing a folk club onto a larger stage, and it didn't work.' John introduced Nick, admonishing the audience to shut up and listen. Inevitably, however, Nick had to play as people milled around, chatted, bought drinks and found their seats. Herman Gilligan, who'd seen him at Cousins three months earlier, vividly remembers him playing 'Mayfair' on this occasion.

By David's oddly candid account in Nick's subsequent Island biography,

> He came on with his guitar, sat on a stool, looked at the floor and sang a series of muffled songs punctuated by mumbled thanks for the scattering of bewildered applause from the audience, who didn't really know who the hell he was nor care too much. At the end of his last song his guitar was still holding the final notes as he got up, glanced up, then walked off, his shoulders hunched as if to protect him from the embarrassment of actually having to meet people.[22]

For Joe, Nick's turn was 'not as magical as the Fairport show at the Royal Festival Hall, but I remember him doing at least okay.' David Franklin reviewed the evening for *Top Pops & Music Now* and felt 'he should endeavour to vary the tempo and setting of his songs rather more. Likewise, whilst his intricate guitar picking is superb, it would be something of a joy to hear him let rip with a simple free strum.'[23]

Letting rip, however, was not Nick's style, and Alex Henderson admits: 'If we hadn't been his friends and known the songs already, I suspect he wouldn't have made any impression on us at all.' Nick felt the set had gone badly and when David Sandison complimented him backstage he muttered thanks and immediately moved away. 'In a room of about fifty or sixty people it would have worked and it would have been very intimate, but he never came to grips with playing to two thousand people in big rooms,' David reflected in hindsight (though not in specific reference to Nick's Queen Elizabeth Hall performance).[24]

It's hard to understand why, as he gained experience, Nick didn't imbue his act with more stagecraft. Although he was certainly introverted, a few good-humoured words to the audience surely wouldn't have been beyond him. Robert was convinced that he had no problem with the basic notion of performance:

> I think he got a great kick out of performing live, I think he liked people hearing him play, I think he knew he was good, he thought his material should be performed . . . As to whether he found all the audiences he performed to suitable . . . Maybe that's what the problem was.[25]

Anthea Joseph, who was also at the QEH show, fundamentally disagreed:

> He just hated performing. If you had him in your own sitting room, he'd sit in the corner and take up the guitar and play you something and it was lovely, no problem. He did do that for me a couple of times. But *performing* was totally different. Joe knew Nick was difficult, because he was, but I don't think he realised how paranoid Nick was about gigging.[26]

It seems he had an almost obdurate determination to present his songs as polished jewels whose sparkle alone should command attention. As Robert put it:

> Nick thought he could turn up anywhere with his guitar and play, but you can't really do that in the Queen Elizabeth Hall – you need a sound person who's going to make sure that you've got everything set up properly. So I think that was possibly a weakness – that there wasn't the guidance there for the live performance.[27]

Irrespective of the sound system, his voice – either speaking or singing – was insufficiently commanding to cut through to an inattentive audience. As Gabrielle puts it, 'His voice was small. Always through his schooldays he'd say he had a bad voice, and even allowing for the usual self-deprecation, he wasn't entirely wrong. Of course, it's the imperfections in his voice that make it unique and appealing, but it's not a classically beautiful voice, and it's not a large voice.'

'Sorry to hear you were dissatisfied with your performance, but I'm sure your audience was pleased with you,' Rodney wrote to

Nick a few days later.[28] 'Gay thought so.'* It was scant consolation, but Nick was more preoccupied by his next album, sessions for which began at Sound Techniques the following week.

---

* 'Gay heard you on Radio 2 at 1 a.m. the other night,' he added. '"'Cello Song", I think.'

19

A Little Uncertain

———

J OHN WOOD HADN'T clapped eyes on Nick since work ended
on *Five Leaves Left* the previous April. He had been busy fitting
De Lane Lea studio in Wembley – a massive £200,000 contract –
and had also rejigged Sound Techniques. 'I made a few alterations
to make it a more controlled environment,' he says. 'It had been a
very "live" space and we needed to change the acoustics to suit the
changing needs of musicians.' For Joe, 'John loved Nick and took
tremendous care, which you can hear in the way [his second album]
stands up. I think the sound he got on Nick's voice, the sound on
the acoustic instruments, is just very, very good.'[1]

Despite his mixed fortunes on stage, Nick had a positive attitude
throughout the sessions, which ran through February and into March.
'I didn't notice any difference in his appearance or enthusiasm,' says
John. 'Certainly his attitude and performances were of the same
high standard. He was always professional and easy to work with.
For example, it wasn't uncommon to see people smoking joints
during sessions, but Nick certainly didn't.' Like Joe, John found
himself actively looking forward to recording Nick: 'It was always
rewarding – his performances were always a hundred per cent, so
the success of a take never depended on him. He was completely
reliable every single time.'

'The sessions were close together,' says John.

They tended to start at around 2 p.m. and we would work on
through, depending on who was available. The first I heard of the
material was at each session – Nick didn't play the songs to me in
advance or make demos. He laid them down with a live rhythm
section and out-takes just got dumped.

Joe emphasises that 'guitar-and-vocal tracks for it don't exist. John didn't want to put Nick in a booth, so there's no separation – he was a great believer in creative spill between mikes.'

As John reiterates, 'The clear intention was that this would be his breakthrough, no two ways about it. It was made in a more conventional way. We went out of our way to do it.' He is referring not only to the more intensive sessions compared to the slow genesis of *Five Leaves Left*, but also to the fact that backing tracks were largely recorded first and then overdubbed onto, rather than having Nick perform live with the other musicians.

'One reason for the shift in approach was the presence of the drum kit on most tracks,' explains Joe.

I don't recall ever deciding that as a conceptual change, but I was certainly conscious of trying to shift the sound a bit to give Nick a better shot at success. While John was great at recording full ensembles at Sound Techniques, which had worked well on *Five Leaves Left*, things change once you have a drum kit. There wasn't a drum booth at Sound Techniques, or at least not a purpose-built one, and John liked to record drums out in the room, so it would have been hard to lay down live flute tracks or backing vocals or strings.

The first tracks to be recorded were 'Introduction', 'Hazey Jane I', 'Hazey Jane II', 'Bryter Layter' and 'Sunday', all featuring Peggy and Dave Mattacks. 'It was a noticeable development from learning the stuff at the Angel, which was skeletal,' according to Peggy.[2]

It all went down fairly quickly. There were never any occasions where stuff was never going to work, where we had to completely redo the track in a different way or try for a different feel. The only thing was, you never really knew what Nick thought about it, whether he was happy or not, because he would never communicate.

Several of the songs seem to concern himself, despite using the vocative. He appears to mention the abandonment of his past life in 'Hazey Jane II': 'And all the friends that you once knew are left behind / They kept you safe and so secure amongst the books and all the records of your lifetime'. The same song concludes with a candid acknowledgement of his social unease: 'If songs were lines in a conversation / The situation would be fine'. In 'Hazey Jane I' he poses existential questions such as 'Do you curse where you come from?', 'Do you like what you're doing?' and 'Do you feel things are moving just a little too fast?', all of which applied to him. Beyond their titles, a link between the two songs is hard to discern, but 'Hazey Jane' seems more likely to be a metaphor than a specific individual. Their numbering probably indicates the order in which they were written.

Discomfort with the urban environment is evident in some of the songs; in Hazey Jane II he asks: 'What will happen in the morning when the world it gets so crowded that you can't look out the window in the morning?' while his advice in 'At The Chime Of A City Clock' seems borderline paranoid: 'Stay indoors, beneath the floors / Talk with neighbours only'. For Molly – herself closely attuned to both lyrics and melancholy –

> The imagery [in 'At The Chime Of A City Clock'] is very strong – you can feel someone rather alone and with very few possessions, living like that in rather a tragic sort of way, like he lived in London, when he was terribly alone, and he wanted to be alone.[3]

Conversely, the refrain of 'Poor Boy', 'so sorry for himself', reflects the wry humour familiar to many who knew Nick, though its verses cut deeper, with lines like 'Nobody cares how steep my stairs' and 'Nobody feels the worn-down heels'. His mother certainly did; she later recalled of this time that he had 'just one pair of shoes, which was completely worn out. He wouldn't have anything different. He wanted to be totally without material possessions at all, I think.'[4]

'Fly' appears to reference William Blake's poem, with Nick characterising himself – perhaps with humour – as a fragile, unnoticed creature akin to Blake's, albeit aspiring to an unattainable partner like those mentioned in his earliest songs.* 'Northern Sky' speaks of the thrill of new love and its accompanying sense of rebirth, though if it was directed at someone specific, its sentiment appears

---

* Few of Nick's songs underwent lyrical changes between his home recordings and the studio versions, but in early versions of 'Fly' he refers to 'my big white car' and 'my merry car' rather than 'my streetcar'.

to have been unrequited or unfulfilled. Its title perhaps refers to North London, and it's easy to envisage him sitting in the window at Danehurst as he wrote it. Its hymnal quality doesn't surprise Paul Wheeler: 'Christianity was woven into our generation, even if you were an atheist, and we all knew the same hymns and psalms.'

The instrumentals were hard to get right in the absence of the strings that were to be added under Robert's baton. Their very existence vexed Joe, who considered them less original and interesting than Nick's songs:

I was very sceptical about the idea, and I was very resistant. I said, 'Well, we can record them, but only at the tail-end of a session where we're doing a proper song,' because the idea of having instrumental tracks seemed to me to be sort of Chinese for 'Nick couldn't think of any lyrics'. I was putting him under a lot of pressure to come up with lyrics for them – and again, he was adamant. He said, 'No, these are not songs, these are instrumental pieces, and I want one at the beginning and one at the end, and that's the way the album is going to be.'[5]

John was also perplexed by Nick's determination to include them: 'I thought it was odd. I could understand two – one at the start and one at the end – but three seemed excessive.' He remembers Nick being especially particular about Dave Mattacks's use of mallets during the recording of 'Introduction'. 'Nick's time-keeping was so good,' according to Dave:[6]

I remember distinctly he was playing this constant arpeggio, running sixteenth notes on the guitar pattern, and it was apparent there wasn't any point in reproducing that on another part of the drum set so I chose to do more of a colour thing with timpani beaters on the drums and cymbals, and play more colours rather than play time as such (though hopefully it is in time).

'If anything,' John felt,

Nick was a little more confident at the sessions for his second album – he had always been assertive about what he wanted, but he was more overtly so. He always got what he wanted and was very quick to say if he didn't like something. He was polite but firm – he had a way of stating his view in the studio that put you off answering back.

An example arose when they attempted 'At The Chime Of A City Clock'. 'Nick wasn't happy with the way the rhythm was sounding,' continues John. 'He didn't think Dave's drumming was right on it, so he put his foot down. It was no insult to Dave, he just wanted a different feel.'

Joe asked Mike Kowalski to drum on it instead. Mike was American and had recently drummed on tour with the Beach Boys, whom Nick admired.

> The New Nadir had recorded an album [still unreleased at the time of writing] at Sound Techniques and I first met Nick when he popped into one of the sessions. Our album was in a crazy mix of styles and when Island turned it down Joe offered us some studio work just to keep us going. One job was for Nick. I hadn't heard any of the songs until the session, when Nick played them through on his guitar. He was quiet, calm and respectful, but you could tell at once that he knew what he wanted. He told me he wanted it played straight, with no fills, which was fine by me – the last thing his music needed was someone overplaying.

In Mike's memory,

> Joe hardly said a word – Nick was very much in control, he did all the communicating. He was very demonstrative. He'd let you know just what he wanted in the studio and let you groove with it, but he wouldn't let the improvisation get out of hand. There were quite a few takes – he would recognise certain accents, he would hear you playing embellishments and ask you to accentuate them. 'At The Chime Of A City Clock' was like that.

'Poor Boy' also featured the Pegg-Kowalski rhythm section. A surviving home recording is in a straighter style, but the studio version tilts towards bossa nova. Immediately before Nick arrived for the session Joe had been working with Chris McGregor, who was still smoking dope in the control room. He stuck around and, says Joe, 'jumped in spontaneously', playing an immaculate piano part in one take. Simon Nicol, Fairport's rhythm guitarist, happened to be there too: 'As the arrangement came together it was decided that Nick should play an electric guitar, so he borrowed my Gibson L-7C archtop "jazz" guitar, which I had with me.'*

The sunny piano part on the jazzy 'One Of These Things First' was supplied by Paul Harris on another visit to London. Peggy wasn't always available, so Ed Carter – another American and also a member of the New Nadir – played bass on it. Mike was primarily a drummer but 'I had brought my 1954 Fender Precision bass to England to play on the New Nadir recordings, and Ed used it on that track.'

Most overdubs, including the strings and brass, were recorded in March. Joe enjoyed fleshing out the songs.

> The material was so rich that it lent itself to contributions, which in a way is more fun for a producer. It feeds your ego, I suppose . . . There was something so rewardingly rich about the music, the melodies and the guitar parts, that it was incredibly exciting and fulfilling to hear what happened when really good musicians began to play . . . The thing already fits together so well just with the guitar and the voice, it's just so well-constructed, that the more [instruments] you add, the better it gets.[7]

As with *Five Leaves Left*, the sessions were well underway before Nick informed Robert. 'I didn't know they'd been doing this album for quite a few [weeks] before. I really was just called in at the end to put on those arrangements on those tracks that I did.'[8] Also as with *Five Leaves Left*, Robert's parts offer counter-melodies and drama rather than just dressing. Unlike *Five Leaves Left*, however, Nick heard them for the first time in the studio, despite having collaborated closely on them. Again, they were taped in a single session, but without him playing and singing as they went down.

Top players were booked; for example, although they weren't credited on the cover, the celebrated jazzmen Kenny Wheeler and Henry Lowther played trumpet on 'Hazey Jane II'. John Wood was

---

* Simon has long since sold the guitar.

absent for the morning session at which backing vocals were over-dubbed onto 'Poor Boy', so his assistant Roger Mayer took over. The song's soul-funk stylings are unique in Nick's oeuvre, but Robert was at pains to emphasise that everything was done with his approval.

He was there to oversee Pat Arnold and Doris Troy and remembered them 'wailing away, Nick sitting there at the back, seeming quite happy'.[9] As he explained, the refrain of 'so sorry for himself' was 'supposed to mock Nick's self-pity, it is supposed to be viciously sarcastic. I was there, and Nick actually told them what to sing and how to sing it.'[10] Pat confirms this: 'He knew exactly how he wanted us to sound . . . He wanted the sarcasm to come across.'[11]

Richard Thompson dropped in to overdub lead guitar on 'Hazey Jane II'. '[Nick] is a very elusive character,' he said in 1974.[12] 'I asked him what he wanted, but he didn't say much, so I just did it and he seemed fairly happy. People say that I'm quiet, but Nick is ridiculous.' Dave Pegg is dismissive of any suggestion that there was any rivalry or animosity between them: 'I can't imagine Richard ever being anything other than supportive or encouraging towards Nick – he wasn't competitive and had no desire to be a star himself.'

The saxophonist Ray Warleigh, who worked closely with Scott Walker at the time, was booked to play on 'Hazey Jane II', 'At The Chime Of A City Clock' and 'Poor Boy'. 'I remember Nick well,' he recalled. 'He was softly-spoken but knew exactly what he wanted. His reputation is for being shy and introverted, but I remember going to the pub over the road with him during breaks and he was open and friendly.' John Wood also has fond memories of everyone heading over to the Black Lion for lunch and a game of darts.

Despite Joe's best efforts, Nick remained determined to bookend each side with instrumentals. They didn't argue, but their difference of opinion was stark. 'I think Nick might have become annoyed with me,' Joe reflects.

There were two clear areas of conflict. First, he wanted instrumentals to open and close each side, and I hated the idea. I thought they were stupid and lowered the tone. I dug my heels in and said we shouldn't be wasting our fucking time on instrumentals and couldn't afford to record a fourth one anyway.* Secondly, I said we should record 'Things Behind The Sun' instead. He told me it wasn't finished, even though I'd previously heard the whole thing. In the end we didn't record either.

By the end of March every song had been recorded but, says Joe, 'I didn't feel we had a complete album.' This was partly due to his dissatisfaction with the instrumentals, but was mainly because, as John puts it, 'Fly' and 'Northern Sky' were 'sitting there without a clear idea of what to do with them'. It seems puzzling that Nick hadn't worked on arrangements for them with Robert but, suggests Joe, 'We were trying to make less of a "string" album and more of a "rock" album.' As such, John says, 'The arrangements weren't set in stone when the basic tracks were put down.'

Occasionally Joe drove him home. 'We would talk about music in my car – I remember him saying he liked Django Reinhardt, but I wish I'd spoken to him about João Gilberto, as they were so similar – shy, fussy, quiet, understated.' Nick did not unburden himself, however: 'I got along well with Nick but a lot of the dialogue was not outside of specific, concrete stuff to do with production. There was a lot of one-way traffic.'[13]

By mid-March the bulk of the album had been recorded and Nick returned to live work. On Thursday, 12 March, Witchseason had arranged for him to travel 250 miles north to provide entertainment for a group of drunken students in the Common Room at Cartmel College, part of the University of Lancaster. Nick had come to dread such bookings. Quite apart from the unpredictable audiences, says Paul Wheeler, 'The actual musical side of being a gigging musician was quite limited, and he didn't like the surrounding business – the trains, the meeting strangers, the bed-and-breakfasts, the hustling.'

Joe had asked Bob Squire to keep him informed about Nick's gigs.

I had a phone call from Bob in which he reported that Nick was depressed because the audiences wouldn't stop talking and clinking

---

* John Wood has no memory of a fourth instrumental.

beer glasses. I don't think he had stage-fright – he knew perfectly well that he could sing and play – he just didn't have the right arena in which to do so and was unable to project his personality in noisy clubs. In those days people really had to project! Also, his tunings were complicated and seemed to take ages. He needed more than one guitar, which would have involved having an assistant . . . and it all required records being sold first.

Much of the material Nick had just recorded was specifically written for wider instrumentation than just him and his guitar. It's possible that he would have found it easier to project with a band or just a rhythm section behind him, but it was never discussed. 'It probably wouldn't have been possible for him to tour with the people he'd recorded with,' suggests John Wood. 'Also, the financial and logistical requirements of playing live become very different if you have more than just you and your guitar to think about.'

Self-promotion of any sort was anathema to Nick, and he concluded that he was achieving little by performing in random venues around the country. Always decisive where his music was concerned, he decided to pull the plug on the remaining club dates Witchseason had booked. 'Shortly after my talk with Bob I got a call from Nick,' says Joe. 'I remember it vividly. He said he was sorry for letting us down, but he couldn't carry on. He was devastated, ashamed.' He still had dates in the diary, though – later that month he was due to support Sandy Denny's new band, the much-hyped Fotheringay, on a short national tour.

In the meantime he was prevailed upon to attend a party given by the pop group Design in their new flat in Rosary Gardens, South Kensington. 'Nick knew he had written some really strong songs but was frustrated by the lack of interest in him,' recalls Tony Hill Smith.

> He was open about that with us, and clearly in need of a lot of encouragement (which we tried to give). Our friend Alec Reid was coming to the party, and he was a BBC Radio producer, so I told Nick to come along and talk to him because he was calm and sympathetic, not showbizzy. They got along well – but I do remember Nick left the party quickly.

Nick's Cambridge contemporary Iain Cameron also knew Alec and lent him *Five Leaves Left*. Alec admired it and invited Nick to record his second *Night Ride* session. However, he says, 'I wasn't aware that Nick had already recorded one with Pete Ritzema, otherwise I might very well not have offered him another.' Iain was still at Cambridge, but playing music wherever possible. Alec suggested he accompany Nick on the session, which was set for Monday, 23 March, so he arranged to go to Danehurst and rehearse.

Iain hadn't hung out with Nick since the previous summer and was struck by the change in him.

> He was more untogether – I didn't get the impression that he was progressing well with his self-organisation. When I arrived he offered to make me a cup of tea. Even in those days, when you accepted a cup of tea you had a reasonable expectation of what you were going to get, but he departed from the normal sequence and it ended up being just warm water with leaves in it. It was as if he had forgotten how to do it.*

Nick's chat was desultory and he didn't mention that he had almost finished recording his second album.

> If you're working with somebody you have to establish a good rela-tionship, get comfortable with them, and I found that difficult with him. At Cambridge, in Paul's room, we'd be kicking songs around, I'd play a bit of flute on that, he'd play some guitar there, 'Oh, I really like that . . .' Whereas I found him much harder to work with in London. There was a strange atmosphere. It's hard to put into words, but when you're trying to work like that, you detect quite readily. He wasn't giving anything.[14]

When Iain put down his cuppa and took up his flute, however, their interaction came into focus. 'He was able to demonstrate things to me purposefully and accurately and when we came to "Sunday" and "Bryter Layter", where the flute was the main feature, he was precise about my playing the lines exactly as he wanted them, with

* Brian Wells also recalls Nick's incompetent tea-making at Danehurst; on one occasion he burned his finger on his whistling kettle.

no extemporisation.' For Iain, the newer songs were 'really good. They were harder to follow, actually, than the *Five Leaves* stuff . . . More intricate, more considered, more minutely engineered.'[15]

Ahead of the BBC recording, Nick had the Fotheringay tour to face up to. He now had no more enthusiasm for large halls than small clubs and was reluctant to see the commitment through. Fittingly, the souvenir programme carried his picture but no supporting information. The first night was Monday, 16 March; Rodney and Molly proudly bought tickets, presumably without telling him, but to no avail. As Rodney recalled: 'He was booked to come to the Town Hall in Birmingham and never turned up.'[16]

The second show was at Leicester's De Montfort Hall on Wednesday the 18th. This time Nick – presumably under pressure from Witchseason – did make the journey. Also on the bill was the whimsical Scottish duo the Humblebums, consisting of Billy Connolly and Gerry Rafferty, but his involvement or interactions with the other musicians was minimal. 'He didn't seem to care about fame or any of those things,' recalls Billy. 'He didn't travel with us and wasn't pushing to play on the tour. He wasn't pushing at all.'

According to Joe, 'Sandy and Nick regarded each other with respect, but from a distance. Sandy couldn't relate to Nick, and Nick was as reticent towards her as he was towards most people.'[17] Audience member Dave Crewe says Nick broke a string halfway through a song, soldiered on and ended to an ovation – but ignored calls for an encore.[18]

It seems that Nick did not play at the Manchester Free Trade Hall on 20 March, but at Bristol's Colston Hall two days later, on Sunday the 22nd, the Humblebums' manager Mick McDonagh recalls him 'sitting down and playing delicately and quietly. His songs sounded beautiful, and one did engage with them as he played.' After the show Mick drove him back to London.

> He sat in the back with his guitar upright next to him. I found him hard work, as he didn't speak unless spoken to, so the silences seemed uncomfortable until I grew used to them. As he was hungry and had no money, I bought him a late-night meal in Membury services on the M4.

The next day Nick presented himself at Studio 2 in the sub-basement of Broadcasting House. 'I remember looking at Nick through the glass as he sat with his hair over his face, playing his guitar,' says Alec Reid. 'He was very quiet and didn't give much out. My abiding memory is that the session was rather dull, if anything. There was no interview and Colin Nichol, who presented it, never met him.'

Nick and Iain recorded eight songs. Five were relatively old: ''Cello Song', 'River Man', 'Saturday Sun' (with Nick on celeste), 'Time Of No Reply' and 'The Thoughts Of Mary Jane'. Nick had recorded three of them for his previous *Night Ride* session. The others were newer: 'Brighter Later' (as the BBC spelled it), 'Green Sunday' (Nick's working title for 'Sunday') and the otherwise undocumented 'Hillside' (lasting 3 minutes and 35 seconds).* Perhaps it was the fourth instrumental Joe remembers Nick having mooted. Two of the songs have surfaced as off-air recordings. Following an apparently extemporised guitar opening, ''Cello Song' (which might as well have been retitled 'Flute Song' here) is faithful to the rendition on *Five Leaves Left*, and 'Bryter Layter' is almost identical to the version he'd recently recorded in Sound Techniques. After the recording Nick showed no camaraderie towards Iain as they went their separate ways.

As Nick pondered how to complete 'Fly' and 'Northern Sky' – and hence his album – the first cover of one of his songs finally appeared on 26 March. It was a bizarre rendition of 'Mayfair' by the Jamaican singer Millie Small – whose global success with 'My Boy Lollipop' in 1964 had boosted Island's growth – on the reggae label Trojan. It came about through her friend Will van Zwanenberg, who'd been at Caius with Robert, and had appeared in Nick's backing ensemble at one or two Cambridge concerts. He remembered the song fondly and suggested Robert arrange it for her. She promoted 'Mayfair' with a topless spread in the adult magazine of the same name, but the few reviews it received focused on its B-side, the topical 'Enoch Power'. According to Robert, Nick was 'very

---

* The only song by Nick in which the word 'hillside' occurs is 'Voices'.

pleased' with the record, but it wasn't a hit and he certainly had no intention of revisiting it himself.*

On Easter Monday – exactly a week after the BBC session – Nick played at the Royal Festival Hall for the second time, opening the final show of Fotheringay's tour. Iain would happily have accompanied him but Nick chose to be supported by a double bassist, echoing the set-up for his first ever gig with Micky Astor back in December 1967. 'I think he'd heard of me through musicians I'd worked with at Sound Techniques,' says Chris Laurence, who had recently recorded with Elton John, Tom Paxton and numerous British jazzmen.

> He rang me out of the blue and asked if I wanted to play with him. I went to rehearse in his flat, with my bass on my back. It felt like a student's place, with a slightly bygone feel – blankets, peace-and-love stuff, as I recall. He was a really nice, gentle bloke. He was shy and his voice was extremely quiet. We just started playing. He was a lovely, understated guitarist who knew what he wanted to do but wasn't pushy – you had to listen. He was open to my ideas and not fazed by anything I did. I was there for a couple of hours and wrote a few bass parts down on paper.

They met again at the venue on the night. 'There were a lot of egos flying around backstage and we were both nervous,' continues Chris. John Martyn was there and recalled: 'Nick was cripplingly nervous. I mean, he was distraught before the gig. It was rather embarrassing, in fact, to see him. He was distinctly uncomfortable on stage – the music was fine, but he just didn't like being there at all.'[19]

Audience member John Etherington remembers that 'Nick sat on a stool with his head hung down. He didn't engage with the audience at all and only sang about five songs. I wasn't very impressed.'† Chris, however, says:

---

* 'Mayfair' also appeared on Millie Smalls's album *Time Will Tell*, issued in April, where it was misattributed to Desmond Dekker (under his real name, 'Dacres'). According to *Record Buyer* of June 1970, 'The material is thankfully more varied than [on] most reggae sets, "Mayfair" having a very unusual atmosphere, for instance.'

† John became what he calls 'a devotee' of Nick's when *Bryter Layter* came out, and had a tribute letter printed in *Sounds* of 11 January 1975.

I don't know if having me behind him gave him confidence, but he didn't play nervously. His manner was humble and reticent, but we went down well, perhaps because his soft approach was such a contrast to the other acts on the bill. We played for maybe twenty minutes.

By now Nick had a decent amount of live experience, including appearances in a disproportionate number of large venues for an artist of his standing – but the consensus among critics was that he was nowhere near ready for them. Reviewing this concert, the *NME*'s Nick Logan stated that Nick 'hunches over acoustic guitar and sings his own songs in a pleasant voice that seems to slide out of the corner of his mouth. The songs themselves are good but the fact that they are all in the same low key tended to send me to sleep.'[20]

Mark Williams wrote in *International Times* that

There was a short burst of applause for his first number, 'Time Has Told Me', which must prove something about the sales figures for his album,* but his act lacked presence or vitality and the beautiful arrangements that made the album so memorable. It seemed he felt a little uncertain as to whether or not he wanted to make public performances, there being little or no communication with the audience, who nevertheless gave his basically excellent music a basically well-deserved reception.[21]

Karl Dallas, who had damned Nick's showing in Croydon the previous October, covered the concert for *The Times*, stating:

It seems somewhat unfair on him to pitch him straight into concerts without the grassroots training he'd get humping his guitar around the country from club to club. This is the third time I have heard him in concert, and each time more of his music has got through to me – but still he remains a performer more for the intimate club or the recording studio, I feel.[22]

In the same review Dallas commented upon Billy Connolly's 'almost unintelligible Scottish humour and appropriate gesticulations' and

---

* Or, more likely, the sales figures for *Nice Enough to Eat*.

Sandy Denny's 'rumbustious good nature'; in halls of this size such things mattered.

Anthea Joseph was on both the Fairport and Fotheringay tours, and was convinced that Nick simply disliked gigs:

Nick needed more nannying than most of them because he loathed live performing . . . I remember him sleeping on my floor in Islington, 47 Thornhill Road, because he didn't want to go home [after a gig]. He crashed there a couple of times. We'd sit up all night. He didn't talk, you didn't even get that – and in those days the meaning of life was all. We'd sit there, I'd be rolling joints, and again, nothing – cups of tea, endless cups of tea . . . The next day he'd shamble forth and vanish into the morning.[23]

20

Going Downhill

DETERMINED TO FOLLOW his own ascetic path, by the spring of 1970 Nick had been living in London for six months, alone and penurious. He hadn't exactly cut himself off from his parents, but they had little idea what he was up to. They often wrote to him, whether offering him tickets to the Chelsea Flower Show, asking him to *Hamlet* at Stratford, gently rebuking him for having not replied to a wedding invitation or commiserating about his latest motoring mishap.

On Friday, 24 April, he met his father, who reiterated his willingness to offer any support he might want. Nick, however, restated his determination to be independent. '*Very* nice seeing you and having a talk,' Rodney wrote to him that weekend.

> Whatever your next move is, we hope it turns out well – there doesn't seem to be anything I can do to forward your plans, and anyway I know you want to go your own way and 'do it your way' so I'll stop buzzing around you. Keep us informed of how you're getting on and we shall look forward very much to your next visit.
>
> Masses of love,
>
> Mum and Dad

'Doing it his way' was not yielding much reward. His second album was almost finished but there was little momentum behind it. His second *Night Ride* session had aired shortly after midnight on the 14th, billed in the *Radio Times* as 'swinging sounds on and off the record, featuring tonight Nick Drake', but his profile remained stubbornly low.

Joe's hopes for him as a live act were evaporating, but he had more pressing concerns: his attempts to shore up Witchseason were not working. Aside from Fotheringay's enormous overheads, most of its resources were being gobbled up by *U*, the Incredible String Band's so-called 'surreal parable in song and dance', which had opened at the Roundhouse on 8 April, in the teeth of his strenuous advice to the contrary. Chaotic, under-rehearsed and ruinously expensive, the three-hour, Scientology-inspired show confirmed what Joe had long feared: the Incredible String Band's glory days were behind them.

Nick was spending much of his time at Danehurst, where Diana Soar and Andy Matheou visited him one day. 'It was a typical young man's room, untidy and not well-lit, but not smelly,' she recalls.

> There was a bed in the corner and a Chinese screen. Through the window was a laburnum tree in bloom, and I remember us talking about how it was so beautiful and yet so poisonous. Nick had a huge piece of pure Afghani hash – he was so pleased with it, we all smelled it and he said, 'Jungle fresh!' We sat cross-legged on the floor, smoked some, listened to music and enjoyed each other's company.

He continued to hang out with Bev. One late spring afternoon they went to the cinema to watch Ken Loach's *Kes*, which made a strong impression on him. According to Bev: 'He had never really seen what normal country people were like. He lived in cotton wool.' The Martyns were in fact growing disenchanted with the city. 'Life in London is wholly deranged,' John complained at the time.[1] 'The pace, the bustle and the price of everything has gone quite crazy. It's all one great hoax. All these clerks, secretaries and typists flood to London from the provinces thinking they'll find a swinging city, and they spend their lives in bedsitters, being hopelessly miserable.'

It was therefore serendipitous that an architect friend offered them the use of his weekend home at 10 Cobourg Place in Hastings for a few weeks as of May 1970. 'We invited Nick to stay,' says Bev. 'He was often playing and singing and I was running around after Wesley or trying to catch my breath, rather than focusing on what he was doing – but there was a hatch between the kitchen and the living room, so I could hear everything.' Nick was still preoccupied by how to finish the remaining songs for his new album: 'I remember him singing "Northern Sky" on his guitar, and from where I stood it looked like he was sitting at the top of this big tree you could see out of the living room window.'

One weekend he visited Mike Kowalski at Herons Wake, the cottage in Chilham, Kent, where he lived with his wife Dawn and their baby daughter. 'The idea was just for him to get away from London and have a break,' says Mike.

> We picked him up from the station, smoked a bit, drank some wine, chatted about what was going on in the States and on the London scene and went for walks in the woods. The hoarse sound the herons made really freaked him out! We also listened to music – I played him Pharoah Sanders, as he liked jazz and blues.* I was in awe of his talent, so I probably just thought his quiet manner was all part of his genius.

Sometimes he dropped in on Keith Morris in St Mary's Mansions, Paddington. Keith:

> He'd appear, knock on the door. It'd be, 'Nick! Come in, have a cup of tea and a chat!' But he was never with anyone – I didn't know a girlfriend or anything like that. Normally if you meet people you start getting the detritus of their life, but with Nick you didn't – you just got Nick.[2]

He would not always be talkative: 'If he was up, you could have a normal conversation with him. If he was down, there'd be a knock on the door, I'd let him in, he'd sit there, have a cup of tea, and he wouldn't have said a word before leaving.'[3]

Nick also called on David Ward in Knightsbridge.† 'He would ring the bell, come up with his guitar, all six-foot-whatever of him, concertina his legs under him, then they'd play all night,' says David's then girlfriend Sarah Coates. 'He'd play songs he'd just written, hot off the press, or they'd just jam away. I might bake them some potatoes or roll a joint, then go to bed and leave them to it.' On

---

* John Martyn also visited Mike in Chilham in 1970 and vividly remembered the impact Sanders's *Karma* had on him when he heard it there.
† David had become Viscount Ednam upon the death of his grandfather, the Earl of Dudley, in December 1969, but he remains David Ward here.

one occasion a few others were there, including David's cousin Stella Astor, who says, 'We were all stoned. Nick went up to the piano, flicked his long fingers nimbly across the keys, played a couple of complex phrases, stopped abruptly and left.'

Despite some of his recent lyrics, Nick continued to show no apparent interest in having a girlfriend or sex life. As Bev summarises: 'I never questioned Nick's sexuality, I just understood that he didn't know women in that way. He was naïve and though he felt comfortable with some women he couldn't handle relationships. Love was too much for him, his head wasn't strong enough.' Ben Laycock puts it starkly: 'I've no knowledge of any romantic or sexual relationship he ever had with anyone.'

By the spring of 1970 Joe's on-off girlfriend Linda Peters had got to know him a little. She grew up in Glasgow (where she knew John Martyn) and had been immersed in London's folk scene since 1967. Outgoing and forthright, she had a very different personality to Nick's ('He was the most spectral kind of person I ever met – he was very grand actually, and there was a line you definitely couldn't cross'[4]) but was drawn to him. 'He was the type I liked: very quiet and cool and obviously very bright. Even if he didn't talk, you knew he was very bright.'[5]

Linda was sharing a place in Holland Park Avenue with a yoga teacher named Barbara, and he would visit, probably combined with a trip to the Squires', just up the road. 'Nick would drink macrobiotic tea and I'd put on records for him,' she says.[6] She found his silence frustrating: 'I used to get quite cross with him because he didn't talk enough.' She was close friends with Sandy Denny and remembers Nick especially liking 'The Sea', which Sandy had written for Fotheringay. Nonetheless, 'Every time Sandy came round and saw him she gave him very short shrift indeed. She just couldn't be doing with this at all. "Nick! Speak to me, Nick! Talk to me!" So I think he was scared of her.'

Linda can only recall one occasion on which he gave much reaction to anything:

> I had reddish hair and one day I dyed it jet-black. It was frightening-looking, so awful it was beyond belief. Nick never registered anything

that ever happened, never ever remarked about anything, but he walked in and was absolutely flabbergasted . . . He just kept saying, 'Your hair! Your hair!'[7]

She had hopes of taking their relationship further but found him physically remote too. 'We'd have a bit of a cuddle, but it was always strangely detached.' On one occasion he stayed, but it was hardly a night of passion: 'We tucked him up and I slept on the edge of the bed.' At the end of his visits, says Linda, 'I would go to the end of the road with him and give him a ten-shilling note for a cab, because he never, ever had any money.'[8]*

Certainly no royalties were due for *Five Leaves Left*, making Nick's weekly Witchseason advance his only regular source of income. It was supplemented by the occasional gig. On 11 April he was at Les Cousins alongside the Third Ear Band, but now that he'd asked Witchseason to stop arranging dates, his few bookings came via Marcus Bicknell. On the 13th he was booked to support Genesis at Friars in Aylesbury (though it's unclear whether he did), and Molly later mentioned him having played in the 'Upstairs' space at Ronnie Scott's in Soho, where Genesis had a Tuesday residency that month, but his attendance was becoming erratic.

On Friday, 8 May, he was part of an improbable all-night bill at Bedford College in Regent's Park, headlined by Graham Bond's Initiation and featuring John Martyn, East of Eden, the Climax Chicago Blues Band and hard rockers May Blitz. Once he would have savoured appearing alongside the mighty Bond, but he was coming to detest such events, and David Ward remembers that 'reports began to arrive via mutual friends that Nick was beginning to lose faith in the validity of public performance'.[9]

Witchseason had intended his new album to be a May release, so it was optimistically included in *Music Business Weekly* – without a title – in a list of Island LPs due to appear that month.[10] At the same time the independent publicist Frances van Staden, whose sister Oonagh worked at Witchseason, issued a press release about him, offering basic background information and tentatively stating: 'The

---

* This was perhaps due to Nick's long-held dislike of carrying change in his pockets, though he did keep a small purse for that purpose.

second album is almost completed and veers away from the highly acoustic sound of the first. Response to Nick has been steady. His introverted, extremely personal music takes time and consideration to appreciate fully.' Extracting coherent statements from Nick was becoming increasingly hard, though, and he was barely quoted in it.

Nonetheless, it seems to have prompted his first known interview. Squarely aimed at adolescent girls, *Jackie* magazine billed itself as 'Britain's brightest teenage weekly' and sold a remarkable half-a-million copies a week. Its cheaply printed pages were dominated by romantic fiction, pin-ups and skincare tips, but – thanks to Frances – also incorporated some surprisingly hip music coverage. Witchseason acts including Fairport, the Incredible String Band, Fotheringay, and John and Bev were all given valuable *Jackie* column inches.

The feature was written under the pseudonym 'Samantha' and appeared in the regular 'Sam Meets the Goodlookers' column. (Her true identity – whether male or female – is unknown and probably unknowable.) The interview took place in Frances's flat in Swiss Cottage, Nick wearing 'a green open-neck shirt with a black sweater and black donkey jacket, his brown hair curling over his shoulders'. Illustrated by one of the shots Keith Morris had taken the previous April, it began by announcing: 'Nick Drake is tall, gentle, modest and very, very shy.' The author had seen him perform, stating that he played 'almost embarrassingly alone in a spotlight, nervously tuning his guitar before each number. He says the title of the song, but apart from that he rarely speaks – his is a very private world.'

Nick provided a brief synopsis of his life and career and mentioned liking the Beatles, Donovan and Debussy, but stopped short of calling them influences. The piece emphasised his lack of interest in politics, although he did express enthusiasm for the zeitgeist: 'Things have reached the stage where anything can happen in the development of pop culture – art, music, poetry, writing, politics are all coming together, and I would like to be in on it.' Gabrielle doubts these were his exact words, but Paul Wheeler can identify with the sentiment: 'I was writing a novel at the time Nick was working on his second album and I remember an excited sense of post-sixties possibility, as if we were all poised for take-off.'

Longing to help Nick take flight, in late May his parents gave him a Uher 4-track reel-to-reel tape recorder as an early birthday present. 'It's certainly a very fine thing to suddenly have in one's possession, and I really am grateful,' he wrote in the courteous, considered tone he used in letters home. 'I know it's going to come in very useful in various ways, be it for recording new things to hand in to the publishing woman [i.e. Brenda Ralfini] or entertaining British Rail passengers with rural sounds etc. Thank you very much indeed.' Rodney replied with a number of technical recommendations about the device, which he had thoroughly researched. Perhaps its most useful function for Nick was the 'transfer from one tape to another plus the addition of another instrument or voice. One can go on doing that indefinitely, apparently.'

Rodney also informed Nick that he and Molly had only just bought their first stereo system:

> We have been enjoying your record so much on the stereo – the first time we have ever heard it properly. You really must hurry up and do another one – it was such a delightful work of art and it's high time there was another like it! You've got it in you, all right.

His encouraging tone suggests that he and Molly had inferred that all was not well with their son's career, and they were apparently unaware that his second album was all but finished.

Rodney did not tell Nick of their growing concern for his well-being, both physical and mental. Rodney was a *Times* reader, and on 9 May the paper had published a long article entitled 'A Case of Schizophrenia', in which the journalist John Pringle candidly described the sad situation of his own son, who had gone downhill at Oxbridge, becoming steadily more antisocial, unreliable and emotionally detached. 'There is a distressingly high incidence among young adults, including those of beyond average intelligence,' he wrote, prompting considerable correspondence. 'I am sure my dad read the article, and it must have rung peals of bells with him,' says Gabrielle.

The *Jackie* article, meanwhile, appeared in the 30 May issue and claimed Nick's new album was finished – but 'Fly' and 'Northern Sky' remained unresolved. Joe had recently been in the US, where he was working on *Desertshore* by Nico while the Incredible String

Band baffled audiences on both coasts with *U*, and in Ireland, recording Dr. Strangely Strange's second LP. He was back at Sound Techniques in early June, mixing *Desertshore* with John Wood and its co-producer John Cale, who had played with Nico in the Velvet Underground. At the end of one session Joe played John some of his other recent recordings and he 'went nuts for Nick', as Joe puts it.

Joe explained that 'Fly' and 'Northern Sky' were works in progress, upon which the headlong John insisted that Joe immediately call Nick. Joe recalls: 'I called Nick up and said, "Look, John Cale's here and he'd like to talk to you."' Joe explained that John was proposing to help finish the outstanding tracks.

> Nick was very hesitant. He said, 'Oh, oh, really? Well, ah, ah . . .' My impression was that he hadn't the faintest idea who Cale was, though it might have been just his habitual diffidence. Cale was sitting next to me, so I tried to communicate by tone of voice that this was not something he should refuse. And then John said, 'Give me his address, tell him I'll be over there in fifteen minutes!' So I said, 'Well, you heard that – he's coming over,' and Nick said, 'Oh, well, uh, uh . . .' After John left to hail a taxi, I may have called Nick back to explain more fully who he was . . .

John went straight to Danehurst, where the blindsided Nick let him in. For Joe, their meeting was 'an absolute collision of two separate, disparate personalities – the tornado of Welsh energy from a working-class background in Merthyr Tydfil and the shy and diffident public schoolboy . . . I think Nick was kind of overwhelmed.'[11] According to John,

> He was a very quiet guy. It was very difficult to figure out what was going on in his mind . . .[12] I had a twelve-string and he had never seen a D12 before, a Martin. And you know that very complicated picking that he had? He just picked up the guitar and it was just like this orchestral sound coming out. He went nuts. He was sitting there, stunned by it.[13]

Spurred by John's infectious vitality, if nothing else, they swiftly devised arrangements for the two songs. The following morning, says Joe, 'We were booked to do more work on *Desertshore* but John

rang me and said, "Cancel it, we're doing 'Fly' and 'Northern Sky'."
He ordered instruments: organ, celeste, harpsichord, an amp for his
viola pickup, etc.' They arrived together that afternoon, 'John with
a wild look in his eyes and Nick trailing behind. Despite his domin-
eering manner, Cale was solicitous towards Nick, who seemed to
be guardedly enjoying himself. His only choice was to relax and be
carried along.'[14]

   John Wood also remembers the contrast between them, but says
the session was harmonious. 'Cale was dogmatic but there was no
friction. Nick was quite happy. All the overdubs were done by Cale
within three hours. Nick's Hammond organ on "Hazey Jane I" –
just a subtle pulse, not an obvious part – was the very last thing we
recorded for the album.' The recording sessions had finally come to
a close.* 'There were no out-takes – we recorded everything Nick
wanted to be on it, and that was that,' says John. 'I wiped the unused
takes – that was standard practice back then.'

   John and Joe now set about mixing at Sound Techniques, though
Joe feels 'balancing' might be a more accurate term because John
had been so meticulous about microphone placement during the
sessions. 'What's on the record is what it sounded like in the studio,'
emphasised Robert Kirby.

> There was no tarting about, changing EQs, taking bits out, changing
> levels; I mean, the volume that something was playing at when it
> came in was the volume it was playing at when it finished, and you
> didn't touch it. So that was the whole essence of the way John and
> Joe worked together – they got the sound correct to start with.[15]

Nonetheless, it presented more of a challenge than *Five Leaves
Left* had. 'We mixed *Five Leaves Left* in one long sequence of several
days,' according to John.

> This time, however, it was eight-track. Mixing eight-track could be
> quite complicated because you'd probably record the basic set-up on

---

* By John Cale's various accounts, he worked on the tracks in Nick's absence, but
Joe says he 'would never have started overdubbing John Cale on those tracks
without Nick there'. Precisely dating the session is impossible, but on 10 June
Molly wrote to Nick stating: '*Very* glad to hear you got two more things recorded.'

about four tracks, and on those you'd probably have bass, drums, acoustic guitar, and vocal . . . Then on something like 'At The Chime Of A City Clock' you'd end up with two or three string tracks and the sax and maybe something else. Sometimes you'd end up with more than one thing on one track, so you'd have to start sorting out different options, with changing cues, throughout the song.[16]

Their first attempt wasn't satisfactory so they decided to take the tapes to New York and try again at Vanguard. John explains: 'I really liked the way the echo-plates worked at Vanguard so Joe indulged me by sending me off there.* Nick didn't come.' Alas, that mix also failed to meet John's standards:

It wasn't hanging together the way I felt it should. At the outset of a recording I have a mental sound picture, and I wasn't satisfied that I was putting it across. It's not technical, it's visceral. I didn't feel the perspective was right, I felt there was more on the tapes than we were getting across. I really dug my heels in until I had the result I wanted. My motto has always been: 'Every record gets the sound it deserves.'

As such, it was back to Sound Techniques, where a new pair of monitor speakers had been installed. Using those, they started from scratch again. John wasn't being pedantic; he emphasises that 'I'd never done more than two mixes on anything before and haven't since. "At The Chime Of A City Clock" and "Poor Boy" were the most complicated – getting the sound to knit together so it had depth and feeling.' Joe recalls spending an entire day on 'At The Chime Of A City Clock', underlining the meticulousness they applied to Nick's work.

As with *Five Leaves Left*, Nick stayed out of decisions about the mix and running order (though, as John says, 'The running order was simpler because to an extent the instrumentals dictated it'). He

---

* 'An echo-plate is an electro-mechanical device – a sheet of steel hung within a metal frame inside a wooden box – through which you played a recording to give the impression that it had been made in a more reverberant setting,' explains John Wood. 'Every studio set them up slightly differently, so you'd get a unique sound from each.'

did go to Sound Techniques to hear the album before it was mastered, with a view to objecting to anything he might wish to – but by general agreement it sounded wonderful. 'I finally got the whole thing to work the way I wanted,' says John, 'and it's the only album I've ever recorded where I wouldn't want to change a thing.'

Joe had the same feeling:

I think it's the [Witchseason album] on the whole that I was happiest with. It's one I can sit down and listen to without ever thinking 'I wish we'd mixed that differently', or 'We shouldn't have done that'. It just seems to work as a record. I can appreciate it beyond worrying about any aspect of the production. It was a record where everything fell together pretty well. It ended up as a good reflection of Nick's music [and] what we tried to accomplish.[17]

Opening with the short, shimmering 'Introduction', the stylistic departure from *Five Leaves Left* is made clear with the punchy, brass-laden 'Hazey Jane II' – the only rock song Nick ever recorded. His guitar playing throughout is startlingly original and immaculate, whether on the upbeat pop of 'One Of These Things First' or the jazzy stylings of 'At The Chime Of A City Clock', while the emotional depth of 'Northern Sky' is leavened by the irony of 'Poor Boy'. The album succeeded in having a more broadly appealing sound without being blatantly commercial (though Joe's bêtes noires 'Bryter Layter' and 'Sunday' stray close to library music), and Nick again powerfully communicates his observant, cryptic, wry persona.

Those involved in its creation remember him being delighted with the finished product. David Sandison stated that 'Nick personally supervised every aspect of Kirby's arrangements, working with him and mainly getting Kirby to chart out what he had in the main already planned.'[18] However, Nick remarked the following year: 'I'm not altogether clear about this album – I haven't got to terms with the whole presentation.'[19]

He seems to have been referring to its range of instruments and styles, but according to Joe, John and Robert, he was fully involved in every choice. Joe is willing to speculate that

Nick liked control over how his work sounded and was always very closely involved with Robert's arrangements, but the contributions by McGregor and Cale were unplanned accidents. Everyone loved the way they turned out, which maybe made it difficult for him to dissent. He never complained to me about their contributions, but perhaps he felt the album had slipped away from him.

Robert, however, rebutted any suggestion that Nick had been railroaded towards a finished product that he wasn't entirely satisfied with: 'Nick always had the final word, he made the decisions. The arrangements I did were worked out with him over time . . . He never seemed in the least displeased . . . [The album] is a hundred per cent Nick's work and how he wanted it at that time.'[20] Paul Wheeler concurs: 'Nick and I used to meet in a Greek restaurant in Charlotte Street called Anemos. I had lunch with him there after the album had been completed and I remember he was pleased with it.'

As it was readied for release, Witchseason still had the challenge of turning Nick into a viable commercial proposition. He wasn't gigging, so having him write for others was an obvious area to explore. The *Jackie* article had mentioned that his 'songs are widely admired by singers like Françoise Hardy'. She had indeed been struck by *Five Leaves Left*. By her account, 'The "soul" that emerged from his songs touched me deeply – romantic melodies, poetic but at the same time refined – as well as the so-individual timbre of his voice, which added to the melancholy of the whole thing.'[21]

When Joe and Brenda Ralfini got wind of her enthusiasm they decided to follow up. Joe had already observed similarities between Nick's work and French *chanson* and, as he puts it, 'Getting covers of Nick's material was one way out of the dead-end of his not performing, and I thought it would make the whole thing more concrete and interesting if he wrote one specially for her.'

Nick was cautiously open to the idea of writing something for her, so Joe set up a meeting through the arranger and producer Tony Cox, who was often in Sound Techniques and was interested in the possibility of arranging and producing Françoise. One day in June the three of them flew to Paris.

'We checked into a hotel, then went to meet her in her fabulous apartment in an old tenement in the Île Saint-Louis,' says Tony. According to a contemporary report, the top-floor flat was 'cool and moody, with white walls and black carpets'.[22] The encounter was no more colourful. 'I don't think Nick had a guitar with him, and he didn't take my cues to speak,' says Joe. 'She didn't say much either, which left me doing most of the talking. The whole meeting was awkward. We left it that she would let us know if she wanted to record anything of his, and didn't hear from her again.'*

Silent though Nick had been, the meeting gave him certain bragging rights. As David Sandison put it, 'I wouldn't be at all surprised if he weren't deeply in love with Françoise Hardy, because anybody around during that time with a reasonably normal level of testosterone would have followed her to the end of the world.'[23] Upon returning to the UK, Nick went to Cambridge during May Week and met Rick Charkin for a drink in their old haunt, the Criterion. As Rick recalls, 'I said to him, "Where have you been?" and he replied, "In France with Françoise Hardy. She's interested in recording my songs." I was speechless.'

The visit to Cambridge, teeming with undergraduates celebrating the end of their final exams, was a powerful, almost masochistic reminder for Nick of what he had abandoned. Had his album appeared on schedule it would have acted as a neat substitute for his degree – but its cover wasn't even yet designed. A photograph taken at Witchseason that month shows him studying the back cover of Fairport's *Full House*; it surely hadn't escaped him that theirs and Fotheringay's albums had been recorded at the same time as his, and had both come out swiftly.

'I had the sense that we'd released too many Fairport albums too quickly, and maybe felt that releasing another by Nick too soon would tread on whatever momentum *Five Leaves Left* was generating,' explains Joe.

* She has since stated: 'It never occurred to me to record any of his songs, because my vocal and rhythmic limits, as well as my whole personality, make me prefer to sing simpler songs.'

Also, Fairport and Fotheringay were touring and were well-known. As soon as an album of theirs was done, Island would have wanted it in the release schedule, as they were guaranteed sellers – unlike Nick. They didn't want to just throw Nick's second album out there to sink or swim, they wanted to think it through. We were looking for ways to build up his career.

Nick, meanwhile, was in limbo. One day Richard Thompson bumped into him:

> I was on the Tube platform at Hampstead, heading into central London . . . He must have thought it would be more embarrassing to walk past without acknowledging me before waiting further down the platform, so he came and sat down next to me. This was now awkward for both of us, so I had to strike up a conversation, or what would have to pass for one, between two socially inept introverts.

At Richard's instigation they discussed Delius and Debussy until their train came. 'We both got on and sat opposite one another; it was noisy enough to stem conversation, to our mutual relief. Fifteen minutes later he got off at Goodge Street.'[24]

It was the closest stop to Charlotte Street and Witchseason. One day in June Nick sat down in Joe's office and surprised him with a decision he'd taken.

> He came to me before the cover was done or anything and said, 'The next record is just going to be me and my guitar.' I know he liked [the new album] but I was probably distracted during the process of making it and I think he felt, 'Okay, we've done this, now I'm going to do something completely different.'

Nick's motivation was almost certainly artistic, if partly pragmatic, but Joe says: 'I took the way he told me that he wanted his next album to be just guitar-and-voice as a criticism.' He also considered it misguided. 'Right from the start, my vision for Nick's songs had been about the embellishments, the interactions between instruments – but I wasn't going to argue with him about it because I knew that Nick wasn't somebody you really argued with.'

Unbeknown to Nick, Joe took the news as another indication that Witchseason wasn't working.

My relationships with the artists had always been what got me out of bed in the morning, but when those started collapsing, I lost enthusiasm. There was the Fairport crash, the Incredible String Band had become Scientologists, Sandy had left Fairport, Fotheringay was expensive and difficult, Richard and I had argued over what to include on *Full House*, Nick had flopped and his mental state was going downhill . . . I felt overworked because I was taking on more and more, I still had my own obligations, and things were dividing in an amoeba-like fashion. Instead of producing Fairport, I now had Fairport and Fotheringay to produce, Mike Heron was doing a solo album at the same time as the Incredible String Band were doing more recordings, Chris McGregor led on to Dudu Pukwana at the same time as the Brotherhood of Breath . . .

It just mushroomed, and all of it was produced by me. It got so I was just block-booking weeks at a time at Sound Techniques, getting up at 8.30 in the morning, going into the office for two or three hours, trying to make a one o'clock session at Sound Techniques and staying there until one o'clock in the morning, then doing the same thing again the next day, sometimes having one group down from one till seven, then another from eight till midnight, and kind of running people in and out of the studio. It also got to the point where, from being very appreciative of the lack of pressure to produce or to work or tour, groups or artists became very upset at the lack of money that was coming in.[25]

Nick certainly fell into this category. Instead of rushing out his album, Island had decided to push it back and try to generate interest in him via another sampler LP. On Friday, 12 June, they released a double set entitled *Bumpers*. Side three closed with 'Hazey Jane I' (here titled plain 'Hazey Jane'), whose gentle power, sustained by Nick's rippling guitar and Robert's delicate strings, was experienced by music fans all over the country, so low was the purchase price. The cover explained that the song came 'from his album to be released Autumn '70'.

Bumpers was distributed internationally, and separately issued in

France, Germany, Holland, Italy and Greece.* As David Betteridge explained at the time:

> If you use [samplers] in the right way and don't flood your market
> with too many at one time, they can be of enormous assistance in
> introducing little-known names like Nick Drake to the public . . .
> If you can sell five hundred copies of an album because of a sampler,
> you're doing well.[26]

Nick was uninterested in such strategising; his frustration at the slow progress of his career was starting to overwhelm him. On the evening of Sunday, 21 June, he played a gig at Westfield College in Northwest London, alongside John Martyn, Stefan Grossman, the Humblebums and Elton John, who was on the threshold of stardom.† A voracious consumer of pop, Elton had strongly connected with *Five Leaves Left*: 'I loved that album so much – the melodies, the nonconformity of the songs, their bleakness and their beauty. I found solace in them.'[27]

He and Nick did not connect that night, however. The World Cup Final was on and the show began after the game, in front of a well-refreshed audience. Football had never remotely interested Nick and he did not share in the camaraderie. A stripper was on hand and strutted down the aisle, gyrating her tasselled breasts to lusty cheers. John Altman was there to back John Martyn:

> Nick was dispirited by the fact that the students spent his entire set
> drinking and talking. John and I talked to him backstage, urging him
> to ignore them. We told him that everyone was having the same
> experience, and that no one could get through to people like that.
> Billy Connolly and Gerry Rafferty were chipping in too – we were
> all trying to convince him, but it didn't have much effect.

The following Thursday Nick appeared at Ewell Technical College for the second time, this time supporting Ralph McTell. They met for the only time in the dressing room: 'He was monosyllabic. At

---

* Nick's track was omitted from the Australasian and Scandinavian releases.
† His debut album, *Empty Sky*, had been released at the same time as *Five Leaves Left*. His second (self-titled) album had appeared in April 1970, and he was gigging relentlessly to promote it.

that particular gig he was very shy. He did the first set, and something awful must have happened. He was doing his song "Fruit
Tree" and walked off halfway through it, just left the stage.'[28] Ralph's
brother Bruce was also there: 'Nothing went wrong at the concert,
but something *was* wrong – Nick was unwell and should not have
been there. I ran into him backstage but he was anxious only to
run away. My abiding and haunting memory of that night remains
Nick's fearful, despairing stare.'

By all accounts Nick's social energy was all but depleted by the
summer of 1970, as his personality turned ever more inwards. John
and Bev's flat in Denning Road remained a retreat. A seventeen-
year-old New York music fan named Brian Cullman was crashing
there, having befriended John on the folk circuit. He was nominally
'London correspondent' for the American music paper *Crawdaddy!*,
and by his account the usual order of play was 'listen to music, drink
tea, get stoned and watch the sun set over the heath'.[29]

One afternoon, after an hour of music and chat,

> something by the window stirred and started to rise. I hadn't noticed
> anyone there, and it gave me a fright . . . I could see it was someone
> fairly tall with the physique of a tennis player, all arms and legs and
> elbows. A curtain of dark and uncombed hair hung around his face,
> hiding everything but his eyes.[30]

Intrigued by Nick, Brian listened to *Five Leaves Left* (with Bev's
advice not to praise it too much in front of John) and was stunned.
He saw Nick again in their kitchen later that week.

> I tried to tell him how much I liked his album . . . I mentioned a
> few songs – "Cello Song' and 'River Man' and 'Saturday Sun' – and
> he nodded and stared at the table. After a few minutes he started
> fumbling through his coat pockets. There was a smell of mint and
> tobacco, maybe cloves, and he was pulling out scraps of paper, guitar
> picks, rolling papers and such. He looked up.
>
> 'Do you like chocolate?' he asked. He held an unopened bar of
> Cadbury's Dairy Milk.[31]

Andy Matheou was also there, so Brian – himself an aspiring
singer-songwriter – took the opportunity to play a couple of songs

on his Gibson Hummingbird, an instrument not often seen in Britain. When he'd finished John played it, then handed it to Nick. Brian was curious to hear him but says that Nick stood ('He had an odd way of sitting that made him seem smaller and frailer than he was – it was always a surprise, when he stood up, that he towered over John and nearly everyone else'[32]), took the guitar and went next door.

It was characteristic of Nick not to be willing to play an unfamiliar instrument in front of others. Brian recalls:

I could hear the faint sounds of finger-picking, like the ocean, far away. Ten, maybe fifteen minutes later, the sound stopped and he walked back in, nodding to himself. 'Nice,' he said, handing it back. Then he studied the front, as if he'd just noticed the design on the pickguard. 'Gibson,' he said.[33]

On Saturday, 1 August, Nick was again billed at Les Cousins alongside John James. The date had probably been arranged at John Martyn's urging, and he was there too. Brian had been offered a slot and says: 'There was a large though not capacity crowd there.'[34] Nick came on after him. The billing had stated that he would be appearing 'with bassist friend', meaning Danny Thompson, but it was probably a case of John over-promising, and John James says that 'Danny didn't show, and probably didn't know about it'.

Nick had not worked up solo arrangements of newer material for gigs, and remained reliant on *Five Leaves Left* and other songs of its vintage, such as 'Time Of No Reply' and 'Mayfair'. By mid-1970 those who had seen him repeatedly surely felt his repertoire was growing stagnant. Although his new album was complete, it appears that the only song from it he performed live was 'Hazey Jane I' – and even that had been in repertoire since the spring of 1969.

Brian recalls Nick playing 'Time Has Told Me', 'Three Hours', "Cello Song', 'The Thoughts Of Mary Jane' and 'Things Behind The Sun', but was most struck by 'Hazey Jane I'. The audience was perhaps familiar with it via *Bumpers*, but on this occasion, says Brian,

He sang the first few lines over and over again, almost like a mantra, against safe and rolling chords. The effect was chilling. Nick made no eye contact with the audience and shrank into himself, looking smaller and more lost and fragile than usual . . . I've never seen a performer as deeply unhappy or uncomfortable on stage.

As at Ewell Technical College, Nick did not complete his set; audience member Steve Aparicio remembers him 'leaving the stage in some sort of distress and being looked after by John Martyn'. Without announcing it or perhaps realising it, after a few more than thirty confirmed performances Nick's live career was over.

'There were only two or three concerts that felt right, and there was something wrong with all the others,' he reflected a few months later.[35]

I did play Cousins and one or two folk clubs in the north, but the gigs just sort of petered out. I was under some obligation to do them, but it wasn't the end of the world when I stopped. If I was enjoying the gigs, it would have made much more sense.

It might not have been the end of the world, but Nick had cut off a vital route to success. As David Ward puts it: 'Discontinuing public performances in those days spelled curtains for an artistic career.'[36]

21

A Different Nick

E VERYONE WHO KNEW Nick agrees that he had become worry-ingly uncommunicative by the summer of 1970. Months of unstructured, frugal solitude, coupled with his lack of recognition and career momentum, seem to have precipitated a change in his personality. By Joe's account, after he stopped gigging he 'retreated to his room in Hampstead. He had always smoked hashish but that now became the pattern of his days: play guitar and smoke joints, go out for a curry when he got hungry.'[1]

His few visitors found him silent and introspective, lacking his previously leavening humour. He later told his mother that he 'had realised that his joie de vivre was slipping from him in Hampstead days and was being "taken away from him" by the people surrounding him, from whom he could not break away as he was "up to the neck" with them'.[2] This was surely a reference to Witchseason and its related circles, and the pressure he felt to generate and promote new material.

His friends in Chelsea had seen little of him since 1969. 'By 1970 our group was fragmenting – not the friendships, but the amount we saw each other,' says Alex Henderson. 'People were getting jobs, getting married, having children . . . Nick might disappear for two or three months at a time.' One day Ben Laycock, who was busy setting up a removals business, took it upon himself to visit Danehurst for the first time. 'It was a grim place,' he says.

> A cell, is my memory of it – not a pleasant memory. There was nothing in it other than the bare essentials – a chair and a bed, no pictures or carpets. I hadn't seen him for a longish time and he looked dirty, like he wasn't looking after himself. That was the first time I realised something was wrong.

Ben reported back to Alex, who then visited with Sophia. 'Haverstock Hill seemed a long way from Chelsea!' she says. 'We sat in the garden. He was quieter, but not silent.' Alex recalls that 'His room was large and square, a perfect cube, like a cell, looking out over an unkempt garden':

> It had a bed and an electric fire and there was mess everywhere. It would've done my head in, and I certainly wasn't very tidy! The place itself wasn't squalid, the wallpaper wasn't peeling, but it wasn't at all homely and he obviously wasn't eating well or looking after himself. It was all rather sad – not at all what we wanted for him.

Disturbed, Alex and Ben returned together soon afterwards. 'We just wanted to check that he was okay,' says Alex. Nick's untidiness didn't trouble them nearly as much as the apparent transformation in his personality. 'We were nonplussed that he wouldn't talk,' says Ben.

> If we asked something he'd reply, but there was no conversation and the silences were long, with no proper responses or back-and-forth. I don't remember him even playing his guitar on those occasions. It wasn't the old Nick, it was a different Nick. I can't explain it; I've never been able to. I would ask him why he was so down – things seemed to be going well – and he wouldn't say, or couldn't say.[3]

It seems that his father's fears about his dope smoking were being realised. 'I suspect his problems were exacerbated by spending too much time alone and by the amount of dope he was smoking,' continues Alex. 'I think it became a crutch for him.' Stella Astor also links his introspection to his dope smoking:

> We used to smoke Afghani hash without realising what a strong drug it is – very taxing to the nervous system. Being creative, Nick needed to spend time on his own, and smoking strong dope by yourself can make a shy person paranoid. You don't realise how crazy the dope's making you till you stop.

Nick spent part of the summer with Paul Wheeler. They'd seen little of each other since Nick had dropped out of Cambridge, and Paul noticed that by now he 'seemed monastic, with very few possessions or even a favourite guitar'. Paul had himself just dropped out, after deliberately failing his Part I exams. For him, 'The utopia of the sixties morphing into the reality of the seventies was a heavy crash.' He continued to feel a kinship with Nick; like him, he was uncertain about the present, let alone the future.

Paul's girlfriend Diana was working from Tittenhurst Park, John Lennon's Georgian mansion outside Ascot, twenty-five miles west of London. 'Paul and I moved into a little workman's cottage on the estate,' she says. 'Nick would turn up without warning. He wasn't physical – he wouldn't have instigated a hug but might have returned a kiss in a perfunctory way.' Paul says they passed 'a lot of time wandering around the grounds – we wouldn't have gone into the main house with him, and even if we had Nick would have been far too discreet to snoop. The house was subsidiary to the trees, anyway.'

In the evening, says Diana, 'Paul and Nick would play their guitars together':

> There was a gentle power to Nick's style that always made people listen. It seemed instinctive and sounded rather lovely even when he was tinkering away. I think the guitar was a useful prop for him, too – it distracted attention from him personally. He spoke softly and not very much. It felt like there was a shield around him. I wanted to look after him but he never asked for anything. He was so thin that I always tried to feed him, but he was a tea-and-toast sort of eater.

Like Paul, Brian Wells had seen little of Nick in recent months: 'I'd scraped through my last year at Cambridge, then got a place to do clinical training at Middlesex Hospital in Goodge Street.' Upon moving to London Brian often hung out with Nick at Danehurst, and they occasionally visited Paul at Tittenhurst. As Brian recalls: 'They were idyllic summer afternoons – Nick and I would eat hash brownies and wander around the grounds or row a boat around the lake.'

Music was, of course, a frequent subject of discussion: 'I remember Nick being disparaging about the fact that Paul McCartney was playing everything on his first solo album when he could have had his pick of musicians,' says Brian. 'We also listened to *Sweet Baby James* – he liked James Taylor's very clean picking, although it was different to his.' Paul, meanwhile, remembers Nick listening repeatedly to the stark '4 + 20', performed solo by Stephen Stills on *Déjà Vu* by Crosby, Stills, Nash and Young.*

In contrast to these giants, Nick's career was inert. It occurred to Brenda Ralfini that the reason his material (and that of other Warlock artists) wasn't being widely covered might be down to its being deemed too 'folky'. She therefore suggested to Joe that they make a demonstration album to send out to anyone who might be interested. 'She felt there was a lot of potential in the songs, but the way we'd recorded them was not exactly going to show a straighter singer how to do them,' explains Joe.[4]

One Saturday morning in July 1970 he convened a session at Sound Techniques to record deliberately straightforward arrangements by Del Newman of songs by Nick, the Incredible String Band, the New Nadir and John and Bev.† They were sung by Elton John (in his dying days as a voice-for-hire) and Linda Peters, with backing from Andy Fernbach on piano and guitar, and three members of Fotheringay (guitarist Jerry Donahue, bassist Pat Donaldson and drummer Gerry Conway).

Nick was not present but four of his songs were included, all from *Five Leaves Left* – 'Day Is Done', 'Saturday Sun', 'Way To Blue' and 'Time Has Told Me' – and all sung by Elton. Despite the personal connection Elton had made with Nick's music, his renditions were characterless, as the task demanded, and John Wood was unimpressed. For Joe, 'They're not spectacular but they're workmanlike and presentable.' Ninety-nine white label copies of the album were duly pressed and sent out.

Simultaneously, moves were being made towards finalising Nick's new album. He hadn't mentioned a title while it was being recorded, but when the time came to design its cover he announced it was

---

* *Sweet Baby James* had been released in February 1970 and *McCartney* in April. Nick was also an admirer of Taylor's debut album, with arrangements by Richard Hewson, released in December 1968. *Déjà Vu* was released in March 1970.
† Newman had just recorded arrangements for Cat Stevens's breakthrough album *Tea for the Tillerman*, issued on Island that November.

to be called *Bryter Layter*, the name of one of its instrumentals. 'Brighter later' was a phrase as familiar to students of the weather forecast – such as his father – as *Five Leaves Left* was to dope smokers. Weather reports often included phrases such as 'dull and overcast but brighter later' or 'cloudy at first but brighter later', and borrowing the term was in keeping with Nick's streak of droll self-awareness.

He seems never to have explained why he chose to change its spelling, but it was likely a nod towards the Romantic poets (for example, William Blake's 'Tyger' or Samuel Taylor Coleridge's 'Ancyent Marinere'), a jokey tribute to John and Bev (whose name was frequently misspelled 'Martin'), or even a homage of sorts to the Byrds, one of his favourite bands. Whatever the reason, the consensus among his friends was that it seemed cool and enigmatic, like him.*

Joe commissioned Keith Morris to take more photographs of Nick for artwork and publicity. Having discussed some ideas with Nick, Keith came to Danehurst one fine afternoon in the middle of August, bringing Nikon and Hasselblad cameras with him. Using both black-and-white and colour film, he took the first shots in the garden. Brian Wells had recently left his new Yamaha classical guitar at Nick's, so Keith photographed Nick with it, playfully ducking under the washing line and fiddling with the Hasselblad. When he went indoors Keith snapped him through the open window. Other shots were taken in the hallway and show Nick moving about and posing at his piano, which they'd dragged out of his room in order to take advantage of the sunshine streaming through the front door.

Next they drove fifteen miles southeast to Maryon Park in Charlton, where Nick was captured standing, sitting and walking with the River Thames and Blackwall Point Power Station in the distance. The shots capture the album's intermittent theme of the tension between nature and industrialisation. Nick looks thoughtful but not preoccupied; in some shots he is broadly smiling. They then went to Regent's Park in central London, where Nick was photographed with his guitar and a large (and unidentified) hardback book.

---

* Genesis took the same approach with *Nursery Cryme*, issued in November 1971.

When darkness fell they furtively climbed onto the newly opened Westway, an elevated dual carriageway that ran past Keith's Paddington flat. It was strictly closed to pedestrians but they crossed the barrier and picked their way to the roadside, where Keith photographed Nick watching the sparse nocturnal traffic speed by. It was a superbly composed variation on the image on the back of *Five Leaves Left* – Nick as solitary observer – but with an urban twist that reflected another theme of his new recordings.

When Keith reviewed the images, he concluded:

> We got a few gems but visually we were marking time, and ideas did not fully develop. There was a need for Nick's music to reach a wider audience and we probably took it all a bit too seriously. There wasn't the same spontaneity [as the previous year's session].[5]

In particular, no clear front cover concept had emerged. According to Keith:

> We did a whole series of ideas, which is why we'd never got on with the front – double exposures, shots looking out over a desolate city, which we did in black-and-white. I never got around to sorting how it could work cover-wise. '*Bryter Layter*' – how do you illustrate that?[6]

A surviving sketch by Nick suggests that he envisaged the Westway shot being on the front, but it was deemed insufficiently striking.

Attempts were made to kick other ideas around but the process was hampered by Nick's decreasing ability or willingness to articulate his thoughts. 'I clearly remember one meeting at Witchseason, sitting around the table with Joe, Keith and Nick,' says Island's Tim Clark.

> We were meant to be discussing concepts for the sleeve but Nick simply sat there, looking down, making no eye contact and giving monosyllabic answers. He expressed no feelings on the subject at all. As a result, the meeting was short and uncomfortable. I felt sorry for him because all he seemed able to do was mumble.

Eventually Joe asked his friend Nigel Waymouth – whose cover for John and Bev's *Stormbringer!* had attracted widespread admiration a few months earlier – to come up with a design. As Nigel remembers:

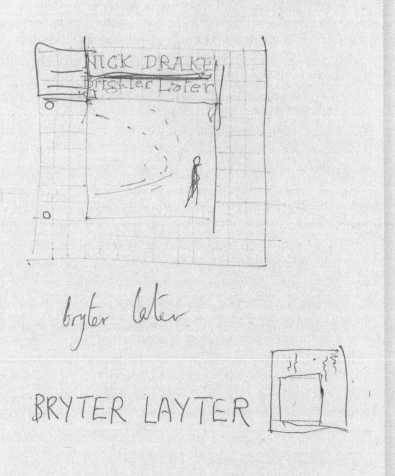

Nick's concept for the cover of *Bryter Layter*, August 1970.

I hadn't met Nick and knew nothing about the music, but was told the title and the fact that it was to have an odd spelling. That wasn't explained, but it's any artist's prerogative to have quirks like that. There was nothing preconceived about the artwork, though it was never suggested that it could have been a painting. It was always assumed I would design it around a photograph I'd take.

My studio was in Farm Place in Holland Park. It was a great room with a wooden floor, wonderful light from a skylight and practically no furniture – just my easel, a table and an old captain's chair I'd picked up in an antiques shop in the New King's Road. It had a brass plaque on the back saying Dickens had owned it and sat in it when he lived in Doughty Street. On the arm were lots of little pit-marks, as if a nib had been repeatedly stabbed into it. Joe and Nick came along one morning in the late summer, just the two of them. I'd put the chair on some blue photographic paper, which was the backdrop, and as props I'd brought along a pair of blue suede brothel-creepers I'd had made in the Chelsea Cobbler in a fit of nonsense sometime in the late sixties (and hardly ever worn) and a pretty little Guild guitar that Martin Sharp had given me.[*]

Nick was a man of very few words. I asked him to take off his overcoat and shoes, then I put my shoes in front of him. He sat down and immediately tuned up the guitar and began to play. He didn't sing, just finger-picked beautifully. It was a treat to hear him as I took the pictures. It was a short session, an hour or less, and we didn't say much – he played, I took photographs, then he and Joe left. He was the most passive subject you can imagine, but very sweet. He was the perfect model, really – he did exactly what I asked.

Nigel quickly came up with some artwork:

I chose the photo I wanted, designed and painted the lettering in an art-deco style, then did the layout. I wanted it to have some 'brightness' to it, hence the shoes and the lilac colour. I didn't have

---

[*] Martin Sharp was a renowned Australian psychedelic artist. Nigel: 'Eric Clapton, Martin and I had lived together in the Pheasantry in the King's Road a couple of years earlier. When Eric moved out he gave it to Martin, and Martin then passed it on to me.'

as much input into the back cover – that photo was taken by Keith Morris, and I heard later that he was put out that he hadn't done the front cover too.* I don't remember any mention of a gatefold or a lyric sheet and had no input into the card it was printed on. Once I'd finished it I sent it off to Island and had little else to do with it. I subsequently lost all my transparencies in a move, so as far as I'm aware, the only surviving fruit of the session is that cover image.†

Nick's initial views on the finished artwork are not known, but one night after its release he and Nigel found themselves at the same London gathering: 'He materialised by my side and quietly said, "I just want you to know that I now understand what you meant by your cover for *Bryter Layter*, and I really like it." It was sweet but puzzling.' Joe Boyd, however,

> wasn't thrilled with the cover, but I was too busy to think very long or hard about it. It was the usual story with many of my productions – by the time there's a mock-up and you don't like it much, starting over is out of the question, for budget and scheduling reasons.

Island were apparently ambivalent too, as they created their own mock-up design in-house, using a colour close-up of Nick smiling (taken by Keith) on the front and a variant of Nigel's design for the back.‡

Nick had nothing left to do regarding the album but await its release in the autumn. Brian Cullman continued to see him around North London but never got anything out of him:

> I'd run in to him at John and Beverley's or sometimes see him on the streets of Hampstead. He'd appear and disappear from rooms, from restaurants (I had dinner with a group of musicians [including

---

* Keith bore no grudge, later telling Patrick Humphries: 'I've got a lot of time for [Nigel] as a designer.'

† As with *Five Leaves Left*, the cover credits are imperfect: the list of musicians is incomplete, and Robert later admitted to being peeved to be credited with 'bass' arrangements rather than 'brass' ones.

‡ Nigel had nothing to do with the mock-up, which resurfaced in a London record shop many years later. The image on its front cover is unique; most of Keith's colour shots of Nick are lost.

the Martyns and Paul Wheeler] at an Indian restaurant once and only realised that Nick was there with us when he got up to go) – always by himself, always quiet, deep in his own world.[7]

It seemed obvious that he wouldn't submit to an interview ('It never occurred to me to try to interview him, as it was nearly impossible to get him to answer questions even in safe and private situations'), but Brian nonetheless decided to write about him for *Crawdaddy!* – the first US coverage he ever received. 'In John Martyn's house in Hampstead, Nick Drake sits over in a corner playing my guitar and smoking a very badly rolled joint,' the article began:[8]

> Sometimes he smiles, almost from behind his face, for he is incredibly shy. 'He's known us for over a year,' Beverley Martyn says, 'and only now will he say things like, "How are you?"' Everyone has their own opinion about why no one is buying Nick's album. Those who like him say it's because he's too good for public taste. Others aren't as kind. Selling records in England is hard because of the terrible radio situation, and so continual performances, perpetual gigs, are necessary to sell your album. 'Nick has no stage presence – he just gets up and sings, and he seems very self-conscious, very shy,' is the explanation of a friend who has toured with him.* 'Someone like Ralph McTell has incredible presence – he draws your attention, makes you focus on him. Nick doesn't do this, he's too fragile . . .'

The piece contained no comments from Nick and concluded with a shower of praise:

> Nick Drake is a gentle, happy surprise, a smile from a passing stranger. He is a writer and singer of soft, rhythmic songs that are neither self-conscious nor self-pitying: a rarity . . . His songs are of love, of friendships, of indecision, and of faith – faith in himself and faith in the ways of the world . . . He loves people and treats them in his songs the same way Truffaut handles all of the characters in his movies: with incredible tenderness . . . The arrangements and strings

---

* Brian: 'It's safe to say this was John, though he wasn't usually that analytical.'

are exceptional, the feeling of the album is like someone scratching your back; you don't want it to stop, and so you let it play over.

Brian assured the paper's American readers that 'His album is worth hunting around import stores for', but Nick was more preoccupied with its successor. Island finally put *Bryter Layter* into production in September, with its copyright registration dated the 25th and November given as its month of release on internal paperwork. At long last Nick could look forward to seeing a finished copy, though how willing or able he would be to promote it was unclear.

Vashti Bunyan was presenting Witchseason with a similar problem. She had been living in the Outer Hebrides since recording her own album, *Just Another Diamond Day*, the previous December, but visited London in September to discuss its impending release.* Joe had a brainwave: perhaps these two singular, single-minded talents would be kindred spirits and spark ideas off each other, even collaborate! It was the sort of notion he'd had in mind when founding Witchseason.

'It was a strange idea because we were both so reticent,' says Vashti.

I went to Nick's place with my partner Robert and my baby, Leif, and Christopher Sykes. Nick was hunched over this old upright piano, dressed in black, not saying a word, and Leif cried every time I picked up my guitar. My memory is that Nick's shoulders went higher and higher until I could tell nothing was possibly going to come of it. It was never going to work, and I don't know why Joe ever thought it could.

Vashti had been lucky to get into his room; Pete Russell got no answer when he visited, nor did Rick Charkin, who had just finished at Cambridge and moved to London. After knocking he walked around the side of the house and was taken aback to see Nick through the window, staring at the wall. Feeling that tapping on it would be intrusive, he withdrew.

David Sandison's attempts to contact Nick on behalf of Island rarely succeeded.

---

* Island had passed on it, so Joe had placed it with Philips.

Even if Nick had got into conversation with [another tenant] and told them his name, when you [phoned] nobody was really sure whether he was there. Somebody would tramp off and come back about ten minutes later and say, 'Well, I've knocked on the door and there was no reply.' But that didn't mean anything. You didn't know if he was there or not.

Nick rang Far Leys on 5 October and mentioned his frustration at the non-appearance of his album. When asked what he was up to he replied, 'Observing life in its various facets,' and his tone disquieted his parents. 'From our short talk on the phone on Monday evening I rather gathered that things are a bit sticky for you at the moment,' Rodney wrote to him the next day.[9]

> Try not to let things get you down. If your record is held up for some reason and you can't see how to get it going again or – still worse – if the whole thing comes to a sticky end, try to get a bit of a change to sort yourself out. Speculate for a while on the fact that most disastrous and exasperating situations always have their humorous side in retrospect, and therefore must contain the elements of humour even while they're happening. I have found this a helpful reflection in many dire and seemingly hopeless situations.
>
> Come home for a bit and listen to my new records and cheer me up in my temporary depression over the impending end of my career as a (not so) hard-boiled businessman . . . Cheer up, Nick, and don't lose belief in yourself – you're one of the few who've got something.

The advice was loving and well-meant, but is unlikely to have chimed with Nick, whose aptitude to see the humorous side of life was much diminished. 'I am free to pop up to London any day if there is suddenly a chance of hearing a recording session (or even meeting your Joe Boyd!),' Rodney ended, indicating how little Nick had explained of his current activities.

Nick did little but keep his own company at Danehurst in the latter months of 1970. Efforts to engage him in performance were futile; John Altman was closely involved with the music scene at Sussex University and was helping to organise a 'Grand Benefit

Festival' there, which took place on Saturday, 31 October, and Sunday, 1 November: 'John Martyn and Bridget St John were on the bill, and according to my diary I rang Nick on Saturday, 17 October to ask him to participate, but he told me he'd given up gigs.'

What Nick's family and friends were slow to realise was that he was suffering from a depressive illness rather than a temporary slump. As Linda Peters puts it, 'He wasn't well, but we didn't realise that – we just thought he was incredibly cool. One didn't see the signs in those days. If we had been older or more knowledgeable . . .'[10] Joe summarises the contemporary popular attitude as:

> He needed a girlfriend, he needed some success, he needed to get out, [he needed] *something* – you didn't think of it at the time as a *condition*. That was the atmosphere in Britain at the time . . . Analysis of people's behaviour and personality was not what people did.[11]

In any case, Joe was heavily preoccupied with Witchseason's ever-precarious finances. While Nick was exasperated by the delay in *Bryter Layter*'s appearance, Joe was simply pleased to have it off his agenda and to be able to submit another invoice to Island, because 'we never sold enough records. As long as Island continued to advance money, we were okay, but one of two possibilities was always around the corner: a hit or a day of reckoning.'[12]

As winter came around the latter seemed ever more likely, and Joe was worn out by the grind of keeping the show on the road. 'In 1970 I finished sixteen LPs: I was working myself to a frazzle. In Charlotte Street the financial wolves were circling; we owed money in every direction and the more we achieved, the more we seemed to spend. Break-even was a horizon that kept receding.'[13] As John Wood summarises, 'Joe didn't think enough about where the money was going – he had too much on his plate, the expenses were adding up and there was no overall business model.'

As such, he was receptive to an invitation from Mo Ostin to have breakfast at the Dorchester Hotel in mid-October. As President of Warner Bros. Records, Ostin was one of the most powerful and influential men in the business. He knew and respected Joe's work, having encountered him late the previous year when Joe had produced Geoff and Maria Muldaur for Reprise and Warners had picked up John and Bev for North America.* At the meeting he took Joe aback by asking if he'd be interested in working for Warners in Los Angeles, specifically to oversee the use of contemporary music in their movie division, where forthcoming projects included John Boorman's *Deliverance* and Stanley Kubrick's hugely anticipated *A Clockwork Orange*.

Joe scented a solution to all the company's problems: 'I was excited at the idea of drawing a line under it, not having to worry about money constantly, and doing something different.' What he didn't immediately appreciate was that Mo wasn't only interested in his talent; he was looking for ways to undermine Island, having recently had a takeover bid parried by Chris Blackwell. Joe told him he'd think about it and get back to him.

> Chris was on tour with Traffic in America and I was there for Thanksgiving, so on a Sunday morning I drove through the snow to see him in a motel in Northampton, Massachusetts. Despite being in charge of a multi-million-pound business he was adding up receipts for hamburgers and taxis when I went into his room. I told him about the offer, and there and then he said it sounded like a great opportunity and that he'd buy Witchseason and Warlock. I don't know why neither of us suggested keeping me in-house on a salary to work with Nick, Sandy and Fairport, but it didn't arise – maybe I wouldn't have wanted it anyway.

Joe flew on to Los Angeles, where he was interviewed, toured the film studios, and accepted the job. He was troubled by the notion that he was letting down his artists, but confident they would be secure under Island's stewardship, and excited at the prospect of trading freezing London for sunny California.

> There was a general feeling everywhere I turned within Witchseason that basically people were going to do what they were going to do their way . . . I just had this very strong feeling that everyone would be much better off with a clean broom, and people were by that time ready to produce their own records anyway . . . I also thought

---

* As of July 1970, Warners also owned Elektra, to which the Incredible String Band were signed.

that my laissez-faire style of management was never going to make anyone any money, myself included.[14]

By Anthea's account: 'Joe rang me up and said would I meet him at [Heathrow] Airport . . . We sat down on those awful plastic seats and he said, "I've taken a job in Hollywood" . . . And that was it, that's when we all broke up. That was the end of Witchseason.'

Nick took the news hard. Anthea felt that Joe underestimated the unique place he occupied in his estimation:

> He trusted Joe, trusted him implicitly, and I think that was really the basis of their relationship. Nick relied enormously on Joe, he was emotionally tied to Joe. It was a mental thing, a brain thing. Neither of them were homosexuals by any stretch of the imagination, but Joe rang a bell in Nick, I think, and vice versa. Joe really did care about him and tried to look after him as best he could – as much as [anyone] could.[15]

Nick was of course prominent in Joe's thinking, but he'd made it clear that his next album was to be pure voice and guitar, so Joe inferred that his absence wouldn't prove too problematic. In hindsight, he can see how unsettling the news of his departure was for Nick:

> Witchseason was a home-from-home of a kind for him, regardless of whatever unhappiness he might have felt about the delays with *Bryter Layter*. I was his manager, publisher and producer, I had provided a (barely) living wage for him, and I'd recorded a pair of albums with him for Britain's hippest label. It seems reasonable to me that he would have viewed me as an anchor, the one person who had actually delivered on promises and transformed his life.

At the time, he had more pressing thoughts. 'When you're twenty-eight years old and your main concern every day is how to rescue your production company from bankruptcy, you're not thinking so much about the psychological profiles of your artists.'[16] In any case, he was already wondering whether writing songs for films could be another avenue for Nick to explore. According to David Sandison,

> Nick was very lucky to have Joe Boyd, because nobody else I can think of would have persevered with that state of affairs. It made no

commercial sense; it made artistic sense to very few people . . . He sold Witchseason to Island for £1, I think it was, and the condition was, 'Look after everybody, but especially Nick.' Nick especially was to be persevered with.[17]

Joe set about arranging the terms of the handover with Island.

A central point in my discussions with Blackwell was that Nick should be properly looked after. I have a vague memory that the sales figure for *Five Leaves Left* at the time was around two thousand, but I was obsessed with the idea that it was only a matter of time . . .

In the immediate term, the complications surrounding Joe's departure put the release of *Bryter Layter* back on hold. Whilst arranging its absorption of Witchseason, Island was also grappling with national power cuts, a major rebranding exercise (from its familiar pink label design to a palm tree image) and a printers' strike. *Bryter Layter*'s supposed 24 November release date came and went, with 18 December being announced as the new date in the music press.[*]

Amidst the chaos was a glimmer of optimism: in October Chris Blackwell had concluded a licensing deal with Capitol in the US for Island product that hadn't been assigned elsewhere, effective from 1 January 1971. According to *Record Mirror* of 14 November, '*Five Leaves Left* is among the very first LP releases to be issued by Island in the United States under the new arrangement.'

Vashti Bunyan's album was finally released in late November, and she encountered Nick when she went to Witchseason to collect copies.

There would be lots of people there, trailing down the stairs. He was clearly finding things very difficult and when I said hello he literally turned to the wall, which I found hard because I took it personally. I thought, 'Oh dear, he really doesn't like me.' He seemed mysterious and unknowable to me – a beautiful boy, almost unreal.

---

[*] November did see the release of John and Bev's second and final album together, *The Road to Ruin*, which included Paul Wheeler's signature song, 'Give Us a Ring'. Nick has been claimed as its inspiration, but Paul says: 'I wrote it before I met him.'

Nick had by now given up his car (or perhaps it had given up on him) and, cold, broke and unoccupied, he retreated further into himself. Paul Wheeler remembers him being shaken by John Lennon's *Plastic Ono Band* album, which appeared in the run-up to Christmas and included – amongst much else – the blunt message 'the dream is over' in the song 'God'. 'It was relatively stripped back, and it seemed shocking for someone to show vulnerability in that way.' Nick later told his parents that his own music-making was suffering towards the end of 1970 because he 'couldn't synchronise' – in other words, play and sing simultaneously, something he had effortlessly accomplished before.[18]

On Thursday, 10 December, his father took him out for lunch. It had been over a year since Nick had left Cambridge, and he and Molly knew less than ever about his life. The meeting was unenlightening and Rodney went home perturbed. The following day he wrote another letter to Nick.

> It is rather strange for me to reflect as I sit writing this how very little indeed we know about your life and how it is developing. This, I think, however, is how you want it – to some extent it is perhaps that you do not know yourself, and anyway you want to keep your options open – and, I presume, your independence of action without commitment of any sort to anyone.

Nonetheless, he continued,

> we are hoping very much that if at any time you are considering a change of course, or are confronted with a problem that greatly worries you, or find yourself in an *impasse* that you can't see any way out of, you will not regard us as only a last resort for consultation and help . . . As you said yourself, both your generation and mine have had enough disillusionments to bring them within range of each other.

Nick continued to spurn his parents' offers of consultation, but did call upon their help in at least one way. He had managed to accumulate a remarkable thirty-five unpaid parking fines, indicating not only a casual attitude towards regulations but a paralysis about taking responsibility for his affairs. They were automatically sent to

Far Leys, where Nick's car had been registered, and Rodney did his best to field them.

Rodney wrote again on 15 December, in the gently ironic tone that had defined their correspondence in Nick's schooldays: 'In reflecting upon the problem of how I am going to keep myself occupied after my retirement, I am disturbed to think that you no longer have a car, because paying your parking fines has become quite a part-time occupation lately.' Far from remonstrating, the generous solution he proposed was to 'shoulder the burden myself as a contribution to your career – and I shall expect a free record of *Bryter Layter* in return'.

Nick went home for the usual family Christmas, but was unable to give his parents a copy of *Bryter Layter* because it had not appeared on 18 December; according to *Record Mirror* it was now due for release 'in late January'. Nor did he give them a taster in person: the era when he proudly played his songs to his family was over. 'In the early days when he came home from London he occasionally used to play us some of his early compositions, but he became less and less disposed to do that,' as Rodney wistfully put it.[19]

In contrast to the sluggish progress of Nick's career, Gabrielle's star was in the ascendant. She was in the popular sci-fi TV series *UFO*, sporting a purple wig, and her latest film, *There's a Girl in My Soup* – in which she appeared alongside Peter Sellers and Goldie Hawn – was a hit. The glamour and camaraderie of her world was far removed from the grey isolation of her brother's. He returned to London as soon as he could, taking with him the portable black-and-white television he had been given for Christmas; his parents had guessed he'd appreciate its company.

22

A Second-Division Act

— —

Joe Boyd flew to his new life in Los Angeles on Sunday, 24 January 1971, after a leaving party at the Speakeasy,* during which he says he experienced 'major doubts' about the wisdom of the move. Before departing he reiterated to Nick that he would make time to continue producing him, but according to Rodney, Nick 'was very upset when Joe Boyd left to go over to the States', and for Molly his departure 'was a very big thing in Nick's life'.[1]

'I think we all felt a bit abandoned when he went to America – Sandy, Fairport, John and I, we all relied on him and didn't know what our future held when he left,' reflects Bev. 'Being musicians, we were all needy, always asking Joe for things.'

'Of course, we are delighted to continue the association with the artists and the Witchseason staff, but it is a great pity that Joe Boyd is leaving the country because we have always worked together so well,' commented Island's David Betteridge that week.[2] Witchseason retained its Charlotte Street base, with Marian Bain its new head, and Nick still turned up intermittently, though his weekly advance was now paid by standing order.

Soon after Joe's departure he met Chris Blackwell at Island's headquarters in Basing Street to discuss his future: 'We agreed that he would continue to record with John Wood, with him acting as his own producer and me reimbursing him for any finished albums. It was a gentlemen's agreement and I suspect there was no paperwork. We did it on a handshake.' At the same time, Nick had his only encounter with David Betteridge: 'He barely sat down or said anything. He didn't seem terribly interested.'

* Joe can't recall if Nick was there, but thinks it unlikely.

Despite Island's pledge to keep releasing his music, Nick felt adrift without Joe acting as a buffer. According to Rodney,

> When he got involved with Witchseason, [it was] a new, small firm – he was very keen on that and he felt that was a place for him to go, and I think he liked the people at Witchseason and got to know them. Then of course there was an upheaval there and Joe Boyd went and it was taken over by Island, and that was too big an organisation for him to cope with.[3]

Bryter Layter was caught in Island's machinery. Its latest release date had been torpedoed by a nationwide postal strike that hamstrung the record industry and much besides. As David Sandison wrote at the time, it 'has disarranged the best-laid plans of mice, men and record companies'.[4] As the strike rumbled on, Island dreamed up a promotional campaign to be entitled 'El Pea', centring on the tenuous concept of its forthcoming LPs being 'peas in a pod'. It was cold comfort to Nick that *Bryter Layter* was to be featured, and therefore had to be postponed again whilst a sampler album was sequenced and designed. In the meantime a separate sampler was sent to radio stations and included 'Hazey Jane II' and 'One Of These Things First', suggesting that they might have been under consideration as a 45.*

In mid-February *Record Mirror* announced yet another release date for the album: 'After several months of apparent inactivity, Island has prepared a five-album release for March.' A press ad for *Bryter Layter* was required, so a photo session was set up with Tony Evans, who did a lot of work for Island at the time. 'We had a studio in our house in Dartmouth Park,' says his wife and assistant Caroline.

> Nick arrived alone and by taxi on the afternoon of Friday, 19 February. I'm pretty sure it was raining. Tony sensed his quiet and gentle character right away and took the time to chat with him over a cup of tea before he put any film in the camera. He took half a dozen polaroid shots to check lighting etc. and make sure Nick felt comfortable with the set-up. Five rolls went through the Hasselblad, and that was pretty much it.

---

* Another unassigned Island catalogue number (WIP 6099) from March 1971 could have been intended for Nick.

The images show Nick looking tired, even haggard. He's unshaven, with extremely long hair, wearing a V-neck jumper and collared shirt. In several shots he's holding Brian Wells's Yamaha guitar, which was still in his possession. His fingernails on both hands are strikingly long, suggesting that fretting would have been difficult at this point, not to mention a falling-off in his personal grooming. The length of his nails strikes Paul Wheeler as 'certainly very odd. I *suppose* he could have been experimenting, but it more likely indicates neglect and indifference.' In some shots he looks preoccupied and distant but in others he smiles. Caroline says: 'I got the impression that he found the whole business of coming to the studio and being photo-graphed a bit of a challenge, but Tony's calmness and sense of humour helped to ease him through. I don't think he stayed for more than an hour.'

His glum disposition was partly due to a letter Hampstead Homefinders had slipped under his door that week: 'Our client, Mrs Vanger, has now decided to demolish this property and will erect a block of flats. Accordingly, we are instructed to give all tenants notice to quit . . .' He was asked to be out by Friday, 26 March, with the return of his deposit being conditional upon leaving 'the landlord's furniture and fittings in reasonable condition'.* This would leave him without a London base, compounding the sense of rootlessness Joe's departure had created.

Tony's images were rapidly delivered to Island, where one was selected to illustrate the ad spaces they had booked. In it Nick gazes steadily into the lens, the ghost of a smile on his features. His unset-tlingly long nails are clearly visible around his guitar, over whose soundhole Island had superimposed a cartoon Sun as a nod towards the album title. 'Nick Drake is a folk singer who writes and sings all his own songs,' ran the vague accompanying copy. 'He was discovered a little while back by the Fairport Convention. *Bryter Layter*, his second album, has been a long time in the making. It's been worth the wait.'†

---

* The house was sold to Camden Council, which demolished it in 1974.
† The half-page ad appeared in different orientations in *Melody Maker*, *Time Out*, *Sounds* and the UK edition of *Rolling Stone*.

Just ahead of its release David Sandison made his way from Island to Charlotte Street 'with the intention of telling Nick how much I liked the album and that I wanted him to do a couple of interviews', he wrote later that year, continuing (with remarkable candour for a press release):[5]

> He arrived an hour late, shuffled in, and shrugged disinterestedly [sic] when I suggested a coffee round the corner. When we got there (it was about lunchtime) I asked him if he wanted a cup of tea, something to eat, anything? He looked down at the dried ring of saucer-stain on the table, and smiled to himself, meaning 'no'. For the next half-hour he looked at me twice, said maybe two words (one was to agree to an interview, which was [later] done and was a total disaster), while I rattled on at him about every kind of nonsense, trying to get some reaction, until I ran out of voice, paid the bill for my coffee and sandwich and walked him back to Witchseason.

The interview in question was with Jerry Gilbert, for the music weekly *Sounds*. Jerry had helped launch the paper in October 1970 and was intrigued by Nick. He'd admired *Five Leaves Left* and seen him play live a few times, and was mystified by his low profile. They had never met, even though, he says, 'The folk scene at that time was very sociable, with an awful lot of drinking going on.' As with the previous year's encounter for *Jackie*, the meeting took place in Frances van Staden's flat in Swiss Cottage.

Jerry was aware of Nick's reputation for taciturnity but wasn't expecting quite so little interaction:

> I'd love to say that there was this huge charisma that came with him when he walked into the room, but there was absolutely not – just a chap with his head down, stooped, very shy, very self-effacing, not wanting to talk much about himself, really uneasy. I don't remember what he was wearing – he had long hair, which he played with all the time . . . Normally in an interview there's a bit of chat before and after the tape was rolling, but there was none of that with Nick.[6]

As the exchange got underway, continues Jerry, 'I got the clear impression that he was being made to do it. Because I used shorthand, I was able to maintain eye contact and not have to fiddle with a tape recorder, but there was no symbiosis; he looked at the ground throughout.' For David, who was also present,

> We finished up like two idiots sort of blithering at him. Jerry would spend two minutes asking a question that demanded an answer, and Nick would say 'yes' or 'no', and then hum a bit and stir his tea, and maybe then sort of start a sentence and then kind of give up . . .[7]
>
> We sweated through three-quarters of an hour trying to get three words out of him that weren't 'yes' and 'no' or 'um'. You had to wait for a good minute or two for him to come back with more than a 'yes' or a 'no'. A full sentence that moved the conversation on was a rare gem . . . It didn't strike me as depressive, it was just incredibly vague.[8]

Jerry says: 'I faithfully reported his exact words but a lot of his statements were unfinished or left hanging, so it wasn't by any means fluent. I extracted every last word from my notes, trust me.'

The short result appeared in *Sounds* dated 13 March, on sale late the previous week. 'Nick Drake is a shy, introverted folk singer who is not usually known to speak unless it is absolutely necessary,' it began. Jerry's admiration for him was clear, though his choice of words was cautious: 'Placed in the right context, his songs produce quite a stunning effect over a period of time.' Asked to comment on *Bryter Layter*, Nick was unwilling to commit himself: 'The album took a long time to do. In fact, we started doing it almost a year ago. I'm not altogether clear about this album – I haven't got to terms with the whole presentation.'

Asked whether he would be playing gigs to promote it he gave a vague but unpromising reply:

> I don't think that would help unless they were done in the right way. I'm just not very sure at the moment, it's hard to tell what will turn up. If I could find making music a fairly natural connection with something else, then I might move on to something else.

This might have been a reference to writing songs for films, which Joe had mentioned. Nick also indicated that his aversion to gigs was not rooted in stage-fright or objections to certain types of venue: 'I think the problem was with the material, which I wrote for records rather than performing.'

As the encounter staggered to its end Jerry asked what Nick's next move would be. 'I think there'll be another album and I have some material for it, but I'll be looking around now to see if this album leads anywhere naturally,' he said. It's not clear what material he was referring to, but 'Things Behind The Sun' was long finished and surviving home recordings indicate that 'Place To Be' and 'Parasite' were also written well in advance of being recorded. He then repeated what he had already told Joe: 'For the next one I had the idea of just doing something with John Wood, the engineer at Sound Techniques.'

Bryter Layter was finally released on Friday, 5 March 1971, priced at £2.15 (in the new decimal currency).* Its cover was printed on reversed card, lending it a textured effect similar to canvas. 'The reason it didn't have a gatefold or an insert is that it simply wasn't warranted by our expectations of its sales,' explains David Betteridge. It was promoted as part of Island's eccentric 'El Pea' campaign, alongside *Dive Deep* by Quintessence, *Be Glad for the Song Has No Ending* by the Incredible String Band, *Wildlife* by Mott the Hoople and *Aqualung* by Jethro Tull.

The 'El Pea' push involved placing inflatable peas in shop windows, alongside display stands that showed the album covers inside giant pods and promised they were 'both unusual and tasty'. They were described in print ads as 'the full pod', with their covers bursting out of a lurid pea-shell, and *Bryter Layter* and the Incredible String Band and Quintessence LPs were also featured on a poster as 'three from a pod of five'. What Nick made of all this is not known.

It fell to David Sandison to drum up media interest, but if he produced a press release to accompany promo copies, no copy has yet resurfaced. Either way, reviews soon began to appear. 'On their own merits his songs are not particularly strong, but Nick has always been a consistent if introverted performer, and placed in the cauldron Joe Boyd has prepared for him, things start to effervesce,' Jerry wrote

---

* *Five Leaves Left* was re-pressed on Island's new label design at much the same time. They asked Nigel Waymouth to redo its cover but, he recalls, 'I mischievously put together a design involving Rizla papers and a block of hash and they never did anything with it.' This artwork appears not to survive.

in the same issue of *Sounds*. 'Late night coffee'n'chat music,' said Andrew Means of *Melody Maker*, exemplifying the hastily written, superficial nature of most reviews of the time. 'The tracks are all very similar – quiet, gentle and relaxing. Drake sends his voice skimming smoothly over the backing.'

Disc and Music Echo was more laudatory: 'He sings his own very personal songs in a strange, deep vaseline voice, probably more suited to crooning, accompanied at times by really funky backing, with an amazing array of faces featured. An extraordinarily good, hefty folk album'. *Record Mirror's* Lon Goddard set a precedent by praising his guitar playing:

> A beautiful guitarist – clean and with perfect timing – accompanied by soft, beautiful arrangements by Robert Kirby. Nick isn't the world's top singer, but he's written fantastic numbers that suit strings marvel-lously. Definitely one of the prettiest (and that counts!) and most impressive albums I've heard . . . Happy, sad, very moving.

Record & Tape Retailer – aimed at the industry and trade rather than consumers – had nothing but admiration, saying that 'An intricate tapestry of sounds surrounds Drake's guitar and vocals . . . Production is excellent . . . Drake's first album went pretty well unnoticed by the general public; hopefully this one will create the interest it deserves.' Closer to home for the Drakes was the *Birmingham Daily Post*, whose reviewer felt it was 'beautifully arranged and produced. His singing is precise and sensitive, and his songs carefully written and often quite memorable.' The *Daily Mail* – Molly's paper – concurred, with Michael Cable calling it 'One of the nicest albums of its type I have heard. Gentle, thoughtful songs with soft, acoustic guitar and piano backings.' Ominously, however, he concluded: 'Probably not commercial – but then, most of the best things in pop aren't.'

Like all of Nick's friends, Paul Wheeler listened to *Bryter Layter* as soon as he could: 'To me it was a more positive set of songs than *Five Leaves Left*, and a better representation of his personality – "At The Chime Of A City Clock" was the exception rather than the rule, I felt.' Simon Crocker had long since fallen out of touch with Nick but bought the LP right away. 'I was disappointed, not with the songs but the arrangements,' he says. 'They felt schmaltzy, as if an effort were being made to commercialise Nick and had gone too far.'

Alex Henderson had a similar response:

I loved the songs – 'Northern Sky' is my favourite of all his songs – but I thought the arrangements eclipsed the distinctiveness of his guitar playing as the music's main feature. They didn't overwhelm it, but I thought they took away from it. And I was rather amazed at the sleeve – it wasn't psychedelic, in the style you'd expect from Nigel Waymouth, and nor was it eye-catching, to attract the attention of people in shops who'd never heard of him. I didn't think it was anything.

One influential admirer was Jeff Dexter, who'd been running the popular Implosion gatherings at the Roundhouse on Sundays starting in June 1969.

Bryter Layter was the most fantastic LP for me, and I would use it in every set I ever did – all the concerts and pop festivals. When Nick was living in Hampstead he used to turn up at Implosion, always towards the start, when I'd play gentle records, including his. I can remember him listening to Bryter Layter as it played over the speakers there but scuttling away if anyone tried to speak to him. I tried really hard to get him to play there himself . . .

Copies of Bryter Layter were sent to Joe in Los Angeles, where he was not finding his new job as rewarding as he'd been led to expect. Shortly after he'd moved into the Chateau Marmont hotel the San Fernando earthquake of 9 February had rocked Los Angeles, which he took to be an ill omen. Sure enough, 'My whole interaction with film people about music was not creative. I'd had the idea that I could place some of Nick's songs in movies, but after arriving there and seeing how it worked that quickly seemed like a fantasy.'

Capitol had decided against releasing Five Leaves Left in America, but Joe did what he could to generate interest in Nick:

I did introduce quite a few people in LA to his music, and they liked it. I gave a copy of Bryter Layter to David Geffen, whom I knew through

Joni Mitchell and others, knowing that he was thinking of starting a label and thinking it would be a great home for Nick. He liked it but said he had to see him perform before he could make an offer . . .*

Nick was invited to play a third BBC session, in support of *Bryter Layter*, so a junior member of Island's promo team, Garrell Redfearn, was despatched to Danehurst to discuss it with him.

> Maybe because we were about the same age, I was asked to see if I could chat to him and persuade him to do [the] session . . . I remember the flat being extremely grotty, all dark inside, with tatty, filthy bits of fabric covering the windows as curtains, keeping the light out. There was a big, heavy old Victorian sideboard. He sat in a chair, head down, with very long hair falling over his face.[9]

Garrell made some small talk but all he got back were 'a few mumbled responses. He wasn't being difficult or unpleasant, he really just had difficulty talking to anyone, just making that contact.' Garrell explained to Nick

> how it would really help if we could get him to do a session because it would mean a lot more exposure for the album. He said something like, 'I don't think so at the moment, maybe in the future.' It was almost down to nods and shakes of the head, grunts.

Garrell was astonished:

> I remember saying to him, 'Do you *want* the album to sell?!' It seemed illogical to me that you take all this trouble to record your music and yet don't make any effort to try and help it get exposure, for people to hear it. But I remember feeling afterwards that he may have got to a stage where it almost didn't matter. If it was important, it wasn't important enough for him to overcome whatever the inhibitions were . . . I don't think I spent more than fifteen minutes there. I came away very depressed at the state in which he was living, quite shocked, and reported back to Chris Blackwell, who was taking an interest in Nick.

---

* Geffen had recently signed another brilliant but complicated singer-songwriter, Judee Sill. She, however, performed widely to promote her work.

'I didn't expect Nick to behave differently in promotional terms from how he was normally,' says Chris. 'I felt that his shy persona fitted his music perfectly.' This wasn't much help for his sales team, and Muff Winwood found it exasperating:

> No matter who you were or how talented you were, it was tough getting your music across and it took hard work. As far as I was concerned, promoting Nick was a hopeless task because he wouldn't allow it. He wanted to make music but he couldn't go out and front it, and that made him a nuisance, from my perspective. I remember going home on two or three occasions and complaining to my wife about what a pain in the arse he was. My perspective in my twenties was probably different to what it is today, but all I saw was a guy who was too stoned to be bothered. And I only cared because he was so good!

It appears that Nick was in fact prevailed upon to do the session, as Anthea Joseph vividly recalled:

> It was in the Paris Studios, in [Lower] Regent Street. I got Nick there, took him out, gave him dinner, and we went down there and he said, 'I don't want to do this. I'm not playing.' It was just in the studio, there wasn't an audience . . . [John Peel and his producer John Walters] were wonderful, endless patience and kindness – and every now and again Nick would get up and say, 'I'm going now,' and head for the door, and I was like a whipper-in. I'd crack the whip on the door, going 'Back, back!' and he went back. We did actually finish it, but it was absolutely exhausting.[10]

The results, however, were not broadcast and appear neither to have been documented nor kept.*

Nick's reluctance to perform his songs in a friendly environment that offered maximum exposure with minimum demands is striking. Unlike the other acts featured in the ongoing 'El Pea' campaign, he

---

* Nick's 1970 session (featuring Iain Cameron) was repeated on *Night Ride* on Tuesday, 6 April 1971, and John Peel played 'Hazey Jane I' on his show on 18 May. When asked about Nick in later years John Peel did not mention the session described by Anthea, and did not mention having met him.

had no promotional plans. In fact, as soon as *Bryter Layter* became available he belatedly heeded his father's advice to have 'a bit of a change' and headed alone for Paris, in the second-hand Riley he had recently acquired. It was as if he were fleeing the reality of the album's existence and any demands that might be placed upon him as a result.

'I was most interested to hear that you had popped over to Paris for a change of scene – what a good idea,' Molly wrote to him on 19 March, enclosing the *Daily Mail* review. She left him in no doubt as to the pride and pleasure she and Rodney took in the album, whose contents were evidently completely new to them:

> I have been meaning to write this since the day the postal strike ended to tell you how very impressed and delighted I am with your record. I love it all and each different song grows on you the more you play it – fresh subtleties come to light with each hearing. I particularly love 'Sunday', which is so haunting, and I find it continually running through my brain. I am becoming very fond too of 'Northern Sky', and as for 'Poor Boy', I think it is splendid and deserves to be a great hit.*

The record-buying public did not share her view, and no single was extracted. ('I always rated "Poor Boy", or they could have gone with "Northern Sky" – but nothing ever happened,' said Robert Kirby.) Even allowing for the kudos of Nick being Joe's protégé and on Island, in the absence of personal visibility he was seen as just another in a long line of long-haired young men putting out self-written albums. Singer-songwriting remained a huge growth area, and at much the same time as *Bryter Layter* a blizzard of major label albums were recorded and released in the UK by aspiring male artists including Pete Atkin, Jimmy Campbell, Keith Christmas, Mike

---

* Molly wrote a song of her own called 'Poor Mum', seemingly inspired by 'Poor Boy'. Gabrielle: 'It would have been written, I am sure, after *Bryter Layter* came out. I think it was a gentle, probably undeclared (certainly to Nick) but definite push-back by my mum, and is typical both of her ability to stand up for herself and to view herself with a certain objective irony.' In later years Molly expressed especial admiration for 'At The Chime Of A City Clock', even though it bore unhappy reminders of Nick's decline.

Cooper, Marc Ellington, Dave Evans, Gary Farr, Bill Fay, Ernie Graham, Mick Greenwood, Rick Hayward, Tony Hazzard, Tim Hollier, John James, Al Jones, Dave Kelly, Paul Kent, Rab Noakes, Andy Roberts, Mick Softley, Meic Stevens and Allan Taylor.

Many of them were touring hard, giving interviews and appearing on TV and radio, yet none had anything approaching a whiff of chart action. Records were expensive, and competing for sales in the same area were popular acts (Cat Stevens, Ralph McTell, Al Stewart, Roy Harper and others) as well as equally obscure female artists (Vashti Bunyan, Shelagh McDonald, Bridget St John, Anne Briggs, Gillian McPherson and others) and huge-selling Americans and Canadians (from Leonard Cohen, James Taylor and Neil Young to Carole King, Joni Mitchell and Carly Simon).

'We just didn't have faith in Nick at the time,' admits David Betteridge.

> But even if we had really believed in him commercially, he would've had to be involved, and he was legendarily shy. I can't remember any promo materials being produced for him – certainly it was a very limited marketing spend. He was a low priority, a second-division act in the company. We recognised there was something special there, but we didn't know what to do with him.

Bryter Layter wasn't exactly doomed to fail, but no one at Island was expecting a hit. 'If *Five Leaves Left* had sold better or generated more buzz we might have decided to push it harder and press something like 25,000 copies – but as it was I think we pressed 5,000 at most, and didn't sell all of them at that,' says David.

Like Nick, John Wood had hoped that its sheer quality would translate into sales, and was taken aback when it made no impact at all. 'I was very surprised – I can't remember anybody who wasn't bowled over by it,' he says. 'In retrospect the relationship Witchseason had with Island may have been a disadvantage, as [Island] were producing so much of their material in-house.'[11] In Anthea's blunt view: 'Nobody was interested in Nick at all, it was just Joe's passion.'[12] Joe, however, wasn't anywhere near: 'When it actually came out and didn't sell, I wasn't around as a manager. I guess I feel badly that I couldn't follow through on it. I think he did feel abandoned.'

Back from France, Nick was given a two-week extension to his eviction. His parents encouraged him to visit Far Leys, but he was finding it hard to motivate himself to do anything. On Monday, 29 March, his father wrote to him in unusually direct terms:

> I really must take you to task for the *very* casual and inconsiderate treatment we have had from you the last two weekends. The weekend before last you had Gay wasting three hours driving to Coventry and back to meet you whilst you lay in bed [in London] and this Sunday, having told me on Saturday that you would be coming up by car, you apparently never gave the matter another thought.
>
> This was not just inconsiderate, it was also cruel, for we spent the morning looking forward to your arrival and the afternoon worrying increasingly about what had happened to you. I have not seen Mum so upset for a very long time as when we eventually discovered that your failure to come was due to just not bothering . . . Now I begin to wonder if I can depend on you.

What Molly and Rodney did not yet appreciate was that, as Gabrielle puts it, 'Nick's illness turned him into someone thoughtless.'

The storm blew over; Nick went home a few days later, bringing with him some of his possessions ahead of leaving Danehurst. 'So nice having you here last week, and you did a most useful evening's work [in the garden], despite your ecological reservations!' Rodney wrote to him on 4 April. It seems that the subject of drugs had come up again, as he concluded: 'I enclose a short article on the subject of cannabis smoking,[13] which seems to be a pretty strong argument against the school which says the drug is harmless.'

'Four Oxford scientists making a laboratory investigation have found strong evidence that the drug is unsafe and in some cases may be highly dangerous,' stated *The Times* piece, explaining that Professor William Paton believed 'cannabis smoking is at least as habit-forming as heavy cigarette-smoking. He urged any chronic user of cannabis to break the habit, however difficult it might be, and even if psychiatric help was necessary.'[14]

23

Nick-Lack

———

U PON QUITTING DANEHURST in April 1971 Nick had no alternative but to return to Far Leys. Since leaving Cambridge he
had deliberately kept his parents at arm's length, tending to disregard
their letters and phone calls and spurn their entreaties to visit or
meet in London. Now that they could observe him for longer
periods they were alarmed at his restlessness and unhappiness, as
well as the fact that he was experiencing dizzy spells.

Molly welcomed the opportunity to talk to him about his problems to whatever extent he was willing or able.

> I once said to him, 'When do you think things started going wrong,
> Nick?' . . . And he said, 'I think about a month after I went to
> Hampstead.' When he went to Hampstead was the time when he
> cut himself off from all his friends and was very, very much alone,
> and this was when things started to go wrong.[1]

His angst almost certainly had no single cause, but Molly suspected
creative frustration lay at its heart: 'I think he felt that he had got
something, but other people didn't realise what it was. That was the
basis of all his troubles and sadnesses, really.'[2]

It was obvious that he was both unwilling and unable to promote
Bryter Layter. 'I think Nick both wanted to be left alone and at the
same time desperately wanted to communicate and be recognised –
but I have never known anyone do less about actually courting
recognition,' reflects Gabrielle.[3] It had perhaps dawned on him that
expecting his albums to sell on merit alone was unrealistic. For David
Sandison, 'I don't think the word "career" ever occurred to Nick's
mind's vocabulary. It was just whatever he did, and the next album
wasn't going to lead anywhere, it was just going to be the next album.'[4]

ROYAL FESTIVAL HALL

Gen. Man.: John Dennison

FAIRPORT CONVENTION

AND FRIENDS

WEDNESDAY

24th SEPTEMBER

Tickets: 25/-, 21/-, 17/-, 13/-, 10/- and 8/-

Box Office: (01) 928 3191

The small ad for Nick's prestigious launch as a solo performer – as one of the 'friends'.

The only known image of Nick in concert, shot during his short gigging career between September 1969 and August 1970.

John and Beverley Martyn with her son Wesley in 1970. John and Bev separately met Nick in 1968 and became important friends to him in different ways.

Joe Boyd and John Wood hard at work in Sound Techniques, 1970.
Their unconventional dynamic suited both them and Nick very well.

Nick playing Brian Wells's Yamaha guitar in the garden at Danehurst, 112 Haverstock Hill, August 1970.

Posing in the hallway outside his flat in Danehurst on the same day.

Trespassing on the newly opened Westway that night.

Evidently relieved not to have been caught.

Nick's bedroom at Far Leys, where
he was based from late 1971.

Nick often sat in silence in the drawing room.

The music room, with Nick's preferred orange armchair to the left and the *Encyclopaedia Britannica* he'd bought in the summer of 1971 to the right.

Nick would occasionally make himself a snack when he couldn't sleep.

Françoise Hardy, who represented something important but unfathomable for Nick as his creative powers withered. His first two albums can be glimpsed in this photo, taken in September 1973.

Louisa Raynes House, part of Central Hospital in Hatton, Warwickshire, where Nick stayed intermittently following his breakdown in April 1972.

In the words of her husband John, Sheila Wood had 'an unconscious bond' with Nick from 1971.

Guy Norton, an old friend of the Drake family, who did all he could to reverse Nick's decline in the last months of his life.

Dave and Kirstie Lodder, who reconnected with Nick when they moved back to Warwickshire in late 1972.

Sophia Ryde, at whose London flat Nick would spontaneously appear between 1971 and 1974. Like all his friends, she wished she could have done more to help him.

The Revd Edward Wilmot's tribute to Nick in the Tanworth-in-Arden
parish newsletter, December 1974.

Molly and Rodney in 1976, coming to terms with their appalling loss and
starting to realise how meaningful Nick's work was to so many.

Some people were connecting strongly with his work, however. In mid-April a Swiss schoolboy named Rolf Vasellari wrote to him from Zurich:

Dear Nick,

I am a fanatic for your music and love your first and second LPs so much. You are really unique and incomparable. Perhaps you would be so kind as to tell me something about your next records and concerts. I really hope to meet you one day.

Island forwarded the letter and Nick kept it, but did not reply. As Rolf recalls, 'Island wrote to me saying that I was the first person from outside of the UK who'd written to him, that no one could tell them where he was and that he was suffering from psychological problems, and that was why he did not answer letters.'*

Nick's confidence was not boosted by the surprise announcement in mid-April that Chris Blackwell was resigning as Island's managing director, with David Betteridge taking his place. 'Reason given for Blackwell's decision to step down is that he wants to become more involved with record production and securing new talent for development on the label,' reported *Record Retailer*.[5] 'It is also suggested that he will spend more time living in America, where he has just launched the Island label through Capitol.'

Chris, however, did not insist that Capitol pursue their intention to release *Five Leaves Left*, and they also spurned *Bryter Layter*. Joe says: 'I thought, "The second record's going to be so incredible, we'll release it in America, he'll be famous in America!" But nothing ever happened and by the time the second record was out he was in much worse shape.'[6] Instead, it was decided to introduce Nick to this potentially vast new audience by condensing the two albums into a compilation. 'I tried to persuade them to release both, but when it was clear they would release only the combination, I put in my suggestions about what to include,' says Joe. 'I don't believe Nick was involved.'

While that was in motion, the *El Pea* double album came out in

---

* Rolf visited England in late 1973 and tried again to reach Nick (with Island's help), but to no avail.

the UK and across Europe at the end of April, as the culmination of Island's campaign. As well as tracks by Traffic, Free, Jethro Tull and others, it included 'Northern Sky' – a last-minute substitution for 'One Of These Things First', which is listed on the cover and labels. The sleeve offered caricature drawings of the featured artists but no accompanying information. David Betteridge again singled Nick out in an interview as an example of an artist in need of a leg-up: 'A lot of people are saying that samplers are no good. I don't believe this. How can it be bad if a new artist like Nick Drake is exposed to the 60–70,000 people who will buy the album?'[7] (In fact, despite heavy promotion, it sold fewer copies than Island's previous samplers.)

A couple of months after the release of *Bryter Layter*, all that the record-buying public had to go on were a press ad, a brief interview, some scattered reviews and a misnamed track on a sampler LP. Unsurprisingly, few people were buying it. Paul Wheeler remembers discussing it with Nick at this time. 'He said he'd assumed that it would be much more successful than it was, and I remember being surprised, because I didn't think he was in it for that . . .'[8]

John Martyn expressed a similar thought:

> I never realised Nick was ambitious until he confided to me that he was, and it took me greatly by surprise . . . It crushed him that he was ignored, because he was used to excelling at everything: as a student,* as an athlete. It was the first time he'd ever failed at anything. It astonished me that he valued commercial success.[9]

'It amazes me that people express surprise or shock about Nick wanting to sell records,' says Joe. 'Of course he wanted to sell records – how else was he supposed to earn a living?'

To Brian Wells's way of thinking, 'It wasn't about stardom; it was more about recognition and feeling fulfilled and appreciated and admired in some way.'[10] Molly agreed: 'I don't think he ever wanted to be a star or to make a lot of money, but he terribly wanted to get through and speak to the people of his own age.'[11] Either way, he was pained by the sense that his songs were being released into

---

* All of Nick's friends assumed he was academically successful.

a void, and that he might as well not be bothering. 'I think that really did knock him back a long way,' Robert came to feel.[12]

Finding Far Leys and his parents' concern claustrophobic, in mid-May he embarked on another road trip, driving with his guitar down through France and into Spain in his Riley. His purpose was not social, but Joe remembers hearing that, passing through Paris, he 'rang Françoise Hardy's doorbell and a secretary or maid came to the door, and he stammered and didn't say anything, left a message but never came back'.[13]

His destination was a newly built apartment Chris Blackwell had recently bought as an investment (but never visited) in the village of El Cuartón, not far from Algeciras on the south coast. Chris seems to have had it in mind that his artists could use it as a song-writing retreat − members of Spooky Tooth and Mott the Hoople went there for the purpose − and he made it available to Nick if he ever wanted a change of scene. Nick had last been in the area four years earlier, on the way back from Tangier, and had fond memories of it. 'Nice flat here in a big block in the hills overlooking the sea − very cold up there at the moment, but warm down here in the town,' he wrote on a postcard home. 'Morocco just across the sea. Will let you know any further plans.'

It's likely that his intention was to focus on writing songs, but − in keeping with his increasingly hermitic world − their genesis was completely private. 'We never saw him writing a song,' said Molly.[14] 'He was terribly quiet about it − whether it all happened in his head or not I don't know.' As Rodney put it, 'Where and how and when he wrote [his third album] is difficult to say. He was beginning to get very withdrawn and depressed then.'[15]

He got back as the English summer got underway. Steve Tilston saw him with Andy Matheou outside Les Cousins one afternoon in June, shortly after his debut, *An Acoustic Confusion*, had appeared.

He startled me by saying that he liked my album, and I said some-thing along the lines of that being good, given that I was supposed to sound like him . . . I asked him about a news snippet I was convinced I'd seen in *Sounds* about him doing some recording with one of the old black American blues legends, and feeling really envious.* He laughed at the somewhat bizarre prospect. I liked him a lot; my recollection is of us getting along pretty well.[16]

Nick returned to his peripatetic habits, and sometimes crashed with Robert Kirby at Cranley Gardens. 'I knew friends he'd had from Cambridge and I knew his friends in Hampstead, and it was the same with all of them,' recalled Robert.

> They would have an intense period of a week or two when they would see Nick and talk to Nick and be with Nick, and then not hear anything from him for two or three months, and you wouldn't know where he was or what he was doing at all.[17]

It was clear to Robert that a change had come over him.

> Between *Bryter Layter* and [his last album] he would come round, stay for a week and not say anything. Nothing. If we were in the front room, enjoying listening to sounds, he'd come and sit down and enjoy listening. If we went to the pub or a restaurant, he might come with us. But he would quite often not say anything. Sometimes he would actually stand in the corner, facing out on the room but looking down. He looked haggard, unkempt. I don't think he was eating, which didn't help.[18]

Robert was eager to emphasise that there was no correlation between Nick's silences and the profundity of his utterances:

> He would talk sometimes, when he wanted to, when he had some-thing to say. People think that if Nick spoke, the words he said would somehow be like the words of Muhammad or the words of Jesus Christ, that everything would have meaning – but he'd say, 'Terrible weather we're having,' just like anybody else would.[19]

Robert was becoming established as an arranger (especially in the folk-rock field)† and continued to make recordings of Nick, but

---

* 'Son House sings on new Nick Drake double album,' ran the line in *Sounds* of 17 October 1970, intending to refer to Stefan Grossman's *The Ragtime Cowboy Jew*.
† The artists for whom he supplied arrangements in 1971 include Audience, Shalom Chanoch, Steve Gibbons, Tim Hart and Maddy Prior, John Kongos, Shelagh McDonald, Gillian McPherson, Ralph McTell, Andy Roberts, and Spirogyra.

there was no talk of collaborating on further arrangements. Nick barely played new material to him.

> He might get the guitar out and play, and it was like an exercise. What he'd do is play for fifteen or twenty minutes, non-stop, moving from figure to figure – and the figure that I'm thinking of is the introduction to 'Things Behind The Sun'. That was going for years before he recorded it.

When the educational publisher Longman commissioned Robert to provide music for a classroom aid, he asked Nick to help. 'We practised during the thirty-minute train journey from Liverpool Street to Harlow Town Station, where the Longman offices were located, to the amusement of fellow passengers.'[20] Nick contributed to three of the basic recordings: settings of Shakespeare's 'Full Fathom Five' and the American standard 'I Wish I Was a Single Girl Again', both with Vivien Fowler singing, and the Australian folk song 'With My Swag All On My Shoulder', with Robert singing. 'I was asked to make sure of clear enunciation, so it's in my best Cantab choral-scholar baritone – somewhat bizarre, considering the lyrics. Nick was highly amused by the incongruity of the culture clash.'*

More importantly for Nick, the American *Nick Drake* compilation was released in a gatefold sleeve in late July, with one of Keith Morris's 'running man' shots on the front and a large colour image of Nick reclining on Wimbledon Common in April 1969 inside. It contained only eight tracks (three from *Five Leaves Left*), when more could have been accommodated, and nowhere on the sleeve was it indicated that it consisted of tracks from different albums. No lyrics, sleevenotes or biographical information were included. 'Liner notes were very uncool in the seventies,' as Joe drily puts it.

'It was launched with a 6 p.m. cocktail party/press reception at the Troubadour in Los Angeles,' he continues. The Troubadour was America's premier venue for singer-songwriters, where Elton John had spectacularly kick-started his US career the previous August – but Nick

---

* Consisting of a book, a set of three filmstrips and a double LP, *Interplay One* was distributed to schools in 1972 and never made commercially available. Nick's contributions are simple and not recognisably his work.

was thousands of miles away. 'I'm sure he would have been asked,' Joe contends. In his absence, 'I introduced the record before they played it.' As Nick's music filled the room a spotlight was trained on a life-sized cut-out of him onstage. 'The balladeer sounded fine, though he looked a little flat,' snickered *Billboard* the following week.[21] 'I thought it was a bit silly, but I was glad they were doing *something*,' says Joe.

'Nick Drake has two English albums produced by Joe Boyd,' proclaimed full-page adverts in the US trade press. 'Both have received airplay in this country. Now he has a domestic release which is a combination of those albums. It's for people who have time to be quiet.' Reviews were scant but complimentary. 'Nick Drake has stolen Sinatra's lead for the dim-light music man,' improbably stated the *Arizona Republic*. 'His words are lost in the melodies – but not one song is lost in this album.' For the *Tampa Bay Times*, 'He has a soft, winning voice that might make itself heard above many of those with more volume but less talent.' The *Honolulu Advertiser* felt it was 'a set that gets better each time you put it on the turntable', while according to the *Morning News* of Wilmington, Delaware, 'Drake has a strange, evasive quality to his voice, but it is most effective in his own musical context . . . It really is a fine album.'[22]

The longest review he'd received anywhere to date was in the influential *Phonograph Record Magazine*, whose prosaic name concealed a hip sensibility. Colman Andrews called the set 'one of those elusive but tenacious LPs that simply won't stay off the turntable for very long'.[23] He inferred that behind Nick's cool, controlled persona 'lurks a wise heart, a well-educated soul', and that his lyrics hinted at 'a spirit, a feeling, a sense of wise mystery, of shrewd delineation of time and place and character'. In conclusion, he called it 'an album of great depth, great variety and yet great unity, and great importance as an extension of a tradition of music-making that has not been articulated so consistently beautifully since that wondrous Van Morrison album of three years ago'. Nick would have been thrilled by these words, especially the suggested parity with *Astral Weeks*, but probably never saw them.*

---

* The album was also reviewed at length in *Rolling Stone*, by Stephen Holden (who also compared it to *Astral Weeks*), but not until its issue of 27 April 1972.

Tumbril, a student paper at Brown University, Rhode Island, felt the selection of tracks was imperfect, yet still declared it 'Probably the finest album of the year'. However, the piece continued, 'it's almost impossible to get without specially ordering it'. Indeed, most surviving copies are promotional (designated by having holes punched through their covers), indicating that it had a limited commercial circulation. As Island had already found in the UK, trying to break an artist who wasn't visible was a fool's errand.

'*Bryter Layter* sold no better than *Five Leaves Left* had,' says Tim Clark. 'My memory is that they both did around 3,000 in fairly short order, then stagnated.' By general consensus, this crushed Nick. 'I don't think he gradually sank from 1967/68 to 1974,' Robert later remarked. 'I think he sank rapidly from halfway between *Bryter Layter* and [his last album].[24] I think there was a great deal of embarrassment around his peer group that what he – and we – thought was going to happen hadn't really happened.'[25]

His career appeared to have reached an impasse, but he was not forgotten. On 31 July *Melody Maker* published an overview of folk rock in which Karl Dallas declared: 'His records have been very nice but his stage presence has been virtually nil, a private communion which is very hard to join.' Nonetheless, he cautioned that Nick 'has never explored his full potential'. As if to emphasise the fact, that same week Alexis Korner – the gravel-voiced *éminence grise* of the British blues scene – released a cover of 'Saturday Sun' on his latest album, possibly through Nick's friend David Ward (who had four songwriting credits elsewhere on the album).* Korner's reworking of 'Saturday Sun' was exactly the sort of thing Joe had always had in mind, and even featured Chris McGregor, but did little for Nick's profile.

Busy as ever, John Wood hadn't seen Nick since they'd finished *Bryter Layter* a year earlier, but he took an interest in his welfare. 'I heard odds and ends about Nick through John Martyn,' he says, and decided to ask him to stay in Suffolk. 'I can't remember how it arose, but he must have been at a loose end.' John and Sheila lived with their daughters Vickie and Annagh, aged seven and nine, in a

---

* *Alexis Korner*, produced by Jean-Paul Salvatori and recorded in September 1970.

modern, four-bedroom detached house in Farrows Close in the village of Chevington.

According to Annagh, 'It was an odd home to be brought up in because musicians would often drop in or stay for a few nights – Sandy Denny, Richard and Linda Thompson, Nick and various others.' 'Some made an impact on us, some not so much,' says Vickie. 'Nick made a very big impact. I loved him and loved being around him. He had a gentle, patient and unassuming way about him – a serene, unimposing magnetism that I was drawn to. He had a calming influence on me.' Annagh remembers him as 'enormously tall – a gentle giant'.

Nick hadn't met Sheila before, but she loved his records and they swiftly bonded, despite her being over eleven years his senior.* 'She got along with artistic people,' says John.

> She liked music but had always wanted to act and was a clever mimic. She was what you might call a cheerful depressive herself, and had her own demons. I think that perhaps created an unconscious bond between them. She would interrogate Nick more than I would, and virtually force him out of silence.

'They sat and talked for hours,' Annagh adds, 'no one knew what about. She was a wordsmith, she loved crossword puzzles and so on, so maybe they partly enjoyed each other on that level.'

Nick had his guitar with him and both girls vividly recall him playing it. 'He'd play and sing his own songs in the living room while we sat cross-legged on the floor in front of him,' recalls Vickie. 'To me his hands were massive, with very long fingers. They mesmerised me.' Although he played and sang, the purpose of the visit was social. 'He didn't make any recordings with me at home – I didn't even have a basic tape recorder there,' says John. In fact, as far as John was concerned Nick wasn't intending to make a new record: 'While he was staying with us, I certainly asked him if he had any recording plans but he gave me no information on that at all.'

Nick had never been an autodidact – beyond the guitar, at least

* She was born Sheila Harris on 21 March 1937.

– but he surprised his parents by ordering a new set of the *Encyclopaedia Britannica*, payable in instalments, which he kept, along with its accompanying bookcase, in the music room at Far Leys. For a time he used the cheap Oxford Hotel in Penywern Road, Earl's Court, as a base, but his movements had no apparent focus. He continued to visit Paul and Diana at Tittenhurst Park, where Paul remembers him enthusing about Joni Mitchell's newly released *Blue*. From time to time they went further afield. 'Nick liked driving, so occasionally we'd go on an excursion,' says Paul. 'For example, we drove to Rye for the day, had lunch in a local café, wandered around and drove back.'

One afternoon the Loungers had a reunion, catching up over a picnic in a London park. In that context Paul was struck by the change in Nick: 'He had always seemed comfortable in himself and not awkward. We were throwing a plastic football around and he couldn't catch it. It wasn't like him not to be highly co-ordinated, but he seemed disorientated. He looked awkward at first, then scared that it might come towards him.'

Despite his parents' clearly expressed concerns, Nick was still smoking hash when the mood took him. One day, relates Paul, 'Nick told me that someone had held out a blackberry in their hand at a party and said it was a bunch of grapes – and that it unquestionably had been. I began to wonder whether dope was affecting his perspective, almost in a hallucinatory way.' However, Robert felt, 'It's possible that [dope] didn't help, but I believe the demons he fought came from deeper within his soul rather than his brain.'[26]

As the summer progressed Nick suffered increasingly acute stomach pain, to his parents' distress. A nadir was reached at Far Leys in August, when he rolled around on the drawing-room floor in such agony that – relates Gabrielle – he implored Molly to help him end his life. Sleep was induced in hospital for days on end while tests were carried out. Tuberculosis was suspected but it was discovered to be a kidney stone, possibly psychosomatic, or possibly caused by a poor diet and low fluid intake over the preceding couple of years. The diagnosis came as a relief to his parents, as it suggested that his worsening mental state might have a physical cause.

He passed the stone without surgery, and in the course of monitoring him their GP told Rodney and Molly that he suspected Nick
was showing symptoms of schizophrenia – a biological or chemical
disturbance in the brain that can present in a variety of ways. The
most obvious manifestation is psychosis – delusions and hallucinations
– which Nick is not known ever to have experienced. However,
his disorganisation, lethargy, introspection and taciturnity did point
towards so-called 'simple-type' schizophrenia, which frequently
comes on in early adulthood and can be triggered by stress, amongst
other things. 'There was a lot of pressure around and I suppose I
sort of cracked up,' Nick later wrote of this time.[27]

Molly and Rodney already had concerns of their own and now
passed them on to Nick's specialist, Dr Vivian Weinstein, who gave
them the name of a local psychiatrist. However, Gabrielle – who
was busy with her career and not closely involved in Nick's welfare
at the time – explains that 'Nick refused to accept that there was
anything wrong with him mentally and certainly rejected the idea
of any psychiatry.'[28]

Casting about for ways to get through to him, Molly and
Rodney obtained Joe's number and telephoned him in Los Angeles.
Joe hadn't spoken to Nick since his departure in January. By his
account, they 'said they really wanted Nick to seek help but that
he was afraid that everyone would look down on him if he went
to a psychiatrist. He was reluctant, and they would appreciate it
if I would speak to him because they said he respected me so
much.'[29]

Joe – who had himself been under a lot of pressure the previous
year – did his best to reassure Nick that there was no shame in
seeking help. 'I spoke to him and said, "I don't want to tell you
what's right or wrong, but you should never feel people are judging
you. You have to deal with things from your own point of view,
and if you need help, you should get help."'[30]

The exchange left Joe unsettled:

Nick sounded terrible on the phone. His hesitant manner had always
seemed to shield an inner core about which he was certain, even if
he had little ability to communicate it other than through his music.

Now it felt as if both core and shield had been shattered. He sounded frightened.[31]

Molly and Rodney could only offer him any support he might want as he decided on his next steps. In mid-September they took a holiday in the South of France, from where his mother sent him a postcard at Far Leys that typifies their love and concern: 'I do hope you are well, Nick darling, and that all is well with you – don't forget to drink plenty! Hope all is well at home, if you are there – longing to see you again. Dad sends very much love and so do I.'[32]

Upon their return at the end of the month they were astonished to discover that he had moved out, without saying a word to Naw or anyone else. 'Suddenly he took off and went away, and we didn't know where he'd gone at all,' recounted Molly.[33] 'He was very casual, in a way, [but] although he'd quite planned to go away and disappear, he left a letter lying on his desk from the landlord saying exactly where he was.'

Nick had found himself a room at 138 Muswell Hill Road, probably whilst visiting Cranley Gardens, and Robert was apparently the only person he informed:

> His very last place in London was a very grim bedsit on Muswell Hill Road, only about a hundred yards from where I lived. It was a nasty house, there were other nasty bedsits, there was a nasty landlord. It wasn't a slum, but it only had the very basics.[34]

David Sandison remembered Nick taking it under an assumed name, and others recall him keeping its address to himself. On one occasion, recalls Diana Wheeler, 'We were all in the car and I was going to drop him somewhere, but he was secretive about exactly where he lived. He wanted to be dropped on a street nearby.'

Molly and Rodney were disconcerted, but knew how resistant he was to apparent meddling in his affairs. Gabrielle explains: 'My parents didn't want to be seen to interfere with his life, but they were worried because of his physical health.' As such, after a couple of weeks of silence they decided to drive to London and talk to him. With the help of another resident they worked out which was his room, but he wasn't there (or didn't come to the door). Molly therefore scribbled a note to him, which he kept:

> Dad and I are dead of Nick-lack. It does seem such a terribly long time since we saw you. We have lots to tell you about, and Dad wants a last game before we put the croquet hoops to bed for the winter. Do please try to find time to come and see us, Nick darl, please please – even if only for one night. We do miss you dreadfully. All love, Mum.

He did not respond.

At a loss, they enlisted Gabrielle, who did something she knew her brother would deplore:

> I rang up Island. We thought that he was deeply depressed because Island weren't supporting him, that he'd brought out [Bryter Layter] and they'd never give him dates and things like that, but they said, 'We'd do anything for Nick, give him publicity, but he won't do it!' Chris Blackwell said, 'If he doesn't want to do public performances, fine! We'll keep him on a stipend of however-much-it-was a week.' And I suddenly realised that, quite on the contrary, Island were prepared to do anything, and that that was not where the problem lay.[35]

This was a revelation for Molly, Rodney and Gabrielle. The alarming fact appeared to be that whatever Nick was grappling with did not have an immediate cause, either in his kidneys or his career; it ran deeper. The reticence and self-containment that had always been components of his personality were squeezing out the other characteristics that had until recently allowed him to enjoy life, albeit on his terms.

His parents resigned themselves to not hearing from him until he felt like it, and on 12 October Rodney wrote him a note:

> As it seems that you want to be on your own at the moment, we shan't of course give anyone your address or bother you ourselves – but please, Nick, at least give us a ring now and then if you feel you can't come and see us – which we so much want you to do, of course. Very much love from all of us here, Dad.

Nick did not reply, so his father wrote again on 20 October:

Dear Nick, aren't you ever going to ring us up here? I am going up
to London tomorrow for the Bombay Burmah dinner, returning on
Friday. It would be very nice to hear from you – perhaps you would
feel inclined to give me a ring at the Oriental club. We are very
anxious to know how you are, to hear from you and see you. Very
much love from here, Dad.

This also elicited no response.

It wasn't only Nick's parents who wanted news of him. Admirers
of his music had virtually no means of establishing even the most
basic facts about him – as was the norm by 1971, his record covers
offered no background information, while Island's promo handouts
were circulated in tiny numbers and generated barely any press. On
22 October a fan named Helen, of Fishponds Road, Bristol, wrote
to him, care of Island, having bought and admired *Bryter Layter*.
'Forgive me please for being so rude in asking, but who are you?'
she asked. 'If you could find a time to reply and tell me who you
are, I would be grateful. Look after yourself, the man with big shoes,
love Helen.'

Nick kept the letter but is unlikely to have answered it. Without
explaining himself to anyone, he had in fact resolved to hide away
until he had perfected a set of new material. One afternoon he
appeared at Alex Henderson's flat in Edith Terrace, wanting to ask
a favour of Sophia Ryde. She now had a job at the Jeremy Maas
Gallery in Clifford Street, but sometimes worked from home. Nick
knew she could type and he needed to submit his new songs to
Warlock:

I used to sit at the little desk under the bunk Nick had slept in and
type out manuscripts for Jeremy on an old typewriter of my grandfather's. He turned up and asked me to type out a pile of handwritten
pages.* They were the words to his next album, though I didn't
know it at the time.

---

* This was probably for publishing purposes, as Nick didn't need the lyrics as
prompts.

If any of the lyrics – especially 'Free Ride', with its references to 'All of the pictures that you keep on the wall' and 'a carpet that's so thick on the floor' – were aimed at Sophia, she was oblivious.

> It didn't occur to me that 'Free Ride', or any of his other songs, might have referred to me. Even though I was interested in pictures, I don't think there were any on the wall at Edith Terrace, let alone a thick carpet, and he didn't ask me to type the words out in any pointed way. I don't think he had any particular reason for asking me, it was just because he'd seen me typing things for other people.

At much the same time, the Woods' telephone in Suffolk rang. 'To my surprise, it was Nick, saying "I want to go back into the studio",' says John. He wasn't talkative, but he did make a couple of things clear:

> I knew it was an album we were talking about, not demos, and when I asked if he wanted me to get Danny Thompson or anyone else down, he was clear that it was to be just him. I fitted him into the diary as soon as I could – I felt I needed to strike while the iron was hot, or else it might not happen at all.

24

A Small Reel

～

NICK'S THIRD ALBUM was recorded in Sound Techniques over
two consecutive nights in the week of Monday, 25 October
1971. He made his way to Chelsea from Muswell Hill Road,
carrying his guitar, and both sessions took place between 11 p.m.
and 2 a.m. They were the only slots John Wood could find, but
he adds that in any case, 'I suspect I also knew I'd get the most
out of him with no one else there. He wasn't in good shape, he
didn't look healthy.'

John was the only other person in the building throughout, and
meticulously organised the equipment before Nick's arrival.

> Even though it sounds like a simple recording, it wasn't a case of
> just sticking a microphone under his nose and pressing the start and
> stop buttons. There were two mikes on his guitar, two room mikes
> and a separate vocal mike, and it was recorded onto a 16-track
> machine – so fairly elaborate. To compensate for the fact that it was
> just guitar-and-voice, I wanted the recording to have a larger-than-
> life immediacy and presence, to draw the listener into it.

There was little preliminary chat and Nick performed with the
efficiency John had come to expect, sitting on a chair (as always)
on the studio floor and singing from memory as he played. 'All the
songs were recorded on one guitar – I think it was a Martin, but I
couldn't swear to it.' Some sound like they're played on nylon strings,
but John insists none were: 'I have absolutely no doubt that all the
tracks are played on the same guitar, and I never ever saw Nick
change a single string, which is pretty extraordinary.'

John sat up in the control room as Nick played and sang:

The multi-track tape machine was on my left, the console was in front of me, and the window looking down towards Nick was on my right. Most of the time I was focused on my monitors, meters and tapes, but I'd glance down at him and we'd have occasional communication through the talkback. We were able to discuss whatever we needed to, but there wasn't a lot else to talk about. He had perfected the songs and his performances were very together.

Opening with a beautiful, unorthodox chord sequence, on the brief 'Pink Moon' Nick comes across as a prophet of doom, employing unorthodox syntax ('Saw it written and I saw it say') and a curious blend of archaism and modern contraction ('Pink moon gonna get ye all') to heighten his words' foreboding effect. What he meant the central image to stand for is obscure, but he surely intended the contrast between the unsettling words and the lovely melody. 'Place To Be' is a song of emotional self-reconciliation, acknowledging past naïveté and confronting an overwhelming need for love. It references 'Day Is Done', apparently as evidence of a changed perspective. Here he sings 'When I was strong, strong in the sun / I thought I'd see when day was done'. A surviving home recording is finger-picked with Nick's customary perfection, but for the album he strummed it. 'Road', by contrast, has a complex and fitful guitar part and comes across as a declaration of independence and self-reliance, an assertion of Nick's need to follow his own inclinations, whether in terms of his career or in the light of the concern others were expressing about his life.*

The lovely tune of 'Which Will' forms the background for another series of rhetorical questions that can be taken to imply a disappointment in love, or to invite answers about wider issues. In almost comic contract to the lush instrumentals on *Bryter Layter*, the instrumental 'Horn' is raw, its power and beauty lying in its restraint. It sounds simple, yet there's an unfathomable feeling and musicality underpinning it. The ensuing 'Things Behind The Sun' is a virtuoso performance, Nick's copious, cryptic words flowing seamlessly against his relentless guitar pattern, the whole being so perfectly rendered

---

* It's possible that Nick was deliberately countering his mother's song 'The Road to the Stars', which emphasises the need for companionship and support.

that the complexity of its syntax is barely apparent. Its words are an apparent stream-of-consciousness that can be interpreted as a series of profound existential statements or just happy turns of phrase that appealed to him as he played the guitar figure over and over (as described by Robert). It too references 'Day Is Done': 'Don't be shy, you learn to fly / And see the sun, day is done'.

'Know' is similarly nebulous, its repetitive guitar part growing in power as Nick hums and then sings his starkly equivocal lyric: 'Know that I love you / Know I don't care / Know that I see you / Know I'm not there'. As with other parts of the album, it can be interpreted as a love song (perhaps an imagined dialogue between an unrequited lover and the object of his affection), or as spiritual (though Nick was not religious), or even a reference to schizophrenia.

'Parasite' is overwhelmingly sad, and listening to it is a bleak and vicarious experience, akin to eavesdropping. Like 'At The Chime Of A City Clock', it speaks of urban alienation, yet with none of that song's leavening touches, and offering a central image suggestive of profoundly low self-esteem. It opens with the easily imaginable image of Nick riding a Tube escalator deep underground, looking down, as was his habit, and overhearing the complaints of his fellow travellers, for whom he feels helpless empathy. The next verse is more opaque, though its alliteration and internal rhyming indicate the deliberateness of the words. 'Falling so far on a silver spoon' hints at failing to live up to the privilege he was born to, while 'making the moon for fun' and 'Changing a rope for a size too small / People all get hung' defy obvious interpretation.* If Nick literally considered himself parasitic, an obvious host is hard to point to.

'Free Ride' appears to reiterate some of the ideas expressed in 'Parasite', with an insistent guitar part that – alone among the songs on the album – could have lent itself to a rock arrangement. The words appear to have a sardonic overtone, as if suggesting contempt for middle-class comforts and values but also a desire to benefit from them. 'Harvest Breed', like 'Pink Moon', appears to accept or even welcome the inevitability of fate, even death. Its central image of

---

* In one of the two known home recordings, Nick sings 'Changing a *shirt* for a size too small'.

'falling fast and falling free' feels disturbingly immediate and personal, and Nick sounds reconciled to it.

The 'harvest breed' itself can be seen as a reference to the human race as no more than another crop, sown to be reaped, yet the effect is not morbid or cynical. 'I think "Harvest Breed" is an important song in understanding Nick's state of mind at that time,' says Paul Wheeler. 'It's reminiscent of certain words in the Christian funeral service.'* 'From The Morning' is so beautiful and calming that its elliptical lyric is easy to mistake for life-affirming catharsis after its frequently despondent predecessors. Nick may very well have intended it as such, but like all of the songs he intended to record, it resists any one analysis.

'We did five the first night and the rest the next night,' says John.

> I might have screwed up a take or two, but every time one was okay he'd put down his guitar and come up and listen, until we'd agreed on one to keep. Some were done on the first take, but none took more than three. I don't recall what the very first one he played was, but 'Parasite' was second and I thought, 'Uh-oh. This is something different . . .' The songs were no longer observational, they seemed to come from a much more personal place, but I didn't ask him to explain them − it obviously wasn't going to be a good idea to start turning them over. I think part of the reason he felt comfortable working with me was that he knew I wouldn't challenge him about his lyrics.

The last thing they recorded was an instrumental version of the ancient French chestnut 'Plaisir d'amour', which John says Nick played 'almost as an afterthought', perhaps intending its simple beauty as an antidote to the turmoil of the other material. Naturally enough, continues John, 'I assumed he was going to want the tracks augmented, so it was a surprise when he told me on the first night it was going to be just as it was.' The only other instrument Nick wanted was a piano on the title track:

> He overdubbed it using the studio's 1930s Steinway B grand, whilst listening to his guitar and vocal on headphones. It was the only

---

* 'As for man, his days are as grass: As a flower of the field, so he flourisheth. For the wind passeth over it, and it is gone' (Psalm 103).

instrument we kept there, and it was hired. You can hear it on all his albums, and many others. I have no idea what became of it . . .

At the end of the second session John was still unclear as to exactly what Nick had in mind for the project. 'After we had finished I asked what I should keep, and he said, "All of it," which was a complete contrast to his former stance,' he stated in 1974.[1]

Nick was adamant about what he wanted. He wanted it to be spare and stark, and he wanted it to be spontaneously recorded . . . He would sit in the control room and sort of blankly look at the wall and say, 'Well, I really don't want to hear anything else, I really think people should only just be aware of me and how I am.'[2]

The stance mirrored his increasingly spartan lifestyle.

To John's bemusement, the sessions were over almost as soon as they'd begun: 'I'd assumed he was going to re-record some of them, but when he said "No", it made sense – we both knew he'd nailed them.' Although the album was created in close collaboration with John, and its sleeve credits 'Witchseason Productions Ltd' as producer, Nick considered himself to have produced it. 'I made three albums, two produced by an American, Joe Boyd, and the third produced by me,' he later stated.[3]

Nick returned to Sound Techniques on Saturday, 30 October, to mix and sequence the tracks with John, who explains:

The mix was quick and straightforward, and we played around with the sequencing together at the same time. Nothing was already set in stone, not even starting with 'Pink Moon' or ending with 'From The Morning', but obviously the sides needed to be roughly equal in length. The decision to leave off 'Plaisir d'amour' was taken when we were working out the running order – I wasn't bothered that it was only twenty-eight minutes of music, because you don't want something that intense to last any longer.

The album's approach can be interpreted simply as a rejection of its predecessors' elaborateness, and some detected a streak of petulance in Nick's determination to keep it so plain. Robert Kirby later speculated that it amounted to a demo of a series of unfinished masterpieces, absolutely perfect in this raw state, but unfinished. Each of the songs on it contains a wealth of material that earlier he would have spent time developing . . . I think he felt that he could trust nobody to help him, or just couldn't be arsed and wanted rid of the weight of all those potential masterpieces.[4]

Another interpretation is that Nick perfectly understood his own artistry. The album not only holds attention throughout, it becomes more engrossing and more deeply mysterious upon repeated plays. His bearing is profoundly introspective, his lyrics more inscrutable than ever, yet the songs artfully bridge despair and hope, carrying a substantial emotional charge. His guitar playing is startlingly deft and distinctive, made all the more immediate and striking by John's consummate recording. The album's overall economy and power is remarkable; Nick's genius was in full flower.

With the album completed to both their satisfaction, John compiled the master reel and ran off a 7½-inch copy for Nick, which he took away with him. 'I would never have let the master tape out of my hands,' says John. He then made arrangements to master it with Malcolm Davies, who had mastered Nick's previous albums at Apple but was now at Pye. Incredibly, Nick hadn't informed either Witchseason or Island that he was making a new album, but of course expected Chris Blackwell to honour the verbal agreement they'd made at the start of the year. 'After we'd made it I spoke to Marian Bain at Witchseason, but it was all a bit loose,' says John.

On Monday, 1 November, Nick presented himself at Island in Basing Street. David Sandison was on his way back in from lunch and was surprised to see him in reception, 'smiling that weird little smile, half-mocking, half-bewildered'.[5] By David's later account,

He came and sat in my room for half an hour or so. He didn't say much. I got him a cup of tea, the phone was ringing, people were coming in and out, and he hadn't said what he wanted. After a while he said he'd better go, so I said, 'Okay' – still couldn't figure out why he was there.[6]

Nick made his way back to reception and asked to see Chris, who happened to be there:

Someone got hold of me in the studio and said, 'There's a guy downstairs who wants to see you.' I asked who he was and was told that he hadn't given a name, he was just sitting in reception. I asked them to find out, and when I was told it was Nick I immediately went down and sat next to him. He clearly wasn't in good shape and had no energy. He barely looked up, just stared at the floor. I asked after him but he just muttered a couple of words and handed me a small reel, the sort of thing people used for demos. I asked what it was and he said it was his new record. I asked what I owed him and he told me it was five hundred pounds.*

Chris wrote him a cheque, then 'asked if there was anything else I could do for him': 'He said "No" and left. I remember the encounter vividly because it was so sad. It moved me a lot. I didn't know what I could do for him, and even now I wonder what I could or should have done to help him.' Chris went back upstairs and spoke to David. Puzzled, they rang John, who explained that the tape was indeed Nick's new album, which he was in the process of mastering. They made another copy, then played it. 'I liked it, but not as much as the others,' was Chris's reaction.

Island was increasingly focused on rock: as 1971 drew to a close their biggest sellers were the likes of Jethro Tull, Free and Emerson, Lake & Palmer, with Cat Stevens flying the singer-songwriter flag to great heights. The starkness of Nick's album baffled everyone there, but – to their credit – quietly setting it aside was never considered. In fact, they unhesitatingly accepted it as it was. 'I was waiting for Island to get on to me to complain about its length, but they never did,' says John Wood. 'I think everyone thought, "Well, if that's what his music is as of now, that's fine." I invoiced them about £400 for the recording costs – nothing.'

David knew that an unconventional approach would be required to sell such a personal, esoteric record, and decided on a teaser campaign. The following week he composed an unusually frank press release:

---

* Chris's payment of £500 (around £5,500 in 2022) was the agreed advance payable upon delivery of a finished album; Nick's weekly advances were against publishing income.

Nobody at Island is really sure where Nick lives these days. We're pretty sure he left his flat in Hampstead quite a while ago. We have a bank agreement for him so that he's always got his rent money and some spending bread . . . The chances of Nick actually playing in public are more than remote.

So why, when there are people prepared to do anything for a recording contract or a Queen Elizabeth Hall date, are we releasing this new Nick Drake album, and the next (if he wants to do one)? Because we believe that Nick Drake is a great talent. His first two albums haven't sold a shit, but if we carry on releasing them maybe one day someone in Authority will stop to listen to them properly and agree with us, and maybe a lot more people will get to hear Nick Drake's incredible songs and guitar playing. And maybe they'll buy a lot of records and fulfil our faith in Nick's promise. Then. Then we'll have done our job.

Simply dated 'November 1971', it generated no coverage. Island was in fact unclear how to proceed; they didn't even know the album's title and Nick had expressed no views as to artwork. Chris therefore summoned Island's art director, Annie Sullivan: 'Chris said to me, "You're going to do the album sleeve for Nick Drake, but it's going to be difficult." And I thought, "Well, I've got a quite good, sensitive manner . . ." But it *was* difficult.'[7]

Annie met Nick to discuss it but he was virtually silent:

He just sat there, hunched up. Even though he didn't speak, I knew the album was called *Pink Moon*. I can't remember how he conveyed it, whether he wrote it down. He couldn't tell me what he wanted, but I had *Pink Moon* to go on, so I decided to go about it by a process of elimination . . . I got lots and lots of pictures of moons – I got someone to photograph the moon and put a pink light over it, I got historic old pictures of the moon . . .

When that didn't work she decided to commission original artwork. Surrealist painter Michael Trevithick had worked for various newspapers, magazines and book publishers, and wanted to diversify into album art. As such, he submitted his portfolio to Island in early 1971 and designed a memorable sleeve for an

American repackaging of the first Spooky Tooth LP.* Annie thought his style might be a good fit for the abstract feel of Nick's lyrics.

'I was given a copy of *Bryter Layter* and the lyrics for *Pink Moon*, without the music,' he says. He quickly came up with a small draft design in acrylic paint. 'I incorporated items mentioned in the songs – flower, hill, deepest sea, local clown, shine of the shoes, rope, broken cup. The cheese and moon rocket were added for fun.' Another meeting was arranged at Basing Street, at which Annie and Nick could discuss the concept with Michael and request any changes.

'He looked dishevelled as he shuffled in,' continues Michael.

> I gave him the artwork to scrutinise but he merely stood hunched, gazing down upon the design which he was holding, without a single utterance. He was totally uncommunicative and non-committal. We just stood there. I suspect he was bemused by the imagery. After a short, uncomfortable time the meeting was terminated, with no input from him, and he shuffled out. It was a bizarre meeting – it was clear something was perturbing him, but Annie hadn't mentioned the state of mind he was in.

Michael assumed that was the end of that, but Annie subsequently asked him to proceed to a finished design, for a fee of £90. He took around a week to paint the picture (again in acrylic) that the final cover was photographed from. He had hand-painted Nick's name, but it was deemed illegible and replaced with type. Annie had decided that a gatefold was merited, in order to reproduce the lyrics (not entirely accurately) alongside a photograph of Nick.

As such, Annie commissioned Keith Morris to take a third set of pictures of Nick one cold winter's afternoon. The shoot was organised at short notice. 'I got a phone call saying, would I do this session with Nick?' recalled Keith. 'I was really surprised because I hadn't seen him for months. They came round in a car to pick me up, then to go and get Nick, and out to Hampstead Heath.'[8] This

---

* *Tobacco Road*, released in May 1971.

time there was no prior discussion about ideas, and Keith only brought black-and-white film.*

Nick was wearing a roll-neck jumper and a grey anorak with a pen clipped into its top pocket. He was clean-shaven, but Annie still thought he resembled 'a tramp': 'He looked very shabby. He wasn't fashionably down-at-heel, he was kind of sad.' Also in the car was a golden retriever named Gus, whom she was dog-sitting. 'I'd brought him along because everybody liked Gus, and dogs sometimes have a way of getting through where people don't. Nick didn't talk to Gus but he obviously liked him.'

When they reached Hampstead Heath Annie focused on walking Gus: 'I left them to it – there was no point in me being there and saying, "I think you ought to do this" or "Smile!". Keith was brilliant with people.' Keith shot Nick sitting on a bench and wandering around. In some frames his expression is grim, in others he has a half-smile on his lips. According to Keith: 'The biggest problem I had was trying to get a shot of him actually looking into the camera, or even in the vague direction of the camera. His tendency was really to look down or away – anything but at the camera – and that dictated the whole session.'[9]

> Certain sessions you remember for their colour. I remember that one because I don't remember a single colour. Everything about it was grey. I don't remember green – I remember grey. It was the quickest session we ever did, barely an hour. We didn't talk about any ideas, I just snapped away. I had seen him before when he'd been very introverted, but that day he wouldn't even look at me, let alone do anything. It was just, 'Stand there! Stand there! Look over there!' He just did it . . . I think there's a tragic simplicity to those pictures. Anyone could have taken them, I just happened to be the person.[10]

The circumstances under which *Pink Moon* had been created were highly unusual. An obscure artist with no commercial track record had gone into a top studio with a world-class engineer and made an album precisely the way he wanted, with no one else's input.

---

* A solarised headshot from this session was used in the eventual artwork (the negative also reversed, perhaps unintentionally).

Next, he had it mixed and mastered to the highest standard, and delivered it to a prestigious label who had no idea it had even been conceived of. They then unquestioningly paid him and set about packaging and promoting it, with the help of one of London's top photographers.

The fact that Island had no expectation of it selling is testament to the extraordinary atmosphere Chris Blackwell had fostered there, and the fact that Nick created it whilst barely being able to speak makes its existence all the more remarkable.

Nick was on a downward spiral throughout the period in which he crafted *Pink Moon*, and mustering the energy and discipline to bring it into being had cost him dearly. As soon as it was completed and delivered and its artwork was organised, he quit his bleak bedsit and returned to Spain. Once again, his parents had no idea of his whereabouts and were gravely concerned about his welfare. When their old friend Wilfrid Russell* visited for lunch on 14 November, they told him of Nick's condition. He offered to write to his acquaintance Dr John Flood, director of The Priory – a private mental hospital in Roehampton – to see if an appointment could be arranged.

'At Marlborough and Cambridge he seemed quite normal,' he wrote to Dr Flood the same day,

> but during the last few years since coming down from university he has become very withdrawn and his parents have found it increasingly difficult to communicate with him. It has now got to the stage where the boy seems to have deliberately cut himself off from them . . .
> I feel sure that if he could be persuaded to see you a start could be made to get to grips with the problem. Of course, he has to be found first, and they are understandably hesitant to bring in the police.

To their great relief, however, Nick materialised at Far Leys in December, telling them nothing of his recent activities but seeming finally to accept the need to live at home.

---

* A businessman, author and philanthropist who was closely involved with Leonard Cheshire.

PART FOUR

25

Teetering On The Edge

'On the one hand, going back to live with your parents feels like a terrible defeat, but on the other hand it's a welcome retreat, a sanctuary,' suggests Paul Wheeler, who was struggling with his own mental health at the time. 'Good,' he remembers thinking, 'Nick's safe, with people who care about him, I don't have to worry about him.'

Life at Far Leys was indeed secure, and Molly and Rodney were relieved to know Nick was safe, but their concerns about his condition were only amplified by his return. 'I have believed all along that you are basically a strong person,' Rodney had written to him two years earlier, but his fragility was now all too clear. He kept his own hours, his moods and behaviour were unpredictable and unreliable, and he was silent and surly, sharing few of his thoughts other than that he remained dead set against psychiatry.

In the words of John Pringle's powerful May 1970 article in *The Times*, concerning his own son, the challenge Molly and Rodney faced was 'how best to cope with this strange, new member of the household, whose moods alternate impossibly between sullen lying on his bed in the dark to wild fits of aggression, with social manners regressed to an almost animal level . . . Should he be persuaded to get up, dress, keep himself clean, encouraged to work or study, or just be left alone – which course was best for him?'[1]

They were indeed uncertain how to proceed, but had endured much adversity during the war and were not defeatists. Crucially, they saw no shame in his condition, and focused on doing whatever they could to understand and ameliorate it. This was by no means a typical response to mental illness at the time, and they were frustrated by how little support or instruction was available. 'If someone breaks a leg,' Molly later reflected,

> you know exactly what to do, or you can be told what to do, but with this you didn't know what the treatment was, and whatever you did seemed to be the wrong thing to do. The only thing that mattered to either of us was that we should try and make him a little happier, bring something into his life. One just longed to do something to help Nick and felt so impotent that one could do little to help him.[2]

Nick continued to interpret his family's need to collaborate in pursuit of his welfare as simple meddling. It was a vicious circle for them all, but worst for Molly and Rodney, who were always at home. Rodney was reading Nina Bawden's 1966 novel *A Little Love, A Little Learning* and made note of her observation that 'unhappy people often hate those who love them the most'.[3] As Gabrielle puts it, 'At times our parents became the enemy for him, and at times his closest cohorts. The difficulty was that they could never predict which mantle had descended on them in their son's eyes.'[4]

His animosity was provoked more by frustration with his predicament than any obvious fault with life at Far Leys or his parents, now sixty-three and fifty-six respectively. 'Although very much of their generation, they were far more open-minded than most of the people that surrounded them – and interested in new developments,' says Gabrielle. 'My mother loved new fashions, my dad was into any new gadget going. They listened to a great deal of music – and not just classical. They were much into *Top of the Pops*, for instance.'

They contributed to village life and were intermittent churchgoers, but – if set in their ways – were not inflexible. 'They could not have coped with Nick if they had been,' as their daughter points out, but acknowledges: 'Life at Far Leys, though safe and cosy, could feel suffocating if one was trying to spread one's wings. It was the wing-spreading that Nick had come to find so difficult.'

Nick showed little appreciation for his parents' constant support, but its availability was the most important benefit of living at home.

Although Molly and Rodney were occasionally exasperated by his caprices and outbursts, they recognised them as symptomatic of his illness, rather than youthful thoughtlessness or selfishness, and understood that his condition made it difficult for him to think straight, let alone consider life from others' perspectives.

He had come to question his privileged upbringing but remained fond of Naw, whom Gabrielle describes as 'more a member of the family than a servant, the much-loved, gentle, silent, ever-loyal, ever-staunch third member of the Far Leys team'. They were all unswervingly devoted to Nick and committed to making sense of the tangle his life had become.

Communication was difficult, though. He had never been loquacious, and now even basic exchanges were challenging. 'At first my parents and I thought it was just us he wasn't communicating with, and it was a great shock to discover it was the same with his friends and record company,' says Gabrielle. 'When he was in this very down state he just couldn't talk at all, and it was only during those rare moments that he did open up that you could get him to clarify a little what he was feeling.'[5]

Even when he was minded to articulate his thoughts, he struggled.

> Often one couldn't get the flow of what he was saying and if you tried too often to say 'What do you mean by that, Nick?', he'd clam up again . . . I found it unbearably painful to be standing outside him and not to be able to reach into his mind to help him.

When Nick wanted a change of scene he spontaneously visited friends, in London or elsewhere. 'He'd just appear at the door,' says Beverley Martyn.[6] 'Sometimes he'd stay, sometimes he'd go, sometimes he'd be silent, sometimes he'd talk. That was what we expected of him, and he knew we wouldn't reprimand him for being the way he was.'

He paid John and Bev one such visit at Christmas 1971. They were now living in Hastings full-time and had a baby daughter, whom Bev fondly recalls him holding. She made mince pies for the first time, which Nick pronounced 'scrumptious'. It was one of the only things he did say. 'After he'd made *Pink Moon* things got worse and worse,' she says.

We'd go for a walk and he'd just stare into the sea, or stare into the night. It was just silence, hanging there. It wasn't awkward, I got used to it. Sometimes he'd mutter something under his breath and you'd want to hear it, because, really, you wanted to hear *anything* he had to say.

Nick also visited Paul and Diana at Tittenhurst Park. For Paul, 'He was like one of those cats which turn up at many households, all of which are under the impression that they have a unique role in providing food, shelter and company.'[7] Diana remembers: 'He looked a bit grubby. His clothes seemed slept in, his hair looked greasy, he was really thin.'

He'd largely stopped writing songs after *Pink Moon*, but playing and listening to music remained a focal pastime when he was with Paul. 'After *Pink Moon* I don't think he ever played any new material to me, but he was very moved – more than usual – by a song of mine called "Easy Time",' Paul recalls. Its lyric candidly acknowledges: 'It's just not that easy to be strong.'

'He'd sleep on the sofa and be gone when we woke up,' Diana continues. 'He had the same sort of alertness that a wild animal has – he'd prick up his ears and bolt if someone said something or made a noise that he didn't like.'

London was his most frequent destination. Ben Laycock and Rose Cuninghame had married in June 1971, Alex Henderson and Sophia Ryde had just split up, and there was a general sense of shifting priorities in their circle, but he could usually find someone to pass the time with. 'He would ring up to check if you were there,' says Robert Abel Smith, 'and we'd urge him to come over. By then he wasn't carrying his guitar around. We just let him sit in silence. He would literally not speak for the whole evening.'

His desire for company and inability to communicate made for a painful combination. 'He became quieter and quieter until eventually he'd just sit staring at his knees, saying nothing at all,' as Sophia Ryde puts it. 'We were all too young to know how to help, and we didn't realise how bad things were.'

At one gathering, he 'just leaned against the wall beside the front door with his overcoat on, hovering', remembers Victoria

Ormsby-Gore. 'His sweet, happy smile had been replaced by a look of regret and disturbance,' adds Julian Lloyd. 'I spoke to him but he couldn't maintain a conversation.'

Ben and Rose had moved to Wandsworth. 'Nick would appear out of the blue,' says Ben. 'The doorbell would ring, it was always late at night, and it was terribly difficult to know how to deal with him because he wouldn't say anything, and we'd soon run out of things to say. He'd just sit in the corner – sometimes not even that.'

On one occasion, remembers Rose, 'He just stood beside a chair, as if he couldn't summon the energy to sit.' Ben says: 'I asked him what the matter was and I clearly remember he muttered something about a black dog.'*

Sophia had moved into a basement flat at 72 Ifield Road. No one had ever got the impression that Nick took an especial interest in her, including Sophia herself, but he began to call on her too. 'The minute I left Alex he began to visit quite often, so I had an inkling. It was quite a shock the first time he turned up.' Alex wonders if 'it had suited him that Sophia was unavailable, as unrequited love kept him in his comfort zone'.

If he harboured such feelings, it was beyond him to express them. 'He wouldn't speak, so all the time I spoke I was trying to think of what to say next,' she says. 'I would clatter about, making myself seem busy so the silence wasn't so obvious.'

He also took to turning up at the gallery where she worked. 'I'd see him looming through the door, with his long hair and donkey jacket. I'd jump up, say I had to go out to lunch and usher him round the corner to the Coach and Horses pub. When we got there he wouldn't talk, he'd just sit.' Someone less compassionate might have found his behaviour unnerving, but she felt only helplessness.

Island were finalising *Pink Moon* with no further input from Nick. In mid-January 1972 they faced a deadline for a back-page advert they'd booked in a new monthly music paper, *Record Collector*.† Keith Morris and Annie Sullivan both felt that the best shot from their

---

* 'This was well before the song "Black-Eyed Dog",' he adds.
† Launched as *Record Bargains* in July 1971, and nothing to do with the more familiar *Record Collector* magazine (which began publication in 1980).

recent photo session was of him rounding a corner by Hampstead Number 1 Pond, with his back to the camera as Gus the dog came towards it. 'I thought, "This picture says more about Nick . . ."' she says. 'I thought it was an enigmatic image.'[8]

David Sandison decided to double down by including nothing to identify either Nick or the album, just the teasing caption 'WAIT FOR IT'. It appeared in the February 1972 issue, and within Island, recalls David Betteridge, 'We all laughed about the promo photo of the back of his head.' Their amusement wasn't unkind; it was just that everything about Nick seemed surreally counter-intuitive to them at a time when, say, Cat Stevens was touring hard to support his huge-selling *Teaser and the Firecat* and the first Roxy Music LP was nearing release.

In stark contrast to *Bryter Layter*'s lengthy gestation, *Pink Moon* was scheduled for 25 February, a mere four months after it had been recorded. Island printed a poster showing its cover on a dartboard, alongside other new releases, but there was no dedicated promo material. They put 'Pink Moon' and 'Things Behind The Sun' (mis-titled 'Thing Beyond The Sun') onto a compilation LP sent to radio stations, but there was no commercial sampler LP this time, let alone talk of a single.

To coincide with the album's release they placed another full-page ad in *Melody Maker* and the *NME*, using the same image of Nick from behind, this time with the candid text from November's press release, under the headline 'PINK MOON – NICK DRAKE'S LATEST ALBUM: THE FIRST WE HEARD OF IT WAS WHEN IT WAS FINISHED'. David Sandison subsequently called this 'a bit of an admission of failure – but I don't know what else I could have done. It was a statement of faith as much as anything: we'll stay here as long as he wants to make records.'[9]

Island knew Nick wasn't going to tour in support of *Pink Moon* but, as Chris Blackwell concedes, 'It was hard to put pressure on someone who wouldn't tour when their record only cost five hundred quid,'[10] and they remained happy to have him. 'Chris's vision, which we all bought into, was that we only signed artists we believed in,' explains Muff Winwood. 'We wanted quality artists that would deliver over time. That meant we would allow them the freedom they needed to develop into a commercial success. If one album failed to sell, we would happily stick out another. It took Free three albums before they made it.' Chris goes further: 'I was never driven by sales, with Nick or anyone else – if I liked the person and the music and felt I could help with it, that was that.'

Nick's relationship to the finished album is unknown, and it's likely that his family and friends were unaware of its existence until it was released. Brian Wells is convinced that Molly and Rodney didn't listen to it closely, and Gabrielle doesn't recall doing so either; by the time it appeared they were more focused on Nick's day-to-day condition than on his musical output.

Rodney later wrote that it was made 'when Nick was getting pretty bad, and it's rather "way out", as they say'.[11] In another letter he admitted: 'The material on *Pink Moon* has always bewildered us a little (except "From The Morning", which we love).'[12]

Joe Boyd had nothing whatsoever to do with *Pink Moon*. The first he knew of it was when Island sent a copy to him in Los Angeles.

> When I saw the cover I was horrified, and when I played it I was even more horrified. I interpreted its starkness as a rebuke to me. I thought it was self-destructive, a capitulation, as if he were saying, 'Fuck it, I don't care whether people listen to it or not.' I listened to it once.

Nick's close friends were upset by it too. Brian Wells says: 'I wasn't around when he was making *Pink Moon*, and when I heard it I found it bleak. I remember a friend from Cambridge describing it as "music to commit suicide to".' Alex Henderson and Ben Laycock were taken aback by it after *Bryter Layter*. 'We found its atmosphere dark and depressing, knowing how Nick had become,' remarks Alex. 'We had no idea what musical direction he would or could take after that.'

Paul Wheeler goes further: 'I was appalled by *Pink Moon*. I found it incredibly upsetting. I thought the songs were frightening. To this day I cannot ever imagine listening to it for pleasure. It's like opening some terrible Pandora's box.'

Bev had similar concerns.

I thought, 'This boy's gone, we've lost him. We can't reach him anymore, and he can't reach us.' I wondered why he'd bothered to record some of the tracks, and who had thought it was a good idea to let him go into the studio and do so. They were so dark and sad, and telling about the state of his mind – doom, gloom and despair, with apocalyptic elements.

People listen to it and say, 'That's a great line!', and talk about the songs and the surreal cover like they're a puzzle they can solve, but *Pink Moon* is like the Book of Revelation. It doesn't make sense and it's a manifestation of illness, of madness. When people are really ill they don't know what they're saying, they don't hear what's coming out of their own mouth. I thought those songs, those words, were the product of a sick person. I don't think Nick himself knew what he was driving at.

Richard Thompson heard it when John Wood played it to him in Sound Techniques:

I was disturbed. Part of what had made Nick's earlier music so appealing was a balance between dark and light. The sadness inherent in the music had been veiled behind beautiful arrangements and an intriguing voice that drew you in. However, his third album seemed a stark cry for help, the voice of a man teetering on the edge of sanity.[13]

Not everyone felt that way. 'A lot of people think it's a very depressing, down LP, yet I find it's got some of the most optimistic songs of his,' said Robert Kirby.[14] 'I think *Pink Moon* is in fact my favourite, as far as the songs are concerned.' Despite his disappointment at not having worked on it, he supported Nick's prerogative in eschewing arrangements and later stated: 'I think it's his greatest work, by far. I think it's one of the definitive albums of all time.'[15]

In keeping with Island's commitment to Nick, the album was at least widely reviewed. *Melody Maker* was perplexed: 'The more you listen to Drake, the more compelling his music becomes – but all the time it hides from you.'[16] *Record Mirror* felt that 'a very fragile but beautiful talent has been captured',[17] while *Record Retailer* called him 'one of the most underrated of British singer-songwriters', with 'a maturity and depth of perception often lacking in other artists of the genre',[18] and *Time Out* remarked: 'He writes striking and evocative songs, and always has done, but most of the magic is in the delivery.'[19] *Records and Recording* felt its effect was 'like intruding upon a private dream world',[20] and *Penthouse* hailed Nick as 'a genuine talent', calling *Pink Moon* 'denser and more emotional' than its predecessors.[21]

Not everyone had the patience to plumb its depths. 'It sounds as if he is singing more for his own entertainment than that of the record buyer,' observed the *Reading Evening Post*,[22] while Jerry Gilbert commented in *Sounds* that 'his songs necessarily require further augmentation, for whilst his own accompaniments are good [they] are not sufficiently strong to stand up without any embroidery at all'.[23] Recalling his frustration at Nick's taciturnity a year earlier, he tartly ended with: 'Maybe it's time Mr Drake stopped acting so mysteriously and started getting something properly organised for himself.'

Jerry now regrets writing the piece ('aside from the fact it's an appalling piece of journalism, I really grew to like many songs on that album'), but Muff Winwood would certainly have welcomed proper organisation from Nick. Looking for a way to gain him the maximum of exposure with the minimum of demands, he had booked him onto BBC TV's influential *Old Grey Whistle Test*, presented by Richard Williams of *Melody Maker*. 'It was a big break for Nick,' says Muff.

> It took me ages to get them to agree to have him on – a lot of schmoozing, taking the producer out to lunch and so on. On the morning in question we were talking about it in the office and I was told that I'd better personally make sure he was ready, so I went to the house he was staying in, in Notting Hill [presumably 3 Aldridge Road Villas]. It was an upstairs flat so I rang the bell. Nothing. I stood there ringing and ringing. Still nothing. There was no phone number, so all I could do was wait as time ticked on.
>
> Eventually a bloke came out of the front door, so I explained I was looking for Nick and he let me in. I went upstairs and hammered on the door. Nothing. Eventually Nick opened it, in a complete and

utter state, and said he couldn't go. I explained how important it was, but he simply refused and got back into bed. I couldn't drag him off with me, so I walked out, went down to the studio and explained that he had fallen ill. It was a joke but it was also sad, because that appearance would've made a big difference.

Nick's Cambridge acquaintance Ian MacCormick seized the chance to praise the album to him shortly after its release:

He dropped by with Paul Wheeler and I collared him and told him I thought it was fabulous, a classic. Characteristically, he sort of floated back slightly without physically moving, then smiled – partly out of mild amusement and partly out of genuine diffidence – and said, 'Thank you.' I kept telling him how great the record was, because I didn't think he believed me. Although this must have begun to seem fairly mad after a few minutes, he stayed irreproachably patient and polite.[24]

Nonetheless, MacCormick – by then writing for the *NME* as Ian MacDonald – did not interview him. His colleague Nick Kent explains that, even if Nick had been willing,

Right around the time of *Pink Moon* David Bowie took off and changed a lot of priorities for the music press. All the oxygen in the pop atmosphere was inhaled by him and a few other sixties musicians who'd worked hard to become stars: Elton John, Rod Stewart, Marc Bolan. Nick didn't stand a chance of getting coverage alongside them.

In the absence of gigs or interviews, *Pink Moon* had to generate its own momentum – but Nick certainly had existing fans. 'In places he is a cult figure, and among the new younger sixth-form and college audience there are pockets that go overboard to catch the latest glimmer of news,' *Melody Maker* asserted on 26 February 1972.

One such pocket contained the fifteen-year-old Nick Carter and his friends, who lived in and around Maidenhead, west of London. In 1971 they had attended a gig by John Martyn, who recommended Nick, so they bought all three of his albums and played them repeatedly. 'Themes of the counterculture were instantly recognisable in his words and compositions,' says Nick.

We regarded him as one of us. He wasn't seen as a 'folk singer' at all, he was seen as 'progressive' – but the term meant something different during his lifetime. It applied to all musicians who pushed musical ideas away from the mainstream and towards more innovative and consciousness-expanding forms, which were often less commercial. We saw Nick Drake as a siren and a soothsayer, a voice of the British counterculture who spoke to our own feelings of anxiety, alienation, love, dreams and sometimes depression in the context of the times.*

Nick would have been thrilled to learn his work was making such an impact – but even if he had been aware, he was in no state to build on it.

* In 1978 Nick Carter recorded his own 'innovative and consciousness-expanding' album, *Abstracts and Extracts*.

26

This May Be A Long Job

ON TUESDAY, 21 March 1972, three months after Nick had moved back to Far Leys, his father began to keep a diary. Far from being an intimate account of his own thoughts and experiences, it meticulously documented his son's life as he witnessed it (with the occasional aside about the garden). In Gabrielle's words, Rodney 'knew that the collection of data was of vital importance',[1] and – as he surely anticipated – his straightforward but often wry entries, scrawled in pencil before turning off his light at night, both documented and helped predict the direction Nick's illness was taking at any given time.

The first month's entries alone paint a bleak portrait. On Tuesday the 21st Nick was 'very silent', on Friday the 24th Rodney 'found Nick asleep in his car', and on Saturday the 25th, 'after grapefruit he returned to his room where he stayed for the remainder of the day, lying on the floor and ignoring all attempts to rouse him'.

On Tuesday the 28th Nick 'seemed well and played his guitar most of the day'. This was hopeful, except for the fact that (unbeknown to Rodney) he was scheduled to be recording a session for Bob Harris's *Sounds of the Seventies* on BBC Radio 1. The corporation's paperwork coldly recorded: 'Unreliable – did not appear for recording. Has a habit of disappearing without trace.'

Thus ended his relationship with the BBC, and as if to prove their point, the following Monday morning he took off on a bicycle, leaving his parents to worry about him until he rang in the evening, wanting to be picked up: 'Went to fetch him and also his bike which he had left in a ditch some four miles south of Shipston. No conversation.'

Another, more worrying indication of his unpredictability came that Saturday, as Molly and Rodney prepared to go to a local tombola party and wondered if he wanted to come along. 'Found him locked in upstairs loo,' wrote Rodney.

> After half-an-hour tried to talk to him through the door but could get no reply. After some time we became alarmed and I broke the lock and opened the door, to find him seated with head down but refusing to talk and apparently unwilling (or unable) to move. Suddenly, however, he showed himself perfectly well, swearing loudly at Molly, which angered me and caused us to leave him.

Ringing home later, Rodney found he was fine: 'He had a good supper, watched TV. Extraordinary chap!'

There was 'no mention of yesterday's absurd display' the following morning, though Nick admitted he was 'going through a difficult time' and expressed his dislike of 'being at home and the way of life here (and presumably us too) but it was at least a roof over his head (gratifying reflection for us). However, he at least talked a little – first time for weeks.'

On Wednesday, 12 April Nick wordlessly departed Far Leys with a rucksack, headed for Paris. It is tempting to think that his trip might have been connected to an ecstatic review of *Pink Moon* in the latest issue of the influential French pop magazine *Best* – the first to call him 'a genius'[2] – but is more likely to have related to Françoise Hardy, who continued to loom large in his mind.

By her account,

> He telephoned to let me know he was visiting Paris. I already had plans to go out with some friends for dinner that evening and to see Véronique Sanson at the restaurant in the Eiffel Tower. I had no choice but to bring him with me, which seems surreal when I think about it now . . . Being in a public place where strangers were knocking back champagne and talking too loudly was the last thing he would have wanted.[3]

Françoise's neurotic temperament was unlikely to put Nick at ease either, but even by her standards he was difficult company.

> It was so odd that he would show up like that without warning, and without once abandoning his total silence (which I instinctively,

maybe mistakenly, respected). He knew nothing about me and I knew nothing about him, and we didn't try to get to know each other better. Did he expect something? A word, a gesture, a step? What had brought him to Paris? Could he have come because of me? This last possibility never crossed my mind . . .

His spontaneous visit may indeed have represented a last-ditch attempt to salvage momentum for his career. The idea of his writing especially for Françoise had come to nothing thus far, but she was preparing to record another album in Sound Techniques. If he was hoping she would include one of his songs, however, he never broached the subject − or any other.

His parents heard nothing from him until he reappeared at Far Leys a week later, and

> revealed that he had been to Paris, where he had eaten 'pig's foot'. The only other item of news we extracted was that he had returned by hovercraft . . . He seems to have even less use for us than ever − but has he for anyone else?

At this juncture, he later told his father, he felt that he was 'finished, and the sooner the better'.[4]

To Molly and Rodney's increasing alarm, he spent the next forty-eight hours in bed, pale, silent and barely eating and drinking. It was a pattern that was to become all too familiar: frustration, a sudden venture away from home, then an extended period of unresponsive lethargy. On Monday, 24 April, he appeared insensible, so Rodney took decisive action and rang Dr Weinstein, who had dealt with Nick's kidney trouble. He agreed to come to Far Leys at 12.30, but while awaiting his arrival, 'Nick suddenly appeared downstairs fully dressed and announced that he was about to leave for London!'

Persuaded to stay put, Nick had a 'longish talk' in the music room with Dr Weinstein, who

> emerged looking very serious and grim. Said Nick was obviously in grave need of psychiatric help (had talked amongst other things of suicidal thoughts), but Nick would have none of it. Weinstein considered it his duty to see that Nick was examined in a hospital and that he *must* agree to the necessary action being taken.

Weinstein was hinting at having him sectioned, something Rodney and Molly desperately hoped to avoid. Nick ultimately capitulated ('pretty much against my own will', he later wrote[5]) and was driven by Dr Weinstein to Central Hospital, a gloomy NHS psychiatric institution in Hatton, eleven miles southeast of Tanworth-in-Arden.

There he was seen by the sympathetic Dr Gerald Dickens, whose firm view it was that he should remain as an in-patient. Returning to the hospital with a suitcase of clothes later that afternoon, Rodney and Molly met Nick walking along the drive. 'He sat in the car with us – very low, of course, and very upset about being "forced" to come.' They explained that his admission was entirely voluntary, upon which he 'seemed to make up his mind, took the suitcase and strode purposefully back to the hospital'.

Central Hospital had long been criticised for its overcrowding and understaffing, not to mention its oppressive Victorian atmosphere. Recent attempts had been made to make it more efficient and to create a more positive ambience for its patients. Nick was accommodated in Louisa Raynes House, named after one of the hospital's nineteenth-century nurses. The block had been designed 'to embody a new approach to the treatment of mental illness' by offering 'light, airy, one-storey buildings where patients have such amenities as individual strip reading lights over their beds'.[6] 'We hope your stay will be as pleasant and comfortable as possible and that you will soon be well and home again,' trilled the welcome leaflet.

As his parents left, Nick desperately told them he just needed another six weeks to 'sort himself out'. 'Poor old Nick,' wrote Rodney. 'He's been trying to sort himself out for the last two years and, as Molly says, it's time someone else tried to help him.'

He remained in hospital for the next month, silently accepting his parents' regular visits. 'His trouble is psychotic and will need fairly long and careful handling,' Rodney recorded on 27 April after another conversation with Dr Dickens. 'Nick appears very introverted and shows some paranoid tendencies. Looks as though this may be a long job.'

As they reconciled themselves to the severity of his condition, Rodney and Molly found a useful contact in the amiable Duty

Officer, Aniya, who reported that he was 'settling down' but seemed 'muddled' as to his relationship with his parents, had some sort of 'guilt complex about leaving Cambridge', and also 'talked a lot about his music'.

Aniya recommended they visit less frequently, advice they heeded, though they maintained contact with Dr Dickens. He stressed the importance of regular medication in addressing Nick's 'deep anxiety complex' and restoring his equilibrium.

Putting a name to Nick's condition was and remains vexed, but Dr Dickens explained in a letter to Rodney that simple-type schizophrenia, 'as described over the years, tends to occur in late adolescence and in people of all types, including intelligent young people coming from stable family backgrounds':

> The symptoms are usually those of progressive deterioration in intel-lectual ability, with loss of the ability to comprehend new information and think abstractly. There is also loss of initiative, loss of the ability to concentrate, and a tendency to withdraw from the world of reality into a world of more comforting fantasy.
>
> The outcome of treatment is variable. With the drugs available to us, and other methods of treatment, there can be no doubt that some patients can be helped considerably. Others, however, cannot.[7]

From the start, Nick was suspicious of anti-depressants, though he never categorically explained why. According to Brian Wells – who, virtually alone among Nick's friends, knew of his hos-pitalisation, and himself became a psychiatrist – Nick was 'a classic non-compliant patient. You've got to get an adequate and consistent blood-level of anti-depressants in order for them to be effective, but it's evident that Nick wanted to be in control of when he took the pills and when he didn't.'[8] Brian remains adamant, however, that 'medication alone, whether anti-psychotics or anti-depressants', could never have solved Nick's problems.[9]

Three options were proposed for Nick's treatment: to continue with the in-house programme at Louisa Raynes House; to undergo a course of electroconvulsive therapy (known as ECT); or to transfer to London for psychotherapy under the supervision of Leon Redler. Born in 1936, Redler was an American doctor who had worked closely with the celebrity psychiatrist R. D. Laing and espoused his unconventional approach.

When Molly and Rodney sought the advice of their psychiatrist friend Toby McDowall (the older brother of Nick's uncle Chris), he said ECT was 'nothing to be afraid of at all and might do a lot of good', 'expressed profound disagreement with idea of sending Nick to Redler', and suggested he see a psychiatrist in London instead. According to Rodney's diary, Nick 'was not unduly worried about electric shock treatment, but did *not* want "psychiatric" treatment' – an intransigence that continues to puzzle Gabrielle: 'Was [psychotherapy] too humiliating – a final admission of defeat? Or did he fear that by revealing the inner recesses of his mind to another human being he risked the final destruction of his already ailing muse?'[10]

In Brian's view, Redler's approach was the more likely to succeed. 'Grand old Harley Street psychiatrists were anathema to Nick,' he explains. 'They would've thought Laing and Redler were mavericks whose treatments leaned on belief systems rather than scientific evidence. The idea with Redler was to provide asylum – in the true sense of the word – in a non-judgemental environment, rather than treatment for the actively suicidal.'

Brian explained this to Molly and Rodney on the phone, and they valued his input: as a trainee doctor he formed a bridge of sorts between them and Nick. 'I think they thought I might be a catalyst for improving things, and my opinion was that Nick was eventually going to come out of it – but I underestimated how ill he was.'

Nick agreed to a visit from Brian on Monday, 22 May, but it did not go well.

> It was a typical NHS psychiatric ward, and he was clearly depressed. I took Anthony Scaduto's *Bob Dylan* book as a present, but he wasn't very interested in it. His main preoccupation was with emphasising that it wasn't a 'nuthouse' or a 'loony bin' and that he wasn't a 'nutcase'. He also made occasional short statements like: 'I can't cope'.

After their short encounter Brian drove to Far Leys for the night, meeting Molly and Rodney for the first time.

They were very welcoming, and there was no 'best behaviour' around them. Rodney was gentle and had a self-deprecating sense of humour. I think Molly was more attuned to the emotional side of things with Nick, and to his music, but they were both always understanding and supportive of him in every way.

As he got to know them better, he came to admire their united front. 'I never saw them disagree. There wasn't any stiff-upper-lip, shove-mental-illness-under-the-carpet with the Drakes. I think they were very practical, very sensible.'[11]

Dick Mills, the young social worker handling Nick's case, visited Far Leys the following week to borrow copies of his albums, and recommended that Nick meet Redler. Nick, however, couldn't make up his mind what to do. He told Rodney he wanted to stay on the ward for at least another fortnight, then 'proposed to discharge himself as he was convinced now that he was getting no better – rather worse', then said he wanted to stay another night. With his usual restraint, Rodney described this indecision as 'disconcerting', and no meeting with Redler was arranged.

Nick was home for the last weekend in May, without medication. On Friday he played guitar a little and sat with his parents in the evening to watch *The Brothers*, a BBC drama featuring Gabrielle as ex-model and goodie-goodie Jill Hammond. Centring on the struggle for control of a family haulage business, it had begun in March and become an unlikely hit, making her a household name.* Watching the long-running series became a ritual at Far Leys, though one from which Nick increasingly opted out. On this occasion he had an early night. 'Back to square one,' Rodney glumly concluded.

The wearying pattern of silences and changes of mind resumed. Nick began to flit morosely between hospital and home, where a supportive phone message from Chris Blackwell elicited no response. The very act of speech seemed beyond him, until the opening of

---

* She featured in the series throughout the remainder of Nick's life, and her character was killed off (at her request) in a car crash in an episode broadcast in December 1974.

a letter on 3 June elicited the exclamation, 'Oh God, it's from my publisher!'* After reading it, he 'appeared all upset'.

Early on Monday, 5 June, Rodney drove him back to Louisa Raynes House, but the following day he walked out and made his way home, determined not to return. His parents collected his belongings and medication, returning 'to find poor old Nick very depressed – tears at lunch'.

That afternoon he approached Molly and asked if he could talk to her. The result, wrote Rodney, was 'the first long conversation with him we have either of us had for years. He spoke of his great worries, his fear of London, anxiety about the future and much more.'

Nonetheless, he announced his intention to go to London the next day. Fearing he wasn't in a condition to be behind a wheel, Rodney offered to drive. They set off at 9.30 a.m. but only got as far as Stratford before Nick asked to be dropped back at Louisa Raynes House, conceding that he was attempting to run away from his problems. Rodney left him there at 11.30, but a couple of hours later he rang Far Leys asking to be collected.

Dr Dickens 'agreed that Nick should not stay if he was unhappy, but extracted a promise from him that he must go on taking pills for the time being' and scheduled a weekly consultation at Louisa Raynes House. Once home, Nick immediately got into his car and set off for London, only to return a few minutes later.

Despite the foul weather, Nick did exactly the same thing the next morning. The timing was frustrating, as Dick Mills had turned up in the interim to return the LPs he'd borrowed. In no time Dick – who was not a doctor – was well-meaningly informing Nick that pills were a waste of time compared to psychotherapy with Leon Redler.

After lunch Nick reiterated that he wanted to go to London, so Rodney drove. Their destination, he explained, was Sound Techniques: Françoise Hardy was recording there, with Tony Cox producing.† The possibility of Nick submitting material to her had been the subject of Brenda Ralfini's letter.

---

* Brenda Ralfini at Warlock.
† The resulting album came out later in 1972, under various titles and in various territories, but not the UK. None of Nick's songs were included.

Upon arrival, Rodney waited outside in the car as Nick hesitantly approached the entrance. Françoise was happily 'surprised' to see him, she relates,[12] but he barely spoke to her. 'The language barrier prevented us from communicating, unless that was a convenient screen to disguise deeper blockages . . . Nick's excessive introversion bordered on autism.'

Jerry Donahue was there to play guitar: 'He came up and sat next to me in the control room . . . He wasn't unfriendly, you just really felt like you were putting the guy on the spot when you'd ask the most simple, harmless questions.'[13]

After a short while, wrote Rodney, Nick 'came out again and said he would go back':

> Did so three more times without making further contact – obviously lost his nerve. Very depressed and unhappy. I could do nothing with him to make him try again. Changed his mind several times – once ten miles out of London – but eventually asked to go home and seemed ill. Couldn't drive.

In mid-June Nick declared his intention to abandon music in favour of a conventional career, possibly in a bank, or at Davenports, a local brewery. He surprised Molly by informing her 'he had twice tried to get into the Army but had been turned down by Colonel Whittaker as unsuitable'. 'It was as if he were unwilling to explore the havoc within,' comments Gabrielle, 'preferring instead to seek a discipline that could be imposed from without.'[14] Nick also told an astonished Robert Kirby that he'd been to 'an Army recruitment office' and 'was quite seriously considering it'.* For Robert,

> Underneath it all I think Nick did have a wish, a hankering, that maybe he should have got a proper job, been able to do something else. It seemed as though he was burning his bridges rapidly unless he did . . . I'm sure his father suggested things, and he did try to please his father – but I don't believe his father pressured him . . .

---

* The idea of joining the Army was perhaps inspired by his aunt Gwladys's second husband, Major-General Jack Harman, who had recently been appointed Commandant of the Royal Military Academy, Sandhurst.

I can't see that any problem was ever caused by family pressures, unless [it was] something that he felt he had to live up to.[15]

On the afternoon of 14 June Rodney chose a moment to talk to Nick:

I judged him to be well enough to have a chat about his future and my helping him financially to get going in some sort of job *eventually*. Did not go down well, and I was told that he and I had nothing to offer each other (rather shattering).

Brian Wells vividly remembers Nick's ungenerous interpretation of his father's attempts to gee him up.

It frustrated Rodney that Nick had this athletic body and was so lacking in energy, so he encouraged him to take more exercise, running or going for walks – but it wasn't because he was trying to order him around, it was because he thought it might help shake him out of his lethargy.

Molly also did her best to prevent Nick spending too much time in bed. She thought simple gardening tasks might offer a refuge from his depression, but he never showed any interest. They took him on a few outings – to the garden centre, to Birmingham to see the Spaghetti Junction, to the shops in Solihull – but he remained almost entirely self-contained. There were occasional signs of engagement – helping with the washing-up, contributing to the crossword or playing Scrabble – but whenever he talked, wrote Rodney, 'He is exclusively preoccupied with himself and his problems and unable to think or talk about anybody else.'

Despite his promise to Dr Dickens, Nick now described pill-taking as being 'against my principles'. It was exasperating for his parents, who clearly saw the benefit when he did take them. 'Hopeless situation,' wrote Rodney on 16 June, after he'd been refusing medicine for several days. Nick spent the following morning 'moaning and groaning and obviously in great distress', saying he'd 'been an idiot', but with no further explanation.

Nick turned twenty-four on Monday, 19 June 1972. At 8.30 a.m. he presented himself in his parents' bedroom and made the unconvincing announcement: 'You must understand that things are much better with me and that I want to get this new feeling across to people.' He didn't explain what he meant and quickly fell silent.

That afternoon he had his weekly appointment with Dr Dickens, who – by Nick's account on the way home – urged him not to hide away from people. Molly and Rodney accordingly suggested they swing by Ward Leys in Wootton Wawen to see his childhood friend Janie Lodder, who was visiting her parents.

She had barely seen Nick since she'd left home in 1965, and was happy to accept the Drakes' spontaneous invitation to a birthday tea. 'My parents spoke frequently about their concerns for Molly and Rodney, who were despairing,' she says. 'They were clutching at straws and thought perhaps I could talk to him.'

Back at Far Leys Nick disappeared to his bedroom, so she followed:

> He was clean-shaven and didn't appear unkempt, but was monosyllabic and staring into space. Rather than having a general conversation about his life, I wanted to engage with his thoughts and feelings at that particular moment, but very little came out. He was clearly in a deep, deep place and just looked sad – really, really sad. I hated it for him because he hated it too.

Unusually, the following evening Nick rang Gabrielle and – to an extent – unburdened himself. She was immersed in rehearsals for *Po' Miss Julie* at the Hampstead Everyman Theatre, but found some time to herself in the dressing room to write him a long, loving and supportive letter that powerfully conveys the depth of feeling that existed between them.

> Darling Nick,
>
> I thought I'd write to you to tell you how glad I am that you rang me yesterday. For what it's worth, I want you to know that I *firmly* believe this bad scene *will* end for you, that despite the terrible despair I could hear in your voice, I believe you are at last on the threshold of the road that will lead you to a life that will be bearable, even happy for you. *My* despair for you is ending because at last you have been able to communicate *your* despair to me. And that is the first step towards the end of despair.

You have some *fine* qualities to help you through. You have the rare ability to make other men admire, respect and *love* you: on the rare occasions I've met your friends I have been forcibly struck by their obvious love and admiration for you . . . You have your talent, your music, even though it counts as nothing for you now – maybe it never will again, that doesn't matter.

What *does* matter is that you were able to get a large commercial company to believe in you to such an extent that, even when you refused public appearances, missed appointments, disappeared unpredictably – they *still* wanted to represent you, to promote you, to help you. In the cut-throat world of show business, overcrowded and swimming with talent as it is – well, Jesus, Nick, that's pretty incredible. What I'm saying is, even if you never sing another song in your life, the quality of inspiring faith will always remain with you, whatever life you lead.

Above all, you have a stoic, obstinate strength – you've had it ever since you were a tiny child. Maybe it will be the quality you will most need in the immediate future – the will to come through the bad time, the strength to ask for and accept help from friends and strangers.

That's what I feel you're doing now, and that's why *I feel sure you will come through*. Well, Nick, as I said, that's what I think, for what it's worth to you. Very little, I expect. But I wanted to tell you, anyway, because I too love, respect and admire you.

God bless, Nick – I'm thinking of you a lot.

Although he had come to fear London, Nick now announced his intention to move back there, explaining that Island had offered him accommodation even though he had no musical plans. He set off, leaving his car at the station, but when Rodney went to check he noticed that his guitar was still in the back, and he was home by late afternoon.

At 5.30 the next morning he appeared in their bedroom to explain that he had to go to Paris, but when Molly took him downstairs for a cup of tea, he told her he had decided he wanted psychiatric help – and a haircut. This took his parents aback, since his long hair was, they assumed, an important aspect of his identity, but he was insistent, so Rodney took him into Stratford, 'where Ladds gave him a real short, back and sides'.

If he had hoped that adopting a conventional appearance would improve his condition, he was mistaken, as he seemed 'full of self-hate when we got back' and grew a beard over the ensuing weeks, as if to compensate.

Mindful of the need to act swiftly upon Nick's apparent openness to psychiatry, Rodney made an appointment with Dr Myre Sim in Queen Elizabeth Hospital, Birmingham, for that very afternoon. Dr Sim considered Nick 'a very sick boy', Rodney wrote later, and 'badly in need of treatment'. He proposed daily consultations (excepting Sundays) for the next month but was insistent that Nick should concurrently undergo a course of electroconvulsive therapy (ECT), starting the following day, 23 June.

Nick had grave misgivings and came into his parents' room at three in the morning to express them. Unconvinced by their reassurances, he tried to flee by car (but couldn't find the keys), then allowed himself to be driven to the hospital, only to change his mind upon being dropped off. The next morning he said he was feeling better, then that he had decided to have the ECT after all, then that he was going to have a bath. He set off for London instead. As Rodney summarised: 'His vacillations are impossible!'

This time, Nick did not reappear after a few minutes. Instead, the telephone rang at 3.15 p.m. It was the police, explaining that he had been found on a zebra crossing in Swiss Cottage, unable to muster the wherewithal to cross the road. Upon questioning, he had told a policeman that his car had broken down and he was 'unable to cope'.

With Gabrielle immersed in rehearsals, de Wet – who didn't drive – fetched him from Marylebone Lane Police Station and took him to 28 Campden Hill Gardens. Being an artist himself, de Wet had an instinctive empathy with Nick's temperament. 'He understood Nick better than most,' says Gabrielle. 'I feel there is much in his own work that makes a connection with Nick's.'

Rodney and Molly soon joined them, made arrangements for his car to be towed, and drove him back to Far Leys. Nick was 'very silent and pretty unfriendly' on the way home, and it was well past midnight when they wearily arrived. For all the recent efforts to engage with his condition, it was clear that he was getting worse, not better.

27

Don't Douse The Grouch

— —

NICK'S ILLNESS WAS ravaging his creativity, but his existing work was at least starting to receive wider circulation. Under arrangements Island had made in 1971, foreign territories had less discretion as to what they put out, meaning that *Pink Moon* was released in France, Spain, South Africa, America, New Zealand and Australia. At the same time *Five Leaves Left* and *Bryter Layter* received second British pressings and were belatedly issued or distributed in certain other countries.*

The American release of *Pink Moon* in late May 1972 prompted reviews that were largely sensitive, if somewhat bemused. David F. Wagner of the *Post-Crescent* in Appleton, Wisconsin, was a lone voice of contempt, damning the album as a 'bland bunch of trash . . . Everything is dull, he can't sing and his lyrics are stupid.'[1]

Jim Conley of the *Abilene Reporter-News* in Texas was more representative of the general response, identifying Nick's 'private world which you are made to share through his convincing sincerity' and concluding: 'I think he's where 1972's music is going, maybe where 1973's will be. At least, I hope so.'[2]

Ideally Nick would have been promoting the album in America, where *Billboard* had just written of a 'definite Nick Drake cult',[3] but in reality he was confronted by the impossibility of reconciling his desire for an audience with the demands it would impose on him. As his mother put it, 'If he'd been a wild success, with people

---

* A British singer-guitarist named Andrew Johns had found *Five Leaves Left* in a shop in Denmark: 'I really loved it and began to cover some of the songs on it. My first album, *The Machine Stops*, was released on CBS in April 1972 and included "Time Has Told Me".'

424

clamouring for him, I think he couldn't have stood the pressure of it.'[4] Instead his work stood independently of him, as if having no tangible creator, while he languished in Warwickshire.

His constantly shifting positions towards his own condition made helping him virtually impossible. He refused to take his pills, then did so; he said he had no interest in Dr Dickens, then asked to return to his care; he opened up to his parents, then told them 'he regretted everything he'd told us about himself'; he said he wanted to go and live with his aunt Nancy and uncle Chris in Hampshire, then changed his mind upon arrival.* 'One can only feel that he is slipping back into the shell from which we have all made such efforts to extract him,' wrote Rodney.

Rodney also observed that all Nick's energies were being expended in 'coping with these strange waves of depression which seem to knock him over physically as well as mentally'. Appearing in the garden in tears one morning, he accepted Rodney's suggestion that they go out for lunch for a change of scene, only to insist on eating his in the car because he now couldn't stand public places. That evening he 'spoke of Christianity and probably becoming a Catholic to control forces of evil', and twice the next day he inexplicably laughed.

Psychosis appeared to be rearing its head, as Dr Dickens had warned. Nick began to make such pronouncements as 'I'm not a chap anymore' (by which he meant a decent or reliable person), and 'I will make it one day, but I don't know if you will live to see it'. He expanded on these themes to Rodney: 'Talked despondently to me about being insane and [how] nothing could be done. Said he'd finished his life's work and had done more than many in a lifetime. One day people would realise[†] . . . Sat with closed eyes, or head in hands.'

Such openness was increasingly rare, however, and though he seemed to enjoy lying outside on the lawn in the sunshine, he came

---

* It is indicative of the closeness of Nick's family that the McDowalls unhesitatingly agreed to have him move in with them.
† It is tempting to infer that he was reflecting on his lyrics to 'Fruit Tree': 'They'll stand and stare when you're gone'.

in to tell his parents that 'the atmosphere [at home] restricted him from exploiting this good feeling'. In an attempt to escape it he cycled off early one morning and caught a train to London. Rodney mobilised Gabrielle, de Wet and Brian to meet trains at Euston and Paddington, but he bypassed their attention, returning that afternoon with Desi Burlison-Rush. She explained that he had checked into a hotel and then called on her. Seeing the shape he was in, and despite being bedridden with bronchitis, she had prevailed upon him to accept a lift home.

Gabrielle came to Far Leys that weekend, and Nick disclosed to her that, for all that he loved John and Bev, he felt that their 'great influence over him' (as Rodney put it) was 'working against his submitting to medical treatment'. Gabrielle duly contacted them, in the hope they might clarify their position to Nick. John rang on Wednesday, 12 July, and arranged to come and stay that very night. 'Nick seemed very pleased about this at first,' Rodney wrote, 'then predictably was overcome with misgivings and worry.'

Such misgivings were partly on account of how John would respond to him, but also because of the necessary overlapping of his carefully maintained parallel 'worlds'. 'Nick always went on about his two worlds,' Molly later explained, and imagined him thinking, 'John Martyn's one world and you're another world, and it simply won't work.'[5] Nick perhaps underestimated the extent to which Molly - being a songwriter herself - could empathise.

John rolled up with his guitar on the 8.30 p.m. train, met by Rodney and Nick, but seems to have been more bent on impressing Molly and Rodney than on engaging with his friend. 'He was a consummate actor, really,' reflects Paul Wheeler. 'He could switch between characters and was terribly good with people's parents. He charmed Nick's parents to death.'

Rodney described him as 'very charming and cheerful', and Nick as being 'in good form and, for him, very talkative and responsive', though he 'ran out of steam soon after supper, leaving us to have a very pleasant chat with this very likeable young man'. In fact, they sat up into the small hours and, said Rodney, 'had a very amusing time'.[6]

Early the next morning Nick made it clear that 'he did not feel he could cope with John and would like him to go', so Rodney woke him at 1.20 p.m. and politely suggested he have some lunch and depart. 'Nick spoke hardly at all at lunch and responded very little to John's efforts to have a chat with him afterwards, but he was not hostile – rather, apologetic.'

Seeking to make sense of Nick's condition, John devised a new song on the way home. Back in Hastings that night, he rang Paul Wheeler. 'He said he'd written a song about Nick and sang "Solid Air" to me there and then, unaccompanied.' The gesture was well-meant, but Paul says:

> I don't think the song was helpful to Nick in any way, or showed any understanding of his condition. 'I'll follow you anywhere' would have been anathema to Nick.* Nick was like a delicate deer, with John running towards him shouting, 'I understand you!' John thought depression was a weakness and couldn't begin to engage with Nick or me about our problems with it. Bev had a more instinctive under-standing of what it meant.

Bev wearily concurs: 'John never acknowledged that Nick had depression or other mental health problems.'

Striving to understand what treatment would be in Nick's best interest, Rodney again sought the view of Dr Dickens, who now dismissed ECT, telling him 'it would perhaps add unbearably to his anxiety, possibly to the point of suicide'.

At the start of July Nick's uncle's brother, Toby McDowall, had recommended another psychiatrist, Dr John Pollitt, 'the "top man" in his profession'. A consultant at St Thomas's Hospital with a private practice in Harley Street, Pollitt was the highly regarded author of *Depression and Its Treatment* (1965). An appointment was fixed for Friday, 14 July.

Nick was dreading it and made numerous attempts to flee the

---

* 'Solid Air' was released on the album of the same name in February 1973. 'It was done for a friend of mine, and it was done right with very clear motives, and I'm very pleased with it, for varying reasons,' John told *ZigZag* magazine (April/May 1974). 'It has got a very simple message, but you'll have to work that one out for yourself.' Its 'message' is in fact hard to discern, and it is not known if Nick knew it was written with him in mind.

treatment in advance, stating that 'he had decided to become an exile and disappear'. He finally agreed to attend, partly because – at Gabrielle's request – Joe Boyd had rung him at Far Leys and urged him to go through with it.

He spent the journey to London lying across the back of his father's car, and was 'in a fearful state in [the] waiting room – made one attempt to leave, flung himself about the place at one stage, threatened to undress', but 'pulled himself together the moment Pollitt appeared'.

Pollitt found Nick to be deeply depressed and prescribed four different medications: Stelazine, Tryptizol, Disipal and Valium. Stelazine was an antipsychotic to help with anxiety, and Tryptizol was the trade name for amitriptyline, aimed at improving moods by increasing serotonin levels in the brain. Its side effects included drowsiness (meaning it could also be used as a sleeping aid), palpitations and a loss of libido. An overdose could cause respiratory paralysis, leading to heart failure – but it was a relatively new drug so this was little known.

Disipal countered the possible tremors and restlessness caused by Stelazine and Tryptizol, and Valium was prescribed as a sedative. The regimen was two Stelazine and three Tryptizol, distributed through the day, with two more Tryptizol at bedtime (increasing the likelihood of deep sleep); once their effect was gauged, Dr Pollitt would reconsider the necessity of ECT. The Valium and Disipal were to be discretionary.

Having collected enough for a three-month course, the Drakes returned home, upon which Nick 'seized the parcel of pills and we had to remove them', then grudgingly took two Tryptizol, but 'refused to take any water with them and seemed not to have swallowed them'.

He passed much of the ensuing week in bed, apparently taking the pills his mother meted out, which Dr Pollitt had warned might take ten days to take effect. He ate heartily, as usual, but remained lethargic, keeping the radio on at a low volume and occasionally listening to classical records.

Marian Bain, from Witchseason, 'offered to send up any records Nick might want to hear', noted Rodney on 19 July; 'usual lack of response'. In fact Rodney took to writing down any utterances at all from his son; 'all right' and 'not particularly' were typical.

Nick showed no interest in music-making, but his creativity found remarkable expression on the evening of 22 July, when Rodney and Molly went out for the first time in months. In their absence he borrowed his father's typewriter and concocted a long, untitled free-form poem.

Spread across five pages, it begins with the full lyrics to 'Harvest Breed', suggesting its especial importance to him, then veered into a series of freely associated images and conceits that evoke his thoughts in the moment; a reference at its start to '625 lines, VHF, Channel 8, give me the clue!' suggests that he regarded himself – for this purpose, at least – as both a receiver and transmitter of messages on different frequencies. Internal rhymes and alliteration suggest an enjoyment of language for its own sake, but a sprinkling of profanities ('horseshit', 'cunts', 'arseholes') implies a degree of vitriol too.

Some lines are perplexing ('give me linseed oil', 'skewered by a coathook yanked from the door', 'onus is in line for President'), while others appear to refer to himself, whether autobiographically, to his life in Hampstead ('Grove End Road marks the perimeter of all that is dear to me', 'Sunday's the day for a trip to the pond'),* or psychologically (repeated references to a 'silent cacophony', perhaps describing his interior monologue, and the poignant archaism of 'Don't send me out of reach again / For I must needs play my lute').

It carries echoes of Symbolist and Modernist writers – there are oblique references to works by Arthur Rimbaud, Henry Miller and T. S. Eliot, as well as Dylan Thomas, Bob Dylan and others – and also indicates that he was incorporating elements from the evening's TV in 'aleatoric' style, perhaps the means by which he had found earlier lyrical inspiration. These include references to *Gunsmoke* and showjumping, while 'salvaged at last by the Good Ship Lollipop' was likely prompted by Shirley Temple's appearance on *Parkinson*, during which vintage footage of that song was broadcast.†

---

* Respectively, a short walk from Haverstock Hill, and a possible reference to Hampstead Ponds.
† A line from the Bee Gees' 'Lonely Days' implies that was aired too.

Certain words or themes recur, most strikingly capitalised references to 'THE GROUCH', which appears to represent himself or his muse, or both. At one point he writes, 'Elusive, miraculous, DON'T DOUSE THE GROUCH', as if fearful that psychiatric treatment or medication might extinguish his creative flame.

Midway through he again quotes 'Harvest Breed', whose fatalistic tone is quickly challenged by the ominous: 'July is the lonely month but come August I may scream again. Scream I must.' The tone alternates between playfulness and anger, making for puzzling and unsettling reading, but its survival suggests that Nick did not object to its being read – or that Rodney rescued it before Nick could destroy it. In any case, no other such works appear to exist.

When no upturn in his condition took place in the fortnight following his prescription from Pollitt, Nick resumed what Rodney called 'his normal sunk-in-gloom position' in bed or in the music room, refusing to come to the phone when friends rang and even stopping listening to the radio. At the end of July, however, he told Rodney that his depression had 'completely gone', attributing his lack of energy to 'my present environment'. Rodney asked if he wanted to go away. 'Not particularly,' he replied.

As he absorbed his parents' time and energy, the parameters of their lives shrank too. 'I literally didn't really think of anything else at all during that time,' Molly later explained; 'I never went out for eight months [except to] the garden, I never left him at all.'[7]

Gabrielle suspects that Nick's illness caused their mother to abandon her own songwriting, though she continued to play the piano. 'Molly gets greatly discouraged and distressed by his failure to respond to all her efforts to get through to him,' Rodney observed. 'A poor return for all she does for him.'

Despite having claimed that he intended to abandon his musical career, Nick told his parents that he had 'a thing' about helping out in the kitchen 'because he wanted to keep his hands in condition for his guitar'. Indeed, he began to play again, and even tinkered with the piano and clarinet, suggesting that the pills were starting to restore some equilibrium. But he remained borderline hostile to Rodney, and in the middle of August the question of psychosis resurfaced when he confessed to Molly that he'd 'got the horrors' and 'feared to turn off the radio'.

Unlike Dr Dickens, Dr Pollitt was confident that ECT would help, but Nick remained opposed, so in August he switched him from Tryptizol to another, stronger 'tricyclic' anti-depressant named Allegron, re-emphasising the importance of taking it daily.* Nick expressed reservations about the new prescription, stating (perhaps with a flash of mordant wit) that he 'ought to have his head examined' for agreeing to take it.

When Gabrielle came to visit a few days later he withdrew, claiming that he couldn't 'do with more than a certain number of people'. However, he told Molly that he struggled with their relative levels of success and acclaim, adding that one of his reasons for going into the entertainment business had been 'the challenge from Gay' – a measure of his illness, since she had never wished him anything but success and took obvious pride in his achievements.

She managed to speak to him, and he made a characteristically random series of remarks that she repeated to Rodney. 'Talking to people made him feel physically sick,' he wrote, so he was grateful 'just to sit and feel relatively all right'; 'he thought it would take him two years to get right', and anticipated moving back to London, but not as an 'escape'. In this country, he said, people could never 'break away from their background', whereas in America they had to, but he had 'nothing to build on'.

When Gabrielle raised the subject of his medication, he told her 'he had decided to give up taking pills and nothing would induce him to change'. That evening he accepted his pills from Molly, who 'stayed with him until (she thought) they had dissolved, but he spat them out and she tried to get them back into his mouth'.

The problem, Nick told Rodney, was that he wanted to be more active, but anything he did 'must be "on the spur of the moment" as this is how he always does things'. As he saw it, his pills hampered this by regulating his moods and imposing a routine on him.

Eventually the cauldron bubbled over, and what his father termed

---

* Tricyclics prevent the neurotransmitters norepinephrine and serotonin from being absorbed, so they remain in the brain for longer.

'smash-ups' began. Rodney was out and Nick was upstairs on 22 August when 'there was an explosive sound and a crack which alarmed both Naw and Molly'. Molly rushed up to the nursery,

> and to her astonishment found Nick in a fuming rage, having vented his spleen on a chair and broken it. A long tirade followed about hating everything – having to say thank you, his upper-class voice, our way of life, the oppression of the poor, Molly's 'failure to mix' and much more.

It wasn't an isolated incident (he also smashed his radio and tore up a pair of trousers around this time), but when Rodney asked if 'he felt restless and frustrated', Nick replied that 'he wasn't wanting to leave home, if that was what I meant', then that he wanted to return to hospital.

The events of the ill-fated Munich Olympics were engaging his attention on TV, and Rodney noticed that he had to squint to watch. When asked about it, Nick said he wasn't 'yet ready to accept that he ought to wear glasses all the time, and this ranked with a number of other problems he has to deal with'.

This typified a trend: 'He seems to work up different worries and anxieties to a peak and then suddenly drop them,' observed Rodney. These included smoking, the state of his teeth and the unlikely prospect of growing overweight. On one occasion he fretted over a live engagement he hadn't fulfilled for some friends earlier in the year,[*] then abruptly dropped the subject.

By the end of the month he had resumed taking his pills. In the ensuing days he put on his tracksuit and went for a run (an activity he had spurned since leaving Marlborough six years earlier), took his car out for a spin with Rodney (driving for the first time in three months), and accompanied his parents and sister to *Julius Caesar* at Stratford. He even took Rodney out for a pint at the Beoley Cross Inn, a few minutes' drive away, where he defined his main problem as 'having no goal in life, which affects everything'.

Feeling better than he was, in mid-September he slipped out of the house and caught a train to London. He visited his old Charlotte

* Andy Matheou and Diana Soar at Les Cousins.

Street haunt, the Greek restaurant Anemos, but found its ownership changed, then called at Island Music in Oxford Street, where he barely responded when an astonished Anthea Joseph greeted him.* From there he made his way to his sister's house to borrow his return fare, telling her he 'felt trapped at home'.

She and de Wet saw him onto a late train, which Rodney met, returning to Far Leys in the early hours. 'We thought he had got over these secret disappearances,' Rodney noted. 'He knows of course that he could go to London with our help if he wanted to . . . The inconveniences suffered by others seem to be of little concern to him.'

In fact Nick did feel guilty, and a couple of days later he told Rodney that he had reconsidered ECT and intended to discuss it with Dr Pollitt at their next meeting. Rodney gratefully recorded his recognition 'that his great difficulty over all this was his inconsistency'.

Gabrielle, meanwhile, observes that

> whenever Nick's behaviour had been particularly antisocial, difficult or even cruel, his mind turned to ECT. Was it remorse? Throughout Nick's life, remorse was an emotion that came easily to him. He hated cruelty. To find himself hurting those he undoubtedly loved – or had loved – perhaps made him feel invaded by an alien being. Did he think that with ECT he could jolt this being out of his body?[8]

No immediate decision was taken on ECT, but Dr Pollitt thought Nick slightly improved and told Rodney he doubted he was schizophrenic. He encouraged him to meet friends but warned of the danger of recreational drug-taking, which he termed 'most dangerous to recovery'. In fact, it seems that Nick had long since stopped smoking dope; Rodney was under the impression that he had given it up in mid-1971, and he was not naïve. 'Our parents would have surely smelled it in the house,' reasons Gabrielle.†

---

* Brenda Ralfini had recently moved on, and Warlock had been subsumed into Island Music.
† Rodney annotated a *Reader's Digest* article on the subject in December 1974 with the marginal comment: 'Nick "smoked" not at all during his last 3 and a half years.'

The general outlook seemed promising, but an unfortunately timed article about the nineteenth-century painter Richard Dadd in the *Sunday Times* magazine of 24 September played into Nick's worst fears and 'convinced him he was mad'.[9] It described how Dadd had undergone a dramatic personality shift aged twenty-four, changing him from being 'gentle, pleasing in voice, looks and manner' to paranoid: 'His frank and engaging manner had been exchanged for one of increasing suspicion and hostility. Without warning, he would rush away from his companions to hide . . . He rarely spoke even to close friends . . . His behaviour became erratic and unpredictable.'

Dadd's devoted father had sought psychiatric help, something Dadd greatly resented and sought to prevent by murdering him. In the aftermath of his crime and with the diagnosis of his madness, the article stated, the public felt 'regret that a brilliant talent should so soon be extinguished. For there was no doubt in anyone's mind that this was the end of his artistic life.'

Nick was not exhibiting symptoms of paranoid schizophrenia – the condition Dadd likely suffered from – but the parallels were striking enough to distress him, not least because Dadd had spent the remainder of his life in mental hospitals. Nick was 'very despondent' after reading the article, wrote Rodney; 'Molly had a long talk with him – he felt he ought to be back at Louisa Raynes, but was scared of it.'*

He had not lately been making music, instead expending his limited creative energy on assembling model aircraft from kits; it's easy to imagine his long fingers deftly putting them together. He finally took up his guitar in October, but in place of the easy fluency of old he would play a single phrase over and over, a habit that unnerved his parents (and had perhaps already informed 'Know' on *Pink Moon*).

He was doing just that when the phone rang on Friday, 6 October. Unexpectedly it was Joe Boyd, who encouraged him to think in

---

* According to the article, at Nick's age Dadd 'chose to live exclusively on eggs and ale'; Nick announced he now intended to eat nothing but bread and cheese, but soon returned to his usual broad diet.

terms of making another album. The call 'put life into Nick', wrote Rodney, noting how 'obviously pleased' he was to receive it. 'Evidently Joe urged him not to give up his guitar and afterwards Nick talked about buying a "good one" – seems to have sold his old "good one"' [presumably his Martin D-28].

Probably prompted by Joe, Chris Blackwell also phoned, asking after any progress on a new album, 'which obviously cheered Nick up considerably . . . It seems that he has in fact some material, and he talked to him about getting going again soon. All very surprising but very excellent that he should have something to think about.'

Soon afterwards John Wood rang Far Leys and told a surprised Rodney that he wanted to book a new session with Nick. Chris confirms that he would have released any recordings 'if Nick had continued making them', but Nick was almost certainly overstating his readiness. He had barely touched his guitar or the piano in 1972, and hadn't been observed using his tape recorder, so whatever material he was referring to is likely to have been left over from the time of *Pink Moon* or before.

Nick had hardly seen Robert Kirby since leaving London a year earlier, but suddenly announced that he wanted to visit him, then that he wanted him to come to Far Leys. This may have been with a view to renewing their collaboration, but Robert was about to depart for California. Disappointed, and faced by his inability to generate new songs, within a few days Nick was back in the music room, 'sunk in unresponsive gloom with eyes shut'.

It was therefore greatly to Molly and Rodney's surprise when, on Thursday, 9 November, he resurrected his desire to go to Paris, that very day, as he urgently wanted to see Françoise Hardy. She evidently represented a vital link in his sense of relevance as a musician, and it is striking that Joe's recent encouragement had led to thoughts of her.

His parents had misgivings but felt that encouragement was their best policy, not least as 'it is of course a great boost for us to have Nick in discursive, friendly and adventurous mood'. He did not tell them what he hoped to achieve, and was unable to contact Françoise in advance, but caught the 4.30 p.m. plane from Birmingham with a return ticket and enough pills for three days. Upon reaching Paris he went straight to the Île Saint-Louis and climbed the stairs to her flat. Alas, she was not there, so he went straight back to Orly and bought a new one-way ticket home.

His impulsive mission had failed, and with it evaporated his burst of dynamism. On Monday afternoon, wrote Rodney, 'he was playing his own records and then suddenly retired to bed without a word and declined to come down for supper or to give any explanation why'. Thereafter he shut both his guitars away in their cases and stated that 'he had no spark of music in him at the moment'.

Once again refusing his medication, he passed the ensuing days silently staring into the middle distance. On Friday he took a train to London but found himself unable to leave Euston station. Maddened by his indecision, he called Dr Pollitt's office from a payphone to request hospital admission for ECT that very day.

28

Confusion

⁓

IT HAD BEEN over a year since Nick had recorded *Pink Moon*, and the recent talk of a new album had sharply focused him on the need to improve his condition. He had been havering about ECT for six months. Dr Dickens was against, Dr Sim and Dr Pollitt were in favour; all were wise and experienced. Nick had been vigorously opposed, but now saw it as a possible shortcut to recovery.

ECT tended to be reserved for the seriously depressed, who either refused or didn't respond to drugs. It involved the administering of electric shocks to the head whilst under general anaesthetic, inducing a brief seizure. There was a good response rate, though the science of it was (and is) vague. It was agreed that Nick should take a week to confirm his willingness to undergo it.

Fluctuating between eagerness and anxiety, he 'suddenly emerged from the music room' mid-week, Rodney wrote, 'rang up and fixed an ECT appointment for 1 p.m. next Monday'. This calmed him, and the next few days saw a marked increase in his musical activities. Brian Wells visited at the weekend to reassure him, and they spent much of their time in the music room, where Nick played guitar and they listened to records including Mahler songs and piano works by Debussy and Satie.

On 27 November his parents drove him to St Thomas's Hospital in London, where he signed the necessary forms before being led off to a preparatory ward. Having been anaesthetised, electrodes were placed on his head and split-second electric shocks passed into his brain.

It seems a horrific scenario, but Nick's readiness to see it through felt like a breakthrough. Back home after the short session he had some whisky and 'seemed all right but complained of painful jaws and some loss of memory . . . said he thought the treatment had done him good. Quite relaxed and friendly and a good deal of amusement over an attack of hiccoughs.'

Brian rang for an update, but none of Nick's other friends ever knew of it. 'I was amazed when I found out much later that he'd had ECT – he certainly never told us,' says Bev.

Alas, its apparently positive effect quickly wore off. Nick spent Tuesday evening lying fully dressed on his bedroom floor and decided against the second session, scheduled for Thursday. He changed his mind at the last minute but upon reaching St Thomas's he refused it. Once home he expressed regret, but not to the extent that he ever made another appointment.

He was despondent in the aftermath of the abandoned treatment and shaken by the death of his formidable maternal grandmother on 7 December, but agreed to attend Liv Lodder's wedding reception a couple of days later. Clad in a suit and black T-shirt – his preferred outfit at the time – he surprised his parents by staying until well past midnight, catching up with figures from his past, including Jill Bennett, the sympathetic widow of his headmaster at Hurst House, who offered to set up a meeting between Nick and her friend Canon Peter Spink, of Coventry Cathedral. Nick vaguely agreed.

Most notably, he reconnected with his former girlfriend Kirstie and Liv's brother Dave, neither of whom he'd seen for over three years, and who were now married with a two-year-old son, Jo. Dave and Kirstie had been together since 1969, 'but there was no awkwardness between Nick and me about that', says Dave.

They knew that Nick had made some albums and had been struggling with depression, but they were taken aback by his changed demeanour. When Rodney discreetly requested their help with Nick they were only too happy to give it, and began to drop in to Far Leys.

Kirstie felt powerless: 'His eyes had lost their brightness. For a lot of people, going out and doing something energetic like digging the garden can help shake off depression, but I could see that Nick was far beyond that.'

Dave did, however, manage to get him to play in a local hockey match – like running, an activity he had spurned since leaving school. He enjoyed it, but at Far Leys, continues Dave:

> He would be largely silent, with his parents jollying the conversation along. On a good day he'd play – to himself, rather than to us – in the music room. He would react to Jo, though. The first thing Jo ever said was 'Ni . . . Ni . . .', trying to say Nick's name.

Nick had next to no social energy, but Dave occasionally persuaded him to go to the pub. 'We'd talk about this and that over a drink and a game of darts. He looked gaunt and you could not get a smile out of him, but he was never unkempt – the funny thing was, even when he was ill, he was always cool.'

Dave's sister Liv disagrees:

> Where his reserve had previously seemed cool, he now came across as defeated. In one pub near Tanworth someone made a comment about Mick Jagger and Bianca and he suddenly became fired up and said, 'Everybody deserves to have a private life!' I only remember it because he was usually so withdrawn.*

Nick couldn't face his grandmother's funeral on 14 December, but in his parents' absence he decided to attend Julian Lloyd and Victoria Ormsby-Gore's wedding reception in the Welsh borders. Ben and Rose Laycock drove him there and back. 'He was jolly,' says Ben, but being asked by so many old friends when they might expect another album had drained him, and after they left Far Leys he sank back into gloom.

His silence lasted for three days, at the end of which he told his parents he had abandoned both his medication and his music. By the end of the same conversation, however, he was saying he still wanted to take his pills 'sporadically', move back to London and resume his musical career. At Paul Wheeler's instigation he travelled to London to inspect a new guitar – perhaps to replace the Martin he had apparently sold – but decided against paying £125 for it

---

* Nick's remark echoes the disgust he had expressed to *Jackie* magazine about media coverage of Brian Jones's death in July 1969.

(around £1,200 in 2022), explaining that he remained undecided about whether to pursue music.

'I'm glad to have said goodbye to the worst year of my life,' he told his parents on New Year's Day, but the outset of 1973 seemed to bring little change. In early January Peter Spink came for tea at Far Leys. Nick was not in favour of organised religion, but the forty-six-year-old canon – broad-minded and mystically as well as musically inclined – was far from a conventional churchman. They had a wide-ranging discussion centring on Nick's fundamental dilemma: whether to recommit to music or seek a different path.

Music was what he wanted to do, he explained, but he was struggling to generate material, and stagnating at home was exacerbating his depression. The canon suggested a short-term compromise of finding work in a music shop whilst renting a room in Coventry or Birmingham. Nick saw the sense in his advice but was unable to act upon it.

He fell silent again, and when he did speak on Monday, 15 January, it was unexpectedly to revisit his idea of working in a bank or the Army, and to propose a new one: the growing field of computer programming. He had shown no previous interest in it, but Rodney swung into action, contacting a former colleague named Roger Slater at Nu-Way (a company in the Wolseley-Hughes portfolio).

Being his father's son, Nick was immediately invited for an informal interview at their office in Droitwich the following week. The prospect of actually getting a job catapulted him back into trepidation. Needing to air his worries beyond Far Leys, late on Wednesday night he slipped out to visit Dave and Kirstie in their cottage – a very rare instance of his wishing to unburden himself to friends.

Dave tactfully withdrew, leaving Nick with Kirstie. 'He was in despair,' she says.

> He said that he'd come to the end of what he had to offer musically, that something he didn't understand was preventing him from going further and he didn't know what to do about it. I tried to advise him, but I could see he was out of reach.

Knowing how troubling Molly and Rodney found Nick's unexplained disappearances, in the early hours Dave surreptitiously called them to say Nick was safe and would stay the night. Sleep-fogged, Rodney thought he was being asked to collect him in the morning, so he turned up at 8.30, just as he was sitting down to a boiled egg. 'We were mortified,' says Dave. 'We felt that Nick would have seen my having rung Far Leys as a breach of confidence, and he was less receptive to us afterwards.'

Nick loathed the notion of his parents keeping tabs on him and didn't speak to them for several days. They feared he would pull out of his Nu-Way interview, but he went through with it, filling in a formal application* and taking intelligence, maths and aptitude tests. He was promptly offered a six-month traineeship, paying £700 (around £7,000 in 2022), which he immediately accepted, to his parents' delight.

The enormity of the commitment was yet to sink in. Abuzz, he took off to visit the Wheelers. 'I was amazed,' says Paul, who was diplomatic enough to congratulate him. When Nick called Bev, however, she was direct: 'I advised him not to walk away from music unless he was sure he was ready to. There was nowhere for him to go when he started to lose the dream.'

Suppressing the thought, Nick continued to prepare for a career at Nu-Way – filling in tax forms, choosing a new suit, submitting to another haircut (this time from Molly), and even buying a second-hand Austin 1100 from the local garage. This ate up the bulk of his bank balance; Island had stopped paying his weekly retainer, so he called them to see if any royalties were due. They weren't.

On his first day at work – Thursday, 1 February 1973 – he learned that he was required to take a course in London the following week and had been booked into a hotel for its duration. Gabrielle dropped him there on Sunday evening, and over dinner on Monday he assured her that he planned to see the course through, despite finding it hard to follow. During Tuesday's lunch break, however, he walked out, took a train to Ascot and made his way to Tittenhurst Park.

---

* He named Dennis Silk, his old Housemaster at Marlborough, as a referee, though they'd had no contact in almost seven years.

'I was staggered when he turned up in a suit, with glasses and a short back and sides,' Paul remembers. 'He seemed to have joined the world he resented. It was almost like a betrayal.' Nick asked for a lift to the station early on Wednesday, so he'd be in time for that day's course, but the lure of music proved too great to resist and he actually went to Robert Kirby's flat in Cranley Gardens.

There he met Mick Audsley, another young singer-songwriter, whose debut album Robert had just produced.* 'Robert was working on a musical entitled *Man of Destiny* that was being put together by a producer called John B. House,' Mick explains.[†]

> He asked Nick and me to record demos of some of the material, so we spent a couple of afternoons rehearsing – Nick was shy to the extent that he played guitar facing the wall. We then recorded them at Marquee Studios. Nick was a far faster learner than me, so he did the fingerstyle parts. At the same time, sitting side-by-side on stools, he and I recorded 'Money Honey' and 'How Can You Keep On Moving?' from Ry Cooder's *Into the Purple Valley*, a favourite at Cranley Gardens.[‡]

Concerned that she hadn't heard from Nick as arranged, Gabrielle rang his hotel and was told he had checked out that morning. She wasn't surprised: 'Nick would occasionally try to suppress his artistry and talent, but it would always bubble up again.' It took Molly and Rodney until Saturday to establish that he was at Robert's, and he was brusque when Rodney called to ask if he had enough pills.

Returning to Far Leys on Sunday, he explained that he did not intend to return to Nu-Way. 'With hindsight, the idea of Nick

---

* *Dark and Devil Waters* came out in May 1973. Robert remembered Nick playing on it, but according to Mick, 'That's definitely not the case. I kept details of who played on every track, and whilst various friends did drop by and maybe contribute, that was very much not Nick's style. And if he had been there, we would certainly have featured him more prominently.'
† As Robert later told Patrick Humphries, House 'had a lot of money and a friend who wrote lyrics, and they needed twelve songs to go with them, which I wrote and linked together. I was trying to turn it into a medieval mystery play – it started with birth and ended with death. We had this grand design – it was going to be the new *Hair*.'
‡ None of this material has surfaced.

becoming a computer programmer could be seen as risible,' says Gabrielle. 'Let there be no doubt, however, that Nick, who set the whole machine in motion, wanted it to succeed. But perhaps he was also the first to come to his senses and see what a hopeless venture it was.'[1]

Awkward as extricating himself proved, the affair at least clarified to Nick the impossibility of seriously pursuing anything other than music. Following his sessions with Robert and Mick he was playing more guitar than he had in months and, unbeknown to his parents, was planning a return to recording his own material. On Saturday, 17 February, he abruptly departed for Suffolk, to stay with John and Sheila Wood.

'He behaved normally,' remembers John:

> He had his guitar with him and fiddled around on it, but not playing complete songs. He'd have a glass of wine but didn't drink a lot, and certainly never smoked dope. He spent a long time looking out of the window. The TV seemed to grab his attention in a way that things going on around him didn't, and he focused on it in a way that prevented you from chatting. I remember Sheila asking him who he'd like to appear on TV with and he said, 'Olivia Newton-John,' which was a surprise.

The Woods' young daughters, Annagh and Vickie, then at primary school, adored Nick. 'I was small for my age,' says Annagh,

> and my abiding memory of him is that when I walked in he would scoop me up, with his massive hands under my armpits, spin me around for just one rotation and say: 'Hiya, Titch!' It was a gentle, lovely thing. My mum always told us to leave him alone as he needed time to come out of himself.

For Vickie, 'I was probably asking him a shedload of questions, but he never got tetchy with my babble.'

'What the attraction was of coming to stay with us I don't know, as he didn't really participate in whatever was going on,' continues John. 'My best guess is that he felt comfortable around Sheila and enjoyed being in her environment. Nick wouldn't start conversations, but she would push him into talking. She had a rapport with him.'

At one point she bluntly asked: 'If you're so unhappy, Nick, why haven't you killed yourself?', to which he replied: 'It's too cowardly, and besides, I don't have the courage.'[2]

The following Wednesday evening, 21 February 1973, Nick had his first session at Sound Techniques since October 1971. As with *Pink Moon*, John was the only other person present. 'We'd probably discussed it when he came to stay, but I didn't know what he had in mind.'

Nick put down fluent and competent guitar parts for four unnamed songs, but John was taken aback that he didn't want to sing. 'He told me that he was having a problem writing lyrics and didn't have any ready. He had the songs sketched out but hadn't refined them – they were clearly unfinished. It was unheard of for Nick to go into the studio to record something unfinished.' John ran a tape off for him and, with misgivings, agreed to a second session at midnight the following Monday.

Nick hoped to come up with the lyrics at short notice, but seems not to have rated the material too highly in the first place. By his own account three months later, 'I still write songs but they have become a little too "far out" for comfort and don't stand up very well in the studio.'[3]

He 'must have been desperate to prove that the job debacle was for a reason', suggests Gabrielle, 'that if he could get back to his music, if he could just go into a studio – even unprepared – he would once more find himself able, assured, and in command. What a devastation it must have been to find that this was not so.'[4]

Back at Far Leys he told his parents he had been sleeping in his car in London – a sure sign that he was in a serious slump; they also suspected he was taking too much Valium. He continued to play his guitar in anticipation of Monday's session, but words stubbornly refused to come.

On Sunday evening, after watching *The Brothers*, Molly and Rodney noticed he seemed bleary and unsteady. They put him to bed, upon which he fell into a comatose sleep from which they could only rouse him by shouting. In a daze he told them he had taken twelve Valium. They managed to reach their GP, Dr Ackroyd, who said the dose was not life-threatening and that he should sleep it off.

They monitored him overnight, with Rodney at one point sticking a pin in his back to make sure he was alert. In the morning he seemed comfortable, and admitted to Molly that he had in fact swallowed an entire new bottle's worth – thirty-six pills – with the intention of killing himself. He explained that 'everything was in a mess, that his music wasn't coming properly, that he couldn't get on with people, that he didn't like being at home but couldn't stand being anywhere else'.

These were longstanding problems, but suicide had been the extreme to which Molly and Rodney hoped he would never resort. They now took care to lock away Aspirin, Valium and other sleeping pills, though Nick still had access to his anti-depressants, which they were unaware could also be dangerous. His suicide attempt was kept secret – even Gabrielle wasn't told – but his parents could never again be sure what value he placed on his life.

Later that morning Nick rang Sheila, and at the weekend he returned to the Woods'. On Sunday they visited Danny Thompson in nearby Grundisburgh. Vickie has never forgotten that afternoon:

> I was aware that Nick was sad, I could sense that. He went off to the boundary of the property and was looking out, with his back to me. All I wanted to do was stand with him and hold his hand, but Mum told me to leave him alone.

Nick was almost certainly unaware of his growing international reputation: in early April the Italian magazine *Sound Flash* carried an impassioned profile by Stefano De Marchis that called him 'assuredly one of the most sensitive and genuine folk singers on the current global pop scene'.[5] Whether this would have gratified or unnerved him is questionable, though.

Molly and Rodney knew he was struggling to complete new material, but he disregarded her suggestion that Paul Wheeler write lyrics for him; he was never a collaborative songwriter. At the same time Paul suggested that Nick might consider joining a four-piece group he was forming: 'I thought playing with others might unblock something in him, and that it would be like Neil Young joining Crosby, Stills and Nash – a fully formed talent being integrated into an existing group – but nothing happened.'

Nick did at least buy an electric guitar, as if experimenting with a new instrument might stimulate his muse. 'A lot of electric guitar playing – simple theme repeated ad nauseam,' Rodney wearily recorded on 5 April. It was in theory a positive sign, but he told his mother that 'music was the only thing for him and that wasn't going particularly well', and when his uncle Chris visited he explained 'he was doing some recording but only found it possible to compose in the studio'. This was in stark contrast to his former practice, albeit probably no more than an impromptu remark.

On top of his illness, his fitful pill-taking was leading to restlessness, dizziness and what Rodney called 'alarmingly unreasonable' behaviour. He asked his parents to leave him alone yet resented it when they went out; he wanted to eat alone, stood for long periods in his bedroom, slept in his clothes with the light on, disregarded personal grooming, declined to attend appointments with Dr Pollitt, and for a time only communicated in 'grunt language'.

Eventually his father called the Woods to establish what Nick's musical plans were, if any, and learned that he was hoping to make further recordings in May, when Joe Boyd would be back in London. John doubted Nick would be ready, and so did Rodney.

As the date neared, Nick told his parents he was looking for a room in London; a few days later, in a drastic reversal, he told them he wanted to return to Louisa Raynes House. This required an initial referral, but he refused to see Dr Pollitt, so it was left to his parents to attend and outline his recent history. Dr Pollitt told them that, on the basis of all he now knew, he considered Nick to be schizophrenic.

Rodney and Molly had long been aware of the possibility, and began to read up on it. Although Nick showed some classic symptoms – silence, catatonia, emotional disengagement, indecision, unpredictability – they had not presented in childhood or adolescence, which is often the case with schizophrenics; nor was he ever known to have endured hallucinations, or attributed events to delusional causes, other common symptoms.

446

Rodney was aware of the role that dope could play in triggering psychosis, but Dr Pollitt assured him that 'he did not think that Nick's cannabis smoking had materially affected' his condition, and Dr Dickens agreed.

The Drakes seem not to have told Dr Pollitt of Nick's suicide attempt, but they were ever alert to the possibility of its recurrence. On 17 April Rodney found that Nick had been hoarding sleeping pills from the cabinet in which he usually kept them locked, but under questioning from Molly his only response was to laugh.

In place of treatment, in the spring of 1973 Nick adopted the habit of racking up aimless mileage in his Austin. 'I think driving was a sort of therapy to him,' his mother reflected. 'It gave him tremendous comfort.'[6] Brian Wells considers it characteristic of 'the mindset of someone who felt lost, miserable, and didn't know what else to do'.[7] It was also preferable to being so visible to his parents, and Molly suspected he hoped it would prove a source of musical inspiration.

London continued to draw him like a malign magnet. Rodney took to monitoring his mileage, and on two consecutive days he clocked up 229 and 227 miles respectively. It was an easy statistic to interpret: 'It seems he must just drive to London and straight back – a rather pointless and expensive form of therapy.' When asked where he had been on such occasions, his response tended to be: 'Around and about.'

Sometimes he did visit people. One morning he surprised Gabrielle by turning up at the BBC's rehearsal studios in Acton, where he sat silently in the canteen with her. Upon occasion he would sit with de Wet as he painted in his studio in Campden Hill Gardens; de Wet appreciated his wordless companionship, and felt no need to attempt to speak himself.

More often Nick dropped in on friends. 'He would simply go to friends' houses unannounced and knock,' says Paul Wheeler, who had just moved from Tittenhurst Park to 30 Albert Square in Stockwell, South London, with his wife and baby daughter.

Presumably if nobody was at home he would simply go away. We wouldn't expect him to contribute much conversationally – his presence was enough. We spent a lot of time listening to music. He would maybe bring an album for us to listen to, or we'd play ourselves. Music was our only real currency.*

One day Paul was driving Nick somewhere when Nick took the unusual step of 'asking me something about depression. I said, "I thought you were the one who knew all about that!" It was disorientating for us to realise that neither of us had the answers . . .'

Christopher Sykes hadn't seen Nick since 1970 and was delighted when he 'rang out of the blue, asking if he could come around to my flat in Prince of Wales Drive'. However, he found the two hours of his visit, during which Nick 'spoke barely a word', a 'shattering' experience.

Jo Dingemans hadn't seen him for years either and was likewise 'shocked' when he visited her flat in Sinclair Road, near Olympia, albeit more by his 'thin and unkempt' appearance than his behaviour.

> He chatted about the music he was writing but was vague about where he was living. He was rude about my record player being crap (which it was), and I bought him a drink in the Beaconsfield pub. It was crowded and he wasn't relaxed. He didn't really reply when I asked what was wrong, but when I asked if he was taking hard drugs he vehemently said he wasn't.

David Ward had been warned by mutual friends of 'the changes in him' but was still 'very surprised' to experience Nick's 'monosyllabic replies and avoidance of eye-contact' when he called.[8] At least Sophia Ryde knew what to expect: 'I'd moved from Ifield Road to Elm Park Gardens and he'd turn up there too. He was pretty incommunicable but was sweet with my two cats. One day I'd had a bed delivered and, as he was quite practical, he helped screw on the legs.'

Less helpfully, she says, he would sometimes appear late at night. 'I had to tell him I was going to bed as I had work the next morning,

---

* Among the albums Paul recalls playing most frequently at the time are Laura Nyro's *New York Tendaberry* (released in September 1969), the Beach Boys' *Sunflower* (August 1970), David Bowie's *Hunky Dory* (November 1971) and Ry Cooder's *Into the Purple Valley* (January 1972).

and he would stay sitting there or sleep on the sofa, but always be gone in the morning.' He was secretive about his pills with most friends, but Sophia remembers him apologetically going to the kitchen to take them. One evening he turned up when she was with her new boyfriend, who 'had no idea how to deal with him. I couldn't wait for Nick to leave, it was so awkward.'

Alex Henderson cautions: 'It wasn't unrelentingly grim – there were occasional holes in the clouds where a bit of the old Nick would shine through. I'd get a phone call when he sounded OK and I'd think things were back on track for him.'

It was hard for Nick's friends to unite in support because he'd always kept his circles separate and his contact was so sporadic. David feels they each 'assumed that Nick was obtaining from other people the moral support he didn't get sufficiently from us alone'. In any case, most of them were too young and uninformed about mental illness to offer meaningful help, though the extent to which Nick would have responded to it is questionable.

'He was loved by all his friends, but they didn't really seem to know him, and I think he felt that very much,' Rodney later reflected.[9] He once went so far as to tell his parents that he had no real friends at all, but on the other hand, as Molly put it: 'He didn't ever put himself out particularly for his friends, and yet they continued to love him – and revere him too, in a way.' As Jo Dingemans summarises: 'Everyone liked Nick and everyone wanted to help him. Everyone he visited felt helpless.'

The bureaucracy of daily life was another challenge. He mislaid his passport and birth certificate, fell behind with the instalments for his *Encyclopaedia Britannica*, ignored so many tax reminders that an official came to the door, and after driving a remarkable 10,000 miles in his Austin since February without checking its oil, was stopped by the police on 23 April because of the noise it was making and ordered to produce the relevant documents within twenty-four hours. 'Everything is pissed up!' he announced that night, taking the unusual step of drinking whisky.

That month he received a new passport, supposedly in order to take a holiday to Spain with Brian while his parents went to France. The photo in it is the first known to have been taken of him since the *Pink Moon* session in December 1971, and also the last. Even allowing for official strictures, it is haunting; he is gaunt and unshaven, his hair long and straggling, his eyes dark and piercing, his gaze unnervingly intense yet somehow vacant too.

On 24 April – a year to the day since his admission to hospital – he set off from Far Leys for the airport. Rodney wrote that he left with his 'guitar, tape recorder and kit bag', and 'seemed very determined and composed, for him, and we felt much happier about him than we have done for some weeks'. Alas, he hadn't organised a trip, and as soon as Molly and Rodney departed for France he signed himself back into Louisa Raynes House.

When they returned a week later the duty sister rang to say he'd just gone missing. As such, wrote Rodney, 'we unpacked and went to bed in the state of uneasiness that Nick seems to have perfected the method of inducing'. Knowing they were due back, Nick had driven to London without any money. Quickly running out of petrol, he had abandoned his Austin at the start of the motorway and hitchhiked onwards. Without any sleep, he spent the day in London, then hitchhiked back to Birmingham and began walking home.

Exhausted and miserable, he rang Far Leys at 7.15 a.m. and Rodney fetched him from the outskirts of the city. He told his relieved parents that he couldn't stand Louisa Raynes House, but returned that evening, impressing upon them that he didn't want to be visited. He stayed for a fortnight, refusing medication and intermittently hitchhiking to Far Leys, before checking out for good. He remained uncommunicative but was still playing a good deal of guitar; evidently he still had it in mind to impress Joe.

Much of his time was spent reading, in his favoured orange armchair in the music room. Books he tackled included a history of Europe, *War and Peace*, novels by Somerset Maugham and Graham Greene, a compendium of horror stories, the *Oxford Musical Companion* and his trusty *Encyclopaedia Britannica*. He also watched a lot of television, often tuning into music coverage, whether opera or the *Old Grey Whistle Test*, and especially enjoying a BBC2 documentary entitled *Man of Letters*, about the simple, fulfilling life of a postman in rural Yorkshire.

One evening in mid-May he called at the flat in Chiltern Street, Marylebone that Brian Wells shared with his girlfriend, Marion Stevens, at whose twenty-first birthday party in Cambridge he had performed four years earlier. A trainee doctor like Brian, she was sensitive and intelligent, and Nick enjoyed being around her.

They were so concerned by his condition that, with Molly and Rodney's blessing, Brian made fresh efforts to have him admitted as an inpatient at the Philadelphia Association, under the care of Leon Redler. Nick was cautiously acquiescent. By coincidence, the social worker previously assigned to him, Dick Mills, was now working there and recommended that he write a letter setting out his case history and current position as he saw it.

On Tuesday, 22 May, Molly and Rodney spent a rare night at Rodney's London club, the Oriental, in order to attend the Chelsea Flower Show. They clandestinely met Brian and Marion to discuss the plan over a drink. At Far Leys, meanwhile, Nick composed his letter to Redler, which he left open on the hall table for them to find.

It's been a long time since I wrote a letter so I hope it won't seem strange. I'll try and briefly outline what's been happening to me, as I suppose that's what this letter is meant to be about. At 18 I got into Fitzwilliam College, Cambridge, and a year later went up there to read English. While there I did read English but spent much time playing music and writing songs.

After two years I left to go to London, where I made three albums, two produced by an American, Joe Boyd, and the third produced by me. (If they would be of interest, I would be happy to send them.) There was a lot of pressure around, and I suppose I sort of cracked up.

After completing them I went to Spain for a while and then came home here to my parents' place, where I have been for about the last year and a half. Fairly soon after arriving I was placed by a local doctor in the Louisa Raynes Ward of the Warwick Central Hospital, pretty much against my own will. I spent six weeks there under a Dr Dickens, during which time I met Dick Mills, who I think is now working with Ron Laing, and he suggested that I should come and see you.

However, what with one thing and another I didn't, and ended up seeing a Dr John Pollitt, of St Thomas's Hospital. He treated me for depression, and to tell the truth he was pretty helpful, although I never really understood the word and felt that 'confusion' was more apt. Just lately I went back to Louisa Raynes as a voluntary patient but didn't stay there very long. I could probably go into detail about what's going on now, but I don't think this is the place.

I still write songs, but they have become a little too 'far out' for comfort and don't stand up very well in the studio. My parents seem anxious to help but when I try to communicate with them I get completely tongue-tied, which is a problem. Come to think of it, it's getting harder to talk to everyone now. I don't know too much about your work, so I've just said what springs to mind about me. I'm sorry if it all sounds trite or presumptuous or anything, but I would really like to hear from you.

Yours, Nick Drake.

Rodney and Molly were impressed with his evident self-knowledge and ability to articulate it, and though he 'seemed pleased' when they complimented him, he remained silent, 'standing aimlessly' in the drawing room.

Objectively examining and describing his condition had in fact been excruciating. His inability to write new songs or finish old ones was panicking him; since 1967 his identity had been bound up in his creativity, and to find it inaccessible was agonising. It was as if a flowing tap had been abruptly turned off and, try as he might, he couldn't get it going again.

It was perhaps fortuitous that Joe had cancelled his plan to visit London. The day after writing the letter, in what Rodney called 'a fit of frustration and despair', Nick violently smashed his Levin and Brian's Yamaha, leaving him only with his Estruch, bought way back in 1964, and his electric.

29

In A Terrible Mess

～～

WITHOUT ACKNOWLEDGING IT, the Drakes were all tensely awaiting Leon Redler's reply, which arrived on the last Thursday of May 1973. He offered to meet Nick that Saturday, and mentioned that a trainee might sit in. Nick read it and wordlessly drove off. When he didn't return for the night Rodney rang Louisa Raynes House.

Nick wasn't there, and Dr Dickens explained that they could do nothing for him until he engaged seriously with treatment, and that he might get worse in the interim. Rodney took the opportunity to ask if he considered Nick schizophrenic, to which Dr Dickens robustly replied that it 'was a meaningless word covering a whole host of psychic maladies' and 'all we could do was to soldier on as we were and hope that Nick would soon come round to accepting treatment'.[*]

Nick returned home the following evening but, after several false starts, did not attend the appointment with Redler the next day. When asked why he'd decided against it he simply drove off again. 'Perhaps it was the request for another person to be present at the interview that defeated Nick,' suggests Gabrielle.[1] 'Perhaps it was the reality of an actual session. But he never attempted psychotherapy again.'

Instead he reverted to 'inactive silent gloom' (in Rodney's phrase), wearing the same clothes day and night and reacting with hostility when addressed. He ate well but alone and kept his own hours,

[*] According to the *Lancet* of 21 November 1970, a total of only £96,000 (equivalent to around £1.2 million in 2022) had been spent on researching schizophrenia in the previous year.

sitting up long into the night or, when unable to sleep, going downstairs for cornflakes.

Molly, who was a light sleeper, often joined him, but when he spent the entire night of 7 June sitting in his car Rodney tried to persuade him up to bed at 4.45 a.m. He responded with a laugh before driving to London at dawn. When he had a puncture he didn't get it fixed, using his worn spare until that too became useless. A few days later Rodney despairingly wrote: 'What is one to do? . . . He seems unable to face up to anything.'

Much of his time was spent asleep, although he didn't appear to be taking Valium or anything else. 'Can't imagine how he can sleep so much,' wrote Rodney. He still watched a lot of television, especially enjoying *The Two Ronnies* and *Look, Mike Yarwood*. Brian Wells remembers Nick's enjoyment of comedy: 'Even when he was feeling miserable, he did like *Monty Python*. He wouldn't necessarily laugh while he watched it, but he enjoyed talking about it afterwards.'

He continued to spurn his spectacles, so for his twenty-fifth birthday his parents gave him expensive new contact lenses. On the day, however, he pointedly left them in his room and wore sunglasses. He opened his presents (including a jumper from Molly that he didn't put on) but wanted to eat his cake alone in the music room. It was, as his father put it, 'Not a very happy birthday'.

Turning twenty-five was significant for Nick in one respect: it qualified him for access to a trust that Rodney's sister Pam had set up in 1963 to benefit her niece and nephew. Through his father's canny investing, Nick's half had grown to the substantial sum of £4,277 (around £40,000 in 2022), and Rodney now set out the financial options open to him. 'To have a little money behind you at your age is a tremendous advantage,' he concluded.

The first purchase Nick made after his birthday was not expensive, though: a number of books about drug addiction. When his disquieted parents asked about them he told them to 'shut up and piss off'. It seems he was wondering whether hard drugs might cure his ills.

One evening he visited Brian and announced: 'Look, I really want to try smack.' Brian, who was not averse to reckless experimentation, remembers: 'I said, "Are you sure?", because neither of us had ever done any.' Brian half-seriously rang a user he knew, but as the call connected, 'I put the phone down and we fell about laughing . . . And so that was that. As far as I know, Nick never took heroin. He wasn't really a big drug user.'[2]

Nick showed no interest in his trust fund, so Rodney pointed out that he could at least now well afford a new guitar. On 13 August Nick drove to Ivor Mairants Musicentre, in the West End of London, and treated himself to a brand-new Martin 000-28, costing £235 (around £2,250 in 2022). His parents took it as a good omen, not least since Sheila Wood had told Rodney that Joe Boyd was shortly moving back to London.

The instrument, however, sat untouched for the next couple of days. When his uncle Chris visited, the two of them went for a walk during which, Chris divulged, Nick 'talked quite a lot about his music, which at present he can't get very far with, and his hope for a "leap" out of his present troubles'.

The next day Nick put on clean clothes and polished his Chelsea boots before driving off with his guitar and a suitcase. By examining his cheque stubs, his parents established that he had paid a week's rent for a room in 21 Cranley Gardens, South Kensington (not to be confused with the Cranley Gardens in Muswell Hill where Robert Kirby lived). They nervously inferred that he was hoping to move back to the city, but he was home again the same night.

At the start of September he made another 'leap' at life beyond Far Leys, this time staying away for a fortnight – the longest stretch he had spent away since his hospitalisation the previous year. He first called on Paul Wheeler, who was perplexed by his new habit of carrying a half-bottle of whisky around with him: 'I wondered whether he'd decided to move towards alcohol from dope as part of the general change he was considering in his life.'

After a few days with no word from Nick, Rodney called Paul, who said he had been with him in Stockwell but was now with Robert Kirby in Muswell Hill. Robert explained that Nick had just left, under the impression that – as Rodney wrote in his diary – 'no one wanted to see him now'.

From Robert's he drove to the Martyns' in Hastings. John was often away gigging, meaning Bev was likely to be alone with the children. This may well have been Nick's hope: John was increasingly dependent on alcohol and cocaine, and it had become clear that his ebullient exterior masked aggressive insecurity. He tended to conceal his brutish tendencies from visitors, but Nick was no fool. 'He had seen John doing things such as flicking me with tea towels in the past, and always left the house when anything like that happened,' says Bev, who had turned from an ambitious singer-songwriter into a timorous drudge since marrying John.[3] 'Nick was one of the few people allowed to visit me.'

On this occasion he didn't even announce himself:

> One baking hot summer's day some young kids came over and said, 'Your friend's on the beach wearing a suit,' so I told them to tell him to come to the house, and they dragged him back with them. He hadn't wanted to knock on the door. I would feed him and he would sit drinking tea and looking out at the sea for hours.

They might go for a drink in the evening, or walk the dog, or compose music; Bev was working on a song called 'Reckless Jane' and recalls Nick throwing out words that rhymed with the name.*

After a couple of days he returned to London, where his car broke down again. 'He blew it up, he just ran out of oil,' says Brian, whom he made his way to. 'I'm sure he did it deliberately, impulsively – "Fuck it, I'm just going to keep driving it! I'm not going to put any oil in it!" – almost out of frustration, bloody-mindedness.'[4]

Brian offered him a bed, but he preferred to sit in Brian's car. The next day he checked in to a hotel in Haverstock Hill – a stone's throw from his former base – and wrote a short letter to Rodney, asking that all his trust money be transferred into his current account. 'It's not that I plan to spend it all or anything, but I just would like it there,' he wrote, signing off with the oddly formal 'Yours, Nick'.

Rodney and Molly were disturbed by this development, but Rodney immediately replied to say he would make the necessary

---

* Nick was adept at word games, and had carried out a similar exercise on his own 'Day Is Done'.

arrangements. 'Best of luck, Nick, from us both, in whatever it is you are doing,' he signed off. 'We think of you all the time and you know how we welcome anything you can manage in the way of a letter or phone call. Yours, Dad.'

Before the letter had been posted, however, Nick was back at Far Leys, where Rodney persuaded him to limit the immediate transfer of funds to £1,000 – still a significant sum (around £10,000 in 2022). He had apparently already offloaded his new Martin, but occasionally played his electric guitar or the piano. Otherwise he passed the days watching TV or listening to records. He was not a collector, though, and his albums were well-played, with worn covers. Brian says he enjoyed Carly Simon's *No Secrets* (released in November 1972), Sophia Ryde remembers him liking Jim Croce, and he had recently bought *Tubular Bells* by Mike Oldfield (released in May 1973), but mostly he favoured classical.

After a week of silence Molly attempted to get him to open up, upon which he exclaimed: 'There's no outlet to say what I think about this bloody place!' A week later he was hovering in the hall late at night when Rodney suggested he go to bed. 'Something is burning me up and I can't stand it!' he replied.

The consequences of his refusal to accept professional help or take his medication were clearer than ever. He was enervated, hid from visitors and declined to come to the phone. He also took to wearing his old clothes, including the shabby coat that had been a mainstay of his Hampstead days. He was confounded by trivial matters, such as a choice of puddings, and remained incapable of organisation; with his father's encouragement he exchanged his Austin 1100 for a three-year-old 1300, but continued to run out of petrol or forget to take money or his house key, necessitating assistance at antisocial hours.

He also showed hints of psychosis, bursting into giggles over afternoon tea in late September, then lapsing into gloom. His parents were now well aware of the symptoms of schizophrenia, and it seems Nick wanted to learn more about it too, having been found in his father's dressing room one afternoon searching for a book on the subject. He thrust it under the bed when approached, but the incident led to his first conversation with Rodney in months:

He told me (with long gaps of silence in between) that he expected that the time had come when he would suddenly be better, and then he would leave home; that he had no wish now to go back to London; that he has tried some religious meditation in London recently but it hadn't appealed to him; that he didn't want to replace his guitar.

Said he wouldn't now consider a routine job under any circumstances whatsoever. Didn't want to be a down-and-out – had tried it once and found it very frightening. Dreaded possibility of being me when he was forty. Said he couldn't write because he couldn't observe or be impersonal.

Rodney was encouraged by his openness, but – as so often when he unburdened himself – he fell silent in the ensuing days, and resumed his aimless driving. 'It was as though Nick had been imprisoned by an invisible captor who allowed him an occasional appearance at a barred window but snatched him back and muffled him before he could cry out in communication,' says Gabrielle.[5]

Paul and Diana Wheeler arranged to visit for lunch on Saturday, 20 October. They were late, and Nick nervously sank three beers as he awaited them. At 2 p.m. he cracked and drove off. 'We certainly weren't offended that he wasn't there, just disappointed not to have seen him,' says Paul, who had not met Molly and Rodney before. 'They were warm and welcoming, as well as open-minded and sympathetic about his problems.'

According to Rodney's diary, Paul and Diana assured them that Nick 'was still a real name in the pop or folk world, and that plenty of people would be delighted to get him on their books for a record'.* It's striking that Nick evidently no longer regarded himself as an Island artist.

'I can't swear that we would have released a fourth album by him,' admits the label's production manager Tim Clark,

---

* In 1978 David Geffen told Arthur Lubow: 'I thought his records were fabulous, and yet he met with complete indifference in this country. I thought Nick Drake should have been a star, and that I could help him. I kept asking Island Records about him, and they kept putting me off.' (*New Times*, 1 May 1978.)

but Chris Blackwell was willing to plough on with certain artists even if their sales weren't brilliant, and Nick fell into that category. The idea was that this is what Island did – we believed in our artists and we didn't give up on them. It was part of what set us apart.

Nonetheless, Nick had had no contact with them in almost a year and – though he dreaded obsolescence – he remained in wilful ignorance about his standing with them. The company and its personnel had changed a good deal since he'd last known it, and in all his trips to London he hadn't once visited their new headquarters in St Peter's Square, Hammersmith.

'We were a more commercial operation than had been the case in 1969, but Witchseason was still a strong part of our identity,' contends Richard Williams, Island's new Head of A&R. Indeed, Fairport, Sandy Denny, John Martyn, Richard Thompson and the Incredible String Band were still on its roster, if middling sellers – but Nick had apparently sunk beneath the waves.

'I can't remember any conversations about Nick,' Richard continues. 'If a shop put in an order, I assume it would have been sent out, but I doubt there were copies of his albums in the office. By 1973 he was regarded as a back catalogue artist.'

David Betteridge, Island's managing director, reflects:

We could have given Nick more respect and support, but he had no management – Joe was long gone – and people simply weren't buying the material. We were busy with Cat Stevens, Roxy Music, Bob Marley and goodness knows who else, and Nick was never a priority for us. I think the perception was that he'd had his shot, and he just got put out to pasture.*

Even if Island had been pressing Nick for a new album, and he had been in a position to make it, the fundamental question remained as to whether he still wanted to pursue music. According to Rodney,

---

* One of Nick's songs did make it out via Island that month, at least: *Strong in the Sun* by Tír na nÓg opened with a rock treatment (with some lyrical additions) of 'Free Ride', that album's title evidently having been subconsciously suggested to singer-guitarist Leo O'Kelly by 'Place To Be'.

the Wheelers 'seemed to think he didn't want to do anything at all now – but I doubt this'.

Following the Wheelers' visit Rodney extracted a few more perplexing words out of Nick:

> He said he had no alternative at present to going back and forth to London regularly, because he had things to do there which I wouldn't understand, and moreover he couldn't stay in London before he had got something going because London 'ate one up' in such circumstances. He said little likelihood at present of the situation changing.

As if to illustrate his point, he immediately drove there and back, accumulating another 227 apparently senseless miles. Chris Blackwell had reiterated that Nick was always welcome to use his flat in Spain, so on 24 October he impulsively bought himself a return ticket to Malaga – but instead of catching his connecting flight in Paris he bought a new one-way ticket and came home, having first retrieved his Martin from London.

Monday, 5 November, was Molly's fifty-eighth birthday, but Nick had forgotten. Upon seeing her cards and presents he departed for London without a word. 'One sometimes thinks he lives to be as unpleasant as he can,' conjectured Rodney, though he understood, of course, that Nick's thoughtlessness was not calculated.

It was a time of even greater stress than usual for the Drakes, since Rodney's sixty-six-year-old sister Pamela, who had emigrated to Canada in 1946 and had no family of her own, was suffering from dementia. The decision was made to bring her to Far Leys.

Nick did not accompany his parents and sister to meet her at Heathrow on 7 November, and barely acknowledged her upon arrival at home. Like her nephew, but for different reasons, she was restless and confused and needed careful management. When Rodney tried to discuss her situation with Nick the following morning, he put on his coat and left. On his return he told Molly he was 'in a terrible mess', but wouldn't elaborate. That week alone he drove over a thousand miles.

Inspiration remained elusive, and it was months since he'd spoken to John Wood. He was sporadically tickled by *Some Mothers Do 'Ave 'Em* and the *Benny Hill Show*, but spent most of his time lying on his bed, awake and fully clothed, or standing vacantly outside, rarely picking up his guitar.

'Nick appears to be in a permanent suppressed rage,' observed Rodney a fortnight after Pam's arrival. On the last Friday in November he went outside and attacked his car until he had destroyed the rear passenger window. Molly then found him in the music room 'leaning over one side of his chair in seeming physical distress. However, he would say nothing.'

It was six months since he had received professional care, and this latest 'smash-up' was some sort of breaking point for Rodney. The following morning he urged Nick to accept psychiatric help and, in the absence of meaningful NHS support, took steps to join the National Schizophrenia Fellowship.* In doing so he aimed to learn more about Nick's condition, and to derive practical and emotional support from the many others in his and Molly's predicament.

Slade were at Number 1 with the relentless 'Merry Xmas Everybody', but its optimistic message was at odds both with Nick and the country at large. As well as an ongoing IRA bombing campaign, major strikes were causing power cuts (dodged at Far Leys by a back-up generator) and a looming three-day week that threatened inconvenience and discomfort for many.

Nick was antisocial over Christmas, but when his uncle Chris joined him in the music room – where they listened to *Desertshore* by Nico (produced by Joe Boyd) – on 28 December, he said he thought he had 'rounded a corner'. It didn't seem that way to his parents. He had a streaming cold but – as if to prove his stated distrust of the medical profession – he refused to take anything for it and 'opened the window (which he never normally does) and lay with bared chest, as though courting pneumonia'. He sat up with Molly and Rodney to see in 1974 with the BBC, but Rodney noted that he didn't say 'Happy New Year' to them – or anything else.

Nick had called 1972 'the worst year of my life', but 1973 had, if anything, been worse. In his sister's words, the last twelve months

---

* The National Schizophrenia Fellowship was founded by John Pringle, author of 'A Case of Schizophrenia', the influential article that appeared in *The Times* on 9 May 1970.

had simply been 'a long list of false starts and dead ends'.[6] Things seemed equally unpromising at the outset of the New Year. 'We feel we are both in the doghouse in a big way and that he is in a very paranoiac state,' wrote Rodney.

On the afternoon of Friday, 4 January, the weather was filthy and Nick had a nasty cough, but he still drove to London. This time there was a purpose to the trip: Joe Boyd had just returned, and they were to meet for the first time in three years.

Since moving to Los Angeles Joe had produced the huge-selling 'Duelling Banjos' single from *Deliverance*, co-produced Maria Muldaur's smash hit solo debut and overseen the well-received *Jimi Hendrix* documentary, but Warner Brothers had given him less autonomy than he'd been led to expect so he had resigned.

He now regarded himself as more of a film producer than a record producer, but had rung Nick at Far Leys upon reaching the UK. 'I got in touch out of friendship and a sense of personal responsibility, rather than anything professional – I had no music industry deals or infrastructure anymore, but I knew he had been having a hard time and I wanted to get a feel for how he was.'

They agreed that Nick would visit his first-floor flat at 24 Ladbroke Gardens, Notting Hill at 5.30. 'He rang the bell and came up. The first thing I thought was that he didn't look like the same Nick. He looked far worse than I had ever seen him: his hair was greasy, his hands dirty, his clothes rumpled.'[7] His mood was correspondingly grim: he had evidently been brooding en route.

Joe says:

> I made him a cup of tea, and fairly quickly he said: 'You say I'm a genius, other people say I'm a genius, so I don't understand why I haven't sold any records and I don't have any money! Why didn't Island promote me more?' He was upset, but this was Nick – he wasn't shouting or anything close to it, and he wasn't pointing the finger directly at me. It was more a vehement, frustrated 'why, why, why?' than a 'j'accuse'. It was sad.

When Nick had finished, Joe spoke. 'I just said, "We're all shocked that your records haven't been picked up on – but if you don't tour it's very hard." I tried to steer the conversation towards the future and asked if he had any songs.' By Joe's account that year, 'John Wood had previously told me that Nick had said that he had some tunes but no words, and I mentioned this to him. He just looked at me and said sadly: "I haven't got any tunes anymore."'[8]

Joe persevered, assuring him of his willingness to work with him whenever he felt ready. 'I had no idea if it would lead to an album, but I felt Nick needed somebody to say to him, "I believe in you – let's go into the studio!" That was all I could offer, anyway.'

Joe felt the Nick he'd seen that evening 'was not fulfilling some gloomy romantic fantasy, he was in a hell of bitter loneliness and despair'.[9] The meeting appears to have been more galvanising for Nick, who returned to Far Leys at around nine that night 'seemingly in considerably more human form', according to Rodney, who had no idea where he'd been.

As ever, the prospect of resuming work with Joe had perked him up, and he spent Saturday playing in the music room. Rodney was astonished when he agreed to come to church on Sunday, still more when he 'made the odd light-hearted remark about the service'. He got up early and worked hard over the next few days; one evening he went to bed early, then came back down and listened to *Pink Moon*.

Creative block soon intervened, however, and within a week he was stuck 'playing his electric guitar in the old single-phrase-repeated-ad-nauseam style. We thought this rather ominous.' Rodney took to referring to the dreaded phrase as 'the note', and eventually checked whether Nick had smashed his Martin, but found it safe in its case.

Having spoken to Joe, John Wood – who was also entirely sensitive to Nick's condition – rang on 12 February to see if Nick wanted to book some studio time. It had been a year since Nick had recorded the four guitar tracks at Sound Techniques, and he had to concede that he still wasn't ready to add to them.

He 'seemed ultra-low' thereafter, but continued to spurn his medicine. His parents noticed that he had dug out his letter from Leon Redler, received eight months before, but rather than following it up, after another solid week of 'the note' he impulsively drove to Louisa Raynes House. Upon learning that the sympathetic Dr Dickens had moved to a new post elsewhere, he abandoned any idea of staying there. 'A tragedy, of course,' wrote Rodney.

Brian and Marion were due for the weekend, but – as with the Wheelers' visit the previous October – Nick drove off just before their arrival, so lunch was eaten in his absence. Upon his return he and Brian repaired to the music room. 'I got him to play *Pink Moon* and show me some of his tunings,' says Brian. 'We then played *Bryter Layter*, and I said, "God, if I'd made that and it hadn't sold, I'd be so pissed off!" And he said, "Well, now you know how I feel." I remember it because normally he was so unforthcoming.'

Marion later joined them with her flute, and the three of them jammed. Brian: '"The Peter Gunn Theme" was about my level, so I began to play it on Nick's electric guitar and he picked up his saxophone. It was a laugh.' The trio then strolled up to the pub, after which (as Rodney noted) 'Nick and Brian were up till nearly 3 a.m., talking and playing music – v. good.'

During their conversation Nick told Brian that he felt 'rejected' by his parents. The truth was that they remained unceasingly devoted to him. 'Molly and Rodney's patience with him was amazing,' says Gabrielle's old friend Joanna Lodder, who sometimes saw them when she visited her parents.

> They tried so hard to understand and never gave up on him for a moment, just constantly provided love and support. I can picture Rodney now, and I can hear his voice saying 'Poor old chap' with such humanity. They loved that boy, they really did.

At the end of February Rodney and Molly finally found a suitable care home for Pam. On the morning of her departure Nick was 'playing a phrase repeatedly on the piano', then drove off without saying goodbye. Joe had returned to Los Angeles for a few weeks and Nick was considering visiting him there, so he filled in a visa application (giving his occupation as 'musician' and the purpose of his trip as 'visiting friends'), but the effort seemed to overwhelm him and he spent the rest of the day 'on the sofa with his duffel coat over him'.

What was on his mind at such times is unknowable, but creative block was a constant preoccupation, and he continued to seek ways around it. On Monday, 4 March, he made several abortive attempts to drive off, eventually disappearing into the snowy darkness just as Molly brought in dinner. His destination was Flat 39, 5 Elm Park Gardens, Chelsea – Sophia Ryde's address.

She remembers the encounter vividly:

> He turned up and, as usual, we were sitting in silence on sofas opposite each other, with the coffee table between us. Suddenly he asked me to marry him. He said it in an apologetic way but had clearly worked out what he wanted to say. I think he imagined us living in a country cottage or something . . .

Nick had known Sophia for over six years, but not especially well, and if he'd been harbouring feelings for her, he'd kept them carefully concealed. He had certainly never made any sexual advance. 'I was never remotely aware of him being keen on Sophia,' says Alex Henderson, who had long since split up with her but remained in touch with them both, and Brian Wells – the friend with whom Nick was most often in contact at this time – was 'unaware of Sophia Ryde's existence'.

Nick had taken to dropping in on her unannounced, but she was far from unique in that, and if she had inspired any of his songs, she was unaware. Possibly relevant are some perplexing but evocative lines that he wrote on the back of an envelope around this time – 'I have a giant love / That grows like a mountain bear / Who scrapes the bark from the edge of the trees / And hugs my past to death' – but it's impossible to assess whether he was in love with her or had simply seized upon marriage as another possible route out of his rut.

Either way, he was in no position to proceed, and appears not to have discussed the notion with anyone. 'I was so surprised that all I could say was "I'll think about it", which in hindsight was stupid and insensitive,' says Sophia.

Molly heard Nick coming in at 2.15 a.m. and the next day, wrote Rodney, he 'seemed very low'. Bruised by Sophia's equivocation, that morning he wrote her a tart note: 'Dear Sophia, I'm really sorry to have taken up so much of your time, thinking there might be something in it. But I was wrong. You're really SO FAR BEHIND ME. Lots of love, Nick.'

Deciding it was intemperate, he set it aside and wrote another, asking her to come and stay the weekend after next.* After posting it he 'seemed relaxed and much more expressive than usual', though he also struck his parents as unusually restless.

That Friday afternoon Molly and Rodney drove to the Solihull cinema, to watch *The Hireling*. Nick accompanied them, but as soon as they'd found their seats he got up and left. Arriving home after the film, they found he'd walked all eight miles back, through the cold and darkness. He had perhaps used the time to think: over the weekend, to his parents' delight, he spoke about himself for the first time in months.

'Said he'd been "on the hook" so long and couldn't get off,' Rodney recorded:

> His plans were always being exploded – his own fault. Said he had his life planned up to when he was old . . . Thought he was coming through his difficulties (2 years up in 3 months)† – pressures of his recording life, trying to get his two lives together. Now was the 'crunch' – wanted to go on with music, thought his contacts still intact, and much more.

He continued on Monday, saying that 'his girl friend [*sic*] had said she was coming this weekend':

> We tried to talk him out of a delusion he seems to have built up that we are trying to get him back to being a 'straight-up-and-downer'. Said he was all set to enjoy himself, and (as usual) various other non-sequiturs and rather incomprehensible remarks – but the GREAT thing was that he talked. Feel the talk did him a lot of good.

Reflecting his apparently positive attitude, he had resumed taking his pills, though he still refused to see Dr Pollitt. It fell to Rodney to control the complicated rationing of Stelazine, Disipal and Tryptizol. They were easily distinguishable, so Nick kept them in

---

* In early January 1975 Molly found the sealed, unaddressed envelope containing Nick's original letter, and sent it to Sophia. Sophia had already discarded his second letter.
† For some reason, this would date his 'troubles' to June 1972.

one bottle. He knew that Tryptizol was powerful and had soporific effects, but whether he was taking the others responsibly was another question.

On Wednesday he was again 'in discursive mood – seemed relaxed', going so far as to tell his startled parents that 'all his difficulties were resolved'. When he visited Robert Kirby in London, by Robert's own account, 'He was the happiest I'd ever seen him.'[10] On Thursday, 14 March, however, he received a letter from Sophia, explaining that she had decided not to come to Far Leys for the weekend, and effectively declining his proposal. 'I should have just said "No" straight away,' she reflects.

Upon reading it he drove off, returning later with a smashed windscreen. He then drove Molly's car to London, but if he was planning to visit Sophia, he thought better of it and returned that night. 'Something has evidently gone wrong,' Rodney surmised. He and Molly attributed the downturn in his mood to apprehension about their impending trip to Canada, to wind up Pam's affairs. Just before their departure on 25 March Nick surprised them by arranging to part-exchange his clapped-out Austin 1300 for a more dynamic 1969 Sunbeam Rapier. Rodney considered the deal 'rackety' (it had 64,000 miles on the clock) but was pleased Nick had managed all the arrangements.

He drove them to Heathrow on Monday, 25 March, and waved them off. They had resolved not to contact him in their absence, and upon their return twelve days later they were dismayed to find that he had stopped taking his pills and was hostile, uncommunicative and sleeping badly. He still hoped to visit Joe in America, he said, but at a time when it took over a week of false starts to renew his car registration, the prospect of making a new album seemed more distant than ever.

As if to symbolise the fact, when Rodney lit a bonfire on Tuesday, 16 April, 'I found to my surprise that yesterday evening Nick had taken his two old broken guitars and thrown them on the heap ready for burning. Duly cremated them. Nick came out just before but said nothing.' Instead, he stood in silence, watching his mangled instruments turn to smoke and ashes.

30

Struggling Musically

—◦—

NICK'S PARENTS COULD only look on helplessly as he haphazardly self-medicated. No sooner did his pills take positive effect
than he abandoned them, as if expecting the benefit to endure. On
6 May he rounded on Rodney, unjustly accusing him of having 'left
him with nowhere to go to, having rung up all his friends and
interfered with his life and much more'. To the suggestion that he
contact Leon Redler again, 'He said he didn't want to talk to anyone,
and certainly had no wish to go to London.'

The very next day, however, he did just that. His plan was to
see his schoolfriend Simon Crocker for the first time since 1969.
'Sometime towards the start of 1974 I met Robert Kirby,' explains
Simon, who was managing the singer-songwriters Pete Atkin and
Juliet Lawson. 'He told me that Nick wasn't in good shape, so I left
a note for him at Island.' They forwarded it, and – to his surprise
– Nick rang him. 'I don't know why, honestly. Perhaps I represented
something solid to him, from happier days. We arranged to meet at
Juliet's parents' house at 20 Chelsea Square.'

Upon his arrival, says Simon,

> It was distressing to see him so changed. He wasn't dirty but he was
> dishevelled, and he never took his coat off. I thought he was stoned
> but realised it was more like he was on medication. Juliet made him
> a cup of tea and we sat in the huge, empty ballroom where she
> worked. He was monosyllabic and almost incoherent, but told us
> things hadn't been going well.
>
> There was an ironing board in the middle of the room, and he
> kept flicking the iron's on/off switch, which was distracting. We
> asked if he wanted to play something on Juliet's guitar or the piano,

but he declined. It occurred to me that perhaps I could get him performing again, so I asked if there was anything I could do to help, but he said there wasn't. He gave the impression of being lost and I felt terribly sad after he left.

Nick remained conflicted over a return to music and racked by the challenge songwriting had become, but interest in his work continued to ripple. *Ciao 2001*, Italy's leading rock magazine, had just run a feature that indicated his legend was well underway.[1] 'Nick Drake is among the most stimulating British singer-songwriters of the last generation, but his name is neglected even in England,' lamented Enzo Caffarelli, concluding: 'Maybe he's a pioneer, a maestro, and no one has yet noticed – including him.'

Nick almost certainly didn't see the article, but at the end of May he told his father that 'he could not adapt himself to anything but his music, which he was really scared to return to'. Still, with Joe Boyd's encouragement, he agreed to a session at Sound Techniques a few weeks ahead. Joe was no longer formally his manager, but was happy to facilitate anything Nick aspired to.

Having a date in the diary invigorated him, and in early June he assured his parents that he was taking his pills 'religiously' and was 'really all right now'. He was heard humming, spoke of taking up the violin, helped prepare his parents' balloon stall for the village fête (though he declined to attend) and even acted as host at a dinner party when Rodney was bedridden with back pain.

Characteristically overestimating his fitness, he announced his intention to move back to London after his twenty-sixth birthday, on 19 June. The reality of finding a billet there, however, coupled with a card from Sophia ('This comes with much love for a very happy birthday,' she wrote), threw him; after breakfast he retreated, and the afternoon 'found him sitting disconsolate in music room'.

When John Wood rang a few days later to confirm his booking at Sound Techniques, he was again forced to confront the fact that he had barely anything new to present, and predicted, as Rodney sadly noted, that 'he would just have to go on living here until we died'.

At this time of raw self-doubt it was serendipitous that he was featured in the highly regarded British music magazine *ZigZag*,[2] a copy of which he bought on Wednesday, 26 June. Connor McKnight's lengthy piece called *Five Leaves Left* 'one of the best first albums ever made', praised the 'literally fantastic empathy' between Nick and Robert Kirby, described *Bryter Layter* as 'altogether brilliant' and 'near-perfect', hailed the 'searing sensibility' of *Pink Moon*, and concluded that Nick's oeuvre was 'the complete affirmation of what music is about'.

Connor's praise was tempered with candid references to Nick's continued musical silence and 'depressed' and 'insecure' personality, and he stated that Island 'didn't know where Nick Drake was, what he was doing or what he intended to do'.

There were warm, if double-edged, comments from Richard Thompson ('he is extremely talented, and if he wanted to be he could be very successful') and Joe (asserting his constant willingness to 'work with Nick if he wants'), but one voice was conspicuously absent. 'Connor tried to get in touch with Nick but it was impossible to pin him down to do anything,' recalls *ZigZag*'s editor, Andy Childs.

Rodney was still laid up with back trouble, so Nick wordlessly deposited the magazine on his bed. 'Most interesting and impressive,' he wrote in his diary. 'It seems clear that the article has given him a boost.' Molly subsequently emphasised that 'He didn't say much, but I knew it meant a terrific lot to Nick that he wasn't forgotten, although he'd disappeared from the world for three years.'[3]

Connor conjectured that Nick 'seems to have retired into a world in which music doesn't exist as a form of expression anymore'. As if to disprove him, late in the afternoon of Sunday, 30 June, Nick set off for London with his Martin 000-28, saying nothing to his parents.

He had arranged to stay with Joe, and on Monday evening they met John at Sound Techniques. John had declined to charge for studio time. 'That way we could get an idea of where things stood before setting other wheels in motion,' explains Joe. 'We both knew he was very fragile.'

It was an intense moment for Nick – a scenario he had both aspired to and dreaded for over two years. Joe emphasises that embarking on a new album was not the object of the exercise: 'We had no plan. The results might have been demos or masters, we were just going to see what emerged.'

'We were treading on eggshells,' adds John. 'Nick was very withdrawn, even more so than when we made *Pink Moon*. He barely said anything or responded to anything.'

They began by listening to the four unnamed guitar tracks he had recorded in February 1973, which he had since titled 'Rider On The Wheel', 'Hanging On A Star', 'Black-Eyed Dog' and 'Tow The Line'.* He now had lyrics and wanted to re-record them with vocals, along with another song named 'Voices'. When John had arranged the microphones, he and Joe went up to the control room, leaving Nick alone on the studio floor. He sat down and, at John's signal, began to perform.

'He stumbled trying to play and sing at the same time,' says Joe. 'John and I exchanged anguished looks, and we decided to record the guitar first, then overdub the vocals.'[4] The guitar tracks were accordingly recorded on Monday, before they reconvened on Tuesday night to record the vocals. For John,

> It was a sad experience because you could see he was struggling musically – he wasn't happy with what he was doing, or in command of his material as he always had been before. I mean, on *Pink Moon* he knew exactly what he wanted and was satisfied with the result. These sessions weren't like that.

'Voices' seems to concern the conflicting advice he was receiving, and indeed giving himself: 'Where can it end, it end?' he asks. 'Rider On The Wheel' is addressed to an outside agent that spins 'round and round' – the Earth? The wheel of fortune? Karma? A roulette rack? It implies resignation to fate but, as with so many of Nick's lyrics, resists any single interpretation.

'Black-Eyed Dog', by contrast, feels unambiguous; it's a horrifying personification of the illness that had bedevilled him for so long, wouldn't leave him alone and was wearing him out. 'I vividly recall

---

* Nick perhaps intended the title to be 'Toe The Line'; his spelling had never been perfect.

471

watching and listening to those chilling words coming out of his mouth,' says Joe. 'When John and I heard them, we were just crushed.' Its guitar part – built on harmonics rather than strumming or plucking – is equally eerie and unsettling.

Nick refers to his identity in all three songs ('I know my name' in 'Voices', 'You know my name' in 'Rider On The Wheel', and 'He knew my name' in 'Black-Eyed Dog'), as if assuring himself of it. 'Hanging On A Star' also touches on his status, rebuking those who had led him to believe that he was assured of fame, fortune and renown, only to abandon him.

That was certainly Joe's reading, not least after their discussion in January.

> I've always assumed it was directed at me, and everyone else who told him he 'couldn't miss' being successful, even to the critics and the audiences who cheered him, as at the Royal Festival Hall, but didn't buy his records. But I'm probably top of that list.

Nick's high vocal makes his rhetorical questions all the more powerful, and his raw and soulful guitar part – strikingly different to the 1973 recording – shows him still to be a master of the instrument.

Set to a familiar descending guitar pattern, the words to 'Tow The Line' also appear to be directed at Joe, but in a more conciliatory spirit: 'And now that you're here you can show me the way / And now that you're here we can try make it pay / And while you were gone it was hard, it was cold . . .' Joe, however, did not hear it at the time. John surmises that Nick returned to tape it with him alone, shortly after the other four tracks, perhaps because he had not yet finalised the words. Either way, John quickly forgot about it, and it was not considered part of the session thereafter.

All the songs contain clear echoes of Nick's past work, but – good as they are – they offer little in the way of innovation beyond the harmonics of 'Black-Eyed Dog' and the relative directness of certain lyrics. 'They don't have the lyrical and musical depth of his previous work,' contends John:

> They lack the immediacy and feeling he projected on *Pink Moon* and aren't as convincing. The overall quality is lower, other than

maybe 'Black-Eyed Dog', which just doesn't sound like a Nick song to me, maybe because it's more directly personal. I wasn't taken with it, whether because of the structure or lyrics I don't know.

Nick gave no indication as to whether he wanted to have the tracks arranged, though Robert (whom he hadn't seen since March) was under the impression that their collaboration would eventually continue. 'I never got that far in my mind,' says Joe. 'I was far more concerned with what would happen to Nick as a person.'

Joe arranged to play the four recordings he had overseen to Island later that week, but felt they were 'pretty devastating – I had little confidence that he could come up with enough tracks for an LP.' Nick surely knew that he couldn't; only 'Voices' was – possibly – under eighteen months old.

He returned to Far Leys on Wednesday evening and did not mention what he'd been doing, instead telling his parents yet again that he was 'unable to reconcile his two worlds' – a notion that was bound to surface whenever he sought to resurrect his career. He seemed dejected on Thursday, but drove back to London to accompany Joe to a meeting at Island in Hammersmith.

Upon arrival he couldn't face going in, so, according to *Melody Maker*'s facetious gossip column:

> Boyd entered the hallowed halls and walked into the office of David Betteridge, the managing director, to whom he promptly announced the return of Nick Drake . . . Mr Drake, whose last album on Island was released at least two years ago, has not been seen by any member of the label in that period.
>
> Boyd said that Drake was now ready to do another album, so he and Betteridge sat down for an hour to discuss the deal. In all that time the taxi was waiting outside, and in the back seat – Nick Drake. And when the taxi drove away, the staff at Island had still to see the man they call the Elusive Pimpernel.[5]

The reason for the meeting was to discuss the status of Nick's previous recordings, not least because no contract existed to cover *Pink Moon*, and to discuss the possibility of Nick receiving an advance. No deal was done, but Joe left behind a copy of the four new recordings he was aware of, which Richard Williams played on the office Revox. He remembers being especially struck by 'Black-Eyed Dog'.

David Betteridge cautiously mentioned the new recordings at Island's next sales meeting. 'I remember very well how excited we all were that Nick was recording again,' says Neil Storey, a sales rep. 'We were all massive fans, so this was serious news! There was a feeling of joy throughout the company.'

Nonetheless, if Nick had made a fourth album it is not easy to see where it would have fitted into the mid-seventies music scene. The commercial heyday of singer-songwriting was passing, and established stars of the genre such as Cat Stevens and Donovan had sharply changed gear of late, while John Martyn's most recent record, *Inside Out*, was easily his most experimental. Still, Richard maintains: 'I would have been delighted to commission a new album by Nick. Had we proceeded I don't think the sound of the songs would have been a problem – we always had room for esoteric artists.'

Pepped up by Joe, Nick seemed more optimistic at home that night, telling his parents that 'he was starting on another record, that he thought he was going to be able to work for Island again, and that there was a chance of staying in the flat of Joe Boyd (who was shortly going away)'.

Rodney and Molly remained dubious about Nick's ability to live in London. He departed on Saturday, but after dropping him at the station Molly waited a little in the car. He came back out twice before finally buying his ticket. That night he went to a rock concert* but walked out early and took a train to Birmingham and a taxi home.

Morose, hostile and confrontational over the next few days, he took out on his parents his frustration at his unreadiness to live independently, his inability to generate new material and his dissatisfaction with his recent recordings.

Molly recalled:

He said they should have been a lot better and that they were substandard, and I said, 'Well, Nick, do they think they're substandard

---

* It is not known whose, nor with whom (if anyone) Nick went.

at Island?' and he said, 'No, they think they're all right.' I said, 'Well, what the hell, then? What does it matter?' Well, they didn't suit him, he had got to have everything absolutely exactly right.[6]

Joe was back in America for a few weeks, so there were no further sessions booked, and as July progressed and no new songs came, his musical activity petered out. Joe had persuaded him against visiting Los Angeles, convinced it would be a poor environment for him. One day John Martyn rang and afterwards Nick mentioned that he was 'hoping to form a supergroup' with him and Bev, but the idea went nowhere – and nor did he, despite talk of a European package holiday or even travelling to India with Brian and Marion.

Instead, he passed the long summer days sunbathing on a chaise-longue, feeding sugarlumps to the horses in the neighbouring field, or sitting at the wheel of his car before 'returning disconsolately to the music room'. He continued to drink whisky in unpredictable quantities and at odd hours. 'Tried to impress upon him the dangerous consequences of solitary drinking of this nature,' wrote Rodney. Not the least of these was combining it with such pills as he was taking – but he gave no indication of having even heard.

Given their scant communication, his parents were delighted when Nick agreed to come to lunch at the Trout Inn in Lechlade on Wednesday, 7 August. There they met his cousin Virginia, his aunt Gwladys and her husband Jackie.

The next day Gwladys wrote to Molly and Rodney to describe 'the really fantastic improvement' she had observed 'in our poor old Nick's condition' during their long conversation. The letter emphasises what a collaborative effort his welfare was, and what a loving and concerned family he belonged to:

I do really feel he has broken through AT LAST. He tore my heart (a condition to which yours have been subjected all these last years, I know well, my darlings) all the time he was talking to me, as he was trembling and I could see the enormous effort he was making, and it's obvious there's still a long way to go. BUT all he said was strong and thoughtful and responsible and made a deep impression on me, for I felt that for the first time in I simply forget how long I was through to him.

I started by asking him about the songs he's already done, and about the remaining six or so that are needed to make up a new long-playing record. I asked him if working on these brought him satisfaction or even pleasure; his answer was no, not at present – he found it the most terrible effort, but thought the satisfaction or pleasure would return, and that he was absolutely determined to press on and get himself back.

He then said (heart-rendingly) 'It's the only thing I know I can do well.' I rejoined, 'And how,' or words to that effect, and went on to rub in how, in spite of him having been out of things for so long, he hadn't been forgotten, as proved by the *ZigZag* article. I got the impression that the article had really been the starting-point of his beginning to surface from the slough of despond.

I was afraid Joe Boyd might be pressing him for the next batch of songs, but he assured me strongly that this wasn't so, that he's very understanding and is ready to wait. He then spoke of having 'so much to fill in' . . . He finished up by saying that he is worried about not making any money, to which I replied that I was pretty sure this was the very *last* thing that either of you cared about, and that all you wanted, and ever had wanted, was his happiness, first and foremost. And so our talk finished.

He declined to accompany his parents to stay with his aunt Nancy and uncle Chris for the weekend. Instead he drove to London and appeared on David Ward's doorstep in Carlyle Square on Sunday morning. 'I was going to a hippie-ish but down-to-earth spiritual gathering with some friends in Harston, just outside Cambridge, so I suggested Nick came along,' says David.

Nick enjoyed the meeting but was sceptical about their teetotal hosts' ideology,[7] craftily revealing a bottle of whisky in his pocket when they got back to the car. 'We roared with laughter,' says David. 'On the journey back to London he was the old Nick for an hour and a half.'

Nick perhaps felt he could speak more freely to an old friend than to an aunt. David remembers him expressing 'specific frustration about two people':

Joe Boyd, because he hadn't been more successful, and his father, from whom he felt an undercurrent of pressure to do something else

476

with his life, or commit to a course. He hated the feeling that he'd let his parents down. On our return – it would have been at about 6.30 p.m., and still sunny outside – I'm not sure Nick even came back into the house. I just remember cursorily watching him rambling off down the pavement.

David hoped the conversation had been therapeutic for Nick, but – as ever – articulating his problems confronted him with their harsh reality. After two 'tired and subdued' days during which he seemed 'unable to get cigarettes for himself although he is craving them', Rodney and Molly returned from dinner with friends to find evidence of 'a real smash-up – electric guitar apparently smashed down onto piano, breaking music holder, vase and Perspex cover of tape recorder'. He had also damaged the tape recorder itself, further sabotaging his efforts to write.

Attempts to discuss the incident with him the following day were fruitless: instead, he 'settled down in the music room to take the electrical section of the guitar he'd broken completely to pieces, cutting all the wiring'. This left him with only his Martin.

He had yet again stopped taking his pills. Gabrielle did her best to get him to resume, and to open up, but it wasn't until the end of the month that he felt ready to express himself. In obvious distress one evening, he told Rodney that he had reached 'the end of the line'. The next morning he elaborated on this to Molly in the drawing room.

'He had always longed to get through to young people, particularly young people who had difficulties in life like he did, and he just thought he hadn't,' she recalled.[8]

> He just felt that he had totally failed. I remember him striding up and down saying, 'I've failed in every single thing I've ever tried to do.' It was the most terrible, heart-rending cry, and I said, 'Oh Nick, you haven't! You know you haven't!' But it wasn't any good – he had the feeling that he was a failure, that he hadn't managed to achieve what he'd set out to do.

He then drove off, intending to visit the Woods in Suffolk, but only got as far as Cambridge, which he wandered around for the first time since leaving almost five years earlier. Back home he was silent and surly, and his parents could only urge him to resume his medication. By the evening of 7 September he was 'clutching his head and exclaiming loud and long about the condition he was in', as Rodney noted: 'Couldn't go on living like this. All very distressing . . . Said he would go to Pollitt – told me he would go to hospital if he could go now.'

By the morning he was calmer and sought out his father on the terrace, telling him that he couldn't now envisage Island wanting to maintain a relationship with him, but had 'decided he must either go ahead with his musical career or chuck it all'. Indeed, over the following week he perked up and began to play his guitar again. He was perhaps buoyed by having been placed second (to Kevin Ayers, but just ahead of one of his favourites, Tim Buckley) in the 'neglect' section of *ZigZag*'s readers' poll, in September's issue.

Inspiration remained elusive, so he formulated a new album on paper, as if that exercise might provide the required alchemy. His handwritten list contained ten titles, divided into two sides. The first five have ticks next to them, because he had already demoed them at Sound Techniques; the second five – 'Saw You On A Starship', 'Old Fairytale', 'Even Now', 'On This Day' and 'Long Way To Town' – survive only as lyrics, though instrumental fragments on tapes made at Far Leys might belong to them. As Rodney later explained: 'It was not his practice (as far as we know) to write lyrics without music.'[9]

On Sunday, 15 September, he borrowed Rodney's typewriter and typed out the words to all ten – his usual practice when preparing to submit songs to his publisher. Their language was simple yet impenetrable, its unorthodox syntax familiar from *Pink Moon*.

'Saw You On A Starship' runs in part: 'Saw you with the dragon between your knees / Said, Hey you, won't you help me please / You can travel, I can travel too / We can travel, travel two by two' (this last line echoing 'Parasite'). 'Old Fairytale', meanwhile, declares: 'The days go by, you're looking for a theme / The night come down, you go to bed to dream / While the people there they change from blue to green / It's an old fairytale'.

In addition to the unrecorded songs on the draft running order,

Voices ~
Black-eyed dog ~
Rider on the wheel ~
Hanging on a star ~
Toe the line. ~

Saw you on a starship
Old fairytale.
Even now
On this day
Long way to town.

Draft running order for Nick's fourth album, September 1974.

he typed out lyrics to two more, 'Paid Brain' and 'Sing A Song'. The former evokes his dread at becoming a wage-slave ('Well they's paying him in gold / And they's paying him in smiles / And they's payin' for his brain / And they's payin' for his wiles'), while the latter is an uncharacteristically direct love song: 'You are my treasure trove / You are my stars above / Hold on tight, let me prove / I am yours from now on'.

When he'd finished he withdrew into silence, no longer able to fool himself about the progress of the putative album. Late that night Rodney found him in the drawing room, 'sitting with head bowed': 'He did not indicate by any movement or gesture that he was even aware of my presence.'

For the next few days most of Nick's time was spent 'incarcerated' (as Rodney put it) in the music room, reading Galsworthy or T. E. Lawrence's *Seven Pillars of Wisdom*. His musical activity was limited to 'a series of strident chords repeated ad lib on the piano for about five minutes'.

Although new music was eluding Nick, his records continued to find devotees. That month David Belbin, a fifteen-year-old schoolboy in Burnley, was in a local junk shop:

I found a white-label compilation for 50p, and fell in love with two of the tracks on it.* Their lyrics were enigmatic, brooding, and seemed to speak of some secret wisdom. Who was singing? I had no idea, but I was a convert. Eventually, with the help of an Island catalogue, I discovered the singer was Nick Drake and the tracks were from *Pink Moon*. I tried to find out anything I could about him, but there was no information out there. Soon afterwards there was a school trip to London. I immediately hit the record shops and asked for Nick Drake in each. In one the guy said, 'Afraid not, but I admire your taste.' I finally found *Bryter Layter* in Dobell's (at full price). I took it home and loved it.[10]

Having been at Far Leys every night since early July, on Monday, 23 September, Nick visited the Martyns for the first time in over a

---

* This was the promo sampler Island had given to sales reps and sent to radio stations in February 1974.

year. John was there and dominated the visit. Restlessly energetic, brilliant new material came to him easily and he couldn't understand how Nick could be so passive and ponderous. He teased him as 'Nick Drag' and tried to force him out of himself.

'He'd started getting fed up with Nick being this precious commodity,' explains Bev.

> He felt he had to be 'honest' with him and told him that he had to get on with life, that you can't be withdrawn if you want to be a musician or an actor or any sort of performer. He asked him what he ever expected to happen if he had that attitude.

'John was into deep-sea fishing at the time and he used to go out with the trawlermen overnight,' according to David Sandison of Island.[11] 'He tried to persuade Nick to go, but Nick wasn't going to have any of that.' Instead they went to the nearby Lord Nelson pub, a fishermen's haunt, while Bev – who was pregnant and tired – stayed at home. After a few drinks John informed Nick that if he wanted to 'fuck' Bev, that was fine by him.* Nick was shocked and walked out. Bev sensed a 'bad mood' when they returned:

> John went into the kitchen and started cooking, and I heard Nick say, 'I always trusted you, John, but now I see you're really devious.' Then he asked me if I thought John was 'devious'. I couldn't answer the question, certainly not in front of John.
>
> I had never seen Nick like this before. He was always such a romantic, gentle man, and here he was being angry and confrontational with me. It was as if he had seen something in John he had not known was there, and was challenging me to look closely at the man I had married . . . Then he asked me, 'What do you think of me?' Before I had time to answer, John shouted from the kitchen: 'She fucking loves you, man! She's always worried about you.' By now I'd had enough. The pregnancy was making me feel sick to my stomach and I couldn't handle whatever was going on, so I made my excuses and went to bed.

---

* Arthur Lubow: 'John refused to talk to me for my *New Times* piece in 1978 and forbade Bev to do so. Years later she told me the cause of [John and Nick's] quarrel was simpler and cruder than I'd imagined.'

Nick was still upset in the morning: 'I made him marmalade on toast and a cup of tea,' said Bev. 'He was sullen and didn't want to speak. When he got up to go, I went to hug him but he pushed me away.'[12]

Back at Far Leys he barely spoke and played no guitar, and when his cousins visited for the weekend he studiously hid from them. Despondent, after their departure Molly drafted a letter to a Mr Edwards:[*]

> Your name and address have been given to me by a friend. I hope so much therefore that you will not mind my writing to you to tell you a little of the story of the sad problem of our son Nick.
>
> He is twenty-six years old and had a severe nervous breakdown in April 1972. At least, that was when matters came to a head, although we suspect that things had begun to go wrong for him two or three years before this (when he left Cambridge in 1969), as he had become increasingly withdrawn and unapproachable. When the breakdown happened he spent five weeks in hospital, but discharged himself as he hated it so.
>
> Since then he has been living at home with us. He has seen two psychiatrists but paid scant attention to their recommendations and seems to have no belief in them. One of his troubles is, I think, that he has no faith or trust in anyone or anything, which makes things harder for him than they might otherwise be.
>
> He is artistic and creative and has a very strong musical talent, particularly in the field of 'folk music'. He has brought out three long-playing records and the company for whom he records evidently thinks highly of his work, as they have said they will publish anything he likes to produce. He has started on a fourth record but seems to have lost the courage and the drive to proceed with it.
>
> In fact, he has really lost the courage and confidence to do anything at all. He will not consider any other form of work, nor can he make himself help us in the house or garden, and indeed sometimes finds it impossible even to go to a shop to buy small things like shaving cream or to go to the garage to get petrol for his car.

---

[*] Gabrielle cannot identify him.

He seems to have a terrible fear of people and to be unable to meet or communicate with them any longer. This last weekend his young cousins came to stay, and Nick could not make himself face them and stayed in his room the whole time. I don't think this was because he didn't *want* to see them, but he just couldn't find the courage to confront them, even though they love him and are very sympathetic and understanding.

My husband and I at times feel near to despair because, being the two people in all the world who most want to help him, we seem to be the least able to do so. He cannot speak to us and seems hardly to be able to bear to be in the same room with us.

I pray every day for him, and also for ourselves, that we may be given the wisdom to help him, for so often whatever we do or say seems to turn out to be wrong. I'm afraid this is a very long letter and I do hope you will forgive me. But if there is anything you could do to help our son – or anything that you could suggest whereby we may help him ourselves – we would both be so deeply grateful.

31

Watching The Water Going By

—◆—

A S IF IN answer to her prayers, that very afternoon – Monday, 30 September – Guy Norton visited Far Leys. He hadn't seen Nick since they'd formed a friendly bond over maths tuition at Easter 1963. Now thirty-four, he had been living abroad for years and had just moved back to London with his wife, Noel. They were visiting his widowed mother Mildred at the family home – Carpenters Hill, three miles from Far Leys – so he arranged to pop over for a game of croquet with Rodney, whom he had always looked up to.

Rodney asked Nick to join them, but he declined. Guy was dismayed to learn of his condition. His own personality was almost comically different – jolly, energetic, pragmatic – and he immediately offered to talk to him. Rodney demurred, for fear of seeming to pressurise him, but Guy was determined to help.

'I rang the next afternoon and asked to speak to him,' he relates. 'My immediate objective was literally to get him out of his bedroom, nothing more than that. Rodney was amazed that he even came to the phone.' He was even more amazed when Nick agreed to join Guy for a drink in a local pub.

Guy had no interest in pop and was more or less unaware of Nick's music. He simply wanted to help a family friend. His manner was light and gregarious, but he also possessed a sensitivity that the similarly dynamic John Martyn lacked. Expecting the worst, he was pleasantly surprised:

> When someone's been withdrawn for as long as him, you don't expect a ball of fire, but I wouldn't have thought he was at all unwell from his appearance or manner. I was pretty amazed by how long his hair was, but he wasn't unkempt and he was immaculately behaved.

We had a gin and tonic and chatted away. There were no long silences. I was anxious to keep things superficial and friendly, and not be seen to delve. He told me that he regretted leaving Cambridge and had no idea why he had. I told him that people can't always explain their actions and shouldn't feel they have to. He seemed pleased by that.

They stayed for dinner, and Guy dropped him home at 9.45. His impression was that rather than being mentally ill, Nick was still struggling to reconcile himself to the demands of adulthood: 'Nick certainly wasn't spoilt, but his childhood had no rough at all, only smooth, and I think he had been insulated from a lot of things. Cumulatively I don't think he'd had sufficient preparation to cope in the wider world.'

'We had no chance to find out or try to assess how his evening had gone,' wrote Rodney, but the next day Guy sent them a letter, aware that if he telephoned Nick might overhear and feel betrayed. 'Nicky [sic] talked a great deal,' he wrote. 'I don't think that there is anything "wrong" with him at all. In fact, I am sure there isn't. It's just that he thinks and feels things deeper than most people.' The upshot was:

I think I can help him. This sounds terribly arrogant, but I do think that I have a tremendous advantage: I am not a psychiatrist and therefore do not start from his resentment . . . Please do not mention this letter. I want it to be a casual relationship in which I ring him up and ask him for a drink.

Long and bitter experience kept Rodney and Molly from sharing his conviction that Nick had nothing wrong with him, but they were glad when he arranged to take him out again later in the week. The prospect buoyed Nick ('rather less clam-like', wrote Rodney), and he had a haircut in Birmingham and dressed smartly for the evening.

'Over dinner,' says Guy,

I told him that Noel and I were going to Paris for a few days that weekend, and asked if he'd like to come with us. When someone's in Nick's predicament, you need to strike while the iron's hot and keep the momentum up, so I would have asked him to join in whatever we were planning.

The timing was neat: Nick badly needed a change of scene and had always liked Paris. To his parents' amazement, he agreed to go. The prospect daunted him, though. Friday found him in agonies of indecision, and even as he awaited his train to London he was torn between taking his old anorak or newer duffel coat, both of which he thought were dirty. (He finally opted for the former.) Despite a panicky phone call home from Coventry station, he completed the journey.

'He stayed the night in our little doll's house at 44 Bourne Street,' remembers Guy, 'and the next morning we drove to Dover in my Fiat 126 to catch the car ferry. I was driving, with Noel in the passenger seat and Nick and his guitar and sports bag squashed in the back.'

Their hosts were Guy's great friends Alan and Sue Holt,* who lived on a large, comfortable 1920s houseboat called *Myosotis* ('forget-me-not'), moored at the Place de la Concorde. 'I had introduced them to each other,' Guy continues. 'Alan was much older than Sue and had four kids from a previous marriage. He was a practical joker, light-hearted and friendly. They weren't bohemians, but there was a relaxed, welcoming atmosphere on board.' As you entered there was a large living room to the left, while a series of bedrooms led off a passage to the right. Nick had one, with its own bathroom.

Guy had telephoned ahead to tell the Holts that he was bringing a friend who was a musician, but he made no mention of Nick's current situation, not least because he 'didn't feel that there *was* anything to prepare them for, as he'd been perfectly behaved in all the time I'd spent with him'.

'Nick slotted in very easily,' he remembers, and the atmosphere was 'light-hearted and friendly. Nick was with us all the time and they both liked him very much.' They would go for a stroll or have dinner in a restaurant, 'and there was always work to do on the boat, so Nick helped with that'. After three nights, he says, 'Alan

---

* Sue had in fact visited Far Leys with Guy in the 1960s, and Molly had, by coincidence, known her father in Burma. Alan died in 2016.

sidled up to me on the wheelhouse and said, "Nick's a bit of a lost soul, isn't he?" He was a sensitive person, so I told him some of the background.' The Holts often had lodgers to stay, earning their keep by helping to maintain the boat, so over dinner Alan asked Nick if he'd like to stay on when Guy and Noel left in the morning. 'He readily accepted,' says Guy.

As Sue remembers it, Nick said he wanted to increase his knowledge of Paris, and had a specific project in mind: 'He was apparently writing an album for Françoise Hardy, whom he admired very much.' Nick, it seems, had fallen back on that stale notion.

Guy and Noel departed on Wednesday, 9 October. 'I would never have left him there if I'd thought he was mentally ill,' reflects Guy, but Sue saw an immediate change: 'Guy's enthusiasm had kept Nick on top of the world, but the moment he left Nick changed. His shyness became very evident [and he] became very introverted.'

She and Alan left for work at eight the following morning.

> We left him alone on the boat, drinking coffee and smoking. He was responsible for looking after himself – there was hot water, a washing machine and a drier, and we always had a full fridge, so I told him to help himself to lunch. When we got back that evening, he was in exactly the same position.

Rodney and Molly were hugely encouraged by an exuberant phone call from Guy that same evening, but in truth, as Gabrielle puts it, 'Without the dynamo of Guy's presence, Nick's battery was running out of charge.'[1] He hadn't taken medicine with him and his sedentary first day established a pattern. 'We quickly realised he was going through a very serious depression,' says Sue.

> We were moored right in the centre of things, a few minutes' walk from the Eiffel Tower, the Champs-Élysées, the Opéra and so on, but he didn't take advantage of it. The only variation was when he very occasionally told us he'd gone out. He seemed to be in a better mood afterwards, but we didn't know what he'd been doing. His great desire and passion was to meet Françoise Hardy.

He did not, however, see her at this time.

On Tuesday, 15 October, the Holts travelled to London for a

week, leaving Nick on the boat with Alan's eighteen-year-old son Marc,* who 'apparently gets on very well with Nick', Rodney recorded via Guy, 'and they are going about together. It all sounds extremely good.' Guy relayed to Rodney that Nick was 'talking volubly' on the Holts' return – and in French. 'Excellent news,' wrote a relieved Rodney on Thursday, 24 October, by which time Nick had been there for nineteen days.

The reality was different. Talk of Françoise Hardy had ceased, and by now, says Sue, 'He literally spent the days watching the water going by.' Arriving home after extremely long working days, she and Alan 'simply didn't have the time to make him our focus or to entertain him. We'd have a bit of limited conversation over dinner, but that was that.'

Eventually they told Guy that Nick was doing little but sit around and occasionally roam the streets. Guy spoke to Nick on the boat's phone on Monday the 28th, suggesting it might be time to find a job. 'Nick agreed,' Guy reported to Rodney, 'and said he was looking into something in Paris this evening.' To Guy's counterproposal that he seek work in London, Nick 'said he didn't want to have anything to do with music', but acknowledged Guy's suggestion that he was perhaps 'being lazy'. 'We await events with great interest,' Rodney wrote.

It was beguiling to imagine that three weeks in Paris had solved Nick's problems, but – in Gabrielle's words – Guy 'might have been painting a rather rosier picture than the reality of what was actually happening'.[2] Of course, Molly and Rodney were shrewd and experienced enough to perceive this, wondering 'if Nick really would be able to carry it through or if it really meant he was running out of steam'.

A couple of days later, says Guy, 'Sue rang me in London and asked, "Do you have any idea how long Nick's planning to stay?" She wasn't trying to get rid of him, but he obviously couldn't stay forever. I spoke to him and suggested he come back.' Sue explains: 'He simply seemed pissed off towards life in general, and his depression had started getting *us* depressed. Eventually Alan – perhaps

---

* Marc died in May 2016.

rather brutally – said it would be better for him to return to England, which he did straight away.'

After an overnight stay with the ever-supportive Guy, Nick returned home by train on Thursday, 31 October. His plan was to pick up his car and a few possessions before returning to Paris the very next day, supposedly to pursue his vague plan of working there. His parents were delighted to find him 'more communicative' and 'more together' than in years, even organising his own car insurance, while Molly patched up 'all his old clothes. He wouldn't have anything new.'[3]

Seeing him off in his Rapier that afternoon, his parents were apprehensive about the practicalities ahead, but encouraged by his 'initiative', as well as Guy's confidence (in a quick phone call) 'that Nick will make it now in some way or another'.

After another night with Guy – who reported on his 'good form' – Nick crossed the Channel and motored back to Paris, where the Holts had found him a cheap hotel. 'It was absolutely wonderful,' said Molly. 'We felt as if a terrific weight had been taken off our shoulders – it was a marvellous feeling, to feel that he was happy.'[4]

He didn't call home, but this year he did remember his mother's birthday and sent her a French-language paperback of Albert Camus's 1942 essay *Le Mythe de Sisyphe*, a meditation on the meaning – or meaninglessness – of life. Molly was a student of the language and no stranger to existential thoughts, but the book's concern with suicide made for a puzzling choice of present. If the subject had been on Nick's mind and he was obliquely communicating the fact, or hoping to discuss it upon his return, he was to be frustrated: a French postal strike delayed its arrival for over two months.

The next his parents heard of him was on Wednesday, 6 November, when they came home to the perplexing news from Naw that he had rung to say he was back in the UK and on his way to visit the Woods. John was in America with Joe; it seems Nick simply wanted to talk to Sheila.

He sat up with her for much of the night, before strolling into Far Leys the following afternoon. Despite the uncertainty of his movements and plans, to Rodney he seemed 'very different and vastly improved', partly because of the relish with which he described his sojourn in Paris: 'He had evidently enjoyed his time on the boat very much. Said he tried to get a job but failed – though probably because he didn't really want one.' He also told his parents that he 'felt he was "nearly there" now and that he must keep going', and was 'veering towards going back to music'.

He disclosed similar plans to Guy: 'He said he wanted to start making a new album and needed a base in London.' Guy made him a standing offer to stay in Bourne Street. A few minutes' walk from Sloane Square, it was a familiar and congenial location, and he gave the clear impression of wanting to work: 'The new album was very much his focus, there was no vacillation about that. He was talking a lot about needing to see his manager. This person was clearly very important to him.'

'This person' was, of course, Joe, who had just written what Molly considered a 'rather businesslike' letter to Nick from New York, after failing to reach him on the telephone:

Dear Nick,

I'm sorry things didn't work out for me to be in London this Autumn. I know I got you started on thinking about doing some more recording and then didn't really follow it up. All I can say is that I still would really like to do another album with you, and I hope I will be back in London long enough this winter to get something done with you.

I know you want to get things straightened out with Island. I will be glad to help when I get back, but in the meantime Richard Williams is the man to speak to if you need anything. I'm sure they would be willing to give you an advance, but it must be under a proper contract. I told him that you wanted an accounting for the first three LPs, and he will be trying to get that brought up to date.

See you soon, Joe.

Further sessions would obviously not be happening that year, but the letter was still en route when Nick set off for London on Friday, 8 November, taking his guitar and newly repaired tape recorder with him, apparently in good shape.

'He looked fine, he was natural and relaxed, he was shaving and so on,' says Guy. 'It didn't bother us at all if he played his guitar in

joe boyd

24 ladbroke gdns london W.11 tel 727 5957

8430 santa monica blvd suite 100 hollywood california 90069 tel. 213 656 1544

November 6, 1974

Dear Nick,

I'm sorry things didn't work out for me to be in
London this Autumn. I know I got you started on thinking
about doing some more recording and then didn't really
follow it up. All I can say is that I still would really
like to do another album with you and I hope I will be
back in London long enough this winter to get something done
with you.

I know you want to get things straightened out with
Island. I will be glad to help when I get back, but in
the meantime Richard Williams is the man to speak to if
you need anything. I'm sure they would be willing to
give you an advance but it must be under a proper contract.
I told him that you wanted an accounting for the first three
LP's and he will be trying to get that brought up to date.

See you soon,

Joe

16 East 96th Street Apt. 4H New York New York 10028 till 12/31/74

Joe Boyd to Nick, 6 November 1974.

the house, we didn't much notice. I was just delighted that he'd found a safe haven and was back to his music and seemed busy and occupied.'

Guy's understanding was that Nick was going out to meet Joe every day, but that was impossible. Instead, he seems to have spent much of the time wandering around or calling on friends, including Bob and June Squire in Princedale Road. One day, 'looking pretty bad', he bumped into Rick Charkin, whom he hadn't seen since 1970, in South Kensington.

He returned to Far Leys on the afternoon of Monday, 11 November, because Guy and Noel's friend Janie Mackenzie was visiting from South Africa and needed his bed. 'There simply wasn't room for both Janie and Nick in Bourne Street,' explains Guy,

> but I think he took it as a rejection, which it wasn't at all. I was aware that he had latched onto us and was becoming dependent on me, but when I told him that he wouldn't be able to stay that week I felt I was cutting the cord and knew that he would take it badly. When people are feeling insecure, the tiniest rejection can seem monumental.

He seemed 'reasonably responsive' back at home, according to Rodney, and was 'playing very attractive stuff which we didn't remember hearing before'. ('What swansong might this have been?' wonders Gabrielle.)

Joe's letter arrived on Tuesday. 'I think it scared Nick to death somehow,' Molly later said, wondering if 'all the business of another album, and all the contracts, was just more than he could cope with'.[5] Its immediate effect seemed beneficial, with a 'very well together' Nick renewing the Rapier's front tyres at the village garage and borrowing Molly's Linguaphone course to help with his French.

By Wednesday, though, he had retreated into glum reticence, confronted again by the impossibility of having another batch of songs ready in time for Joe's impending return. 'We are *most* worried that he may be slipping back into his old misery,' wrote Rodney.

Early the next morning, while Rodney was shaving, Nick declared his intention of returning to Paris and trying to get a job there. Before Rodney had dressed, he was gone, but he was back by evening, having 'got halfway to Dover' – an inadvertent metaphor for his plight. He was at least still willing to talk:

> Said his difficulty was he was halfway to getting back to his music and halfway to getting a job, and kept switching from one to the other. Of course, the truth is he can't find the resolution or inspiration to do either, and unless he does we are back to square one of miserable silence.

He spent a bad night, groggily telling his parents when he surfaced at lunchtime that he'd taken Tryptizol instead of requesting a sleeping pill as usual. Guy and Noel came for drinks that evening, bringing Janie. Guy suspects Nick might have resented her presence, and he remained in his room until Guy managed to coax him down, 'looking very rough and not at all communicative', by his father's account.

Gabrielle arrived shortly afterwards. She was in the middle of rehearsing Terence Rattigan's *French Without Tears* in Bristol, due to open on Tuesday, 26 November, but wanted to catch up with her brother after his French sojourn. Guy asked them both for lunch at Carpenters Hill the next day, but the event was not a success, Gabrielle reporting that Nick had been 'very silent' – as he remained.

He spent Monday, wrote Rodney, 'more or less just sitting in the music room – very little music going on', and was 'inactive' again on Tuesday. Wednesday saw a glimmer of positivity when he told Molly he wanted to drive to London the next day to buy a violin.* She suggested he borrow her car, but he had seemingly forgotten the idea by morning, or been dissuaded by the grim weather. Instead, he passed another 'very inactive day', and that evening, 21 November, he confessed that he 'couldn't make it' to the local Co-op to buy some beer.

He spent Friday sequestered in the silent music room. 'At teatime Molly mentioned to him our dismay at his seeming return to his old inability to do anything, but her comments were received in silence,' reported Rodney.

Guy, Noel and Janie were back at Carpenters Hill for the weekend.

---

* He had floated the idea of learning the violin as far back as Christmas 1966, and more than once that June.

On the Saturday morning of 23 November Guy rang to invite Nick to join them for lunch. Despite his parents' apprehension, 'after a couple of false starts he strode off to his car and off he went'. Guy remembers:

> I wanted to make sure he felt especially welcome, to compensate for any hurt he felt about us not having been able to have him to stay that week. I was probably over-attentive to him, because I felt I'd let him down and wanted him to know that he was a priority for me.

At 4.45 Guy rang to say that Nick, Noel and Janie were walking through the gloaming to Far Leys for tea, with Guy following in his car to drive them all back to Carpenters Hill (where Nick had left his car) for supper. 'Guy said on the phone that Nick had been fine and talking a lot,' wrote Rodney, 'but he was very silent with us.'

Guy went to bed that night having agreed to put Nick up at Bourne Street again on Tuesday, an arrangement he says Nick 'was clearly intending to continue indefinitely, into 1975'. Nick sat downstairs watching TV with Guy's mother before driving home after midnight.

She later remarked that she had found him 'so interesting and alive with us all',[6] but on the morning of Sunday the 24th, wrote Rodney, he was 'completely silent and wouldn't answer when we asked him how he had got on'. Before lunch, however, 'he did open up a little, pacing the drawing-room floor and saying what an extraordinary chap Guy was for getting people to do things'.

At lunch he got up and down from the table – an old habit – and in the evening he declined to join his parents as they watched the news. Instead, he wandered in and out of the music room's outside door more than once. Rodney and Molly were not disconcerted; they had witnessed such behaviour many times before. He went up to his room at around 10.30, a little earlier than usual. Molly remembered him 'standing at the door, and I said to him, "Are you off to bed, Nick?" I can just see him now . . .'[7]

His parents went up nearer midnight and were soon fast asleep, but Nick was restless, as was often the case. In the middle of the rainy night he made his way downstairs, had a bowl of cornflakes in the kitchen and listened to an album of Bach's Brandenburg Concertos on headphones in the music room. Naw heard him moving about at around 5.30 a.m., but Molly happened not to.

Back in his cold bedroom, he picked up his current bottle of Tryptizol, which contained around sixty pills. Tired, dejected by his musical stagnation and unable to envisage a fulfilled future, he swallowed them all. Then, having shrugged off his dressing gown, he lay on his back on top of his bed, wearing only a pair of briefs, his long legs stretching towards the door, and awaited oblivion.

32

A Very Special Person

A MIDST THE TERRIBLE events of Monday, 25 November, Rodney and Molly's top priority was Gabrielle. Inopportunely, *French Without Tears* was previewing that very evening, with the opening night on Tuesday. De Wet was in Berlin and, wanting to tell her in person, they sent her a telegram announcing that they would visit on Wednesday, and took the phone off the hook.

Molly's sisters came to Far Leys on Tuesday. That afternoon Rodney wrote to Guy Norton, to say thank you 'for your great kindness to Nick, for the help you gave him, and for the visit to Paris in particular, which was such a happy time for him in the midst of all the anxiety and unhappiness which always surrounded him, and which we seemed quite powerless to protect him from'.

Molly and Rodney made the melancholy trip to Bristol on Wednesday morning, and broke the news to the unsuspecting Gabrielle over lunch. 'The moment they told me, it was no surprise,' she says. She was due to promote her play on the local BBC station immediately afterwards, and used all her professional acumen to retain her composure for the interview, the ensuing performance and cast drinks, before finally having some time to herself late that night.

Nick's death was announced in *The Times* on Thursday, 28 November:

> DRAKE – on November 25, Nicholas Rodney (Nick), aged 26 years, beloved son of Rodney and Molly, dearest brother of Gabrielle. Funeral service Tanworth-in-Arden Church, Warwickshire, on Monday, December 2nd at 1.15 pm. No flowers, please.*

---

* The time given was wrong, so the announcement also appeared the following day, correcting it to 12.15 p.m. The error perhaps caught out Robert Kirby and others.

Rodney rang the Woods that day, and the distressed Sheila explained that John was working in Los Angeles with Joe Boyd. He rang them too. 'The call didn't come as a complete surprise,'[1] admits Joe, adding: 'I was frightened by "Black-Eyed Dog", but you can be frightened by something yet not expect it to happen.'

At her father's request, Gabrielle rang Brian Wells, then on his shift at St Bartholomew's Hospital in London. Brian rang Robert Kirby, who was stunned, having inferred that Nick was getting better when he'd last seen him, in March. As the truth sank in, he admitted: 'I was a bit angry. I thought, "What am I going to do now?"'[2]

The news carried an additional charge for Paul and Diana Wheeler because, as she explains, 'At the same time that Nick was dying, I was in labour with our son at Westminster Hospital – one dear person leaving as another arrived. Poor Nick. It didn't feel like he was ever quite of this world.' They named their baby Benjamin Nicholas, in Nick's memory.

Paul found a moment to ring the Martyns. 'I was lying in my bed in Hastings and the phone went,' recalled John. 'I laughed! For which my wife never forgave me.'[3] Paul vividly remembers the sound: 'I know it might have been instinctive, but I found it chilling.' Bev, by contrast, says she 'just went to pieces. I took it very badly and got very ill.'[4]

Sophia Ryde hadn't seen Nick since his awkward proposal in March, and was tactlessly informed by her mother, who saw *The Times* announcement and rang her at work. 'Luckily, Robert Abel Smith was working in the same building,' she recalls, 'so we were able to sit on the stairs and take it in together.'

She immediately sent a note to Molly and Rodney:

> I just had to write to say how sad I was to hear about Nick today. He was such a gentle person and so very talented. I wish I had understood more and been able to help in some small way. I will always remember him as he was – a very special person who meant a lot to me.

She informed Ben Laycock and Alex Henderson. 'It felt almost inevitable by that point,' says Alex. 'It was the last thing I'd have imagined when I'd first known him, but he'd really declined since *Pink Moon*.'

Flat 39
5 Elm Park Gdns
London. S.W.10.
28th November.

Dear Mr and Mrs Drake and Gabrielle,
    I just had to write to
say how sad I was to hear about
Nick today. He was such a gentle
person and so very talented. I wish
I had understood more and been
able to help in some small way.
I will always remember him as he
was - a very special person who
meant a lot to me.
        With love
            Sophia Ryde.

Condolence letter from Sophia Ryde, 28 November 1974.

As the word spread, Rodney and Molly faced the bleak task of making funeral arrangements with their vicar, Edward Wilmot. He visited Far Leys on Friday to discuss the service. He also composed a brief tribute for the parish newsletter:

Nick, as all his many friends knew him, had been very far from well for a considerable time, but his untimely death came as a shock to many. He was a musician, both composer and performer, of an exceedingly high standard, and his loss to the world of folk music is very great.

Gabrielle arrived home on Sunday, 1 December, the eve of her brother's funeral. That night she couldn't get the 1930s song 'I'm in a Dancing Mood' out of her head – an absurdity he might have enjoyed. Monday morning was cold, but the rain held off as she, Rodney, Molly and Naw made their way to St Mary Magdalene to await the congregation.

There was a decent number of mourners, but several of Nick's friends – including Joe Boyd, John Wood, Bob Squire, Desi Burlison-Rush, Mike Hacking, Jeremy Harmer, Jo Dingemans, Marcus Bicknell, David Ward, and Julian and Victoria Lloyd – were abroad, and most of them had yet to hear the news.

Other important figures in his life – Andy Murison, Simon Crocker, David Wright, Jeremy Mason, Rick Charkin, Keith Morris and Anthea Joseph, among others – were unaware too. In fact, no one from Marlborough, Witchseason or Island was there, reflecting how compartmentalised he had kept his relationships. Sheila Wood was unable to attend, as were the new parents Paul and Diana Wheeler, but Robert Abel Smith drove Sophia, Ben and Alex up from London.

'It was a horrible day and a long way,' remembers Sophia, while Robert adds that they 'didn't know any of the other people there'. 'I think Nick's was the first funeral I ever went to,' says Alex, 'and we didn't really know how to deal with the situation.' 'I couldn't look at his coffin,' says Sophia.

Despite the many absentees, Joanna Lodder says: 'The church was very full, I think mainly with local friends, and all their family.' The service was short and simple. To Alex, the Revd Wilmot's address felt remote: 'There was barely any mention of Nick's music. The vicar seemed more focused on how good he'd been at running at school . . . We thought, "Is this the same Nick?"' Joanna remembers him explaining 'how Nick had been overwhelmed by the struggle to get his music out, despite having so much talent'.

Brian and Marion had driven from Wales but got lost around Birmingham and missed the service. Gabrielle was waiting at the church and directed them to the Solihull Crematorium, a few miles up the road. 'Robert missed the funeral too,' remembers Brian. 'I sat next to him at the crematorium. He was crying, I was in a daze.'

Lunch was provided at Far Leys, where Gabrielle was 'surprised that so many of Nick's friends didn't know each other'.[5] Rodney and Molly hadn't met many of them either. For his cousin Grania, 'All these young people were obviously huge admirers of Nick's. They were drinking whisky and I remember thinking: they need it.' To Ben the occasion felt 'unreal', and Alex was 'amazed at how gracious and friendly his parents and Gabrielle were, when they must have just wanted everyone to leave'.

In fact, the presence of a handful of Nick's friends was a source of comfort to Nick's distraught parents, not least because their re-assurances dispelled the notion that 'the generation gap' had played a role in Nick's struggle to communicate with them. 'We could never get through to him either,' Rodney remembered them saying.[6]

Nick's friends were shown up to his room, Alex recalls, but were 'too shell-shocked to take it in'. Brian casually asked after the Yamaha classical guitar he'd left with Nick in 1970, upon which, to his discomfiture, Rodney 'insisted on giving me Nick's Martin 000-28, which was a much better instrument'.

The gathering broke up mid-afternoon. 'We'd spoken about Nick all the way there but were silent on the way back, just desperately sad,' says Robert Abel Smith. Brian recalls a similar atmosphere when he and Marion gave Robert Kirby a lift back to London afterwards. He wrote to Molly and Rodney, telling them: 'Although it's little consolation, you are the only people that Nick could ever *really* come to during his sufferings, even though he probably couldn't make his love for you that obvious.'

In the days after the funeral Rodney and Molly busied themselves with replying to such letters. Almost all were from their friends, not

Nick's. Paul Wheeler's was an exception. 'I am quite sure that Nick appreciated your kindness, even in his darkest moments,' he wrote. 'We were proud to know him, and his gentleness is something which stays with us, through his music as well as his memory.'

Jeremy Harmer, with whom Nick had taken some of his first steps as a guitarist, belatedly heard the news from his parents. He was the only person explicitly to assure Rodney and Molly of Nick's artistic standing in the wake of his death:

> He was a guitarist of consummate skill – a fact recognised, I can assure you, by all in the profession and many outside it . . . Because he never catered for a 'mass' audience his records never sold a million, but there are very few of my friends who do not possess copies, and who do not feel, as I do, a deep attachment to his music and the feelings expressed in his songs.

Following the funeral, Molly and Rodney spent a few days at the Grand Spa hotel in Bristol, where Gabrielle was based. They were there when the first tribute to Nick appeared, in *Sounds* of 14 December. Its author was Jerry Gilbert, who had interviewed him for the same paper almost four years earlier. He remembers having to battle for the piece's publication, and though it was heavily edited he says it prompted substantial feedback, indicating that 'Nick certainly had a decent number of admirers by then'.

Headlined 'Death of a "Genius"', it opened with the sad misapprehension that Nick's 'enthusiasm had never been as high, for he was totally immersed in the prospect of completing his fourth album'. Robert Kirby was then quoted saying, 'He was a genius. There was absolutely no one to touch him in England', and evoked him in private, 'sitting back relaxing and playing blues and ragtime pieces like you wouldn't believe'. Robert also shared the view that by the end of his life Nick had 'had enough, there was no fight left in him . . . Yet I get the feeling that if he was going to commit suicide, he would have done so a long time ago.'

There would be no room for such conjecture at Nick's inquest, scheduled for 3 p.m. on Wednesday, 18 December. 'We spent the morning dreading it,' Rodney wrote in his diary. 'It turned out to be a much less formal affair than we had expected, in a small room on the first floor of Henley-in-Arden police station. One press man there, we thought.'*

The coroner, Dr Hubert Stephen Tibbits, was renowned for his courtesy and had also conducted Rodney's mother's inquest in 1963. He gently talked him through Nick's life at Far Leys since 1971, then asked Molly about the level of pills in the Tryptizol bottle when his body was found. Next the pathologist, Dr Kenneth Holly, stated that he had found evidence in Nick's body of a 'serious overdose' – a minimum of thirty-five pills' worth from stomach samples and up to a further fifty from blood samples. This had led to respiratory paralysis and heart failure. Even allowing for residue from recent days, there was no way Nick could have taken even the lower estimate by accident. The verdict was therefore inevitable: 'Acute amitriptyline poisoning – self-administered when suffering from a depressive illness. (Suicide)'.

'We were fairly shattered at first by this,' wrote Rodney, who sought a private meeting with the kindly Dr Tibbits later that day. Tibbits told him that even the provable minimum number of pills Nick had taken would likely have proved fatal, causing Rodney to muse in his diary: 'Perhaps it was better that Nick should have taken his life deliberately rather than just made a terrible mistake.'

Molly resisted accepting the verdict because of her faith that his condition would have improved.[7] 'He was a great chap of impulse,' as she later put it, 'he was having a bad night, and he [thought], "Oh, what the hell!" and took some extra ones.'[8]

Gabrielle draws comfort from her belief – shared with de Wet – that 'Nick wanted it to work . . . I believe the actual act of taking the pills was an impulsive one, but I believe the will was a deep one . . . I sort of always knew it was on the cards.'[9]

Brian Wells agrees that Nick acted on impulse, not least because there was no suicide note, but adds that, given his history and the size of the overdose: 'It was difficult for [the coroner] to record a verdict of misadventure.'[10]

Rodney wrote to Brian on 19 December to say: 'We are finding

---

* The short resulting article appeared in the *Stratford Herald* on 20 December, and reported that Nick had 'committed suicide by taking about 85 drug tablets . . . Such a massive overdose could not have been taken accidentally, said the coroner.'

it very difficult to come to terms with what has happened, and keep on asking ourselves what we should have done that we failed to do.' He repeated that 'we had never realised that Tryptizol was a dangerous drug' and that he and Molly had been 'completely off our guard' following Nick's apparently cheerful return from Paris, adding that they derived a modicum of comfort from recalling the depths of Nick's suffering and 'the fact that all that is over for him now'. 'I suppose the improvement in his condition was the very thing which enabled him to accomplish the act when an urge suddenly came upon him,' he later speculated.[11]

On the same day, Richard Williams wrote from Island, to express their 'profound respect for Nick's talent and love for his music. He never made us money, but somehow it never mattered because being involved with his music was its own reward.' Chris Blackwell adds: 'I felt really guilty that I hadn't spent more time with him and tried to help him more. I still do.'

Joe Boyd asked himself tough questions in the aftermath of the tragedy: 'The months after his death brought anguished thoughts. Was it my phone call which gave him the reassurance he needed to start the treatment that led to the fatal pills? Would he still be alive if I had stayed in London?'[12]

Robert also felt a degree of self-reproach:

My memories of Nick are predominantly happy, but stained with guilt and remorse . . . I wish that between 1972 and 1974 I'd rung him up and said, 'Are you working on anything?' And if he'd said, 'Well, yes, I'm working on this on my own,' I'd have said, 'Well, can't we try a few ideas and see if it works?' He would almost certainly have said yes – but I don't think people ever pushed him, because they always thought [the impetus] was going to come from him . . . I was always overawed by Nick.[13]

Thanking Molly and Rodney for forwarding Nick's unsent note from March, Sophia Ryde echoed their own thoughts: 'The more I think, the more I accept what has happened as being the best for him in many, many ways,' she wrote. 'Nick really was a very special person, and I know how important you were [to him], and all that you must've been through – you are really wonderful people.'

David Ward was stunned when Sophia told him the news upon his return from a spiritual retreat in India. 'It's a shame he didn't travel with me, since that would have re-established more of a balance in his mind,' he ventures. 'He would have coped just fine with me in India.' Kirstie Lodder feels that nothing more could have been done, because 'Nick was in a place inside himself where no one could help – least of all his parents, who were just lovely. I feel that the price Nick paid for his talent was the depth of his depression.'

Rodney registered Nick's death on Christmas Eve, giving his occupation as 'musician'. Nick had died intestate and Rodney wound up his affairs, such as they were, selling his car and acquainting himself with how royalty payments worked. Otherwise, he wrote, 'driving about seems to be the best therapy'.

During a long walk after a quiet family Christmas with Nancy and Chris McDowall, Chris's psychiatrist brother Toby ventured that Nick 'would never have recovered and that his illness, having gone on for three years, must have impaired his brain irreparably'. Seeking further answers, on 7 January Rodney met the pathologist, Dr Holly, who told him that 'kidney trouble was observed but not considered as contributing in any way, and his heart was sound'. He assured Rodney that even if Nick had been found earlier, the outcome would have been the same, since 'about 40 Tryptizol would constitute a dangerous, probably lethal dose', and he had taken 'a very large overdose'.

The Drakes chose a gravesite under an oak tree at St Mary Magdalene. 'Sad little ceremony this morning at the churchyard,' Rodney wrote on Tuesday, 14 January.

> Molly and I and our beloved Bird attending the interment of poor Nick's ashes. The vicar presided and said the few prayers. Molly had brought up a little flower arrangement – all from the garden – and put it on the grave . . . At 4 p.m. we went back to the churchyard and found the grave neatly covered over and the flowers in place – beautiful evening light.

A headstone was later added, reading 'Nick Drake 1948–1974 / Remembered With Love'. After much thought, in October 1976, Molly, Rodney and Gabrielle had a line from 'From The Morning' inscribed on its reverse: 'Now we rise and we are everywhere'.

Probate was granted on 24 January 1975, with Rodney as Nick's sole executor. The gross value of Nick's estate stood at £4,394.26 (around £30,000 in 2022), the bulk of it deriving from his aunt's trust. Molly and Rodney immediately signed everything over to Gabrielle. Royalty income was barely a consideration – at the end of 1974 he was due £1,771.50 (around £15,000 in 2022), but this included belated accounting for earlier periods; *Bryter Layter*, the best-selling of his albums at the time, had total sales of around 15,000.[14]

Brian Wells came to stay at Far Leys that week. 'We had a very interesting evening with him and heard a great deal about Nick,' wrote Rodney. 'After dinner we played Nick's old tapes . . . His visit did us a lot of good, and I think perhaps it did him some good too.'

Molly drew further solace from the late arrival of Nick's birthday present to her, Camus's *Le Mythe de Sisyphe*. It seems that its possible significance was never apparent to her. 'I'm not sure she ever read it,' says Gabrielle. 'I think it just touched her very much that he had remembered.' The Drakes kept it on a side table in the drawing room.

Another source of succour was a fulsome tribute in *ZigZag* by David Sandison, who had departed Island in July 1972 but remained an evangelist for Nick's work.[15] Headed 'The Final Retreat', it saluted Nick as 'a man of sincerity, an artist of tremendous calibre and one of the few entitled to be called unique'.*

At much the same time the huge-selling *NME* published a heart-felt two-page article by Nick Kent, headlined 'Requiem for a Solitary Man'.[16] 'I felt it was ridiculous that he hadn't had any proper obituary apart from the pieces in *Sounds* and *ZigZag*,' he says. 'I'm not especially proud of the article and I've never wanted to reprint it, but I'm glad I wrote it and had the chance to recommend his music to a large audience.'

He was sensitive to Rodney and Molly's grief but emphasises

---

* David sent the Drakes the original *Pink Moon* artwork in November 1983, with a letter explaining that he had rescued it from a pile of items about to be discarded by Island just after the album's release.

that he didn't leave anything out as a result; for example, he says, 'I don't think Nick used heavy drugs, and no one told me he had at the time.' His most striking contention in the article was that the 'suicide verdict seems ludicrous'. This was based, he explains, on a conversation he had with Brian Wells, who assured him Nick had only taken three Tryptizol pills. 'He was a doctor, so I accepted what he told me, but I now realise that he was trying to protect Nick's parents from having to see more stuff about their son taking his own life.'

The piece praised Nick's 'overwhelmingly gentle, hypnotic music' and called his death 'pitifully under-publicised'. Rodney described it as 'sympathetic and appreciative' in his diary, albeit containing 'a few inaccuracies', and Nick himself would surely have relished having his work placed within the same 'echelon of creativity' as two albums he esteemed: Love's *Forever Changes* and Van Morrison's *Astral Weeks*.

The article made reference to 'four new tracks' Nick had recorded the previous July, and suggested they might now form part of a compilation. Rodney and Molly had only just heard the songs themselves, on a tape Richard Williams had supplied,* and the consensus was that they should remain unreleased. 'Nick was clear that they were unfinished,' John Wood reiterates. 'At best he saw them as works in progress, at worst something never to see the light of day in any form.'

As such, the next issue of the *NME* carried a letter from Richard stating that 'John Wood has destroyed the 16-track master tapes, with our full approval'. John says: 'It was a fib, I have to admit – but my allegiance has always been to the artist.'

As the shock of losing Nick subsided, his parents sought to understand what had caused his decline, rather than his death. On 27 September 1975 Rodney wrote to Gerald Dickens, the NHS psychiatrist who had worked so sympathetically with Nick, explaining that 'My wife and I are finding some comfort in gathering together

---

* Island was never given a copy of 'Tow The Line'. Rodney played the other songs to Gabrielle and de Wet on Sunday, 6 July 1975, recording in his diary how 'tremendously' 'Black-Eyed Dog' had 'moved and impressed' de Wet (who 'explained its significance to us').

as much information as we can about Nick', and asking: 'Could you tell us what, in your view, the nature of his illness was?'

Gabrielle feels that Dr Dickens's long and compassionate reply was 'one of the foundation stones on which they were able to start rebuilding their lives'.[17]

'Many people assume doctors become hardened in their responses to such tragedies, but I can assure you that this is not so,' he began:

I believe that Nick was suffering from an illness which is called (in the textbooks) 'simple schizophrenia', but I must add that I think such labels are meaningless, and to a large extent cover our lack of understanding of such illnesses . . .

I think the problem in treating Nick was what would be called his 'lack of motivation to treatment' – his inability to see himself as being a sick man . . . I have but little doubt in my own mind that you, as his parents, did all that you possibly could to encourage Nick to seek the help he required . . . I am afraid that we all must accept that Nick posed an insoluble problem.

I can well understand your concern over the use of the word 'suicide', with all its implications. Again, I think that this is a mean-ingless word, part of an often-meaningless legal jargon. It would be quite impossible for anyone to understand what was in or on Nick's mind when he took the overdose of tablets. I think it would be absurd, knowing Nick, to believe that he killed himself in order to revenge himself upon others or upon society at large.

All I can tell you is, first, that I believe that in no way at all did you or your wife in your handling of Nick over the years contribute to or exacerbate his illness, and, secondly, your lack of understanding in no way reflects upon you as parents. People who have studied this illness all their lives have no better understanding of patients than you had of Nick. I must emphasise that neither you nor your wife have anything at all to reproach yourself about.

The final point that I would make is that whatever behaviour Nick indulged in after the onset of his illness should be seen as being the outcome of that illness, and not in any way should moral judge-ment be passed upon what he did. I think his flirtation with drugs was simply a manifestation of the need he had to try and understand the changes that were taking place within him. I do hope that you and your wife will in due course of time be able to come to terms with this tragedy.[18]

Gabrielle was a huge consolation to her parents as they sought to do just that, as was visiting Paris (where they met the Holts) and compiling a scrapbook about Nick by going through his papers, letters and photos. It was a bittersweet but cathartic process that, as Rodney wrote, 'took us back to the days when he was active and enjoying life'.

Rodney also devoted time and effort to transferring Nick's various early home recordings onto a single reel, from which he could make copies. The first recipient was Gabrielle, whose Christmas present it was in 1975.

Epilogue

D ESPITE ISLAND'S PRIDE in Nick's work, they made no immediate plan to repackage it. Nonetheless, says Nick Kent, interest
in him 'snowballed quite quickly after his death':

> 1976 was the time of punk, when everyone hated sensitive singer-
> songwriters like James Taylor and Joni Mitchell, but for some reason
> that crowd did like Nick. I remember Joe Strummer, the Damned
> and Paul Weller all liking him in those days, and it wasn't because
> he'd died young – it was because his music spoke to them.

Five Leaves Left was finally released in America in March 1976,
on Island's mid-priced Antilles imprint, with ardent sleevenotes by
Bruce Malamut that praised Nick's 'masterful musicianship',
described him as a 'visionary' and 'the John Coltrane of folk singers'
and stated: 'Life speaks for itself through Nick Drake.' They were
written barely a year after Nick's death and indicate how his reputation was growing.

Molly and Rodney were in France at the start of that month.
Upon their return to Far Leys they were intrigued to hear from
Naw that a twenty-one-year-old American girl named Melinda
Cullen had been telephoning in their absence, and had even come
to the door.

'I saw *Pink Moon* in a store in Houston, Texas in 1974,' she explains.
'I'd never heard of Nick Drake, but I thought the cover was intriguing,
so I bought it. And when I got home and played it, I thought it
was magical and dreamlike.'

Nick's music cast such a spell on Melinda – a troubled soul at
the time – that she resolved to come to England and learn as much
about him as possible. She rang Far Leys again on 11 March, and

what she told Rodney and Molly took them aback. 'Nick is evidently the most important thing in her life and she thinks about him all the time,' Rodney wrote that night. 'She wants to know many details of his life, and also his death.'

She was based in a hotel in Stratford, so they asked her to stay instead. 'They were the loveliest people you could imagine,' she says. 'Melinda gave us a lovely picture of Nick printed from one of his record sleeves,' wrote Rodney.[*] 'After lunch we put her in the music room to play Nick's tapes and records, which seemed to be an endless source of pleasure and comfort to her . . . Molly took her up to show her Nick's room, which she had asked to sleep in.' The next day, he continued, 'Molly gave her Nick's address book, watch and black jumper and took her to Solihull to catch the 12.40 to Paddington.'[†]

In the ensuing days the Drakes rather missed Melinda. They little realised that she was but the first of many fans who would find their way to Far Leys from all over the world in the months and years to come. They would not remain so liberal with Nick's possessions, but always offered a warm welcome, refreshments, and lifts to and from the station. Eventually Rodney made a supply of cassettes from his reel of Nick's unreleased material, which he handed to visitors, unwittingly fuelling illicit releases. Gabrielle remembers her mother determining that the family remain at Far Leys 'until we have made it a happy house again', and visits from Nick's fans played an important part in easing the pain and bafflement they felt at his fate.

In April 1979 Island repackaged all three of Nick's albums and four of his final recordings[‡] as *Fruit Tree* – one of the first retrospective boxed sets accorded an artist of Nick's generation, and another indication of his increasing renown. It was followed in May 1985 by a compilation entitled *Heaven In A Wildflower*, while in 1986 Joe Boyd oversaw a collection of previously unreleased material entitled

[*] A positive print from the negative image supplied inside *Pink Moon*.
[†] Melinda says they gave her Nick's copy of George Eliot's *The Mill on the Floss* and not an address book.
[‡] John Wood was strongly opposed to their inclusion; 'Tow The Line' had yet to be rediscovered.

Time Of No Reply. Nick's work has never lost momentum since, its popularity growing with each reissue or use in film and TV.

Joe's respect for Nick's artistry has never wavered:

> I listen to the music now and it sounds the same as when I first heard that first demo. I thought his songs were genius and I still do. He was a unique and brilliant talent and it's heartbreaking for me that I didn't think of a way to make him happy and famous.[1]

He has, however, come to understand that the short-term obscurity of Nick's work has yielded a long-term benefit: 'The fact that Nick's music failed to find an audience during his lifetime means it's not identified with a particular time and place, which allows each generation to create its own connection to it.'

In despair, Nick had told Rodney in July 1972 that 'he'd finished his life's work and had done more than many in a lifetime. One day people would realise.' The fulfilment of those words helped his parents and sister reconcile themselves to his absence.

In 1977 the Drakes decided to spend some of Nick's royalties on a new Sesquialtera stop for the organ in St Mary Magdalene, Tanworth-in-Arden, and an accompanying bronze plaque in his memory. They were unveiled during the morning service on Sunday, 8 May, when – to their great pleasure – the organist played his own arrangement of Nick's 'Sunday'.

Rodney Drake died on 6 March 1988, aged seventy-nine. He was, according to his obituary, 'a constant source of innovative ideas and a wise counsellor to those with personal problems'.[2] 'I am totally lost without my beloved Rodney,' Molly wrote on the anniversary of Nick's death that year. 'But I am so profoundly grateful for the privilege of having been married for so many years to such a very wonderful man.'[3]

The unfailingly loyal and much-loved Naw had preceded Rodney, dying in January 1988. In early 1989 Molly sold Far Leys and moved to a smaller house in the village. 'It's wonderful to know that Nick is not really dead, because with people listening to his music he lives on,' she stated shortly before her own death on 4 June 1993, aged seventy-seven:[4]

It's been the most immense joy and comfort, always . . . Since he's died, large numbers of young people have written and actually come to see me and told me that Nick has helped them through terrible black periods of their lives. This is what he would have liked. That is why he said to me, 'I've failed in every single thing I've tried to do' – because he thought he hadn't been able to help anyone and get through to them. But he has, and I hope he knows.

Acknowledgements

THIS BOOK COULD not have been written without the support, generosity and hospitality of Nick's devoted sister Gabrielle, who has answered my many questions about her family with unfailing grace, candour and good humour, as well as making many important introductions.

It also owes its existence to Cally Callomon, who manages Nick's musical estate. His commitment to broadening the understanding of Nick's life and the reach of his work has been inspirational to me, as have his wise counsel and profound love for music of many sorts.

Neither Gabrielle nor Cally sought to influence a single word I wrote, nor asked me to conceal or downplay any aspect of Nick's life. Their encouragement has underpinned the entire project, despite its painful personal resonances, and I consider myself very fortunate to have their trust and friendship.

Joe Boyd – who instantly recognised Nick's artistry, and without whom he might never have recorded professionally – has been unflaggingly co-operative and open to revisiting the past, despite being more focused on the future. The speed with which he responded to my hundreds of abstruse queries puts me to shame.

John Wood – who painstakingly ensured that Nick's records sounded as Nick wished, as well as being a good friend to him – has also given up an especially large amount of time to me. His celebrated commitment to detail, which benefited so many recordings, has richly informed my work.

Whilst researching I spent a good deal of time with Sophia Ryde, who was increasingly unwell but did her best to conceal the fact. I am very grateful for the kindness she showed me and sincerely hope she would have approved of the finished book.

Many other people have contributed, by sharing memories, making introductions or supplying important information. In particular, Patrick Humphries lent me all the materials he gathered when working on his pioneering biography of Nick in 1997. Without them my research would be much the poorer, not least because several people he interviewed or corresponded with have since died. Not all writers would have been so generous-spirited.

David Barber shared precious transcripts of interviews he conducted for an unproduced documentary in 1995, and Pete Paphides sent me the various interview recordings he made when writing about Nick over the years. Neil Storey shared the fruits of his long experience as an employee and historian of Island Records. He, Richie Unterberger and John Venning made many helpful suggestions about the manuscript, and Adam Foster shared his insights into Nick's guitars. I am indebted to them all.

I am also grateful for the help of Jørn R. Andersen, Dr Donnah Anderson, Colman Andrews, Larry Ayres, Silvio Badillo, Dominic Benthall, Samantha Blake (at BBC Written Archives Centre), Chris Brazier, the British Library, Catherine Brumwell (at the Marlborough Society), Douglas Buchanan (at Eagle House), Jane Cowburn, Dr John Cleaver (at Fitzwilliam College, Cambridge), Jason Creed, Brian Cullman, Alan Fitzpatrick, José María Pérez García, Sam Giles, Antony Harding, Colin Harper, Chuck Harter, Chris Healey, Colin Hill, Harriet Hughes, Charles Kitson, Mark Lewisohn, Arthur Lubow, Joseph McGrath, Alex Marshall, Eleanor Marshall, Sevrin Morris, the Museum of Rural Life, Gorm Henrik Rasmussen, Nancy Sandison, Chris Sirett, Mike Stax, Gareth Thomas, Fernando Soto Trujillo, Vincent van Engelen, Professor Richard Vinter, Adam Waymouth, Louis Waymouth, Geoffrey Weiss, Harvey Williams and Brian Wolfe.

As well as Nick's sister, the following people shared their memories and reflections with me, often at considerable length; any unattributed quotes in the book are from my interviews with them. Both here and in the text, I have used the names Nick knew them by.

Robert Abel Smith, John Altman, Dawn Aston, Micky Astor, Stella Astor, Mick Audsley, Edward Bailey, David Betteridge, Marcus

Bicknell, Christopher Bishop, Chris Blackwell, Joe Boyd, Chris Bristow, Alan Brookes, Lindsay Brown, Vashti Bunyan, Res Burman, David Burnett, James Calvocoressi, Iain Cameron, Steve Cardy, Peter Carey, Andru Chapman, Richard Charkin, Tim Clark, John Cleaver, Joe Cobbe, Chris Cobley, Billy Connolly, Tony Cox, Simon Crocker, Melinda Cullen, Paul de Rivaz, Jeff Dexter, Hugh Dickens, Jo Dingemans, Lyn Dobson, John Downie, John Du Cane, Phil Dudderidge, Hugh Dunford Wood, Sue Dunnett, Caroline Edwards, Antony Evans, Alan Fairs, Andy Fernbach, Derek FitzGerald, James Fraser, Robin Frederick, Fred Frith, Howard Gannaway, Adrian George, Jerry Gilbert, Ed Gilchrist, Herman Gilligan, Lon Goddard, Oliver Goode, Michael Hacking, Virginia Harman, Jeremy Harmer, Tom Hayes, Alex Henderson, Diana Hicks, Mike Hill, Tony Hill Smith, Michael Hodge, Sue Holt, John James, Chris Jones, Wizz Jones, Oonagh Karanjia, Nick Kent, Helen Kirby, Stuart Kirby, Caroline Knox, Mike Kowalski, Chris Laurence, Ben Laycock, Rosie Laycock, Nick Lewin, Robert Lewis, Julian Lloyd, Sarah Lloyd, Tod Lloyd, Dave Lodder, Janie Lodder, Joanna Lodder, Kirstie Lodder, Liv Lodder, Clare Lowther, Mick McDonagh, Michael Maclaran, Beverley Martyn, Jeremy Mason, Phillip Matthews, Bruce May, John Molony, Andrew Murison, Grania Murphy, Lois Murphy, Martin Nelson, Simon Nicol, Sarah-Jane Norman, Guy Norton, Leo O'Kelly, Victoria Ormsby-Gore, Jane Parker-Smith, Ivan Pawle, Dave Pegg, Linda Peters, Tom Poole, Huw Price, Jean-Louis Pujol, Julian Raby, Nicolae Ratiu, Alec Reid, Colin Reynolds, Peter Rice, Rich Robbins, Diana Robertson, Chris Rudkin, Peter Russell, Sophia Ryde, Dominique Saint-André Perrin, Martin Shelley, Nick Sibley, Diana Soar, Bridget St John, Oliver Stapleton, Nick Stewart, Christopher Sykes, Allan Taylor, Colin Tillie, Martin Trent, Michael Trevithick, John Venning, David Ward, Ray Warleigh, Mick Way, Nigel Waymouth, Paul Weinberger, Chris Welch, Brian Wells, Paul Wheeler, Martin Wilkinson, John Williams, Mark Williams, Richard Williams, Mark Wing-Davey, Muff Winwood, Annagh Wood, John Wood, Vickie Wood and David Wright.

I am grateful to my agent Matthew Hamilton, and am lucky indeed to have had Nick Davies as my editor. Thanks too to Caroline Westmore, Nick de Somogyi, Howard Davies, Alice

Herbert, Amanda Jones, Sara Marafini, Sarah Arratoon and the rest of the wonderful team at John Murray, who have worked tirelessly to create the best book possible. Any remaining errors are mine, and I welcome corrections.

Picture Credits

Images within the text. Page ii: Photograph by Victoria Waymouth, Reproduced by permission of Adam Waymouth. Pages 105, 161, 345 and 479: Reproduced by permission of Bryter Music – The Estate of Nick Drake. Page 258: Artist unknown. Page 273: Reproduced by permission of Fitzwilliam College, Cambridge. Page 491: Reproduced courtesy of Joe Boyd. Page 498: Reproduced courtesy of Charles Kitson.

Section 1. Page 1 left, right and below, Reproduced by permission of Bryter Music – The Estate of Nick Drake. Page 2 above © Alan Fitzpatrick. Page 2 below, Reproduced by permission of Bryter Music – The Estate of Nick Drake. Page 3 above left and below left, Reproduced by permission of Bryter Music – The Estate of Nick Drake. Page 3 right © Melinda Cullen. Page 4 above, Courtesy of Eagle House Digital Archives. Page 4 below left, Eagle House Digital Archives courtesy of Patrick Kirwan. Page 4, below right, Reproduced by permission of Bryter Music – The Estate of Nick Drake. Page 5 above, Author's collection. Page 5 below left, Courtesy of Simon Crocker. Page 5 below right, Reproduced by permission of Bryter Music – The Estate of Nick Drake. Page 6 above left and right, Photographer Unknown. Page 6 below left, Reproduced by permission of Bryter Music – The Estate of Nick Drake. Page 7 above left, Courtesy of Michael Hacking. Page 7 above right, Courtesy of Andy Murison. Page 7 centre left and below left, Photographer unknown. Page 7 centre right, Courtesy of Jeremy Mason. Page 7 below right, Courtesy of Simon Crocker. Page 8 above left and above right, Courtesy of David and Kirstie Lodder. Page 8 centre left, Courtesy of Michael Hacking. Page 8 below left, Reproduced by permission of Bryter Music – The Estate of Nick Drake. Page 8 below right © Simon Crocker.

Section 2. Page 9 above © Dr J. R. A. Cleaver. Page 9 below left, Reproduced by permission of Fitzwilliam College, Cambridge. Page

517

9 below right, Courtesy of Brian Wells. Page 10 above left, Courtesy of Richard Charkin. Page 10 above right, Courtesy of Marcus Bicknell. Page 10 below, Reproduced by permission of Bryter Music – The Estate of Nick Drake. Page 11 above left, Photographer unknown. Page 11 above right and below, Courtesy of Marcus Bicknell. Page 12 above left, Courtesy of Ben Laycock. Page 12 above centre, Courtesy of Charles Kitson. Page 12 above right and centre left, Courtesy of Alex Henderson. Page 12 below left © Nigel Waymouth. Page 12 below right, Reproduced by permission of Bryter Music – The Estate of Nick Drake. Page 13 above left and centre right, Photographer unknown. Page 13 above right, Courtesy of John Wood. Page 13 below left, *Billboard*, 25 May 1968. Page 13 below right, Watson/Daily Express/Getty Images. Page 14 above left, Courtesy of Paul Wheeler. Page 14 above right, Courtesy of Beatrice Schutzer-Weissmann. Page 14 below left, Reproduced by permission of Bryter Music – The Estate of Nick Drake. Page 14 below right © Treld Pelkey Bicknell. Page 15 above © Keith Morris Archive, reproduced with permission. Page 15 below © Estate of Keith Morris/Getty Images. Page 16 above, *ZigZag*, No. 3, July 1969. Page 16 below © Ben Laycock.

Section 3. Page 17 above left, *Melody Maker*, 13 September 1969. Page 17 above right, Photographer unknown, *Dark Star*, May 1979. Page 17 below, Photographer unknown. Page 18 above, Photographer unknown. Page 18 below, Photograph by Willi Murray, courtesy of John Wood. Page 19 above left and right © Estate of Keith Morris/ Getty Images. Page 19 below left and right © Keith Morris Archive, reproduced with permission. Page 20 above left, right and below, Reproduced by permission of Bryter Music – The Estate of Nick Drake. Page 21 above, centre and below © Alan Fitzpatrick. Page 22 above, Wojtek Laski/Getty Images. Page 22 below, Photographer unknown. Page 23 above left © John Wood, reproduced with permission. Page 23 above right, Courtesy of Guy Norton. Page 23 below left, Courtesy of David and Kirstie Lodder. Page 23 below right, Courtesy of Charles Kitson. Page 24 above, Tanworth-in-Arden parish newsletter, December 1974. Page 24 below © Melinda Cullen.

Every reasonable effort has been made to trace copyright holders, but if there are any errors or omissions, John Murray will be pleased to insert the appropriate acknowledgement in any subsequent printings or editions.

Discography

A catalogue of Nick's officially released work, covering most of the songs referred to in the text.

Five Leaves Left
Island ILPS 9105, 4 July 1969 (UK)
Time Has Told Me / River Man / Three Hours / Way To Blue / Day Is Done / 'Cello Song / The Thoughts Of Mary Jane / Man In A Shed / Fruit Tree / Saturday Sun

Bryter Layter
Island ILPS 9134, 5 March 1971 (UK)
Introduction / Hazey Jane II / At The Chime Of A City Clock / One Of These Things First / Hazey Jane I / Bryter Layter / Fly / Poor Boy / Northern Sky / Sunday

Nick Drake
Island/Capitol SMAS 9307, July 1971 (US)
Cello Song / Poor Boy / At The Chime Of A City Clock / Northern Sky / River Man / Three Hours / One Of These Things First / Fly

Pink Moon
Island ILPS 9184, 25 February 1972 (UK)
Pink Moon / Place To Be / Road / Which Will / Horn / Things Behind The Sun / Know / Parasite / Free Ride / Harvest Breed / From The Morning

Interplay One
Longman LG 0582 24136, 1972 (UK)
Nick plays guitar on 'With My Swag All On My Shoulder', 'Full Fathom Five' and 'I Wish I Was a Single Girl Again'.

Time Of No Reply
Hannibal HNBL 1318, July 1986 (UK)
Time Of No Reply / I Was Made To Love Magic / Joey / Clothes Of Sand / Man In A Shed / Mayfair / Fly / The Thoughts Of Mary Jane / Been Smoking Too Long / Strange Meeting II / Rider On The Wheel / Black Eyed Dog / Hanging On A Star / Voice From A Mountain

Made To Love Magic
Island ILPS 8141, May 2004 (UK)
Rider On The Wheel / Magic / River Man / Joey / Thoughts Of Mary Jane / Mayfair / Hanging On A Star / Three Hours / Clothes Of Sand / Voices / Time Of No Reply / Black Eyed Dog / Tow The Line

Family Tree
Sunbeam, SBR2LP 5041, July 2007
Come In To The Garden / They're Leaving Me Behind / Time Piece / Poor Mum (*Molly Drake*) / Winter Is Gone / All My Trials (*Nick Drake and Gabrielle Drake*) / Kegelstatt Trio (*Nick Drake, Chris McDowall, Nancy McDowall*) / Strolling Down The Highway / Paddling In Rushmere / Cocaine Blues / Blossom / Been Smoking Too Long / Black Mountain Blues / Tomorrow Is A Long Time / If You Leave Me / Here Come The Blues / Sketch 1 / Blues Run The Game / My Baby So Sweet / Milk And Honey / Kimbie / Bird Flew By / Rain / Strange Meeting II / Day Is Done / Come Into The Garden / Way To Blue / Do You Ever Remember? (*Molly Drake*)

Plaisir D'Amour (45 rpm single, one-sided)
Antar, No. 11, November 2012

The John Peel Session
Antar, ANTARMP003, November 2014
Time Of No Reply / River Man / Three Hours / Bryter Layter / 'Cello Song
[*The first three songs are from Nick's first BBC session, recorded in August 1969. The last two are from his second BBC session, recorded (with Iain Cameron) in March 1970.*]

Nick Drake's Guitars

A chronological list of the guitars Nick is known to have owned or played, and some basic information about them and his likely use of them.

Estruch

The first guitar Nick owned, bought in Marlborough High Street for £13 in December 1964 and now in the possession of his estate.

Levin LS-18

Nick's first 'serious' guitar, with back and sides made from maple and a spruce top. Bought in Chas. E. Foote in Denman Street, London for £53 11s. in September 1966. The receipt erroneously states 'Levin De Luxe'. Nick took it to Aix in February 1967 and used it in early recordings made at home and at Cambridge. It can be heard on *Five Leaves Left* and *Bryter Layter*, and possibly on his February 1973 instrumental session at Sound Techniques. He smashed it on 23 May 1973 and its remnants were burnt on 16 April 1974.

Martin D-28

Acquired in the second half of 1967 – provenance unknown. Its back and sides were made from rosewood with a spruce top. Nick used it on home recordings, on all three albums and at gigs (he's playing it in the only known live photo of him). In early October 1972 his father remarked that he appeared to have sold it.

Robert Kirby's Spanish guitar

Make and model unknown, described by Robert as 'naff'. Possibly used by Nick on recordings made in Robert's room in Cambridge in the spring of 1968.

Gibson L-7C
Whilst recording 'Poor Boy' in Sound Techniques in March 1970, Nick spontaneously borrowed this archtop 'jazz' guitar from Simon Nicol of Fairport Convention, who happened to be present. Simon has long since sold it.

Yamaha G50
This classical guitar was bought by Brian Wells for £35 in London in the summer of 1970. He left it in Nick's flat soon afterwards and never got it back. Nick was photographed with it by Keith Morris that August, and again by Tony Evans in February 1971. He smashed it on 23 May 1973 and its remnants were burnt on 16 April 1974.

Guild M-20
This all-mahogany guitar was owned by Nigel Waymouth, who was given it by the artist Martin Sharp (who had himself been given it by Eric Clapton). Nick can be seen holding it on the cover of *Bryter Layter*, but only ever played it during the brief shoot, circa September 1970. It is now in the possession of Nick Laird-Clowes. There is no evidence that Nick ever owned a Guild.

Unknown electric
Nick acquired an electric guitar circa early 1973, make and model unknown. His father stated it had been 'imported' and Brian Wells recalls its colour as red. Nick is not known to have made any recordings with it, and he destroyed it in August 1974.

Martin 000-28
Nick's final guitar, with back and sides made from rosewood and top made from spruce. Bought from Ivor Mairants Musicentre in Rathbone Place, London for £235 on 13 August 1973. He used it on his final studio recordings in July 1974, and his father gave it to Brian Wells after his funeral that December. 'It was still in standard tuning but I never found it easy to play – the action was elevated,' says Brian. It is now in Gabrielle's possession.

Notes

Abbreviations

GD	Gabrielle Drake
ND	Nick Drake
MD	Molly Drake
RD	Rodney Drake
RD Diary	Diary kept by Rodney Drake from 21 March 1972
RFAW	*Remembered For A While*, ed. Gabrielle Drake and Cally Callomon (John Murray, 2014)
RMJ	Richard Morton Jack

Chapter 1: A Very Cosy World

1. GD, interview with David Barber, 2 December 1995.
2. *Farm Implement and Machinery Review*, 1 September 1962.
3. *RFAW*, p. 23.
4. Ibid., p. 20.
5. *Daily Telegraph*, 9 June 2004.
6. *RFAW*, p. 24.
7. *TV Times*, 18 May 1985.
8. GD, Introduction to *The Tide's Magnificence: Songs And Poems Of Molly Drake* (Fledg'ling Records, 2017).
9. *RFAW*, p. 20.
10. GD, interview, *De Mysterieuze Drake*, VRT Radio 1, Belgium, November 2004.
11. GD, audio interview with Pete Paphides, March 2007.

Chapter 2: A Totally Warm And Communicative Kid

1. *RFAW*, p. 21.
2. GD, 'Dear Nick . . .', *Family Tree* (Island, 2007), booklet, p. 6.
3. *RFAW*, p. 21.
4. GD, Introduction to *The Tide's Magnificence: Songs And Poems Of Molly Drake* (Fledg'ling Records, 2017).
5. GD, interview with Patrick Humphries, 1994.
6. RD, interview with Gorm Henrik Rasmussen, November 1979.
7. Ibid.
8. MD, interview with David Barber, 9 November 1992.
9. RD, interview with T. J. McGrath, 1981.
10. Ibid.
11. Diana Hicks to Patrick Humphries, 23 February 1998.
12. *RFAW*, p. 27.
13. Facebook comment, 18 October 2021.
14. *RFAW*, p. 27.
15. Ibid.
16. MD, interview with Gorm Henrik Rasmussen, November 1979.
17. *Stratford Herald*, 8 April 1988.

Chapter 3: Recognised As Efficient

1. RD, interview with T. J. McGrath, 1981.
2. MD, interview with Gorm Henrik Rasmussen, November 1979.
3. MD, interview with David Barber, 9 November 1992.
4. Ibid.
5. RD, interview with Gorm Henrik Rasmussen, November 1979.
6. Ibid.
7. Paul Wootton to Maxine Watts, 14 February 1987.

Chapter 4: A Rather Dreamy, Artistic Type Of Boy

1. Interview for Humphries (1997).
2. MD, interview with Gorm Henrik Rasmussen, November 1979.
3. Robert Peel to Patrick Humphries, 10 December 1997.

4. 'Confidential Statement' for university entrance, 6 October 1966. By permission of Fitzwilliam College, Cambridge.
5. Interview for Humphries (1997).
6. Ibid.
7. Ibid.
8. Island Records, press release, May 1970.
9. Arthur Lubow, 'Remember Nick Drake', *New Times*, April 1978.
10. RD, interview with T. J. McGrath, 1981.
11. MD, interview with Gorm Henrik Rasmussen, November 1979.
12. Michael Maclaran to Patrick Humphries, 15 December 1996.
13. *Melody Maker*, 4 July 1987.

Chapter 5: No One Can Claim To Know Him Very Well

1. *RFAW*, p. 379.
2. Interview for Humphries (1997).
3. Mark Phillips to RMJ, email, 8 January 2021.
4. Ibid.
5. ND to his parents, 18 May 1965.
6. Interview for Humphries (1997).
7. Ibid.
8. Dennis Silk to GD, 2 April 2002.
9. Interview for Humphries (1997).
10. GD, *The Times*, 8 June 2007.
11. ND to his parents, 6 February 1966.
12. Reference for Nick's Cambridge application, quoted by permission of Fitzwilliam College, Cambridge.
13. Interview for Humphries (1997).
14. Ibid.
15. Ibid.
16. Ibid.
17. Ibid.

Chapter 6: A Genuine Late Developer

1. Michael Maclaran to Patrick Humphries, 15 December 1996.
2. Ibid.
3. Interview for Humphries (1997).

4. *S2* magazine, *Sunday Express*, 28 November 2004.
5. Interview for Humphries (1997).
6. Ibid.
7. *S2* magazine, *Sunday Express*, 28 November 2004.

Chapter 7: Young And Discovering The World

1. GD, interview with David Barber, 2 December 1995.
2. Interview for Humphries (1997).
3. Ibid.
4. Island Records, press release, May 1970.
5. *RFAW*, p. 79.
6. Interview for Humphries (1997).
7. Ibid.
8. Ibid.
9. *The Times*, 8 June 2007.
10. Robin Frederick, privately circulated memoir, October 1997.
11. Ibid.
12. *The Times*, 8 June 2007.
13. Robin Frederick, privately circulated memoir, October 1997.
14. ND to his parents, 6 April 1967.
15. Facebook post, 2 July 2020.

Chapter 8: A Natural Progression

1. Interview for Humphries (1997).
2. *S2* magazine, *Sunday Express*, 28 November 2004.
3. Interview for Humphries (1997).
4. Betts (2007), p. 90.
5. The tape is now in the possession of Nick's estate. Several tracks on it are on the *Family Tree* album.
6. MD, interview with T. J. McGrath, 1981.
7. *RFAW*, p. 126.
8. GD, interview with Patrick Humphries, 1994.
9. Robert Kirby, interview, *De Mysterieuze Drake*, VRT Radio 1, Belgium, November 2004.
10. Boyd (2006), p. 262.
11. Betts (2007), p. 93.

12. *RFAW*, p. 337.
13. *A Stranger Among Us: Searching for Nick Drake*, BBC TV, 1999.
14. *RFAW*, p. 104.
15. Bowie (2000), pp. 19–20.
16. RD, interview with Gorm Henrik Rasmussen, November 1979.

Chapter 9: Casting Around

1. *Varsity Handbook: The Undergraduate's Guide to Cambridge 1968–69*, p. 114.
2. Letter to Rodney and Molly Drake, 17 October 1967.
3. RD, interview with Gorm Henrik Rasmussen, November 1979.
4. Ibid.
5. Brian Wells, quoted in Taylor and Taylor (1992), p. 144.
6. Maurice Hussey, Michaelmas 1967 report, by permission of Fitzwilliam College, Cambridge. John Venning explains: 'End-of-term reports were seen by Fitzwilliam, but were written for the Director of Studies, Dominic Baker-Smith, whose job it was to review academic performance.'
7. GD, interview with Gorm Henrik Rasmussen, November 1979.
8. Interview for Humphries (1997).
9. *Uncut*, October 2014.
10. Interview for Humphries (1997).
11. Ibid.

Chapter 10: A Remarkably Original Singer

1. Thompson (2021), p. 27.
2. Boyd (2006), p. 191.
3. *ZigZag*, No. 42, June 1974.
4. Boyd (2006), p. 191.
5. Joe Boyd, interview with Trevor Reekie, RNZ Music, New Zealand, broadcast 30 June 2019.
6. *Joe Boyd: A World of Music*, BBC Radio 2, 5 March 1997.
7. Joe Boyd, interview with Trevor Reekie, RNZ Music, New Zealand, broadcast 30 June 2019.
8. *Kaleidoscope*, BBC Radio 4, 20 December 1997.
9. Simpson (2020), p. 225.
10. MD, interview with Gorm Henrik Rasmussen, November 1979.

Chapter 11: My Musical Friend

1. Joe Boyd to RMJ, 24 September 2020.
2. Robert Kirby, interview with David Barber, 15 July 1995.
3. Ibid.
4. *RFAW*, p. 156.
5. Ibid.
6. Petrusich (2007), p. 33.
7. Interview for Humphries (1997).
8. This is drawn from Robert's introduction to *The Nick Drake Song Collection* (Wise Publications, 1998), the notes to *Family Tree* (Universal, June 2007), and *Kaleidoscope* (BBC Radio 4, 20 December 1997). Robert told David Barber in July 1995: 'I believe the first song he ever played to me was "Day Is Done".'
9. *New Musical Express*, 8 February 1975.
10. Robert Kirby, interview with David Barber, 15 July 1995.
11. *Kaleidoscope*, BBC Radio 4, 20 December 1997.
12. Petrusich (2007), p. 33.
13. Robert Kirby, interview, *De Mysterieuze Drake*, VRT Radio 1, Belgium, November 2004.
14. Robert Kirby, interview with David Barber, 15 July 1995.
15. Pete Paphides, 'Stranger to the World', *Observer*, 25 April 2004.
16. *Family Tree* (Island, 2007), booklet, p. 13.
17. Robert Kirby, interview with David Barber, 15 July 1995.
18. *RFAW*, p. 157.
19. Robert Kirby, interview with David Barber, 15 July 1995.
20. Ibid.
21. Robert Kirby, interview with Gorm Henrik Rasmussen, November 1979.
22. *RFAW*, p. 157.
23. Robert Kirby, interview with Gorm Henrik Rasmussen, November 1979
24. *Kaleidoscope*, BBC Radio 4, 20 December 1997.
25. Robert Kirby, interview with Gorm Henrik Rasmussen, November 1979.
26. *A Stranger Among Us: Searching for Nick Drake*, BBC TV, 1999.
27. Robert Kirby, interview with Gorm Henrik Rasmussen, November 1979.

28. Interview for Humphries (1997).
29. ND to his parents, 12 February 1968.
30. *Kaleidoscope*, BBC Radio 4, 20 December 1997.
31. Ibid.
32. Ibid.
33. GD, audio interview with Pete Paphides, March 2007.
34. Joe Boyd, interview with Trevor Reekie, RNZ Music, New Zealand, broadcast 30 June 2019.
35. *RFAW*, p. 201.
36. Robert Kirby, interview with Gorm Henrik Rasmussen, November 1979.
37. Interview for Humphries (1997).
38. Robert Kirby, interview with Cally Callomon, August 2004.

Chapter 12: Happy Moments

1. GD, audio interview with Pete Paphides, March 2007.
2. *Kensington Post*, 17 May 1968.
3. GD, audio interview with Pete Paphides, March 2007.
4. Boyd (2006), p. 204.
5. Ibid., p. 124.
6. Ibid., pp. 205–8.
7. Joe Boyd, interview with soundonsound.com, June 2006.
8. *RFAW*, p. 368.
9. *RFAW*, p. 369.
10. Boyd (2006), p. 193.
11. Joe Boyd, interview with Rob O'Dempsey, *Musin' Music*, No. 4, 1986.
12. Boyd (2006), p. 186.
13. Ibid.
14. *RFAW*, pp. 28–9.
15. By permission of Fitzwilliam College, Cambridge.
16. Ibid.
17. Interview for Humphries (1997).
18. *Billboard*, 25 May 1968.
19. MD and RD, interview with Gorm Henrik Rasmussen, November 1979.
20. Ibid.
21. Heron and Greig (2017), p. 173.
22. Interview for Humphries (1997).

23. Ibid.
24. Ibid.
25. Ibid.
26. Boyd (2006), p. 210.
27. Ibid., p. 211.
28. *Kaleidoscope*, BBC Radio 4, 20 December 1997.
29. RD to ND, 31 January 1969.

Chapter 13: Developing A Purely Professional Approach

1. 'Memoirs', pwheelermusic.wixsite.com, 2019.
2. *RFAW*, p. 201.
3. MD, interview with T. J. McGrath, 1981.
4. *New Musical Express*, 8 February 1975.
5. Interview for Humphries (1997).
6. Ibid.
7. Ibid.
8. Ibid.
9. Martyn (2011), p. 40. John, meanwhile, recalled: 'this very sexual lady with a big hooter and great big brown eyes was playing away, and I thought, I'd love to fuck that' (*Supersnazz*, No. 2, September 1973).
10. Martyn (2011), p. 42.
11. John Martyn, interview with Rob O'Dempsey, *Musin' Music*, No. 5, 1986.
12. *Saturday Live*, BBC Radio 1, 24 May 1986.
13. The Free Appreciation Society newsletter, No. 27 (February 1986).
14. Interview for Humphries (1997).
15. Ibid.
16. Ibid.
17. Boyd (2006), p. 196.
18. Interview for Humphries (1997).
19. Joe Boyd, interview with musicradar.com, 26 April 2013.
20. Boyd (2006), p. 196.
21. *Mojo*, June 2009.
22. *Beat Instrumental*, November 1968.
23. Thompson (2021), p. 95.
24. Interview for Humphries (1997).
25. Ibid.
26. *Mojo*, March 2018.

27. Dann (2006), p. 66.
28. By permission of Fitzwilliam College, Cambridge.
29. Interview for Humphries (1997).
30. Joe Boyd, interview with musicradar.com, 26 April 2013.
31. Clare Lowther to RMJ, email, 20 February 2020.

Chapter 14: The Record Of The Year

1. Joe Boyd, interview with Rob O'Dempsey, *Musin' Music*, No. 4, 1986.
2. Robert Kirby, interview with David Barber, 15 July 1995.
3. Ibid.
4. *Mojo*, June 2009.
5. Letter to *New Musical Express*, 15 February 1975.
6. Interview for Humphries (1997).
7. *Pynk Moon*, No. 17, September 1998.
8. MacDonald (2003), p. 210.
9. *Tatler*, 3 March 1965. Its premises had in fact been built in 1863. As of 2022 it shares them with a branch of Pizza Express.
10. Interview for Humphries (1997).
11. Ibid.
12. Letter to ND, 11 March 1969. By permission of Fitzwilliam College, Cambridge.
13. *Mojo*, June 2009.
14. Robert Kirby, interview with David Barber, 15 July 1995.
15. Interview for Humphries (1997).
16. *Kaleidoscope*, BBC Radio 4, 20 December 1997.
17. Interview for Humphries (1997).
18. Robert Kirby, interview with David Barber, 15 July 1995.
19. Boyd (2006), p. 194.
20. Joe Boyd to GD, 8 April 1999.
21. Boyd (2006), p. 197.
22. Calder (1967).
23. Interview for Humphries (1997).
24. Ibid.
25. Keith Morris, interview with David Barber, 1995.
26. Ibid.
27. Martyn (2011), p. 43.
28. John James to RMJ, email, 16 June 2020.
29. Boyd (2006), p. 207.

30. Ibid.
31. Joe Boyd, interview with Rob O'Dempsey, *Musin' Music*, No. 4, 1986.
32. *Word* magazine, August 2005.
33. *Record & Tape Retailer*, 6 March 1971.
34. Interview for Humphries (1997).
35. Robert Kirby, interview with Gorm Henrik Rasmussen, November 1979.
36. Interview for Humphries (1997).
37. *Uncut*, October 2014.
38. Interview for Humphries (1997).
39. Robert Kirby, interview with David Barber, 15 July 1995.
40. *Pynk Moon*, No. 17, September 1998.
41. Interview for Humphries (1997).
42. By permission of Fitzwilliam College, Cambridge.

Chapter 15: Lost In The Shuffle

1. *Kaleidoscope*, BBC Radio 4, 20 December 1997.
2. RD to ND, 28 May 1970.
3. *RFAW*, p. 79.
4. Mick Brown, *Sunday Telegraph* magazine, 12 July 1997.
5. Interview for Humphries (1997).
6. John Wood, interview with Vincent van Engelen, *Walhalla*, KRO (Katholieke Radio Omroep), Netherlands, 27 August 1980.
7. Interview for Humphries (1997).
8. Barry Partlow, interview with Neil Storey, April 2019.
9. Interview for Humphries (1997).
10. Beverley Martyn, interview with Simon Holland, Folk Radio UK, 15 April 2014.
11. 'He went berserk. He started shouting and throwing things at me, including a fork that hit me under the eye. I thought he had gone mad. It was terrifying.' (Martyn (2011), p. 47.)
12. Bizarrely, a 1971 German press release about Nick claimed: 'At the last Isle of Wight Festival over a million people had been waiting far too long for Bob Dylan. A young man named Nick Drake appeared on stage, stepped up to the microphone with his guitar and started playing simple songs. After the second one the ice was broken and applause drowned out the unknown Nick.' [Translation by RMJ.]

13. *RFAW*, p. 97.
14. Joe Boyd, interview with Rob O'Dempsey, *Musin' Music*, No. 4, 1986.

Chapter 16: No Backward Glances

1. *A Stranger Among Us: Searching for Nick Drake*, BBC TV, 1999.
2. Interview for Humphries (1997).
3. MD, interview with David Barber, 9 November 1992.
4. *Dark Star*, May 1979.
5. Boyd (2006), p. 198.
6. *Mojo*, June 2009.
7. GD, interview with Patrick Humphries, 1994.
8. MD, interview with Gorm Henrik Rasmussen, November 1979.
9. *Record Mirror*, 4 October 1969.
10. *A Stranger Among Us: Searching for Nick Drake*, BBC TV, 1999.
11. RD, interview with T. J. McGrath, 1981.
12. MD, interview with David Barber, 9 November 1992.
13. MD, interview with T. J. McGrath, 1981.
14. Interview for Humphries (1997).
15. *Record Mirror*, 4 October 1969.
16. *Daily Telegraph*, 13 October 1969.
17. *Jackie*, 30 May 1970.
18. MD, interview with T. J. McGrath, 1981.
19. Paul Wheeler, interview with David Barber, 15 July 1995.
20. *RFAW*, p. 431.
21. *Croydon Advertiser*, 17 October 1969.
22. *Record Retailer*, 25 October 1969.
23. *Melody Maker*, 18 October 1969.
24. Ray Kelly to RD, 13 November 1969. By permission of Fitzwilliam College, Cambridge.
25. ND to Ray Kelly, 13 October 1969. By permission of Fitzwilliam College, Cambridge.
26. RD to Ray Kelly, 10 November 1969. By permission of Fitzwilliam College, Cambridge.
27. Ray Kelly to RD, 13 November 1969. By permission of Fitzwilliam College, Cambridge.
28. Robert Kirby, interview with David Barber, 15 July 1995.

Chapter 17: Two Different Worlds Coming Together

1. *Brighton Argus*, 14 January 2010.
2. MD, interview with T. J. McGrath, 1981.
3. RD, interview with T. J. McGrath, 1981.
4. RD to ND, 3 March 1970.
5. *Fruit Tree: The Complete Recorded Works* (Island, 1979), booklet.
6. *Jackie*, 30 May 1970.
7. *Sounds*, 13 March 1971.
8. Interview for Humphries (1997).
9. Robert Kirby, interview with David Barber, 15 July 1995.
10. *Fruit Tree: The Complete Recorded Works* (Island, 1979), booklet.
11. *RFAW*, p. 399.
12. Thomson (2020), p. 78.
13. *Jackie*, 19 September 1970.
14. Boyd (2006), pp. 199–200.
15. Speech at the Nick Drake Tribute Concert, Cockpit Theatre, Marylebone, London, May 2009.
16. Interview for Humphries (1997).
17. *RFAW*, p. 431.
18. *Pynk Moon*, No. 19, 2000.
19. Facebook comment, 2020.
20. Interview for Humphries (1997).
21. John Martyn, interview with Rob O'Dempsey, *Musin' Music*, No. 5, 1986.
22. *Saturday Live*, BBC Radio 1, 24 May 1986.
23. MD, interview with Gorm Henrik Rasmussen, November 1979.
24. Interview for Humphries (1997).

Chapter 18: People Didn't Really Listen

1. *Record Retailer*, 7 March 1970.
2. Newsletter, joeboyd.co.uk, 28 June 2020.
3. Joe Boyd, interview with Patrick Humphries, 1994.
4. Boyd (2006), p. 200.
5. Interview for Humphries (1997).
6. Ibid.
7. Ian Anderson, interview for jonwilks.online, 26 September 2017.

Ian's debut album was briefly set to be released on Island in early 1969.

8. *fRoots*, No. 377, November 2014.
9. *fRoots*, No. 328, October 2010. In the same piece he stated: 'On a recent TV feature about Drake, Joe – a man who I greatly respect and with whom I'd rarely argue – came out with some statement about how Drake was so original and unlike anybody else at the time. "No he fucking wasn't, Joe," I bawled at the screen. "If you thought that, you didn't get out enough!"'
10. Ian Anderson, interview with Philip Ward, brushondrum.blogspot.com, September 2015.
11. Interview for Humphries (1997).
12. Iain Cameron to Patrick Humphries, 4 December 1997.
13. Interview for Humphries (1997).
14. Interview for Humphries (1997).
15. Paul Donnelly to Patrick Humphries, 2 February 1997.
16. *Pynk Moon*, March 1997.
17. Ibid.
18. *Time Out: A Guide to the North West*, 11–25 April 1970.
19. Robert Kirby, interview with David Barber, 15 July 1995.
20. Interview for Humphries (1997).
21. Island Records, press release, November 1971.
22. Ibid.
23. *Top Pops & Music Now*, 28 February 1970.
24. Interview for Humphries (1997).
25. Robert Kirby, interview with David Barber, 15 July 1995.
26. Interview for Humphries (1997).
27. Robert Kirby, interview with David Barber, 15 July 1995.
28. RD to ND, 3 March 1970.

Chapter 19: A Little Uncertain

1. Joe Boyd, interview with Patrick Humphries, 1994.
2. Interview for Humphries (1997).
3. MD, interview with Gorm Henrik Rasmussen, November 1979.
4. MD, interview with Vincent van Engelen, *Walhalla*, KRO (Katholieke Radio Omroep), Netherlands, 27 August 1980.
5. Joe Boyd, interview with Rob O'Dempsey, *Musin' Music*, No. 4, 1986.
6. DVD, *Nick Drake: Under Review* (Chrome Dreams, 2007).

7. Joe Boyd, interview with Patrick Humphries, 1994.
8. Robert Kirby, interview with Gorm Henrik Rasmussen, November 1979.
9. Interview for Humphries (1997).
10. Robert Kirby, interview with Matt Hutchinson, nickdrake.com, 2008.
11. Arnold (2022), p. 255.
12. *ZigZag*, No. 42, June 1974. Richard has subsequently said Nick was not in fact present.
13. Joe Boyd, interview with Patrick Humphries, 1994.
14. Interview for Humphries (1997).
15. Ibid.
16. RD, interview with T. J. McGrath, 1981.
17. Boyd (2006), p. 265.
18. Dave Crewe to Patrick Humphries, 21 January 1997.
19. *Saturday Live*, BBC Radio 1, 24 May 1986.
20. *New Musical Express*, 4 April 1970.
21. *International Times*, 9 April 1970.
22. *The Times*, 1 April 1970. Dallas had also seen him at the Royal Festival Hall in September 1969 and at Croydon's Fairfield Halls in October 1969.
23. Interview for Humphries (1997).

Chapter 20: Going Downhill

1. *Jackie*, 19 September 1970.
2. *A Stranger Among Us: Searching for Nick Drake*, BBC TV, 1999.
3. Interview for Humphries (1997).
4. *A Stranger Among Us: Searching for Nick Drake*, BBC TV, 1999.
5. Interview for Humphries (1997).
6. Ibid.
7. Ibid.
8 Ibid.
9. *RFAW*, p. 104.
10. *Music Business Weekly*, 25 April 1970.
11. *Kaleidoscope*, BBC Radio 4, 20 December 1997.
12. *HoboSapiens*, EMI press release, 2003.
13. The *Wire*, September 1996. Nick had certainly handled a twelve-string before, if not this model.
14. Boyd (2006), p. 201.

15. *Pynk Moon*, No. 18, April 1999.

16. *Fruit Tree: The Complete Recorded Works* (Island, 1979), booklet.

17. Joe Boyd, interview with Kevin Ring, *Zip Code* magazine, 1992.

18. *ZigZag*, No. 49, January 1975; his remark perhaps subconsciously echoed what Nick had told *Sounds*.

19. *Sounds*, 13 March 1971.

20. Robert Kirby, interview with Matt Hutchinson, nickdrake.com, 2008.

21. Interview for Humphries (1997).

22. *Rave*, January 1971.

23. *Pynk Moon*, No. 6, April 1996.

24. Thompson (2021), pp. 95–6.

25. Joe Boyd, interview with Rob O'Dempsey, *Musin' Music*, No. 4, 1986.

26. *Music Business Weekly*, 18 April 1970.

27. *Sunday Times*, 29 January 2006.

28. Interview for Humphries (1997).

29. Fax to Patrick Humphries, 6 March 1997.

30. *RFAW*, p. 231.

31. Brian Cullman, 'Things Behind the Sun', *Paris Review*, 27 December 2012.

32. Interview for Humphries (1997).

33. Ibid.

34. Ibid.

35. *Sounds*, 13 March 1971.

36. *RFAW*, p. 104.

Chapter 21: A Different Nick

1. Boyd (2006), p. 199.

2. RD Diary, 12 September 1972.

3. Mick Brown, 'The Sad Ballad of Nick Drake', *Sunday Telegraph* magazine, 12 July 1997.

4. Joe Boyd, interview with Patrick Humphries, 1994.

5. Keith Morris, introduction to 'Three Days: An Exhbition of Nick Drake Photographs', June 2004.

6. Interview for Humphries (1997).

7. Ibid.

8. *Crawdaddy!*, September 1970.

9. RD to ND, 26 October 1970.

10. Interview for Humphries (1997).

11. *Kaleidoscope*, BBC Radio 4, 20 December 1997.
12. Boyd (2006), p. 183.
13. Ibid., p. 229.
14. Joe Boyd, interview with Rob O'Dempsey, *Musin' Music*, No. 4, 1986.
15. Interview for Humphries (1997).
16. *Mojo*, March 2018.
17. *Pynk Moon*, No. 6, April 1996.
18. RD Diary, 3 November 1972.
19. RD, interview with Gorm Henrik Rasmussen, November 1979.

Chapter 22: A Second-Division Act

1. RD and MD, interview with T. J. McGrath, 1981.
2. *Music Business Weekly*, 30 January 1971.
3. Ibid.
4. *World Pop News*, March/April 1971.
5. Island Records, press release, November 1971.
6. Interview for Humphries (1997).
7. *Pynk Moon*, No. 6, April 1996.
8. Interview for Humphries (1997).
9. Ibid.
10. Ibid.
11. *Uncut*, October 2014.
12. Interview for Humphries (1997).
13. *The Times*, 19 March 1971.
14. Ibid.

Chapter 23: Nick-Lack

1. MD, interview with Gorm Henrik Rasmussen, November 1979.
2. MD, interview with David Barber, 9 November 1992.
3. Mick Brown, *Sunday Telegraph* magazine, 12 July 1997.
4. *Pynk Moon*, No. 6, April 1996.
5. *Record Retailer*, 24 April 1971.
6. *A Stranger Among Us: Searching for Nick Drake* (BBC TV, 1999).
7. *Record & Tape Retailer*, 13 March 1971.
8. Interview for Humphries (1997).
9. *The Word*, October 2005.

10. *RFAW*, p. 370.
11. MD, interview with Gorm Henrik Rasmussen, November 1979.
12. Petrusich (2007), p. 39.
13. Joe Boyd, interview with Patrick Humphries, 1994.
14. MD, interview with T. J. McGrath, 1981.
15. RD, interview with T. J. McGrath, 1981.
16. Interview for Humphries (1997).
17. Robert Kirby, interview with David Barber, 15 July 1995.
18. Interview for Humphries (1997).
19. Robert Kirby, interview with Gorm Henrik Rasmussen, November 1979.
20. Robert Kirby to GD, 10 April 2008.
21. *Billboard*, 7 August 1971.
22. *Arizona Republic*, 26 September; *Tampa Bay Times*, 6 December; *Honolulu Advertiser*, 4 November; *Morning News*, 4 December 1971.
23. *Phonograph Record Magazine*, November 1971.
24. Interview for Humphries (1997).
25. *Observer Music Monthly*, April 2004.
26. Petrusich (2007), p. 35.
27. ND to Leon Redler, 23 May 1973.
28. *RFAW*, p. 327.
29. Joe Boyd, interview with Patrick Humphries, 1994.
30. Interview for Humphries (1997).
31. Boyd (2006), p. 237.
32. MD to ND, postcard, 19 September 1971.
33. MD, interview with T. J. McGrath, 1981.
34. Interview for Humphries (1997).
35. GD, interview with Patrick Humphries, 1994.

Chapter 24: A Small Reel

1. *ZigZag*, No. 42, June 1974.
2. John Wood, interview with Vincent van Engelen, *Walhalla*, KRO (Katholieke Radio Omroep), Netherlands, 27 August 1980.
3. ND to Leon Redler, 23 May 1973.
4. Petrusich (2007), p. 55.
5. Island Records, press release, November 1971.
6. Interview for Humphries (1997).
7. Ibid.

8. Ibid.
9. Keith Morris, interview with David Barber, 1995.
10. Interview for Humphries, 1997.

Chapter 25: Teetering On The Edge

1. John Pringle, 'A Case of Schizophrenia', *The Times*, 9 May 1970.
2. MD, interview with Gorm Henrik Rasmussen, November 1979.
3. RD Diary, 31 May 1972.
4. *RFAW*, p. 327.
5. *Melody Maker*, 4 July 1987.
6. *RFAW*, p. 212.
7. Thomson (2020), p. 79.
8. Interview for Humphries (1997).
9. Ibid.
10. Dann (2006), p. 170.
11. RD to Helen Vinter, 22 December 1975.
12. RD to Scott Appel, 12 December 1986.
13. Thompson (2021), p. 97.
14. Robert Kirby, interview with Gorm Henrik Rasmussen, November 1979.
15. Robert Kirby, interview with David Barber, 15 July 1995.
16. *Melody Maker*, 1 April 1972.
17. *Record Mirror*, 4 March 1972.
18. *Record & Tape Retailer*, 11 March 1972.
19. *Time Out*, 17 March 1972.
20. *Records and Recording*, April 1972.
21. *Penthouse*, April 1972.
22. *Reading Evening Post*, 14 April 1972.
23. *Sounds*, 25 March 1972.
24. Ian MacCormick to Patrick Humphries, 13 January 1997. Paul has no memory of this meeting and questions the account's reliability.

Chapter 26: This May Be A Long Job

1. *RFAW*, p. 328.
2. *Best*, May 1972 (review by Hervé Muller).
3. Hardy (2018), pp. 144–5.

4. RD Diary, 7 September 1972.
5. ND to Leon Redler, 24 May 1973.
6. *Coventry Evening Telegraph*, 13 March 1968.
7. Gerald Dickens to Rodney Drake, 29 September 1975.
8. *RFAW*, p. 372.
9. Ibid.
10. *RFAW*, p. 330.
11. Interview for Humphries (1997).
12. Hardy (2018), p. 146.
13. Unterberger (1998), p. 117.
14. *RFAW*, p. 332.
15. Interview for Humphries (1997).

Chapter 27: Don't Douse The Grouch

1. *Post-Crescent* (Appleton, Wisconsin), 23 July 1972.
2. *Abilene Reporter-News* (Texas), 18 June 1972.
3. *Billboard*, 27 May 1972.
4. MD, interview with Gorm Henrik Rasmussen, November 1979.
5. MD, interview with T. J. McGrath, 1981.
6. RD, interview with Gorm Henrik Rasmussen, November 1979.
7. MD, interview with Gorm Henrik Rasmussen, November 1979.
8. *RFAW*, p. 335.
9. Patricia Allderidge, 'Midsummer Nightmare', *Sunday Times Magazine*, 24 September 1972, pp. 52–8.

Chapter 28: Confusion

1. *RFAW*, p. 340.
2. *New Times*, 1 May 1978.
3. ND to Leon Redler, 24 May 1973.
4. *RFAW*, p. 341.
5. *Sound Flash*, No. 25, 8 April 1973 [translation by RMJ]; De Marchis was unaware of the existence of *Five Leaves Left*.
6. MD, interview with Chris Brazier, 1985.
7. *RFAW*, p. 372.
8. Ibid., p. 105.
9. RD, interview with Chris Brazier, 1985.

Chapter 29: In A Terrible Mess

1. *RFAW*, p. 344.
2. Interview for Humphries (1997).
3. Martyn (2011), p. 64.
4. Interview for Humphries (1997).
5. *RFAW*, p. 347.
6. Ibid., p. 349.
7. Boyd (2006), p. 259.
8. *ZigZag*, No. 42, June 1974.
9. Boyd (2006), p. 261.
10. *Sounds*, 14 December 1974.

Chapter 30: Struggling Musically

1. *Ciao 2001*, 26 May 1974. [Translation by RMJ.]
2. *ZigZag*, No. 42, June 1974. According to the same magazine's December 1974 issue, the article prompted 'many letters' from Nick's admirers.
3. MD, interview with Gorm Henrik Rasmussen, November 1979.
4. Boyd (2006), p. 259.
5. 'Raver', *Melody Maker*, 3 August 1974.
6. MD, interview with Gorm Henrik Rasmussen, November 1979.
7. See *RFAW*, p. 105.
8. MD, interview with T. J. McGrath, 1981.
9. RD to Gorm Henrik Rasmussen, undated draft, c. 1979.
10. A few months later, David Belbin wrote one of the first posthumous articles about Nick's work – an appreciation of *Pink Moon* for the Autumn 1975 issue of *Liquorice* magazine.
11. Interview for Humphries (1997).
12. Martyn (2011), p. 65.

Chapter 31: Watching The Water Going By

1. *RFAW*, p. 359.
2. Ibid.
3. MD, interview with Gorm Henrik Rasmussen, November 1979.

4. Ibid.
5. MD, interview with T. J. McGrath, 1981.
6. Mildred Norton to MD and RD, 27 November 1974.
7. MD, interview with Vincent van Engelen, *Walhalla*, KRO (Katholieke Radio Omroep), Netherlands, 27 August 1980.

Chapter 32: A Very Special Person

1. Boyd (2006), p. 259.
2. Robert Kirby, interview with Vincent van Engelen, *Walhalla*, KRO (Katholieke Radio Omroep), Netherlands, 27 August 1980.
3. Munro (2010).
4. *Mojo*, May 2001.
5. *Melody Maker*, 4 July 1987.
6. RD, interview with T. J. McGrath, 1981.
7. MD, interview with Gorm Henrik Rasmussen, November 1979.
8. MD, interview with Chris Brazier, 1985.
9. *Kaleidoscope*, BBC Radio 4, 20 December 1997.
10. *RFAW*, p. 372.
11. RD to Helen Vinter, 22 December 1975.
12. Boyd (2006), p. 261.
13. Interview for Humphries (1997).
14. *New Musical Express*, 8 February 1975.
15. *ZigZag*, No. 49, February 1975.
16. *New Musical Express*, 8 February 1975.
17. *RFAW*, p. 364.
18. Gerald Dickens to RD, 29 September 1975.

Epilogue

1. *Mojo*, March 2018.
2. *Stratford Herald*, 8 April 1988.
3. MD to Scott Appel, 25 November 1988.
4. MD, interview with David Barber, 9 November 1992.

Bibliography

Arnold, P. P., *Soul Survivor: The Autobiography* (Nine Eight Books, 2022)

Barry, Lee, *John Martyn: Grace and Danger* (Lulu.com, 2006)

Bean, J. P., *Singing from the Floor: A History of British Folk Clubs* (Faber, 2014)

Betjeman, John, *Collected Poems* (John Murray, 2006)

Betts, Colin, *Frozenlight* (Floating World, 2007)

Blackwell, Chris, *The Islander: My Life in Music and Beyond* (Nine Eight Books, 2022)

Bowie, Angela, with Patrick Carr, *Backstage Passes: Life on the Wild Side with David Bowie* (Cooper Square Press, 2000)

Boyd, Joe, *White Bicycles: Making Music in the 1960s* (Serpent's Tail, 2006)

Calder, Julian, ed., *Aspect* (Guildford School of Art, 1967)

Cleaver, John, *Fitzwilliam: The First 150 Years of a Cambridge College* (Third Millennium Publishing Ltd, 2013)

Creed, Jason, ed., *Nick Drake: The Pink Moon Files* (Omnibus, 2011)

Dann, Trevor, *Darker Than the Deepest Sea: The Search for Nick Drake* (Portrait, 2006)

Drake, Molly, *The Tide's Magnificence: Songs And Poems Of Molly Drake* (Fledg'ling Records, 2017)

Drake, Nick, *The Nick Drake Song Collection* (Wise Publications, 1998)

Green, Jonathon, *Days in the Life: Voices from the English Underground, 1961–1971* (Heinemann, 1988)

Hardy, Françoise, *The Despair of Monkeys and Other Trifles: A Memoir* (Feral House, 2018)

Heron, Mike, and Andrew Greig, *You Know What You Could Be: Tuning into the 1960s* (Riverrun, 2017)

Hicks, Andrew, Robert Brown, and Andrew Clive, *Arden House, 1869–1962: Memories of a Warwickshire Prep School* (privately printed, 2021)

Hogan, Peter, *Nick Drake: The Complete Guide to His Music* (Omnibus, 2009)

545

Humphries, Patrick, *Nick Drake: The Biography* (Bloomsbury, 1997)

Johnson, B. W., *Unwillingly To School? A Brief Account of Eagle House from 1820 to the Present Day* (privately published, 1995)

MacDonald, Ian, *The People's Music* (Pimlico, 2003)

Martyn, Beverley, *Sweet Honesty* (Grosvenor House Publishing, 2011)

Munro, John Neil, *Some People Are Crazy: The John Martyn Story* (Birlinn, 2010)

Petrusich, Amanda, *Pink Moon* (Bloomsbury, 2007)

Pettinger, John W., *Tanworth in Arden: An Introduction to the History of the Ancient Parish* (Brewin Books, 2005)

Pickford, Chris, and Nikolaus Pevsner, *Warwickshire* (Pevsner Architectural Guides, Yale University Press, 2016)

Rasmussen, Gorm Henrik, trans. Bent Sørensen, *Pink Moon* (Rocket 88, 2012)

Simpson, Rose, *Muse, Odalisque, Handmaiden: A Girl's Life in The Incredible String Band* (Strange Attractor Press, 2020)

Smith, Naomi [Helen Vinter], *The Tangled Web: My Son, a Schizophrenic* (Johnson, 1975)

Taylor, Joan, and Derek Taylor, *Getting Sober . . . And Loving It!* (Vermilion, 1992)

Thompson, Richard, with Scott Timberg, *Beeswing: Fairport, Folk Rock and Finding my Voice 1967–75* (Faber & Faber, 2021)

Thomson, Graeme, *Small Hours: The Long Night of John Martyn* (Omnibus, 2020)

Unterberger, Richie, *Unknown Legends of Rock'n'Roll: Psychedelic Unknowns, Mad Geniuses, Punk Pioneers, Lo-Fi Mavericks & More* (Backbeat, 1998)

Whittaker, Adrian, *Dr. Strangely Strange: Fitting Pieces to the Jigsaw* (Ozymandias, 2019)

Index